SZASZ
Under Fire

The Under Fire™ Series

General Editor: Jeffrey A. Schaler

SZASZ
Under Fire

The Psychiatric Abolitionist Faces His Critics

EDITED BY

JEFFREY A. SCHALER

OPEN COURT
Chicago and La Salle, Illinois

To order books from Open Court, call toll-free 1-800-815-2280, or visit our website at www.opencourtbooks.com.

Open Court Publishing Company is a division of Carus Publishing Company.

First printing 2004
Second printing 2005

The correspondence between Thomas Szasz and Karl Popper, reproduced on pages 134–38, appears by kind permission of Melitta Mew, the Estate of Sir Karl Popper, Surrey, England. Permission to reproduce these letters must be secured from the Estate of Sir Karl Popper. The Hoover Institution on War, Revolution, and Peace, Stanford University, is the repository of the Popper Archive. Thomas S. Szasz Cybercenter for Liberty and Responsibility, www.Szasz.com. Copyright © 1998–2010 by the author of each page, except where noted. Cover photograph of Thomas Szasz by Jeffrey A. Schaler.

Printed and bound in the United States of America.

Library of Congress Cataloging-in-Publication Data

Szasz under fire : the psychiatric abolitionist faces his critics / edited
by Jeffrey A. Schaler.
      p. cm.
   Includes bibliographical references and index.
   ISBN 0-8126-9568-2 (pbk. : alk. paper)
   1. Psychiatry—Philosophy. 2. Szasz, Thomas Stephen, 1920- 3. Antipsychiatry.
 I. Schaler, Jeffrey A.
   RC437.5.S94 2004
   616.89—dc22
                                             2004006826

To Renée

Many looked upon the abolitionists as monsters.

THOMAS CLARKSON (1790)

It is the union of Church and State that has caused all persecution.

LORD ACTON

Contents

About the Authors

MARGARET P. BATTIN, Ph.D., is Professor of Philosophy and Adjunct Professor of Internal Medicine, Division of Medical Ethics, at the University of Utah. She has authored, co-authored, edited, or co-edited twelve books, including *The Least Worst Death* (1994) and *Praying for a Cure* (with Peggy DesAutels and Larry May, 1999).

RICHARD BENTALL, Ph. D., was appointed to a chair in Experimental Clinical Psychology at the University of Manchester in 1999. His books include *Sensory Deception: Towards a Scientific Analysis of Hallucinations* (with P.D. Slade, 1988) and *Madness Explained: Psychosis and Human Nature* (2003).

H. TRISTRAM ENGELHARDT, Jr., Ph.D., M.D., is Professor, Department of Philosophy, Rice University, and Professor Emeritus, Department of Medicine and Community Medicine, Baylor College of Medicine. His recent publications include *The Foundations of Bioethics* (1996) and *The Foundations of Christian Bioethics* (2000).

K.W.M. FULFORD, D. Phil., F.R.C.P., F.R.C. Psych, is Professor of Philosophy and Mental Health, University of Warwick, and Honorary Consultant Psychiatrist, University of Oxford. He is editor of the journal, *Philosophy, Psychiatry, and Psychology*.

MARGARET A. HAGEN, Ph.D., is Professor of Psychology at Boston University. She is the author of *Whores of the Court: The Fraud of Psychiatric Testimony and the Rape of American Justice* (1997) and *Varieties of Realism: Geometries of Representational Art* (1986).

ROBERT EVAN KENDELL, C.B.E., M.D., F.R.S.E., was appointed Professor of Psychiatry at Edinburgh Medical School in 1974, and became Chief Medical Officer at the Scottish Office in 1991. He was President of the Royal College of Psychiatrists from 1996 to 1999. Dr. Kendell died after writing his contribution to this volume.

E. JAMES LIEBERMAN, M.D., M.P.H., is Clinical Professor of Psychiatry, George Washington University School of Medicine. He is author of *Acts of Will: The Life and Work of Otto Rank* (1998), and host of the website, www.ottorank.com.

STANTON PEELE, Ph.D., J.D., has published nine books, including *Diseasing of America* (1995) and *The Truth about Addiction and Recovery* (1992).

RAY SCOTT PERCIVAL, Ph.D., is Assistant Professor in the College of Humanities and Social Sciences, United Arab Emirates University. He is President and Founder of Karl Popper Forums. In 1999 he was named by *Baron's Who's Who* as one of the five hundred leaders of the new century.

RONALD W. PIES, M.D., is Clinical Professor of Psychiatry at Tufts University School of Medicine and Lecturer in Psychiatry, Harvard Medical School. He is author or editor of several psychiatric textbooks, including *The Difficult-to-Treat Psychiatric Patient* (with M. Dewan, 2001), and author of *The Ethics of the Sages* (1999).

JEFFREY A. SCHALER, Ph.D., is Assistant Professor of Justice, Law, and Society at American University's School of Public Affairs in Washington, D.C. He is editor of *Drugs: Should We Legalize, Decriminalize, or Deregulate?* (1998) and author of *Addiction Is a Choice* (2000).

RITA J. SIMON, Ph.D., is University Professor, School of Public Affairs and the Washington College of Law, at American University, Washington, D.C. Her more than fifty books include *Abortion: Statutes, Policies, and Public Attitudes the World Over* (1998) and *The Insanity Defense* (with David E. Aaronson, 1988).

RALPH J. SLOVENKO, Ph.D., J.D., is Professor of Law and Psychiatry at Wayne State University Law School. He is author or editor of forty books, *including Psychiatry in Law—Law in Psychiatry* (2002) and *Psychotherapy and Confidentiality* (1998).

RYAN SPELLECY, Ph.D., is Assistant Professor at the Center for the Study of Bioethics in the Medical College of Wisconsin. He has published several scholarly articles on bioethics.

THOMAS S. SZASZ, M.D., is Professor Emeritus of Psychiatry at the State University of New York Health Center in Syracuse. His recent books include *Pharmacracy* (2001) and *Faith in Freedom* (2004).

Introduction

JEFFREY A. SCHALER

Thomas Stephen Szasz[1] has challenged conventional thinking about freedom, responsibility, madness, sexuality, medicine, and disease. He has come to be regarded by psychiatrists and psychoanalysts as the most controversial living psychiatrist and psychoanalyst. As Arnold Rogow has put it,

> Of all critics of psychiatry in recent years, Thomas S. Szasz is undoubtedly the best known and he has aroused the most controversy. . . . Szasz has attacked psychoanalysis and psychiatry at their roots by arguing, in a number of books and articles, that mental illness, with the exception of certain organic diseases, is itself a myth, and that therefore psychiatry is more related to moral philosophy and social theory than to medicine.[2]

Szasz is best known for his insistence that "mental illness" is a metaphor, and that we go astray if we take the metaphor literally. Yet belief in mental illness is not his main target. In Szasz's view, people are free to believe in mental illness, exactly as they are free to believe in God, witchcraft, alien abductions, or psychokinetic spoon-bending, to mention a few of the other common beliefs about which Szasz is skeptical.

Szasz is certainly concerned to expose the false beliefs of psychiatrists, but what drives him is the conviction that people should be free to engage—or not engage—in the ceremonies and rituals involved in going to a psychiatrist or a psychotherapist, just as people are free to partake of Easter communion or a Passover seder. Indeed, Szasz holds that there

---

[1] Hungarian is a phonetic language with an alphabet containing forty letters, many of them compounds of what would be two letters in English, for example "cs," "gy," and "ly." "Sz" is such a compound letter. It is prounounced as a sharp "s," as in "sand." The letter "á," with the accent, is prounounced as a long "a," as in "father."

[2] Arnold A. Rogow, *The Psychiatrists* (New York: Putnam's, 1970), p. 28.

is a close kinship between psychiatry and what is commonly recognized as religion. As a thinker in the tradition of classical liberalism, influenced by Thomas Jefferson, John Stuart Mill, and Ludwig von Mises, Szasz believes in the separation of religion and state, the separation of medicine and state, and the separation of psychiatry and state.

In Szasz's view, individuals should be free to devote themselves to any variety of psychiatric belief and practice. What Szasz objects to is *forcing* people to see (or not see) a psychiatrist, to reside or not reside in a mental hospital, to partake (or not partake) of drugs, and to believe (or not believe) in any specific set of ideas.

Though Szasz has been called an "anti-psychiatrist," he rejects this label, closely identified with the ideas of R.D. Laing and David Cooper, ideas which Szasz detests. Szasz is against coercion, not "psychiatry between consenting adults." Just as Szasz defends everyone's right to believe in God, so too, he defends everyone's right to believe in alien beings beaming messages to him or her through the fillings in his or her teeth. The state has no business inside a person's head, according to Szasz.

Szasz is a psychiatrist, and yet he is highly critical of psychiatry. He maintains that there is no contradiction. A professor of medicine comments on the nature and practice of medicine. A professor of theology or comparative religion comments on the nature and practice of religion. Just as an atheist can teach theology, the theory of God, angels, demons, and the like, so a psychiatric abolitionist can teach psychiatric theory, the theory of mental illness. Szasz has also been a practicing psychotherapist. When practicing psychotherapy, Szasz claims that he is not doing what "mental health professionals" usually claim to be doing. As Szasz prefers to describe it, he is having conversations with people about their problems.

Szasz has advocated a number of social policy changes, with mixed results to date. He argued against the classification of homosexuality as a disease when this classification was the overwhelmingly predominant view. He alone spoke out against the pretence that circumcision is a medical procedure, and Szasz's position has now become generally accepted. Together with George J. Alexander and Erving Goffman, Szasz founded the American Association for the Abolition of Involuntary Mental Hospitalization in 1970. This organization published a journal, *The Abolitionist*, and provided legal help to mental patients; it was dissolved in 1980 because political opinion was running so strongly in the other direction, yet ironically the Reagan administration's eviction of mental patients from mental hospitals, known as "deinstitutionalization," is often attributed to Szasz's influence. In *Ceremonial Chemistry* and other works he has fought against the War on Drugs and called for the removal of all drug prohibitions, a view which has gained adherents but is far from its goal. Szasz was the first to criticize the "sexual surrogate therapy" of Masters and Johnson as medicalized procuring and prostitution and he has spoken out against much "sex research" and "sex therapy," which he views as pornography masquerading as "mental-health education."

Szasz supports the right to suicide—but is a sharp critic of "physician-assisted suicide." Szasz opposes what usually passes for "drug legalization," which he sees as a further step toward giving physicians control over people's lives. Yet he advocates the complete and total repeal of drug prohibition and believes that medical licensure ought to be abolished along with prescription laws.

Just as priests were once empowered by the state—the theocratic state—to do certain things to certain people, doctors, and in particular, psychiatrists, are now empowered by the state—the therapeutic state[3]—to do certain things to certain people. As Szasz sees it, doctors have now assumed the role in society once occupied by priests and other religious leaders. The theocratic state, says Szasz, has been supplanted by the therapeutic state; the political power of priests has been replaced by the political power of doctors.

What can doctors do now that is possibly so horrid? They can, as agents of the therapeutic state, deprive people of liberty because of their deviant, aberrant, abnormal, and socially-unacceptable behavior. Just as negroes were once defined by the state as three-fifths persons in order to maintain the institution of slavery, people diagnosed as mentally ill are defined—in effect—as three-fifths persons in order to maintain the institution of "psychiatric slavery." The U.S. Constitution protects individual citizens against deprivation of their liberty without due process of law. That protection is circumvented when psychiatrists are empowered by the state to deprive citizens of liberty by diagnosing them as mentally ill and committing them to prisons called "mental hospitals."

Today, people are declared a danger to themselves and others by psychiatrists and deprived of liberty via commitment to a mental hospital. Though these individuals have often committed no crime, they have

---

[3] This now widely-employed phrase was coined by Szasz in 1963: "Although we may not know it, we have, in our day, witnessed the birth of the Therapeutic State." *Law, Liberty, and Psychiatry* (Syracuse: Syracuse University Press, 1989), p. 212.

committed a metaphorical crime called "being a threat to self and others." While suicide is currently not forbidden by criminal law, it is effectively forbidden by mental health law, as well as being opposed by most of the churches and other branches of organized religion.

While no one, including psychiatrists, can reliably predict dangerousness towards self or others, psychiatrists are empowered by the state to do just this very thing. As in the Tom Cruise movie *Minority Report*, crimes are punished before they occur, and therefore punished though they never occur. Persons considered a "threat to self and others" effectively lose their entitlement to a trial without being tried, and are deprived of liberty by the state when committed to a mental hospital after being examined by a psychiatrist. If they object to being examined or reject the concept of mental illness, this stance is itself taken for a sign of their mental illness, exactly as disbelief in witches used to be taken as evidence of being a witch. According to Szasz, this whole psychiatric procedure conflicts with the liberal principle of the rule of law.

When a person is accused of committing a crime and is denied his constitutional right to a trial, a psychiatrist may be called in by the court to examine and declare a defendant mentally healthy or mentally ill in what is referred to as a pretrial psychiatric examination. A person who is clearly guilty of a crime may be exculpated and sent to a mental hospital as a result of psychiatric testimony. Psychiatrists who examine a defendant in the present are credited by the court with the competence to assess whether a defendant lacked the necessary intent or *mens rea* in the *past*, when he or she committed the crime. In Szasz's view, the insanity defense is tantamount to denial of justice, just as involuntary commitment is tantamount to unconstitutional deprivation of liberty.

A psychiatric pretrial examination is frequently used to declare a defendant incompetent to stand trial even though the defendant may be fully competent according to normal legal standards. Even when defendants understand the charges brought against them by a prosecutor, are able to assist counsel with a defense, and understand the proceedings of the court. Szasz fully accepts the principle of legal competency, yet as he points out, demonstrable competency may be set aside when a psychiatrist is brought into the picture. For if defendants are diagnosed as mentally ill, legal competency is usually over-ridden by this diagnosis.

Szasz does not advocate the use of illegal drugs—far from it. He argues that drug use and addiction are moral, ethical and political issues, not medical issues, and that the state has no business interfering in such private matters. Drugs are nowadays considered safe and dangerous, good and bad, on account of their alleged potential for addiction, supposedly a public health issue. Szasz argues that drugs themselves are neither safe nor dangerous, neither good nor bad—again, drug use is an ethical issue. Good, bad, safe, and dangerous are not qualities to be found within the physical properties of any drug. It all depends on how drugs are being used and who considers them good or bad, safe or dangerous. Drugs are considered "good" when doctors and society label them as such. Antibiotics, for example, and psychiatrically-prescribed drugs, are considered "good." Marijuana and psychedelic drugs are supposed to be "bad." Just as the government should not interfere with the beliefs or ideas a person puts inside his or her mind, Szasz holds that the government should not interfere with the foods, drugs, or other substances a person puts inside his or her body.

Szasz carefully discriminates between legitimate public and private health matters. An example of a legitimate public health matter is the control of contagious disease. Smallpox is a matter of public health concern, and it may be right for the government to coerce smallpox carriers, if this is necessary to prevent harm to other people. A decision to see a doctor about controlling one's weight, or a decision to smoke cigarettes, is a private matter, and none of the government's business.

Szasz advocates that psychiatrists and doctors be stripped of the power the state now bestows upon them. The state entangles itself with medicine when it uses force to deprive citizens of basic constitutional protections. Psychiatry and medicine become an extension of law and government. The state entangles itself with medicine when it is instrumental in excusing criminal behavior. It entangles itself with medicine when the government gives financial support to psychiatrically-based treatment programs for "bad" behavior. And it entangles itself with medicine when it interferes in what should be an entirely contractual relationship between doctor and patient, therapist and client.

Thomas Szasz's autobiographical statement which immediately follows this Introduction ends where *The Myth of Mental Illness* begins. (Important episodes from Szasz's subsequent life are described in some of his replies to the critical essays in this book.) Although *The Myth of Mental Illness* is still (some thirty books later) the work for which he is best known, it was not Szasz's first book, nor was its publication the first time the title had appeared in print. Szasz's first book was *Pain and Pleasure: A Study of Bodily Feelings*, published in 1957. The title "The Myth of Mental Illness" first appeared on an article published in *American Psychologist* in 1960. As the bibliography of Szasz's writings at the back of this book shows, he published a number of articles before he became famous for challenging institutional psychiatry.

The "Szasz Affair" at Upstate Medical Center

The battle over Szasz's position at Upstate Medical Center is a watershed event in the history of international thinking about psychiatry, an event which dramatically changed the lives of many individuals, some of them to become influential thinkers and writers. No full account of this stormy and fateful conflict has yet been published anywhere. Here I give a brief outline of what occurred. An appendix to this book reproduces some of the relevant documents.

In 1961, when *The Myth of Mental Illness* appeared, Szasz was a tenured professor of psychiatry at the State University of New York's Upstate Medical Center in Syracuse. Friends and colleagues of Szasz were well acquainted with his views on psychiatry and mental illness, and were generally sympathetic. This did not immediately change following publication of *The Myth of Mental Illness* in 1961.

That book, however, attracted a lot of attention. It was widely and favorably reviewed. Matters were then brought to a head by Szasz's testimony at the *habeas corpus* hearing for John Chomentowski on April 12th, 1962. Chomentowski was held at the Mattewan State Hospital, in Mattewan, New York after firing a gun in the air when a big real estate developer tried to take over a property Chomentowski had owned and refused to sell. State psychiatrists asserted that Chomentowski was mentally incompetent to stand trial for the incident. Accounts of this case are given in Chapter 4 of Szasz's book, *Psychiatric Justice*, published in 1965 and in a 1997 article by Ronald Leifer.[4] Szasz protected Chomentowski's identity by naming him "Louis Perroni."

The Chomentowski hearing was later described by Leifer as "a highly anticipated event in psychiatric circles, since for the first time Szasz was in an adversarial confrontation with conventional psychiatrists in a public forum." State psychiatrists, distressed by Szasz's testimony, complained to Paul Hoch, New York State Commissioner of Mental Hygiene. Newton Bigelow, director of the Marcy State Hospital and editor of the then prestigious psychiatric journal, *The Psychiatric Quarterly*, published an article in his journal condemning Szasz.[5] This was the begin-

---

[4] Leifer, "The Psychiatric Repression of Thomas Szasz: Its Implications for Modern Society," *Review of Existential Psychology and Psychiatry* XXIII, Nos. 1, 2, 3 (1997). At the time, Szasz gave Chomentowski the fictitious name "Louis Perroni" to protect his privacy, but his real name has subsequently been made public.

[5] N. Bigelow, "Szasz for the Gander," *Psychiatric Quarterly 36*, No. 4 (1962), pp. 754–767.

ning of what Szasz's admirers perceive as a concerted campaign by institutional psychiatry to silence Szasz, discredit him, and deprive him of his livelihood.

Dr. Hoch wrote a letter to Marc Hollender—who, in addition to being Chairman of the Department of Psychiatry was also Director of the Syracuse Psychiatric Hospital, a state mental hospital—ordering that Szasz be banned from teaching in the state hospital. Szasz was thereby punished for denying the existence of mental illness. Hoch cited *The Myth of Mental Illness* and Szasz's disbelief in "mental illness" as evidence of his incompetence as a psychiatrist and his unfitness to teach psychiatry. (It was never disputed that all that was wrong with Szasz was his dissenting beliefs and his readiness to propagate them.) Szasz responded that if he could not teach in the hospital, he would no longer attend faculty meetings in the hospital. Thus, Szasz rejected the punishment imposed by Hoch and Hollender and filed a complaint with the university authorities.

The Syracuse Psychiatric Hospital, then located adjacent to the Medical Center, was a state mental hospital, a part of the New York State Department of Mental Hygiene. (The hospital, located elsewhere in the city, is now called Hutchings Psychiatric Center.) The Department of Psychiatry of the Upstate Medical Center (now Upstate Medical University), was a part of the State University of New York. When Hollender and Szasz had come to Syracuse, in 1956, Hollender had assumed two positions: one, as professor and chairman of Psychiatry at the medical school, and another, as director of the state mental hospital; and, because of superior physical facilities, he located his office and all official functions of the department at the state hospital. Szasz, was appointed professor of psychiatry in the medical school. His office was located in a small building housing the department of psychiatry staff. Hollender not only located his office at the Syracuse Psychiatric Hospital, he also moved all psychiatry department faculty meetings and conferences to the site of the state mental hospital.

Szasz and Hollender had known each other in Chicago, were close friends, and saw eye to eye on many issues. They had co-authored several articles. Hollender had voiced the opinion, for example, that there should be no involuntary commitment of the mentally ill.

Hollender loyally carried out Hoch's wishes, communicating to Szasz that he was banned from teaching in the hospital. Szasz's workload and supervision were increased and his secretarial staff reduced, in a concerted effort to make his professional life difficult. Many psychiatry residents and colleagues were outraged at Szasz's being "censured" and complained to the university administration. The medical school administration as well as the American Association of University Professors (AAUP) investigated the conflict and both found that Hollender's actions violated Szasz's academic freedom.

As the matter dragged on acrimoniously, month after month and year after year, Szasz became concerned that his position was being eroded, and retained George J. Alexander, a law professor at Syracuse University College of Law (now, Professor of Law, Santa Clara University School of Law, Santa Clara University), to defend him against further defamation [6] and possible removal. In the end, Hollender was asked to step down as chairman. He and Szasz retained their positions as professors of psychiatry. However, none of the non-tenured faculty members who supported Szasz had their appointments renewed, while those who opposed Szasz or remained uncommitted kept their jobs.[7] Hollender left the Upstate Medical Center in 1966,[8] while Szasz remained there, becoming emeritus in 1990, and is now highly respected by the present faculty.

Among the many individuals involved in or influenced by the events at Upstate, it's worth mentioning Ron Leifer, later a psychiatrist in private practice and author of *In the Name of Mental Health* and other works; Robert Seidenberg, a distinguished psychoanalyst who has argued against the labeling of any behavior, including homosexuality, as a disease; Peter Breggin, outspoken critic of psychiatry and opponent of the forced drugging of children; Abraham Halpern, a leading expert on psychiatry and law, who at the time pressed for Szasz to be thrown out of Upstate but who now characterizes his own outlook as much more in agreement with Szasz; Julius B. Richmond, Dean of the Medical School in the 1960s, and first Director of Headstart; Frederick K. Goodwin, who was to become Director of the National Institute of Mental Health; and E. Fuller Torrey, author of several notable books on psychiatric topics.

---

[6] Among actively disseminated mendacities was the association of Szasz with the John Birch Society. Szasz had no connection with this organization, which had however reprinted something he had written. See the last item in the Appendix below.

[7] For detailed documentation of these events, see the papers in the Thomas Szasz Collection in the Special Collections at Syracuse University Library, Syracuse, New York. For a few selected documents, see the Appendix below.

[8] Hollender was Professor of Psychiatry at the University of Pennsylvania, 1966–69, then Professor and Chairman of the Department of Psychiatry at Vanderbilt University School of Medicine, 1970–78. He was President of the American College of Psychiatrists fom 1977 to 1978 and President of the American Board of Psychiatry and Neurology in 1980. He died in 1998 at the age of 81.

Paul Hoch had led the attempt to destroy Szasz's career and reputation. Shortly afterwards, in 1964, Hoch died suddenly of a heart attack at his home in Albany, aged 62. He had originally been appointed Commissioner of the State of New York Department of Mental Hygiene by Governor Averell Harriman, and was subsequently re-appointed as Commissioner by his (Hoch's) "warm friend and admirer," Governor Nelson A. Rockefeller.

Depending on one's point of view, it may be significant, interesting, merely ironic, or of no relevance whatsoever, that it came to light that Hoch had been deeply involved in lucrative Central Intelligence Agency experiments using psychoactive drugs on unsuspecting subjects. Among the many illegal activities, for example, as reported by John D. Marks, Hoch along with Dr. James Cattell poisoned and killed New York tennis professional Harold Blauer. In the words of the illustrious Dr. Cattell, "We didn't know whether it was dog piss or what it was we were giving him." [9]

Hoch is remembered warmly by mainstream psychiatry. A 1996 tribute to him characterizes him as

> one of the most respected and honored psychiatrists of his generation. A bronze plaque prominently displayed in the lobby of the New York Psychiatric Institute with a bust of Hoch is inscribed as follows: "Compassionate physician, inspiring teacher, original researcher, dedicated scientist, dynamic administrator." Then, as now, over three decades later, it distils the essence of the man. [10]

---

[9] John D. Marks, *The Search for the Manchurian Candidate: The CIA and Mind Control* (New York: Times Books, 1979), p. 67. For other background on Hoch, the CIA illegal activities, and Hoch's involvement in them, see Nolan C. Lewis and Margaret O. Strahl, eds., *The Complete Psychiatrist: The Achievements of Paul H. Hoch* (Albany: State University of New York Press, 1968); Joseph B. Treaster, "Mind-Drug Tests a Federal Project for Almost 25 Years" (*New York Times*, 11th August, 1972, pp. 1, 13); *Commission on C.I.A. Activities: Report to the President* (Washington, DC: Government Printing Office, 6th June, 1975); Boyce Rensberger, "C.I.A. in the Early Nineteen-Fifties Was Among Pioneers in Research on LSD's Effects" (*New York Times*, 12th July, 1975, p. 11); Joseph B. Treaster, "Army Discloses Man Died in Drug Test It Sponsored" (*New York Times*, 13th August, 1975, pp. 1, 13); Thomas Szasz, "Patriotic Poisoners," *Humanist* (December 1976, pp. 5–7); Philip Shenon, "C.I.A. Near Settlement of Lawsuit by Subjects of Mind-Control Tests" (*New York Times*, 6th October, 1988, p. A14); Anon., "U.S. to Pay $750,000 in Suit on LSD Testing" (*New York Times*, 12th October, 1988, p. 12); Leonard S. Rubenstein, "The C.I.A. and the Evil Doctor" (*New York Times*, 7th November, 1988, p. 12); Leonard S. Rubenstein, "The C.I.A. and the Evil Doctor" (*New York Times*, 7th November, 1988, p. A19); Albert C. Higgins, "On Psychiatry's Paul Hoch" (www.albany.edu/~ach13/soc325/notes/notes7.html).

[10] Sidney Malitz, *American Journal of Psychiatry* 153: 10 (October 1996), p. 1339.

A Polarizing Figure

Szasz Under Fire is the first in a series of Open Court books which will confront controversial writers with their intellectual critics. Szasz is particularly suited to this project because of his unusually polarizing influence. Szasz's writings have provoked both extraordinary praise and extraordinary denunciation. Critics have been invited based both on their knowledgeability and their strong disagreement with Szasz, at least on the specific topics of their articles.

Szasz has been the target of both scathing criticism and fulsome praise. His ideas have inspired both warm adherence and bitter opposition. There have also been some notable changes of mind, in both directions. Karl Menninger's life and work seemed to be a denial of everything that Szasz stands for,[11] yet Menninger eventually ended up a convert to Szasz's general position. E. Fuller Torrey became known as an enthusiastic proponent of Szaszian ideas, most notably in his book, *The Death of Psychiatry*, published in 1974. Torrey subsequently changed his mind and is now one of Szasz's harshest critics. He has become a hero of the National Alliance for the Mentally Ill, a powerful political lobby funded by the pharmaceutical industry. The cases of Menninger and Torrey are discussed by Szasz below, in his Reply to Slovenko.

As a final contrast I will cite a couple of recent occurrences. When I began the work of organizing and compiling this book, I sent letters to various individuals I thought would be interested in writing essays for it. I sought contributors who would definitely have a strong disagreement with Szasz on at least one issue (though they might agree with him on other issues), and who would mount a strong case against Szasz from a reasoned and knowledgeable perspective.

One of the people I believed would fall into this category was Thomas G. Gutheil, M.D., a Professor of Psychiatry at Harvard and a recognized expert on psychiatry and law. I sent him an invitation on September 6th, 2000. He promptly declined, and that, I assumed was the end of the matter. I proceeded to solicit other promising candidates. I invited Dr. Harold Bursztajn, who also declined. However, he volunteered that he would ask around for other possible contributors, something I had not asked him to do.

On April 18th, 2001, I received the following letter out of the clear blue sky from Dr. Gutheil. The spelling and other mistakes are all in the original.

---

[11] See for instance, Menninger, *The Crime of Punishment* (New York: Viking, 1968).

HARVARD MEDICAL SCHOOL
DEPARTMENT OF PSYCHIATRY
MASSACHUSETTS MENTAL HEALTH CENTER
74 FENWOOD ROAD
BOSTON, MASSACHUSETTS 02115
TELEPHONE: 617-734-1300 EXT. 476
THOMAS G. GUTHEIL, M.D.
PROFESSOR OF PSYCHIATRY
DIRECTOR OF MEDICAL STUDENT TRAINING
CO-DIRECTOR, PROGRAM IN PSYCHIATRY AND THE LAW

April 18, 2001
Jeffery A Shaler, Ph.D.
School of Public Affairs
American University
4400 Massachusetts Ave. NW
Washington DC 20016

Dear Dr. Shaler:

Dr. Harold Bursztajn passed on to me the invitation to write for
Szasz under fire and I in turn have tried to interest others in this, alas,
without success. The reasons given are listed below, which may or
may not be helpful to you.

Most of Szasz's ideas of the mythical nature of mental illness have
been rendered obsolete by genetic studies, imaging, cross-cultural
anthropology and the like. While many legal scholars see him as
important to that field, the damage he has done to care of the mentally
ill has not been carefully assessed and cannot be overestimated.
Well-meaning but misguided advocates following his leads have
trashed mental health delivery systems in state after state and have
clearly contributed to the adversarialization of the mental health
advocacy systems. More clearly venal forces from Ronald Reagan
to Scientology have been able to draw on his "teachings" to support
their causes, again to the detriment of patients.

My own view is that he was popular as a sixties kind of guy, an anti-
establishment rebel where the facts he distorted were not a problem for

the political force of his claims; any smidgin of value he could have had is long eclipsed, and, except as a trip down memory lane, I can see no reason whatsoever why he deserves a book like this, even a mixed one with opposing views. Dr. Szasz is simply no longer worth it.

I regret that neither I nor Dr Bursztajn was able to help, nor were our recruiting attempts successful to get any one else to care enough to do it.

Regretfully,
(signed)
Thomas G. Gutheil, MD.

Readers can study the intelligent and knowledgeable criticisms of Szasz in the present volume, followed by Szasz's replies, and make up their own minds as to whether Dr. Gutheil's opinion is right or wrong.

By way of contrast, on May 20th, 2001, Robert L. King, Chancellor of the State University of New York, bestowed upon Thomas S. Szasz the degree of Honorary Doctor of Science (http://www.szasz.com/upstatedegreeremarks.htm). The citation read as follows:

State University of New York

Thomas S. Szasz, M.D.

You have raised the level of academic, scientific and societal discourse by putting forth views that have challenged the premises and assumptions of all the various health care professions. Indeed, the vigorous debate you began and still oversee has helped shape society's views on an individual's liberty and responsibility. Your thirty-four years on the faculty of the College of Medicine at the State University of New York Upstate Medical University were extraordinarily productive. During those years you became known as one of the world's best known and widely read mental health professionals. Your twenty-five books and approximately seven hundred scientific papers have profoundly shaped the theory and practice of psychiatry and psychology. Titles such as "The Myth of Mental Illness," "Law, Liberty and Psychiatry,"

"Psychiatric Justice," "The Meaning of the Mind" and "The Ethics and Politics of Suicide," have stood the test of time and are noted as among the influential works of their kind over the past half-century. Strong ideas can be best embraced and debated within a strong institution. The SUNY Upstate Medical University has been proud to stand with you and provide a forum for your ideas. The State University of New York and your colleagues at the SUNY Upstate Medical University salute you and confer upon you the Honorary Degree, Doctor of Science.

Upstate Medical University
May 20, 2001

An Autobiographical Sketch

THOMAS SZASZ

Homo sum: nil a me alienum puto. (I am a man: nothing human is alien to me.)

— TERENCE

Nil sine magno vita labore dedit mortalibus. (Life grants nothing to us mortals without hard work.)

— HORACE

I was born in Budapest, Hungary, on April 15th, 1920, the second son of Lily (Livia) Wellisch and Julius (Gyula) Szász. My name in Hungarian, a language in which the family name comes first, followed by given names, was Szász Tamás István. Tamás was a popular name in Hungary in those days. I always felt very pleased with it. My family and friends called me "Tomi," the diminutive of Tamás, similar to the English "Tom." My third (in English, middle) name, István (Stephen), has deep roots in Hungarian history.

St. Stephen (975–1038) Christianized the Magyars and, in A.D. 1000, with the blessing of the Pope, founded Hungary as a Catholic Kingdom. One of the most important Hungarian national holidays is August 20th, celebrated with fireworks over the Danube, much as July 4th is in the United States. The date commemorates the transfer of St. Stephen's supposedly incorruptible, miraculously preserved right hand—the most sacred Christian relic in Hungary—from the village where it was buried to Buda.

Buda is on the right, western side of the Danube, and is very hilly. It may be of interest to mention here that, in the first century A.D. most of the area that is now Hungary became a part of the Roman empire. A few miles north of Buda stood the Roman settlement of *Aquincum,* so named on account of the many artesian wells in the area. At one time *Aquincum*

1

was home to thirty thousand people; numerous ruins of it remain and are one of the tourist attractions of Budapest. For centuries, Buda and Pest were separate cities, divided by the Danube, the largest river west of the Volga. Buda and Pest were united into a single city, Budapest, only in 1873.

II

My brother, who has played an exceptionally important role in my life, was born on January 11th, 1918. He was named Szász György János (George John), and was called "Gyuri," the Hungarian diminutive of George.

My mother, Lily—like other upper-middle-class married women—was a housewife. This did not mean that she had the duties we now associate with that word. All housewifely duties were then delegated to domestics. My brother and I were raised first by a nurse and, from the time I was a year old, by a governess. Other housework was done by a cook and maids, and by help hired for special occasions. We lived in a large apartment, in downtown Budapest, only a block or so from the Danube river. My mother's duty was to manage the domestic help, entertain, and generally support her husband as breadwinner and head of the family.

I loved my mother dearly and was, all my life, very attached to her, and she to me. She was an exceptionally beautiful woman who remained handsome even in her old age. She enjoyed good health and died, in 1990, at the age of ninety-six. (Her younger sister lived to be 101.) She was a quiet and soft-spoken person, gracious and sociable. There was always an air of elegance about her. She lay great importance on being well groomed and well dressed, as did my father also. I "inherited" these traits.

My father, trained as a lawyer, was a successful agricultural businessman. This description fails to convey to the contemporary American reader what his work actually consisted of. However, a precise account and understanding of his occupation would require familiarity with economic and social conditions in Hungary following World War I. He was a squat, compactly built man. My mother was a little taller than he. He was an exceptionally honest man, with a reputation for fairness and integrity. Occasionally, he served as an arbitrator for businessmen who wanted to settle their conflicting claims out of court and save the time and expenses of litigation.

My parents' marriage was extremely harmonious—idyllic would hardly be an exaggeration. This impression has only gained weight in retrospect, when I compare that relationship with the majority of modern marriages. My father adored my mother. My mother looked up to my father and, when speaking about him, would always say there has never been a better husband in the world. I do not recall a raised voice, much less a quarrel, between them. Credit for the harmoniousness of their relationship belongs largely to my parents, and partly to the traditional character of the marriage relationship, a clear role allocated to husband and wife.

My father was comfortable in the role of *pater familias*: he felt responsible for his family's welfare and provided generously for everyone's needs. He was a dependable person, a man of his word. Our governess, Kisu—about whom more in a moment—idolized him. She thought he was the most wonderful man in the world. He was, indeed, a *very good man*. Under a veneer of conventionality and sternness, there beat a heart of gold and lurked a skeptical mind. He was well-informed, especially about economic and political matters. At the same time, he was a modest and very private person. Besides business, his main interest was his family. Both he and my mother were atheists. We celebrated Christmas.

Until I was about ten years old, the most important person in my life was "Kisu," the governess. The word "kisu"—which might have been a name made up by my family—was a contraction of the Hungarian "kisasszony," literally "little woman", meaning an unmarried woman. In most upper-middle class homes, the governess had a double role: she took care of the children and ensured that they would become bilingual, Hungarian being a useless language outside of Hungary. Most often, her native language was German or French; in a few families, the governess was English-speaking.

Kisu—whose name was Prém Jolán (Yolande)—spoke only Hungarian. She came from a family of German descent and was a Lutheran. She went to church on Sundays and observed the major Christian holidays but was not, certainly by the Hungarian standards of the time, very religious. Born in Budapest, she lost both parents and her brother to tuberculosis when she was still young, was uneducated, and accepted the role of governess as her occupation as if it were the natural order of things.

In the highly stratified social order that still prevailed in Hungary between the wars, there was a fair measure of dignity in the status of a governess. She was entrusted with the everyday care of the child, had virtually complete control over disciplining him, and was formally treated as a part of the family. When we were little, George and I would have our meals with Kisu. The family table was for adults and older children. When I was seven—perhaps a bit younger—we joined the adult world of meals. Kisu's status was then symbolized by her having the noon and evening meals at the family table, eating food prepared by a cook and served by a maid. She was not expected to do any cleaning or other housework. Her only duty was to care for and be the child's protector and companion, and often the teacher, by conversation, of a second language.

Kisu's whole life was taking care of and loving George and me. Literally, she had no one else in the world. Once in a while, on her day off, she met a distant "cousin" in a coffee house. She loved me dearly and I loved her in return—more and differently than I loved my parents.

I was a "sickly" child. I contracted every contagious disease of childhood, from chicken pox and whooping cough to measles, scarlet fever, and diphtheria. I was probably about seven when I had diphtheria and well remember a period when I was breathing with difficulty, followed by a dramatic development: if I drank a glass of water, the liquid ran out of my nose. My fifth cranial nerve was paralyzed. I did not then realize how close to death I came.

My illnesses taught me some valuable lessons. One was a clear realization of the advantages of being ill: I enjoyed the languorous passivity of lying in bed and dozing, the anxious concern of my parents and governess, the visits of the kindly pediatrician, the choice of whatever food I wanted, and, during recovery, the opportunity to occupy myself with drawing, coloring, assembling puzzles, and, last but not least, learning to sew—from Kisu—and becoming quite skillful with needle and thread. Missing school was an added benefit. I intensely disliked going to elementary school, especially during the first two years. I preferred staying at home. I knew what "secondary gain" was decades before I heard the term.

The second valuable lesson was that I learned to malinger. As I mentioned, I disliked being away from home, being separated from Kisu. So I had a powerful motive to malinger. If Kisu and my parents thought I was ill, I didn't have to go to school. I learned not only how to lie about feeling ill, but how to cough, how to vomit, and how to have a fever, by surreptitiously placing the thermometer close to a lighted light bulb. I was well aware of the difference between being ill and occupying the sick role decades before encountering these terms.

It was some time during these early years that the pediatrician—considered the best in Budapest—who took care of George and me informed my parents that I had "heart trouble." This, as I was able to reconstruct later, was both a correct and an incorrect diagnosis. I had a pronounced systolic murmur. In elementary school, I was exempted from gym. When I entered the Gymnasium,[1] I rebelled against this restriction, based on an "illness" which, as far as I could see, had no observable basis in fact.

This semi-real, semi-fictitious heart disease played a significant role at various points in my life. It was something of a medical curiosity during my internship in Boston, when the top cardiologists concluded it was due to a small interventricular defect (hole between the left and right ventricles) and wanted to prove it by the then primitive and dangerous methods of angiography. It was not easy to reject their "help." This diagnosis seemed to me most unlikely to be correct: I was twenty-four years old and my heart was not enlarged. In any case, confirming the diagnosis would not have done me any good. In my seventies—when my heart was still not enlarged, indicating that there was no significant leakage—echocardiography established the exact nature of the pathology responsible for the murmur: it is due to a thickening of the aortic valve.

For a while George too was exempted from gym, because the pediatrician declared him to be too thin and advised that he not engage in strenuous sports. We both soon rebelled against these restrictions. We had a ping-pong table in our spacious apartment. George and I spent untold hours in fiercely competitive combat and both of us became very good players. In our teens, we also played tennis, soccer, and in the winter went ice skating and skied in the mountains in Buda. I would also go on long walks all over Budapest, with Kisu when I was younger, and, later, with my mother. One of my happiest memories from my teens is the almost daily stroll with my mother—from home, near the *Erzsébet hid* (Elizabeth bridge), north on the *Korzó* on the Pest side of the Danube, across the *Lánchid* (Chain bridge), then south on the Buda side, returning either by way of the Elizabeth bridge or, if we wanted to make our stroll longer, by way of the *Ferenc József hid* (Franz Joseph bridge, now *Szabadság hid* [Freedom bridge]). I have repeated this walk every time I returned to Budapest, first in 1979, and three or four times since then.

As I grew older and was approaching the age of ten—which was the beginning of serious education—I spent more time with my parents and became much closer to them. My mother and I often went for long

---

[1] EDITOR'S NOTE: In central Europe, a secondary school or high school is called a *Gymnasium*.

strolls and our relationship became more intimate. My father loved to go hunting on the farms he owned and managed—mainly for rabbits, partridges, and pheasants—and I was eager to join him on these outings. When I was eleven or twelve he bought me a .22 caliber rifle. I often accompanied him on his hunting trips and became a good shot. My father had a beautiful, hand-crafted, Belgian double-barreled shotgun. I fired it a few times, but its kick was far too powerful for me to handle. I also enjoyed target shooting with my cousin Bandi's Colt revolver.

III

Some brief comments about the Hungarian educational system in the 1920s and 1930s are in order here. Education was compulsory only to age twelve. Children whose parents expected them to become laborers or farmers or what we would call "blue-collar" workers would attend elementary school for six years, from six to twelve, when their formal schooling ended. In contrast, children whose parents expected them to become "educated persons"—bankers, doctors, engineers, whatever— began their serious education at age ten.

Parents and children had a choice among several types of secondary schools, some oriented toward business and commerce, others toward engineering, and still others—the so-called "classical *Gimnázium*" (Gymnasium)—oriented toward providing the most broadly based education, giving the young person, graduating at eighteen, the option to continue with any university study he chose.

My father, the youngest of three children, and his brother, Ottó, both attended classical Gymnasiums. My father then studied law and received a degree of doctor juris. My uncle studied mathematics, received a doctor of philosophy degree, and became an internationally known mathematician.

I had nothing to do with the decision about which Gymnasium to attend. By the time I was ten, I had long looked up to George as a model whose example I should follow. George was a real *Wunderkind,* very smart and quick-witted, and an omnivorous reader from an early age. He was incredibly well informed when he was a child, and he is still incredibly well informed, on a wide range of subjects, at the age of eighty-six. For example, in his early teens, he would send long letters to our parents when they were away on vacation, expressing his views about the changing political climate in Europe and Mussolini's role in it. He also did something that was unusual in the rigid, Hungarian educational system: he entered the Gymnasium a year early, when he was nine. As a result, although I was only two years younger, I was three years behind him in school.

Although George and I were extremely competitive, he was always exceptionally good to me. He was precocious, while I was plodding. However, he never looked down on me and always treated me as an equal, which I was in ping-pong and tennis, but not in other ways. He encouraged me to read, helped with my homework, and was then—and has been ever since—unfailingly supportive of my aspirations and work. I owe him—as well as Kisu and my parents —a very great deal.

Hungarian secondary schools were sex-segregated. Hungary was a Catholic country. Most secondary schools were "parochial" schools, that is, run by the major religious organizations. Some of the best schools were Catholic. The Lutheran and Jewish Gymnasiums and the Minta, a state school, were also among the top-ranking Gymnasiums. Admission to the Gymnasiums was open. The student did not have to belong to the religion represented by the school. Any child deemed capable—by parents and elementary school teachers—could enroll.

The open enrollment policy—characteristic also of admission to university, provided the applicant completed the requisite preparatory schooling—did not mean that the student could stay in the school. It was easy to flunk out on account of failure to perform academically or because of misbehavior. I should add that, regardless of which type of school the student attended, instruction in religion was compulsory: the students were split into three groups, Catholics, Protestants, and Jews, instructed in their respective faiths by priest, minister, and rabbi.

In an important sense, religion was compulsory for adults too. Every official document—from birth certificate and passport to the most trivial—required listing the person's religion. The subject had to choose one of the officially recognized religions; choosing "no religion" or "atheist" was not an option. My family was nominally Jewish. I attended classes conducted by a rabbi, an experience that only intensified my aversion to religion, which seemed to consist of conceited beliefs, senseless rituals, and terrifying threats. Only as an adult did I begin to understand religions as important cultural-symbolic manifestations of human nature, and appreciate that most people value dependence on authority and the illusory security it provides more highly than they value independence and having the courage to face the uncertainties of the human condition, unaided by gods and their deputies.

The official name of the Minta—its real name was long and meant something like the Royal Hungarian Training Institute—was one of a handful of schools in the country that educated not only its students, but also teachers who aspired to excellence and better employment opportunities. Many of the teachers were scholars. Some, after many years of service, rose to become faculty members at the University of Budapest.

George went to the Minta, so I went to the Minta. The school was about a fifteen to twenty minute brisk walk from our house. This was considered a short distance. Walking was considered the normal mode of transportation. Or, for boys and young men, standing on the steps of streetcars and jumping off when the ticket-collector approached. This was not a matter of saving money. It was a matter of honor, a sport, a kind of initiation ceremony into the adult male world.

The school consisted of eight grades. Classes were small, from about twenty-five to thirty-five students for each grade, for a total student body of well under 250. The director of the school was an imposing figure—stocky, bordering on being obese. He always wore a dark suit and a white shirt with a stiff, high collar that made the flesh of his neck bulge. There was a threatening air about him. Regardless of the weather, he stood, with a stern visage and pocket watch in hand, at the front door of the school building ten or fifteen minutes before eight o'clock, watching the students arrive and greeting them. A student who was late, even by a few seconds—indeed, even if he made it by eight o'clock, but had to do so by running down the block—was severely reprimanded. If the offense was repeated, the student's parent was summoned for an interview and warned about the dire consequences of breaking the rules of conduct, which he enforced with fanatical zeal and absolute fairness.

At the end of the eighth grade, the student had to take a difficult comprehensive examination, the *matura*. If he passed, he was qualified to enroll in any university, engineering school, or other higher level institution.

School began at 8:00 A.M. and ended at 1:00 P.M. six days a week. The main meal of the day was around 2:00 P.M. With one exception, that I will mention presently, the student had no choice about what courses to take. The prescribed curriculum included Hungarian language and literature, Latin, and mathematics, one hour, six times a week. History, geography, German, art, and gym, and physics made up the rest of curriculum. At the end of the fourth grade, the student had a choice between taking Greek or French. I chose French.

I found school work demanding and was, especially the first few years, a plodding student. The expectation to excel was thick in the air, in the family as well in the school. The first year, I had a mixture of A's and B's. (A to C was passing, D was near-failure, F was failure.) After that, I had straight A's. However, I had to work very hard to maintain this level of achievement and received a great deal of help, both with schoolwork and homework from George, and also from my cousin Bandi, who lived with us for many years.

I learned many important lessons in the *Minta Gimnázium*. One was summed up very succinctly in the saying, "Megszöks vagy megszoksz." "Grammatically, the phrase is descriptive; loosely translated, it means: "Get used to it or get out." The actual impact of the phrase is injunctive, a warning or threat: "Perform as expected or flee (before you are expelled)."

Initially, this threat was a source of anxiety. But I quickly adapted to it. I learned that behaving properly—being polite, doing what is expected—is a good thing, and that it is enough to pretend to conform; my private life—what I thought—remained my own, of no concern to the school authorities. Sadly, in this great country, the United States, these principles are inverted: students are allowed to behave incredibly badly, but their private lives are invaded by professional soul-murderers, poisoning their bodies with drugs and their minds with deceptions. In Budapest in the 1930s, most students behaved properly and did their school work as expected, and the teachers did not care if some of the youngsters were depressed, failed, or committed suicide, which was by no means rare, especially before and after the *matura* examination. We managed very well without grief counselors.

By the time I reached my early teens, I had formed a passionately held career choice, or, more precisely, choice for higher education: I wanted to go to medical school. There were no physicians in my family. In Hungary in the 1930s, becoming a physician was not economically rewarding, nor did the career of a practicing physician have the prestige of a university professor or a successful businessman. My father strongly opposed my desire to pursue medical studies.

Perhaps because I had many childhood illnesses—or, more likely, for other reasons—it seemed to me imperative that I become knowledgeable about my most important possession, my body. It seemed to me astonishing, and it still seems to me astonishing, that intelligent, educated people can go through life without having the faintest understanding of how the machine they inhabit works. It was like driving a car and not knowing what's under the hood. This curiosity, which is pervasive, has characterized my life ever since. I wanted to go to medical school not because I wanted to practice medicine but because I wanted to know medicine.

If, for some reason, I could not go to medical school, my second choice was to become a writer. As the years passed after 1933, the career of a writer became highly impracticable, as it seemed increasingly unlikely that I would spend many more years of my life in Hungary.

George finished the Gymnasium in 1935 and entered the University of Budapest to study chemistry. Politically sophisticated, he had one foot out of Hungary as Hitler rose to power in Germany. He had spent several summers in England studying English and became a passionate Anglophile. After the *Anschluss*, in March 1938—I was to graduate in June of that year—neither George nor I planned to remain in Hungary. George was planning to settle in England. I was planning to go to medical school in France. I spoke German and French fluently.

On March 12th, Hitler—who was Austrian, not German—marched into his homeland, not as a conqueror but as an adored Leader. Vienna is only about 150 miles from Budapest. The sirens had been sounded. Momentous decisions followed in quick succession.

IV

My uncle, Otto, had been a distinguished professor of mathematics in Frankfurt. Within months of Hitler's accession to power, he was, as the new Nazi law required, fired: He was a foreigner and a Jew, although he had converted to Catholicism as a young adult—when he and my father changed their names from Schlesinger to Szász—and hence was so identified in his passport. My father did not take this step, partly because he was too averse to all religions, and partly because he correctly assumed that conversion was no protection against virulent anti-Semitism.

Otto's having to leave Germany so soon proved to be very fortunate for him and my whole family. He quickly received invitations to teach from some of the most prestigious American universities and, by the fall of 1933, he was teaching at MIT. After spending some time as a professor at Brown University, he settled in Cincinnati. As a research professor of mathematics at the University of Cincinnati, he had virtually no teaching duties, except for supervising a few Ph.D. students. He could spend most of his waking hours devising mathematical problems and trying to solve them, which was his life's work.

My father and Otto were very close. Every spring, Otto would leave America as soon as the academic year ended and stay in Europe, mostly in Budapest, until school started again in September. His emigration to and settling in the United States was a palpable reminder of a course of action to seriously consider. However, the immigration quota for Hungarians was minuscule. In 1938, the quota was, for all practical purposes, filled: the waiting list for a visa was measured in decades. So how did I and my family manage to gain entry to this promised land?

The quota system allocated a certain number of immigration visas per year to persons from each European country. The system was not based on the individual's nationality or place of residence, at the time of his application for a visa. It was based on the country of his birth, as that country was politically defined after 1920. Both Otto and my father were born, in the late 1800s, in northern Hungary, that is, what was then a part of the Austro-Hungarian empire. After the Treaties of Versailles and Trianon in 1920—which dismantled the empire and under which Hungary lost two-thirds of its territory—the northern and northeastern parts of what had been Hungary were incorporated into the newly created state, Czechoslovakia. That meant, as Otto discovered in 1933, that, from the point of view of American immigration law, my father was a Czechoslovakian. The Czechoslovakian quota was larger than the Hungarian and was not filled in 1938. My father could thus come to the United States and, once on American soil as a legal immigrant, his wife and minor children could jump the queue and receive a so-called "preference visa."

There was no time to waste. The political situation was deteriorating rapidly. The outbreak of World War II was predictable. Only the exact moment of when this would occur was in doubt. Moreover, on January 11th, 1939, George would reach the age of twenty-one, and would no longer qualify for a special visa.

In July 1938, George was in Paris, staying with my mother's French cousin, "Uncle" Louis (Wellisch), a wealthy stockbroker. (One of my grandfather's brothers had emigrated to France as a young man, in the late 1800s.)

I was in Grenoble investigating the possibility of going to medical school there in the fall. It was there that I received a letter from my father informing me that he and George were going to America, and leaving to me the decision whether to go ahead with my French plans or go with them to the United States. The decision was difficult in principle, but easy in practice. It was difficult because throughout my teens I had been steeped in French literature, poetry, history—the whole nine yards of French *gloire*. I didn't know a word of English. My knowledge about the United States was slight. I was familiar with the history of the First World War and learned that

America was an economic and military colossus that no European power could have hoped to best. I read the works of Mark Twain and learned the usual tales about America as the land of movies, money, and the mistreatment of blacks, with the history of slavery and the Civil War as background.

Those negatives were overwhelmed by the advantages of going to America. In France, I would have been not only alone, but exposed to the dangers of Naziism looming from across the border. In the United States, I would be with George and, probably my parents, who were then still somewhat undecided about the move. And I would be safe from the turmoil of Europe. I immediately returned to Budapest to make preparations for leaving the country for good. I spent my last six or seven weeks in Budapest learning a few words of English—and, with time on my hand and because in America everyone knew how to drive a car—learning how to drive. Since I wanted to know what is under the hood of a car, as well, I also worked, as an unpaid apprentice in a garage. I enjoyed every minute of it. When I arrived in the United States, I didn't speak English, but I alone in my family knew how to drive.

There were many harrowing moments between August, when my father and I joined George in Paris, and October, when George and I left for New York. We spent our last six weeks on the Continent in Rotterdam, to escape a possible German invasion of France, which seemed imminent. We had to wait until my father landed in New York, completed the necessary paper work for an application of so-called "preference visas" for George and me, and until the permission to issue us the visas was received by the American consulate in Amsterdam. The intense, widespread Nazi sympathies of the Dutch were palpable and unforgettable.

At the beginning of October, our visas arrived and, October 14th, George and I boarded the Veendam, a small—11,000-ton—Holland-America liner headed for New York. On October 25th—after a stormy 11-day passage—our ship docked in Hoboken, New Jersey. I have come to view that date as a kind of second birthday.

The realization that I had lost my homeland and my mother tongue, both of which I loved dearly, weighed on me heavily. Abstractly, I should have been happy. In fact, I felt miserable. George, who spoke English, was in better spirits. Only after my family was reunited and I learned English far more quickly than I would have imagined possible, did I begin to appreciate that by losing Hungary—and coming to America—I gained the whole world.

As I look back at these events, I am struck by the realization that the year of my my birth, 1920, and the year of my emigration, 1938, bracket some of the most momentous events in modern history. The Versailles treaty, in 1920, marked the formal end of World War I. The *Anschluss* and the Munich pact, in 1938, marked the beginning of the palpable prelude to World War II.

V

In April 1939, my mother and father arrived in the United States and my family was whole again. Many members of the extended family were in America as well. Magda—my mother's beloved younger sister, our "favorite aunt"—and her family left Germany in 1938. My father's older brother, Otto (who had been divorced), was a distinguished professor of mathematics at the University of Cincinnati. His daughter Brigitta joined him in 1939.

Two important members of the family, and Kisu, stayed behind. One was my maternal grandfather, with Kisu caring for him. The other was my cousin (my father's sister's son) Bandi—nickname for Andrew—who was eleven years my senior and was, in many ways, a second older brother to me. About a year later, my grandfather fell, broke his hip, and died of a fat embolus. My mother was uncertain of precisely how old he was. To me he always appeared to be a very old man. He was probably in his middle or late eighties when he died.

Bandi spent some harrowing years in Hungary until he escaped in 1956, came to the United States, studied library science, and settled in the San Franciso Bay area. He had a good job at a small college where he was beloved, enjoyed his life in America, and—despite the fact that he had been a heavy smoker all of his life—lived to be eighty-seven. I traveled to the west coast frequenly and we spent many happy days together.

Otto's presence in Cincinnati greatly facilitated George and me continuing our interrupted education. George, enrolled as a graduate student in chemistry, received a Master's degree in organic chemistry, and after a short stint of teaching at a small college, received a job as a graduate teaching assistant at Pennsylvania State College and earned a Ph.D. in physical chemistry.

To gain some mastery of English, for several month I audited—that is, sat in on—classes, mainly English and physics. I well remember riding on streetcars in Cincinnati months after my arrival and not being able to understand what people were saying to one another. It was not a pleasant experience.

I matriculated as a college student at the University of Cincinnati in February, 1939. My English was still rudimentary. Although my burning ambition was to go to medical school, the prospect of doing so was dim. Discrimination against Jews—not to mention blacks and women—was then perhaps even more intense here than it had been in Hungary. Most schools admitted only a handful of Jews, who were not only good students but had "pull"—thanks to fathers who were alumni, donors, or prominent physicians or businessmen.

With my prospects for going to medical school dim or hopeless, and with my family's economic situation going from wealthy to strained, I had to prepare myself for a career other than medicine. I was keenly interested in physics, had an excellent background in it from the Minta, and was patient, careful, and good with my hands in the laboratory. The university granted me two year's of college credits for my work in the Gymnasium—for German, French, Latin, and mathematics—and I started to take courses satisfying the requirements for a bachelor's degree in physics, as well as so-called pre-med courses required for admission to medical school. I graduated with a bachelor's degree with honors in physics in May 1941.

Besides learning English and the subjects taught in the courses I took, I was also learning about America. One of my memorable learning experiences was the following. I became superficially friendly with one of my fellow students. One spring day I suggested we go to lunch together in the cafeteria. He gently explained that that was not possible: he was black and we could not eat at the same table. Cincinnati was then still an essentially "southern" city, with restaurants, hotels, movie houses, and so forth closed to blacks. Kentucky, just across the Ohio river, was thoroughly segregated, with separate drinking fountains for blacks and whites. Huck Finn and Jim were becoming flesh and blood. Years later, I had a different, yet similar, experience, that I shall mention presently.

All my college grades were A's, except for the required Freshman English class, which I had to take as soon as I began my studies. I still knew very little English. The other courses I took were in math or the sciences and did not require great competence in the language. In English, I received a D, which was a gift to a foreign-speaking student. I deserved an F minus. I was planning to work my way to a Ph.D. in some branch of experimental physics.

Because of a series of unexpected events, it became possible to reconsider my going to medical school. In the fall or winter of 1940, I applied to twenty-six medical schools. My educational qualifications could hardly have been better. In those days, it was extremely rare for applicants to medical school to have qualifications beyond completion of the required premed courses. I had a college degree in physics, spoke German and French fluently, and had a solid background in Latin. I received tentative acceptance from virtually all of the schools to which I applied, final acceptance conditional on a personal interview. The purpose of the interviews was to make sure that no "undesirable" applicants—for example, persons suffering from serious physical deformities or handicaps, children of parents from a low economic class, or Jews—were permitted to become physicians. The interview for admission to the Johns Hopkins medical school, which I remember especially clearly, was typical.

The interviewer was a prominent Cincinnati surgeon, an alumnus of the Johns Hopkins medical school. After an exchange of some polite platitudes, he made some complimentary remarks about my academic qualifications, after which the conversation went approximately like this:

> Mr. Szasz, you were not born in the United States. May I ask you some personal questions?
> TS: Of course.
> Szasz. That's a very unusual name. What kind of name is that?
> TS: It's a Hungarian name.
> That doesn't sound like a Jewish name. Are you Jewish?

Although I thought of myself as an atheist, I knew what he was asking and said yes. That was the end of every one of these interviews, except one. I was admitted to the University of Cincinnati College of Medicine. Having gone to the university as an undergraduate was an advantage. Receiving exceptionally strong recommendations from college instructors known to the medical faculty probably helped. And so did being a resident of Ohio and having an uncle who was professor of mathematics at the University.

My dream of going to medical school was coming true. During the summer of 1941, I worked as a chauffeur and in a VD (venereal disease) clinic to earn some money and, in August 1941, became a freshman medical student at the University of Cincinnati. Although I never quite overcame the feeling that there was something repellent about dissecting a cadaver, I was entranced by learning anatomy, and everything else that followed.

On September 3rd, 1939, World War II began. Except psychologically, it had little practical impact on my life. On December 7th, 1941, the Japanese bombed Pearl Harbor and the United States was at war. Physicians of draft age were quickly called up. Medical students were declared to be pursuing studies necessary for the war effort, were drafted *en masse*, given the provisional rank of lieutenant in the Army and then sent back to continue their studies. Physicians considered my heart murmur and abnormal electrocardiogram as evidence of heart disease and I received a medical deferment.

I should mention here that soon after the attack on Pearl Harbor, to increase the production of physicians, the customary three-month summer vacation between academic years was abolished. Medical schools and residency programs were put on a continuous nine-month schedule, with only a few days off between one term and the next.

I enjoyed medical school thoroughly. Ever since I was an adolescent, I felt driven by a need to find out "what is under the hood," the metaphor that best captures my eagerness to learn, motivated in part by intellectual curiosity, and in part by fear. I felt that anything I did not understand posed a potential threat to me, that acquiring information and understanding was a matter of prudent self-protection. I wanted to know how radios worked, how cars worked, how the body worked, how the law and society worked, how the economy worked, how history worked — in short, how life worked. I made the best of my opportunity to learn how the body worked.

In June, 1944, I graduated from medical school, ranking first in my class. My parents were proud. I was proud.

V

I was now comfortably trapped in the lock-step machinery of medical education. After medical school came the internship. I would have been satisfied with doing it in Cincinnati. I was well liked by the faculty and could have stayed close to my parents. However, several of my prominent teachers were eager to show off their prize pupil by securing one of the coveted internship slots for him. At their urging, I applied for an internship at the Harvard Medical Service of the Boston City Hospital. My application was accepted and I spent nine months in Boston, at "Harvard."

My internship was an excellent learning experience. However, the workload was so absurdly heavy that, as a personal experience, it was a period of unremitting, severe hardship, made tolerable only by the realization that it lasted only nine months. During virtually all of that period, interns were "on call" for thirty-six hours at a stretch, followed by twelve hours off. I could count on sleeping, undisturbed by a ringing telephone and a new admission or some medical crisis, only every other night. The nights I was on call, I got no sleep at all or dozed restlessly for a few hours.

During my internship, as in medical school and the Gymnasium, I was an eager and good student and reliable worker. I was offered coveted residencies at Harvard as well as a research fellowship with a prominent endocrinologist. A career in basic medical research appealed to me, but was foreclosed by the fact that, in 1945, it was a path open only to young physicians who did not have to support themselves for many years to come. As an intern, I received only room and board at the hospital. The fellowship stipends were mere pocket money. I had had enough of poverty and was anxious to complete my training and start making money. Why didn't I stay in Boston for a medical residency? Because I found the human atmosphere vaguely repellent: the Harvard arrogance, the New England anti-Semitism, the pervasive cultural snootiness.

I applied for a medical residency at my *alma mater*, the Cincinnati General Hospital, where I was welcomed back with open arms. My residency—which was another excellent learning experience and which I enjoyed very much—had barely begun when I had to face a difficult decision. I was rapidly moving in the direction of becoming a specialist in internal medicine, with only one option for making money: practicing medicine. This did not appeal to me. It is not why I had gone to medical school. I did that to learn medicine. I had fulfilled that aspiration. It was time to give up medicine and start all over, in another direction.

Although I had an abiding interest in and love for medicine and the hard sciences, my true passion was literature, history, philosophy, politics—or, put more plainly, how and why people live, suffer, and die. Thanks largely to my brother's influence, I too had become an omnivorous and fast reader. In the 1930s, psychoanalysis was in the cultural air of Budapest. I read some of the writings of Freud and Ferenczi before I left Hungary. I read more about psychoanalysis while I was in college. As a medical student, I knew more about the history of psychiatry and psychoanalysis than did my teachers in psychiatry, who always wore white coats and presented themselves to students and faculty alike as sophisticated "clinicians."

Having read some of the perceptive essays on psychiatry and psychoanalysis by the popular writer Karinthy Frigyes, I realized, even before I left Hungary, that psychiatry and psychoanalysis had nothing to do with real medicine or with one another: psychiatrists locked up troublesome persons in insane asylums for the benefit of their relatives; psychoanalysts, who were not supposed to touch their patients, engaged in a particular kind of conversation with them. Incarcerating people and talking to them were not medicine. Any intelligent child would have known that. Of course, such simple-minded clarity had to be "educated" out of people to make them normal members of society, especially American society.

Although Ferenczi had been a forthright advocate of lay or nonmedical psychoanalysis, and Anna Freud and many of the leading European analysts were not physicians, in the United States psychoanalysis was defined as a medical activity, a special kind of psychiatry. I knew this was bunk long before I finished medical school.

On July 1st, 1945, I began my medical residency in Cincinnati. In the fall or winter, I decided to bite the proverbial bullet: I decided to quit medicine. I planned to finish my residency, which lasted until March 31st, 1946, and then continue with a residency in psychiatry. I went to see the chairman of the department of medicine, Marion Blankenhorn, who was a beloved figure in Cincinnati medical circles. His daughter and I had been classmates. I did not know him well, but I liked him very much and he clearly thought well of me. When I informed him that I was not planning to continue as a second-year resident—which was, of course, the expected thing to do—but apply for a residency in psychiatry in Chicago, he was dumbfounded. After a moment's silence, he said: "I am sorry to hear that, Tom. Medicine is losing a good man."

Ever since, that sentence resonates in my mind whenever I hear psychiatrists insisting on their medical identity and witness the unwillingness of real doctors to publicly disown them as quacks. I found Blankenhorn's casual remark instructive. I thought: "But if he knows that, why does he never say it or act as if psychiatrists were not real doctors?" It was a rhetorical question.

Strange as it may sound, just as I wanted to go to medical school to learn medicine, not to practice it, I served a psychiatric residency to qualify as a psychiatrist and be eligible for training in psychoanalysis, not to practice psychiatry. I felt that I would rather earn a living as a psychoanalyst than as an internist; that I would then have more leisure and opportunity to pursue my intellectual—literary, social, political— interests, and that the role of psychoanalyst would provide a platform from which I could perhaps launch an attack on what I had long felt were the immoral practices of civil commitment and the insanity defense.

In the meanwhile, the war ended. On August 6th, 1945, an atomic bomb destroyed Hiroshima, on August 9th, a second bomb was dropped on Nagasaki, and on September 2nd, the Japanese surrendered.

In the fall of 1945, I applied for a psychiatric residency at the University of Chicago, to commence on April 1st, 1946, and was quickly accepted.

VII

I chose the psychiatric residency in Chicago for two reasons: because it was in Chicago, where I could receive training in psychoanalysis at the Chicago Institute for Psychoanalysis; and because it offered no opportunity for contact with involuntary patients. Both of these elements were important. In combination, they made the University of Chicago Clinics the perfect choice.

April 1946 was a long time ago. Psychiatry and psychoanalysis and the cultural and economic climate in America were utterly unlike what they are today. It was a different world. There were, I think, less than two thousand psychiatrists in the country and most of them were state hospital employees. There were only a few dozen psychoanalysts, most of them European refugees.

The University of Chicago Medical School—and the Clinics, the name of the school's teaching hospital—had no separate department of psychiatry. Psychiatry was a small subdivision of medicine. The staff consisted of three psychiatrists. David Slight, an expatriate from England, was the chairman of the department. He was a pleasant, middle-aged man of no special distinction. I never saw him do any work. As far as I knew, he spent a few hours in his office reading the papers and then disappeared. The rest of the department consisted of a young assistant professor, an instructor, and a single resident, me. There were no classes and few duties. It was expected that young psychiatrists and residents would spend a good deal of their time away from the premises, migrating north to the Institute for Psychoanalysis.

I received credit for my residency in internal medicine and started with the rank of a second-year resident. The psychiatric residency at the University of Chicago Clinics was tailor-made for me. Nothing even remotely like it exists or could exist now, as such a program would not meet the qualifications for a psychiatric residency. The hospital contained no separate psychiatric ward for mental patients. The psychiatric services consisted of a small outpatient clinic, catering mainly to students at the university, and a consultation service, about which more in a moment. Strange as it may seem today, in 1946, that was the state of affairs in one of the most prestigious teaching hospitals in America. The circumstances responsible for this arrangement require some explanation.

Chicago, a vast metropolis, was the home of several medical schools and many hospitals. The University of Chicago's teaching hospital was a VIP institution, catering to an upper class clientele. I do not recall seeing a single black patient during my years there. But I do recall walking into an elevator and seeing Thomas Mann in a wheelchair, following his operation for cancer of the lung, by one of the hospital's star surgeons.

Psychiatry at the University of Chicago had a reputation for being psychoanalytically oriented. After Franz Alexander emigrated from Berlin to Chicago, and before he founded the Chicago Institute for Psychoanalysis in 1932, he had served for a short time as professor of psychoanalysis at the university. Faculty and residents alike were expected to be in psychoanalytic training at the Institute. It was during the postwar years—approximately from 1946 until the 1970s—that the prestige of psychoanalysis in America and the influence of psychoanalysts on psychiatry were at their peak.

The selectively upper-class clientele of the hospital accounted in large part, perhaps entirely, for the absence of a "mental ward." In those days, VIPs were not hospitalized for mental illness, unless their misbehavior made the headlines or entailed physical assault on family members. Individuals who were depressed because of marital problems, or had drinking problems, or had a "nervous breakdown" attributed to something else were usually admitted to the GI (gastrointestinal diseases) service of the University of Chicago Clinics, with a false diagnosis, such as "gastroenteritis." (This was the practice in Washington as well, as I later witnessed, first hand, at the Bethesda Naval Hospital.) It was the duty of the resident, and usually of a staff psychiatrist, to "evaluate" the patient. Typically, the purpose of the hospitalization was to facilitate restoring domestic peace by housing, and perhaps sedating, the patient, while arrangements for reconciliation or legal separation or divorce were made. Some patients stayed a few days, some several weeks. The constraint on the patient was family pressure, not legal-psychiatric coercion. It was understood that the main rule governing such "hospitalizations" was discretion and protection of the patient's privacy. Admission and discharge were informal, like to a hotel. It would not have occurred to anyone that the patient's "need for hospitalization" had to be justified to some authority or that anyone but the patient or his family would pay the bill. During my tenure as a junior doctor at this "sanatorium," one of the celebrity patients was the first wife of Robert Hutchins, then Chancellor of the University, whom Hutchins was leaving to marry his secretary.

The residency at the University of Chicago was ideal for me, not least because no one made any attempt to teach me anything. I always preferred to learn, rather than be taught. I read widely, had many intelligent and good friends, played bridge and tennis regularly, and read a lot. Eventually, this idyll came to an abrupt end.

Not long after I began my residency, David Slight was replaced by a freshly demobilized psychiatrist, Henry (Hank) Brosin. Although he was sixteen years my senior, he recognized that I knew far more about psychoanalysis, and much else, than he did and he admired me. We often played tennis together—we were about evenly matched—and had a very good relationship. He treated me like a caring, older brother. As time for the last year of my residency was approaching, Brosin called me into his office for a chat. He told me that he was giving a great deal of thought to my psychiatric training and felt that the program at the University of Chicago was gravely deficient in one respect. I would complete my residency without, as he put it, "having any experience with treating seriously ill patients." He suggested—in fact, insisted—that, for my own good, I take the third year of my residency at the Cook County Hospital. He assured me that I would have special status as a "University of Chicago resident" and would receive my diploma as if I had done all my service there.

I told him that I preferred to stay where I was. I was not about to tell him that the persons he called "seriously ill patients" I regarded as persons deprived of liberty by psychiatrists. I still felt much too vulnerable to let my superiors, or even friends, know what I thought about mental illness and psychiatric coercion. After a moment's hesitation, I thanked him, and said: "Hank, I tell you what, I quit." When he pressed me for an explanation, I told him that if I had wanted to be a resident at the Cook County Hospital—the Bellevue of Chicago—I could have gone there. I would look, I added, for a third year slot elsewhere.

I did not tell Brosin that ever since I was an adolescent, when I set my sights on going to medical school, I had believed that the physician's role is to help relieve the suffering of individuals who ask for and accept his help, and that the psychiatrist is committing a grave moral wrong if he imprisons individuals who neither seek nor want his help. This was one of the things that made psychoanalysis particularly appealing: it dealt with "mental problems," but only if the subject—the "patient"—

sought and accepted what the analyst had to offer. Forced psychiatric treatment was, and is, a tautology: all psychiatric treatment was, and is, actually or potentially involuntary. In contrast, I have always viewed forced psychoanalytic treatment as a self-contradiction. Making such distinctions was psychiatrically incorrect even in the 1940s. Today, contrasting coercive psychiatry with contractual psychoanalysis is considered an unfounded attack on psychiatric benevolence and on biologically based, scientific psychoanalysis.

In medical school, I had seen involuntary psychiatric patients begging to be set free. I didn't relish being in the position of asking a "patient" how I could be of help to him, only to be told, "Doctor, please get me out of here."

Actually, my decision to quit was not as daring or heroic as it may seem. Demobilization was far from complete: there were more residency openings than applicants for them. Also, by that time, I had a very good reputation in the small circle of Chicago psychiatry and psychoanalysis. I completed the requirements for board certification at the Institute for Juvenile Research, an affiliate of the University of Illinois Medical School, seeing families and their troubled or troubling children in the outpatient clinic.

I have to backtrack here to recount my training in psychoanalysis. Before leaving Cincinnati, I applied for admission to the Chicago Institute for Psychoanalysis and was quickly accepted. A few weeks after arriving in Chicago, I began my so-called personal or training analysis (with Therese Benedek), about a year later I began to "take courses" and undertake the "supervised analyses" of patients, and in 1950 I graduated from the Institute. In 1951, I took and passed my examination for certification in psychiatry by the American Board of Psychiatry and Neurology. I now had all the credentials a psychiatrist could have.

Those were exciting and important years. I learned about psychoanalysis, partly by reading, partly by seeing patients, and largely by observing, from the inside, not only what psychoanalysts preached but also what they practiced. Everything I had learned and thought about mental illness, psychiatry, and psychoanalysis—from my teenage years, through medical school, and my psychiatric and psychoanalytic training—confirmed my view that mental illness is a fiction; that psychiatry, resting on force and fraud, is social control; and that psychoanalysis—properly conceived—has nothing to do with illness or medicine or treatment, but is a special kind of confidential dialogue that often helps people resolve some of their personal problems and may help them improve their ability to cope with the slings and arrows of outrageous fortune.

Still, I had to keep my beliefs—or, better, disbeliefs—to myself. I was poor, I was in debt, I had to earn a living. It was obvious that my view of psychoanalysis, as an enterprise separate from psychiatry—indeed, conceptually, economically, and morally antithetical to it—was not shared by my teachers or fellow trainees. The analysts passionately believed that they were treating real diseases, never voiced objections against psychiatric coercions, and believed that criminals were mentally ill and ought to be treated, not punished. These beliefs were an integral part of their self-perception as members of an *avant-garde* of scientific, liberal intellectuals. Psychoanalytic confidentiality was a myth, betrayed not only by training analysis and child analysis, but also by the loose lips of most of the analysts.

The absurdity of medicalizing psychoanalysis was nicely captured in an old spoof about psychoanalytic diagnoses (and, derivatively, psychiatric diagnoses as well): If the patient is early for his appointment, he is anxious; if he is on time, he is compulsive; if he is late, he is hostile. This witticism is a humorous summation of the thesis of Sigmund Freud's famous book, *The Psychopathology of Everyday Life*. Freud, the early analysts, and psychiatrists like Richard von Krafft-Ebing unashamedly declared that their aim was to medicalize life. However, many people were not listening, and most of those who did listen embraced the message as liberation from religious sexual repression.

Psychoanalysts diagnosed not only their patients, they also diagnosed the colleagues they disliked, and the politicians who didn't share their left-liberal "progressive" prejudices. They were all fanatical Democrats and considered Republicans either fascists or sick or both. They seemed not to realize that they were delivering insults, not diagnoses. Many of the analysts hospitalized patients and gave them electric shock treatments. And they made a lot of money. All this was a far cry from my image of psychoanalysis based on the classics, the uncompromising European rejection of psychoanalysis as a medical activity, and my idealization of analytic confidentiality as sacrosanct as the confidentiality of the Catholic confessional.

I couldn't ignore that psychoanalysts were not supposed to touch their patients; some analytic fanatics even debated whether it was permissible for an analyst to shake hands with his patient. Nor could I ignore Freud's book, *The Question of Lay Analysis*, and that many of the most prominent European analysts—Anna Freud, Melanie Klein, Erik

Erikson, Erich Fromm, Bruno Bettelheim, Robert Waelder—were not physicians. Yet, in America, especially in Chicago, psychoanalysts insisted that they were practicing medicine and excluded non-medical analysts from their ranks.

Without intending to, I was becoming a part of a cult—American, pseudomedical psychoanalysis. I wanted no part of it. I did not want to be a training analyst who spies on his analysand. I had no interest in climbing the ladder of the psychoanalytic pecking order, from lowly practicing analyst, to training analyst, supervising analyst, and power broker cum policy-maker in the American Psychoanalytic Association. Except for practicing psychoanalysis as I saw fit, with uncompromising confidentiality as a precondition, all the rest was a fraud and a trap. Once again, I felt I had to escape.

I began to see private patients in 1948, while still a resident. A year later, I was in full-time psychoanalytic practice, often seeing patients as early as 7:00 A.M. and as late as 7:00 or 8:00 P.M. and working a half day on Saturdays. After graduating from the Chicago Institute for Psychoanalysis, I was invited to join its staff, became the fair-haired boy of the Institute, and was viewed as the "Crown Prince," being groomed to inherit Franz Alexander's mantle. I was pleased and flattered by my success and enjoyed earning money by engaging in an activity that came easily to me. However, as I noted, there was a huge fly in the ointment.

Alexander, I might mention here, was an engaging, friendly person, especially towards me. He, too, was born in Budapest and had attended the Minta Gymnasium, some thirty years before I did. His father had been a renowned professor of philosophy at the University of Budapest. He was middle-aged when he emigrated to the United States and, at his suggestion, sometimes we conversed in Hungarian.

In addition to the reasons that I mentioned for being dissatisfied with the direction in which I was heading, there was one more. I disliked living in Chicago. I disliked living in a large city. What attracted many people—especially European refugees—to New York, Chicago, and Los Angeles—repelled me. The big cities were too crowded, too dirty, and there was too much crime. I found the need to commute imbecilic and intolerable; it consumed huge chunks of time and energy that could have been better spent. My desire to live in a smaller city—and as far away from the psychoanalytic centers as possible—greatly increased after I married and my first daughter was born. I was pondering how to get out of Chicago, when fate intervened. I was drafted.

VIII

The Korean War began in 1950 and ended in July 1953. The draft was reinstated. For ordinary draftees, the age limit was twenty-nine. Again, the military needed physicians. The age limit for the "physician draft" was thirty-five. Furthermore, the physical requirements to be drafted were greatly relaxed. The military authorities rightly reasoned that if a young man was able to work as a physician in civilian life, he could also work as a physician in the armed forces, if not overseas then in a military hospital in the United States. Although the Korean war ended in July 1953, the draft remained in effect. In the spring of 1954, just one year short of my 35th year, I was drafted into the United States Naval Reserve. I received the rank of Lieutenant and was assigned to the crown jewel of Navy hospitals, the United States Naval Medical Center in Bethesda, Maryland.

On July 1st, 1954, I reported for duty. Soon, I was promoted to Lieutenant Commander and then to Commander. One of my memorable experiences in the Navy occurred soon after I began my duties. I became friendly with one of the enlisted men who worked on the ward to which I was assigned. One day, as the noon hour approached, I suggested that we go to lunch together. He had to enlighten me: I could not eat with the enlisted men, and he could not eat at the officers' club.

My required tour of duty lasted only two years. In anticipation of my discharge, I was offered plum positions at the National Institute of Mental Health, which was then in its infancy. I turned the offers down. I did not want to be an employee of the federal government's bureaucracy.

Having said that, I must acknowledge that I thoroughly enjoyed my two years in Bethesda. Daily life was far more comfortable than it had been in Chicago. In 1955, my second daughter was born. My colleagues and superiors were decent, intelligent men, easy to work with and talk to. Some were in psychoanalytic training in Washington. Some were traditional psychiatrists. They were more open-minded than the analysts in Chicago. The work load was light. I had to be at the hospital at 8:00 A.M., but could be home by 4:30 or 5:00. I saw a few private patients after hours. I had time to be with my family and to read, think, and write. I wrote several papers while in the Navy, one of which—written with my then closest friend, Marc Hollender—has become a classic essay on the ethics and politics of the doctor-patient relationship.[2] I also finished

---

[2] Thomas S. Szasz and Marc H. Hollender, "A Contribution to the Philosophy of Medicine: The Basic Models of the Doctor-Patient Relationship," *A.M.A. Archives of Internal Medicine* 97 (May, 1956), pp. 585–592.

most of the material for my first book, *Pain and Pleasure*, published a year after my discharge.

Having been drafted was a veritable *deus ex machina* to get me out of Chicago. However, getting away from Chicago was not, by itself, a solution for my problem. Service in the Navy was only a brief respite. I had to have a plan for what to do when I was discharged. Going back to Chicago was the easy, but unpalatable, answer. I was expected to return: my official status at the Institute was "staff member, on leave of absence for military service."

I did not want to resume my previous lifestyle if I could possibly help it. What I really wanted was an academic appointment in a university department of psychiatry, in a small town, where my duties would be mainly teaching, where I was not compelled by economic need to practice full time, and where I could have some time to think and write, in a free, academic environment.

Again, I was lucky. A second *deus ex machina* suddenly offered me exactly the opportunity I was seeking. I made many friends in Chicago. One was Julius (Julie) Richmond, who was then a young assistant professor of pediatrics at the University of Illinois and also a candidate at the Chicago Institute for Psychoanalysis. In 1953, Julie moved to Syracuse to become the chairman of the pediatrics department at the State University of New York College of Medicine, now the Upstate Medical University. The SUNY medical school in Syracuse—recently acquired by the SUNY system from Syracuse University—was beginning a period of rapid growth. A new department of psychiatry had been founded a year earlier. In 1956, its chairman moved to Los Angeles. Because of Julie's influence, the job was offered to Marc, who was as eager as I was to get away from Chicago and full-time psychoanalytic practice, and pursue an academic career. Marc was offered the chairmanship of psychiatry which he accepted.

This was a time when medical school departments of psychiatry were expanding rapidly. Being a fully accredited psychoanalyst was a highly prized commodity in academia. Julie and Marc and I had been good friends. They invited me to come to Syracuse. I visited, was interviewed, and was offered a job as professor of psychiatry. In August 1956, my family of four moved to Syracuse. For the rest of the story I will let my work speak.[3]

---

[3] For additional biographical information, see Keith Hoeller, "Thomas Szasz's History and Philosophy of Psychiatry," *Review of Existential Psychology & Psychiatry* 23 (1997), pp. 6–69; Ronald Leifer, "The Psychiatric Repression of Dr. Thomas Szasz: Its

IX

Before ending, however, I want to add a brief remark. During my years in the Gymnasium, I learned about the famous, nineteenth-century Hungarian obstetrician, Ignaz Semmelweis. I well remember Semmelweis's statue situated in a small park in front of the St. Rochus Hospital, not far from the Minta Gymnasium. He is standing and, at his feet, a mother, cradling an infant, gazes up at him adoringly.

I was deeply moved by the story of Semmelweis's tragic life. It taught me, at an early age, the lesson that it can be dangerous to be wrong, but, to be right, when society regards the majority's falsehood as truth, could be fatal. This principle is especially true with respect to false truths that form an important part of an entire society's belief system. In the past, such basic false truths were religious in nature. In the modern world, they are political and medical in nature. The lesson of Semmelweis's tragedy proved to be extremely helpful, virtually life-saving, for me.

Even as an adolescent, once I grasped the scientific concept of disease, it seemed to me self-evident that many persons categorized as mentally ill and incarcerated in mental hospitals are not sick; instead, they exhibit behaviors unwanted by others, who diagnose them as mad and lock them up; and that this is why, unlike medical patients, mental patients insist that they are not ill. In medical school, I began to understand clearly that my interpretation was correct, that mental illness is a myth, and that it is therefore foolish to look for the causes or cures of the imaginary ailments we call "mental diseases." *Diseases* of the body have causes, such as infectious agents or nutritional deficiencies; often, they can be prevented and cured by dealing with these causes. *Persons* said to have mental diseases, on the other hand, have reasons for their actions; reasons for such actions must be understood and represented the same way that novelists and playwrights understand and depict the motivations of fictional characters and their behaviors.

A deep sense of the invincible social power of false truths enabled me to conceal my ideas from representatives of received psychiatric wisdom until such time that I was no longer under their educational or economic control and to conduct myself in such a way that would minimize

Social and Political Significance," *Review of Existential Psychology and Psychiatry* 23 (1997), pp. 85–106; Jim Powell, "Involuntary Commitment," in Jim Powell, *The Triumph of Liberty: A 2,000-Year History, Told through the Lives of Freedom's Greatest Champions* (New York: Free Press, 2000), pp. 387–394; and Randall C. Wyatt, "An Interview with Thomas Szasz, M.D.," http://psychotherapistresources.com./current/totm/totmframe.html.

the chances of being cast in the role of "enemy of the people" (Henrik Ibsen).

Ever since *The Myth of Mental Illness* was published, interviewers—puzzled by how a psychiatrist can say there is no mental illness—invariably ask me, "When and why did you change your mind about mental illness / psychiatry?" "What experiences did you have that led you to adopt so deviant a point of view?" I try to explain—usually without success—that I did not have any unusual "experiences", that I did not do any "research," that I did not "discover" anything—in short, that I did not replace a belief in mental illness with a disbelief in it. I hope this brief essay makes my explanation more understandable and convincing.[4]

[4] For an appreciative recognition of my view that mental illness is not a genuine medical disease, and that psychiatric incarceration is not like medical hospitalization, see the remark by the respected English medical historian, Roy Porter: "This radical claim that 'mental illness' is itself a delusion commands only a small following even amongst critics of psychiatry. But it does highlight one feature which sets apart the social response to insanity from the handling of any of the other sorts of disease dealt with in this volume. This is the fact that, over the last two or three hundred years, those people suffering from serious mental disturbances have been subjected to compulsory and coercive medical treatment, usually under confinement and forfeiture of civil rights. Sick people in general . . . have typically had the right to seek, or the right to refuse, medical treatment; . . . in so far as they have been cared for in institutions such as hospitals, they have been legally free to come and go as they please." Roy Porter, "Madness and Its Institutions," in Andrew Wear, ed., *Medicine in Society: Historical Essays* (Cambridge: Cambridge University Press, 1992), pp. 277–301; 277.

1

The Myth of Mental Illness

R.E. KENDELL

The Famous Challenge to Orthodoxy

Dr Szasz's views about mental illness were first and most famously expressed in *The Myth of Mental Illness* in 1961, and were reiterated, essentially unchanged, many times over the next twenty-five years. In a nutshell, and in his own words, he asserted that "Strictly speaking, disease or illness can affect only the body; hence, there can be no mental illness" and that "Mental illness is a metaphor. Minds can only be 'sick' in the sense that jokes are 'sick' or economies are 'sick'" (Szasz 1961).

American Psychiatry in the 1950s

The cultural setting in which these heretical views were formulated is significant. *The Myth of Mental Illness* was written in the U.S.A. in the late 1950s. At that time psychoanalysis was the dominant influence on American psychiatry and Szasz himself had recently completed a psychoanalytic training at the Chicago Institute for Psychoanalysis. Psychoanalysis regarded psychiatric disorders as, quite literally, mental disorders. It was only interested in patients' minds, it ignored their bodies, and it regarded the disorders from which they suffered as wholly psychogenic, in the sense that they were assumed to be the product of the meanings attributed to and the conflicts generated by early infantile experiences. It therefore had almost no point of contact with the rest of medicine, which was increasingly losing interest in patients as people as it became more and more fascinated by their biochemistry. As a result, there was an almost unbridgeable gulf between, on the one hand, psychoanalysts and psychoanalytically orientated psychiatrists, the diseases they treated and the therapeutic techniques they employed and, on the other, physicians and surgeons, the diseases they treated and the treatments they employed. Psychoanalysts were also increasingly prone to regard almost the whole of humanity as neurotic, and therefore in potential need of therapy, a dramatic expansion of the traditional concept of mental illness.

Three other features of American psychiatry in the 1950s are also relevant. Large numbers of people were detained in mental hospitals for years on end, usually against their wishes and often in deplorable conditions, and many of them were subjected, without their consent, to treatments of questionable efficacy. The substantial evidence that hereditary factors made a major contribution to the etiology of schizophrenia and manic depressive psychoses was forgotten or ignored, partly because it was incompatible with the prevailing psychoanalytic philosophy, and partly because that evidence had been generated by German psychiatry which had been utterly discredited by its involvement in the racial cleansing policies of the Nazis. The American concept of schizophrenia had also degenerated into a vague synonym for almost any severe form of mental illness, applied indiscriminately to anyone whose behaviour or speech were at all irrational, threatening or difficult to understand.

Against this background, it is not particularly surprising that Dr. Szasz should have come to the conclusion that mental illnesses had nothing in common with other illnesses, that ever increasing numbers of people were being labelled as mentally ill on the basis of little more than a psychiatrist's opinion, that outdated mental health legislation was being used inappropriately to deprive large numbers of people of their liberty and, even worse, to subject them to irreversible treatments like lobotomy without their consent, and that the whole concept of mental illness was suspect.

Contemporary American Psychiatry

The situation now, nearly fifty years on, is very different. The dominant orientation of American psychiatry is wholeheartedly biological and psychoanalysis is all but forgotten in the main university centres. The evidence that genetic factors play a major role in the genesis, not just of what in the 1950s were known as the "functional psychoses" but of the whole gamut of mental illness, is almost universally accepted and the attention of research workers is focused on the brains rather than the minds of psychiatric patients (Eisenberg 1986). Schizophrenia and other diagnostic terms have been given precise meanings (American Psychiatric Association 1994). And there are now far fewer involuntary patients in American mental hospitals, and the legislation under which they are detained pays more attention to their civil liberties. If Dr. Szasz were an independent minded and iconoclastic young psychiatrist now he would, I suspect, be writing a quite different but perhaps equally provocative book.

Are Mental Disorders Diseases?

There are two fundamentally different ways of determining whether it is appropriate to regard mental disorders as diseases: by examining historical and contemporary usage of the term 'disease', particularly in other (non-mental) contexts; or by assessing mental disorders against the criterion provided by a formal and preferably widely recognised definition of the term disease or disorder.

The Evolution of the Concept of Disease

It is central to Szasz's argument that for the last 150 years the concept of disease has been firmly tied to a demonstrable "lesion" of some kind, and that we owe this to the great nineteenth-century German pathologist, Rudolph Virchow. In fact, as Pies (1979) has pointed out, although Virchow argued that the *basis* of disease was local cellular pathology he did not argue that cellular pathology *was* the disease. Indeed, he maintained that "Disease presupposes life. With the death of the cell, the disease also terminates." The lesion, on the other hand, still remains, temporarily in the cadaver or permanently on a histological slide or preserved in formalin.

More fundamentally, it is not the case that there is a single, agreed concept of disease, either now or at any time in the past. There is, it is true, usually a dominant concept, but that changes from generation to generation with developments in medical technology and changing assumptions about the nature of disease. For most of human history disease has been essentially an explanatory concept, invoked to account for suffering, incapacity, and premature death in the absence of obvious injury, and suffering and incapacity are still the most fundamental attributes of disease. Initially, individual symptoms like breathlessness and diarrhoea were regarded as diseases. Then, in the seventeenth century,

Sydenham and his contemporaries developed the concept of a syn-drome—a cluster of related symptoms and signs with a characteristic evolution and outcome. A century later the slow spread of post-mortem dissection of the body led to a realisation that disease was often accompanied by obvious pathological changes in one or more of the internal organs. The development of the microscope in the nineteenth century made it apparent that disease was even more frequently accompanied by pathological changes at a cellular level, and also that many of the great scourges of mankind—typhoid, cholera, tuberculosis, and malaria—were due to the invasion of the body by a micro-organism. Further waves of technological innovation in the twentieth century led, in quick succession, to the identification of a series of other new diseases on the basis first of physiological and then of biochemical abnormalities, and more recently on the basis of abnormalities of chromosomal or molecular (usually genetic) structure. From each of these successive eras in medical history some diseases have survived. A few (migraine, torticollis, and most so-called mental disorders) are still defined by their syndromes and others (mitral stenosis, cholecystitis) are still defined by their morbid anatomy. Many more are defined by their histology (most cancers, Alzheimer's disease) or by the identity of the infective organism (tuberculosis, measles). Other more recently recognised diseases are defined by a physiological (myasthenia gravis) or biochemical (the aminoacidurias) abnormality or by a chromosomal (trisomy 21, Turner's syndrome), molecular (the thalassaemias) or genetic (Huntington's disease, cystic fibrosis) abnormality. This great diversity of defining characteristics is one of the reasons medicine has such difficulty providing a definition of disease in general which includes all individual diseases and nothing else.

Dr. Szasz's claim that a condition is only a disease if a morphological abnormality of some kind—a lesion—can be demonstrated "by post-mortem examination of organs and tissues"(Szasz 1976) is therefore misleading. Indeed, his insistence that structural abnormality is the defining characteristic of disease not only *excludes* many universally recognised diseases; it also *includes* an even wider range of conditions that are not regarded as diseases. Fused second and third toes and dextrocardia are clear cut structural abnormalities which are not regarded as diseases, for the very good reason that they do not involve either suffering or disability. The same is true of several chromosomal abnormalities (mainly translocations and small deletions) and thousands of abnormal DNA sequences, again because there is no associated disability. It is true, of course, that the defining characteristic of many diseases is a structural abnormality, but this is partly a matter of convenience.

Structural abnormalities are stable and easily demonstrated in biopsy specimens or fragments of tissue mounted on slides, whereas functional impairment can usually only be demonstrated in a cooperative, living patient. But functional impairment is still the fundamental criterion, and structural abnormality is only accepted as a criterion if it is already established that it is regularly associated with impaired function.

Like all skillful polemicists, Dr Szasz has always been careful to avoid raising issues that might undermine his arguments. He never discusses whether tuberculosis, small pox, malaria and typhoid were diseases before their underlying pathology was elucidated, and whether physicians were justified in striving to treat them before the causal organisms were identified. Nor does he ever discuss whether conditions other than mental disorders that are still defined by their syndromes— migraine, for example, and movement disorders like essential tremor, torticollis, blepharospasm, and torsion dystonia—are justly regarded as diseases. Presumably, this is because he recognises like everyone else that the obvious suffering and disability associated with these conditions is at least *prima facie* evidence that they should be regarded as diseases, and that physicians are not only justified in trying to treat them but under an obligation to do so.

Dr. Szasz is perfectly justified, though, in drawing attention to the fact that psychiatry does differ from all other branches of medicine (neurology and dermatology are partial exceptions) in the sense that most of the disorders it recognises are still defined by their syndromes; and that at a time when psychiatrists are claiming to recognise an ever widening range of mental disorders, this leaves them vulnerable to accusations of unjustified medicalisation of deviant behaviour and the vicissitudes of everyday life.

Definitions of Disease or Disorder

Partly for the reasons described above, medicine has never had a satisfactory definition of disease in general that was capable of being used as a criterion against which mental disorders could be assessed, individually or corporately. Suffering and disability are fundamental characteristics of disease, and it would be difficult to question the suffering and disability associated with most mental disorders, but on their own they are an inadequate criterion. For one thing, other conditions like poverty, low social class and membership of a minority ethnic group are often associated with suffering and disability, and no one suggests that these should be regarded as a diseases.

1   OFFICIAL DEFINITIONS

The World Health Organisation has always avoided defining "disease", or "illness", or "disorder" in the successive revisions of its International Classification of Diseases, Injuries and Causes of Death (ICD), and in its current (ICD-10) Classification of Mental and Behavioural Disorders it simply states that "the term disorder is used throughout the classification, so as to avoid even greater problems inherent in the use of terms such as disease and illness. Disorder is not an exact term, but it is used here to imply the existence of a clinically recognisable set of symptoms or behaviour associated in most cases with distress and with interference with personal functions" (World Health Organisation 1992a). Like its immediate predecessors, the current edition of the American Psychiatric Association's Diagnostic and Statistical Manual of Mental Disorders (DSM-IV) does provide a detailed definition of the term "mental disorder", but although this runs to 146 words and contains numerous clauses and qualifications it is not intended to be a criterion and is not cast in a format that allows it to be used as one. It does, though, include two important statements. There is an assumed or implied "behavioral, psychological or biological dysfunction" underlying every mental disorder; and "neither deviant behavior nor conflicts that are primarily between the individual and society are mental disorders unless the deviance or conflict is a symptom of a dysfunction in the individual" (American Psychiatric Association 1994).

2   BIOMEDICAL DEFINITIONS

Although official definitions of disease or mental disorder are incapable of resolving the key issue of whether mental disorders fulfill the accepted criteria of disease, many other definitions have been proposed since Dr. Szasz first threw down his gauntlet in 1961. Although none of these has succeeded in commanding wide acceptance they are still worth considering, if only to emphasise the diversity of contemporary views about the nature of disease. Basically, most are either biomedical definitions in which a biological dysfunction of some kind is usually a crucial element, or sociopolitical definitions which explicitly involve a value judgement and usually a utilitarian decision justified by its expected consequences (for instance Sedgwick 1982). Scadding (1967), for example, suggested that disease should be defined as "the sum of the abnormal phenomena displayed by a group of living organisms in association with a specified common characteristic or set of characteristics by which they differ from the norm for the species in such a way as to place them at a biological disadvantage." Although Scadding himself never spelt out what he meant by "biological disadvantage" I argued twenty-five years ago that it must at least embrace both impaired fertility and reduced life expectancy, and that a wide range of mental disorders are associated with a reduced life expectancy and some, including schizophrenia, with reduced fertility as well (Kendell 1975). Since then it has become clear that nearly all mental disorders are associated with a significantly increased mortality (Harris and Barraclough 1998).

More recently, Wakefield has proposed that mental disorders (and by implication other diseases as well) should be defined by the combination of a "dysfunction"—where dysfunction implies the failure of a biological mechanism to perform a "natural function" for which it was designed by evolution—and "harm" or handicap (Wakefield 1992; 1999). His closely argued analysis of the concept of mental disorder has attracted widespread interest and much support, though it has also been argued that too little is known about the evolutionary origins of the higher cerebral functions whose malfunctioning is presumed to underlie many mental disorders for this to be a practical criterion, and that mood states like anxiety and depression may well have evolved as biologically adaptive responses to danger or loss rather than being malfunctions (for example Lilienfeld and Marino 1995).

3 SOCIOPOLITICAL DEFINITIONS

The simplest plausible sociopolitical definition is that a condition is regarded as a disease if it is agreed to be undesirable (an explicit value judgement) and it seems on balance that physicians (or health professionals in general) and their technologies are more likely to be able to deal with it effectively than any of the alternatives, such as the criminal justice system (treating it as crime), the church (treating it as sin) or social work (treating it as a social problem). A definition of this kind is essentially utilitarian. Whether the antisocial behaviour of habitual delinquents, for example, is better regarded as criminal behaviour or as a manifestation of an antisocial personality disorder would be determined by the relative success of the criminal justice system and psychiatry and clinical psychology in reducing the antisocial behaviour; and whether restless, overactive children with short attention spans are to be regarded as suffering from attention deficit hyperactivity disorder (ADHD) or simply as difficult children would depend on whether child psychiatrists were better at ameliorating the problem than parents and teachers.

Definitions of this kind, which have usually been proposed by social scientists rather than by physicians, also imply that a given condition might be a mental disorder in one cultural setting or generation but not in another, depending on the relative efficacy of medical and other approaches to the problem in those different settings and time periods.

Although sociopolitical definitions of disease have rarely commended themselves to the medical profession, it is undoubtedly true that treatability is often a crucial consideration underlying doctors' decisions to regard individual phenomena as diseases. It was the introduction of disulphiram (Antabuse), which was hailed at the time as a highly effective treatment, that finally persuaded the American Medical Association and similar bodies throughout the world that alcoholism was a disease after all, and so led to its inclusion in the ICD. The attitudes of contemporary physicians to obesity, and of psychiatrists to personality disorders and drug dependence, are likewise strongly influenced by their assumptions about treatability, with those who regard these conditions as treatable generally keen to regard them as diseases and those who do not believe there is any effective therapy preferring to withhold this designation.

If mental disorders are judged by this criterion the answer is fairly clear cut. Although few, if any, can be cured by contemporary therapies the symptoms of most mental disorders can be substantially alleviated and the associated suffering and disability reduced more effectively by psychiatrists and other health professionals than by any other profession or institution. This may not always be so, of course, nor can it be assumed even now that all currently recognised mental disorders would be able to pass this test. This socio-political criterion also provides a simple, defensible explanation of why the concept of mental disorder has expanded so much in the last fifty years. Psychiatrists have acquired the ability to control the troublesome behaviour of restless, overactive children, for example, and most parents and schoolteachers have been happy to see the problem taken over by psychiatrists and pediatricians and dignified with the title of ADHD.

4   SZASZ'S DEFINITION

More than twenty years after the publication of *The Myth of Mental Illness*, Dr. Szasz published what were in effect his own criteria for accepting schizophrenia, and by implication other mental disorders as well, as a genuine disease. "I concede the possibility", he wrote, "that some persons now diagnosed as schizophrenic might suffer from such a disease (an 'organic psychosis'). Indeed, research into the pathological anatomy and physiology of schizophrenia, and hence the development of a rational therapy for it, demand such an assumption. . . . In that event, it would be possible to ascertain, by means of objective tests, whether a person suffers from schizophrenia. The term 'schizophrenia' would then no longer designate a mental condition or a form of behavior; it would become the name of a biological abnormality of the human body" (Szasz, in Vatz and Weinberg 1983, p. 93).

Let us see, therefore, whether Dr. Szasz's own criteria, rooted as always in morphological abnormality, can be met. Although no "schizophrenic genes" have yet been identified, and it is increasingly likely that a large number of different genes are involved, each individually of comparatively small effect, the evidence from twin and adoption studies that heredity makes a major contribution to the etiology of schizophrenia is strong (Gottesman and Shields 1982). As genes are simply recipes for the synthesis of proteins, this implies that there must be biological differences, and at a molecular level structural differences, between people with schizophrenic illnesses and other people. Similar genetic differences underlie many other human characteristics, of course, including eye and hair colour, which are not diseases. What matters is not evidence of genetic transmission on its own, but evidence of the genetic transmission of a condition which is consistently associated with suffering and incapacity. Schizophrenia and a wide range of other mental disorders meet this criterion. Poverty and low social class do not. There is also much evidence, both from postmortem examination of the brain and from CT or MRI scanning *in vivo*, that the brains of people with schizophrenia are abnormal. They are smaller than those of matched controls, they have enlarged lateral and third ventricles, and they frequently have local structural abnormalities as well, particularly in temporal lobe structures such as the hippocampus and the amygdala (Lawrie and Abukmeil 1998; Stevens 1999). Though well established, these structural abnormalities are, however, only characteristic of populations of people with schizophrenia compared with matched controls. They cannot be demonstrated in every individual, and so cannot yet be used as a diagnostic test in individuals.

Although his initial onslaught used hysteria as a (highly atypical) paradigm of mental illness (Szasz 1961), Dr. Szasz and his opponents have both chosen to debate whether or not mental illnesses are properly so called by using schizophrenia as a paradigm, mainly, I suppose, because it is part of the "heartland" of psychiatry and underlies both the judicial concept of insanity and the layman's understanding of madness. There are other equally good exemplars, however. Depressive illnesses

(which, curiously, are almost never mentioned by Szasz) are far com-
moner than schizophrenia and probably occupy a higher proportion of
the professional time of psychiatrists, and the evidence that they are
appropriately regarded as diseases is equally strong. As with schizophrenia, there is extensive evidence from twin and family studies that
genetic factors make a major contribution to the etiology of the whole
range of depressive illnesses from the most severe to the relatively mild
(Andreasen et al. 1986; Kendler et al. 1992). As before, this implies the
existence of an underlying biological, and at a molecular level a structural, abnormality. There is other, more direct, evidence of this biological abnormality. Antidepressant drugs alleviate the symptoms of the
depressive syndrome (not always, it is true, but commonly) but have no
effect on mood in normal people, or indeed in people who are merely
despondent (Paykel et al.1988), implying that there is a crucial difference between raising mood, which a euphoriant drug like amphetamine
achieves, and alleviating the symptoms of a depressive illness. It is also
possible to precipitate a depressive mood in people with a history of
recurrent major depression, but not in other people, simply by giving
them an amino acid drink containing no tryptophan (Delgado et al.
1990). (Tryptophan is the precursor of the neurotransmitter serotonin
and there is indirect evidence that serotonin neurotransmission is abnormal in people prone to major depression.)

5   CONCLUSIONS

In summary, it is not a straightforward matter to decide whether or not
individual mental disorders are justly so regarded, mainly because there
is no agreed definition either of disease in general or of mental disorder.
If disease is regarded as a biological dysfunction associated with suffering and incapacity there is strong *prima facie* evidence of a biological
dysfunction underlying most of the main groups of so-called mental disorders, but this is not necessarily true of all mental disorders and certainly not of all individuals said to be suffering from a mental disorder.
If a sociopolitical definition of disease is adopted, response to treatment
is a key consideration and again there is evidence that contemporary
therapies for most of the main groups of disorder, but not all, are effective even though they are rarely if ever curative. If Szasz's chosen criterion of a demonstrable structural abnormality is accepted, Alzheimer's
disease and other common dementias clearly qualify and there are
sound, mostly genetic, reasons for believing that a structural abnormality must be present, at least at a molecular level, in most of the other

main groups of disorders. But even in schizophrenia a structural abnormality can only be demonstrated in populations, not in all, or even most, individuals.

The Response to Szasz's Challenge

If Szasz had restricted himself to arguing that new mental disorders were being "identified" nearly every month without any adequate justification, and the term mentally ill applied to an ever growing proportion of the population with equally inadequate justification, he would have attracted a great deal of support, including that of many psychiatrists. He chose, though, to try to debunk the whole notion of mental illness; and he failed. Broadly speaking, the only people who were convinced by his arguments were antipsychiatrists like Laing and Cooper, social scientists with no understanding of biology or medicine, and left wing students keen to overthrow established dogma across the board—none of them groups for which Szasz himself had a conspicuously high regard. As he himself admitted fifteen years after *The Myth of Mental Illness* was published, "every modern authority—religious, political, judicial, medical, scientific—now ceaselessly affirms that the word schizophrenia names a disease in exactly the same sense that the word diabetes names a disease" (Szasz 1976). His own explanation for the "popularity and persistence of the so-called medical model of schizophrenia" was that "no other model of comparable scope and power has ever been offered for it"; and he is almost certainly correct because, as he goes on to say, "once it has achieved the status of a paradigm (in Kuhn's sense), a scientific theory is declared invalid only if an alternative candidate is available to take its place" (Szasz 1976).

More prosaically, it simply made no sense to most people familiar with the basic phenomena of so-called mental illness, least of all on humanitarian grounds, to reject the whole concept of mental illness if the only alternative on offer was to assign it to the undifferentiated ragbag of deviant behaviour. It was also straining credulity to suggest that the human brain and mind, with all their staggering complexities, were only prone to a few gross disorders like tumours, strokes, and fits, while all the other, far simpler, organs of the body were subject to myriads of different disorders. The evidence that psychiatric diseases are justly so-called is still less solid than that for most other diseases. But it is considerably stronger than it was in 1961, and the likelihood of some alternative paradigm emerging to replace the "medical model" is much lower than it was then.

Disease of the Mind and Disease of the Brain

Dr Szasz has always conceded the possibility that, in time, "significant physicochemical disturbances will be found in some 'mental patients' and in some 'conditions' now labelled mental illnesses"(Szasz 1961). He goes on to argue, though, that "If all so-called mental disease is brain disease, if all mental disease is really only the 'mental symptoms' of conditions such as paresis or pellagra—then it makes no sense to have two classes of brain diseases: one neurological, the other mental. Instead, it would be necessary to insist . . . that brain diseases are brain diseases, and that mental diseases are not diseases at all"(Szasz 1976, p. 110).

This statement raises two issues, the first a relatively trivial one of how diseases should be classified, the second a philosophical issue of profound importance. Szasz is quite right to point out that, as more and more so-called mental disorders are shown to have a cerebral pathology, there may be increasing pressure to reclassify them as brain disorders. Indeed, this is already happening. In the discussions leading up to the production of the current (tenth) revision of the International Classification (ICD-10) there was pressure from neurologists for conditions like Alzheimer's disease to be reclassified as "diseases of the nervous system". It was eventually decided that Alzheimer's disease should be so classified unless it resulted in dementia—which, of course, it invariably does—in which case it should continue to be classified as a "mental and behavioural disorder"(World Health Organisation 1992b). Parkinson's disease was accorded the same dual status, while vascular dementia and the post-encephalitic and post-concussional syndromes continued to be classified as mental and behavioural disorders. In reality, the distinction that is being drawn in ICD-10 is still between conditions normally treated by neurologists and those normally treated by psychiatrists, rather than between "diseases of the nervous system" and "mental and behavioural disorders", but this may not be so in ICD-11.

The Distinction between Mental and Physical Diseases

The second, much more important, issue concerns the distinction, not merely between diseases of the brain and those of the mind, but the more fundamental distinction between diseases of the body and diseases or disorders of the mind. From the beginning Szasz has drawn an absolute distinction between the two and has never wavered from this position. As he put it in *The Myth of Mental Illness*, "Strictly speaking, disease or illness can affect only the body; hence, there can be no mental illness" (Szasz 1961). This assumption, or philosophical position, underpins all Szasz's subsequent arguments and is, in my view, profoundly mistaken. Neither minds nor bodies suffer from diseases. Only people (or, in a wider context, organisms) do so, and when they do both mind and body, psyche and soma, are usually involved. Pain, the most characteristic feature of so-called bodily illness, is a purely psychological phenomenon, and the first manifestation of most acute bodily illnesses, from influenza to plague, is also a subjective change—a vague general malaise (Cantor 1972). Fear and other emotions play an important role in the genesis of myocardial infarction, hypertension, asthma, and other somatic illnesses, and bodily changes like tachycardia, weight loss and increased cortisol production are commonplace in psychiatric disorders. There is also unassailable evidence—some of which is summarised above—of somatic abnormalities in schizophrenia, major depression, obsessional disorder and panic disorder.

Indeed, it is impossible to identify any characteristic feature of either the symptomatology or the etiology of so-called mental illnesses which consistently distinguishes them from physical illnesses. Nor do physical illnesses have any characteristics which distinguish them reliably from mental illnesses. If pathological changes and dysfunctions are restricted to organs other than the brain, as is often the case, effects on mentation and behaviour are relatively inconspicuous, but this is an inconstant and purely quantitative difference, and in any case does not apply to diseases of the brain or situations in which there is a secondary metabolic disturbance of cerebral function. There are many differences between "mental" and "physical" diseases, of course. Hallucinations, delusions, and grossly irrational mentation and speech, for example, are a conspicuous feature of the former. But they only occur in a small proportion of mental disorders, and also feature in the confusional states that often complicate physical disorders. The mechanisms underlying hysterical amnesia or paraplegia are very different from those underlying the amnesia of dementia or the paraplegia of spinal injury and are commonly described as "psychogenic". But a myocardial infarction precipitated by fear or anger is equally "psychogenic", and in both cases there are good grounds for assuming that the emotional predicament generates neuronal or endocrine changes which play a critical role in producing the loss of access to memories, loss of voluntary movement, or inadequate oxygenation of the myocardium. In reality, the differences between mental and physical illnesses, striking though some of them are, are quanti-

tative rather than qualitative, differences of emphasis rather than fundamental differences, and no more profound than the differences between
diseases of the circulatory system and those of the digestive system, or
between kidney diseases and skin diseases.

Dr. Szasz was therefore quite right to assert that mental illness is a
meaningless term, a myth, and a dangerous metaphor. But the concept
of physical or somatic illness is equally meaningless, equally mythical,
and equally dangerous. Illnesses afflict people, not isolated bodies or
disembodied minds. As Szasz himself once observed, "brains, or livers,
cannot be treated—only persons, or patients, can" (Szasz 1976).
Moreover, as Pies (1979) pointed out, Virchow's insistence that disease
terminates with death makes it clear that, despite his preoccupation with
cellular pathology, even he realised that diseases afflict people rather
than their bodies. The distinction between mental and physical illness is
ill-founded and damaging to the interests of patients themselves, whatever kind of illness they are suffering from. Most illnesses have psychological as well as bodily manifestations and all but the most trivial have
psychological consequences. Emotional arousal and the meanings
attributed to past and current events also contribute to the genesis of
many illnesses, from myocardial infarction to panic disorder. To divide
illnesses into two arbitrary groupings, mental and physical, is to invite
physicians, research workers and patients themselves to overlook what
may be important causal factors, potentially effective therapies, and serious consequences like persisting invalidism. The distinction also—by
implying that there is a fundamental difference between mental illnesses and illnesses of other kinds—helps to perpetuate the profound stigma
that is still attached to mental illness.

The Origins of the Distinction

Szasz argues, or at least seems to assume, that the concept of mental illness was invented by psychiatrists in the second half of the nineteenth
century: "Until the middle of the nineteenth century, and beyond, illness
meant a bodily disorder whose typical manifestation was an alteration of
bodily structure," he asserts, and "physicians distinguished diseases
from nondiseases according to whether or not they could detect an
abnormal change in the structure of a person's body. . . . Modern psychiatry—and the identification of new psychiatric diseases—began not
by identifying such diseases by means of the established methods of
pathology, but by creating a new criterion of what constitutes disease: to
the established criterion of detectable alteration of bodily structure was

now added the fresh criterion of alteration of bodily function; and, as the former was detected by observing the patient's body, so the latter was detected by observing his behavior . . . Thus was hysteria invented and thus were all the other mental illnesses invented . . . And thus was a compelling parallel constructed between bodily and mental illness" (Szasz, in Vatz and Weinberg 1983, pp. 62–63).

In fact, the concept of hysteria is three thousand years old and was frequently diagnosed and discussed by Sydenham and other seventeenth-century physicians. And the concept of disease of the mind originated in the latter half of the eighteenth century before there were any psychiatrists. Conditions that are now regarded as psychiatric disorders, like mania and melancholia (and hysteria), have figured in classifications of disease since the time of Hippocrates, and for over two thousand years were treated by physicians with much the same range of potions, medicaments, and attempts to correct humoral imbalance as they employed for other disorders. Although Plato attributed some forms of madness to the gods, and medieval theologians like Thomas Aquinas attributed hallucinations and insanity to demons and other supernatural influences, from the Renaissance to the second half of the eighteenth century melancholia and other forms of insanity were generally regarded as bodily diseases, not differing in any fundamental way from other diseases. When the mid-century *belle lettriste* Lady Mary Wortley Montague commented that "madness is as much a corporeal distemper as the gout or asthma" she was simply expressing the "commonplace of high and low, lay and medical opinion alike" (Porter 1987).

The idea that insanity was fundamentally different from other illnesses, that it was a disease of the mind rather than the body, developed towards the end of the eighteenth century. The scene was set by Cartesian dualism, the dominant philosophical influence of the time, but medical opinion and medical impotence also played crucial roles. The development first of private mad-houses and later of large, purpose-built lunatic asylums took the management of the insane out of the hands of the general run of physicians; and because the managers of these new institutions were only concerned with insanity it was relatively easy for them to regard it as different from other illnesses which did not concern them. At the same time it was becoming clear that insanity was not accompanied by the obvious pathological changes that post mortem examination was revealing in other diseases. It was also increasingly apparent that although the armamentarium of eighteenth-century medicine—special diets, bleeding, purging, emetics, and blistering—was as effective in the management of hypochondriasis and hysteria as it was in other disorders, it had little effect on madness. In England the success of the clergyman, Francis Willis, in curing the King (George III) of his madness after the conspicuous failure of his physicians to do so, and the remarkable success of the York Retreat (opened by the Quaker, William Tuke, in 1796) in calming and curing its inmates despite using few medicaments or restraints, both had a considerable influence on public opinion. It was in this climate that the terms "disease of the mind," "disorder of the mind," and "mental illness" first began to be widely used. Indeed, the York Retreat was explicitly for "persons afflicted with disorders of the mind" (Hunter and Macalpine 1963).

The implication of these new terms was that madness was a disease of the mind, not of the body, and there was some debate whether diseased minds might not be better treated by philosophers than by physicians. "Moral treatment"—a benevolent, ordered regime based on moderation and religious observance rather than medication—became the mainstay of the new asylums that were built in the early years of the nineteenth century and initially several of them had no physician. It was not long, though, before the medical profession reasserted itself. In Philadelphia Benjamin Rush (1812) insisted that the fundamental pathology of what he himself referred to as "diseases of the mind" was somatic (he suggested it lay "primarily in the blood vessels of the brain") and in 1845 Wilhelm Griesinger, the first professor of psychiatry, convinced most of his German contemporaries when he argued in his influential textbook that *"Psychische Krankheiten sind Erkrankungen des Gehirns"* (mental illnesses are diseases of the brain). But despite this return to the traditional unitary view of disease, the terms mental illness and mental disease survived, partly because they clearly implied that what had previously been called madness or insanity was medical territory. The doubts about causation also survived, even within the medical profession itself; and the school of psychoanalysis which emerged at the end of the nineteenth century regarded all mental illnesses as entirely psychogenic disorders to be treated by purely psychological means. In the last forty years, however, the situation has changed irrevocably. Understanding of the complex etiology of so-called mental illnesses has increased, effective treatments, somatic and psychological, have been developed, and both medical and lay attitudes to these conditions have changed.

Why then do we still talk of "mental" illnesses and "physical" illnesses? The answer is given in the introduction to the American Psychiatric Association's Diagnostic and Statistical Manual of Mental Disorders (DSM-IV): "The term *mental disorder* unfortunately implies a distinction between 'mental' disorders and 'physical' disorders that is a reductionistic anachronism of mind/body dualism. A compelling literature documents that there is much that is 'physical' in 'mental' disorders and much 'mental' in 'physical' disorders. The problem raised by the term 'mental disorders' has been much clearer than its solution, and, unfortunately, the term persists in the title of DSM-IV because we have not found an appropriate substitute" (American Psychiatric Association 1994). It is easy to sympathise with the American Psychiatric Association's dilemma. Even so, the consequences of continuing to use the terms mental illness and mental disorder are so insidiously damaging that we would all do much better to avoid them and to refer instead to psychiatric illnesses or disorders. If we do continue to refer to "mental" and "physical" illnesses we should preface both terms with "so-called", to remind both ourselves and our audience that these are archaic and misleading terms.

Psychiatry's Debt to Dr. Szasz

I have often wondered whether Thomas Szasz foresaw the howl of outrage from the psychiatric establishment that greeted the publication of his first book, *The Myth of Mental Illness*, or indeed the glee of those who, for a variety of reasons, were delighted to see the establishment discomforted. For the most part the book consisted of an original and perceptive analysis of the role of the behaviours associated with a diagnosis of hysteria, together with a rational plan for their management. But, with what can only be described as a daring sleight of hand, Szasz argued that in demolishing the pretensions of hysteria he had also demolished the foundations of mental illness as a whole, and livened his argument with a series of barbed comments about psychoanalysis and psychoanalytic institutes, psychiatrists and their therapies, and Christianity and other religions. Almost overnight, he became the *enfant terrible* of American psychiatry and, whether with pride or resignation, he has continued to occupy that role ever since. He has also stuck to his guns, and elaborated on his original arguments in a long series of further books, illustrating his claims with a wealth of (carefully selected) quotations and historical incidents. In doing so he has probably become the most widely known psychiatrist of his generation.

However, despite his fame and the world-wide sales of his books, he has largely failed to convince his readers of the truth of either of his most important contentions—that mental illness is a myth or a metaphor, and that there is no medical, moral or legal justification for involuntary psychiatric hospitalisation or treatment. He has intrigued his readers, and convinced many of them that there were good reasons to be suspicious of psychiatric diagnoses and the uses to which they were put, but he has been unable to persuade most of them to adopt his own radical alternatives, and as a result he has failed to bring about any major change in either medical or legal practice. But although his core arguments have not, broadly speaking, been accepted, he has made many psychiatrists, social scientists, and jurists think about crucial issues they might not otherwise have considered and key assumptions they might never otherwise have questioned. He has certainly made me think deeply about the nature of mental illness and the ways in which it differs from other kinds of illness, and I am grateful to him for this. Had I never been confronted by his provocative assertions I might never have explored the meaning of fundamental concepts like disease and illness, and the implications of the persisting semantic distinction between mental and physical disorders. I am sure, too, that I am not alone in this. Medicine is a practical art, learnt until recently largely by serving an apprenticeship. Few physicians bother to explore the philosophical and ethical assumptions underpinning their profession's activities and few twentieth-century psychiatrists questioned the inexorable expansion of the concept of mental illness they were contributing to, or the fragile empirical basis of that expansion. Thomas Szasz has compelled us to do so, because we could not explain to ourselves or other people why he was wrong without doing so. His provocations have made us better and more thoughtful psychiatrists than we would otherwise have been and for this we surely owe him a debt of gratitude.

REFERENCES

American Psychiatric Association. 1994. *Diagnostic and Statistical Manual of Mental Disorders: Fourth edn. (DSM-IV).* Washington, D.C.: American Psychiatric Association.

Andreasen, N.C., W. Scheftner, T. Reich, et al. 1986. The Validation of the Concept of Endogenous Depression: A Family Study Approach. *Archives of General Psychiatry* 43, pp. 246–251.

Canter, A. 1972. Changes in Mood During Incubation of Acute Febrile Disease and the Effects of Pre-exposure Psychologic Status. *Psychosomatic Medicine* 34, pp. 424–430.

Delgado, P.L., D.S. Charney, L.H. Price, et al. 1990. Serotonin Function and the Mechanism of Antidepressant Action: Reversal of Antidepressant-induced Remission by Rapid Depletion of Plasma Tryptophan. *Archives of General Psychiatry* 47, pp. 411–18.

Eisenberg, L. 1986. Mindlessness and Brainlessness in Psychiatry. *British Journal of Psychiatry* 1148, pp. 497–508.

Gottesman, I.I. and J. Shields. 1982. *Schizophrenia: The Epigenetic Puzzle.* Cambridge: Cambridge University Press.

Griesinger, W. 1845. *Pathologie und Therapie der Psychischen Krankheiten.* (English translation by The New Sydenham Society, London, 1867.)

Harris, E.C. and B. Barraclough. 1998. Excess Mortality of Mental Disorder. *British Journal of Psychiatry* 173, pp. 11–53.

Hunter, R. and I. Macalpine. 1963. *Three Hundred Years of Psychiatry, 1535–1860.* London: Oxford University Press.

Kendell, R.E. 1975. The Concept of Disease and Its Implications for Psychiatry. *British Journal of Psychiatry* 127, pp. 305–315.

Kendler, K.S., M.C. Neale, R.C. Kessler, et al. 1992. A Population-based Twin Study of Major Depression in Women: The Impact of Varying Definitions of Illness. *Archives of General Psychiatry* 49, pp. 257–266.

Lawrie, S.M. and S.S. Abukmeil. 1998. Brain Abnormality in Schizophrenia: A Systematic and Quantitative Review of Volumetric Magnetic Resonance Imaging Studies. *British Journal of Psychiatry* 172, pp. 110–120.

Lilienfeld, S. and L. Marino. 1995. Mental Disorder as a Roschian Concept: A Critique of Wakefield's "Harmful Dysfunction" Analysis. *Journal of Abnormal Psychology* 104, pp. 411–420.

Paykel, E.S., J.A. Hollyman, P. Freeling, et al. 1988. Predictors of Therapeutic Benefit from Amitriptyline in Mild Depression: A General Practice Placebo-controlled Trial. *Journal of Affective Disorders* 14, pp. 83–95.

Pies, R. 1979. On Myths and Countermyths: More on Szaszian Fallacies. *Archives of General Psychiatry* 36, pp. 139–144.

Porter, R. 1987. *Mind-forg'd Manacles.* London: Athlone Press.

Rush, R. 1812. *Medical Inquiries and Observations upon the Diseases of the Mind.* Philadelphia: Kimber and Richardson.

Scadding, J.G. 1967. Diagnosis: The Clinician and the Computer. *Lancet* ii, 877–882.

Sedgwick, P. 1982. *Psychopolitics.* New York: Harper and Row.

Stevens, J.R. 1999. Neuropathologies of Schizophrenia. In W.F. Gattaz and H. Hafner, eds., *Search for the Causes of Schizophrenia,* Vol. IV (Darmstadt: Steinkopff), pp. 221–234.

Szasz, T.S. 1961. *The Myth of Mental Illness: Foundations of a Theory of Personal Conduct.* New York: Hoeber-Harper. (1972 Paperback edn. London: Paladin Press.)

———. 1976. *Schizophrenia: The Sacred Symbol of Psychiatry.* New York: Basic Books. (1988 Paperback edn. Syracuse University Press.)

Vatz, R.E. and L.S. Weinberg, eds. 1983. *Thomas Szasz: Primary Values and Major Contentions*. Buffalo: Prometheus.

Wakefield, J.C. 1992. The Concept of Mental Disorder: On the Boundary between Biological Facts and Social Values. *American Psychologist* 47, pp. 373–388.

———. 1999. Evolutionary versus Prototype Analysis of the Concept of Mental Disorder. *Journal of Abnormal Psychology* 108, pp. 374–399.

World Health Organisation. 1992a. *The ICD-10 Classification of Mental and Behavioural Disorders: Clinical Descriptions and Diagnostic Guidelines*. Geneva: World Health Organisation.

———. 1992b. *International Statistical Classification of Diseases and Related Health Problems*. Geneva: World Health Organisation.

Reply to Kendell

THOMAS SZASZ

I

I wish to express my gratitude to Kendell for a carefully wrought and thoughtful critique of the myth of mental illness—the book as well as the ideas to which the term refers—and for his sympathetic presentation and understanding of my views. I shall do my best to identify and articulate the issues on which we agree and disagree.

II

Kendell begins by focusing on the psychiatric scene of the immediate post-World War II period, when *The Myth of Mental Illness* was written. In those days, he reminds the reader, most people, including most physicians, did not look upon psychoanalysis as a medical activity. Yet it was precisely at this point that psychoanalysts were most eager to emphasize that psychoanalysis was a medical treatment for mental illness whose practice ought to be restricted to psychiatrists. This point of view was epitomized by the title of Franz Alexander's book, *The Medical Value of Psychoanalysis* and by the medical posturings of psychoanalysts such as George Engel.[1]

I agree with Kendell's characterization of that psychiatric scene, particularly with his contentions that: 1) psychoanalysts were "increasingly prone to regard the whole of humanity as neurotic, and therefore in

---

[1] Franz Alexander, *The Medical Value of Psychoanalysis* (New York: Norton, 1932); and George L. Engel, "The Need for a New Medical Model: A Challenge to Biomedicine" [1976], in Arthur L. Caplan, H. Tristram Engelhardt, Jr., and James J. McCartney, eds., *Concepts of Health and Disease: Interdisciplinary Perspectives* (Reading, Massachusetts: Addison-Wesley Publishing Company, 1981), p. 607.

potential need of therapy, a dramatic expansion of the traditional concept of mental illness"; 2) "large numbers of people were detained in
mental hospitals for years on end"; and 3) "the American concept of
schizophrenia had also degenerated into a vague synonym for almost
any severe form of mental illness, applied indiscriminately to anyone
whose behavior or speech were at all irrational, threatening, or difficult."
Every one of these features—some more, some less—still characterizes
the American psychiatric scene. Kendell suggests that it was this background that inspired my view that mental illness is a myth:

> Against this background, it is not particularly surprising that Dr. Szasz
> should have come to the conclusion that mental illnesses had nothing in
> common with other illnesses, that ever increasing numbers of people were
> being labelled as mentally ill on the basis of little more than a psychiatrist's
> opinion, that outdated mental hospital legislation was being used inappro-
> priately to deprive numbers of people of their liberty and, even worse, to
> subject them to irreversible treatments like lobotomy without their consent,
> and that the whole concept of mental illness was suspect.

This is a far more honest acknowledgment of psychiatric misdeeds
during a relatively recent period of American history than has ever been
offered by a leading American psychiatrist, and I thank Kendell for his
candor. Although Kendell's hypothesis about the origin of my ideas
sounds plausible and persuasive, it is, as I describe in my Autobiographical Sketch, completely inaccurate. The circumstances he identifies
played no role in my writing *The Myth of Mental Illness.* To be sure,
Kendell had no way of knowing that I had come to view mental illnesses as nondiseases and involuntary mental hospitalizations as forms of
imprisonment long before I entered medical school or, for that matter,
entered the United States.

While the social scene Kendell describes did not inspire my writing
The Myth of Mental Illness, probably it contributed to its favorable
reception. Today, the situation of the psychiatric patient is essentially the
same as it was fifty years ago. However, the public attitude toward psychiatry is very different indeed. At present, unrelentingly and univocal-
ly, three powerful institutions spread the new "scientific" understanding
of mental illnesses as brain diseases, effectively treated with neuroleptic
drugs: namely, the American government, the American mental health
establishment (that now includes, in addition to psychiatrists, psychologists, social workers, and an assortment of counselors), and the
American media. Every educated person now "knows" that mental ill-

nesses are brain diseases. Hence, although my views on psychiatry are even more relevant today than they were fifty years ago, they fall, for the most part, on deaf ears.

Kendell agrees that "The situation now, nearly fifty years on, is very different." Psychiatry is biological and psychoanalysis "is all but forgotten." Psychiatrists are focusing on the brain, not the mind. Indeed. Kendell offers a modest, historically-based defense of the idea of mental illness, but graciously praises me for emphasizing that psychiatry differs from medicine. He writes: "Dr. Szasz is perfectly justified, though, in drawing attention to the fact that psychiatry does differ from all other branches of medicine (neurology and dermatology are partial exceptions) in the sense that most of the disorders it recognizes are still defined by their syndromes; and that at a time when psychiatrists are claiming to recognize an ever widening range of mental disorders, this leaves them vulnerable to accusations of *unjustified medicalization of deviant behavior and the vicissitudes of everyday life*" (emphasis added).

I wish to add two brief comments here. Today, dermatology is based on dermatopathology just as solidly as cardiology and nephrology are based on the pathology of their respective organ systems. Secondly, the megalomaniacal expansiveness that characterized psychiatry in the 1950s still characterizes it, as Kendell himself acknowledges. Moreover, that megalomania did not start in the post-World War II days. It started more than sixty years earlier, with Richard von Krafft-Ebing's *Psychopathia Sexualis* and with Sigmund Freud's *Psychopathology of Everyday Life*.[2]

Much as I would like to see more agreement between Kendell and me, we differ on a number of issues. For example, he defends the concept of mental illness by asserting that "medicine has never had a satisfactory definition of disease" and advances "suffering and disability" as criteria relevant to the concept. Regarding the first point, suffice it to say that Rudolf Virchow's classic criterion has served medicine well as a kind of polestar by which to steer its professional voyage. Regarding the second point—that "it would be difficult to question the suffering and disability associated with most mental disorders" —I respectfully disagree. It is easy to question it. It seems self-evident to me that *many, perhaps most* people whom psychiatrists characterize as "severely mentally ill" do not suffer; they make others suffer. After all, how do we know

---

[2] Thomas Szasz, *Pharmacracy: Medicine and Politics in America* (Westport: Praeger, 2001).

that a person suffers? We know it because he says so and because he asks for help. The "paranoid schizophrenics" beloved by the tabloid headline writers do neither. If such persons were suffering it would not be necessary to incarcerate them and treat them against their will.

When Kendell entertains definitions of mental illness "which have usually been proposed by social scientists rather than by physicians," and when he endorses alcoholism as a disease, we part company. But here again, Kendell—in contrast to American psychiatrists—is candid: he acknowledges that he has abandoned the pathological criterion of illness and has replaced it with a socio-political criterion of it. He writes:

> The socio-political criterion also provides a simple, defensible explanation of why the concept of mental disorder has expanded so much in the last fifty years. Psychiatrists have acquired the ability to control the troublesome or restless behavior of overactive children, for example, and most parents and school teachers have been happy to see the problem taken over by psychiatrists and pediatricians and dignified by the title ADHD.

I have devoted several books to criticizing this trend. There is no need to repeat here my often-stated arguments against the Therapeutic State and social control by pharmacracy.[3]

The differences between Kendell's views on psychiatry and mine come more clearly into focus when he turns to considering "The Responses to Szasz's Challenge." He writes: "If Szasz had restricted himself to arguing that *new mental disorders* were being 'identified' nearly every month without any adequate justification, and the term mentally ill applied to an ever growing proportion of the population with equally inadequate justification, he would have attracted a great deal of support, including that of many psychiatrists" (emphasis added).

I did *all* that, but I did not restrict myself to doing *only* that. Kendell suggests that I would have been more successful if I had been satisfied with aiming to reform psychiatry. But I did not want to reform psychiatry. Why? Because it was clear to me then—and it ought to be painfully clear to everyone today—that psychiatry and coercion are locked in a deadly embrace, that psychiatry is synonymous with psychiatric slav-

---

[3] Thomas Szasz, *The Therapeutic State: Psychiatry in the Mirror of Current Events* (Buffalo: Prometheus, 1984).

ery. Psychiatry and coercion are like conjoined twins sharing a single heart: they cannot be separated without killing at least one. Coercion (the use of force) is here to stay. The impulse to use force is reflexive; it can be domesticated, but it cannot be destroyed. The use of force against enemies within and without is an integral part of the function of the state. My goal has always been to reconcile psychiatric practices with other consensual, cooperative social practices, characteristic of relations between buyers and sellers, parishioners and clergymen, medical patients and medical doctors. Inasmuch as psychiatry is, and has always been, represented by psychiatrists unwilling to relinquish coercion, psychiatry cannot be reformed. It must be destroyed. Kendell continues:

> He [Szasz] chose, though, to try to debunk the whole notion of mental illness; and he failed. . . . it simply made no sense to most people familiar with the basic phenomena of so-called mental illness, least of all on humanitarian grounds, to reject the whole concept of mental illness.

Kendell is right, and he is also wrong. Most people believe in mental illness and it makes no sense to them when they hear someone say there is no such illness. I know that now and knew it fifty years ago. That is why, from the very beginning of my criticism of psychiatry, I compared contemporary peoples' beliefs in mental illness to past peoples' beliefs in witches; and that is why, also from the beginning of my criticism of psychiatry, I compared psychiatry as an institution indispensable for the society it serves to slavery as an institution indispensable for the society it serves. I consider being able to articulate that viewpoint—and attracting a hearing for it—as much success as I ever hoped for.

With respect to the relations between what we call mental illnesses and the brain, Kendell's remarks seem to me—in the main, but not completely—compatible with mine. For example, Kendell writes: "Indeed, it is impossible to identify any characteristic feature of either the symptomatology or the etiology of so-called mental illnesses which consistently distinguishes them from physical illnesses." This is true, but not enough.

- Typically, physical illnesses are identified by observing the patient's *body*: he has a fever, he vomits blood, he is jaundiced, his white cell count is elevated. Typically, mental illnesses are identified by observing the patient's *verbal pronouncements*: he claims to be Jesus, the FBI sends him messages through his teeth, voices tell him that he ought to kill his wife.

- There are objective, physical-chemical markers to ascertain that a person has, or has not, a particular brain disease, say *subdural hematoma*. There are no such markers to ascertain that he has, or has not, a particular mental disease, say *schizophrenia*. Hence, there is no way a person can disprove the "diagnosis" that he "suffers" from schizophrenia.

- The typical medical patient seeks medical help and is hospitalized and treated *with his informed consent*. The typical mental patient does not seek psychiatric help and is hospitalized and treated *without his consent*.

III

In the end, Kendell agrees that mental illness is a myth and seeks to blunt the force of this observation by asserting that physical illness is also a myth. He writes: "Dr. Szasz was therefore quite right to assert that mental illness is a meaningless term, a myth, and a dangerous metaphor. But the concept of physical or somatic illness is equally meaningless, equally mythical and equally dangerous." I disagree. The "concept of physical illness" demarcates a category, the same way that, say, "the concept of element" demarcates a catgory. Atoms are not molecules. Physical illnesses (paresis) are not mental illnesses (panic reaction). Every concept or idea can be used or abused, help people or harm people. Finally, it is an error to say that I assert that mental illness "is a meaningless term." On the contrary, I show that it has important *strategic* meanings and uses: for example, it justifies civil commitment and the insanity defense.[4]

When Kendell uses conventional psychiatric terms, the differences between our views are clear. He refers to "hallucinations" and "delusions." I prefer to view hallucination as a type of disowned self-conversation: the "voices" the patient allegedly hears are his own thoughts. And I prefer to view delusions as stubborn errors or lies, that the patient

---

[4] Thomas Szasz, *Insanity: The Idea and Its Consequences* (Syracuse: Syracuse University Press, 1997 [1987]), and *Cruel Compassion: The Psychiatric Control of Society's Unwanted* (Syracuse: Syracuse University Press, 1998 [1994]).

is not interested in correcting.

Kendell's essay helps to clarify the empirical and moral issues we increasingly face as medicine and politics become more closely intertwined in their aims and methods. I thank him for acknowledging that my work has merit and for writing:

> He [Szasz] has also stuck to his guns, and elaborated on his original arguments in a long series of further books, illustrating his claims with a wealth of (carefully selected) quotations and historical incidents. In doing so he has probably become the most widely known psychiatrist of his generation. . . . He has certainly made me think deeply about the nature of mental illness and the ways in which it differs from other kinds of illness, and I am grateful to him for that.

I am grateful to Professor Kendell for these kind words. His appreciation of my work contrasts sharply with the unremitting denigration of it as well as of my persona by leading psychiatrists in my own adopted country. England and America, observed George Bernard Shaw, "are divided by the same language." They are divided, and also united, by much more than that, and we ought to be thankful for that.

2

Values-Based Medicine: Thomas Szasz's Legacy to Twenty-First Century Psychiatry

K . W . M . (B I L L) F U L F O R D

It is an honour and a pleasure to contribute to this critical volume on the work of Thomas Szasz. I will be concentrating on one particular strand of Szasz's wide-ranging and scholarly contributions to our understanding of the nature of psychiatry, viz. his work on the concept of mental illness, and, in particular, the significance of value judgements for our understanding of the nature of mental illness and the differences between it and physical illness.

Szasz has rightly resisted the description "anti-psychiatrist"[1] He is not an opponent but a *sceptic* of psychiatry. Others have opposed psychiatry on the grounds of its sometimes adverse effects. Szasz, too, has attacked and continues to attack psychiatry on such contingent grounds,[2] and I will be considering this important aspect of his work later. But his deeper criticism goes to the very logic of the subject, to the meaning and implications of the concept of mental illness itself. In his seminal work on what he famously called the "myth" of mental illness (Szasz 1960 and 1961), he made the essentially sceptical claim that there is, literally, no such thing as mental illness—"literally", because, where physical illnesses are defined by scientifically-established *factual* norms

---

[1] Szasz, T.S., *Schizophrenia: The Sacred Symbol of Psychiatry* (New York: Basic Books, 1976).

[2] See, among many other publications, Szasz 1963; 1965; 1970; 1984; 1994; 2001; and 2002.

of anatomy and physiology, those conditions we call mental illnesses are defined by *value* norms, norms which are "psychosocial, ethical and legal " in nature (Szasz 1960, p. 114).

Scepticism has an honourable place in the histories of both philosophy and science. Scepticism provokes debate and thus drives our ideas forward. As a professor of psychiatry, Szasz's scepticism provoked particularly robust defences of the scientific credentials of the discipline from his peers (for example Kendell 1975; Roth and Kroll 1986; Wing 1978). The ensuing debate has indeed driven our ideas forward. It has led to much detailed research on the meaning, not just of mental illness, but also of physical illness, of disease, and of related concepts of disorder in general. An important theme in this research has been whether, and if so where and how, values come into the definitions of these terms. This theme, in turn, has connected our local conceptual difficulties, in medicine and in psychiatry, with wider debates in ethics and the philosophy of science about the relationship between fact and value in general (Fulford 1989). Both debates, in medicine and psychiatry and in philosophy, continue to attract new contributions.[3] Such is the richness of the sceptical attack! And such is the richness of the sceptical attack that from these debates is emerging a new understanding of concepts of disorder, an understanding in which fact and value are in various ways combined, and from which psychiatry, precisely in being more value-laden than physical medicine, provides a model for a more values-based approach to medicine in general in the twenty-first century.

In this article I will show how this new understanding of concepts of disorder, or values-based medicine (VBM) as I have called it elsewhere (Fulford 2004), provides a response to Szasz's sceptical claim. I will first outline the nature of VBM, its connections with Evidence-Based Medicine (EBM), and its origins in philosophical value theory. I will indicate how VBM and EBM stand side by side in clinical decision-making. I will then connect VBM with the analytic grounds of

---

[3] For a recent collection of articles focussing particularly on the concept of mental illness, see the special issue of *Philosophy, Psychiatry, and Psychology* (PPP) , volume 5:3, 1998 (published by Johns Hopkins University Press). This issue includes an important article by Szasz (1998). Recent debate about the roles of fact and value in defining concepts of disorder has been polarised between reductive (values can be reduced to facts) and non-reductive (values cannot be reduced to fact) extremes. In an article in this issue, the English philosopher, Tim Thornton, draws on recent work in the philosophy of mind on the "space of reasons" to indicate the lines along which a non-reductive and yet value-free approach to defining these concepts might be developed (Thornton 1998).

Szasz's sceptical attack on psychiatry. This in turn will lead to a more extended account of the theory and practice of VBM, which, I will argue, provides at least a partial response to the contingent grounds on which Szasz and others have attacked psychiatry. I will conclude with an indication of how Szasz's sceptical attack on the concept of mental illness has led, paradoxically, not to the demise of psychiatry, but to the potential for it to emerge as a lead discipline in twenty-first century medicine.

TABLE 2.1: Ten Principles of (VBM)

THE PARADIGM

1st Principle of VBM	All decisions stand on two feet, on values as well as on facts
2nd Principle of VBM	We tend to notice values only when they are diverse and hence likely to be problematic
3rd Principle of VBM	Scientific progress, in opening up choices, is increasingly bringing the full diversity of human values into play in healthcare
4th Principle of VBM	VBM's "first call" for information is the perspective of the patient or patient group concerned in a given decision
5th Principle of VBM	In VBM, conflicts of values are resolved primarily, not by reference to a rule prescribing an outcome, but by processes designed to support a balance of legitimately different perspectives

THE PRACTICE

6th Principle of VBM	Careful attention to language use in a given context is one of a range of powerful methods for raising awareness of values
7th Principle of VBM	A rich resource of both empirical and philosophical methods is available for improving our knowledge of other people's values
8th Principle of VBM	Ethical Reasoning is employed in VBM primarily to explore differences of values, not, at in quasi-legal bioethics, to determine "what is right"

9th Principle of VBM	Communication skills have a substantive rather than (as in quasi-legal ethics) a merely executive role in VBM
10th Principle of VBM	VBM, although involving a partnership with ethicists and lawyers (equivalent to the partnership with scientists in EBM), puts decision-making back where it belongs, with users and providers at the clinical coal-face.

(Adapted from Fulford, K.W.M. (2004) *Values-Based Medicine: Effective Healthcare Decision-Making in the Context of Value Diversity*. Cambridge: Cambridge University Press.)

Section I   Values-Based Medicine (VBM)

Values-based medicine (VBM), like evidence-based medicine (EBM), is a response to complexity. EBM is a response to the growing complexity of the *facts* relevant to decision-making in all areas of healthcare. VBM is the corresponding response to the growing complexity of the *values* relevant to decision-making in all areas of healthcare.

The need for values-based medicine arises directly from the way in which, at the turn of the millennium, values have been pushed, willing or no, to the top of the medical agenda. This is most evident in the current feeding frenzy of ethical and medico-legal issues in medicine. But the values agenda is much wider. It includes, among other developments, the appearance of new institutions challenging doctors' traditional self-regulation,[4] the publication of government blueprints prescribing standards for healthcare,[5] and, most significant of all, the rapid growth in the number and influence of patient advocacy groups, the very *raison d'être* of which is to represent patients' values against those, equally, of professionals and of the executive.

Medicine's response to this pandemic of value issues has been largely negative. Perplexed and demoralised by its growing failure, despite

---

[4] In the U.K. such institutions include the Commission for Health *Improvement* and the National Institute for Clinical *Excellence*. Corresponding institutions in the U.S.A. include the National Institute of Health's National Institute of Mental Health, Medicare, Medicaid, and the rules governing tort (malpractice) litigation.

[5] In the U.K. we have the Patients' Charter, for example, and a series of National Service Frameworks covering each major area of healthcare, including mental health.

the many triumphs of medical science, to win hearts and minds, medicine has reacted with a combination of denial and of outright *mea culpa* breast beating. Small wonder, then, that ethicists and lawyers have stepped into the ethical breach. Small wonder that they have become established—in the tabloid "spin"—as moral guardians, protecting the public from what has become widely represented as a somewhat predatory profession.

VBM offers an alternative response to the growing complexity of values in healthcare. VBM, while drawing readily on the expertise of lawyers and ethicists (much as EBM draws on that of scientists and statisticians), nonetheless relocates values where they belong, at the heart of the clinical encounter, in the relationship between professional and patient. It is in showing the importance of values in *all* areas of medicine, that, as we will see later, VBM provides a response to Szasz's sceptical attack on psychiatry. First, though, we need to consider in more detail the role of VBM in respect of clinical decision-making, and its relationship, in this respect, with EBM.

VBM, EBM and Clinical Decision-making

VBM is based on the premise that decision-making in all areas of healthcare stands on two feet, on values as well as on facts. This premise is derived from the notion of practical reasoning, viz. the reasons we have for anything we do (not just in healthcare). Practical reasoning, as Aristotle first pointed out, is always based on some combination of facts and values (Aristotle wrote of beliefs and desires. The importance of values as well as facts in decision-making has been reinforced in modern times through the development of decision theory, which combines probabilities (facts) with utilities (values). Sometimes in healthcare the values involved in a particular decision are not immediately visible. I return to why this should be so in a moment. But the values are there nonetheless.

Case Example: Diane Abbot, the artist who "saw" colours

Diane Abbot was a 50-year-old artist and art historian of considerable distinction. After a year's successful treatment with lithium for a manic-depressive illness, she decided, somewhat abruptly, to stop her medication. The problem, she explained to her general practitioner, Dr Robertson, was that, successful as the lithium had been in controlling her mood swings, it had stopped her being able to see colours. She did not mean "colour blind," she continued. It was that colours had lost their emotional intensity. The loss of her ability to really see *colours outweighed, for her, as an artist, the risks of a further manic episode.*

Diane Abbot's story illustrates a number of the key features of VBM and I will be returning to it at several points in this article. Here, it shows the way in which deciding what to prescribe, in a particular case, depends on values as well as facts.

The facts were certainly essential in Diane Abbot's case. Before starting lithium, she was assessed by the local psychiatric team. The psychiatrist, Dr Kirk, spent some time with her explaining the advantages and disadvantages of different ways of managing manic-depressive disorder, and detailing the effects and side effects particularly of lithium. Being an academic, Diane Abbot was perhaps better placed than many to process all this information. Being a woman of strong character, moreover, there was no question of her being bullied into taking lithium. So this is not an "ethics case", conventionally understood (about patient autonomy, and the like). Fact and value, at the stage of Diane Abbot's initial assessment, all pointed one way, to taking lithium. All the same, the key clinical variable, the deciding factor, when it came to discontinuing treatment, turned out to be an unexpected (though not wholly unprecedented, Jamison 1994), side effect of lithium as judged from the perspective of Diane Abbot's *values as an artist.*

Prescribing is an increasingly evidence-based area of clinical decision-making. Prescribing, that is to say, is an area in which there is a growing body of facts, derived from high-quality scientific research, on which we can draw to supplement our individual knowledge and experience in coming to a decision in a particular case. This is why EBM is important practically. The essence of EBM is to make the facts relevant to a given decision, and the processes by which we come to acquire and then use these facts, explicit. Prescribing was of course "evidence based" long before the invention of EBM. But with ever accelerating progress in medical science and technology, we have had to develop more sophisticated ways of drawing on the growing body of evidence available to us in individual cases.

But this growing body of evidence, and corresponding development of EBM, does not exclude values. To the contrary, without values, there is nothing (*literally* nothing) by which the facts about this or that treatment option can be weighed in coming to a decision "on the evidence."

Diane Abbot's values as an artist, as I noted at the end of the last section, led her to stop taking lithium. But her values were also operative at an earlier stage in her story. In "processing," as I put it, all the information she was given by Dr Kirk (her psychiatrist) about lithium and other treatments, it was her *values* which were critical. For Diane Abbot, at this stage, the risks, say, of thyroid disorder or kidney damage from lithium, were outweighed by the benefits of stabilising her mood, so that she could work more effectively, be less likely to embarrass her family or colleagues during a manic episode, and so forth. I focused above on the critical influence of her values as an artist in deciding to *stop* taking lithium. This is where her values became visible, as it were. But her values were nonetheless there, woven together with facts, in her original decision to start treatment.

Once we start looking for values, once we start thinking in terms of values as well as facts, it is immediately evident that values are operative even further back in Diane Abbot's story. For of course her decision was not taken in isolation. Her decision to start lithium was, at the time, a product of her values combined with the facts about lithium as presented to her by Dr Kirk, the psychiatrist. But the possibility of Diane Abbot making this choice depended on a whole series of earlier decisions, overtly factual or evidence-based, covertly (though crucially) based also on values. These earlier decisions included,

the decision by her General Practitioner (G.P.),[6] Dr. Robertson, to refer Diane Abbot to Dr. Kirk. This decision was based overtly on the evidence of her clinical condition. But as a G.P., Dr Robertson had a budget to balance; and every G.P. is familiar with difficulties about whether a referral is worth making, "worth" in this context being the operative (value) word;

multiple decisions, further back still, of hospital administrators, health authorities and other healthcare providers, to make lithium available as a treatment. Again, these decisions are "evidence-based". But it is here that issues of rationing arise perhaps most acutely, reflecting competing values;

the policy decisions taken by those at a national level[7] to recommend lithium in clinical practice guidelines for the treatment of manic-

---

[6] A family doctor providing primary care.

[7] Such as medical Royal Colleges and NICE (the National Institute for Clinical Excellence) in the UK; and in the USA, the National Institutes of Health, American

depressive disorder. The problems faced by those with responsibility for issuing clinical practice guidelines are often more about how to balance competing perspectives on the benefits and disbenefits of the effects and side effects of a given treatment, than to agree what, as a matter of fact, the effects and side effects are!

the on-going decisions of those concerned with audit and clinical governance, which keep lithium "in play". Such decisions are (or should be) evidence based. Again, though, it is by reference to values that the evidence is weighed in coming to a decision.[8]

even further back, the decisions, by individual researchers, drug companies, ethics committees, and others to pursue the research from which new drugs, and our knowledge of their effects and side effects, are derived. The traditional paradigm of science is of a value-free "objective" activity. But much of the work in the history and philosophy of science in the final decades of the twentieth century was concerned with showing the extent to which values are woven into the fabric of science itself (Fulford et al. forthcoming).

But now a question arises. If values are so important in medicine, if they are woven, along with facts, right through the very fabric of the subject, why has this not been more evident before now? Why have we been so much more aware of the evidence-base than of the values-base of prescribing? This question brings us to the theory supporting VBM.

VBM and Philosophical Value Theory

VBM draws particularly on the work of R.M. Hare and others in what has become known as the Oxford School of analytic philosophy. Writing in the 1950s and 1960s Hare was concerned with the logic, with the meanings and implications of value terms ("good," "bad," "right,", and so forth).[9]

Medical Association, American Psychiatric Association, and the current Diagnostic and Statistical Manual for the Mental Disorders (DSM), defining "standard of care" for the treatment of particular diagnostic entitities.

[8] The key audit criteria for clinical governance in the U.K. is the aptly named evaluative concept of "best practice".

[9] R M Hare died recently. His considerable output included later contributions to "bioethics" one important theme of which was to show how work on the logic of values,

Work of this kind in ethics is called philosophical value theory (or sometimes "metaethics" or just "moral theory"[10]). Although somewhat abstract in orientation, philosophical value theory has a wide range of practical applications in medicine and psychiatry (Fulford 1990; 2001) and I will be returning to Hare's work, and the work of other Oxford philosophers of this period, below. A key observation of Hare's, though, for our present purposes, is that values tend to become visible only where they are divergent, and, hence, are likely to come into conflict. We only notice values, that is to say, when they cause trouble!

Thus, in Diane Abbot's case we did not initially notice her values at the stage of her original assessment because, at this stage, her values were (broadly) concordant with everyone else's (her family, friends, doctors, and so on). It was only when it came to discontinuing treatment that a gap opened up. It was only at this stage that Diane Abbot's values diverged from those of others concerned. At the stage of her initial assessment Diane Abbot was more concerned about the risk of relapse than about possible side effects of lithium, and so was everyone else. Her values, then, although indeed one of the "feet" on which the original decision to start lithium stood, went unnoticed. We had to reflect on them to see that they were there. It was only when Diane Abbott's values diverged from those of others, that they became visible. Her need to be able to "really see" colours, although a value with which we might empathise, is not one that for most people would outweigh the hazards of a relapse of a manic-depressive illness. But the ability to "really see" colours was the critical value for Diane Abbot.

---

combined with reasonable assumptions (and/or actual information) about the needs and wishes of human beings, leads to substantive moral conclusions: see for example his two collections, *Essays in Ethical Theory* (1989) and *Essays on Bioethics* (1993). His first and most abstract book, however, *The Language of Morals* (Hare 1952), is fast becoming a classic of twentieth century philosophy. See also his *Essays on the Moral Concepts* (Hare 1972) for further examples of his work in philosophical value theory. Hare's opponents, philosophically speaking, included Philippa Foot (Foot 1958–59) and G.J. Warnock (Warnock 1971). Foot, Warnock, and others argued, *contra* Hare, that value judgements could sometimes be derived from exclusively factual (or descriptive) premises. Hare followed the eighteenth-century British empiricist philosopher, David Hume, in arguing for a logical separation of description and evaluation. For an outline of the implications of these two positions in the so-called "is-ought" debate for the language of medicine, see Chapter 3 of my *Moral Theory and Medical Practice* (Fulford 1989).

[10] This is the sense of the term "moral theory" as used in the title of my book, *Moral Theory and Medical Practice*. I explore in detail the applications of philosophical value theory of the Oxford School to the language of medicine. Much of the material on VBM in the present chapter is based on ideas developed in this book.

This is why her values suddenly became fully visible at this stage in her story.

Hare's observation, then, is that the *visibility* of the values in a given situation is a function of their *diversity*. The more diverse the values bearing on a given situation, the more likely there is to be disagreement and conflict, and the more visible the values concerned will be. Conversely, the more uniform or homogenous the values concerned, the less they will be in conflict, and the less they will be noticed. Values are in this respect like children: if they are well behaved, they are at risk of going unnoticed!

This observation about values, taken from Hare, is, as we will see, an important part of the explanation from philosophical value theory for the growing visibility of values in healthcare in recent decades. Before returning to this, though, we need a second observation about the logic of values, also taken from the work of Hare and his colleagues,[11] viz., that where the values expressed in a given situation are largely settled and agreed upon, the language used to express these values may come to look, not like evaluative language at all, but like *descriptive*, or *factual*, language.

Hare's work gives us a particularly clear account of how evaluative language can become disguised in this way, camouflaged to look like descriptive language. Thus, Hare pointed out that all value terms, including such general purpose value terms as "good" and "bad," are made up of at least two distinct elements of meaning, a descriptive element and an evaluative element. Hare called the latter element, the "prescriptive" element. This element, he said, is the *action guiding* part of the meaning of a value term. But the value judgement expressed by a value term is made on the basis of criteria which are not as such evaluative (or prescriptive) but *descriptive (or factual)* in nature. This is what Hare called the descriptive element of the meaning of a value term.

The two-pronged, descriptive + evaluative nature of value terms will be important to us shortly when we come to respond to Szasz's scepticism about the concept of mental illness. It is important, though, first, to see that this is a *general* feature of the logic (the meaning) of such terms. It is nothing to do specifically with psychiatric, nor indeed with medical, terms.

This is clear from the examples that Hare and others used. These were drawn from everyday, some would say mundane, uses of value terms such as "good strawberry" (Hare 1952). The use of "good" in such contexts is

---

[11] See, for example Hare 1952; 1963; also Warnock 1971; Urmson 1950.

clearly evaluative in the sense that it prescribes (in Hare's sense) the strawberry in question as one that is good for eating. Yet the meaning conveyed by "good strawberry" is, in everyday usage, not overtly evaluative but descriptive: it implies that the strawberry in question is "red, sweet, grub-free, etc." This, Hare and others argued, is because people's values in respect of strawberries are very similar; hence the descriptive criteria for the value judgement expressed by "good strawberry" will be very similar from one occasion of the use of the term "good strawberry" to the next; hence these descriptions ("red, sweet, grub-free, etc.") will become attached by association to the meaning of "good strawberry"; and hence the meaning of "good strawberry" comes, by way of these contingent considerations, to carry the descriptive meaning "red, sweet, grub-free, etc." But contrast "good strawberry" with, say, "good picture," a value judgement for which there are no widelysettled descriptive criteria, a value judgement, that is to say, the criteria for which vary widely and legitimately, and a value judgement, consequently, the meaning of which, correspondingly, remains overtly evaluative.

FIGURE 2.1: Good Strawberry versus Good Picture

STRAWBERRIES	**PICTURES**

Agreement *over what makes* *a good strawberry* *(= sweet, clean skinned, etc.)*	*Disagreement* *over what makes* *a good picture* *(= ?????)*
Hence *The term "good strawberry" has acquired the factual meaning "red, sweet, grub-free, etc."*	*Hence* *The meaning of "good picture" has acquired no consistent factual meaning*

We now have two observations about the logical (meaning-carrying) properties of value terms taken from the work of Hare and others in philosophical value theory: 1) that values tend to become visible where they are divergent and hence are likely to be contested, and 2) that where values are shared, the language in which they are expressed, including value terms such as "good", may convey descriptive or factual meaning.[12]

In Diane Abbot's case, then, extending Hare's observations to medicine, the original decision to start on lithium appeared evidence rather than value based, not because values were not there, but because they were *shared* values. Correspondingly, values became visible at the later stage of stopping treatment, because at this stage they were *not* shared. In Hare's terms, the value judgements expressed by "good treatment" at the stage of the initial assessment, were made on the basis of shared factual criteria (the probable curtailment of Diane Abbot's manic episodes, set against the risk of possible thyroid or kidney damage, and so forth); but when it came to stopping the treatment, Diane Abbot's criterion of being unable to "really see" colours was particular to her. It was no less legitimate a value for that, of course; but it was at variance with the (also legitimate) values she had formerly shared with everyone else.

Similar considerations apply to the further values (the above list) which, once we had started to look for them, we found supporting Diane Abbot's original decision to start on lithium. These decisions—to refer, to make lithium available locally, to license its use nationally, to continue its use, and, right back at the beginning, to do the research which led to its discovery in the first place—tend to be thought of as scientific, or evidence-based, where the operative values are shared (for example, the shared value of advancing knowledge of disease in medical-scientific research), but as ethical, or values-based, where the operative values are contentious (for instance, where there are issues of competing demands on limited resources). But in each and every decision, fact and value, description and evaluation, were both necessary.

VBM has a good deal to say about where one goes with these observations in practice when legitimately different values are in play. I will be returning to the theory and practice of VBM shortly. This is important, partly because VBM would be empty practically if it stopped merely at this analytic stage; and partly because, as we will see, the practical implications of VBM are as significant as its philosophical underpin-

---

[12] Though Hare was careful to point out (for example, *Language of Morals*, p 124) that these are only tendencies. In some contexts the descriptive criteria may be widely shared and yet the value term remain overtly evaluative.

nings when it comes to responding to Szaszian scepticism. But we now have sufficient ideas from philosophical value theory to answer the question raised at the end of the last section, viz., the "why now?" question, why values are becoming more visible in healthcare at the present time. It is to the answer to this question that we turn next.

VBM and the Growing Visibility of Values in Healthcare

The answer to the "why now?" question, in a word, is science.[13]. To some, this may seem a surprising, perhaps even unlikely, answer. After all, science and ethics, facts and values, have traditionally been counterposed. But the connection between science and the pandemic of values in healthcare in the closing years of the twentieth century, is straightforward enough. It is that scientific progress, in expanding the "can do" of medicine; increases the choices available to us, as practitioners or patients; and this in turn brings the full diversity of human values into play in healthcare decision-making. Thus, so long as I have no choice between outcomes A or B, it makes no difference whether I value A more than B or vice versa. My values, and hence the potential for conflicts of values, only come into play where I have a choice between A and B.

Although in principle straightforward, it will be worthwhile developing this point, partly because it runs directly counter to the traditional stand-off between values and science, and partly because the link between scientific progress and human values is central to my concluding claim in this article, that Szaszian scepticism about mental illness leads, ultimately, not to the demise but to a strengthening of psychiatry.

Traditionally, then, science and values have been perceived as being, somehow, in conflict. This traditional perception is reflected in talk of scientific advances "challenging our deepest values," about the "sanctity of life," the "traditional family," and so forth. And in this construction science and technology tend to emerge as the villains of the piece, not merely challenging but putting at hazard these "deepest values."

But if the values concerned really were our "deepest" values, there would be no challenge to them! Consider euthanasia, for example. It is precisely because the "sanctity of life" is not, for many people in many circumstances, their *deepest* value, that there is an ethical issue about

---

[13] There are other factors, such as growing individualism, international communications, and so forth, but scientific progress is the key factor internal to healthcare—see Fulford forthcoming.

euthanasia. The issue was always there, to an extent, in principle. But technology has sharpened the issue. It has sharpened it, not by "challenging" the sanctity of life, but by opening up choices, about how long and in what circumstances life is worth living, choices which, as a matter of practical possibility, were simply not open to us before. And this in turn has brought into healthcare decision-making the wide diversity of human values operative in this area.

In VBM, then, science and technology are, in themselves, neutral. Advances in medical science, if they open up choices in areas in which human values are shared (and in this sense "deepest"), do not make values more visible. The first use of penicillin to save a child from dying from an infection did not start a pandemic of values. It was an advance in the "can do" of medicine as radical as any in the closing years of the twentieth century. But a painful and premature death, is, in and of itself, a bad condition for (more or less) anyone, at (more or less) any historical period, and in (more or less) any culture. Technological advance, then, in this context, far from "challenging" our deepest values, was actually in service to them.

Diane Abbot's case, although not as dramatic as a case of euthanasia, was less straightforward, evaluatively speaking, than that of a child with a life threatening infection. Her manic episodes were severe. Judged against her own values (during her periods of remission), as well as the values of others close to her, her condition was one that merited treatment. As such, a short-term intervention with a neuroleptic was more or less equivalent on the values side, to penicillin for the child with a life-threatening staphylococcal infection. This indeed was the basis on which Diane Abbot agreed to be treated after she stopped taking lithium. She worked out, with Dr. Robertson (her G.P.), an "advance directive" according to which, if specified members of her family, or one particular named colleague, reported to him that she was showing warning signs of a further manic episode, he (Dr. Robertson) would contact the local psychiatric team and arrange, if necessary, admission on an involuntary basis under the Mental Health Act.

This was a feasible management plan in Diane Abbot's case because her episodes of manic upswing nearly always started with clear-cut warning signs, notably that she stopped sleeping properly. The difficulty was that her insight was also an early casualty of the disorder (she consistently misconstrued these changes as moving into a "productive phase" even though her work actually deteriorated, as judged by others at the time and herself subsequently). In other cases, the "advance directive" strategy is less feasible, sometimes because the warning signs of relapse are not there or are inconsistent (this is a factor on the fact-side), sometimes because there is less agreement about the severity of the condition (a factor on the value-side).[14]

Fortunately, human values not being wholly chaotic, many clinical decisions in medicine are, and will remain, as with the child with a serious infection, evaluatively straightforward. All the same, the growing visibility of values shows that situations in which the evaluative element in decision-making is not straightforward are becoming more common. And if advances in medical science are as I have suggested an important driver of this change, we must expect, on the assumption that medical science will continue to advance, that such situations will become ever more widespread in the future. In the twenty-first century, then, VBM will become as important as EBM. This is why, I will argue, Szaszian scepticism will prove to have been important for medicine as a whole, not just for psychiatry, in the twenty-first century. Before coming to this, though, we now need to respond directly to Szasz's scepticism. We need to apply Hare's observations about the logic of values, as the basis of VBM, to Szasz's claim that mental illness is a myth.

Section II   Values-Based Medicine and the Myth of Mental Illness

In this section I consider the implications of Hare's work in philosophical value theory, as the theoretical basis of VBM, first for the analytic grounds of Szaszian scepticism about mental illness, and then for the counter-arguments of the critics of Szasz's work from within psychiatry. I will argue that Hare's work, while denying Szasz's claim that mental illness is a myth, also denies the claims of Szasz's critics that mental illness is, essentially, no different from physical illness. This will provide a basis, in Section III, for responding to the contingent grounds on which Szasz and others critiqued psychiatry in the twentieth century.

VBM and Szaszian Scepticism

The basis of Szasz's analytic scepticism about psychiatry, the basis of his claim that mental illness is a myth, is, as I outlined at the start of this

---

[14] In mild mania, indeed, difficulties on the values-side of the decision, may extend to disagreements about which phase of the mood swing is pathological, the up-swing or the down-swing (see Moore, Hope, and Fulford 1994)!

chapter, essentially that "mental illness" is defined by *value* norms whereas "physical illness" is defined by *factual* norms. The (paradigmatic) physical illnesses, Szasz argued in his early and foundational work, are defined by anatomical and physiological norms, whereas so called mental illnesses are defined by norms which are "psychosocial, ethical and legal" in character (Szasz 1960, p. 114). Hence, he concluded, talk of *mental* illness involves a category error. Mental illnesses are different in kind from physical illnesses. Mental illnesses are not, really, illnesses at all, in the sense in which the paradigmatic physical illnesses are illnesses. Mental illnesses, properly understood, are life (or moral), rather than medical (or scientific), problems. Mental illnesses, so called, are, in Szasz's memorable phrase, "problems of living" (Szasz 1960 p. 118).

Now, it is certainly true, consistently with Szasz's analytic sceptical claim, that mental illness is more overtly value-laden than physical illness. As I have described elsewhere (Fulford 1994), the differential diagnosis of mental disorders includes moral or "life" problems (psychopathy is close to delinquency, alcoholism to drunkenness, and so forth). Certain disorders, furthermore, in both ICD-10 (International Classification of Diseases, WHO 1992) and DSM-IV (Diagnostic and Statistical Manual, APA, 1994), are actually defined in part by social-evaluative norms (the paraphilias, for example, and personality disorder).[15] DSM, more remarkably still, has added to the traditional exclusively descriptive (symptom-based) criteria for the functional psychoses, a new criterion making explicit the (in part) evaluative criterion of impairment of social and/or occupational functioning. For schizophrenia the new criterion is Criterion B, of "social/occupational dysfunction" (APA, 1994, p. 285); and there are similar criteria for manic depressive psychoses, as in Diane Abbot's case.[16]

Mental illness, then, consistently with Szasz's sceptical attack, is more overtly value-laden than physical illness; and not just outside of

---

[15] The DSM, unlike ICD includes a definition of disorder. This prohibits a diagnosis being based solely on social-evaluative norms. For a condition to be a disorder, it has to be "clinically significant" (APA, 1994, p. xx1).

[16] The criteria of social-occupational dysfunctioning are presented somewhat differently for schizophrenia and for manic-depressive disorder. In the criteria for "Manic Episode," for example, Criterion D includes impairment of functioning in either occupational or social contexts or in relationships. It also includes, as yet further alternatives for satisfying the criterion, the necessity for hospital admission to prevent harm to self or others, or, simply, but inconsistently with the criteria for the diagnosis of schizophrenia, the presence of psychotic features (APA, 1994, p. 332).

psychiatry, in lay discourse as it were, but in the very heartland of the scientific basis of the discipline, in its official classifications (the ICD and DSM).[17] The more value-laden nature of mental illness, indeed, was common ground between Szasz and many of his critics (in the 1970s). The difference between, for example, Szasz (1960) and Kendell (1975), was that where Szasz considered the value judgments involved in taking a mental condition to be a disorder to be ineliminable (and hence mental disorder to be radically different from physical disorder), Kendell argued (as many others have done[18]) that the relevant diagnostic value judgments could be redefined in purely factual terms (in terms of evolutionary norms of survival and reproduction), and hence that mental disorders were no different in principle from physical disorders (Kendell 1975).

Hare's observations, however, of the logical properties of value terms, suggest a very different explanation for the more overtly value-laden nature of mental illness compared with physical illness.[19] Mental illness, according to Hare's observations, is more overtly value laden, and physical illness more overtly factual, not because mental conditions are part of a moral world of life problems while physical conditions are part of a medical world of scientific theories, but because mental conditions are *evaluatively more complex* than physical conditions. I do not have space here to go into this implication of Hare's work in detail.[20] A full account would have to cover the differences between illness, disease, dysfunction, wound, disability, and other terms in the language of pathology,[21] and it would have to include an examination of each of the (logically) very different areas of psychopathology with which psychiatry has traditionally been concerned.[22] The nub, though, the essence of why mental disorders

---

[17] The importance of values in the diagnosis of psychotic disorders is recognised by neuroscience researchers (Goodwin 2002). This is particularly important because, from the perspective of the traditional medical model schizophrenia is, as Szasz pithily put it, the "sacred symbol" of psychiatry (Szasz 1976a).

[18] See for example Boorse 1975; 1997; Wakefield 2000.

[19] Indeed this approach shows that the critical difference between Szasz and his critics is not, directly, a difference in their respective understandings of the concept of mental illness, but a difference in their respective understandings of the concept of *physical* illness (see Chapter 1 of my *Moral Theory and Medical Practice*).

[20] These implications are worked out in my *Moral Theory and Medical Practice*, together with Fulford 1999 and 2000.

[21] I provide a more detailed treatment of these concepts in Chapters 2–7 of *Moral Theory and Medical Practice*.

[22] I examine the concept of mental illness in general in Chapter 8 of *Moral Theory and Medical Practice*, and specific areas of psychopathology in Chapters 9 and 10.

are evaluatively more complex that physical disorders, is that whereas physical medicine tends to be concerned with areas of human experience and behaviour in which our values as human beings are largely shared, psychiatry is concerned with areas of human experience and behaviour in which human values *differ widely and legitimately*.

I am generalizing here, of course. But the generalizations are *prima facie* credible, nonetheless. Thus, in physical medicine we are often concerned with such aspects of human experience as severe bodily pain and risk of death (as in a "heart attack", or appendicitis, for example). Such experiences are, in and of themselves, *bad* experiences by (more or less) everyone's criteria. In psychiatry, by contrast, we are concerned, typically, with emotion, desire, affect, motivation and belief, all of which are areas of human experience in which our values differ widely and legitimately.

The difference, here, is well illustrated by the DSM's new criteria for psychotic disorders, the criteria of impaired social/occupational functioning noted above. These criteria (B for schizophrenia, D for manic-depressive disorder) are widely thought to be no more than further *descriptive* criteria. Consistently with Hare's observations, this is because they were introduced originally with severe disorders in mind, ie conditions which by (more or less) anyone's values would be *bad* conditions.[23] More precisely, according to Hare's observations, these criteria appear factual rather than evaluative to the extent that they are used of severe *disturbances* of functioning. Such disturbances, by definition, are just those *changes* in functioning that are changes *for the worse* by (more or less) anyone's standards.[24] That these criteria are, nonetheless, evaluative in nature is clear from other more contentious cases. In mild mania, for example, the phase of the cycle that is considered abnormal is overtly a matter of value judgements (see Moore, Hope and Fulford 1994); and the differential diagnosis between delusion and religious/spiritual experience turns critically on evaluative norms (Jackson and Fulford 1997).

For Szasz, then, we need a Criterion B for schizophrenia, and corresponding criteria for manic-depressive disorder, because these conditions are, really, " problems of living"; for Kendell we need these criteria because psychiatry is still at a pre-scientific stage of development; for Hare, we need these criteria because the value judgements which are

---

[23] Criterion B was introduced originally to distinguish schizotypy from "florid" or full-blown schizophrenia.

[24] In Diane Abbot's case, she shared with everyone else the descriptive criteria (including her impaired functioning as an artist) required to satisfy Criterion D.

necessary (though of course not sufficient) for these conditions to be taken, in a particular case, to be *pathological* conditions, are open and contentious. The corresponding criteria are there in physical medicine, too; but they remain implicit because the criteria for the corresponding value judgements are (very largely) shared, hence (largely) unproblematic, and hence (generally) can be ignored.[25]

VBM and Szasz's Critics

VBM, then, building on the work of Hare and others in the Oxford School of philosophical value theory, contradicts Szasz's analytical sceptical claim that mental illness is a myth. According to the VBM approach, there is no (necessary) category error in taking a mental condition to be an illness in the same sense that physical illnesses are illnesses. The term "illness," in both contexts, expresses (in part) a negative value judgement. Mental illnesses are, in general, more overtly value-laden than physical illnesses only because the value judgements expressed by "illness" in respect of mental conditions tend to be open and contentious, while the corresponding value judgements expressed by the use of the term "illness" in respect of bodily conditions tend to be widely settled and agreed upon. In this respect, then, "mental illness" is like "good" used of pictures (in our example derived from Hare above), while "physical illness" is like "good" used of strawberries.

If VBM contradicts Szaszian scepticism, however, by the same token it contradicts Szasz's critics. Kendell, and others,[26] in responding

---

[25] Note that a full treatment of this point would have to include an account of the differences (the differences of meaning) between illness and disease. The American philosopher, Christopher Boorse, was among the first to analyse this difference as a difference between a more value-laden (illness) and less value-laden (disease) term—see for example Boorse 1975; 1997. Boorse employs this distinction to develop a more sophisticated medical model. In Boorse's version of the medical model, disease, as a (supposedly) value-free scientific concept, allows us to distinguish genuine illnesses from other negatively evaluated aspects of human experience and behaviours (such as delinquency). Philosophical value theory generates a model which is in a sense the reverse of this. Philosophical value theory suggests that the negative value judgements by which experiences and behaviours are (in part) marked out as experiences to illness, are the origin of the negative value judgements by which, in turn, the underlying bodily causes of those experiences and behaviours are marked out as pathological, and, hence, as diseases (Fulford 1989, Chapter 4). In Boorse's medical model, then, disease defines illness; in VBM, illness defines disease.

[26] For example Roth and Kroll 1986; Wing 1978.

directly to Szasz in the 1970s, argued, essentially, that with a little more science mental illness would end up looking just like physical illness. VBM suggests that this is not only wrong but dangerously wrong. For if the Hare-VBM explanation of the more value-laden nature of mental illness compared with physical illness is right, then science could only make mental illness look like physical illness by abolishing an important aspect of our individuality as human beings, viz., our differences of values in such areas as emotion, desire, volition, belief, and so forth, the areas of human experience and behaviour with which psychiatry is concerned.

Mental illnesses, then, according to VBM, and consistently with Szasz's sceptical argument, are *not* the same as physical illnesses in respect of values.[27] To assume that they *are* the same is to deny an aspect of diagnosis (the evaluative aspect) which, while legitimately ignored in acute physical medicine ("legitimately" because the operative values are for practical purposes agreed), we ignore at our peril in psychiatry ("at our peril" because the operative values will often be highly problematic).

This connects VBM with Szasz's contingent grounds for scepticism about psychiatry. For VBM coincides with Szaszian scepticism in believing that many of the abuses to which psychiatric patients have been subject are a product, in part, of an illegitimate extrapolation of the "medical" model of illness from physical (or bodily) to mental conditions. Szasz takes the illegitimacy involved in this extrapolation to consist in a category error, the error of taking what are really life problems to be illnesses. VBM takes the illegitimacy to consist in a different category error, the error of taking what are really hybrid fact + value concepts (physical illness, disease, dysfunction, and so forth) to be exclusively factual concepts.

The error, then, according to VBM, is not, as such, the extrapolation from bodily to mental conditions. The error is in what is extrapolated: a false, or at any rate incomplete, model of illness. What flows from this in the two cases is of course different. Szasz seeks to take mental conditions out of medicine. VBM seeks to take values into medicine, or at any rate to recognise fully that they are already there. VBM requires medicine, whether concerned with mental or bodily conditions, to tackle values "head on," to tackle the values operative in healthcare decision-making with the same degree of determination and rigour as, in the past, medicine has tackled the operative facts.

---

[27] Mental and physical illness are of course on a continuum rather than being categorically different.

Section III   VBM and the Abusive Uses of Psychiatry

In this section I outline what tackling the values operative in medicine "head on" means in practice. Once again, I do not have space to go into this in detail. But I will outline a key part of what it means by comparing VBM, first with EBM, then with bioethics. I will also briefly indicate the growing knowledge and skills base of VBM including the implications of these for training and research. This will provide a basis, in the last part of this section, for an outline of VBM's response to the contingent grounds of Szasz's critique of psychiatry, the abuses to which the subject has been so peculiarly vulnerable. This in turn will lead, in a brief concluding section, to the importance of Szasz's work not just for psychiatry but for medicine as a whole in the twenty-first century.

VBM and EBM: Different "First Calls" for Information

First, then, VBM and EBM. In Section 1 of this chapter VBM and EBM ran broadly parallel as responses to the growing complexity of healthcare decision-making.[28] In that section, corresponding with the first three principles of VBM (Table 2.1, pp. 59–60), we found that values and evidence are the two feet on which all decisions in healthcare stand, that we tend to notice the values operative in a given clinical situation only where they are diverse and hence likely to be problematic, and that scientific progress, far from making healthcare decisions less dependent on values, is increasingly bringing the full range and diversity of human values into medicine by opening up to us, as users and as providers of services, an ever wider range of choices.

---

[28] As responses to complexity, VBM and EBM both consist essentially in making explicit, and hence more effective, aspects of clinical decision-making which in less complex times could safely be left largely implicit. Just what is made explicit is different in VBM and EBM, of course. Again, this is a complex area. On the fact side, with EBM, it takes us into the disputed concepts of reliability and validity, and from there into deep questions in the philosophy of science. On the values side, with VBM we are drawn into the 200-year debate, noted earlier, footnote 9, about the relationship between facts and values. These are practically relevant areas, it should be said. In the philosophy of science, for example, key practical issues include the relationship between explicit (or 'codifiable') knowledge, of the kind generated paradigmatically by meta-analyses of research findings, and the intuitive or craft knowledge of individual users and practitioners. I return to the practical implications of philosophical value theory below.

With VBM's fourth principle, though, we come to a key difference between VBM and EBM, a difference in what I will term their respective "first calls" for information. In EBM, the "first call" is highly generalised information derived from meta-analyses of well-designed scientific research. The results of these meta-analyses, generated by pooling sources, provides information which is as objective as possible. EBM sets out, deliberately, to be as independent as possible of the perspective of any particular observer. This coincides with the essence of the scientific process, which, traditionally understood, is to be as *a*perspectival as possible, to aspire to what the American philosopher, Thomas Nagel, called the "The View From Nowhere" (Nagel 1986). Meta-analyses seek to approximate to this by giving us a view from everywhere, or at least from as many perspectives as possible. This is why the results of meta-analyses are at the top of the "evidence hierarchy" in EBM, above the results of individual research trials. Such trials in turn are above case histories and the particular knowledge and experience of individual practitioners, whose (necessarily) perspectival knowledge is at the bottom of the hierarchy.

VBM turns the evidence hierarchy the other way up. In VBM, the first call for information, being information about values rather than about facts, is the perspective of particular individuals. Where EBM seeks *a*perspectival information (about facts), VBM seeks *perspectival* information (about values). Where EBM seeks for information which is as perspective-free as possible, VBM seeks for information which is as close as possible to the particular perspectives of the individuals involved in a particular clinical context.

Turning the "hierarchy" upside down in this way, putting individual perspectives at the top, depends on the claim that human values are often *legitimately* different, ie that in many situations there may be no uniquely "right" value perspective. I return to this claim in the next section. As we will see, it is the key also to the differences between VBM and bioethics. It is based in part on the extent of the differences of values that, once we look for them, are apparent at all stages of the clinical process and in all areas of healthcare (Fulford, Dickenson and Murray, 2002). But the claim is also based on the perhaps stronger analytic grounds of the logical separation of description and evaluation for which Hare and others argued in the is-ought debate in philosophical value theory[29] (Fulford et al. forthcoming).

---

[29] See footnote 20 above. The recognition of legitimately different value perspectives is not a recipe for "anything goes." To the contrary, the principle of respect for individual

EBM and VBM, it is important to emphasise, are entirely complementary in emphasising, respectively, aperspectival and perspectival
sources of information. Their respective strengths—their respective contributions to strengthening the factual and evaluative feet on which clinical decisions stand—depend directly on their differences in this respect.
In Diane Abbot's case, for example, both kinds of information were
essential. In coming to her initial decision to take lithium, Diane Abbot
needed factual information about its effects and side effects, and she
needed this information to be as objective as possible.[30] On the values
side, by contrast, had her decision been based on Dr. Kirk's perspective,
on his evaluation of the pros and cons of lithium, had it been his values
rather than hers by which the effects and side effects were balanced, then
the decision would not have been Diane Abbot's at all. It would have
been Dr. Kirk's.

Of course, Diane Abbot might have deferred to Dr Kirk. As those
working particularly in cross-cultural psychiatry have pointed out, the
emphasis in much bioethics on an individualistic notion of autonomy
reflects "Western" values (Okasha 2000). Diane Abbot happened to be a
fiercely autonomous person. But had she not been, deferring to Dr. Kirk
would have reflected her values. Conversely, however, the user movement in psychiatry has repeatedly pointed out the extent to which
despite signing up to "autonomy" of patient choice, treatment decisions
reflect the values not of the patient but of the professionals. Peter
Campbell (1996), a freelance writer on user issues in the U.K., who has
a manic-depressive disorder, has put the point strongly. It is not, he
argues, that most users resist medical help as such, particularly in crisis
situations. But as the actual *users* of services, they want a far bigger say
in *how* it is used—how they are treated—so that interventions work to
best advantage as judged from the perspective of the particular individuals concerned.

An important principle of VBM, then, is that we should listen to our
patients. Our "first call" for information on the values side of clinical (or
indeed managerial) decision-making, is the perspective of the patient or
patient group concerned. Many doctors will say, "but of course we listen to our patients." Many doctors have said of EBM, "but of course we

---

differences, being a principle of *mutual* respect, generates strong constraints on policy
and practice. Racism, for example, is inconsistent with mutual respect.

[30] I leave aside here, as noted above (footnote 20), the relationship between personal
experience and generalised data; also the extent to which the scientific process itself,
although aspiring to be aperspectival, is driven by the perspectives of those concerned.

listen to the evidence." The gap between practice and the scientific literature, though, shows that, in the growing complexity of modern healthcare, we have not been listening to the evidence carefully enough. Hence the need for EBM. Similarly, the gap between practice and the user literature shows that, in the growing value complexity of modern healthcare, we have not been listening to our patients carefully enough. Hence the need for VBM.

Where one goes with this principle is open to debate. On the fact side, the need to listen more carefully, or at any rate with more sophisticated tools, leads to EBM. On the value side, many would say, it leads to bioethics. But there are a number of key differences between VBM and bioethics, at least as the latter has been expressed in practice in a predominantly quasi-legal form. It is to these differences that we turn next.

VBM and Bioethics: Different Ways of Resolving Disagreements

I have set out the differences between VBM and bioethics in detail elsewhere (Fulford, Dickenson and Murray 2002). As noted above, the key difference between them, the difference from which all the other differences spring is that, where quasi-legal ethics prescribes "right" values, VBM starts from respect for legitimately different value perspectives. This leads to a very different understanding of how disagreements on questions of value should be resolved. How to resolve differences of values is of course yet another of those questions that is subject to long-running philosophical debate. In healthcare practice, though, the difference between VBM and quasi-legal ethics can be thought of as being rather like the difference, in politics, between a liberal democracy and an authoritarian regime.

Thus, bioethics, in the predominantly quasi-legal form it has taken in its interactions with practice, has in effect if not in intent, sought to impose particular values, such as autonomy of patient choice. The ever-more complex sets of rules and regulations covering such areas as consent, confidentiality and research, reflect these "given" values. This is a top-down approach, then, in which the operative values are predetermined by ethical authorities, and in which disagreements on values are resolved, in principle, by reference to the rules and regulations embodying these given values. VBM, by contrast, in being premised on respect for differences of values, seeks to resolve disagreements, not by reference to someone else's values (however enlightened), but by seeking a balance of values among those directly concerned in a given situation. As in a democracy, there are limits to respect for differences of values (see above, footnote 29); but whereas in bioethics (of the quasi-legal kind) the guiding idea is to "lay down the law," to determine the "right" values for practice, to prescribe standards, in VBM the guiding idea is to widen awareness of values, to "extend the limits of tolerance" (Fulford 1996).

VBM's approach to resolving disagreements, through a balance of values, flows, like its "first call" for information, directly from the principle of respect for individual differences of values. That human values differ widely and (often) legitimately requires that the values of the individuals concerned be our "first call" for information. But this same principle means that, where differences of values come into conflict, no one value perspective should have automatic precedence. It is no part of VBM, then, that patient-centred care should mean treating our patients merely as consumers, as customers whose needs and wishes we, as healthcare professionals, exist to satisfy.[31] If the values of the patient or patient group concerned are central, this is not to say that the values of professionals are irrelevant. Far from it, the professional's assessment of the pros and cons of a given intervention, the professional's evaluations of these informed by his or her knowledge and experience, matters. As with all issues of value, there is no *a priori* basis for weighing the two, the patient's and the professional's perspectives. This, indeed, as I will indicate below, is a matter for practical reasoning, for processes driven by knowledge and skills mediated through good communication, rather than by reference to an outcome defined by a set of "given" values. Within VBM, indeed, a plurality of perspectives is to be welcomed. For without at least one balancing perspective, we are at risk of slipping from the traditional abuses of "doctor knows best", one extreme view, one absolute, to the abuses of an equal and opposite extreme of "patient knows best."

A plurality of perspectives is the reality in modern mental health care. In community-based models of service delivery a wide range of individuals, besides the "patient," have a legitimate interest in outcomes: these include other family members, especially if bearing a direct responsibility for care; but also employers, insurers, the state even. The idea that the interests of any of these should automatically "trump" those of the patient is anathema in a liberal democracy. But the most liberal of regimes recognizes situations in which doctors must put others before their particular patients (for instance, obligatory breaches of confiden-

---

[31] "The customer is always right" is the first principle of effective salesmanship!

tiality), and indeed situations in which the interests of "the State" are paramount. The point, then, is not that we should give up the Hippocratic principle of "patient first." It is that, as things actually are, this principle is already balanced by other values; that, as things actually are, we have to make judgments between these values; and hence that, given the growing complexity of the values operative in healthcare, we should make these values more explicit as a first step towards dealing with them more effectively.

In a democracy, then, in the democracy of values of VBM no less than in a political democracy, processes must be in place to support, as far as possible, diversity of view. The form, effectiveness, and indeed appropriateness of these processes, has to be subject to continual review. This indeed is of the essence of a healthy democracy. But our aim in this is not uniformity. It is to support diversity. It is to support what I have called elsewhere, a *dissensus*—a balanced and dynamic interplay of different perspectives, supported by processes which aim, not to close down on a given value, but to support effective decision-making which starts from and respects the legitimately different values of those concerned (Fulford 1998).

I have drawn the contrast between quasi-legal bioethics and VBM in this section rather starkly. There is indeed a key difference between them, the difference between *telling* people what they should do, and establishing processes which allow people to decide *for themselves* what they should do. This in turn leads to a series of less stark, but still important differences of emphasis between them. As Table 2.2 shows, these include very different uses of several of the skills of ethical problem solving in clinical practice—raised awareness of values, knowledge of values, ethical reasoning and communication skills (corresponding with Principles 6–9 of VBM, summarised in Table 2.1 above). These skills underwrite VBM's key shift in the locus of decision-making from ethicists and lawyers to those actually concerned, as users and providers, at the clinical coal-face (Principle 10 of VBM).

New training initiatives in the UK are supporting the development of these "VBM skills": in medical student education (Hope, Fulford and Yates 1996), for example, and, most recently, in CPD workshops for assertive outreach and other mental health teams working in the community (Fulford, Woodbridge and Williamson 2002).[32] Such initiatives are being strongly supported by the National Institute for Mental Health for England (NIMHE), the section of the UK government's Department

---

[32] The Values Awareness Workshop described in this article is a training session in which

TABLE 2.2: Differences between Traditional Bioethics and VBM (Values-Based Medicine)

	QUASI-LEGAL ETHICS	VBM
AIMS	i) Advocacy of particular values	i) Respect for diversity of values
	ii) Regulation	ii) Partnership
SCOPE OF APPLICATION	i) Treatment	i) Whole clinical encounter (including diagnosis)
	ii) Secondary care	ii) Primary (as well as secondary) care
CONCEPTUAL MODEL OF MEDICINE	Medical-scientific Model (Fact based)	Healthcare Model (Fact + Value based)
ETHICAL REASONING	i) Substantive ethical theory	i) Analytic ethical theory
	ii) Value content	ii) Empirical content
PRACTICAL APPLICATIONS	i) Ethical rules	i) Ethical process
	ii) Law as external regulator for self-regulation	ii) Law as framework
	iii) Communication skills executive	iii) Communication skills substantive

Based on the Table in K.W.M Fulford, T.H. Murray, and D. Dickenson, eds., **Many Voices,** *the Introduction to* **Healthcare Ethics and Human Values in Healthcare Ethics and Human Values**: *an Introductory Text with Readings and Case Studies (Oxford: Blackwell, 2002).*

ideas and examples from the work of Hare and others in analytic philosophy are used as the basis of practical exercises for mental health nurses, social workers and others, aimed at raising their awareness of their own and their clients' values, and of the differences between them.

of Health responsible for implementing national policies for mental
health. NIMHE's first action, indeed, was to launch, by Ministerial
Announcement (9th July, 2001), a Values Project Group. This Group is
working on a framework of values that will support and provide cross-
linking between key streams of NIMHE's work. Many of these streams
of work have strong resonances with Szasz's critiques of traditional psychiatry. Thus NIMHE's work includes a new determination to put users
at the centre of policy and practice; an emphasis on more effective
multi- and cross-disciplinary teamwork; a recognition and highlighting
of the importance of positive as well as negative values (in relation to
risk, for example); and the promotion of recovery-oriented practice.[33]
The latter, in particular, resonates with Szasz's positive alternatives to
the traditional medical model of psychiatry, in his emphasis, for example, on positive self-regard (see for example Szasz 1976b), and on taking responsibility for oneself, on being an agent rather than, merely, a
patient (see for example Szasz 1960; 1987; 2001; 2002).

   The importance of values, then, in mental health policy and practice
is already receiving support at the highest level in the U.K. It is to the
significance of this for preventing abusive uses of psychiatry that I turn
in the final part of this section.[34]

VBM and the Abusive Uses of Psychiatry

As noted at the start of this chapter, Szasz's sceptical attack on psychiatry is based on both analytic and contingent grounds. VBM, I have suggested, in the ideas it derives from the work of R.M Hare and others,
provides a powerful response to Szasz's analytic claim that mental illness is a myth. When it comes to Szasz's contingent grounds for scepticism about psychiatry, however, it might be thought that VBM, in being
relativist rather than absolutist in orientation, would be less effective.
For Szasz's contingent grounds are the widespread abuses to which
extending the medical model of illness to psychiatry, however well
intentioned, seems inevitably to lead. And abusive situations, many
would argue, require an absolutist rather than relativist ethic. After all,

---

[33] See for example Ruth O. Ralph, Recovery. *Psychiatric Rehabilitation Skills* 4:3
(2000), pp. 480–517.
[34] Within bioethics as a theoretical discipline, as distinct from in its dominant quasi-legal
form in practice, there is a growing counter-movement to the quasi-legal approach. This
counter-movement offers a rich resource for VBM in both its research and training agen-
das (Fulford, Dickenson, and Murray 2002).

to extend the political metaphor introduced in the last section, even in a democracy "martial law" is declared when a nation is at war!

There are dangers in relativism, of course. Like democracy, relativism is a risky business. Again, on the model of a democracy, there is a need for rules and regulation. In adverse regimes, a "code" is a strong ally for doctors who find themselves under pressure to collude in breaches of human rights (Fulford and Bloch 2000). Closer to home, rights and duties, clear principles, have been widely recognised to be central to the protections that, as a profession, we can offer to disadvantaged groups.

The danger, though, comes when we try to do *everything* we need to do with an approach which is appropriate in these extreme cases. And it is this danger, VBM suggests, which is the greater danger for psychiatry. The danger, that is to say, arises, not so much from intentional abuses as from a failure to recognise that the critical factor behind the vulnerability of psychiatry to abusive uses, is unrecognised differences of values. Differences of values in psychiatry fail to be recognised for what they are because of the dominance of the (supposedly) value free medical model. This model encourages us to focus on the facts while neglecting the values. Focusing on the facts, as noted above, is legitimate up to a point in acute physical medicine, to the extent that the operative values are shared. But it is wholly *ill*egitimate in psychiatry where the operative values are characteristically *not* shared.

The importance of mismatches of values over therapy is evident in the gap between user and provider perspectives. This was illustrated by Peter Campbell's observations, above (p. 79); it is also supported by wider epidemiological studies.[35] Therapeutic "enthusiasms," furthermore, as the seventeenth-century empirist philosopher John Locke would have called them (Locke 1960), were the bane of twentieth-century psychiatry. Psychoanalytic, biological, social, and psychological methods all have a proper part to play in psychiatry, and are often usefully combined. But each of them, in their turn, has been promoted as sinecures, to the disadvantage, ultimately, of patients.

Less well recognised is the importance of mismatches of values in psychiatric diagnosis. The "medical" model suggests that diagnosis, above all perhaps, is a matter exclusively for medical science. VBM, as outlined in Sections I and II, shows that it is also a matter of values, in principle in physical medicine, in practice in psychiatry (because of the

---

[35] See for example Rogers, Pilgrim, and Lacey's classic study, *Experiencing Psychiatry: Users' Views of Services* (1993).

inherent diversity of human values in the areas with which psychiatry is concerned—emotion, desire, volition, and so forth, as outlined above). The importance of mis-matches of diagnostic values in leading to abusive uses of psychiatry of the kind with which Szasz has been especially concerned, was evident in a study I carried out with a Russian colleague (Alec Smirnoff) and a Russian-speaking social worker (Elena Snow), on the scientific literature in the former U.S.S.R. over the period when psychiatry was being used there as a means of controlling political dissidence (Fulford, Smirnoff, and Snow 1993). Notoriously in the U.S.S.R., many dissidents over this period were diagnosed as suffering from "sluggish schizophrenia." But what our study of the Russian-language literature showed was that this was not driven by poor science, as many have supposed. Indeed, the diagnostic criteria in use in the U.S.S.R. at the time were closely similar to those employed in Western democracies (Fulford, Smirnoff, and Snow 1993); and the relevant criteria (the descriptive diagnostic criteria) were applied as widely in New York as in Moscow (World Health Organization 1973). The abusive misdiagnoses were driven rather by the absolute values of the Soviet ethic. By the standards of the Soviet ethic, anyone who believed the state could be better organised *had* to be irrational, hence mentally ill. A number of other factors—bureaucratic, legislative, and so forth—allowed these abuses to become widespread. But the essential vulnerability of psychiatry to abusive misdiagnosis in this way was derived, consistently with the expectations of VBM, from the value judgements involved.

Such abuses, it should be emphasised, have certainly not been confined to the U.S.S.R. (Chodoff 1999). There are growing concerns about China at the present time (Munro 2002). We are at risk of similar abuses of psychiatry as a means of social control in the U.K. with a proposed new mental health act. If this becomes law, dangerousness will be for all intents and purposes a "disease"[36] for which psychiatric services, rather than the police, will be primarily responsible. To such dangers, then, as Szasz has done so much to make clear, psychiatry remains vulnerable. But where Szasz takes this to be a sign that mental distress and disorder, of whatever kind, should be removed from medicine, VBM takes it as a sign that psychiatry urgently needs the skills to work more effectively with the values-base, as well as the evidence-base, of practice.

---

[36] In the U.K. government's 'white paper' (a discussion paper which precedes publication of a draft bill), the disease of dangerousness had its very own acronym, DSPD, Dangerous Severe Personality Disorder!

Conclusion: Szasz and the Future of Psychiatry in Medicine

Szasz's sceptical attack on psychiatry, in the 1960s and 1970s, came at a time of scientific optimism. The textbooks of this period, and the academic journals, were full of high-flown hopes for the emergence of a "medical" model of psychiatry, a model based on the paradigms of such "scientific" areas of medicine as cardiology and gastro-enterology. The vision was of a psychiatry no less "scientific," and (correlatively, as it was supposed) no more value-laden, than the better established (scientifically speaking) areas of bodily medicine. These hopes, indeed, have been perceived by many in psychiatry as being at least partly fulfilled by the remarkable advances in the neurosciences in the 1990s, the "decade of the brain." Through these advances, it has seemed to many, psychiatry is at last showing signs of "catching up" (as they perceive it) with scientific developments in other areas of medicine.

Small wonder, then, as I said at the start of this article, that doctors, not just in psychiatry but in all areas of medicine, have been left perplexed and demoralised by the apparent failure of the medical-scientific model as measured by the increasingly negative public reception afforded medicine over this same period. 'Sod's Law', it seems, has prevailed! Even as scientific medicine has finally started to deliver, so its stock among patients has fallen as never before!

History, no doubt, will show that there have been many factors involved in this perhaps paradoxical, certainly unanticipated, outcome (Fulford, Morris, Sadler, and Stanghellini 2003). But Szaszian scepticism, I have argued, filtered through the insights of philosophical value theory, suggests that there has been a key factor within medicine itself, viz., the blindness of the traditional exclusively scientific model of medicine to the wide range and diversity of human values which, through the choices opened up by science itself, are becoming increasingly central to decision-making in healthcare. Szasz was right. There is, in the terms of his original and most famous sceptical claim, no such thing as mental illness. There is no such thing as mental illness, that is, if physical illness is, as the traditional medical model assumes, defined by exclusively scientific norms. But this in turn, philosophical value theory suggests, is because there is no such thing as *physical* illness, so defined. Physical illness appears "scientific" only because the operative values in this area of medicine (the values by which physical illnesses are in part defined) are widely settled and agreed upon.

To the extent, though, that philosophical value theory contradicts Szasz's claim that mental illness is a myth, it also, as we have seen, contradicts the counter-claim of his opponents among medical psychiatrists, that mental illness is no different from physical illness. The operative values in respect of *mental* illness really are more divergent, hence likely to be more problematic, than their counterparts in physical medicine. And the failure to recognise this, I have suggested, is at the heart of many of the abuses to which psychiatry has proven vulnerable in the twentieth century, abuses to which Szasz, in developing the contingent grounds of his attack on psychiatry, has done so much to highlight.

The outcome of Szaszian scepticism, then, is that medicine must take seriously the values as well as the facts on which decision-making in all areas of healthcare will increasingly turn. We need Values-Based Medicine, VBM, alongside and on an equal footing with Evidence-Based Medicine, EBM. And within mental health, at least, some of the features of VBM, as I have indicated, are already beginning to emerge. Alongside and in parallel with an increasingly sophisticated scientific infrastructure, built on the social sciences as well as the neurosciences, we are witnessing multi-agency models of service delivery, a new commitment to the "user" voice, in research and service development as well as in clinical practice; and to multi-agency models of service delivery; a new emphasis on positive as well as negative values, and on recovery practice; and, most exciting of all perhaps, new educational initiatives aimed at enlarging the skills-base of VBM.

Szasz's scepticism, I have argued, has made a crucial contribution to these developments. There is much to do. Psychiatry, as I have illustrated, remains vulnerable to the abuses which Szasz has highlighted. But a start has been made. And it is a start, VBM suggests, that as scientific progress increasingly opens up clinical decision-making to the full diversity of human values, the rest of medicine will in time inevitably have to follow. Szasz's legacy, then, is a psychiatry, not only enriched and strengthened in its own right, but leading the way in the development of twenty-first century medical science.[37]

---

[37] EDITOR'S NOTE: The author made minor verbal changes in this chapter after Dr. Szasz had written his reply (but before the reply was seen by the author).

R E F E R E N C E S

American Psychiatric Association. 1994. *Diagnostic and Statistical Manual of Mental Disorders*. Fourth edition. Washington, D.C.: American Psychiatric Association.

Boorse, C. 1975. On the Distinction between Disease and Illness. *Philosophy and Public Affairs* 5, pp. 49–68.

———. 1997. A Rebuttal on Health. In J.M. Humber and R.F. Almeder, eds., *What Is Disease?* (Totowa: Humana Press).

Campbell, P. 1996. What We Want From Crisis Services. In J. Read and J. Reynolds, eds., *Speaking Our Minds: An Anthology* (London: Macmillan), pp. 180–83.

———. Campbell, P. 1996. What We Want from Mental Health Services. In J. Read and J. Reynolds, *Speaking Our Minds: An Anthology* (London: Macmillan), pp. 180–83.

Chodoff, P. 1999. Misuse and Abuse of Psychiatry: An Overview. In S. Bloch, P. Chodoff, and S.A. Green, eds., *Psychiatric Ethics*. Third edition (Oxford: Oxford University Press).

Foot, P. 1958–59. Moral Beliefs. *Proceedings of the Aristotelian Society* 59, pp. 83–104. Reprinted in P. Foot, ed., *Theories of Ethics* (Oxford: Oxford University Press, 1967).

Fulford, K.W.M. 1989. *Moral Theory and Medical Practice*. Cambridge: Cambridge University Press.

———. 1990. Philosophy and Medicine: The Oxford Connection. *British Journal of Psychiatry* 157, pp. 111–15.

———. 1996. Religion and Psychiatry: Extending the Limits of Tolerance. In D. Bhugra, ed., *Psychiatry and Religion: Context, Consensus, and Controversies* (London: Routledge).

———. 2001. The Paradoxes of Confidentiality: A Philosophical Introduction. In C. Cordess, ed., *Confidentiality and Medical Practice* (London: Jessica Kingsley), pp. 7–23.

———. 2001. Philosophy into Practice: The Case for Ordinary Language Philosophy. In L. Nordenfelt, ed., *Health, Science, and Ordinary Language* (Amsterdam: Rodopi.

———. Forthcoming. *Values-Based Medicine (VBM): From Evidence to Practice in Healthcare Decision-Making*. Cambridge: Cambridge University Press.

———. 1994. Closet Logics: Hidden Conceptual Elements in the DSM and ICD Classifications of Mental Disorders. In J.Z. Sadler, O.P. Wiggins, M.A. Schwartz, eds., *Philosophical Perspectives on Psychiatric Diagnostic Classification* (Baltimore: Johns Hopkins University Press).

———. 1998. *Dissent and Dissensus: The Limits of Consensus Formation in Psychiatry*. In H.A.M.J. ten Have, and H.-M. Saas, eds., *Consensus Formation in Health Care Ethics* (Dordrecht: Kluwer), pp. 175–192.

———. 1999. Nine Variations and a Coda on the Theme of an Evolutionary Definition of Dysfunction. *Journal of Abnormal Psychology* 108:3.

———. 2000. Teleology Without Tears: Naturalism, Neo-Naturalism, and Evaluationism in the Analysis of Function Statements in Biology (and a Bet on the Twenty-first Century). *Philosophy, Psychiatry, and Psychology* 7:1.

———. 2001. Philosophy into Practice: The Case for Ordinary Language Philosophy. In L. Nordenfelt, ed., *Health, Science, and Ordinary Language* (Amsterdam: Rodopi).

———. 2002. Human Values in Healthcare Ethics. In K.W.M. Fulford, D. Dickenson, and T.H. Murray, eds., *Healthcare Ethics and Human Values: An Introductory Text with Readings and Case Studies* (Malden: Blackwell).

———. 2004. Ten Principles of Values-Based Medicine. In J. Radden, ed., *The Philosophy of Psychiatry: A Companion* (New York: Oxford University Press).

Fulford, K.W.M., and S. Bloch. 2000. Psychiatric Ethics: Codes, Concepts, and Clinical Practice Skills. In M. Gelder, J.J. Lopez-Ibor, and N. Andreasen, eds., *New Oxford Textbook of Psychiatry* (Oxford: Oxford University Press).

Fulford, K.W.M., D. Dickenson, and T.H. Murray, eds. 2002. *Healthcare Ethics and Human Values: An Introductory Text with Readings and Case Studies.* Malden: Blackwell.

Fulford K.W.M, K.M. Morris, J.Z. Sadler, and G. Stanghellini. 2003. Past Improbable, Future Possible: An Introduction to Nature and Narrative. In K.W.M. Fulford, K.M. Morris, J.Z. Sadler, and G. Stanghellini, eds., *Nature and Narrative: International Perspectives in Philosophy and Psychiatry* (Oxford: Oxford University Press).

Fulford, K.W.M., A.Y.U. Smirnoff, and E. Snow. 1993. Concepts of Disease and the Abuse of Psychiatry in the U.S.S.R. *British Journal of Psychiatry* 162, pp. 801–810.

Fulford, K.W.M., T. Thornton, and G. Graham. Forthcoming. Philosophy of Science and Mental Health, Part III. In *The Shorter Oxford Textbook of Philosophy and Psychiatry* (Oxford: Oxford University Press).

Fulford, K.W.M., K. Woodbridge, and T. Williamson. 2002. Revealing Values in Mental Health Practice: A Values Awareness Workshop. Published as 'Values-Added Practice', in *Mental Health Today* (October), pp. 25–27.

Goodwin, G. 2002. Hypomania: What's in a Name? *The British Journal of Psychiatry* 181, pp. 94–95.

Hare, R.M. 1952. *The Language of Morals.* Oxford: Oxford University Press.

———. 1963. Descriptivism. *Proceedings of the British Academy* 49, pp. 115–134. Reprinted in Hare 1972.

———. 1972. *Essays on the Moral Concepts.* London: Macmillan.

———. 1989. *Essays in Ethical Theory.* Oxford: Clarendon.

———. 1993. *Essays on Bioethics.* Oxford: Clarendon.

Hope, T., K.W.M. Fulford, and A. Yates. 1996. *The Oxford Practice Skills Course: Ethics, Law, and Communication Skills in Health Care Education.* Oxford: Oxford University Press.

Jackson, M., and K.W.M. Fulford. 1997. Spiritual Experience and Psychopathology. *Philosophy, Psychiatry, and Psychology* 4:1, pp. 41–66.

Jamison, K.R. 1994 [1993]. *Touched with Fire: Manic Depressive Illness and the Artistic Temperament.* New York: Free Press Paperbacks.

Kendell, R.E. 1975. The Concept of Disease and Its Implications for Psychiatry. *British Journal of Psychiatry* 127, pp. 305–315.

Locke, J. 1960. Of Identity and Diversity. In A.D. Woozley, ed., *John Locke: An Essay Concerning Human Understanding* (London: Fontana).

Moore, A., T. Hope, and K.W.M. Fulford. 1994. Mild Mania and Well-Being. *Philosophy, Psychiatry, and Psychology* 1:3, pp. 165–178.

Munro, R. 2002. [Pamphlet]. In Human Rights Watch/Geneva Initiative on Psychiatry, *Dangerous Minds: Political Psychiatry in China Today and Its Origins in the Mao Era* (New York: Human Rights Watch).

Nagel, T. 1986. *The View from Nowhere.* Oxford: Oxford University Press.

Okasha, A. 2000. Ethics of Psychiatric Practice: Consent, Compulsion, and Confidentiality. *Current Opinion in Psychiatry* 13, pp. 693–98.

Rogers, A., D. Pilgrim, and R. Lacey. 1993.) *Experiencing Psychiatry: Users' Views of Services*, London: Macmillan.

Roth, M., and J. Kroll. 1986. *The Reality of Mental Illness.* Cambridge: Cambridge University Press.

Szasz, Thomas S. 1960. The Myth of Mental Illness. *American Psychologist* 15, pp. 113–18.

———. 1961. *The Myth of Mental Illness: Foundations of a Theory of Personal Conduct.* Revised 1974. New York: Harper and Row.

———. 1963. *Law, Liberty, and Psychiatry: An Enquiry into the Social Uses of Mental Health Practices.* New York: Macmillan.

———. 1965. Toward the Therapeutic State. *New Republic* (11th December), pp. 26–29.

———. 1970. *Ideology and Insanity: Essays on the Psychiatric Dehumanization of Man.* Garden City: Doubleday.

———. 1971. *The Manufacture of Madness.* London: Routledge.

———. 1976. *Schizophrenia: The Sacred Symbol of Psychiatry.* New York: Basic Books.

———. 1976. *Heresies.* Garden City: Anchor Books.

———. 1984. *The Therapeutic State: Psychiatry in the Mirror of Current Events.* Buffalo: Prometheus.

———. 1987. *Insanity: The Idea and Its Consequences.* New York: Wiley.

———. 1994. *Cruel Compassion: Psychiatric Control of Society's Unwanted.* New York: Wiley.

———. 1998. Commentary on "Aristotle's Function Argument and the Concept of Mental Illness." *Philosophy, Psychiatry, and Psychology* 5:3, pp. 203–08.

———. 2001. The Person as Moral Agent. In J. Kirk, James F. Schneider, T. Bugental, and J. Fraser Pierson, eds., *The Handbook of Humanistic*

Psychology: Leading Edges in Theory, Research, and Practice (Thousand Oaks: Sage).

————. 2002. Patient or Prisoner? *Ideas on Liberty* 52 (January), pp. 31–32.

————. 2001. *Pharmacracy: Medicine and Politics in America*. Westport: Praeger.

Thornton, T. 2000. Mental Illness and Reductionism: Can Functions Be Naturalized? *Philosophy, Psychiatry, and Psychology* 7:1, pp. 67–76.

Urmson, J.O. 1950. On Grading. *Mind* 59, pp. 145–169.

Wakefield, J.C. 2000. Aristotle as Sociobiologist: The "Function of a Human Being" Argument, Black Box Essentialism, and the Concept of Mental Disorder. *Philosophy, Psychiatry, and Psychology* 7:1, pp. 17–44.

Warnock, G.J. 1971. *The Object of Morality*. London: Methuen.

Wing, J.K. 1978. *Reasoning about Madness*. Oxford: Oxford University Press.

World Health Organisation. 1992. *The ICD-10 Classification of Mental and Behavioural Disorders: Clinical Descriptions and Diagnostic Guidelines*. Geneva: World Health Organisation.

————. 1973. *The International Pilot Study of Schizophrenia. Volume 1*. Geneva: World Health Organisation.

Reply to Fulford

THOMAS SZASZ

I

Fulford's gracious praise for my "criticism [that] goes to the very logic of the subject [psychiatry]" places me in a difficult position. I respect but disagree with much in Fulford's view of psychiatry and the problems that beset this so-called medical specialty. However, as he correctly observes, it is scepticism "provoking debate [that] drives our ideas forward." In that spirit, I rejoin my long-standing conversation with him.[1] The length of my reply is an expression of my esteem for Fulford's pre-eminent position in contemporary bioethics, medical philosophy, and psychiatry.

II

Fulford uses the term 'Values Based Medicine' (VBM) to denote the use of both facts and values in medical decision-making. Because all deciding is, by definition, based on facts as well as values, I regard the term as an uncongenial slogan affirming a truism. Fulford recognizes that the notion of VBM articulates a tautology: "VBM is based on the premise that decision-making in all areas of healthcare stands on two feet, on values as well as on facts. This premise is derived from the notion of practical reasoning, viz. *the reasons we have for anything we do (not just in healthcare)*. Practical reasoning, as Aristotle first pointed out, is always based on some combination of facts and values" (emphasis added). This

---

[1] For my previous comments on Fulford's views, see Thomas Szasz, "Psychiatric Diagnosis, Psychiatric Power, and Psychiatric Abuse," *Journal of Medical Ethics* 20 (September 1994), pp. 135–38, and *Pharmacracy: Medicine and Politics in America* (Syracuse: Syracuse University Press, 2003 [2001]), pp. 117–19.

admission does not stop Fulford from making abundant use of VBM as if it were a phenomenon, a fact, or even an explanatory scheme. I fear, however, that both VBM and its twin, Evidence Based Medicine (EBM) are merely obfuscatory, self-approbating slogans.

Fulford believes that "EBM is a response to the growing complexity of facts relevant to decision-making in all areas of healthcare. VBM is the corresponding response to the growing complexity of the values relevant to decision-making in all areas of healthcare." He writes:

> In Section 1 of this chapter VBM and EBM ran broadly parallel as responses to the growing complexity of healthcare decision-making. In that section, . . . we found that values and evidence are the two feet on which all decisions in healthcare stand, that we tend to notice the values operative in a given clinical situation only where they are diverse and hence likely to be problematic, and that scientific progress, far from making healthcare decisions less dependent on values, is increasingly bringing the full range and diversity of human values into medicine by opening up to us, as users and as providers of services, an ever wider range of choices.

Of course, it is true, but trivially so, that the larger the menu, the more choice of meals. The more treatment options the doctor offers, the more treatment choices the patient has. However, this "complexity" has virtually nothing to do with the problems Fulford discusses. Nor has increased "medical sensitivity to values" anything to do with it. The source of the problems lies in the destruction of medical relations based on co-operation and contract between private doctor and private patient and their replacement by medical relations based on command and coercion between doctor as *de facto* agent of a health care "provider" (the state, employer, insurance company) and the patient as anonymous recipient of health care services (for which he does not pay directly or at all). Fulford's whole essay suffers from the fatal flaw of ignoring the economic underpinnings of medical care. He writes as if the economic nexus of the doctor-patient relationship were irrelevant to the conflicts of values in medicine and as if the replacement of the capitalist model of the doctor-patient relationship by a socialist model of it were, *prima facie*, a good thing. Whether such a transformation is good or bad as an abstract moral principle—whether it helps or harms particular patients, doctors, or societies—depends on our view of the state as a political organ and on our values about the importance of dignity, liberty, responsibility, health, and medical care in human life. Some persons view the state as an instrument of benevolence. I do not. Persuaded by the views of classic English and American writers on liberty, I view the state as a coercion-wielding organization with a monopoly on the use of power that poses a grave and perpetual danger to individual liberty and personal responsibility. Fulford does not tell us whether he regards the state as a friend or a foe of freedom. He does not tell us whether he holds individuals responsible for their self-harming behavior that is the direct cause of disease and need for health care services. We can, however, infer his values on these subjects from his views, as I shall show.

Prior to World War II, medical care (as it was then called) was a personal service *individual entrepreneurs, called physicians, rendered to individuals, called patients.* The patient (or a member of his family) chose the physician and paid him for the service he provided. The physician was an agent of the patient, free to provide any service (except an illegal operation, exemplified by abortion). The provision of medical services was then a capitalist enterprise, much as the provision of food, housing, plumbing, veterinary, and legal services still are capitalist enterprises. Poor people received medical care *gratis*, from teaching hospitals affiliated with medical schools or from community hospitals.

Today, the provision of health care is a socialist (statist) enterprise, in the U.K. overtly, in the U.S. covertly. The patient may be, but often is not, free to choose the physician; he does not pay him for the service he receives. The physician, in turn, may or may not be free to accept or reject the client as his patient; he is not paid for his services by the patient. Instead, the physician is paid by a third party (an agency of the state or an insurance company controlled by the state). The iron rule of economics and politics—"He who pays the piper calls the tune"—still governs. The physician is *not* an agent of the patient. He is not free to provide the service the patient wants or he, the doctor, considers best for him; his options are severely and punitively limited by drug laws and, if he wants to be reimbursed for his work, by the third-party payer that foots the bill. In short, patient and physician alike have lost the freedom to contract. What Fulford calls "complexity" is a set of phenomena attributable almost entirely to the socialization and bureaucratization of healthcare services, not, as he says, to advances in scientific medicine or to greater sensitivity to ethical issues in medicine.

Consider the evidence. If Fulford's interpretation were correct, then all physicians and all patients would face the same "complexity of values and facts" and have to cope with the same constraints. But they do not. The wealthy and politically powerful patient has the means to command, by money or political power, the kinds of drugs and medical care he wants and/or his doctor recommends. Simply put, he is as free to buy these things as he is to buy bread and milk. The physician who caters to such a patient is free to provide him with the drugs and services the patient wants, with little fear of reprisal from the government.

III

Fulford illustrates the use of the concept of VBM in clinical decision-making with the vignette of a patient, Diane Abbot, an artist. (I assume the scenario Fulford presents is that of a hypothetical patient. He does not make this point clear.) Diagnosed as manic-depressive, Abbot claims to have a special ability to "see colors" (whatever that means). Her general practitioner prescribes lithium. Abbot takes the drug for a year and then stops.

"Diane Abbot's story," Fulford writes, "illustrates the key features of VBM . . . *Here, it shows the way in which deciding what to prescribe, in a particular case, depends on values as well as facts.*" What to prescribe *always* depends on values as well as facts, not just in this particular case. As I see it, the issue here was not *what to prescribe* (a decision by the doctor), but *what recommendation to accept or what drug to take* (decisions by the patient).

Before delving deeper into the case of Diane Abbot, it is important to note that Fuflord does not tell us anything about Abbot's economic status or social position. He does not tell us whether she was a N.H.S. (National Health Service) patient or a patient in the private sector (there still is such a thing in the U.K.). He does tell us that before starting on lithium, Abbot saw Dr. Kirk, a psychiatrist. Again, he does not say how Dr. Kirk was selected. Did Abbot choose him? Or did she have to see him and not someone of her own choice if she expected the N.H.S. to pick up the tab? We don't know. In fact, we hardly know anything at all about Abbot: We don't know if she considered herself ill; if she believed her illness was correctly diagnosed as manic-depression; or if she considered manic-depression a somatic ailment susceptible to treatment with drugs. Was Abbot an informed and skeptical "consumer of mental health services" or did she simply obey, or disobey, doctors' orders? Was she familiar with the history of somatic treatments in psychiatry, with mental health laws? Fulford does not say. Diane Abbot is not a person; she is a "psychiatric case." It seems to me that Fulford's decision to explain VBM in action with the synoptic scenario of a patient with a mental disease is especially ill-considered: instead of doing that job, his account illustrates the difference between the management of mental illnesses and that of bodily illnesses. Let us attend closely to Fulford's account. He writes that

> values tend to become visible only where they are divergent, and, hence, are likely to come into conflict. We only notice values, that is to say, when they cause trouble!
>
> Thus, in Diane Abbot's case we did not initially notice her values at the stage of her original assessment because, at this stage, her values were (broadly) concordant with everyone else's (her family, friends, doctors, and so on). It was only when it came to discontinuing treatment that a gap opened up. It was only at this stage that Diane Abbot's values diverged from those of others concerned.

I repeat: *"values tend to become visible only where they are divergent, and, hence, are likely to come into conflict. We only notice values, that is to say, when they cause trouble!"* This is plainly false. Perhaps Fulford only notices values when they cause trouble. I notice values from everything a person does. A Jew or a Christian or a Muslim need not be in conflict with anyone else's values for us to infer his religious values from his religious observances. Fulford writes:

> Thus, in Diane Abbot's case we did not initially notice her values at the stage of her original assessment because, at this stage, her values were (broadly) concordant with everyone else's (her family, friends, doctors, and so on). It was only when it came to discontinuing treatment that a gap opened up.

As noted above, Abbot's values and those of her family, friends, and doctors were expressed in their behavior. When she decided to stop treatment, values in the abstract were no more or less evident than they had been when she decided to start treatment. She simply made a different decision based on what she regarded as different reasons. Would Fulford say that a wealthy investor's values are not evident when he buys a stock his broker recommends and become evident only when he sells the stock against the broker's advice? Fulford's comments reveals the deep-seated character of psychiatric paternalism and of our culture's general support of it.

Let us go further. Suppose Abbot suffered from melanoma instead of mania. Would the "values" of her family and friends concerning the treatment of melanoma be a relevant issue? Surely, such a matter is none of her friends' business; nor is it her family's business, unless she makes it so. In analyzing the Abbot case, Fulford also misses an opportunity to discuss the differences between the individualist-capitalist style of obtaining medical services and the collectivist-socialist style of doing so. He writes:

> But as a G.P., Dr Robertson had a budget to balance; and every G.P. is famil-iar with difficulties about whether a referral is worth making, "worth" in this context being the operative (value) word; multiple decisions, further back still, of hospital administrators, health authorities and other healthcare providers, to make lithium available as a treatment. . . . But it is here that issues of rationing arise perhaps most acutely, reflecting competing values; the policy decisions taken by those at a national level to recommend lithi-um in clinical practice guidelines for the treatment of manic-depressive dis-order. The problems faced by those with responsibility for issuing clinical practice guidelines are often more about how to balance competing per-spectives on the benefits and disbenefits of the effects and side effects of a given treatment, than to agree what, as a matter of fact, the effects and side effects are!

Once again, I repeat what Fulford writes: *"But as a G.P., Dr Robertson had a budget to balance; and every G.P. is familiar with difficulties about whether a referral is worth making, "worth" in this context being the operative (value) word; multiple decisions, further back still, of hos-pital administrators, health authorities and other healthcare providers, to make lithium available as a treatment."* Every one of these constraints is a result of the insertion of agents of the Therapeutic State into the for-merly dyadic relationship between patient and doctor.

In the capitalist-contractual model of medical practice, the patient does not need a family doctor to refer her to a specialist; she can do that on her own. Similarly, the issue of the "worth" of a referral *to the physi-cian* does not arise; the worth of a referral concerns the patient and depends on his decision based on *his* budget and *his* estimate of the worth of the referral. The only budget that is the doctor's business is that of his own household. The patient's budget and the government's budg-et are not his business.

> multiple decisions, further back still, of hospital administrators, health authorities and other healthcare providers, to make lithium available as a treatment.

In the capitalist-contractual model, the patient does not need to obtain "permission"—a prescription from a doctor or a permit from a rationing-agent of the state—to purchase a drug; she can do that on her own.

Every step of the way, Fulford mistakenly attributes problems in the contemporary doctor-patient relationship to a "pandemic of values" brought about by "science." He poses the question of why values are becoming more visible now, and answers:

> The answer to the "why now?" question, in a word, is science. To some, this may seem a surprising, perhaps even unlikely, answer. After all, science and ethics, facts and values, have traditionally been counterposed. But the connection between science and the pandemic of values in healthcare in the closing years of the twentieth century, is straightforward enough. It is that scientific progress, in expanding the "can do" of medicine; increases the choices available to us, as practitioners or patients; and this in turn brings the full diversity of human values into play in healthcare decision-making. Thus, so long as I have no choice between outcomes A or B, it makes no difference whether I value A more than B or vice versa. My values, and hence the potential for conflicts of values, only come into play where I have a choice between A and B.

Fulford is right that if a person does not have a choice between A and B, he cannot have a conflict about which to choose. But he is quite wrong about the relations between science and the sorts of conflicts that now confront physicians and patients, and especially about the moral problems that beset psychiatry.

Since the end of World War II, advances in scientific medicine have been truly staggering: antibiotics, steroids, novel radiologic diagnostic methods, laparoscopic and laser surgery, transplantation technology, are all new additions to the medical armamentarium. Formerly, a patient with coronary heart disease did not have to choose between medical management and surgical treatment. Now he does. Let us stipulate that a patient facing such a choice wants to live as actively, as long, and as comfortably as he can. That is the value that dictates his choice. Scientific advances in cardiology do not create a fresh value conflict for him. They merely give him more promising options for realizing his goal. The patient who needs cataract surgery or hip replacment faces a catalogue of fresh choices, yet there is no "pandemic of values" problem in ophthalmology and orthopedic surgery. Despite claims to the contrary, there has been no progress in the diagnosis and treatment of mental illnesses comparable to the diagnosis or treatment of bodily illnesses, yet in psychiatry there is a vast problem of "pandemic of values."

Fulford and I look at the same social scene and draw diametrically different conclusions from our observations. He writes: "Although in principle straightforward, it will be worthwhile developing this point, partly because it runs directly counter to the traditional stand-off between values and science, and partly because the link between scientific progress and human values is central to *my concluding claim in this article, that Szaszian scepticism about mental illness leads, ultimately, not to the demise but to a strengthening of psychiatry*" (emphasis added). How, in the face of mental health laws, can Fulford hold this view? By regarding involuntary mental hospitalization not as a moral and philosophical problem of the first order, but as a legitimate form of medical treatment.

Regarding Diane Abbot's treatment with lithium, Fulford completely ignores the role of drug controls and mental health laws. Patients cannot purchase drugs and medical services the same way they can purchase food and computer services. In principle, there is no reason why a person like Abbot could not, if she were so inclined, consult a physician, receive a recommendation to take lithium, purchase the drug as she can now purchase vitamins, and take it or not, as she chooses. Instead, the fact is that Abbot lives in a therapeutic state and is subject to pharmacratic social controls, much as women in Saudi Arabia live in a theocratic state and are subject to theological social controls.

Only after we are well into Fulford's essay do we learn that Abbot is a candidate for psychiatric imprisonment, a.k.a. mental hospitalization. Taking the benefits of psychiatric coercion for granted, Fulford writes:

> Her manic episodes were severe. Judged against her own values (during her periods of remission), as well as the values of others close to her, her condition was one that merited treatment. As such, a short-term intervention with a neuroleptic was more or less equivalent on the values side, to penicillin for the child with a life-threatening staphylococcal infection. This indeed was the basis on which Diane Abbot agreed to be treated after she stopped taking lithium. She worked out, with Dr. Robertson (her G.P.), an "advance directive" according to which, if specified members of her family, or one particular named colleague, reported to him that she was showing warning signs of a further manic episode, *he (Dr. Robertson) would contact the local psychiatric team and arrange, if necessary, admission on an involuntary basis under the Mental Health Act.* (Emphasis added.)

Fulford's last sentence above brings us back to square one, the issue of the moral and political legitimacy of psychiatric coercion. Fulford is aware of my unqualified rejection of such exercise of psychiatric power.

Yet, he does not address the issue; he neither questions nor explains why psychiatrists should have the privilege and duty of depriving *competent* persons of liberty and using the power of the state to forcibly impose their services on them. Instead, he points with pride to Abbot's "right" to voluntarily contract for her own future involuntary psychiatric incarceration and involuntary drugging. He does not say whether she has or ought to have an equally valid and enforceable right to reject any and all future psychiatric examination, hospitalization, and treatment. Because Fulford does not mention the psychiatric will—an instrument indispensable for an evaluation of the Abbot scenario—I briefly summarize my contributions to the subject.

IV

Modern psychiatric opinion holds that "even being under a commitment does not in and of itself make a person incompetent."[2] The view that some time during his life the involuntary hospitalized mental patient is a competent adult, able and entitled to make decisions for himself, framed the context in which, in 1982, I proposed a new legal-psychiatric instrument, the Psychiatric Will (PW).[3] The instrument was intended, as the paper's subtitle indicated, to provide "a new mechanism for protecting persons against 'psychosis' and psychiatry"; and to clarify, mediate, and eventually resolve the conflict between the coercive psychiatrist and the coerced patient.

The avowed desires of patients and doctors conflict far more often in psychiatry than in any other branch of medical practice. Unlike medical interventions, psychiatric interventions are routinely imposed on patients against their will. Hence, the person who voluntarily consults a psychiatrist runs the risk of becoming the subject of unwanted psychiatric interventions. Accordingly, advance directives are most important and most useful for potential psychiatric patients.

As matters now stand (especially in the United States), the contact between patient and doctor is dangerous for the psychiatrist as well. The psychiatrist who gives an appointment to a person-as-patient is at risk

---

[2] "Minnesota Advance Psychiatric and Health Care Directive," www.mnlegalservices. org/publications/MDLC20Fact20Sheets/apd_healthdirective.html. The material on the psychiatric will I cite is a condensation of Chapter 5 of Thomas Szasz, *Liberation by Oppression: A Comparative Study of Slavery and Psychiatry* (New Brunswick: Transaction, 2002). Fulford does not refer to this book.

[3] Thomas Szasz, "The Psychiatric Will: A New Mechanism for Protecting Persons Against

for becoming the defendant in a malpractice suit he cannot win. Thus, like the medical advance directive, which protects both patient and doctor, the psychiatric will, too, would protect both patient and doctor. Prospectively consenting to or refusing involuntary psychiatric interventions, the PW would constitute a legally binding agreement between the potential psychiatric patient and his potential psychiatrist: the contract would protect the patient from becoming the victim of unwanted psychiatric coercion, and the psychiatrist from becoming the victim of malpractice litigation as long as he obeys the terms of the contract. While the protective function of the PW for the patient is obvious, its protective function for the psychiatrist may be less clear. I shall briefly discuss each.

Customary psychiatric practice dictates that a person with a mental illness who is deemed to have diminished decisional capacity must be administered psychiatric treatment against his will. He has no right to reject such treatment: the very act of rejecting psychiatric help is interpreted as a symptom of mental illness, a manifestation of dangerousness to self or others, and a justification for involuntary treatment. In short, the PW offers individuals the option prospectively to choose to receive or reject involuntary psychiatric interventions.

The PW also protects the psychiatrist endangered by his so-called special relationship with the patient. Having to act as both physician and guardian, the psychiatrist may be held legally liable for the deleterious consequences of both coercing and not coercing the patient. The PW would protect him from both contingencies.

Because Fulford mentions (his version of) the psychiatric will as if it were a frequently used legal-psychiatric instrument, I must offer a brief comment about its history. I wrote my paper on the PW in the late 1970s. I submitted it to several major American psychiatric journals. Every one of them rejected it. The paper was eventually published in the *American Psychologist*, the official journal of the American Psychological Association. At that time, American psychologists were still interested in opposing psychiatric power. Now, they are interested only in participating in and sharing the psychiatrists' exercise of it.

Despite or perhaps because of the obvious advantages of the PW for the mental patient who wants to avoid being coerced, as well as for

---

'Psychosis' and Psychiatry," *American Psychologist* 37 (July, 1982), pp. 762–770; "The Psychiatric Will: II. Whose Will Is It Anyway?," *American Psychologist* 38 (March 1983), pp. 344–46; and "The Psychiatric Will," in Szasz, *A Lexicon of Lunacy*, pp. 159–172.

the psychiatrist who wants to avoid coercing, psychiatrists first opposed the PW and then perverted it by turning it into a fresh instrument of psychiatric domination and oppression. To my knowledge, not a single psychiatrist or lawyer supports the PW, that is, a psychiatric advance directive (PAD), similar to a medical advance directive. At the same time, many psychiatrists and lawyers support a perverted form of the PW, that is, a legal instrument giving mental patients the option to prospectively request psychiatric coercion, but denying them the option to prospectively reject such measures.[4] That is what Fulford too has done.

As the validity of the last will is independent of the nature or kind of property the testator wishes to bequeath, so the value of the PW is independent of the conceptual nature of "mental illness" or the therapeutic nature of any particular psychiatric intervention. Being an involuntary mental patient is a social role, like being a victim of religious persecution. The latter role does not require that there be a God, and the former role does not require that there be mental illness. I emphasize this because Paul Chodoff and Roger Peele, two eminent psychiatric ethicists, objected to the PW on the ground that "Szasz's equation of illness with an organic base is stiflingly narrow. In the considerable literature on the concept of illness, there is no consensus on its definition and limits."[5]

I acknowledge that, by preventing the use of civil commitment as a method of preventive detention, the PW entails certain risks for persons other than the patient. Nevertheless, Chodoff and Peele complain: "Carrying out a psychiatric will could mean death for someone other than the signer if the latter is, say, under the influence of a dangerous drug or is a paranoid schizophrenic."[6] Psychiatric coercion is not used primarily to prevent people from being dangerous to others while "under the influence of a dangerous drug." If it were, there would be fewer alcohol-impaired drivers on American roads. Chodoff's and Peele's objections to the PW illustrate the psychiatrists' determination to resist, at all costs, any proposal that would liberate the mental patient from their domination.

---

[4] See for example Paul S. Appelbaum, *Almost a Revolution*; Sidney Bloch and Paul Chodoff, eds., *Psychiatric Ethics*; Alan A. Stone, *Law, Psychiatry, and Morality*; and Thomas Szasz, *Insanity*.

[5] Paul Chodoff and Roger Peele, "A Wary View of a New Testament: The Psychiatric Will of Dr. Szasz," *Hastings Center Report* 13 (April, 1983), pp. 11–13 (pp. 13, 12).

[6] *Ibid.*, p. 12.

It is a truism that no social policy is free of costs, or "externalities," as economists call it. One of the externalities of the PW is that a person deemed committable by conventional criteria but left at liberty might harm others, imposing personal and financial costs on families, insurance companies, and the state. However, the present policy of involuntarily hospitalizing and treating dangerous as well as non-dangerous persons also entails great personal and financial cost to families, insurance companies, and the state. It is not obvious which is more costly, maintaining psychiatric slavery or abolishing it. In any case, in Anglo-American political philosophy, individual liberty is supposed to be priceless, dramatically reflected in the enormous cost borne by the taxpayer for prosecuting each death penalty case.

Other critics of the PW found other things to criticize in it. Robert Keisling, a psychiatrist in Washington, D.C., characterized the PW as an instrument for "turning back the clock" on the psychiatric profession's commitment to freedom: "Szasz ignores one central fact. The average length of stay in state mental hospitals is less than one month. The average length of stay in prisons is measured in months and years. . . . How does this promote liberty and freedom?"[7] First, this is not true. For example, John W. Hinckley, Jr., has been "hospitalized" since 1981.[8] Second, it is revealing of the psychiatric mind-set that a psychiatrist casually compares the average length of stay in mental hospitals with the average length of stay in prisons, instead of with the average length of stay in medical hospitals. By comparing confinement in a mental hospital with confinement in a prison, Keisling conflates doctors and jailers, hospitals and prisons, innocent patients and guilty convicts, and tacitly admits that mental hospitalization is *de facto* imprisonment. Illness, *qua* illness, is never a justification for depriving the ill person of liberty. An institution the person cannot leave, legally or physically, should not be called a "hospital." Other critics objected to the PW on other grounds.[9]

A genuine psychiatric advance directive, like a medical advance directive, must cut both ways. If the PAD lets the subject request invol-

---

[7] Robert Keisling, "Turning Back the Clock: A Response to Szasz," *American Psychologist* 38 (March, 1983), p. 343.

[8] See Thomas Szasz, *Law, Liberty, and Psychiatry: An Inquiry into the Social Uses of Mental Health Practices* (Syracuse: Syracuse University Press, 1989 [1963]; and *Psychiatric Justice* (Syracuse: Syracuse University Press, 1988 [1965]).

[9] J.P. Schmidt, "The Psychiatric Will: Is the Cure Worse than the Illness?" *American Psychologist* 38 (March, 1983), pp. 342–43.

untary psychiatric intervention but doesn't let him reject such intervention, then it is not a real advance directive but a wicked trick.

Indeed, it is precisely the choice to request and reject psychiatric
interventions that psychiatrists are unwilling to offer mental patients;
and it is precisely because my version of the PW offers patients this
choice that psychiatrists reject it. For the slave owner, the very idea of
the slave's self-determination was anathema, an insult to the white man's
obligation as a master ("the white man's burden"). For the psychiatrist,
the very idea of the mental patient's self-determination is anathema, an
insult to the psychiatric master's obligation as a "mad-doctor" ("the psychiatrist's burden"). Not surprisingly, the idea of using PADs only to let
patients prospectively request coerced psychiatric treatment is popular
among mental health professionals: by offering the patient's blessing for
what the psychiatrist would have done anyway, such a PW relieves the
psychiatrist of doubt or guilt.

In a 1996 law review essay, entitled "Advance Directive Instruments
for Those with Mental Illness," Bruce J. Winick, professor of law at the
University of Miami, writes: "Some psychiatrists have responded negatively to the use of advance directive instruments in the *mental health
treatment* context [reference to Chodoff and Peele]. . . . However,
because these may have *therapeutic value*, this negative response is
unjustified."[10] Winick endorses the PW solely as an *instrument to facilitate psychiatric treatment*, thus destroying it as an instrument to enable
patients to *reject the role of mental patient and avoid future psychiatric
interference in their lives.*

Mental patients, Winick declares, "should be encouraged to determine in advance how they would like to be treated during future periods of incompetency."[11] At the same time, he opposes giving mental
patients a choice between receiving and rejecting psychiatric treatment: "When the objection is to a therapeutic intervention . . . [there]
may be reason to at least question whether the refusal of such treatment might be antitherapeutic and inconsistent with their [the
patients'] welfare."[12] In other words, when the psychiatrist's decision
is to treat, the patient's refusal ought to be, *ipso facto*, suspect. For
Winick—and evidently for Fulford as well—this is a solution. For me,
it is a problem.

---

[10] Bruce J. Winick, "Advance Directive Instruments for Those with Mental Illness,"
University of Miami Law Review 51 (1996), pp. 57–95 (p. 95), emphasis added.
[11] *Ibid.*, p. 68, emphasis added.
[12] *Ibid.*, p. 73.

In psychiatry, tradition and law sanction the use of involuntary treatment. Put in computerese, involuntary hospitalization and treatment is the default option. Hence, preparing a document to authorize it is redundant. Persons satisfied with the prevailing rules by which the law distributes a deceased person's estate have no need for last wills. The same is true for mental patients satisfied with the judgment and good will of psychiatrists in their dealings with involuntary patients.

V

With this in mind, let us briefly return to the case of Diane Abbot. Why did she need a psychiatric advance directive? Abbot never "denied" that she was ill. She must have known that her symptoms waxed and waned. According to Fulford, and ostensibly thanks to lithium, *she was mentally and legally competent when she decided to stop taking the drug.* Hence, psychiatrists had no valid reason to question her decision, and Abbot had no valid reason to defer to the doctors' judgment. She knew that she might "relapse."

According to Fulford's account, Abbot's relationship to her physicians resembled the child's relationship to his parents, not the adult's relationship to, say, his stockbroker. It was a relationship based on domination-submission, not on co-operation and contract. I have devoted much of my writing on medical ethics during the past half a century to showing that we ought to reject the view that this arrangement is practically necessary or morally desirable. To the contrary, I have argued that it is morally undesirable because *it lets the patient evade responsibility for his behavior and legitimizes the psychiatrist's assumption of responsibility for the patient's behavior.* Yet Fulford seems unable to view the relationship between Abbot and her doctors in any other way than paternalistically:

> Diane Abbot's . . . episodes of manic upswing nearly always started with clear-cut warning signs, notably that she stopped sleeping properly. The difficulty was that *her insight was also an early casualty of the disorder* (she consistently misconstrued these changes as moving into a "productive phase" even though her work actually deteriorated, as judged by others at the time and herself subsequently). (Emphasis added.)

The term "insight"— as in "lack of insight"—is a psychiatric code word for the view that when doctor and patient disagree, the doctor is right and the patient is wrong; and that, because the patient is wrong, it is the doctor's "responsibility" to treat him as a guardian treats his ward, not as a medical doctor treats his medical patient. I repeat Fulford: "[S]he consistently misconstrued these changes as moving into a 'productive phase' even though her work actually deteriorated, as *judged by others at the time and herself subsequently*" (emphasis added). The implication is that Abbot lacked competence to make appropriate judgments and decisions about her welfare as well as her art.

Let us take Fulford's foregoing sentence seriously. What Fulford is saying here is that judging the merit of a work of art is a measure of competence, indeed a measure accurate and reliable enough to justify depriving a person of liberty. In view of what passes today for modern art worthy of display in prestigious galleries and museums, this is both absurd and comical. Surely, judging the quality of art is not an objective, psychiatric, or scientific measure of "insight." Besides, didn't Abbot have a right to produce inferior work and think highly of it?

Competence, let us keep in mind, is primarily a legal issue. There are no objective tests for competence. A determination of competence may or may not be informed, or misinformed, by medical opinion and testimony. My point is that the practice of psychiatry rests on a coercive-paternalistic ethic: as long as the patient co-operates with the doctor, the patient is assumed to have insight and the doctor acts as if he were the patient's agent. However, if the patient refuses to co-operate, he is said to lack insight and the doctor becomes, *de facto*, the patient's adversary, yet *de jure* is accepted as acting as the patient's agent and protector (from himself).

Fulford's account of Abbot ignores that all this is old hat in the literature of psychiatric apologetics. Kay Redfield Jamison—a psychologist, professor of psychiatry at Johns Hopkins University, and self-declared sufferer from manic-depression—never tires of lauding the doctors who "took care of her" against her will and offers her personal version of the psychiatric will as a model instrument: "I drew up a clear arrangement with my psychiatrist and family that if I again become severely depressed they have the authority to approve, against my will if necessary, both electroconvulsive therapy, or ECT, an excellent treatment for certain types of severe depression, and hospitalization."[13] I support Jamison's right pro-actively to reject self-responsibility and embrace

---

[13] Kay Redfield Jamison, *An Unquiet Mind: A Memoir of Mood and Madness* (New York: Knopf, 1995), p. 113; see also her book *Night Falls Fast: Understanding Suicide* (New York: Knopf, 1999).

psychiatric slavery *for herself.* However, she and her colleagues oppose the right of others pro-actively to accept self-responsibility and reject psychiatric slavery.

It is important to note here that the legal and psychiatric denial of the rights of mental patients whose illness is in remission (say, because of "effective drug treatment") to reject future psychiatric meddling is inconsistent with every mental patient's *civil law* responsibility for the consequences of his actions:[14]

> . . . an insane or mentally ill person can intend or expect the results of his actions. . . . As the term is used in civil law, specifically in the law of torts, the term "intent" is used to denote that the actor desires to cause the consequences of his act. . . . The law will not inquire further into his peculiar mental condition with a view to excusing him if it should appear that a delusion or other consequence of his affliction has caused him to entertain that intent or that a normal person would not have entertained it. . . . A standard jury instruction reads: "An adult who is disabled by reason of mental illness must still observe the same standards of care which a normal and reasonable careful person would exercise under the circumstances which existed in this case."[15]

The psychiatric objections to a true psychiatric will illustrate the coercive psychiatrists' conceited belief that assent to their dogmas is a mark of sanity, and dissent from them a mark of insanity. *A priori*, the psychiatric testator's prospective consent to treatment is valid, while his prospective rejection of it is invalid.

VI

The engine that drives the psychiatrist's proclivity for coercive paternalism and aversion to liberty and responsibility is his deep-seated love of "liberalism," that is, his bias for statism of the leftist totalitarian type. Ralph Slovenko, a contributor to this volume, admires Stalin as a protector of the public health of the Soviet people, a judgment unaffected by the fact that the health of the people in the Soviet Union declined disastrously during Stalin's reign. Slovenko writes:

---

[14] For an in-depth discussion of this important subject, see Thomas S. Szasz and George J. Alexander, "Mental Illness as an Excuse for Civil Wrongs," *Journal of Nervous and Mental Disease* 147 (August, 1968), pp. 113–123.

[15] Ralph Slovenko, *Psychiatry and Criminal Culpability* (New York: Wiley, 1995), pp. 314–15. Michigan Standard Jury Instruction, 2d, 13.03, quoted in *ibid.*, p. 315.

The Therapeutic State is not necessarily evil. Indeed, it is preferable to a non-Therapeutic state. Purists need not be fascists to support campaigns against smoking, or to promote nutritional food, education, sports facilities, parks and walkable and bikeable communities. That would be a truly Therapeutic State. Joseph Stalin was a tyrant but he did two good things: he developed an excellent transportation system and he kept the fast-food (a.k.a. junk food) franchises out of the Soviet Union. For that, all Russians are grateful.[16]

Slovenko does not mention that Stalin destroyed tens of millions of his fellow citizens, incarcerated the rest behind the borders of the Soviet Union, and converted churches into vodka factories. I have made it clear that I use the term "Therapeutic State" ironically. Such a state provides coercions and prohibitions it defines as "therapeutic," not services the recipient considers beneficial. Slovenko either misunderstands this important point or, because of his diametrically opposed, statist political perspective, cannot grasp it.

Like Slovenko, Fulford views the state, except when it "abuses" psychiatric diagnoses, as an agency for "doing good." He is a thoroughly correct academic "liberal." He writes:

> The importance of mis-matches of diagnostic values in leading to abusive uses of psychiatry of the kind with which Szasz has been especially concerned, was evident in a study I carried out with a Russian colleague (Alec Smirnoff) and a Russian-speaking social worker (Elena Snow), on the scientific literature in the former U.S.S.R. over the period when psychiatry was being used there as a means of controlling political dissidence . . . in the U.S.S.R., many dissidents over this period were diagnosed as suffering from "sluggish schizophrenia." But what our study of the Russian-language literature showed was that this was not driven by poor science, as many have supposed. Indeed, the diagnostic criteria in use in the U.S.S.R. at the time were closely similar to those employed in Western democracies . . . The abusive misdiagnoses were driven rather by the absolute values of the Soviet ethic. By the standards of the Soviet ethic . . .

Fulford dwells on the abuses of psychiatry in the Soviet Union but is silent about its even more dramatic abuses in Nazi Germany. Nor does he mention the psychiatric persecution, in the West, of homosexuals in the past and "hyperactive" children and illegal drug users today.

---

[16] Ralph Slovenko, "The Trouble with Szasz," *Liberty* 16 (August, 2002), 25–32; and see my response, "Coercion and Psychiatry," *ibid.*, pp. 33–35.

Elsewhere, I have rebutted the selective condemnation of so-called psychiatric abuses and misdiagnoses and the mistaken view that "the essential vulnerability of psychiatry to abusive misdiagnosis in this way derives from the value judgments involved."[17] "Psychiatric abuses" were a Western invention and continue to flourish in the free, liberal democracies of the West.[18] Soviet politicians and psychiatrists were apt students.[19]

I maintain that psychiatric abuses are intrinsic to the legitimacy of psychiatric coercions and that psychiatric slavery ought to be abolished. Fulford maintains that psychiatrists need more professional skills: "To such dangers, then, as Szasz has done so much to make clear, psychiatry remains vulnerable. But where Szasz takes this to be a sign that mental distress and disorder, of whatever kind, should be removed from medicine, VBM takes it as a sign that psychiatry urgently needs the skills to work more effectively with the values-base, as well as the evidence-base, of practice."

What Fulford calls "the essential vulnerability of psychiatry to abusive misdiagnosis," I regard as the essential function of psychiatry as a tool of social control. The difference between my critics and me go down to the bedrock of the language we use and the values we espouse. Towards the end of his essay, Fulford turns his attention to "resolving

---

[17] Thomas Szasz, "Psychiatric Diagnosis, Psychiatric Power, and Psychiatric Abuse," *Journal of Medical Ethics* 20 (September, 1994), 135–38; and *Liberation by Oppression*, *op. cit.*

[18] See Thomas Szasz, *Cruel Compassion: The Psychiatric Control of Society's Unwanted* (Syracuse: Syracuse University Press, 1998 [1994]); *Ideology and Insanity: Essays on the Psychiatric Dehumanization of Man* (Syracuse: Syracuse University Press, 1991 [1970]); *Insanity: The Idea and Its Consequences* (Syracuse: Syracuse University Press, 1997 [1987]); *Law, Liberty, and Psychiatry: An Inquiry into the Social Uses of Mental Health Practices* (Syracuse: Syracuse University Press, 1989 [1963]); *A Lexicon of Lunacy: Metaphoric Malady, Moral Responsibility, and Psychiatry* (New Brunswick: Transaction, 1993); *The Manufacture of Madness: A Comparative Study of the Inquisition and the Mental Health Movement* (Syracuse: Syracuse University Press, 1997 [1970]); *Psychiatric Justice* (Syracuse: Syracuse University Press, 1988 [1965]); *Psychiatric Slavery: When Confinement and Coercion Masquerade as Cure* (Syracuse: Syracuse University Press, 1998 [1977]); *The Untamed Tongue: A Dissenting Dictionary* (La Salle: Open Court, 1990); and Thomas Szasz, ed., *The Age of Madness: A History of Involuntary Mental Hospitalization Presented in Selected Texts* (Garden City: Doubleday, 1973).

[19] See, generally, Thomas Szasz, *Liberation by Oppression: A Comparative Study of Slavery and Psychiatry* (New Brunswick: Transaction, 2002); also the works cited in note 18, and *Kansas v. Leroy Hendricks*, No. 95-1649. "Excerpts from Opinions on Status of Sex Offenders," *New York Times* (24th June, 1997), p. B11.

disagreements." How does he perceive the nature of the conflicting interests and the identities of the contending parties? He explains:

> That human values differ widely and (often) legitimately requires that the values of the individuals concerned be our "first call" for information. But this same principle means that, where differences of values come into conflict, no one value perspective should have automatic precedence. It is no part of VBM, then, that patient-centred care should mean treating our patients merely as consumers, as customers whose needs and wishes we, as healthcare professionals, exist to satisfy. If the values of the patient or patient group concerned are central, this is not to say that the values of professionals are irrelevant. Far from it, the professional's assessment of the pros and cons of a given intervention, the professional's evaluations of these informed by his or her knowledge and experience, matters. . . . Within VBM, indeed, a plurality of perspectives is to be welcomed. *For without at least one balancing perspective, we are at risk of slipping from the traditional abuses of "doctor knows best", one extreme view, one absolute, to the abuses of an equal and opposite extreme of "patient knows best."* (Emphasis added.)

I disagree.

From a medical point of view—assuming that the doctor is a well-trained physician and the patient a lay person—*the doctor always knows best about what ails the patient and how best to treat him.* (Sometimes the patient is a physician who knows best, but that is not the normal contingency.)

From a political point of view—assuming that we value individual liberty and personal responsibility more highly than we value health—*the patient's body always belongs to him and hence he has always the right to accept or reject medical advice or treatment.*

Fulford misframes the conflict. The issue is not whether doctor or patient "knows best." Instead, it is between coercion and co-operation. Neither doctor nor patient should have the right, authorized by law, to impose his will on the other. The doctor should be on tap, not on top. The core issue before us is the psychiatrist's power over the mental patient and his state-authorized power to coerce him. Fulford steers clear of that hot-button issue. He writes: "In a democracy, then, in the democracy of values of VBM no less than in a political democracy, *processes must be in place to support, as far as possible, diversity of view.*"

The term "democracy of values" is either a meaningless slogan or a rhetorical device to blur value conflicts, for example, to justify the psychiatrist's claim that he deprives innocent persons of liberty because he values liberty, or declares guilty persons not guilty by reason of insanity because he values responsibility. "Commitment can be justified on the grounds of enhancing the individual's future freedom," write Roger Peele and Robert Keisling.[20] "The physician seeks to liberate the patient from the chains of illness," explains Thomas G. Gutheil, professor of psychiatry at Harvard.[21]

The depth of my linguistic disagreement with Fulford is dramatically illustrated by his following statement: "Thus, bioethics, in the predominantly quasi-legal form it has taken in its interactions with practice, has in effect if not in intent, sought to *impose* particular values, such as autonomy of patient choice" (emphasis added). Autonomy is self-rule, that is, self-determination and the willingness to assume responsibility for oneself. Accordingly, you can do many things with autonomy, but the one thing you cannot do is *impose* it on anyone. We cannot impose autonomy on an infant, on a patient in the intensive care unit of a hospital, or, for that matter, on a healthy and intelligent adult who refuses to accept the duties of the adult role.

VII

My disagreements with Fulford notwithstanding, his essay has many virtues. One of its virtues is that it shows us how the observer's uncritical acceptance of the moral and political-economic legitimacy of the N.H.S. shapes his view of value-conflicts in medicine and psychiatry.

The proverb, "He who pays the piper calls the tune," frames the political-economic context and defines the rules of human relations outside the family. Capitalist acts imply and rest on a relationship of equality and mutual need: they satisfy the needs of both parties. For example, a person wants his pet cured, takes it to a verterinarian, and pays for his services. The veterinarian provides the service the client requests. The client needs the veterinarian's services; the veterinarian needs the client's money. The participants are partners. In contrast, socialist acts imply and rest on a relationship of inequality and the absence of mutual need: satisfying the needs of one party frustrates the needs of the other party. The participants are adversaries.

Removing the economic nexus from the relationship between doctor and patient destroys the condition of mutuality. Consider the situation of

---

[20] *Psychiatric News* (5th December, 1980), pp. 1, 28 (p. 28).
[21] Thomas G. Gutheil, "In Search of True Freedom: Drug Refusal, Involuntary Medication, and 'Rotting with Your Rights On'," *American Journal of Psychiatry* 137 (1980), pp. 327–28 (p. 327).

the typical patient, Jones, and the typical physician, Smith, in the N.H.S. system. When Jones gets sick, he needs Smith's services. But Smith does not need Jones as a patient; he needs the state's money. I am restating the basic principles of free-market economics.

The point to keep in mind is that socialized medicine rests on man's basic desire for dependency and susceptibility to temptation. The system offers the potential patient something for nothing or, more precisely, Rolex care for Timex prices. It offers the physician independence from the vagaries of the market and the need to please the patient and promises him a secure salary from the state. This arrangement sets the stage for a host of value conflicts for both doctor and patient, some of which Fulford and I discuss in our respective contributions. For the reader interested in exploring the economic aspects of this vast subject from a classical liberal (libertarian) point of view, I recommend the writings of Ludwig von Mises and Friedrich von Hayek.[22] I apply these views to medicine and psychiatry in several of my books, especially in *The Myth of Mental Illness*, *The Ethics of Psychoanalysis*, *The Theology of Medicine*, *Pharmacracy*, and *Liberation by Oppression*.

There remains for me to comment briefly on the work of the Oxford philosopher R.M. Hare, whose writings Fulford approving cites and on whose views he bases some of his own arguments. Fulford writes:

> VBM draws particularly on the work of R.M. Hare and others in what has become known as the Oxford School of analytic philosophy. . . . Hare was concerned with the logic, with the meanings and implications of value terms ("good," "bad," "right,", and so forth). . . . Although somewhat abstract in orientation, philosophical value theory has a wide range of practical applications in medicine and psychiatry . . . A key observation of Hare's, though, for our present purposes, is that values tend to become visible only where they are divergent, and, hence, are likely to come into conflict. We only notice values, that is to say, when they cause trouble!

I have noted earlier that, in my view, this is altogether fallacious. If we are at all sensitive to values, then we will notice that people exude their values in everything they say and do, in their most ordinary, everyday behavior no less than in the way they respond to moral conflicts.

---

[22] And see, for example, Roger D. Feldman, ed., *American Health Care: Government, Market Processes, and the Public Interest* (New Brunswick: Transaction, 2000).

As it happens, I have had some first-hand exposure to Hare's views about the application of his "value theory" to psychiatry. In 1970 (or perhaps 1971) both of us were invited to participate in a four- or five-day conference on psychiatry and law in Oxford, under the auspices of the Ditchley Foundation. I heard Hare expound his views during the day at conferences, at night during dinner, and in private conversations. He supported psychiatric coercions and excuses as staunchly as I opposed such interventions. We left Oxford without changing each other's minds. Also, having read Hare's writings, I was familiar with his views and they did not impress me. Here I cite two brief items featured on Internet sites that exemplify his morally otiose views:

> If philosophers are going to apply ethical theory successfully to practical issues, they must first have a theory. . . . A philosopher's chief contribution to a practical issue should be to show us which are good and which are bad arguments; and to do this he has to have some way of telling one from the other. Moral philosophy therefore needs a basis in philosophical logic—the logic of the moral concepts.[23]

Hare does not say whether an argument is good because it is truthful or because it is persuasive or because it supports a good cause. In my judgment, a philosopher who prefers a good argument for a bad cause to a bad argument for a good cause is an immoral or amoral philosopher and a bad person. In the following excerpt, Hare applies his philosophical acumen to an analysis of National Socialism:

> To criticize pro-Nazi arguments, we must first get clear on the facts (including the differences between the races, and whether these are genetic or cultural). We must also see if the Nazis argue consistently (for example, if Jews are to be maltreated because they are greedy, then Nazis who are greedy must be maltreated too). Golden rule reasoning will show the inconsistency of most Nazis. Only a few Nazi "fanatics" can desire that, if they and their family were found to be Jewish, then they would be thrown into concentration camps and killed.[24]

In my opinion, we need not know any facts about the "differences between the races, and whether these are genetic or cultural" to criticize

---

[23] R.M. Hare, *Essays on Bioethics* (Oxford, 1999), §10, www.petersingerlinks.com/hare. htm

[24] R.M. Hare, www.google.com/search?hl-en&ie=ISO-8859-1&q=r+m+hare&btnG= Google+Sea

and oppose pro-Nazi arguments, just as Americans did not need to know any facts about the "differences between the races, and whether they are genetic or cultural" to criticize and oppose pro-slavery arguments. Nazis are wicked regardless of whether "golden rule reasoning" shows them to be consistent or inconsistent.

Fulford is keenly aware of the painful dilemmas that persons whose behavior we perceive and conceptualize as "psychiatric emergencies" pose to their families, psychiatrists, and society. And he clearly feels that all is not right about the way present-day English and American societies expect psychiatrists to manage such "crises." When John Stuart Mill struggled with the problem of the subjection of women to men—a problem not dissimilar to that of the subjection of "crazy persons" to psychiatrists—he wisely remarked:

> So long as an opinion is strongly rooted in the feelings, it gains rather than loses in stability by having a preponderating weight of argument against it. . . . the worse it fares in argumentative contest, the more persuaded its adherents are that their feeling must have some deeper ground, which the arguments do not reach; and while the feeling remains, it is always throwing up fresh intrenchments of arguments to repair any breach in the old.[25]

VIII

Much as I would like to, I cannot find any point of agreement with Fulford. I am unable to accept his criteria for what constitutes objective evidence. He writes:

> In EBM, the "first call" is highly generalised information derived from meta-analyses of well-designed scientific research. The results of these meta-analyses, generated by pooling sources, provides information which is as objective as possible. EBM sets out, deliberately, to be as independent as possible of the perspective of any particular observer. . . . This is why the results of meta-analyses are at the top of the "evidence hierarchy" in EBM, above the results of individual research trials.

Citing the so-called meta-analysis of research findings as objective evidence of the existence of mental diseases or the efficacy of psychiatric treatments is the latest fad in the effort to prove that the

---

[25] John Stuart Mill, *The Subjection of Women* (Cambridge, Massachusetts: MIT Press, 1970 [1869]), p. 1.

personally and culturally fashioned judgments of psychiatrists and psychologists are "scientifically valid." In fact, the term is used to refer to a "researcher" reviewing a dozen or more "research papers" written by colleagues—say on the addictive qualities of cigarettes—emphasizing points of agreement among them and declaring these points to be as good as "facts." Agreement among observers, even if it is called the result of meta-analysis, is still only an agreement or consensus.

I prefer Ibsen's view that the compact majority is always wrong. The result of pooling misinformation is more misinformation. Surely, it would be easy to secure meta-analyses of theological studies of transubstantiation, demonstrating the truths of the Eucharistic transformation. It was by a similar method of widespread professional agreement that psychiatrists maintained that masturbatory insanity and homosexuality are diseases in the same sense in which diabetes and lupus are diseases. Similarly, there was enough agreement about the value of lobotomy as a treatment for schizophrenia to persuade the most eminent judges of medical "facts" that Egas Moniz deserved a Nobel Prize in Medicine for his "discovery."

Fulford continues:

> Where EBM seeks *a*perspectival information (about facts), VBM seeks *perspectival* information (about values). Where EBM seeks for information which is as perspective-free as possible, VBM seeks for information which is as close as possible to the particular perspectives of the individuals involved in a particular clinical context.

I disagree.

Information is something that is sought by persons, not by abstractions, such as EBM or VBM.

As Fulford's discussion of the case of Diane Abbot illustrates, the use of these terms does not facilitate acquiring information; it facilitates gaining affirmation, that is, justification for action, for example, to categorize mental illness and dangerousness to self and others as a medical indication for involuntary mental hospitalization, make prescribing heroin a criminal offense, or declare routine neonatal circumcision a procedure devoid of medical value and hence not reimbursed by the N.H.S. In psychiatry, the only way to obtain information is by listening to the patient over long periods of time, a nonmedical activity properly not reimbursed by the N.H.S. or any other system of socialized medicine.

Fulford and I both look at the same psychiatric glass: he sees it as half-full; I see it, not as half-empty, but as completely empty. With an excess of generosity or optimism, he believes the result of my sceptical attack on the concept of mental illness will be a new understanding:

> in which fact and value are in various ways combined, and from which psychiatry, precisely in being more value-laden than physical medicine, provides a model for a more values-based approach to medicine in general in the twenty-first century. . . . I will conclude with an indication of how Szasz's sceptical attack on the concept of mental illness has led, paradoxically, not to the demise of psychiatry, but to the potential for it to emerge as a lead discipline in twenty-first century medicine.

That is exactly the opposite of the conclusion at which I arrive in *Pharmacracy*.

3

Persons and Popper's World 3: Do Humans Dream of Abstract Sheep?

RAY SCOTT PERCIVAL

Introduction

In the film classic *Blade Runner*, the story explores the notion of personal identity through that of carefully crafted androids. Can an android have a personality; can androids be persons? The title of the original story by Philip K. Dick is *Do Androids Dream of Electric Sheep?* The story suggests that our sense of being a person depends on our having memories that connect us with our childhood. In the movie, the androids are only a couple of years old, but have adult bodies. To complete them as persons they are given simulated memories of childhood. Some psychiatrists have decided that even humans dream only of electric sheep.

Modern psychiatry is premised on the reduction of the human person to a complex set of chemical states or processes of the brain. This is implied by its conception of mental problems, or fundamental life problems, as mental diseases. Psychiatry is also committed to a now refuted deterministic view of the physical world, and hence of people's life problems. Roughly speaking, determinism asserts that every event has a cause. More precisely, determinism asserts that any event can be explained in any level of detail given the relevant laws and a sufficiently precise statement of the initial conditions. If you combine this with physicalism, then all causes are physical causes. For psychiatry the world of the person is, therefore, a world closed off from any other type of influence outside the world of the physical.

I need to clarify my claim about psychiatry's philosophical commitments. The ubiquitous use of Freud's talking therapy that attempts to explore and solve the person's problems through a long series of in depth conversations about the person's memories, desires, conflicts, anxieties, and so forth, does not automatically suggest a commitment to a determinist physical reductionism. However, this type of reductionism characterises Freud's original metaphysical programme. Freud confidently expected progress in brain physiology to achieve a complete reduction and for this to then allow both chemical and surgical therapies to take over from what he regarded as a stopgap method.

I would like to illustrate just what this type of reduction would mean in terms of interpreting people's mental life. Suppose a person loves life, but has also adopted a theory (such as a religion or world-view) that seems to him to imply that human life is base, disgusting, or immoral. After many sleepless nights and depression, he decides to take his life. Psychiatry completely ignores the abstract aspect of the case by saying that this person took his life because of some yet undiscovered lesion in his brain. To admit that his theory of human life had any influence would be to open up the deterministic physical world into which psychiatry has placed all humans. From this perspective, the human being is hence no longer a person but a machine that has gone wrong.

The Epistemology of Coping with Life

I want to suggest that Szasz's position is lacking a strong epistemology and is therefore unnecessarily open to attack. Szasz suggests that the term "life problem" more accurately captures the phenomena that the term "mental illness" is meant to denote. I think that Szasz's emphasis on life problems suggests that the most appropriate epistemology for Szasz's perspective can be found in the work of Karl Popper.

As Popper said, "All life is problem solving." He meant this in the most general and abstract way, so that all life is covered by this formula: from the humble bacterium seeking out better conditions of warmth, and so forth, to the highly sophisticated scientist trying to unravel the explanation behind some wonderful phenomenon. In dealing with the problems we encounter in life, we adopt, shape, create, and abandon a host of theories, arguments, plans, and strategies in our attempts to solve or avoid them. This is most powerfully described in terms of a conjecture and refutation model. Popper argued that science should be a matter of different scientists advancing competing bold guesses about the world, guesses which are then subjected to unremitting criticism in the hope that they may weed out the false theories and be left with those that are at least closer to the truth. Thankfully, for us, science has often managed to achieve this ideal.

An analogous model applies to the way we live. We actively try on different lifestyles, approaches, world-views, habits, and so forth, for size, testing them against criteria and standards (such as truth, beauty, moral goodness) that we have adopted or created or have genetically inherited (the need for warmth and food and human contact). The extent to which this is a deliberate and systematic enterprise varies between individuals and it may be more readily practised systematically only in the more developed countries, but its form can be discerned even in the most conservative or traditional societies and the most inept, slothful individual. The process is analogous to the evolution of organisms and to the development of science in so far as there is a population of variants, some of which meet the pressures of selection and some that do not. It has a greater similarity with science as far as language plays a key role through the formulation and arguing about world-views and the myriad less grandiose theories that the person finds important.

Popper proposed the following schema for the most abstract account of problem solving:

Problem → Tentative Theory → Error Elimination → New Problem

I want to say that persons are partly and actively constituted by the theories they have about themselves and the world. Persons actively give themselves unity, individuality, and continuity partly by a web of theories, conceptions, problems, arguments, plans and other abstract non-physical things that they have created, adopted, shaped, and adapted for themselves through life. This web of abstract entities makes a difference to what people do and hence opens up their world to the non-physical. Popper's arguments for the existence of three different types of classes of things, World 1, World 2, and World 3, and how they interact with one another help to bolster the rich conception of the person and defend it against the chemical control imposed by the state.

False Theory versus Category Mistake

I agree with Szasz that humans have life problems, but not mental diseases. The medical establishment has overlooked the fact that all life is problem solving, and it is by no means obvious that all people would

produce the same solution, or solutions that deviate only slightly from
the norm, or that non of these solutions might be undesirable from a
moral point of view. "What should I do?" is a question we face anew
every day. Should I marry? Why should I be good? Why should I conform to what others do or say? What is more important: individual
achievement in science through "obsessive" devotion or raising a family? Should I grow up? If not, how do I avoid doing so?

The word "disease" is defined within medicine as tissue damage or
a condition conducive to damage. However, the mind is not tissue, nor a
purely physical state of bodily tissue. Szasz argues that to apply the
adjective "disease" to the mind is to incur a category mistake, an expression popularised by the philosopher Gilbert Ryle. It is like saying that
numbers are red, or that pain is hexagonal. This approach has the
strength of clarity, but it is vitiated by the fact that our language and its
categories are a reflection of our theories about the world, and thus
change with the advance of our understanding. Hundreds of years ago it
would have seemed to be a category mistake to say that whales are mammals, but now we know that whales are in fact mammals, not fish. Once
we classed mushrooms with plants; but now we regard mushrooms as
belonging to the class of fungi. One could even envisage a sensible use
of the expression "pain is hexagonal". We could interpret this phrase as
describing the shape of the area of skin affected, for example.

Different theories carve up the world in different ways.

Popper's Worlds 1, 2, and 3

A stronger argument for the myth of mental illnesses attacks the theory of
reductionism that lies behind the confusion of these different categories.

Popper's argument for dualism is the strongest case against the
reductionist view. Popper argues that there are at least three radically different classes of thing. More concisely, there are three worlds. World 1
is the world of physics. It includes rocks, stars, protons, computers and
biological bodies. It also includes the worlds of chemistry and biology.
World 2 is the world of our conscious selves, dreams, hopes, pleasures,
pains—the world of psychology. World 3 is the world of abstract products of the human mind. It is the world of numbers, theories, arguments,
and problems. It also includes works of art and music.

Popper's World 3 is like Plato's world of forms, but has important differences. Plato's world of forms is a collection of eternal, perfect
abstract concepts, like beauty, the circle, the good, and so on. In contrast,
Popper's World 3 is the creation of the human mind. It contains every-

thing that Plato's world contains but also contains theories, arguments, problems, and works of art and music. It also contains erroneous theories, invalid arguments and other imperfect abstract productions. It retains the autonomy of Plato's world of forms, in that once a World 3 object, like the natural numbers, has been created, it develops a life of its own with its own laws and relationships that are independent of our psychology. For example, once the natural numbers had been created, it could then be discovered that prime numbers existed and this then brought up new unforeseeable problems, such as "is there a highest prime number?" and "do the prime numbers continue to get more scarce as we look further along the sequence of prime numbers?"

Many philosophers are upset by the use of the plural word "worlds," so let us be clear that they are all simply domains within the one world, that which we call the universe. Popper's three worlds could have been called Domain 1, Domain 2, and Domain 3. Some things such as books belong to both World 1 (on account of the fact that books are physical objects) and World 3 (on account of the fact that they contain abstract objects like theories and arguments).

The Reality of World 2

I would like to briefly state my assumption regarding the reality of a non-physical mental domain.

There are active self-conscious minds. The existence of a mind or self is dependent on the brain, but the mind is the pilot of an important range of brain processes. Its evolutionary function was the integration and co-ordination of activities of the brain and the body for the benefit of survival. However, the mind has developed a life of its own in some respects and some of its goals are independent of survival (for example, searching for a solution to an abstruse mathematical problem.) This is not to undermine the theory of evolution, since organs originally used for one function are often used for new functions later. The philosopher A.J. Ayer once said that the problem with radical physicalism is that it requires one to feign anesthesia. The hypothesis of minds explains a whole range of phenomena that cannot be satisfactorily explained simply by brain processes. In this respect, the hypothesis is on a par with the postulation of unobservable atoms to explain the structure of macroscopic objects, so the fact that the minds of other people cannot be directly observed is irrelevant. Moreover, even though it is not quite as open to falsifying tests as the atomic hypothesis or other physical theories, it can be tested.

Sophisticated and Ordinary Cases of World 3 Influence

The designer of a bridge may become deeply depressed if a fault in his calculations for the design leads to a fatal collapse. (The calculations were wrong only relative to the facts of mathematics, which are clearly not chemical or physical. Thus, the builder's behaviour in following the faulty design is not caused simply by his chemistry.) A mathematician may experience life-long frustration at not being able to derive a whole section of maths from a consistent set of axioms. (A logical inconsistency is not a physical or chemical state, process or relation. Hence, the mathematician's frustrating life-long problem is not a product of his chemistry.)

Someone may dismiss the case of the mathematician in search of the properties of prime numbers as irrelevant to the day-to-day thinking of people, but there are innumerable examples from everyday life. Five people out on the town each have 20 dollars, a total of 100 dollars. They all want to go to a Cantonese restaurant for a meal. When they get there, they find that the minimum charge for the five of them would be 150 dollars. Therefore, they decide not to order the meal there. It is a property of the natural numbers that 150 is greater than 100. Moreover, this is clearly not a physical fact; it is a mathematical fact. The reductionist is asking us to believe that the decision of the group not to eat at the restaurant could have nothing whatsoever to do with the fact that 100 is smaller than 150. A little thought will make it obvious that our life is full of instances of our interacting with and making use of abstract things, laws and relationships.

It is astounding that nearly the whole of psychiatry and even psychology implicitly denies any influence in peoples' lives to the existence of plans, designs, theories, numbers and logical arguments and the various non-physical relations that exist within and between these entities. In many cases abstract structures are simply neglected (a recent example would be the work of Antonio Damasio).

Objections

I intend to confine my defence of the person to an attack on one prominent assumption of cognitive science, the idea that the mind can be reduced to a computer program.

It has been argued that the autonomy of World 3 can be fully accounted for by a reduction of World 3 to technology (Levinson 1993). The most popular version of this is that computer hardware and programs can do all the explanatory work that World 3 is meant to do.

A Technological Version of World 3

A number of attempts have been made to reduce World 3 to psychological or physical states, all of which founder on the infinite richness of at least some World 3 objects. One bold attempt was made by Paul Levinson in his *Mind at Large: Knowing in the Technological Age*.

Levinson argues that technological products, for example a humble nail, consist of a union between World 3 and World 1, since it is a physical object that embodies certain theories (presumably to do with how and for what it can be used). So far Popper would agree. But Levinson says that the autonomy of technology itself gives us all the autonomy that Popper sought in World 3 without our having to concede the existence of unembodied ideas. We have computers and other machines that function quite independently of us once they have been created. Even more fancifully, machines may supplant humans and become the next vehicles for the replication of what Dawkins calls memes.

However, the autonomy of World 3 goes far beyond the autonomy of that part of it that is embodied in technology. The idea that World 3 could be reduced to technology is similar to the idea that World 3 is simply the total library of objective knowledge. This is a suggestive metaphor, but it is also a very misleading error. Think of a theory that gets written down in a book. Some of its implications may be worked out and also written down. Now think of the total class of all the implications of this theory that will ever be worked out and embodied in writing. This perhaps vast amount of written material will still not exhaust the theory's logical content.

The Unfathomable Logical and Information Content of our Objective Theories

One of the strongest arguments for the independence of World 3 from psychology is based on the analysis of a theory's logical and information content. It can be shown that a scientific theory—a typical World 3 object—has an infinite information content. Information here is identified with what a theory denies or rules out. Expressed roughly, if I say that it will rain on at least one day next week, I convey less information than if I say it will rain only on Wednesday, because the second sentence rules out more possibilities. Now a scientific theory such as Newton's rules out not only Einstein's theory, but also an infinite number of other possible theories. Newton's mind obviously did not contain a representation of Einstein's theory, let alone most of the other theories that his theory rules out.

In the *Logic of Scientific Discovery* (1934), Popper put forward the idea that a statement says more the more it forbids. Carnap, accepting Popper's suggestion, defined the assertive power of a sentence as the class of possible cases it excludes (Carnap 1942, p. 151). Carnap attributes it to Wittgenstein, an attribution he later explained as an error of memory. Later Popper (1974) reformulated the intuitive idea in terms of theories rather than possible cases, of both high and low universality. The information content is then defined as the class of all those statements that are logically incompatible with the given theory. Thus since Einstein's theory contradicts Newton's theory, Einstein's theory is part of the information content of Newton's. Newton could hardly have known this, and so it could not have been part of his psychology. Furthermore, there are an infinite number of unknown theories that form part of the information content of Newton's theory, and indeed of any empirical theory.

The argument for the infinite logical content of a theory t can be put thus. Suppose an infinite list of statements that are pair-wise contradictory and which individually do not entail t: $a, b, c. \ldots$ Then the statement "t or a or both" follows from t. The same holds for each and every one of the statements in the infinite list. Since the statements in the list are pair-wise contradictory one can infer that none of the statements "t or a or both," "t or b or both," etc., is interderivable. Thus the logical content of t must be infinite.

The proof of the assumption that no pair of the statements "a or t or both", "b or t or both," etc., are interderivable is as follows. "b or t or both" follows from "a or t or both" if and only if the theory t follows from "a and non-b." But because a and b contradict each other, "a and non-b" says the same as a. Thus "b or t or both" follows from "a or t or both" if and only if t follows from a, which by assumption it does not.[1]

This in itself is not so important, but when combined with the idea of information content, the two notions produce some very interesting ramifications. As Popper shows, when we combine this result with the idea of logical content we obtain a parallel result, for if Einstein's theo-

---

[1] This proof is due to David W. Miller. See footnote 18 in *Unended Quest.*

ry E is part of the information content of Newton's theory N then Non-E is part of N's logical content. Thus both the logical and information content of theories consist of an infinite number of non-trivial consequences. As Popper says, it follows that the task of understanding a theory is infinite.

As Popper used to say, we never fully know what we are talking about. Expressed more generally, when someone creates a theory he creates an object whose properties transcend his psychological make-up.

Barrow and Tipler estimate that the information storage capacity of the human brain is between 10 to the power 10 and 10 to the power 15 bits, with the lower figure assuming that each brain cell stores on average 1 bit. While a colossal figure, this is clearly smaller than the infinite content

The Causal Potential of Logical Standards

Cognitive science, which tries to model the way humans think simply in terms of brain states or computer programs, has yet to come to terms with the causal effectiveness of logical standards. A physical brain state cannot logically contradict a theory, but the logical contradictions between Einstein's and Newton's theories obviously made a difference to the thought of scientists. We know this independently of being able to supply an adequate theory as to how contradictions do make a psychological difference. The same point can be made in connection with technology. In explaining why an engineer rejects a proposed building project (that if adopted would have created a dangerous building) because he noticed an error in the reasoning that it was based on, we have to take into account two things:

(a) the engineer's knowledge of logic and mathematics (perhaps describable in terms of dispositions to carry out certain algorithms), and

(b) the objective fact that there was an error in the reasoning to notice. But this latter fact is neither a physical nor a psychological fact.

I think that one of the most challenging problems is to explain how standards can influence our thought. It cannot be a logical relationship between the standard and the psychological state, but there must be some patterned relationship between the logical relationship and the psychological states. This problem is connected to what has come to be called the problem of the empirical basis of science.

But the point I want to make is that current cognitive science is forced to say that the discovery of a logical contradiction never has anything to do with its actually being a contradiction. It cannot explain the psychological impact that the discovery of an error in reasoning can have on us because a contradiction qua contradiction is impotent. For the cognitive scientist, performing an inference validly or discovering a logical error is either an accident of following certain conventional rules that one has been taught or a mysterious pre-established harmony.

As far as computer models are concerned, we must appeal to logical standards in order to make computers perform logical operations properly; we do not appeal to computers to judge logic. After all, computers break down. In the face of a global computer breakdown caused by a computer virus, we would still have recourse to the notions of validity and invalidity.

There is some truth in the idea that we can use computers to judge logic that must not be confused with the idea that computer programs can constitute validity. We can program a computer to perform according to a given set of axioms and inference rules. We can instruct it to draw out implications to see if any contradictions appear. If they do we can say that the putative logic is in fact invalid. But we would be appealing to an independent standard of validity. In an important sense, the computer is just a glorified pencil that helps us perform and check our inferences and calculations.

You can set up so-called "logic gates" in a computer in order for it to perform "logical inferences". But these structures and operations are only called logical because we interpret them so. The action of electrical impulses in a computer is an all or nothing phenomenon. Because pulses are precisely timed, even the absence of a pulse can be interpreted as a signal. When we want a set of possible combinations of signals to make a logic gate, the signals are interpreted as true or false (true = presence of a pulse; false = absence of a pulse). You can then make a logic gate for each of the logical operations: conjunction, disjunction, implication, and so forth. Each logic gate will be defined by what may be called a pulse-analogue of a propositional truth table.

It is clear that the action of a computer has to be suitably interpreted before we can use it for logic. Indeed, a great deal of logic and mathematics is used in interpreting the action of computers to make them useful tools of our reasoning. The more general point that any structure supporting a repeatable process involving the right conditionalities can be interpreted by us as a "logic gate" and as performing a "logical inference". Whether these interpreted processes can be put to any use is another matter.

World 3 as Linguistic Conventions

O'Hear claims that Popper's World 3 is not needed because we can account for the objectivity of World 3 by referring to linguistic conventions. We are simply drawing out the consequences of a set of rules. Of course, some of them may be unintended and unforeseen, but there is nothing more to what we are doing.

However, the first person to discriminate between a valid and invalid argument was not simply applying a set of conventional rules (or manifesting a set of dispositions) that he had been taught. By what convention was the first valid argument a valid argument?

There is another fundamental objection to O'Hear's view that derived from Gödel. Kurt Gödel showed that we cannot set down once and for all a set of rules that will tell us all the valid rules of inference. There will always be some valid rules of inference that remain undiscovered and not even a consequence of our current set.

Conclusion

My intention in this paper has been to argue that Szasz has left his position unnecessarily open to attack. Szasz has failed to supply an epistemology and a sufficiently elaborate philosophical case to defend his thesis about the myth of mental illness. A great deal has been written on the relation between mind and body, and it is not possible for me to cover even a significant amount of the debate. I have only been able to expound the relevant parts of Popper's epistemology and ontology and offer some introductory defence of this perspective on the mind-brain problem.[2]

---

[2] I am grateful for criticism and moral support from my wife Tamara Lynn Schreiber, my stepson Jacob Schreiber, David Barker, Patrick F. Murphy, and David Ramsay Steele.

REFERENCES

Bartley, W.W. 1985 [1973]. *Wittgenstein*. La Salle: Open Court.

————. 1990. *Unfathomed Knowledge, Unmeasured Wealth: On Universities and the Wealth of Nations*. Chicago: Open Court.

Carnap, R. 1942. *Introduction to Semantics*. Cambridge Massachusetts: Harvard University Press.

Dick, Philip K. 1968. *Do Androids Dream of Electric Sheep?* Garden City: Doubleday.

Levinson, P. 1988. *Mind at Large: Knowing in the Technological Age*. London: JAI Press.

Penrose, R. 1989. *The Emperor's New Mind: Concerning Computers, Mind, and the Laws of Physics*. New York: Oxford University Press.

Popper, Karl R. 1959 [1934]. *The Logic of Scientific Discovery*. London: Routledge.

————. 1963. *Conjectures and Refutations*. London: Routledge.

————. 1972. *Objective Knowledge*. New York: Oxford University Press.

————. 1976. *Unended Quest*. London: Fontana. Originally published as the "Intellectual Autobiography" in Schilpp 1974.

————. 1982. *The Open Universe*. Volume II of the *Postscript to The Logic of Scientific Discovery*. London: Routledge.

Popper, Karl R., and John Eccles. 1977. *The Self and Its Brain*. London: Routledge.

Ryle, G. 1949. *The Concept of Mind*. London: Hutchinson.

Schilpp, Paul A., ed. 1974. *The Philosophy of Karl Popper*. La Salle: Open Court.

Szasz, Thomas S. 1974 [1961]. *The Myth of Mental Illness: Foundations of a Theory of Personal Conduct*. Revised edition New York: Harper Row.

————. 1996. *The Meaning of Mind: Language, Morality, and Neuroscience*. Westport: Praeger.

————. 1974. *Ceremonial Chemistry: The Ritual Persecution of Drugs, Addicts, and Pushers*. Garden City: Doubleday.

Reply to Percival

THOMAS SZASZ

I

Ray Percival agrees with my argument and seeks to perfect it. He does so, moreover, by using the ideas of Karl Popper, a philosopher whose work I also admire. Having said that, I must add that I am uncertain—and leave to the reader to decide—whether Percival's remarks strengthen or weaken my argument about the myth of mental illness, especially as regards its implications for the law. In any case, I thank Ray Percival for his stimulating contribution.

I divide my reply, after this preamble, into two parts. In the first, I offer some brief remarks stimulated by Percival's paper. In the second, I reproduce, without comment, my correspondence with Sir Karl Popper. Percival's references to Popper make these letters of interest in this connection.

II

Percival writes:

> I agree with Szasz that humans have life problems, but not mental diseases. The medical establishment has overlooked the fact that all life is problem solving, and it is by no means obvious that all people would produce the same solution, or solutions that deviate only slightly from the norm, or that none of these solutions might be undesirable from a moral point of view.

I am uneasy about the way Percival goes about supporting my thesis because he treats "mental disease" as if it were a largely descriptive rather than a largely prescriptive term. Clearly, certain psychiatric diagnostic terms have descriptive content. A schoolchild diagnosed as having Attention Deficit Personality Disorder is likely to be more energetic than his lethargic classmate, and a person called "depressed" is likely to be sad. However, I maintain that the principal meaning and use of such terms is strategic, justifying psychiatric coercions and excuses, epitomized by involuntary mental hospitalization and the insanity defense. By focussing on the ontological status of "mental illness," rather than on the medically-masked legal, moral, and social aspects of psychiatric practices, Percival may, however inadvertently, distract attention from psychiatry as a *political phenomenon and moral evil*.

"The medical establishment," he writes, "has overlooked the fact that all life is problem solving." The medical establishment has not overlooked this truism. To say what Percival says is like saying that the Roman Catholic establishment has overlooked that Eucharisatic wine is not blood. These are not acts of overlooking; they are acts of denying. Psychiatry and Catholicism distort and reinterpret the "obvious," each to suit its particular agenda. The ontological statuses of mental states consecrated by psychiatrists and of wines consecrated by priests are clear and need no reinforcement from Popperian philosophy.

"It is astounding," remarks Percival, "that nearly the whole of psychiatry and even psychology implicitly denies any influence in people's lives to the existence of plans, designs, theories, numbers, and logical arguments, and the various non-physical relations that exist within and between these entities." As I show in *The Meaning of Mind*, this is no more astounding than the Soviet leaders' denials of the effects of their policies on the economic "illness" plaguing the Soviet people, the Nazi leaders' denial that their psychiatrists were systematically exterminating mental patients, or the everyday denials that people engage in to justify the destructions they wreak in the name of doing good.[2]

I am mindful of Percival's effort to shore up my argument so that it carries more weight with philosophers and am grateful for it. However, philosophers, too, are persons first, and philosophers only after that. I have lived long enough and have met enough philosophers to recognize that many of them, like most people, believe in mental illness and psychiatric benevolence because they themselves use, and approve of using, psychiatric methods of social control (to dispose of annoying relatives and defendants). This is what makes me fear that logical reasoning, without due attention to issues of power and self-interest, is an inade-

---

[2] Thomas Szasz, *The Meaning of Mind: Language, Morality, and Neuroscience* (Syracuse: Syracuse University Press, 2002 [1996]).

quate response to philosophical support for psychiatric coercions and excuses. Viewed in this light, Percival's following remarks may be valid, but are they forensically valuable? He writes:

> Szasz lacks a sufficiently elaborated epistemology and ontology of the person. His position is therefore unnecessarily left open to criticism from his more philosophical critics. However, this grave deficiency in Szasz's position can be corrected by making use of Karl Popper's theory of mind-brain interaction, specifically Popper's theory of World 3. . . . Only by using Popper's ontology can Szasz effectively defend the person from the most fashionable type of attempted reduction, in which the person is reduced to a computer program. . . . My conclusion is that the person is effectively not wholly reducible to a physical system. However, a materialist psychiatry and pharmacology presuppose such a reduction.

Agreed. However, what is there to prevent people from "reducing" other people—typically, people they don't like and wish to harm—to some lower form of existence or material composition? Since the emergence of modern science, scientists of all kinds have reduced humans and their minds to animals, clocks, brains, computers, "chemical imbalances," molecules and atoms, even to stones. For example, Michael S. Moore, a professor of law and philosophy, characteristically asserts:

> Since mental illness negates our assumption of rationality, we do not hold the mentally ill responsible. It is not so much that we excuse them from a prima facie case of responsibility; rather, by being unable to regard them as fully rational beings, we cannot affirm the essential condition to viewing them as moral agents to begin with. In this the mentally ill join (to a decreasing degree) infants, wild beasts, plants, and stones—none of which are responsible because of the absence of any assumption of rationality.[3]

Popper's philosophy is not likely to change Moore's mind. Exposure of the brutalities and injustices intrinsic to such a reductionist philosophy is more likely to be effective. Indeed, I fear that Popper's ideas about Worlds 1, 2, and 3 are especially unsuitable for understanding that coercive psychiatry is a *problem* only for the patients (and a few libertarians); for everyone else, it's a *solution*. This is where Percival's proposal may weaken rather than strengthen the case against psychiatric slavery.

---

[3] Michael S. Moore, "Some Myths about 'Mental Illness'," *Archives of General Psychiatry* 32 (December 1975), pp. 1483–497; p. 1495.

He writes:

> A stronger argument for the myth of mental illness attacks the theory of reductionism that lies behind the confusion of these different categories. Popper's argument for dualism is the strongest case against the reductionist view. Popper argues that there are at least three radically different classes of things. More concisely, there are three worlds. World 1 is the world of physics. It includes rocks, stars, protons, computers, and biological bodies. It also includes the world of chemistry and biology. World 2 is the world of our conscious selves, dreams, hopes, pleasures, pains—the world of psychology. World 3 is the world of abstract products of the human mind. It is the world of numbers, theories, arguments, and problems. It also includes works of art and music.

Creating the categories of Worlds 1, 2, and 3 was decidedly not one of Popper's good ideas. I recognize only one world, the world of everyday life (which includes all three of Popper's "worlds"). When I write about psychiatric coercions and excuses, that is the only world that concerns me.

III

Fallowfield
Manor Road
Penn
Buckinghamshire

July 20th 1961

My dear Doctor Szasz,

Thank you very much for sending me your truly admirable book, The Myth of Mental Illness. Although my eyesight makes reading difficult, I found it so fascinating that I read it at one go. It is a most important book, and it marks a real revolution. Besides, it is written in that only too rare spirit of a man who wants to be understood rather than to impress.

I feel certain that you will take it as a re-affirmation of my admiration of your great work if I indicate here, though only very sketchily, some criticism.

(1) Although you have been very successful in resisting modern fashions of doubtful value, and especially the terrible ephemerally-modern jargon of modern books in this field, I do think that you have [not] entirely escaped from the seductions and temptations of a school of thought which I have dubbed 'instrumentalism' and described in my article on Berkeley in the *BJPS* IV, 1953, pp. 26 ff. . . .

(2) Role Playing and Game playing. I shall make only quite dogmatic remarks. Role playing is for those who dare not be what they are. It is itself already a shoddy and dangerous substitute for genuine learning, that is, for genuinely changing oneself to become more nearly what one wants to be. This learning new roles is not the kind of learning which is really desirable, and an end in itself. Learning a new role has only an instrumental value—for survival. But none of us survives long; and instrumental values are not enough. Learning—as opposed to learning a new role—and growing up, until we die, is, or can be, a value in itself. To perform constantly the miracle of lifting oneself out of the swamp by one's own shoelaces is, indeed, a purpose. (For the methodology of this miracle, see my *Logic of Scientific Discovery*, Basic Books).

(3) You say, quite rightly on p. 310, lines 2–3, "The limiting factor is man!" and you add, line 2–1 from bottom, that bad teachers may be a limiting factor too. To this one must add: bad philosophies of life and of learning. Now role playing is a bad philosophy of life, and so is the theory of learning by repetition (which is inapplicable in a changing environment anyway). I said a few things on the premature refusal to learn, and its relation to neurosis, in the paper quoted by you, "Philosophy of Science: A Personal Report," p. 175, bottom to p. 176 middle. (I also discussed there the prevalent theories of learning, pp. 166 ff.) What is needed is to interest people early in realizing that we learn from our mistakes: that it is not shameful to err, and a great thing to discover one's own errors. But I must not go on rambling.

With kind regards,

Yours sincerely, Karl R. Popper[4]

---

[4] A handwritten letter reproduced here by permission.

Professor Thomas Szasz
From Karl Popper, 10-8-84

Dear Professor Szasz,

It must be twenty years since we exchanged some letters. I have
been reading your books with the greatest admiration. *The Therapeutic
State* is a monument to you, to your rationality, mental independence
and courage. I admire it. But the reason why I have not written is that
only a very long letter would be adequate. I have written many such
letters in my mind. But I cannot put them on paper. I passionately
agree with everything you write except two points, one practical and
one theoretical. The practical point is free trade in drugs. At the risk of
hurting you: That is just silly. (Principles cannot be taken to their
limit.) Do you wish free trade in hydrogen bombs and cobalt bombs? I
am definitely against free trade in shotguns, even in pistols. Even if I
could be persuaded (I might be) by your argument that it is "none of
the government's business what drug a man puts into his body," it is
precisely the main business of government what he puts into another
person's body (a dangerous drug, a bullet, an electroshock). That is the
practical point. The theoretical point is the Non-existence of mental
disease. Here my difficulty is that I know very little about the subject
and you know a lot. The subject never attracted me as a theorist (but I
read quite a bit about it). Also, I think that you are 95% right!

A third point is the danger of this problem degenerating into a
quarrel about words (or 'definitions'). But I believe that if a man is
heavily drunk, he does lose, as common sense puts it, 'control of
himself'. No doubt there are many other drugs that have similar
effects, including drugs produced by our own body when it is ill.
I read your *Myth of Mental Illness* many years ago and I cannot
remember whether you agree or disagree with this: I am in my 83rd
year, and my memory is getting bad (a mental illness, in my opinion—
but let us not quarrel about words). My mind shows symptoms likely
due to aging—the aging of the body, presumably analogous to the
pains in my joints. (I am happy and grateful that my mind is still
capable of producing new ideas and even new mathematical results.)
This is the kind of thing that I and most people would call 'a mental
illness on a physical basis'; and I am not prepared to quarrel about

words or definitions. I am very ready to believe you when you say that most alleged 'mental illnesses' are *not* real, that most or all neurotics are not really ill (but undisciplined). But my (fortunately not yet catastrophic) loss of memory is not merely a loss of mental discipline; and it seems to me that it has a physical basis (as, perhaps, Parkinson's disease seems to have).

Now I can write this to you; but I am not prepared to write and publish this kind of thing—I mean the *theoretical* point—as a criticism of your views: I know so little, and you have a lot of experience in these matters. Result: I cannot, in my writings, refer to you, even where I should like, in order to support you. Which is very sad. For where I think of you and your views, I am all admiration, and these two points appear to me far less important than all those many, many ideas of yours with which I can agree (especially since there seems to me only a small likelihood that these two points will be widely accepted). I am entirely on your side in your fight against the psychiatrists and their intolerable power; and I am glad that you have written against Freud and against Jewish nationalism and racialism as you did (but this is a very minor point compared to your splendid and urgent fight against the power of the new medical priests—the medicine men—a fight in which you surely need supporters). However, this letter is getting too long.

All the best, yours sincerely,

Karl Popper

State University of New York Upstate Medical Center
750 East Adams Street
Syracuse, New York 13210
College of Medicine, Department of Psychiatry

February 9th, 1977

Prof. Karl Popper
London School of Economics and Political Science
Houghton Street
London WC2A 2AE, England

Dear Professor Popper,

I greatly appreciate the inscribed copy of your autobiography,
which arrived a few days ago. I read it immediately—with the same
pleasure and profit with which I have read your other books. I have for
long counted you (and Hayek and Mill) as among my foremost teachers, and am grateful to you for your instruction, albeit in absentia.
(Perhaps that is the best way, as you yourself hint in *Unended Quest*.)
As you will see from the enclosed review,[5] which just appeared, I am
sometimes criticized—indeed, my moral-political views are dismissed
out of hand—specifically because my work leans so heavily on yours
and Professor Hayek's. Who could ask for a more satisfying reason for
being disliked?
   Again, many thanks.

With kind regards. Cordially,

Thomas S. Szasz, M.D., Professor of Psychiatry

[5] Russell Jacoby, "Schizophrenia: A Split Verdict." Review of Szasz's *Schizophrenia: The Sacred Symbol of Psychiatry*, in *The Nation* (5th February, 1977), pp. 149–151.

4

On Thomas Szasz, the Meaning of Mental Illness, and the Therapeutic State: A Critique

RALPH SLOVENKO

For about a half-century there has been an outpouring of articles and books by Thomas Szasz. Just to cite them would take a volume. They are known worldwide. A review of a biography of the financier and philanthropist George Soros tells us: "Nobody has ever satisfactorily explained the magical accomplishments of the Hungarian Jews. A persecuted minority in a land whose language is unfathomable to all others, they have been fantastically over-represented among high achievers in almost every field of cultural and scientific endeavor. Émigrés from this small community have included John von Neumann, Leo Szilard, Eugene Wigner, Theodore von Karman, and Edward Teller" (Seligman 2002). Though these are only illustrations, admirers of Szasz, of whom there are countless, would think it remiss to omit Szasz. Everywhere, Szasz is the number one weapon in attacks on psychiatry, or at least a gadfly, always stimulating discussion.

With each successive writing, Szasz has advanced or rewritten his key beliefs about (1) the meaning of mental illness and (2) the "Therapeutic State" and its threat to individual freedom. On these issues his thinking has ossified into an ideology. His libertarianism has no room for communitarism.

1 The Meaning of "Mental Illness"

Perhaps the best known and most controversial of Szasz's books is *The Myth of Mental Illness* (1961). The title was catchy, but what did it mean? Szasz writes with exceptional lucidity, but at the end of the day, the title of the book had more impact than its contents. The title gave rise to the impression, rightly or wrongly, that Szasz was denying reality. Thus, for example, prominent psychoanalyst Glen Gabbard commented, "[Szasz says] that mental illness does not exist" (Goode 2000).

Szasz says that what he was objecting to in *The Myth of Mental Illness* is the labeling of the phenomenon as "illness" and the use of the medical model, with all its consequences. In *Pharmacracy* (2001), Szasz explained:

> When I say that mental illness is not an illness I do not deny the reality of the behaviors to which the term points, or the existence of the people who exhibit them, the suffering the denominated patients may experience, or the problems they create for their families. I merely classify the phenomena people call "mental illnesses" differently than do those who think they are diseases. When a lesion can be demonstrated, physicians speak of bodily illnesses. When none can be demonstrated, perhaps because none exists, but when physicians and others nevertheless want to treat the problem as a disease, they speak of mental illnesses. The term "mental illness" is a semantic strategy for medicalizing economic, moral, personal, political, and social problems.[1]

Yet what is to be made of subsequent writings where Szasz compares the problem of "schizophrenia" to the "problem of the ether," that is, there is no such problem. Is he protesting the medical model or the reality of the phenomenon? In an article in the magazine *Liberty* (March 2002), Szasz says, "[The] message [of my book, *The Myth of Mental Illness*] is stated unambiguously in the title: Mental illness is a fiction, a metaphor, a myth—on a par with fictions such as witch, unicorn, mermaid, sphinx, ghost, or, *horribile dictu*, God." Later in the article he says, "My aim in writing *The Myth of Mental Illness* was to demonstrate the error in the belief that 'mental illness' is a medical disease, and to delegitimize its use as a weapon in the unholy alliance of the war of psychiatry and state against the individual—epitomized in the incarceration of innocent persons justified with mendacious euphemisms of 'hospitalization' and 'treatment'."

---

[1] Szasz 2001, p. 115.

Behaviors are not diseases or illnesses, Szasz proclaims, but behavior is controlled by the mind, and mind and body are interrelated. Time and again, Szasz says that what is involved is "problems of living." What is the solution to the "problems"? "Talk therapy" assuredly has not resolved them. What does Szasz suggest by way of solution? Critics wonder what type of problems are resolved by Szasz. Given his objection to the medical model, one must wonder why a department of psychiatry is in a medical school and why psychiatrists get a medical education. Szasz in the byline on his publications tends no longer to use the honorific "Dr." before his name *and* "M.D." following it, although he did so at one time, but he continued to have his office in the medical school. Are people with problems lured by the honorific or the venue?

Does the medical profession—or medication—have any role to play in alleviating the "problems of living"? Does medication or the medical mystique warrant the use of the medical model? Before the advent of psychotropic medication, mental hospitals were populated with demented individuals. Today, with the development of medication, one no longer sees individuals once described as catatonic.

The discipline most effective in dealing with a problem tends to be the way the problem will be classified. It may be called a crime by the police, a social problem by a social worker, a sin by the clergy, or disease by the physician. If treatable, it tends to be called a disease. The question is: which classification is most helpful to one and all?

Over the door of a church-based treatment center in Houston, a sign announces, "Drug Addiction is Not a Disease, It's a Sin." Don Willett, a policy advisor to then-Governor Bush, said "In the view of faith-based providers, addiction is indicative of sinful behavior; it's at root a moral problem that requires a moral solution, as opposed to the therapeutic notion that it's a disease" (Rosin 2000). Willett did not elaborate what would be the moral solution, presumably prayer or exorcism.

Through the years Szasz has railed against categorizing (mis)behaviors as diseases, amenable to treatment—through psychiatry. It is a result, he says, of our love affair with medicalizing life and replacing responsibility with therapy. He writes, "Lawyers, politicians and the public embraced this transformation as the progress of science, rather than dismissing it as medical megalomania based on nothing more than the manipulation of language" (Szasz 2002d). Actually, society turned to psychiatry because of the virtual bankruptcy of the criminal justice system (which seems to elude Szasz), and psychiatry offered hope of alleviating human conflict and distress.

Pedophilia is the most recent illustration of which he is dismissive of categorization as disease. True to form, he condemns psychiatrists—especially the authors of the American Psychiatric Association's "Diagnostic and Statistical Manual of Mental Disorders"—for classifying and treating pedophilia as a disease (Szasz 2002d). Actually, the term "pedophilia" is a term that covers the waterfront. Some individuals who commit pedophilia are mentally retarded, others are senile, tormented or lonely, still others are psychopaths. Some pedophiles may limit their activity to undressing the child and looking, exposing themselves, masturbating in the presence of the child, or gentle touching and fondling of the child. Others perform fellatio or cunnilingus on the child or penetrate the child's vagina, mouth, or anus with their fingers, foreign objects, or penis and use varying degrees of force to do so. Are all of these behaviors equally offensive or harmful, all warranting a penal sanction? A prison sentence may be the equivalent of a death sentence, given the abuse of sex offenders that occurs in prison. Should there be a special institution for sex offenders, as there are in a number of states? In some cases is a psychiatric modality effective or appropriate as a treatment? Is Lady Justice wise in lifting her blindfold in order to look closely at both act and actor? Szasz apparently thinks not, but his reasoning while provocative is hardly satisfying.

In debunking "mental illness" as a disease, Szasz calls "schizophrenia" a "fake disease"—"the sacred symbol of psychiatry" (Szasz 1976). Szasz terms schizophrenia a *panchreston*, that is, a dangerous word which purports to explain everything, but which on the other hand obscures matters. Szasz says, "The problem of schizophrenia which many consider to be the core-problem of psychiatry today, may be truly akin to the 'problem of the ether'. To put it simply: there is no such problem" (Szasz 1957).[2]

A leading and outspoken critic of Szasz, Dr. E. Fuller Torrey, formerly with the National Institute of Mental Health, says:

---

[2] In an invited address, to a symposium on "What is Schizophrenia?", Szasz stated that there was "no such thing" as this "alleged disease." He was prepared to acknowledge differences in behavior and speech in "so-called schizophrenic" individuals, but he demanded recognition, by the "dominant intellectual, economic, moral and political institutions of society" of "the differences between disease and disagreement" (Szasz 1976c, p. 308). If early-nineteenth-century asylum doctors accurately described schizophrenic traits, long before the disorder itself was framed and named, would not that be a particularly powerful refutation of the denial of schizophrenia's objective reality? That is contended in Berrios and Porter 1995, p. 141.

Szasz has produced more erudite nonsense on the subject of serious mental illness than any writer alive. As a historian Szasz is first class, but as a psychiatrist he never moved beyond a strictly psychoanalytic approach to treating schizophrenia. He argues, for example, that schizophrenia is merely a creation of psychiatry and "if there is no psychiatry there can be no schizophrenia." What wonderful simplicity! One wonders whether he has ever seen a patient with the disease. (Torrey 2001)[3]

To be a true disease, Szasz claims, "it must somehow be capable of being approached, measured or tested in a scientific fashion," and, he contends, only diseases lend to diagnosis. Yet what is a diagnosis but a category? We cannot do without categories, of one sort or another. We live by categories. In Philosophy 101, one learns that by necessity we divide up the world by categories. We use those categories that best help to deal with the phenomenon. Jose Ortega y Gasset in *The Dehumanization of Art* (1948, p. 15) writes:

[O]ne and the same reality may split up into many diverse realities when it is beheld from different points of view. And we cannot help asking ourselves: Which of all these realities must then be regarded as the real and authentic one? The answer, no matter how we decide, cannot but be arbitrary. Any preference can be founded on caprice only. All these realities are equivalent, each being authentic for its corresponding point of view. All we can do is classify the points of view and to determine which among them seems, in a practical way, most normal or spontaneous. Thus we arrive at a conception of reality that is by no means absolute, but at least practical and normative.

Yet why arbitrary, as Ortega y Gasset suggests? It would seem that at times we can have reasons for our preferences or categories. Figuratively speaking, Plato suggested that a chicken be cut at the joints because that is the most convenient. We adopt that scheme that makes life most orderly, keeping in mind that the categorization we choose has consequences. What one does about something depends on how one categorizes it.

What counts as disease? Disease, or *dis*-ease, literally means not at ease. In that regard, people are like tightrope walkers, trying to reach a balance and to keep it. Dr. Karl Menninger, the renowned psychiatrist,

---

[3] From his research, Torrey suggests that schizophrenia is caused by a virus. CBS, "60 Minutes" (21st April, 2002). Torrey's sister has been diagnosed as schizophrenic.

called it "the vital balance." Like Freud, he proposed a unitary and gradational theory of mental disorder (not one of discrete entities). In his book *The Vital Balance*, shortly before undertaking *The Crime of Punishment* (in which I had a hand), he set forth his view of "mental illness," to wit, the persistent failure to cope with internally or externally induced stresses. Every individual, constantly exchanging with his or her environment, tries to make the best bargain possible with it, considering its threats, demands, opportunities, and danger. To end a crisis from birth trauma to an ingrown toenail, Menninger suggested, one needs an "anticrisis" in order to achieve that vital balance.

No matter what the complex causality of the disorder may be, it is the particular form of functioning (or of operating) with its content that constitutes the predominant and primary (although not exclusive) essence of the disorder and leads to secondary sequels, both organic and functional. The concept of functional disorder is found useful by many, and therefore continues to be used, but it is certain that the last word has not been said.

To be sure, no matter the causality of a disorder, it is not necessary for treatment to know it. A fire can be extinguished without knowing its cause, but knowing the cause may prevent a recurrence. The cause or causes may be known, or it may be neither known nor knowable. Researchers point to a myriad of causes of schizophrenia, including a virus from a cat (Ewald 2002). What brought about Andrea Yates's state of mind that resulted in the drowning of her five children? According to the evidence, she was stressed out by a domineering husband, homeschooling five youngsters, living in cramped quarters, and discomforted by medication. At trial on a plea of not guilty by reason of insanity, psychiatrists offered diagnoses of depression and schizophrenia (Begley 2002).

Medical science, like all sciences, does not proceed from ignorance to enlightenment in a straight line. In the words of the Spanish philosopher Miguel de Unamuno, it is marked by "a cemetery of dead ideas," with one seeming truth being thrown out for another that fits better with the latest research. Time and again, data are reexamined and reinterpreted (Kolata 2002). To explain the physical workings of the body, Benjamin Rush (1745–1813) updated the old theory of four humors with principles drawn from Newtonian physics and organic chemistry. He believed that all disease processes, including insanity, stemmed from disorders of the vascular system. Like most of his medical contemporaries, he recommended restoring the body's internal balance by opening the patient's veins to allow copious bleeding and by administering purging enemas.

Rush summed up his diagnoses and treatment for insanity in *Medical Inquiries and Observations Upon the Diseases of the Mind* (1812), the first major American medical treatise on mental illness.

For the most part, contemporary psychiatry has endorsed the nosology suggested by Emil Kraepelin, a German psychiatrist born the same year as Freud (1856). Kraepelin viewed mental illness not as a continuum as did Freud and Menninger but as consisting of discrete entities. Kraepelin created a taxonomy of mental illness by studying symptom clusters and final outcomes, and by collecting family histories to trace hereditary traits. Psychiatry today argues, in effect, that psychiatry made a wrong turn by following Freud rather than Kraepelin. The initial work of the neo-Kraepelins come out of Washington University in the 1950s where a group of researchers—notably Eli Robins, Lee Nelken Robins, Samuel Guze, and George Winokur—would describe a disorder and then draft criteria for its diagnosis that were clear enough for different observers to give the same diagnosis to the same patient.

Unlike the first two editions of the American Psychiatric Association's *Diagnostic and Statistical Manual* (*DSM*), the third edition, published in 1980, was Kraepelin. The psychiatrists assembled under the guidance of Dr. Robert Spitzer argued that the "innovation" of *DSM-III* would be a "defense of the medical model as applied to psychiatric problems." The minutes from the first meeting of the Task Force on Nomenclature and Statistics stated:

> The diagnostic manual will be essentially behavioral, with exceptions for conditions of known etiology . . . It was agreed that "functional" is no longer a suitable designation for a group of conditions—schizophrenias and affective disorders—which are no longer seen as purely psychogenic. (Wilson 1993)

In other words, diagnosis in psychiatry should matter. When talk therapy was used for everyone, diagnosis was inconsequential. Now a diagnosis would mean that the diagnosed person was mentally ill, and ill in a way that different psychiatrists could reliably recognize, with treatment in a particular way. The manual listed more than two hundred categories and the number has grown in subsequent *DSMs* (only a few are commonly used). From the vantage point of *DSM-III* and the subsequent *DSMs*, it does not matter how an individual had become ill, but whether the necessary number of symptoms for a diagnosis are met.

The Kraepelin approach connects with insurance and medication. Insurance covers certain entities but not others (to be sure, to achieve coverage, there is manipulation in report writing). Medication has developed which targets specific symptoms. Today, that is the scheme of things. Is it the most orderly or workable? For Szasz's "problems of living," what problems would be covered by insurance—or would none or all be covered? What medication, if any?

In daily life overstresses may build beyond ordinary control and threaten to upset internal balances. To reduce the tensions, a person may get assistance from one's family or friends, pastor, or physician. Sometimes the assistance is medication, or acupuncture. It is often purely happenstance what the manifestations of the imbalances are called and what type of help the individual receives—medical, legal, social, or pastoral. The term "biopsychosocial" would indicate a role for various professions in dealing with a disorder.

The mind-body dichotomy is perplexing. Religion teaches that the soul without the body goes to heaven or hell. *The Oxford English Dictionary* defines "mind" as "The seat of a person's consciousness . . . The soul as distinguished from the body." The Latin *mens* is defined as including mind, soul, reason, thought, and intention. Are there two separate camps: mind (soul) and body? Is it either-or? More and more it is coming to be realized that what is psychological is also biological and what is biological also has a psychological component. Symptoms correlate with alterations in brain function that produce a disorder. Physiologic and biochemical data correlate brain function with mental functions. Considerable progress has been made toward establishing cross-correlations between activity of the mind and activity of the brain (Heath 1996). In the introduction to *DSM-IV* it is stated:

> Although this volume is titled the *Diagnostic and Statistical Manual of Mental Disorders*, the term *mental disorder* unfortunately implies a distinction between "mental" disorders and "physical" disorders that is a reductionistic anachronism of mind/body dualism. A compelling literature documents that there is much "physical" in "mental" disorders and much "mental" in "physical" disorders. The problem raised by the term "mental" disorders has been much clearer than its solution, and, unfortunately, the term persists in the title of *DSM-IV* because we have not found an appropriate substitute.
>
> Moreover, although this manual provides a classification of mental disorders, it must be admitted that no definition adequately specifies precise boundaries for the concept of "mental disorder." The concept of mental disorder, like many other concepts in medicine and science, lacks a consistent operational definition that covers all situations. All medical

conditions are defined on various levels of abstraction—for example, structural pathology (e.g., ulcerative colitis), symptom presentation (e.g., migraine), deviance from a physiological norm (e.g., hypertension), and etiology (e.g., pneumonococcal pneumonia). Mental disorders have also been defined by a variety of concepts (e.g., distress, discontrol, disadvantage, disability, inflexibility, irrationality, syndromal pattern, etiology, and statistical deviation). Each is a useful indicator for a mental disorder, but none is equivalent to the concept, and different situations call for different definitions.

Despite these caveats, the definition of *mental disorder* that was included in DSM-III and DSM-III-R is presented here because it is as useful as any other available definition and has helped to guide decisions regarding which conditions on the boundary between normality and pathology should be included in DSM-IV. In DSM-IV, each of the mental disorders is conceptualized as a clinically significant behavioral or psychological syndrome or pattern that occurs in an individual ant that is associated with present distress (e.g., a painful symptom) or disability (i.e., impairment in one or more important areas of functioning) or with a significantly increased risk of suffering death, pain, disability, or an important loss of freedom. (American Psychiatric Association, 1994, p. xxi)

What about the practice of defining a disease in terms of treatability? Szasz says only the prescientific physician perceived illness in this way. Disease as "treatable," he says, is a perversion of medicine (Szasz 2001, p. 141).[4] But why not consider the response to medication as an indica for a diagnosis? A physician who directs a famous medical center says, "There is nothing organically wrong with 70 percent of the patients who come to us but if a sugar pill helps them to feel better, isn't it really medicine?" In practice, diagnosis is often linked in psychiatry to the efficacy of a medication, but given the variation among individuals, there may be a response to one anti-psychotic medication (for example, Clozapine) but not to another (for instance, Risperidone). In the book *Of Two Minds*, Tanya M. Luhrmann, an anthropologist, points out:

---

[4] Aetna Life and Casualty Company, a major underwriter of health care policies, said, "[A] mental disorder is a disease commonly understood to be a mental disorder whether or not it has a physiological or organic basis and for which *treatment is generally provided by or under the direction of a mental health professional such as a psychiatrist, psychologist, or a psychiatric social worker*" (emphasis added). According to this logic, Szasz says, if there were no mental health professionals, there would be no mental illnesses (Szasz 1996, p. 96).

If a patient doesn't seem to need medication for a particular symptom, he shouldn't be diagnosed with a disorder in which that symptom is prominent. For example, mood swings are necessary (but not sufficient) for the diagnosis of bipolar disorder. If the supposed manic-depressive does not respond to lithium or to another of the mood stabilizers, a psychiatrist will wonder whether after all he's schizophrenic. If a supposed schizophrenic is managed effectively on anti-anxiety agents or even without medication, a psychiatrist will question whether she is, in fact, schizophrenic. (Luhrmann 2000)

Should it matter whether psychotherapy or medication can overcome suicidal ideation? Szasz has been an adamant opponent of efforts to prevent suicide. He observes, "Suicide began as a sin, became a crime, then became a mental illness, and now some people propose transferring it into the category called 'treatment,' provided the 'cure' is under the control of doctors (Szasz 1999). His view about suicide prevention can best be conveyed by his own words:

Why do we now give psychiatrists special privileges to intervene *vis-à-vis* suicidal persons? Because, as I have noted, in the psychiatric view, the person who threatens or commits suicide is irrational or mentally ill, allowing the psychiatrist to play doctor and thereby, like other doctors, to save lives. However, there is neither philosophical or empirical support for viewing suicide as different, in principle, from other acts such as getting married or divorced, working on the Sabbath, eating shrimp, or smoking tobacco. These and countless other things people do are the result of personal decision. . . . Psychiatrist and patient are both lost in the existential-legal labyrinth generated by treating suicide as if it constituted a psychiatric problem, indeed a psychiatric emergency. If we refuse, however, to play a part in the drama of coercive suicide prevention, then we shall be sorely tempted to conclude that the psychiatrist and his suicidal patient richly deserve one another and the torment each is so ready and eager to inflict on the other. (Szasz 1989)

Is it not simplistic to say that committing suicide is comparable to eating shrimp or working on the Sabbath? Those who have been helped by psychiatry to overcome suicidal ideation are grateful that Szasz was not in the vicinity (Jamison 1999). In Szasz's view, if a person "wants" to commit suicide, just get out of the way. Reportedly, Szasz does not see patients who are suicidal, which may be an abdication of his training as a psychiatrist. The psychiatrist, having a license to prescribe medication, may be faulted in a lawsuit for not having prescribed in the event of a patient suicide (it happened to Szasz and it may be the reason he no longer sees individuals who are suicidal). If all psychiatrists were to copy Szasz and not treat individuals who are suicidal, where could they turn?[5]

2 The "Therapeutic State" and its Threat to Individual Freedom

More than anyone else, Szasz has stirred interest in law and psychiatry. In a passage quoted by libertarian fellow travelers, U.S. Supreme Court Justice Arthur J. Goldberg wrote in a review of Szasz's 1963 book *Law, Liberty, and Psychiatry*, "Dr. Szasz makes a real contribution by alerting us to the abuses—existing and potential—of human rights inherent in enlightened mental health programs and procedures. He points out, with telling examples, shortcomings in commitment procedures, inadequacies in the protections afforded patients in mental institutions and the dangers of over-reliance on psychiatric expert opinion by judges and juries" (Goldberg 1964).

The verdict "not guilty by reason of insanity" implies a close connection between "insanity" on the one hand and "criminal responsibility" on the other. In *Law, Liberty, and Psychiatry* Szasz urges, "Let us not consider mental illness an excusing condition. By treating offenders as responsible human beings, we offer them the only chance, as I see it, to remain human" (p. 137). The concept of criminal responsibility, however, has its origin in ethics, philosophy, and canon law, not psychiatry, so it would be more appropriate to call a cleric or a philosopher as the expert witness rather than the psychiatrist, but society now considers their pronouncements too metaphysical. The psychiatrist is summoned by members of the legal profession, and then it is complained that psychiatry is corrupting the administration of criminal justice.

Psychiatrists are also called into the criminal law process over the issue of competency to stand trial. It would appear that the appropriate person to decide whether the defendant is able to assist counsel is the

---

[5] Pediatricians are criticized who decline to treat children who may have been abused so as not to get involved in a reporting or testifying situation. Thus, even when a psychiatrist has not chosen to practice in an emergency setting, emergencies may arise in which the psychiatrist will be obliged to treat patients he or she would ordinarily not wish to treat. Until the care of the patient has been delegated to another, the psychiatrist must continue to treat such a patient until he or she is stabilized and safe to release (Bauman 2001, p. 64).

defendant's counsel, or perhaps the judge. Actually, as Szasz points out in *Psychiatric Justice*, published two years earlier, the rule on triability is often used for purposes other than that for which it was intended. It is used by defense counsel to delay a trial until the emotions of the prosecuting witnesses have calmed, or until their memories have faded, and on the other hand it is used by the district attorney to accomplish the goal of preventive detention or indeterminate confinement. Although defense counsel or prosecuting attorney may make a point of seeking out a psychiatrist, ostensibly for the professional opinion they can bring to bear on the case, the psychiatrist may find himself used as a virtuous cover, behind which various goals are accomplished.

In the rebellious years of the 1960s, Szasz, along with George Alexander, then law dean at Syracuse University, and Erving Goffman, a sociologist at the University of Pennsylvania, organized an association for the abolition of involuntary hospitalization. In speeches to lawyers, Szasz urged filing of lawsuits against anyone who would participate in seeking an involuntary hospitalization (Szasz 1968). In a tribute to Szasz, Dr. A.L. Halpern said, "Szasz is responsible for what can be called libertarian transformation of psychiatrists which has resulted in more and more psychiatrists throughout the world (especially the United States) exercising great restraint when faced with the issue of involuntary commitment of non-dangerous mentally ill persons (personal communication, February 20th, 2002). Alexander has called Szasz the "greatest freedom fighter of the twentieth century" (personal communication, January 5th, 2002).[6]

In the 1960s and 1970s the deranged or demented were portrayed as though they were political dissenters. In the book *Asylums* (1961), Goffman wrote that "chronic schizophrenia" was merely an adaption to the social system of the hospital. Ken Kesey's *One Flew Over the Cuckoo's Nest* (1962) was a fictional version of the ideas promoted by Szasz and Goffman. *Time* magazine called it "a roar of protest against a middlebrow society's Rules and the invisible Rulers who enforce them." Made into a popular movie, *One Flew Over the Cuckoo's Nest* depicted Randle McMurphy mobilizing the patients in the state hospital to challenge Big Nurse Ratchet and the evil psychiatrists who work there. The patients are depicted as oppressed, not sick. Kesey was a guru of psychedelic drugs.

---

[6] Alexander defended Szasz when there was an attempt to have Szasz leave Syracuse University because of his views on mental illness. The chairman of the Department of Psychiatry thought Szasz's views on mental illness were incompatible with a position on the psychiatry faculty.

In *The Manufacture of Madness* (1970), Szasz drew a parallel between the persecution of witches from the thirteenth through the seventeenth centuries and what he terms our persecution of people labeled mentally ill in the twentieth and twenty-first centuries. In his view, modern psychiatry has led not to more enlightenment, but only to different victims for persecution. One of his books is titled *Psychiatric Slavery* (1977), with a drawing on the dust jacket of a person in chains. The theme is expanded in 2002 in his book *Liberation by Oppression: A Comparative Study of Slavery and Psychiatry*, where he writes: "During the past few decades . . . all relationships between psychiatrists and patients, regardless of the nature of the interaction between them, are now based on actual or potential coercion. This situation is the result of two major 'reforms' that deprive therapist and patient alike of the freedom to contract with one another. Therapists now have a double duty: they must protect all mental patients—involuntary and voluntary, hospitalized or outpatient, incompetent or competent—from themselves. They must also protect the public from the patients."

In the 1960s, a number of lawyers formed the Mental Health Bar and dedicated their careers to bringing lawsuits against states to get mental patients released from state hospitals, making it more difficult to involuntarily hospitalize or treat them, and passing legislation to effectively hasten deinstitutionalization (Slovenko 2000). In the foreword to ACLU attorney Bruce Ennis's polemic against mental hospitalization, *Prisoners of Psychiatry* (1972), Szasz praised Ennis for recognizing "that individuals incriminated as mentally ill do not need guarantees of 'treatment' but protection against their enemies—the legislators, judges, and psychiatrists who persecute them in the name of mental health." For Ennis, as for Goffman, hospitals were places "where sick people get sicker and sane people go mad."

Ennis and colleagues—aided and abetted by Szasz—accomplished their goals. The numbers of mentally ill in jail or homeless, with freedom to be perpetually psychotic, are a living testimony to their success. Perhaps the opponents of the mental hospital should be given a mattress in a back alley to experience firsthand what they have wrought. A number of the members of the Mental Health Bar have expressed regret (personal communications). Joel Klein, one of them, became counsel for the American Psychiatric Association (and later attorney general challenging Microsoft), and Bruce Ennis went into the employ of the American Psychological Association. The two APA's needed counsel to defend them from attacks, and who better to hire than those who attacked them? Ironically, one might say, these lawyers created their jobs.

The history of mental hospitals is marked by twists and turns. In the early part of the nineteenth century there prevailed in the United States an era of what was known as moral treatment. Palatial manors to house the mentally ill were built at considerable expense in rustic, attractive (though remote) parts of the states. In 1842 Charles Dickens noted approvingly that American mental hospitals were supported by the state, a fact which made the government, in his view, a merciful and benevolent protector of people in distress. The constitutions of the various states mandated state-sponsored care of the mentally ill. In England, on the other hand, where public charity was minimal, the government offered the mentally ill, as Dickens said, "very little shelter or relief beyond that which is to be found in the workhouse and the jail." Today those hospitals are being razed and the grounds turned over to private developers of subdivisions.

Ironically, in the 1960s and 1970s, with some notorious exceptions, mental hospitals were at their best in staffing and conditions since the era of moral treatment of the early 1800s. Justice Goldberg's comment about abuses in reviewing Szasz's 1963 book *Law, Liberty, and Psychiatry* were not made on the basis of firsthand knowledge. In the 1960s, when the allegations of abuses began to mount, Senator Sam Ervin (later of Watergate fame) held hearings and uncovered no cases of "railroading." The American Bar Foundation also commissioned a field investigation of mental hospitals in six states, and it concluded that railroading is a myth. Professor Gerald Grob, the prize-winning historian of mental hospitals, wrote that during this period the hospitals provided an asylum nowhere else available (Grob 1973).

In *Pharmacracy* (2001), Szasz writes (p. 97): "If a person *guilty* of assault or murder is deemed to be mentally ill, he should be sentenced for his crime, imprisoned, and offered treatment for his 'illness'; that is, he should be dealt with just as we deal with the criminal who has diabetes or tuberculosis" (emphasis by Slovenko). "Guilty"? Traditionally, the law says that "guilt" involves *mens rea* and *actus reus*, that is to say, a criminal intent and a volitional act. One or the other lacking, the law would not proclaim a defendant as culpable. Presumably, for guilt, Szasz would call for proof of *mens rea* or *actus reus*, but he does not say what evidence he would allow to establish or negate them, and he does not say what excuses, if any, he would allow. Excuses humanize or individualize the operation of the law. Centuries ago a person was not held responsible if he "doth not know what he was doing, no more than an infant or a wild beast" (*Rex v. Arnold*, 1724). The history of the insanity defense antedates psychiatry.

In *Ceremonial Chemistry* (1976), Szasz argued against any limitations on the use of narcotics, at least until a crime other than drug use is committed. The apathy resulting from addiction is discounted or ignored by Szasz as is any concept of social responsibility. He advocates free access to illicit drugs but makes no mention of the consequences of this proposal, as though we live in a state of nature. His book *Pharmacracy* expands on the theme expressed in *Ceremonial Chemistry* (1976) where he wrote: "Inasmuch as we have words to describe medicine as a healing art, but have none to describe it as a method of social control or political rule, we must first give it a name. I propose that we call it *pharmacracy*, from the Greek roots *pharmakon*, for 'medicine' or 'drug' and *kratein*, for 'to rule' or 'to control'.. . . As theocracy is rule by God or priests, and democracy is rule by the people or the majority, so pharmacracy is rule by medicine or physicians" (pp. 128–29).

In Szasz's view, the United States has created a contemporary fascist health state. He pronounces psychiatry "the most insidious and, in the long run, the most dangerous form of statism yet developed by man" (Szasz 2002b). His *bête noire* is the Therapeutic State (always capitalized). Time and again, he rails against it, not only in a book by that title (1984). He is oft-quoted. For example, in *The Death of the West*, Patrick Buchanan writes:

> Since the 1960s, branding opponents as haters or mentally sick has been the most effective weapon in the arsenal of the Left. Here is the "secret formula" as described by psychologist [*sic*] and author Thomas Szasz: "If you want to debase what a person is doing . . . call him mentally ill." Behind it all is a political agenda. Our sick society is in need of therapy to heal itself of its innate prejudice. . . . [T]he root of the "therapeutic state" [is] a regime where sin is redefined as sickness, crime becomes antisocial behavior, and the psychiatrist replaces the priest. (Buchanan 2002, pp. 82–83)

To be sure, psychiatric language or psychobabble abounds. Freud's writings left their mark on many endeavors. Without familiarity with Freud, one would fail to appreciate the cartoons of Jules Feiffer, the films of Woody Allen, the novels of D.M. Thomas or Philip Roth. The ordinary citizen says "paranoid," not "suspicious"; "sociopath," not "son-of-a-bitch." Therapeutic language is substituted for moral language: "well" for good," "ill" for "evil" (the concept of "evil" has resurged with Osama bin Laden). Assuredly, though, the explanations of behavior given by psychiatry, however faulty they may be, is an advance over the religious view of demon possession ("the devil made me do it") with exorcism as the remedy. The Church after two thousand years of experience with sin has turned to psychotherapy to deal with its pedophile priests (Dreher 2002, pp. 82–83).

Psychological testing is now pervasive throughout society, including school systems, industry and the military, but what better way is there to identifying and classifying? As a way to solve problems and change habits, people in countless numbers have turned to psychotherapy. Is that a plus or minus? Socrates urged, "Know thyself!" Next to Argentina, the United States has more therapists (and lawyers) *per capita* than other countries to resolve "problems of living." Is that a plus? Some say not. In dissenting to the adoption of a psychotherapist-patient testimonial privilege to protect confidentiality, U.S. Supreme Court Justice Antonin Scalia asked (1996), "When is it, one must wonder, that the psychotherapist came to play such an indispensable role in the maintenance of the citizenry's mental health?" The writer Fay Weldon (1994) claims that while marriage has been a nightmare through the ages, now husbands have psychiatrists to make it worse.

And yet where is the Therapeutic State ruled by psychiatrists? Szasz writes, "[P]sychiatric interventions—in particular, civil commitment and diversions from the criminal justice to the mental health system— are the most common, and most uncritically accepted, methods used by the modern state to deprive individuals of liberty and responsibility" (Szasz 2002b, p. 23). Actually, in every instance in the law-psychiatry intermix, the law, not psychiatry, controls, with psychiatric testimony used mostly for window dressing. In criminal responsibility, the scope of "mental disease or defect" is set by the law, not psychiatry, and it is extraordinarily difficult to establish "not guilty by reason of insanity" (NGRI) (Slovenko 1995). The law sets the parameters on what it considers relevant. Even when the legal conditions are met, they are usually not accepted by the jury. In the rare case when a defendant is found NGRI, the law, not psychiatry, has control over discharge. In establishing triability ("competency to stand trial"), psychiatric testimony is used mainly as a tactic to postpone a trial. In civil commitment, the law sets the criterion of "dangerousness." In the usual scenario, a family in distress files a petition, a psychiatrist or two certify, but the court commits.

Szasz's feelings about the Therapeutic State apparently derives from his heritage as a Jew growing up in Hungary and forced to flee the Nazis. Delusion, not empirical evidence, prompted the Nazis to view the Jew as a cancer on society that had to be removed at any cost. But even bad regimes can do some good things. Nazi Germany was decades ahead of other countries in promoting health reforms that today are regarded as progressive and socially responsible, as Robert Proctor points out in his book *The Nazi War on Cancer* (1999). Nazi scientists were the first to definitely link lung cancer and cigarette smoking. The Nazis' forward-looking health activism came from the same root as their medical crimes, and so anti-tobacco advocates in the United States, for example, have been labeled "health fascists" and "Nico-Nazis." Proctor points out the logical error of arguing that since the Nazis were purists, purists today must be Nazis. That too is Szasz's logical error when he describes the Therapeutic State as Nazi pharmacracy (Szasz 2001, p. 141).

A Therapeutic State is not necessarily evil. Indeed, it is preferable to a non-Therapeutic State. Purists need not be fascists to support campaigns against smoking, or to promote nutritional food, education, sports facilities, parks, and walkable and bikeable communities. That would be a truly Therapeutic State. Joseph Stalin was a tyrant but he did two good things: he developed an excellent transportation system and he kept the fast-food (aka junk food) franchises out of the Soviet Union. For that, all Russians are grateful.

Libertarians, quoting selectively in the defense of Szasz, do not quote the passage from Justice Goldberg's review of Szasz's *Law, Liberty, and Psychiatry* where he states, "[B]ecause of the presence or possibility of abuses, [it does not mean that] government should never seek to be beneficent. . . . [T]he mark of a mature society lies in its ability to help its citizens lead full and productive lives without unduly intruding upon their sacred liberties. . . . [I am confident] that our society is endowed with this maturity. Dr. Szasz, like many others, thinks that it is impossible to maintain this delicate balance and that grave dangers lurk in the effort. He believes that a society which attempts to promote the 'welfare' of its citizens will succeed only in enslaving them" (Goldberg 1964).

Szasz believes that the law has delegated much of its authority to psychiatrists. He urges psychiatry to disavow its aggrandizement of power in the legal system (Szasz, 1957). But, what power? The medical excuse plays an important role in out-of-courtroom situations (for example, excuse from school or work) and the medicals play a vital role in assessment of damages, but the psychiatrist is surely not the decision maker in the legal process. Not only does a psychiatrist have no power in the legal process, but his influence is dubious. The courts—judge or jury—do not pay all that much attention to the psychiatrist (sometimes psychiatric testimony is used as window dressing and is accepted only when, in the words of a famous Bing Crosby song, it is "going my way"). Assuredly, although psychiatric jargon abounds, neither the courtroom nor the country is run by psychiatrists. In fact, more often than not, psychiatry is debunked, as in the oft-quoted proposal in a bill by New Mexico Senator Richard Romero:

> When a psychologist or psychiatrist testifies during a defendant's competency hearing, the psychologist or psychiatrist shall wear a cone-shaped hat that is not less than two feet tall. The surface of the hat shall be imprinted with stars and lightning bolts. Additionally, a psychologist or psychiatrist shall be required to don a white beard that is not less than eighteen inches in length, and shall punctuate crucial elements of his testimony by stabbing the air with a wand. Whenever a psychologist or psychiatrist provides expert testimony regarding the defendant's competency, the bailiff shall contemporaneously dim the courtroom lights and administer two strikes to a Chinese gong.

The proposal passed the Senate by voice vote and the House by a vote of forty-six to thirteen, but Governor Gary Johnson vetoed it (*San Francisco Chronicle* [January 31st, 1996], p. E-8).[7]

---

[7] For the 120th annual meeting of the American Psychiatric Association, Los Angeles, May 4th–8th, 1964, I was invited by the APA to respond to an address by Thomas Szasz. For me, it was a memorable event. In attendance were thousands of members of the APA as well as others. The proceedings appear in the *American Journal of Psychiatry* 121 (1964), pp. 521–548. It seemed redux when I was invited to respond to a presentation by Szasz on April 4th, 2002, at Oakland University, Michigan, but due to illness, Szasz had to cancel. This paper is based on the response that I had prepared.

REFERENCES

American Psychiatric Association. 1994. *Diagnostic and Statistical Manual of Mental Disorders*. Fourth edition. Washington, D.C.: American Psychiatric Press.

Begley, S. 2002. The Mystery of Schizophrenia. *Newsweek* (March 11th), p. 44.

Berrios, G., and R. Porter. 1995. *A History of Clinical Psychiatry: The Origin and History of Psychiatric Disorders*. New Brunswick: Athlone.

Buchanan, P. 2002. *The Death of the West*. New York: St. Martin's Press.

Dreher, R. Feb. 11, 2002. Sins of the Fathers. *National Review* (February 11th), p.27.

Mary L. Durham, "Civil Commitment of the Mentally Ill: Research, Policy, and Practice," in Bruce D. Sales and Saleem A. Shah, eds., *Mental Health and Law: Research, Policy, and Services* (Durham, N.C.: Carolina Academic Press, 1996), pp. 17–40 (p. 17).

Ennis, B. 1972. *Prisoners of Psychiatry*. New York: Harcourt Brace Jovanovich.

Ewald, P.W. 2002. *Plague Time: The New Germ Theory of Disease*. New York: Random House, p. 156.

Goffman, E. 1961. *Asylums*. Garden City: Doubleday.

Goldberg, A.J. 1964. Book Review. *American Bar Association Journal* 50, p. 1073.

Goode, E. 2002. A Conversation with Glen Gabbard. *New York Times* (February 5th), p. F6.

Grob, G.N. 1973. *Mental Institutions in America*. New York: Free Press.

Heath, R.G. 1996. *Exploring the Mind-Brain Relationship*. Baton Rouge: Moran.

Jamison, K.R. 1999. *Night Falls Fast: Understanding Suicide*. New York: Knopf.

Kesey, K. 1962. *One Flew Over the Cuckoo's Nest*. New York: Viking Penguin.

Kolata, G. 2002. The Painful Fact of Medical Uncertainty. *New York Times* (February 10th), p. WK5.

Luhrmann, T.M. 2000. *Of Two Minds: The Growing Disorder in American Psychiatry*. New York: Knopf.

Menninger, K.A. 1963. *The Vital Balance*. New York: Viking.

———. 1996. *The Crime of Punishment*. New York: Viking.

Ortega y Gasset, J. 1948. *The Dehumanization of Art*. Princeton: Princeton University Press.

Proctor, R. 1999. *The Nazi War on Cancer*. Princeton: Princeton University Press.

Rex v. Arnold, 1724. 16 How. St. Tr. 695.

Rosin, H. 2000. Bush Puts Faith in a Social Service Role. *Washington Post* (May 5th), p. 1.

Scalia, A. 1996. Dissenting in *Jaffee v. Redmond*, 116 S. Ct. 1923.

Seligman, D. 2002. Soros: The Life and Times of a Messianic Billionaire. Book review. *Commentary* (April), p. 61.

Slovenko, R. 1995. *Psychiatry and Criminal Culpability*. New York: Wiley, pp. 67–117.

————. 2000. Civil Commitment Laws: An Analysis and Critique. *Thomas M. Cooley Law Review* 17, pp. 25–51.

Szasz, T.S. 1955. *Psychiatric Justice*. New York: Macmillan.

————. 1957a. Psychiatric Expert Testimony: Its Covert Meaning and Social Function. *Psychiatry* 20, p. 313.

————. 1957b. The Problem of Psychiatric Nosology: A Contribution to a Situational Analysis of Psychiatric Operations. *American Journal of Psychiatry* 114, p. 405.

————. 1961. *The Myth of Mental Illness*. New York: Hoeber-Harper.

————. 1963. *Law, Liberty, and Psychiatry: An Inquiry into the Social Uses of Mental Health Practices*. New York: Macmillan.

————. 1968. Science and Public Policy: The Crime of Involuntary Mental Hospitalization. *Medical Opinion and Review* (May), p. 24.

————. 1970. *The Manufacture of Madness*. New York: Harper and Row.

————. 1976a. *Ceremonial Chemistry*. Buffalo: Prometheus.

————. 1976b. *Schizophrenia: The Sacred Symbol of Psychiatry*. New York: Basic Books.

————. 1977. *Psychiatric Slavery*. New York: Free Press.

————. 1984. *The Therapeutic State*. Buffalo: Prometheus.

————. 1989. A Moral View on Suicide. In D. Jacobs and H.N. Brown, eds., *Suicide: Understanding and Responding*, pp. 434–447.

————. 1996. *The Meaning of Mind: Language, Morality, and Neuroscience*. Westport: Praeger.

————. 1999. *Fatal Freedom: The Ethics and Politics of Suicide*. Westport: Praeger.

————. 2001. *Pharmacracy: Medicine and Politics in America*. Westport: Praeger.

————. 2002a. *Liberation by Oppression: A Comparative Study of Slavery and Psychiatry*. Piscataway: Transaction.

————. 2002b. Mises and Psychiatry. *Liberty* (February), p. 23.

————. 2002c. Rothbard on Szasz. *Liberty* (March), pp. 33–34.

————. 2002d. The Psychiatrist as Accomplice. *Washington Times* (April 28th), p. B3.

Torrey, E.F. 2001. *Surviving Schizophrenia*. Fourth edition. New York: HarperCollins.

Weldon, F. 1994. *Trouble*. New York: Penguin.

Wilson, M. 1993. DSM-III and the Transformation of Psychiatry: A History. *American Journal of Psychiatry* 150, p. 399.

Reply to Slovenko

THOMAS SZASZ

I

Ralph Slovenko is one of the most respected American authorities on psychiatry and the law. We have known each other for some forty years, during which time he has closely followed my work, as I have followed his. He first criticized my work in 1964. At the end of my comments on his present contribution, I attach a summary of the context and content of our first encounter.

II

My motives for engaging in a systematic criticism of psychiatry were primarily moral and political, and secondarily epistemological and medical. I wanted to show that the psychiatrist's two paradigmatic procedures—conventionally called "mental hospitalization" and the "insanity defense"—are moral wrongs as well as violations of the political principles of the free society based on the rule of law.

Inevitably, the language we use to describe psychiatric procedures prejudges their medical, moral, and social value. Persons who regard them as helping the recipients speak of patients, diagnoses, diseases, hospitals, and treatments. Persons who regard them as harming the recipients speak of victims, stigmas, deprivations of rights, prisons, and tortures. A critical examination of psychiatry requires keeping this semantic problem in mind. Sir James Fitzjames Stephen, the great nineteenth-century English jurist warned: "Men have an all but incurable propensity to prejudge all the great questions which interest them by stamping their prejudices upon their language."[1] This is especially true when we diagnose

---

[1] James Fitzjames Stephen, *Liberty, Equality, Fraternity* (Cambridge: Cambridge University Press, 1967 [1873]), p. 176.

(mis)behavior as "disease," call coercion "treatment," and impose both "diagnosis" and "treatment" on the subject against his will.

Psychiatrists speak of "civil commitment" and the "insanity defense." I call these interventions "depriving innocent persons of liberty under psychiatric auspices" and "excusing individuals accused of crimes by attributing their illegal (or allegedly illegal) acts to mental illness, and imprisoning them in a mental hospital." Why are these psychiatric sanctions important? Because they result in depriving the subject of liberty and responsibility and because they are imposed on vast numbers of people in the United States and other developed nations. According to the authoritative text, *Mental Health and Law: Research, Policy, and Services*, edited by Bruce D. Sales and Saleem A. Shah:

> Each year in the United States well over one million persons are civilly committed to hospitals for psychiatric treatment. . . . Approximately two-thirds of these admissions are officially identified as voluntary commitments; and the remaining one-third as involuntary actions. . . . It is difficult to completely separate discussions of voluntary and involuntary commitment because voluntary status can be converted efficiently to involuntary status, once the patient has requested release.[2]

In 1972, in a paper published in the *New England Journal of Medicine*, I showed that *all so-called voluntary mental hospitalizations* are, actually or potentially, involuntary incarcerations, instances of an officially "unacknowledged practice of medical fraud."[3]

For almost fifty years, I have argued that civil commitment constitutes the single most important threat to the personal liberty of the American people today; and that the use of psychiatric expertise in the courtroom—epitomized by the insanity plea and insanity disposition—represents the most important example of replacing the rule of law (determining a defendant's guilt and punishment by what he has done), with the rule of psychiatric opinion (determining a defendant's legal-psychiatric fate by what his psychiatric adversaries say about his "mental state").

If my judgment regarding the *political role* of psychiatry in contemporary American society is valid, then the arguments that Slovenko and

---

[2] Mary L. Durham, "Civil Commitment of the Mentally Ill: Research, Policy, and Practice," in Bruce D. Sales and Saleem A. Shah, eds., *Mental Health and Law: Research, Policy, and Services* (Durham: Carolina Academic Press, 1996), pp. 17–40 (p. 17).

[3] Thomas Szasz, "Voluntary Mental Hospitalization: An Unacknowledged Practice of Medical Fraud," *New England Journal of Medicine* 287, pp. 277–78 (August 10th, 1972).

I present are, or ought to be, of great concern to people, regardless of race, religion, gender, economic status, or political orientation.

I have no difficulty understanding what Slovenko writes. He, on the other hand, acknowledges that I write "with exceptional lucidity" but complains that he cannot understand what I mean when I assert that mental illness is a myth: "The title [*The Myth of Mental Illness*] was catchy, but what did it mean?" It means that I contend that mental illness is a fiction; it exists only in the sense in which ghosts exist. The corollary of this view is that psychiatric coercions and excuses—based as they are on the existence of mental illnesses—ought to be abolished.

After perfunctorily praising me as a successful "Hungarian Jew," Slovenko asserts that my "thinking has ossified into a ideology," as if ideology were a term of disapproval. According to *Webster*, an ideology "is a systematic scheme or coordinated body of ideas or concepts, esp., about human life or culture." Psychiatry is an ideology—a body of ideas justifying the psychiatrist's control and coercion of the mental patient. My critique of psychiatry is also an ideology—a body of ideas pleading the case against the psychiatric ideology and a proposal for replacing psychiatric control and coercion with psychiatric cooperation and contract.[4]

Slovenko writes: "His [my] libertarianism has no room for communitarianism." This is not true. *Webster* defines communitarianism as "a communal system of organization based on small *cooperating* communities" (emphasis added). Calling hundreds of thousands of persons crazy and coercing them is not communitarianism; it is psychiatric communism. Debauching the meaning of ordinary words is a characteristic of psychiatric jargon, a language Slovenko speaks fluently. Psychiatrists habitually call prisons "hospitals," people who reject their services "patients," coercion "care," and oppression "therapy." He equates communitarianism with coercion and interprets my plea for consensual psychiatry—similar to consensual dermatology and ophthalmology—as tantamount to a rejection of psychiatric care.

Slovenko identifies all the diverse phenomena and problems we lump together in the category called "mental illness" as if they were a single disease, and challenges me to remedy "it." He writes: "Szasz says

---

[4] "Psychiatry and the Control of Dangerousness: On the Apotropaic Function of the Term 'Mental Illnes'," *Journal of Medical Ethics* 29 (August 2003), pp. 227–230; "The Psychiatric Protection Order for the 'Battered Mental Patient'," *British Medical Journal* 327 (20th December, 2003), pp. 1449–451; *Faith in Freedom: Libertarian Principles and Psychiatric Practices* (New Brunswick: Transaction, 2004).

that what is involved is 'problems of living.' What is the solution to the 'problems'? 'Talk therapy' assuredly has not resolved them. What does Szasz suggest by way of solution?" Slovenko has followed my work and ought to know that, in my view, the term "mental illness" may be applied to almost any human behavior that annoys or upsets other people, especially if the actor is weak, such as a child or old person, and the diagnostician, such as a parent or psychiatrist, has power over him. It is meaningless, then, to ask how I propose to remedy "the problem." The problem is life, in the social, not the biological, sense. "It" is not a discrete entity or disease, such as malaria, although the term "mental illness" implies precisely something of that sort. In contrast, Slovenko approvingly cites the view that schizophrenia might be a viral infection.

I reject the view that the human problems Slovenko calls "mental diseases (or disorders)" are, like medical problem such as malaria or melanoma, *phenomena essentially external to the personality, that is, the self, will, character, and habits of the subject.* Accordingly, I believe that the resolution of such a problem hinges—partly or wholly—on the person called "mental patient" assuming responsibility for his predicament and making a sincere attempt at helping himself. How? The possibilities are too numerous to mention. A person beset by difficulties in his life can reflect on how he lives and change some of his habits. He can educate himself about the sort of problem he is experiencing and seek help from family members, friends, clergymen, mental health professionals, physicians, drugs, religion, faith healing, marriage, divorce, and so forth.

Slovenko considers none of these options. Instead, he "wonder[s] why a department of psychiatry is in a medical school . . ." and insinuates that because I have an M.D. degree and had an office in a medical school, the persons who came to see me professionally were "lured [there] by the honorific or the venue." This argument deserves no answer. The point is that Slovenko disapproves of the way I practiced "listening and talking" for some fifty years, serving a clientele limited to adults who paid my fee out of their own pockets and telephoned me personally for their appointments.[5] In contrast, he approves of the way the conventional psychiatrist—whose true client is the involuntary "patient's" adversary (his relatives or a mental health agency of the state)—practices psychiatric coercion and calls it "hospitalization" and "treatment." *Chacun à son goût.*

---

[5] Thomas Szasz, *The Ethics of Psychoanalysis: The Theory and Method of Autonomous Psychotherapy* [1965], with a new preface (Syracuse: Syracuse University Press, 1988).

III

Instead of providing evidence to rebut my views, Slovenko dismisses them by approvingly citing E. Fuller Torrey's statement: "Szasz has produced more erudite nonsense on the subject of serious mental illness than any writer alive. . . . One wonders whether he has ever seen a patient with the disease [schizophrenia]." Either Slovenko and Torrey honestly believe that in almost fifty years of psychiatric practice and teaching, I have never seen a person whom psychiatrists have diagnosed as schizophrenic, or they are dismissing my work with another *ad hominem* slur.

Slovenko does not cite Torrey's book, *The Death of Psychiatry,* in which Torrey enthusiastically supports every one of my major contentions, as the following quotations illustrate:

"Diseases are something we have, behavior is something we do." On this premise, Torrey develops his theory that the vast majority of people whom we call "mentally ill" have problems of living rather than physical disabilities. They are not 'sick' and therefore must not be 'warehoused' and 'treated' on the basis of a medical model.[6]

At this point, disciples of the medical model may answer: "What we really mean, of course, by mental 'disease' is brain disease." . . . Indeed, there are many known diseases of the brain. . . . But these diseases are considered to be in the province of neurology rather than of psychiatry. . . . None of the conditions that we now call mental "diseases" have any known structural or functional changes in the brain. . . . *This is true not only for conditions with labels like "explosive personality" and "paranoid personality," but also for the behavior we categorize as "schizophrenia."*[7]

We abide by the tenet that it is not justified to lock up people for something they might do, for this is an infringement on our freedom. But not so with mental "patients." They are kept for indeterminate, and often interminable, periods for what they might do. . . . As Szasz points out, a drunken driver is infinitely more dangerous to others than is a "paranoid schizophrenic," yet we allow most of the former to remain free while we incarcerate most of the latter."[8]

Another element which further muddles the scene is the way in which the term "schizophrenia" has come to be used, especially in the United States

---

[6] E. Fuller Torrey, *The Death of Psychiatry* (Radnor: Chilton, 1974), dust jacket.
[7] *Ibid.*, pp. 38–39, emphasis added.
[8] *Ibid.*, pp. 76, 89.

and the Soviet Union. . . . As such the term has become meaningless and its demise, along with that of psychiatry itself, will be a welcome addition to clarity of thought. . . . The term "schizophrenic" will wither away to the shelves of museums, looked back upon as an historical curiosity along with the crank telephone. . . . until we have more precise indicators, it is best that we err on the side of labeling too few, rather than too many, as brain diseased. In other words, a person should be presumed not to have a brain disease until proven otherwise on the basis of probability. This is exactly the opposite of what we do now as we blithely label everyone who behaves a little oddly "schizophrenic." Human dignity rather demands that people be assumed to be in control of their behavior and not brain diseased unless there is strong evidence to the contrary.[9]

When the concept of nonresponsibility is rejected outright, then people who [sic] we have called mentally "ill" are given back some of their dignity. . . . there would be no such thing as depriving a person of his right to stand trial. Everyone would retain this civil liberty as guaranteed by the Constitution and it could not be usurped by a psychiatrist or a judge. . . . It should not be possible to confine people against their will in mental "hospitals."[10]

I provided an endorsement for Torrey's book and he presented me with a copy, inscribed:

To Tom, with many thanks for saying nice things about the book. If it has 1/10th the effect which your books have had, I shall be happy. Fuller.

Now, Torrey claims that there are two kinds of mental illnesses, "severe" and "not severe," and that the mental illnesses he categorizes as severe are brain diseases that ought to be treated by psychiatrists with drugs, with or without the patient's consent. He states: "Schizophrenia is a disease of the brain in the same sense that Parkinson's disease and multiple sclerosis are diseases of the brain," yet acknowledges *"that there is no single abnormality in brain structure or function that is pathognomonic for schizophrenia. All deficits cited above can be found . . . occasionally, in normal individuals. . . . Thus, we do not yet have a specific diagnostic test that points conclusively to and exclusively to schizophrenia as the diagnosis."*[11] Both Parkinson's disease and multiple

---

[9] *Ibid.*, pp. 160, 161.
[10] *Ibid.*, pp. 179, 180.
[11] E. Fuller Torrey, "Studies of Individuals Never Treated with Antipsychotic Medications: A Review," *Schizophrenia Research* 58, pp. 101–115 (2002), emphasis added.

sclerosis can be conclusively diagnosed, especially in the later stages of the disease and at autopsy.

Torrey is the foremost American advocate of forced psychiatric treatment.[12] For Torrey and Slovenko, the fact that neurologists do not forcibly incarcerate or "treat" patients with Parkinsonism does not impair the validity of the claim that schizophrenia is like Parkinsonism.

Slovenko supports his criticism of my views by citing the writings of Karl Menninger, his erstwhile mentor: "Like Freud, he [Menninger] proposed a unitary and gradational theory of mental disorder . . . In his book *The Vital Balance*, shortly before undertaking *The Crime of Punishment* (in which I [Slovenko] had a hand), he set forth his view of 'mental illness'" [*sic*]. If mental illness is like Parkinson's disease, why does Slovenko put quotation marks around the term? In *The Crime of Punishment*, Menninger claimed *that punishment is a crime, but crime is a disease, not a crime.* The logic of the book's title implies that both crime and punishment are diseases. Evidently, Slovenko still believes that.

As in the case of Torrey, Slovenko deliberately omits mentioning Menninger's recantation of his views, an event that Slovenko discussed in a brief essay in 1991.[13] In 1988, Karl Menninger wrote me:

Dear Dr. Szasz:

I am holding your new book, *Insanity: The Idea and Its Consequences*, in my hands. I read parts of it yesterday and I have also read reviews of it. I think I know what it says but I did enjoy hearing it said again. I think I understand better what has disturbed you these years and, in fact, it disturbs me, too, now. We don't like the situation that prevails whereby a fellow human being is put aside, outcast as it were, ignored, labeled, and said to be "sick in his mind."[14]

---

[12] E. Fuller Torrey, "Why TAC Exists: To Reduce Victimization," *Catalyst* (Treatment Advocacy Center) (Summer–Fall, 2002), p. 1.

[13] Ralph Slovenko, "Dr. Karl Menninger and Dr. Thomas Szasz: Were They Apart on 'Mental Illness'?" *American Academy of Law and Psychiatry Newsletter* 16 (April 1991), pp. 21–22.

[14] Karl Menninger, "Reading Notes," *Bulletin of the Menninger Clinic* 53 (July 1989), pp. 350–51 (p. 350); cited in Thomas Szasz, *Cruel Compassion: The Psychiatric Control of Society's Unwanted* (Syracuse: Syracuse University Press, 1998[1994]), pp. 201–02.

In a language at once touching and melancholy, Menninger briefly reviewed the history of psychiatry, the tenor of his remarks illustrated by the following sentence: "Added to the beatings and chainings and baths and massages came treatments that were even more ferocious: gouging out parts of the brain, producing convulsions with electric shocks, starving, surgical removal of teeth, tonsils, uteri, etc."[15] He graciously concluded: "Well, enough of those recollections of early days. You tried to get us to talk together and take another look at our material. I am sorry you and I have gotten *apparently* so far apart all these years. We might have enjoyed discussing our observations together. *You* tried; you wanted me to come there, I remember. I demurred. *Mea culpa*."[16]

From my reply, it is enough to cite here that I noted, also not without regret, that I had long felt that our differences were irreconcilable, "because I realized that you wanted to hold on to the values of free will and responsibility and were struggling to reconcile them with psychiatry. For myself, I felt sure, long before I switched my residency from medicine to psychiatry, that this was impossible, that psychiatry was basically wrong."[17]

Commenting on Menninger's letter, Slovenko, wrote: "For nearly thirty years psychiatrist Thomas Szasz has been the harshest critic of his own field. The publication of his book, *The Myth of Mental Illness*, in 1961, sparked debate over the nature of 'mental illness.' The impact of the book cannot be overstated. With it, the terms of our discussion about mental illness have been totally altered."[18]

For a scholar who has devoted his entire professional life to defending psychiatric atrocities, Slovenko displays an astonishing ignorance of psychiatric history. "Diagnosis in psychiatry," he declares, "should matter. When talk therapy was used for everyone, diagnosis was inconsequential." *Psychiatrists,* as distinguished from *psychoanalysts*, rarely if ever used "talk therapy." For centuries, psychiatrists had only involuntary patients and treated them with tortures, such as incarceration, restraint in straitjackets, cold baths, insulin shock, electric shock, and lobotomy.[19] Today's psychiatrist proudly adds outpatient commitment and forcible drugging to his repertoire of coercions.[20]

---

[15] *Op. cit.*, p. 202.

[16] *Ibid.*, emphasis in the original.

[17] Thomas Szasz, "Letter to Karl Menninger," 12th October, 1988, cited in *op. cit.*, p. 202.

[18] Slovenko, "Dr. Karl Menninger and Dr. Thomas Szasz," pp. 21–22.

[19] Thomas Szasz, *The Myth of Psychotherapy: Mental Healing as Religion, Rhetoric, and Repression* (Syracuse: Syracuse University Press, 1988[1978]).

[20] Thomas Szasz, *Liberation by Oppression: A Comparative Study of Slavery and Psychiatry* (New Brunswick: Transaction, 2002).

Slovenko's enthusiasm for modern psychiatry grows in the telling. He explains: "Now a diagnosis would mean that the diagnosed person was mentally ill, and ill in a way that *different psychiatrists could reliably recognize, with treatment in a particular way*" (emphasis added). However, reliability and validity have nothing to do with each other. The reliable recognition of a fictitious entity or status is evidence that the persons doing the recognizing share the same false beliefs, not that "the thing" they recognize exists or is true. Formerly, priests possessed the expertise to "reliably recognize" and "treat" witches. They still possess the expertise to reliably recognize miracles and perform exorcism. Similarly, psychiatrists possess the expertise to reliably recognize that people who enjoy drinking and smoking "suffer" from the disease called "substance abuse."

Slovenko's statement that "different psychiatrists could reliably recognize [mental diseases], *with treatment in a particular way*," erroneously implies that diagnosis *determines* treatment. In the practice of medicine in a free society, it does not. Diagnosis *informs* the doctor about various treatment options. The patient *decides* which, if any, of the options offered he wishes to accept or reject.

Similar misstatements abound. Slovenko writes: "The Kraepelin approach connects with insurance and medication." In Kraepelin's day, there was neither insurance nor medication for the inmates of insane asylums. The connection among health insurance, psychiatric diagnosis, and (forced) psychiatric drugging is the result of the transformation of an individualist-capitalist health care system into a collectivist-socialist health care system and the consequent disconnect between the persons who receive medical services and the persons who pay for them. As I noted, in a free, capitalist society, the patient determines the kind of treatment he receives, subject to the physician's willingness to provide it. The medical patient still enjoys the freedom to reject unwanted medical treatment. The psychiatric patient does not.[21]

Of course, we have long ago lost our freedom to receive the treatment we want and are willing to pay for, and which our physician is potentially willing to provide; for example, we cannot have our intractable pain treated with heroin.[22] We also cannot contract with health insurance companies for the kinds of coverage we want. Most of

---

[21] Thomas Szasz, *Pharmacracy: Medicine and Politics in America* (Westport: Praeger, 1999).

[22] Thomas Szasz, *Our Right to Drugs: The Case for a Free Market* (Syracuse: Syracuse University Press, 1996[1992]).

us receive our health insurance coverage as part of our contract with our employer and the government determines the kinds of policies the insurance companies are permitted to provide. For example, an employee of General Electric or General Motors cannot choose, for a reduced premium, a policy that would exclude coverage for treating alcoholism, pedophilia, and schizophrenia.

"More and more it is coming to be realized," Slovenko explains, "that what is psychological is also biological and what is biological has a psychological component. Symptoms correlate *with brain function that produce a disorder*." I refuse to believe that "*brain functions produce disorders*." I refuse to give up the idea that leprosy and malaria are caused by microbes, not "brain functions."

IV

Slovenko is indignant about my views on suicide. However, instead of presenting my reasons for rejecting the claim that suicide is a disease and that imprisonment is a treatment for it, he distorts my views: "In Szasz's view, if a person 'wants' to commit suicide, just get out of the way." Elsewhere, he has written: "Szasz has been an adamant opponent of efforts to prevent suicide."[23] This is incorrect. I favor helping a person who wishes to kill himself in every way possible, short of coercing him. My objection to the psychiatric approach to suicide is limited to using force to prevent a person from killing himself. (I also oppose physician-assisted suicide, but that is another matter.)[24]

Like most psychiatrists, Slovenko uses the word "help" as a synonym for coercion. And, like psychiatrists, he smears me by claiming that *I prevent* psychiatrists from "helping" persons they deem suicidal: "Those who have been helped by psychiatry to overcome suicidal ideation are grateful that Szasz was not in the vicinity."[25] I have never had any power over psychiatrists and my being in the vicinity of psychiatrists forcing patients to submit to their tortures has not prevented a single patient from receiving his forced "treatment." Slovenko fails to mention that many persons bitterly resent their psychiatric incarceration justified as suicide prevention and, instead of being grateful for their humiliation

---

[23] Ralph Slovenko, "The Trouble with Szasz," *Liberty* 16 (August, 2002), pp. 25–32 (p. 28).

[24] Thomas Szasz, *Fatal Freedom: The Ethics and Politics of Suicide* (Syracuse: Syracuse University Press, 2002[1999]).

[25] Slovenko, "The Trouble with Szasz," p. 28.

become even more determined than they had been to kill themselves. Sylvia Plath, James Forrestal, Ernest Hemingway, Philip Graham are some of the famous examples. The French writer Antonin Artaud wrote: "I myself spent nine years in an insane asylum and I never had the obsession of suicide, but I know that each conversation with a psychiatrist, every morning at the time of his visit, made me want to hang myself, realizing that I would not be able to slit his throat."[26]

A person determined to commit suicide kills himself, often *after* receiving psychiatric "help." If a person communicates his desire to kill himself—to a relative, friend, clergyman, or physician—he does so for a reason: he may want to discuss his predicament with someone he can trust, or want the other person to help him commit suicide, or talk him out of doing so. Psychiatrists maintain, and Slovenko believes them, that the subject's "true interest" requires that the psychiatrist stop him from killing himself, by force if necessary. Regardless of whether this is true or not, it does not follow that the state should authorize psychiatrists to use force for such a purpose or that the state should, in effect, coerce psychiatrists to assume this duty. Obstetricians can refuse to perform abortions without being accused of medical negligence by their colleagues or patients. I believe psychiatrists should have the same option to refuse to imprison and forcibly "treat" their (suicidal) patients.

Each year, approximately one million Americans are committed; an unknown number of persons accused of lawbreaking are diverted from the criminal justice system to the mental health system. Slovenko does not deny that psychiatrists incarcerate innocent people and excuse criminals. Instead, he blames the procedure, of which he approves, on the law: "The psychiatrist is summoned by members of the legal profession." Not true. As a rule, the psychiatrist is summoned by a family member who wants to dispose of an unwanted relative ("loved one") by giving him (the) "treatment." I trust I will be forgiven for quoting more than once in this volume the procedure tacitly recommended by the National Alliance for the Mentally Ill (NAMI), a large, well-funded organization that works in tandem with the APA. The following text appears on the NAMI web site:

> Sometime, during the course of your loved one's illness, you may need the
> police. By preparing now, before you need help, you can make the day you

---

[26] Antonin Artaud, "Van Gogh, the Man Suicided by Society" [1947], in Antonin Artaud, *Selected Writings*, edited by Susan Sontag, translated by Helen Weaver (New York: Farrar, Straus and Giroux, 1976), pp. 496–97.

need help go much more smoothly. . . . It is often difficult to get 911 to respond to your calls if you need someone to come & take your MI relation to a hospital emergency room (ER). They may not believe that you really need help. And if they do send the police, the police are often reluctant to take someone for involuntary commitment. . . . When calling 911, the best way to get quick action is to say, "Violent EDP," or "Suicidal EDP." EDP stands for Emotionally Disturbed Person. This shows the operator that you know what you're talking about. Describe the danger very specifically. "He's a danger to himself" is not as good as "This morning my son said he was going to jump off the roof." . . . Also, give past history of violence. *This is especially important if the person is not acting up.* . . . When the police come, they need compelling evidence that the person is a danger to self or others before they can involuntarily take him or her to the ER for evaluation. . . . Realize that you & the cops are at cross purposes. You want them to take someone to the hospital. They don't want to do it. . . . Say, "Officer, I understand your reluctance. Let me spell out for you the problems & the danger. . . .*While AMI / FAMI is not suggesting you do this, the fact is that some families have learned to "turn over the furniture" before calling the police.* . . . If the police see furniture disturbed they will usually conclude that the person is imminently dangerous.[27] (emphasis added)

Nevertheless, Slovenko insists that "The psychiatrist is summoned by members of the legal profession . . . , [and] in every instance in the law-psychiatry intermix, the law, not psychiatry, controls, with psychiatric testimony used only for window dressing."[28] The truth is that neither law alone nor psychiatry alone can justify what is in effect preventive detention on "therapeutic" grounds. Both are needed to legitimize this practice. Lawyers and psychiatrists collaborate and collude in implementing the body of principles and procedures called "mental health law," much the same way that lawyers and priests collaborated and colluded in implementing the principles and procedures called the Inquisition.[29]

In most states, a single psychiatrist can detain a person in a mental hospital for twenty-four to seventy-two hours (or longer), and the patient must *request to be discharged in writing to get a court hearing,* at which the judge rubber-stamps the psychiatrist's recommendation and recommits the prisoner-patient. Like all professionals licensed by the state, psychiatrists operate in a sphere allocated to them by law. The law

---

[27] D.J. Jaffe, "How to Prepare for an Emergency" (2000), http://www.nami.org/about/naminyc/coping/911.html. Emphasis added.

[28] Slovenko, "The Trouble with Szasz," p. 29.

[29] See also Thomas Szasz, "Reply to Pies," this volume, pp. 354–363.

authorizes pathologists to dissect corpses, surgeons to operate on patients, and psychiatrists to incarcerate mental patients. I consider the fact that pathologists and surgeons choose to engage in the acts emblematic of their professional identity as evidence that they view the acts as "good," benefiting science, society, patients, or all three. Similarly, psychiatrists incarcerate innocent individuals because they consider psychiatric imprisonment "good," a procedure that benefits the patient, his relatives, or society, or all three.

Slovenko's account of the collusion between law and psychiatry makes it appear as if lawyers command psychiatrists who, in turn, must obey them. This is not so. Psychiatrists are free agents. No one is compelled to be a psychiatrist. If psychiatrists coerce people, it is because they love coercion and get money and prestige for coercing people in the name of mental health. One psychiatrist declares: "Force is the best medicine."[30] Another asserts: "The right to refuse treatment is one right too many."[31]

V

As we saw, Slovenko tries to discredit me and my views by selectively citing the writings of E. Fuller Torrey and Karl Menninger that are critical of my views. He uses the same tactic, in reverse, by citing the writings of Patrick Buchanan, a prominent conservative political commentator, who embraces much of what I say. Slovenko assumes, perhaps rightly, that in the minds of right-thinking liberals, if a right-winger such as Buchanan likes what I write, what I write must be wrong and I must be wicked. Slovenko remarks: "He [Szasz] is often quoted. For example, in *The Death of the West* (2002), Patrick Buchanan writes: 'Since the 1960s, branding opponents as haters or mentally sick has been the most effective weapon in the arsenal of the Left.' . . . Assuredly, though, the *explanations of behavior* given by psychiatry, however faulty they may be, is an advance over the religious view of demon possession." Evidently, Slovenko still regards the diagnostic denigrations of people like Ezra Pound and Barry Goldwater as "explanations."

"Josef Stalin," Slovenko explains, "was a tyrant but he did two good things: he developed an excellent transportation system and he kept the fast-food (aka junk food) franchises out of the Soviet Union. For that, all

---

[30] Sally Satel, "For Addicts, Force Is the Best Medicine," *Wall Street Journal* (January 7th, 1998), p. 6.

[31] Stephen Rachlin, "One Right Too Many," *Bulletin of the American Academy of Psychiatry and the Law* 3 (1975), pp. 99–102 (p. 102).

Russian are grateful."[32] More than sixty years ago, Bertrand Russell, assuredly no right-wing fanatic, melancholically observed: "The terror in Russia, likewise, has been condoned by most of the Left."[33] Slovenko still condones it.

Slovenko repeats the canard, pioneered by John Monahan, that I am responsible for the world-wide deinstitutionalization of mental patients and the disastrous consequences of this policy.[34] In Slovenko's view of the history of modern psychiatry, "[Lawyer Bruce] Ennis and colleagues—aided and abetted by Szasz—accomplished their goal. The numbers of mentally ill in jail or homeless, with freedom to be perpetually psychotic, are a living testimony to their success."[35] Actually, the forcible eviction of chronic mental patients from state mental hospitals was carried out by the psychiatrists in charge of the psychiatric establishment in the 1960s and 1970s, who were my severest critics.

Slovenko canvasses my writings and cannot find a scintilla of good in them. In an essay in 2002, I criticized the collusion between Catholic bishops and psychiatrists in their handling of the pedophilia scandals that beset the Church.[36] Slovenko objects: "Pedophilia is the most recent illustration of which he [Szasz] is dismissive of categorization as disease. True to form, he condemns psychiatrists." The American Psychiatric Association classifies pedophilia as a disease (albeit the APA now uses the weasel-word "disorder"). I maintain that sex between adults and minors—an act the law classifies as a felony, largely because minors, by definition, cannot consent to sex with adults—is *not a disease*.

Slovenko feels no need to explain why I am not entitled to that view. Instead, he praises both the Church and psychiatry: "The Church after two thousand years of experience with sin has turned to psychotherapy to deal with its pedophile priests." The Church has done nothing of the kind. Corrupt bishops have colluded with the corrupt psychiatrists and a corrupt psychiatric system. The Church hid its pedophile priests from

---

[32] Slovenko, "The Trouble with Szasz," p. 31.

[33] Bertrand Russell, *Power: A New Social Analysis* (London: Allen and Unwin, 1938), p. 250.

[34] John Monahan, "From the Man Who Brought You Deinstitutionalization," *Contemporary Psychology* 33 (June 1988), p. 492.

[35] Slovenko, "The Trouble with Szasz," p. 30.

[36] Thomas Szasz, "Sins of the Fathers: Is Child Molestation a Sickness or a Crime?" *Reason* 34 (August 2002), pp. 54–59.

the police in "clinics" run by psychiatrists, until they could be quietly reassigned to new venues to ply their predatory trade.[37]

Slovenko concludes by gratuitously psychoanalyzing my motives for my love of individual liberty and personal responsibility: "Szasz's feelings about the Therapeutic State apparently derives [sic] from his heritage as a Jew growing up in Hungary and forced to flee the Nazis."

Adam Smith's and Lord Acton's love of liberty was inspired by the lofty motive of liberal humanism and a longing for a just society. My love of liberty, says Slovenko, is inspired by the lowly motive of wanting to save my own skin from Nazis, nothing more. Slovenko does not explain why many of the Jewish psychiatrists who left Europe because of Naziism became, in the United States, the leading promoters and practitioners of the worst kinds of modern psychiatric brutalities, such as insulin shock, metrazol shock, carbon dioxide coma, electric shock, and lobotomy, accompanied by life-long imprisonment in mental hospitals. To my knowledge, not a single American or English psychiatrist who left Europe under circumstances similar to mine shared, or shares, my opposition to psychiatric coercions and excuses.

Finally, Slovenko considers my concept and criticism of the Therapeutic State. He states that I describe "the Therapeutic State as Nazi pharmacracy." Not true. In *Pharmacracy*—the latest and most complete account of my views regarding the Therapeutic State—I describe Nazi Germany as *a type* of Therapeutic State.[38] Scoffingly, Slovenko asks: "And yet, where is the Therapeutic State *ruled by psychiatrists*?" (emphasis added). I have never characterized the Therapeutic State as "ruled by psychiatrists." Had I believed that, I would have called it the Psychiatric State.

The Therapeutic State is not ruled by psychiatrists. It is ruled by politicians imbued with the faith of medicine (therapy), much as the Theological State, exemplified by Saudi Arabia, is ruled by politicians imbued with the faith of religion (Islam). In the United States, the Therapeutic State is ruled by a coalition composed of politicians—presidents, vice presidents, senators—and their wives; surgeons general and their retinue of politicized physicians from the American Medical Association, the state medical associations, and the various health lob-

---

[37] See Thomas Szasz, "The Psychiatrist as Accomplice," *Washington Times* (April 28th, 2002), p. B03.

[38] Thomas Szasz, *Pharmacracy: Medicine and Politics in America* (Westport: Praeger, 1999), pp. 145–46.

bies; the public health establishment, NAMI, the APA, and the mental health lobby.

Slovenko seems oblivious of the federal government's wars on drugs, drinking, smoking, obesity, guns, suicide, cancer, heart disease, AIDS, *ad infinitum*. Slovenko's self-inflicted blindness to the very existence of the Therapeutic State stands in sharp contrast to the clear-eyed perception of social critic and humorist Florence King's marvelous satire of pharmacracy in all its fatuous absurdity. "There's a war on," she mocks, "against the unhalt, the unlame, and the unstupid. *You're nobody unless there's something wrong with you.* It's only a matter of time before the E.Q., or 'emotional intelligence,' replaces I.Q., so that people who ought to be in an institution learning how to make brooms can feel good about themselves."[39] Indeed so. We used to call especially gifted athletes or artists "special." Now we call especially ungifted students "special."[40]

I define the Therapeutic State as a type of totalitarian state destructive of liberty and responsibility. Slovenko redefines it as a desirable social polity. "The Therapeutic State," he declares, is "preferable to a non-Therapeutic State." Slavery, declared Jefferson Davis, is "a moral, social, and political blessing. . .[It is] the most humane relations of labor to capital which can permanently subsist between them.[41] That is how Ralph Slovenko views psychiatric slavery: it is, to paraphrase Davis, the most humane relations of psychiatrists and mental patients which can permanently subsist between them.

VI

My dialogue with Slovenko, as I noted at the beginning of my reply, goes back almost forty years, to 1964 to be exact. Following the publication, to very good reviews, of my book, *Law, Liberty, and Psychiatry* in 1963, I was invited to present my views at the American Psychiatric Association's 120th annual meeting in Los Angeles, in May 1964. It was the first and last time I was asked to speak at an American Psychiatric Association convention. Andrew Watson, then a leading young forensic psychiatrist, characterized the event with refreshing candor with this

---

[39] Florence King, "The Misanthrope's Corner," *National Review* (June 3rd, 2002), p. 56, emphasis added.
[40] Maureen Nolan, "Special Student Loves SU," *The Post-Standard* (Syracuse) (November 26th, 2002), p. B1. It is the story of a college student handicapped with Down's syndrome.
[41] Jefferson Davis, quoted in M. Byrd, "Lincoln's Shadow," *New York Times Book Review* (December 3rd, 2000), p. 12.

remark: "The purpose of this session, I gather, is to attempt to corral Tom Szasz."[42]

In my presentation, titled "The Moral Dilemma of Psychiatry: Autonomy or Heteronomy?" I challenged the conventional view of the psychiatrist as a physician who diagnoses and treats diseases.[43] Because the psychiatrist deals with conflicts between people as well as within persons, he must be an agent of the patient or of the patient's adversaries. Every one of the psychiatrists invited to discuss my presentation interpreted this truism as heresy and denounced me as a heretic. They were right. I was attacking the foundational doctrines of psychiatry—that human problems are medical diseases and that the coercive psychiatrist is an agent of his coerced victim.

Henry A. Davidson, then one of the leading forensic psychiatrists in the country, titled his presentation, "The New War on Psychiatry." He stated: "We have just heard a cogent and tightly reasoned challenge to modern psychiatry. The issues which Dr. Szasz here raises so temperately are worthy of our best study."[44] Having said this, Davidson minced no words denouncing me: "However, during the past eight years, Dr. Szasz has been provoking a good deal of anxiety in people by a criticism of psychiatry and psychiatrists which could not be called 'temperate'. . . . The net result of Dr. Szasz's writing has been to make people think that we psychiatrists are a menace to our patients." Davidson correctly named 1956 as the year that my "treachery" began. For the rest of his talk, he disputed the validity of my criticism of psychiatric coercions and denigrated me with *ad hominem* remarks.

"In court," Davidson stated, "the dice are loaded *in favor* of the patient" (emphasis in the original)." Dismissing my message, he attacked the messenger: "I do not challenge Dr. Szasz's sincerity. He really believes that psychiatry is a menace to individual liberty—he has said so many times. It is as if, out of all American psychiatrists, only Dr. Szasz has been given the mission of protecting people from the plotting of the other twelve thousand." Neither psychiatrists nor lay persons need a psychiatric dictionary to translate this language into a diagnosis of paranoid schizophrenia.

---

[42] Andrew Watson, "Discussion," *American Journal of Psychiatry* 121 (December 1964), pp. 542–44.

[43] Thomas Szasz, "The Moral Dilemma of Psychiatry: Autonomy or Heteronomy?" *American Journal of Psychiatry,* 121, pp. 5212–8 (December), 1964.

[44] Henry A. Davidson, "The New War on Psychiatry," *American Journal of Psychiatry* 121 (December 1964), pp. 528–533. All quotations from Davidson are from this source.

Davidson went so far as to imply that my "reality testing" is impaired: "As seen from Syracuse, the AMA appears to be leaning toward socialization of medical care. . . . This is the first time I ever heard the AMA considered a left wing organization." For me, the issue is, and has always been, individualism versus statism, not "right wing" or "left wing." Has the AMA changed since 1964 or was my diagnosis of it then accurate?

Davidson cast himself in the role of the "reasonable" person ready to compromise, and me in the role of an uncompromising fanatic: "Dr. Szasz takes an absolutist position. He should be reminded that nothing is one hundred percent right or wrong. . . . *Invasions of civil liberties can be life saving. The obvious example is the forceful prevention of suicide* (emphasis added). In most states, suicide is not a crime, but we may have to impair a patient's civil rights to prevent it." There were thousands of psychiatrists in the audience. None dissented.

At least indirectly, my colleagues were paying me a compliment. They treated me as if I were Goliath who needs six Davids to slay him. Five more psychiatrists mounted the podium to explain my errors and denounce my heresies to the audience. Howard P. Rome, head of psychiatry at the Mayo Clinic, stated: "Dr. Davidson has charged Dr. Szasz with what he calls 'intemperate behavior' over a period of the past eight years. . . . The indictment here seems to be that to shout 'fire' in a crowded theater extends an unquestioned constitutional freedom to an unpermissible level."[45] Clearly, psychiatrists viewed my criticizing them as an act of *lèse majesté*. "Freedom of speech," Rome continued, "is not, as Dr. Davidson's remarks suggest, a license to calumniate, impugn, derogate, asperse, slander, and malign."

Andrew S. Watson dismissed my concerns and disdained my conclusions as due to lack of understanding of "important legal propositions." He stated: "I cannot share Szasz's anxiety about psychiatric tyranny. . . *I felt I had sustained a treacherous blow when Dr. Szasz's article on "Psychiatry, ethics, and the criminal law" appeared in the Columbia Law Review. . . .* The article was tightly reasoned and very persuasive. Regrettably, it was bottomed on false premises about the law. Dr. Szasz did not then understand several important legal propositions, and he still does not."[46] The editors of the *Columbia Law Review* evidently did not

---

[45] Howard P. Rome, "Discussion," *American Journal of Psychiatry* 121 (December 1964), pp. 539–541.

[46] Andrew S. Watson, "Discussion," *American Journal of Psychiatry* 121 (December 1964), pp. 539–541, emphasis added.

think so.[47] Watson and perhaps other psychiatrists regarded my publishing in such a prestigious law review journal as another act of betrayal. "Washing dirty linen in public" was a charge often leveled against me in those days.

Watson was so carried away by his psychiatric piety that he helped me make my points. "I have found myself wondering," he stated, "what Dr. Szasz *does* with the people who come to his office, if they are *not patients* seeking medical help for emotional illness" (emphasis added). Watson was unable to imagine that someone who went to the trouble of going through medical school and a psychiatric residency could insist, as I have always insisted, that what I do is listen and talk to the people who come to me for help; that neither listening nor talking is a form of medical treatment; and that the people who come to see me or other psychoanalysts, are not sick and know it.

John Donnelly, chief of psychiatry at the Institute for Living in Hartford, Connecticut, pondered my reference to Aristotle and the problem of categories, and then ridiculed my comparing involuntary mental patients with slaves, and psychiatrists with slaveholders: "This is a case of apples and oranges. . . . *Lincoln's public discourses on the Negro were well recognized by Lincoln to be only rhetorical—to convince the electors to support him. . . . Lincoln knew that the Negro could be put in whatever class he chose to set up.*"[48] So much for the moral struggle that faced Lincoln and the country following the Dred Scott decision.[49] Adopting an increasingly patronizing tone, Donnelly concluded:

> Professor Szasz repeatedly in his presentation uses this type of loose argumentation. . . . But despite Dr. Szasz's seeming imperfections in his knowledge of the definitions and meaning of the classical philosophical terms which he scatters in his paper, he is concerned with problems in the field of moral philosophy. . . . Dr. Szasz, who adheres so strongly to the principles of Kantian philosophy, himself has two dilemmas—one professional and one philosophical. The professional dilemma (which he does not appear to recognize) is whether or not to adhere, as a practicing psychoanalyst, to the basic theories of his particular school.

---

[47] Thomas Szasz, "Psychiatry, Ethics, and the Criminal Law," *Columbia Law Review* 58 (February 1958), pp. 183–198.

[48] John Donnelly, "Discussion," *American Journal of Psychiatry* 121 (December 1964), pp. 539–541, emphasis added.

[49] See Thomas Szasz, *Liberation by Oppression: A Comparative Study of Slavery and Psychiatry* (New Brunswick: Transaction, 2002).

Donnelly and many of his contemporaries had not the faintest idea of what I was talking about. They were like slaveholders who devoutly believe that their right to own slaves is legitimized by the Bible and God. They could not imagine that a white man would want to destroy that "peculiar institution."

Henry Weihofen, then the dean of American forensic psychiatry, made short shrift of me: "Dr. Szasz does not discuss anything specific. Instead, he gives us generalizations, wholesale denunciations, and metaphorical name-calling. . . . I don't know whether, in giving us this warning, he was using the metaphor of 'slave' consciously or unconsciously [*sic*]." Weihofen then accused me of being a heartless fascist, an "extremist right winger": "But the fears about what goes on in mental hospitals that Dr. Szasz fosters are seized upon by *the right-wing extremists with whom he has been playing footsie. . .*"[50] Since then, virtually all defenders of psychiatric slavery have leveled this charge against me.

The next commentator was Ralph Slovenko, who chose not to address my paper at all. Instead, he told the assembled psychiatrists that they are doing God's work. Where I saw evil, he saw good:

> History would suggest that psychiatry dignifies mankind rather than denigrates it. . . . The trend in clinical and hospital development is to make civil commitment laws less important. . . . Society has always isolated the people we now label "mentally ill," rarely with their consent. . . . [H]ave we any reason to believe that the afflicted object to this treatment or custody? . . . It must be noted that confinement by itself, even in a woefully inadequate setting, suffices to bring about recovery in a sizable percentage of cases. . . . Charges of railroading are unfounded. If it were left to the hospital, such a patient would be readily released. . . . There is need for more lawyers to be involved in the mental illness field in both the areas of civil and criminal commitment. . . . Critics say that psychiatry is depriving people of their liberty and dignity. But what is psychiatry depriving them of? Their "right" to waste life? To commit suicide?[51]

Plus ça change, plus c'est la même chose.

---

[50] Henry Weihofen, "Discussion," *American Journal of Psychiatry* 121 (December 1964), pp. 539–541, emphasis added.

[51] Ralph Slovenko, "The Psychiatric Patient, Liberty, and the Law," *American Journal of Psychiatry* 121 (December 1964), pp. 534–39. All quotations from Slovenko are from this source.

5

Prescribed Addiction

STANTON PEELE

A Szaszian Disputes Szasz

To discuss addiction in the context of a book on Szasz requires that I clarify my view of addiction as distinct from Szasz's. There are similarities and there are differences, real differences.

The American Psychiatric Association should build a statue of Thomas Szasz. He has done more than any individual to focus on the *papier-mâché* nature of much of modern psychiatry, its often value- and cultural-driven diagnoses, and its circular treatments, which move people from one form of societal dependence to another. Moreover, he has had the guts—and longevity—to present his views effectively and with telling impact for close to half a century.

Finally, at its core, the Szaszian vision is of liberty and independence—understanding one's position in the crazy-making cultural machinery is in itself a cure for it.

At the same time, Szasz, although a brilliant historian of science, and the major debunker of current mental health fads, is hidebound in his notions of medicine, illness, and therapy. Szasz is too accepting of medical illness and treatment as objective, physical, and not much affected by history and culture. It is thus a straw man that he differentiates from diagnoses of mental illness and addiction, which he correctly sees as being largely cultural creations.

Thus, Szasz, denier of categories, finds what he assumes is physical causality to be an all-purpose basis for authenticity. To the extent drugs cause something that Szasz recognizes as physical dependence (and that many people call addiction), he accepts drugs' inevitable, inexorable impact on the body! This, like what Szasz thinks of as *real* medical illnesses, cannot be caused by culture and cognition. He does not examine and critique a notion like physical dependence so much as he accepts and correlates it with comparable dependencies people have to prescribed and legal drugs. For Szasz, the issues are (a) that addiction to illicit drugs is similar to accepted addictions, and (b) that people should be free to depend on—and harm themselves with—whichever objects of addiction they choose. Thus, he displays an odd passivity towards and acceptance of addiction that is opposed to my approach. Szasz really shows little concern for escaping addiction—his philosophy of the liberated self stops at this door.

Yet, whether, when, and how people withdraw from substance use has as much to do with their relationship to society and their understanding of the universe as whether they believe they are—whether they are—drug addicted. Ultimately, Szasz fails to perceive and to understand the complexity of addiction in all of its cultural and cognitive richness.

Like many who deny the existence of something called addiction (and also mental illness), Szasz can be clueless when confronted with real human compulsion and emotional despair. People kill themselves with drugs and alcohol, believing until their last breath that they cannot escape their substance abuse. People roam the streets babbling to themselves, commit suicide, and are lost in delusion and despair. Many of these can benefit from some kind of help—although often not that which modern medicine offers them. Szasz's correct perception of addiction (and to some degree mental illness) as a self-fulfilling prophecy—with society encouraging people to label themselves that way—can be developed, as I attempt to, into a treatment philosophy. Although these experiences, as Szasz explicates, are created by often exaggerated views of the power of drugs and of the concreteness of emotional disorders, people nonetheless experience themselves to be in the grip of addiction and mental illness, and the reality of that experience must be recognized.

People may recapture the ability to function, to exist, when they find social supports (including love), a *raison d'être*, coping skills, and mastery of their minds—which, in some cases (*à la* John Forbes Nash in "A Beautiful Mind"), involves managing delusions. Indeed, a majority of delusional individuals—those with sensory hallucinations—function capably. It is far from a great trick. And people train themselves (as did Nash) to do this on their own, without medications. At the other end of the hope and clarity Szasz brings many, is his failure to accept and cope with human frailty and rejection. His views have more to offer people than simply a vision of sanity and hope. In his critical insights are clues, directions to assist those now not being served well by medicine and therapy. I like to think of myself as more Szazian than Szasz. Above all, of course, his crusade against coercion in the name of illusory medical cures for addiction and mental illness—or even cures that potentially might work—should earn him the Nobel Peace Prize.

The Pharmaceutical Example

Szasz is also, of course, right that addiction does not stop with illegal drugs. And this form of addiction is one of the key illustrations of the wrong-headedness of society's views of addictions. Although pharmaceuticals are the largest class of psychoactive drugs consumed by Americans, and illegal consumption of pharmaceuticals has been identified by the National Institute on Drug Abuse (NIDA) as the fastest-growing form of drug abuse, the NIDA, drug users themselves, and especially physicians are incapable of recognizing the extent of addiction to legally prescribed pharmaceuticals. This is because dependence on the drugs is fostered, while medical conceptions of addiction—suffused with the idea that some drugs are "good" and cannot produce addiction while illicit drugs are "bad"—simply cannot cope with the phenomenon. Elvis Presley's life and death embody this myopia. Presley's addiction to prescription drugs led to an early death, yet he railed against drug abuse and was appointed by President Nixon as a special drug enforcement agent.

Addiction, when properly defined, is an over-attachment to an artificial source of gratification, or mood modification, which comes to dominate an individual's life. Antidepressants are the epitome of this form of prescription addiction. Although vastly overprescribed in the United States (they are the largest category of branded prescription drugs sold here), antidepressant abuse has traditionally been ignored by the NIDA. Nonetheless, addiction to antidepressants (following addiction to benzodiazepines and antipsychotics) has been recognized. This recognition is fostering a redefinition of addiction (as occurred in the 1980s with cocaine) which is not yet complete. While understood to produce withdrawal, but not intense pursuit and craving, antidepressants nonetheless fulfil the criteria for addiction.

Elvis Would *Never* Abuse Drugs!

"It's very wrong to say he was a druggie," said Derry Caughlan, 50, of Ireland. "He died early because of the pressures that were put on him and the unnatural life he was leading. He wasn't getting the proper food." (Associated Press 1997)

The classic case of prescription drug abuse and addiction is Elvis Presley. Presley died in 1977 at the age of 42. The official autopsy listed as cause of death "cardiac arrhythmia"or a "severely irregular heartbeat"—"just another name for a form of heart attack." Although use of prescription drugs was noted, the medical examiner reported no signs of needle tracks, which would indicate heroin use, or inflamed nasal tissue, as would appear in the case of cocaine use. Based on this evidence, the examiner confidently announced, "There was no indication of any drug abuse of any kind." (Buser 1977; Rohter and Zito 1977).

Only later were toxicological reports revealed that identified fourteen drugs in Presley's system, including codeine (at ten times therapeutic levels), methaqualone (Quaaludes), barbiturates, and numerous others (Thompson and Cole 1991). Presley had turned to prescription pain killers early in his career, and his use increased over the years. In 1973, which two authors called "the year of the drugs," Presley was brought back from overdoses four times (Brown and Broeske 1997). In September 1979 Presley's private doctor, Dr. George Nichopoulos, was charged by the Tennessee Board of Medical Examiners with prescribing 5,300 individual pills, tablets, and vials in the seven months before Presley's death. Although Nichopoulos was acquitted of any professional violation, he described an intricate drug-management system he developed for the singer, who was hooked on a myriad of mostly pain medications.

Presley never considered himself a drug abuser. Quite the contrary, he despised drug use—by which he meant use of illicit substances. The most notorious example of this attitude was his unannounced White House visit with Richard Nixon in December 1970 to gain an appointment as a special Drug Enforcement Agency officer. "Apparently, Elvis discussed the nation's drug problem, anti-war protests, and the British invasion spearheaded by the Beatles" (Chadwick 1998). The visit is commemorated by a famous picture of a grinning Nixon shaking hands with a spacey-looking Presley.

Still later, the post-death Elvis industry has forwarded the idea that Presley only *seemed* to be an addict.

The technical answer is that Elvis died of not only cardiac arrhythmia but also from the mixing of incompatible drugs. Obviously, Elvis was a very ill man in the last years of his life. And we are now in the position to know that Elvis's heart disease, enlarged colon and other ailments were in part due to chronic substance abuse over several years, probably most of the 1970s. But our conference is unique in that we are exploring the larger psychological issues surrounding Elvis's death, and finally breaking out of the simplistic explanation of drug addiction and looking at the larger picture of Elvis's mental health throughout his life, particularly in the last downward spiraling years. This morning one of our speakers, a therapist from Greystone Park Psychiatric Hospital in New Jersey, advanced the thesis that Elvis suffered bipolar disorder, which is a more technical name for manic depression. And that Elvis's substance abuse, eating disorders, and chronic depression should be placed in the larger context of a personality disorder. We think that this will shed new light on the issue of Elvis's death and will take it out of the narrow context of suspected overdose and addiction to the larger and more fundamental issues of Elvis's childhood, family history, the cultural influences of the times in which he lived and other factors which contributed to a possible personality disorder. (Chadwick 1998)

Presley's case demonstrates the refusal—not only of Presley and his admirers, but of medical clinicians—to accept that prescribed drugs create addictions just as illicit substances, cigarettes, and alcohol do. Even Chadwick's 1998 analysis is a special pleading. Nothing Chadwick says about Presley doesn't hold for any alcoholic, heroin or cocaine addict, or smoker, including that Elvis's addictions were connected to his "mental health throughout his life" and "the cultural influences of the times." The "simplistic explanation of drug addiction" that disregards these things Chadwick refers to could be the standard medical view of addiction, along with the view held by Elvis, his father, and many of his admirers that Elvis was not an addict, since he didn't buy street drugs.

The Phenomenon of Prescription Addiction

One irony of addiction to prescribed pharmaceuticals is traceable to medical ignorance of the meaning of addiction, in that people are often addicted to drugs acquired entirely legitimately through prescriptions knowingly provided by individual physicians (like Elvis's doctor). This seems to have been true for First Lady Betty Ford (whose main addiction was to Valium, rather than alcohol) and to Kitty Dukakis, who was treated for a long-term diet pill (amphetamine) addiction. That addictions to prescription medicines are commonplace is suggested by the number of prominent show business, political, and athletic personalities who have announced such addictions—a short list includes Green Bay quarterback Brett Favre, comedian Chevy Chase, comic actor Matthew Perry, conservative commentator Rush Limbaugh, and senator's wife Cindi McCain.[1]

In addition to cover stories on cocaine and heroin epidemics and medical cures for addiction, *Newsweek*, *Time*, and the *New York Times Magazine* periodically feature articles on abuse of the latest prescription painkillers, most recently Vicodin and OxyContin.[2] But somehow, these addictions seem less inevitable—as though they could be readily remedied by wiser prescription practices. That is, unlike illicit street narcotics, prescription painkillers are seen as not *inherently* addictive. Thus, *Newsweek* recommended limiting prescriptions for OxyContin to those "patients who need it without being 'diverted' to those who don't." For its part, the drug's manufacturer "says it plans to develop new painkillers that would not be subject to abuse" (Kalb 2001a). We—and the pharmaceutical industry—might wonder why, after centuries of the development of drugs with analgesic properties, we should still be finding that the latest painkilling "miracle" drugs show this same disabling side-effect.

In fact, this futility is due to a primary pharmacological misconception. Consider one strange aspect of the field of pharmacology—the search for a nonaddictive analgesic (Eddy 1958). Since the turn of this century, American pharmacologists have declared the need to develop a chemical that would relieve pain but that would not create addiction. Consider how desperate this search has been: heroin was originally marketed in this country by the Bayer company of Germany as a nonaddictive substitute for morphine! Cocaine was also used to cure morphine (and later heroin) addiction, and many physicians (including Freud) recommended it widely for this purpose.

Indeed, every new pharmaceutical substance that has reduced anxiety or pain or had other major psychoactive effects has been promot-

---

[1] In this list, only Cindi McCain was known to be *illegally* filling prescriptions to obtain her drugs, although Limbaugh is supposedly being investigated on such gounds.

[2] Amusingly, *Newsweek*'s OxyContin abuse article appeared (Kalb 2001a) in the Business section under the heading "Pharmaceuticals." A month earlier the magazine announced that OxyContin was addictive (Kalb 2001b). As usual, the *New York Times Magazine* (Tough 2001) article was both the most alarmist, and the most biologically deterministic—and confused—about addiction: "It takes about five seconds to effect the transformation—and not much longer to create an addict."

ed as offering feelings of relief without having addictive side effects. And in every case, this claim has been proved wrong. Heroin and cocaine are only two obvious examples. A host of other drugs—the barbiturates, artificially synthesized narcotics (Demerol), tranquilizers (Valium), and on and on—were welcomed initially, only to have been found eventually to cause addiction in many people (Peele 1995, p. 151).

There is a further basic reason that this is the case. Among the key insights I provided (with Archie Brodsky) in *Love and Addiction* is that "Addiction is not a mysterious chemical process; it is the logical outgrowth of the way a drug makes a person feel" (Peele and Brodsky 1975, p. 47). That is, people do not take a powerful analgesic substance, and then unfortunately become addicted due to some mysterious molecular bonding that takes place outside their consciousness. Rather, it is precisely the experiential effect they seek and welcome in the drug that is the source of the addictive connection—the object of the addiction. Modern pharmaceutical advances with the goal of creating more efficient and powerful drug experiences will be inherently liable for addictive abuse, and perhaps increasingly so.

Prevalence of Addiction to Illicit Drugs, Illegal Pharmaceuticals, and Prescriptions

The actual frequency of addiction to pharmaceuticals is not known. That is, our knowledge of such addiction comes primarily from individual revelations. There is no special dragnet to detect them. For instance, the National Institute on Drug Abuse's *National Survey on Drug Use and Health* questions only use of illicit drugs—or use of illicitly produced or sold prescription drugs—along with alcohol and tobacco. Such government surveys report the *prevalence* of illicit drug use, rather than addiction. For example, the National Survey tables report no more than monthly use, since there are so few daily users of most illicit drugs found in the survey.[3] Thus, according to the best government data, about 400,000 Americans used crack and about 200,000 used heroin in the last month (Substance Abuse and Mental Health Administration 2001, Appendix G).

---

[3] The exception is alcohol, for which table after table reports any use, binge use, and heavy use.

These numbers are *dwarfed* by the illegal use of pharmaceuticals (called "psychotherapeutics"), of which there were about 4,000,000 users in the last month (about 2.5 million analgesic, 1 million tranquilizer, and 1 million stimulant users—categories overlap). That is, *twenty* times as many Americans have recently used pharmaceuticals illegally as have used heroin. Of course, the "legitimate" prescribed users of these and other pharmaceuticals is off the charts, virtually incalculable. One billion dollars worth of OxyContin alone were sold legally in 2000 (Kalb 2001a). The number one class of drugs by volume are codeine-based drugs, for which over 100,000,000 individual prescriptions were written in 1999 (U.S. Pharmaceutical Industry 2000).

For pharmaceuticals, self-referrals and emergency room visits are the only reported instances of trauma. In its online summary of "National Trends" in drug abuse, the NIDA discussed, in order, cocaine, heroin, marijuana, methamphetamine, Ecstasy, and "emerging drugs." But emerging drugs are all pharmaceuticals—the section on emerging drugs in 2000 reads:

> CEWG [Community Epidemiology Work Group] members identified several legal, prescription drugs as emerging drugs of abuse in 1999. These include clonazepam (a benzodiazepine) and the controlled substances hydrocodone (Lorcet®, Lortab®, Vicodin®), hydromorphone (Dilaudid®), and oxycodone (Percodan®, Percocet®). Abuse of one or more of these drugs was reported in New Orleans, Phoenix, St. Louis, Texas, and Washington, D.C.
>
> Hydrocodone appeared to be the most widely abused of these drugs. From 1993 to 1999, hydrocodone emergency room mentions increased from 6,115 to 14,639. Among marijuana/hashish emergency room mentions, combined use with hydrocodone increased from 8 in 1990 to 840 in 1999. In some areas, hydromorphone and oxycodone pills are substituted for heroin by heroin abusers. (NIDA 2000)

Here abuse can only be determined by disasters like hospital emergency visits—in other words, health care handled outside ordinary consultations with physicians. How many non-emergency adverse hospital and other medical visits are made to deal with overreliance, negative side effects, and full addiction to prescribed drugs? Thus, any list of people who admitted to addictions to pharmaceuticals would include primarily legal users (like Betty Ford and Kitty Dukakis) who would not appear in NIDA surveys or emergency room visits.

More fundamentally, the logic in assessing addiction is completely different with pharmaceuticals and heroin and other illicit substances. That is, prescribed use of pharmaceuticals is frequently *intended* to be daily and uninterrupted. Use of sleeping medications is often assumed to be nightly. Antidepressants are felt to be ineffective if used sporadically or incidentally. And so on.

Voices from the Internet

I have an active Web site devoted to nontraditional approaches to and issues in addiction (http://www.peele.net). I answer questions at my website. One of the largest categories of questioners is people concerned with addiction to pharmaceuticals. This takes several forms. In one, people are concerned to call my attention to addiction to one drug or class of drugs, fearing I give it insufficient attention. In the other, more common form of question, individuals write me for advice about their (or a spouse's or other loved one's) prescription addiction. An example of the former concerned tranquilizers (benzodiazpines). My response was:

Dear _____:

The underlying message in my work is that it is not possible to divide the world into "addictive" and "nonaddictive" drugs. Rather, it depends on the individual's relationship to the substance. I have often discussed benzodiazepine addictions in regards to America's most popular tranquilizer, Valium. In a footnote to my article with Rich DeGrandpre, "Cocaine and the Concept of Addiction" (Peele and DeGrandpre 1998, p. 248), I described some prominent examples of Valium addicts, including an example of one TV personality who was addicted to both cocaine and valium, but whose valium addiction was far more severe.

Benzodiazepine and caffeine addictions are often faceless, since this drug use is so readily accepted in our society and all of us know many nonaddicted users.

Personal pleas for help describe individuals addicted and maintained by physicians, and a growing recognition by the patient that this use is harming them, and has become uncontrollable; the prescribing physician is generally unconscious of the problem or unresponsive.

The Case of Antidepressants

The NIDA seemingly has no interest in the prevalence of either the use or the abuse of the drug most often taken in the U.S.—outside of alcohol and various pain killers—for the explicit goal of changing mood, the antidepressants. Likewise, DSM IV (American Psychiatric Association 1995), lists virtually every type of substance, licit and illicit, which can be abused, but does not include antidepressants. Yet, antidepressants are the largest selling category (by dollar volume) of branded drugs in the U.S. (over $10 billion in 2000), including three of the top ten branded prescription drugs (National Institute for Health Care Management Foundation 2001, Tables 1 and 3).

When the top-selling category of prescriptions is a mood-modifying class of drug, one suspects there is much mood dysfunction in the country. One also wonders about the degree of legal dependence on the $10 billion worth of antidepressants sold. For example, in discussions of massive (legal) narcotics use in the nineteenth century, historical analysts are inclined to figure there was a much higher degree of addiction than recognized, since there was little reason for people to question their constant use of the drug, or to have to withdraw from the drug (Courtwright 1982).

For many, certainly the vast group of physicians in America who gladly prescribe antidepressants for a host of maladies, this class of drugs has no addictive liability. Antidepressants have been found to produce withdrawal, yet not to lead to the kind of intense craving and compulsive use seen with street users of cocaine and heroin (Haddad 1999). However, if dependence means coming to rely on a substance to produce essential feelings of well being, and that these feelings become harder to acquire without the assistance of the drug, the person having increasingly lost the ability to combat depression naturalistically, then antidepressants can readily be seen as addictive.

This kind of redefinition—or refocusing—of the meaning of addiction occurred in the 1980s with cocaine. Cocaine was originally excluded from pharmacology's "addiction" or "physical dependence" category because it rarely produced standard narcotics withdrawal symptoms and because patterns of cocaine use tend to occur in explosive bursts, compared with the more steady consumption of heroin and other drugs. In these regards, antidepressants more resemble narcotics than does cocaine. Pharmacologists came nonetheless to identify the need for and reliance on cocaine as addiction, and the drug as addictive. That is, after centuries of human cocaine use, a hundred years of medical usage with humans, and a half century of animal experimentation with cocaine, in the mid-1980s pharmacologists simply moved cocaine from the "nonaddictive" to the "addictive" drug column. (Peele 1998; Peele and DeGrandpre 1998).

The Recent History of Pharmaceutical Psychotherapeutic Addiction

Alongside the mainstream redefinition of cocaine as an illicit addictive drug has been a sub rosa process which has toyed with defining various pharmaceutical psychotherapeutic agents as addictive. This process began with the recognition of addiction to benzodiazepines. That is, in the late 1970s, several first-person best sellers—including Betty Ford's 1978 *The Times of My Life* and Barbara Gordon's 1979 *I'm Dancing as Fast as I Can*—gave personal accounts of severe cases of addiction to Valium. Although, as industry representatives asserted, such cases are rare, so too are cases of cocaine addiction (Peele and DeGrandpre 1998). It strikes most professionals as ludicrous to speak of tranquilizer and cocaine addiction in the same breath—despite cases like that of New York television newscaster Jim Jensen, who reported readily giving up a cocaine habit in treatment but being unable to shake his valium dependence: "Valium withdrawal soon plunged him into a massive depression that left him unable to eat or sleep. It took two more months in two hospitals for him to regain his mental and physical health" (Jensen 1989, p. 67).

But benzodiazepine addiction did become a medical concern—so much so as to influence prescription practices on a large scale. In particular, antidepressants are now the standard prescription for cases of anxiety where once benzodiazepines were routinely offered. Two competing views of this ongoing historical process are provided by letter writers to the "Ask Stanton" section of my Stanton Peele Addiction Website (http://www.peele.net).[4] One correspondent complained that I was insufficiently concerned about benzodiazepine addiction:

---

[4] By far the largest number of comments and questions concerning prescriptions at my web site are letters from individuals addicted to prescribed pain killers, or their spouses or loved ones, railing against the ignorance of the prescribing doctor while seeking help from a stranger on the Internet.

I was disappointed in your web site. I combed through it but not a word on the most harmful and troublesome drugs, benzodiazepines. It is well known that benzo withdrawal is as bad as heroin but more prolonged in about 40% of long term users. It is far worse than alcohol or tobacco withdrawal and yet no mention on your site? Now why might that be? I'd like to hear from you on this. In case you would like some information on it from the world's expert Heather Ashton who ran a benzo detox clinic for 12 years in London, here is her manual. (Ashton 2001)

Another writer had an extremely negative reaction to this view—although the second writer acknowledged Valium was addictive, she regretted its replacement by antidepressants:

I am annoyed at your reply to the Valium writer. Benzos are the only drugs that make me feel normal. But it's such trouble getting doctors to prescribe them because so many people, like the idiot who commented about Valium, make it seems so horrible. Benzos DO cause physical addiction; but so what? If I am going to take a drug for anxiety for an extended period of time, I would pick Valium 100 times over Prozac, which completely destroys libido among other things.

I live in misery because doctors refuse to prescribe the only drugs that work for me and insist on giving me antidepressants that don't work and cause unpleasant side-effects. Weighing the addictiveness of benzodiazepines against living with chronic anxiety day in and day out should be my choice, not some doctor's. I'm all for drug legalization but I think the people who insist on medical marijuana or marijuana not being as bad as this drug or that legal drug, like benzos, are hypocrites. They also play right into anti-drug crusaders' hands by agreeing that these other drugs are indeed bad and should be illegal.

Welsh psychiatrist David Healy (2001) has most effectively addressed historic questions concerning addiction and psychiatric drugs—among other developments in psychopharmaceutics.[5]

---

[5] Healy is a provocative, lightning-rod figure, although in the British context he is a mainstream psychiatrist who regularly prescribes antidepressants. In 2000, as a respected researcher, writer, and clinician, Healy accepted a senior post at the Canadian Centre for Addiction and Mental Health (CAMH) and the Department of Psychiatry of the University of Toronto. However, before actually assuming the post, Healy (2000) lectured at CAMH on the history of psychiatric drugs. Healy's views—although well-known—seemed to shock his hosts, who rescinded the offer of a faculty position (Birmingham 2001). Healy and others have claimed that his critiques of psychopharmaceuticals offended Eli Lilly, manufacturer of Prozac and a major CAMH funder. Even if

By 1966, a large number of studies had confirmed . . . observations that there was a marked and severe physical dependence on antipsychotics that was present in large numbers of people taking them, even at low doses for a relatively short period of time. . . . This led to the concept of therapeutic drug dependence, a concept that blows a hole in most theories of addiction we have. These drugs produce no tolerance, no euphoria. They produce enduring post-discontinuation changes that are as extensive and long lasting as the changes underpinning current disease models of addiction (Healy and Tranter 1999; Tranter and Healy 1998). But recognition of antipsychotic dependence vanished around 1968, when the War on Drugs was declared.

Psychopharmacology was faced with a political problem. The problem was how to distinguish drugs which restored social order from drugs which subverted the social order. The 'decision' was made to categorise as problematic and dependence producing any drugs which subverted the social order. This political rather than scientific decision set up a crisis a few years later when physical dependence on the benzodiazepines emerged. This broadened to an extraordinary crisis, which led to the obliteration of the anxiolytics and indeed almost the whole concept of anxiolysis. By 1990, physicians in Britain and elsewhere regarded benzodiazepines as more addictive than heroin or cocaine—without any scientific evidence to underpin this perception. . . .

As the 1990s ended, dependence on the SSRIs appeared. Is another group of useful drugs going to be lost to us the way the benzodiazepine were lost? Do we understand enough about what happened to the benzodiazepines to be able to guarantee that the SSRIs will not suffer the same thing? Do we understand how the concept of dependence on antipsychotics could have vanished just at a time when a very obvious dependence syndrome—Tardive dyskinesia—was causing so much grief to the psychiatric and pharmaceutical establishments? If we don't understand what happened here, we can offer no guarantees for the future. . . . (Healy 2000)

This analysis is balanced—or divided—in that is seems to criticize both pharmaceutical companies for ignoring negative side effects of psychiatric drugs, and critics of these drugs for forcing their abandonment even though they have useful functions. Healy also notes an almost formal decision to restrict the concept of addiction to illicit or recreational drugs, while ruling out for this purpose pharmaceutical or therapeutic drugs.

Lilly did not directly axe Healy, Healy's social-historical views of psychiatry and his indifferent attitude towards drug companies (Healy regularly testifies at trials where Prozac is claimed to have caused suicides) put him at odds with North American psychiatry.

This redefinition is now in process with antidepressants. Recently the World Health Organization (WHO) warned of addiction risk for Prozac users (Prozac is the largest-selling single SSRI antidepressant). "Prozac, billed for years as a harmless wonder drug, often creates more problems than the depression it is supposed to be treating, warns the head of the World Health Organisation's unit monitoring drug side-effects. Professor Ralph Edwards says Prozac and drugs similar to it are overprescribed. A league table of withdrawal and dependency side-effects, published by the WHO, shows that drugs including Prozac and Seroxat have produced far more complaints from patients than old-fashioned tranquillisers prescribed by doctors in the 1970s." "World Health Watchdog Warns of Addiction Risk for Prozac Users" (Mendick 2001).

Groups have formed to support members in overcoming Prozac dependence and withdrawal.

> The experiences of Ramo Kabbani on Prozac prompted her to set up the Prozac Survivors Support Group. . . . .She began taking Prozac to combat depression after the death of her 27-year-old fiancée from a heart attack. "The medication stopped me working through the feelings of grief which had caused the depression." she says. "When I came off Prozac I became super-sensitive and very emotional. I found it worse going through withdrawal than going through the depression." (Mendick 2001)

A General Model of Addiction

OxyContin is not a pain reliever that accidentally causes addiction; it is a substance which serves addictive purposes because it offers relief from pain. Such relief is recognized only by some people, or by many people under extraordinary circumstances (for example the Vietnam War and civil wars in the United States, Lebanon, and Afghanistan). For these individuals, or in these circumstances, pain relief is highly desirable, and can be gained no other way. It is *not* true that OxyContin produces pain relief *and also* some kind of unrelated euphoria, as in the *New York Times Magazine*'s perception of the problem:

> Purdue's scientists are looking for. . .a 'holy grail,' a drug that will activate the receptors in the brain that control pain relief and leave alone those that control euphoria. And this isn't a new initiative, it turns out, but one that the company has been working on for many years. Scientists and doctors as far back as Hippocrates have tried to find a way to separate the benefits of opiates from their dangers. (Tough 2001, p. 63)

Addiction is, rather, a direct wedding of an individual's needs in a specific situation with the characteristics of the experience he or she derives from an involvement or chemical—an experience determined by a combination of pharmacological effects and social-cultural learning (Peele 1995; 1998). We can create the following list of five general rules of addiction with special reference to pharmaceuticals.

1. People become directly addicted to the experiential effects of a drug or involvement.

2. The more successful and direct at causing such experiential effects (that is, the more powerful or efficient), the more addictive a substance will be.

3. The two largest categories of experience linked to addiction (neither of which is "pleasure" *per se*) are analgesia (pain relief, CNS depressive action) and *remedial* stimulation and/or mood elevation (that is, antidepressant).

4. Pain relief and remedial mood elevation are two recognized, accepted, and primary goals of pharmaceutical medication.

5. The economics of the pharmaceutical industry will contribute to a never-ending escalation of pharmaceutical addiction.

As pharmaceutical providers improve by intensifying their pain-relief pharmacopoeia, supposedly with the goal or reducing or eliminating addiction, rather than reducing addiction, they will increase it. As the *Times* correctly deduced through its tortured logic, "Opioids, including OxyContin, may remain the double-edged sword they have always been" (Tough 2001, p. 63). What implications does this have when combined with the *Times*'s—reflecting the larger culture's—belief that addiction is a direct and unswervable consequence of the use of such potent substances? It means more drug scares, as is traditional with the *Times*, gradual normalization of each new pain relief substance introduced into the culture, and an America—and increasingly, world—hooked on the horns of the addictive dilemma.

REFERENCES

American Psychiatric Association. 1995. *Diagnostic and Statistical Manual of Mental Disorders*. Fourth edition. Washington, D.C.: American Psychiatric Press.

Ashton, C.H. 2001. Protocol for Treatment of Benzodiazepine Withdrawal. Newcastle upon Tyne, U.K.: University of Newcastle, School of Neurosciences, Division of Psychiatry; http://members.dencity.com/ashtonpapers/.

Associated Press. 1997. Flowers Cover Elvis Presley's Grave on 20th Anniversary of His Death. *Boston Globe Online* (17th August); http://www.boston.com/globe/nation/packages/elvis/.

Birmingham, K. 2001. Dark Clouds over Toronto Psychiatry Research. *Nature Medicine* (June), p. 643.

Brown, P.H., and P.H. Broeske. 1997. *Down at the End of Lonely Street: The Life and Death of Elvis Presley*. New York: Dutton.

Buser, L. Death. 1977. Captures Crown of Rock and Roll—Elvis Dies Apparently after Heart Attack; http://www.gomemphis.com/elvis/presley/stories/elvis1.shtml (17th August).

Chadwick, V. 1998. TIME Visits the Fourth Annual Conference on Elvis Presley; http://www.time.com/time/community/transcripts/chattr081198.html (11th August).

Courtwright, D. 1982. *Dark Paradise: Opiate Addiction in America before 1940*. Cambridge, Massachusetts: Harvard University Press.

Eddy, N.B. 1958. The Search for a Non-addicting Analgesic. In R.B. Livingston, ed., *Narcotic Drug Addiction Problems* (Bethesda: Public Health Service).

Haddad, P. 1999. Do Antidepressants Have Any Potential to Cause Addiction? *Journal of Psychopharmacology 13*, pp. 300–07.

Healy, D. 2000. Psychopharmacology and the Government of the Self. Symposium, Centre for Addiction and Mental Health, Toronto, Canada, November 30th; http://www.nature.com/nm/voting/lecture.html

———. 2001. *The Creation of Psychopharmacology*. Cambridge, Massachusetts: Harvard University Press.

Healy, D., and R. Tranter. 1999. Pharmacologic Stress Diathesis Syndromes. *Journal of Psychopharmacology* 13, pp. 287–299.

Jensen, J. 1989. A Veteran TV Anchorman's Toughest Story Was His Own—He Had to Beat Drugs and Depression. *People* (4th September), pp. 67–73.

Kalb, C. 2001a. Painkiller Crackdown. *Newsweek* (May 14th), p. 38.

———. 2001b Playing with Painkillers. *Newsweek* (9th April), p. 44.

Mendick, R. 2001. World health watchdog warns of addiction risk for Prozac users. *Independent* (29th April); http://news.independent.co.uk/uk/health/story.jsp?story=69366

National Institute on Drug Abuse. 2000. *National Trends: Emerging Drugs*. http://www.nida.nih.gov/Infofax/nationtrends.html.

National Institute for Health Care Management Foundation. 2001. *Prescription Drug Expenditures in 2000: The Upward Trend Continues.* Washington, D.C.: NIHCM Foundation; http://www.nihcm.org.

Peele, S. 1995. *Diseasing of America.* Second edition. San Francisco: Jossey-Bass.

———. Peele, S. 1998. *The Meaning of Addiction.* Second edition. San Francisco: Jossey-Bass.

Peele, S., with A. Brodsky. 1975. *Love and Addiction.* New York: Taplinger.

Peele, S., and R. DeGrandpre. 1998. Cocaine and the Concept of Addiction: Environmental Factors in Drug Compulsions. *Addiction Research 6*, pp. 235–263.

Rohter, L., and T. Zito. 1977. Rock Idol Elvis Presley Dies at 42. *Washington Post* (17th August), p. 1.

Substance Abuse and Mental Health Administration. 2001. *National Household Survey on Drug Abuse*; http://www.samhsa.gov/hhsurvey/hhsurvey.html.

Thompson, C.C., II, and J.P. Cole. 1991. *The Death of Elvis: What Really Happened.* New York: Delacorte.

Tough, P. 2001. The Alchemy of OxyContin. *New York Times Magazine* (29th July), pp. 32–37, 52, 62–63.

Tranter, R., and D. Healy. 1998. Neuroleptic Discontinuation Syndromes. *Journal of Psychopharmacology 12*, pp. 306-311.

U.S. Pharmaceutical Industry. 2000. *20 Leading Product Categories for 1999, Ranked by Prescriptions Dispensed*; http://www.idleb.com/pharmacy-top1001999.html.

Reply to Peele

THOMAS SZASZ

Peele lavishes praise on me for my labors in the cause of liberty, but does not discuss my views on addiction, drugs, and drug policy. He neither refers to nor cites *Ceremonial Chemistry* or *Our Right to Drugs* or my many articles on the subject. In so far as he refers to my views on addiction, he attributes views to me that I have never expressed and do not hold.

For example, Peele writes: "Szasz is too accepting of medical illness and treatment . . . as not much affected by history and culture." The opposite is the case. He characterizes me as a "denier of categories." Again, the opposite is the case. I insist that the category called "disease" be defined precisely and objectively. How could I be a denier of categories and be famous or infamous for insisting that addiction does not belong in the same category as arteriosclerosis?

When Peele writes that "Szasz really shows little concern for escaping addiction," he betrays an utter incomprehension of my contention that addiction is an abstract noun that cannot, literally, imprison a person. Only another person can do that. An individual who, acting on his own behalf, imprisons a person is a criminal. Conversely, an individual who, acting as an agent of the state, imprisons a person is carrying out his duty as a member of the government's law enforcement system. Addiction to drugs is a condition that the addict brings about by his own free will and from which he can "escape" by his own free will, with or without the aid of others.

In short, Peele sees the addict as a helpless victim. I see him as a capable moral agent, sometimes doing and enjoying what he wants to do and annoying others in the process; and sometimes victimizing himself or others by his behavior. "Szasz," writes Peele, "can be clueless when confronted with real human compulsion and emotional despair." How does Peele know this? What is his evidence? "People roam the streets babbling to themselves, commit suicide, and are lost in delusion and despair. Many of them can benefit from some kind of help . . ." Does Peele believe that I oppose *helping* poor people or people who suffer from despair or disease? Or does he play the liberal-psychiatric game, equating helping people with coercing them, casting those who oppose forced "treatment" as the enemies of human dignity and "true freedom"?

People, explains Peele, "experience themselves to be in the grip of addiction and mental illness, and the reality of that experience must be recognized." I recognize that reality. But I ask: If people *suffer* from addiction and mental illness, why don't they seek treatment for these alleged diseases? Addicts spend money, sometimes a lot of money, on drugs. Why don't they spend money on drug addiction treatment?

The examples of addicts Peele cites support my views, not his: "[Elvis] Presley never considered himself a drug abuser. Quite the contrary." Why not? Because he regarded taking drugs as something he liked to do, just as Peele regards playing golf or whatever he does for enjoyment as something he likes to do. How does Peele propose to help someone like Presley? Peele doesn't say.

Enough said. Peele devotes the body of his essay to presenting his own perspective on drug addiction and its "treatment." Since Peele never suggests that addicts who ostensibly suffer from addiction should pay for their treatment—or should seek treatment and provide something of value for the help they receive as an expression of their appreciation for it—it is reasonable to conclude that his true but covert agenda is a plea for expansive and expensive taxpayer-funded "drug treatment programs." Peele plays an active role in the drug abuse industry: he supports the "reality" of drug addiction as a disease and the "need" for its treatment at public expense.

But what is "drug abuse treatment"? It is government-mandated transfer of money from productive persons in the private sector to unproductive persons in the public sector, some called "addicts," others called "drug counselors" and "mental health professionals": the "addicts" receive group therapy and prescriptions for habit-forming drugs and money for their bad habit legitimized as a "no-fault mental illness" and "medical disability"; the "drug counselors" receive prestige as professionals who "treat" the nonexistent disease called "addiction" and get paid by the government for this so-called "service."

6

The Legitimacy of the Defense of Insanity

RITA J. SIMON

Thomas Szasz argues that the insane are no different from anybody else and cannot be separated out from the rest of society. He maintains that it is absurd to assume "that just as human beings can be divided into two classes by gender, one male and the other female, they can be divided into classes of psychiatric criteria, one sane, the other insane."[1]

Barbara Wootin shares Szasz's view and also claims that "the distinction between illness and evil is anything but clear cut. In her view tests that claim to separate illness and evil create a false dichotomy between the responsible and the non-responsible."[2]

Szasz also maintains that the assignment of the label "mad" to the criminal offender robs him of his human dignity. He believes that the criminal justice system should regard all offenders as responsible human beings capable of appreciating and controlling their own actions. In the same view Szasz points out that persons who are exonerated of their crimes by reason of insanity face a harsher penalty than if they had been judged sane, because then, at least, their humanity would have been acknowledged. An example of Szasz's position may be observed in testimony he gave at a trial of a young woman accused of infanticide.

---

[1] Thomas Szasz, *Law, Liberty and Psychiatry* (New York: Collier, 1963), p. 136.
[2] Barbara Wootin, as cited by Alexander Brooks, *Law, Psychiatry, and the Mental Health System* (Boston: Little Brown, 1974), p. 226.

Without having examined the defendant, Szasz testified that she was "simply stupid, evil and bad, not insane."[3]

This writer disagrees with Szasz's position. She believes that the underlying premise of our criminal law is that a person's conduct must generally be in accordance with the acceptable range of norms of conduct adopted by society. An underlying assumption is that a person in the exercise of free will should be held accountable, because individuals do in fact have at least a minimum capacity for making the voluntary and rational choices required for criminal responsibility. Thus, the ordinary criminal defendant is viewed as "culpable" or "blameworthy" or "responsible," because that person could have chosen to abide by the dictates of the law. But there are a few individuals who cannot be held accountable. A mental disability or disease deprives them of even the minimal capacity for rational and voluntary choices on which the law's expectation of responsibility is predicated. Because of their incapacity to comply with the law, such persons are not held culpable, nor are criminal sanctions invoked or applied consequent to their conduct.

The insanity defense, therefore, is the exception that "proves" the rule of free will. Supporters of the insanity defense view it as vital to a healthy society, which uses its criminal law to build and buttress self-reliant action on the part of its citizens. Throughout history, it is this vision of law that has rallied supporters to resist efforts to abolish the insanity defense. Eliminating the insanity defense would remove from criminal law and public conscience the vitally important distinction between "illness" and "evil." There is a deeply entrenched human feeling, as old as recorded history, that persons who are grossly disturbed (whether called "madmen," "lunatics," "insane," or "mentally disordered") should not be punished as ordinary criminals would be.

For these few who cannot be held accountable because of mental disability or disease, social control may be best served by confinement in a secure hospital setting especially in the case of those who are dangerously insane. Similarly, the general deterrence theory underlying punishment is that a person's awareness and fear of unpleasant consequences will restrain him or her from engaging in criminal behavior. But this is effective only with persons who can understand the significance of sanctions imposed on violators. Thus, punishment is not likely to deter seriously disturbed individuals from future antisocial conduct.

---

[3] T.L. Clanon, Louis Shauver, and Douglas Kurdys, "Less Insanity in the Courts," *American Bar Association Journal* 68 (1982), p. 825.

Also, the insanity defense is consistent with the notion of specific deterrence or restraint. If the defense is successfully invoked, the defendant is not merely incarcerated for a fixed period of time, but, instead, can or should be committed until such time as he or she is no longer dangerous.

Although the insanity defense is introduced in less then two percent of all criminal trials, it is one of the most controversial and hotly debated issues in American and British criminal law. Professor Francis Allen said of it, "The issue of criminal responsibility has attracted more attention and stimulated more controversy than any other question in the substantive criminal law."[4]

I conclude with the following quotation from Professor Alan Stone because it captures my views on the insanity defense and in so doing defines my disagreement with Professor Szasz's position:

> The insanity defense touches on ultimate social values and beliefs. It purports to draw a line between those who are morally responsible and those who are not, those who are blameworthy and those who are not, those who have free will and those who do not, those who should be punished and those who should not and those who can be deterred and those who cannot.[5]

---

[4] Francis Allen, *The Borderline of Criminal Justice* (Chicago: University of Chicago Press, 1964), p. 105.

[5] Alan Stone, *Mental Health and Law: A System in Transition* (Rockville: N.I.H.M., 1975). D.H.E.W. Pub. No. (A.D.M.), p. 218.

Reply to Simon

THOMAS SZASZ

I

It distresses me to have to respond to an essay so inadequately prepared and so full of factual inaccuracies as Rita Simon's "The Legitimacy of the Defense of Insanity." I will repeat her principal assertions, in the order in which they appear, and add my rejoinder to each in turn. Then, I will present a precise account of the murder trial in which I appeared as an expert witness for the prosecution to which Simon refers.

II

> Thomas Szasz argues that the insane are no different from anybody else and cannot be separated out from the rest of society. He maintains that it is absurd to assume "that just as human beings can be divided into two classes by gender, one male and the other female, they can be divided into classes of psychiatric criteria, one sane, the other insane."

Nowhere do I assert "that the insane are no different from anybody else and cannot be separated out from the rest of society." I am perfectly capable of telling the differences between, say, unhappy (depressed) persons and happy (not depressed) persons. I use a declarative sentence to do the work of an injunctive one. Simon knows this: her sentence about separating human beings into two classes is recycled from her book, *The Insanity Defense* (co-authored with David E. Aaronson), where she adds: "Most abolitionists believe that the distinction between the mad and bad *should not* be made" (emphasis in the original).[1] Simon omits this sentence from her essay.

---

[1] Rita J. Simon and David E. Aaronson, *The Insanity Defense: A Critical Assessment of Law and Policy in the Post-Hinckley Era* (New York: Praeger, 1988), p. 174.

> Barbara Wootin shares Szasz's view . . .

There is no "Barbara Wootin." Lady Barbara Wootton was a distinguished English jurist and criminologist. Evidently, Simon has not studied Wootton either and relied on a secondary source.

> Szasz points out that persons who are exonerated of their crimes by reason of insanity face a harsher penalty than if they had been judged sane . . .

Simon lets my statement stand without comment, as if it needed or deserved neither agreement nor refutation. Does Simon doubt the validity of my assertion, or does she agree with it?

I regard an institution in which an individual is incarcerated, often for decades or for life, as a prison, even if it is called a "hospital setting." Simon does not address this issue. She does not question that psychiatric incarceration is "hospitalization."

In the Foreword to Simon's book, *The Insanity Defense*, Judge Barrington D. Parker, United States District Court for the District of Columbia, states: "Moreover, commitments following an insanity plea do not necessarily, and as a matter of course, result in early release. Rather, such a defendant may likely be incarcerated for as long a period, if not more, in a mental institution as he would be sentenced to a penal institution, without benefit of an insanity plea."[2] Simon approves of this method of managing criminals declared insane by psychiatrists: "For these few . . . [individuals who cannot be held accountable] social control may be best served by confinement in a secure *hospital* setting . . ."[3]

If such detention is morally wrong, it is wrong even for a single individual. Moreover, we are not talking about a "few individuals." We are talking about many individuals and a social policy formally sanctioned by the Supreme Court, which has held that the Due Process Clause of the Fourteenth Amendment permits involuntary commitment of an insanity acquittee for a period "longer than the acquittee might have served in prison."[4]

---

[2] Barrington D. Parker, "Foreword," in Simon and Aaronson, *The Insanity Defense*, p. ix.
[3] Emphasis added.
[4] Michael Edmund O'Neill, "Stalking the Mark of Cain," *Harvard Journal of Law and Public Policy* 25 (Fall 2001), pp. 31–60, p. 53; *Jones v. United States*, 463 U.S. 354 (1993), p. 369.

That is not all. Today, not only are many persons acquitted (by reason of insanity) deprived of liberty for longer periods than if they had been convicted, many persons who have completed their prison sentences for their crimes are re-imprisoned on the pretext that their new imprisonment is "treatment for mental illness." In 1997, the Supreme Court ruled that "a state may civilly commit a sexually violent predator even after he has served a criminal sentence because of the likelihood that he will engage in further dangerous behavior."[5] The Court's decision reflected the belief of legislators that psychiatrists could predict future dangerousness.[6]

Since involuntary mental hospitalization is a form of imprisonment, the term "insanity defense" is, more often than not, a misnomer. It ought to be called *insanity accusation*. For example, John W. Hinckley, Jr. wanted to plead guilty; the insanity plea was imposed on him against his will. Simon ignores this aspect of the insanity defense. She also ignores the closely related legal-psychiatric tactic, namely, declaring the defendant unfit for trial because of mental illness and incarcerating him in a madhouse, for years or decades. Such was the fate of Ezra Pound and tens of thousands of other unwanted Americans.[7]

> An example of Szasz's position may be observed in testimony he gave at a trial of a young woman accused of infanticide. *Without having examined the defendant*, Szasz testified that she was "simply stupid, evil and bad, not insane" (emphasis mine).

Simon is referring to my testimony in the 1980 trial of Darlin June Cromer—a thirty-four-year-old woman and self-declared white supremacist—who lured a five-year-old boy into her car, strangled him, buried his body, and, after being arrested, boasted about her deed. The charge against Cromer was first-degree murder, not infanticide. Once again, Simon's source is secondary. She had access to a complete transcript of my testimony in court, published in a psychiatric journal.[8] Because of the importance of this trial, I a summarize the story in the second part of my reply.

---

[5] Michael Edmund O'Neill, "Stalking the Mark of Cain," *op. cit.*, p. 54.

[6] *Kansas v. Hendricks*, 521 U.S. 346, 1997.

[7] See Thomas Szasz, *Psychiatric Justice*, with a new preface (Syracuse: Syracuse University Press, 1988 [1965]).

[8] "The Psychiatrist in Court: People of the State of California v. Darlin June Cromer," *American Journal of Forensic Psychiatry* 3 (1982), pp. 5–46.

Instead of familiarizing herself with the facts about this sensational trial, which was widely reported in the press, Simon relies on a paper written by three mental-health professionals bitterly opposed to my views.[9] The senior author, T.L. Clanon, was a former superintendent of the California Medical Facility at Vacaville, a euphemism for institutions for the criminally insane. The second author, Lois Shawver, was a clinical psychologist on the Vacaville staff. The third author, Douglas Kurdys, was a lawyer and a doctoral candidate in clinical psychology at the California School of Professional Psychology. The affiliation of the first two authors identifies them as professional advocates and defenders of psychiatric slavery.[10] These authors slandered me with the claim that I failed to examine a "patient" and then testified about her in court, a charge Simon copied from their paper. As I show below, what Simon describes as my failure to examine a defendant was a deliberate decision, an integral part of the prosecution's strategy, not a "failure to examine a 'patient.'"

> This writer disagrees with Szasz's position. She believes that the underlying premise of our criminal law is that a person's conduct must generally be in accordance with the acceptable range of norms of conduct adopted by society.

The second sentence suggests that I *do not* believe that people should obey the law and am advocating licentious behavior. Nothing could be further from the truth. With that awkwardly phrased sentence, Simon manages to obscure and elide a crucial element of Anglo-American law, namely, that the state can use the criminal law to punish only individuals who have broken the law; it cannot use the criminal law to punish individuals for *ideas* or *inclinations*. That is why the criminal law, often correctly characterized as a "blunt instrument," is supplemented by mental health laws, used to punish "dangerousness to self or others." Mental health law permits, indeed mandates, precisely the kind of preventive detention—as "psychiatric diagnosis, evaluation, and treatment"—that the criminal law forbids.

> The insanity defense touches on ultimate social values and beliefs. It *purports* to draw a line between those who are morally responsible and those who are not . . . (my emphasis).

---

[9] T.L. Clanon, Lois Shawver, and Douglas Kurdys, "Less Insanity in the Courts," *American Bar Association Journal* (July, 1982), pp. 824ff.

[10] Thomas Szasz, *Liberation By Oppression: A Comparative Study of Slavery and Psychiatry* (New Brunswick: Transaction, 2002).

All laws rest ultimately on popular beliefs. This was true for laws sanctioning slavery to laws prohibiting drinking beer and is true today for laws prohibiting the possession of marijuana. Sharing a popular belief does not constitute a refutation of a critic's condemnation, as *unjust*, of social policies based on the belief.

The insanity defense rests on the popular belief that mental illness exists, that some criminals are crazy, and that psychiatrists possess scientific expertise to draw the line between sane and insane lawbreakers. Yet a careful reading of Simon's carelessly chosen, but revealing, words shows that she doesn't believe a word of it. Let me repeat. She writes that "It [the insanity defense] *purports* to draw a line" between who are morally responsible and those who are not," that is, between mentally healthy (sane) and mentally ill (insane) criminals.

The synonyms in *Webster's* for "purported" are "reputed" and "rumored," illustrated with the example: "reputedly foreign spies." However, Simon's thesis is that drawing such a line is a matter of asserting facts, not purporting claims. We do not speak about hematologists purportedly drawing a line between persons who have sickle cell anemia and those who do not, or specialists in tropical diseases purportedly drawing a line between persons who have malaria and those who do not.

III

In part, Simon rests her critique of my views regarding the insanity defense on a slanderous accusation against me that my critics love to cite. In the past, I have made no attempt to answer such charges based on factual misstatements, lest my antagonists interpret it—in characteristically psychiatric style—as a "denial" that only proves the validity of their contentions. Simon's shameless recitation of one of these slanders, in this particular volume, makes this an appropriate occasion to break my self-imposed silence and set the record straight.

* * *

In November 1980, a thirty-four-year-old woman, named Darlin June Cromer, was tried in Oakland, California, for the kidnapping and murder of a five-year-old boy. The charged was "first-degree murder with aggravating circumstances," the aggravating circumstances being racial motives for the killing. Cromer pleaded not guilty by reason of insanity.[11]

---

[11] "The Psychiatrist in Court."

The facts about the case were not in dispute. On February 5th, 1980, Reginald Williams, a black boy, was abducted from a supermarket. Suspicion quickly pointed to Cromer, known for previous attempts to lure black children into her car, making comments about "killing niggers," and for her "strange" behavior. When the police visited Cromer, she eagerly confessed to luring Reginald into her car, strangling him, and burying his body in a shallow grave on the grounds of a water treatment plant near her home.

Who was Darlin June Cromer? She was a thirty-four-year-old white woman who spent her entire adult life as a card-carrying mental patient. Diagnosed "schizophrenic" decades earlier, she was in and out of "treatment facilities." In 1980, she was also on probation for having assaulted a Chinese woman in San Francisco in 1977.

At the trial, three young black children gave vivid testimony about how, the day Williams was killed as well as the day before, Cromer tried to entice them into her car. Two refused. One, Steven Willis, accepted Cromer's offer to drive him to his school, but saved himself. "After the car passed his school and stopped at an intersection, Willis jumped out and ran several blocks to his school, and told a teacher what had happened."[12]

The prosecution argued that Cromer's motive, as she herself claimed, was racial hatred. Assistant Public Defender Dean Beaupre, disagreed. He stated: "There is no question that the defendant did kill this little boy on February 5th, 1980. . . . However, this case does not involve racism, it involves insanity. The defendant *is* insane."[13]

This was patently false. If Cromer had been legally insane when Beaupre uttered these words, she would not have been on trial, because the judge would have declared her mentally incompetent to stand trial. What Beaupre was saying, and what four of the most eminent forensic psychiatrists in California were saying in their testimony, was that Cromer was insane in February, some eleven months earlier. Not having known Cromer then, they could not possibly have known what her mental state was. This contention became the focus of my testimony. But I am getting ahead of the story, which was tragic, yet fascinating.

What evidence did the prosecution have for maintaining that Cromer's act was not "meaningless"—as newspapers like to describe the

---

[12] Ann Bancroft, "Darlin June Cromer: 3 Children Testify at Murder Trial," *San Francisco Chronicle* (2nd December, 1980).
[13] *Ibid.*, emphasis added.

reasons why "mental patients" kill—but was a motivated, goal-directed act? Here is some of the evidence:

> In the third day of the trial, a deputy sheriff recounted a free-swinging jail-house conversation she had with Cromer only hours after Cromer's arrest for the murder of Reginald Williams . . . Deputy Dorothy Soto said Cromer "wanted to talk about niggers," and even though Soto didn't encourage her, began a long, rambling diatribe against blacks. Soto, who wrote it all down later, read her recollections to the jury yesterday. She said Cromer sat on a table, talking lucidly. "It is the duty of every white woman to kill a nigger child," Soto quoted Cramer. "I've already killed mine." She said Cromer urged her to kill a black herself.[14]

Not surprisingly, Beaupre didn't put his client on the stand, to reject these charges. Instead, he explained that "his client killed because she is consumed by schizophrenic paranoia—not hate for blacks."[15]

A jail psychologist testified that Cromer told him "she thought the killing of a black child from Alameda would cause a 'snowball' effect in reaction to 'blacks taking over.'"[16]

On February 23rd, 1981, *Newsweek* ran a feature article on the trial. The reporters characterized Cromer as a "twisted woman," and stated that her attorney, Dean Beaupre, argued that his client was an "acute schizophrenic" who should be acquitted because she was insane.

> "That boy [he told the jury] died because Ms. Cromer was about as psychotic as she could be." . . . Stanford Professor Donald Lunde described her belief that blacks were like animals, meant to be eaten. "If she isn't crazy," he concluded, "who is?" . . . Prosecutor Albert Meloling . . . tried to make light of what he called "the mystic knights of psychiatry." He imported his own gladiator, maverick psychiatrist and professional debunker Thomas Szasz, who contended that the defendant was "suffering from the consequences of having lived a life badly, stupidly, evilly from the time of her teens."[17]

---

[14] Peter Kuehl, "Tale of Racial Hate in Bay Murder Trial," *San Francisco Chronicle* (4th December, 1980).
[15] *Ibid.*
[16] "Jail Psychologist Testifies in Trial of Alameda Black Child's Slayer," *San Francisco Chronicle* (12th December, 1980).
[17] Aric Press and Pamela Abramson, "A Law for Racist Killers," *Newsweek* (23rd February, 1981), pp. 80–81.

On January 17th, 1981, the jury found Darlin June Cromer guilty of first-degree murder because "she knew what she was doing." She was sentenced to life imprisonment without parole.

Different observers drew different conclusions from this outcome. Dean Beaupre maintained that Cromer was so insane "that she thought she was committing a 'positive act' when she killed the boy." Albert Meloling, "noting that the jury returned its verdict in a relatively short time, said, 'It's obvious that these jurors are saying psychiatrists do not belong in the court room.'"[18] *Newsweek* conceded that the verdict "will serve one useful purpose: it will keep Darlin June Cromer off the streets for the rest of her life."[19]

*   *   *

How did I get involved in the Cromer case? Beginning in the middle 1950s, I began to write critical essays about the role of psychiatry in law. In 1963, *Law, Liberty, and Psychiatry* was published. It was widely and favorably reviewed and became required reading in many law schools. In 1965, *Psychiatric Justice* was published. I continued to publish widely in law review journals. Thus, I became known in legal circles as a psychiatrist with a principled opposition against both civil commitment and the insanity defense.

In the 1960s, I testified in court—in a few cases, probably no more than two or three times—on behalf of persons incarcerated in mental hospitals trying to regain their liberty. (My testimony in one of these cases, together with my publishing *The Myth of Mental Illness* in 1961, played important roles in the concerted but ultimately unsuccessful effort, by highly placed psychiatrists, to remove me from my tenured professorship.)

In a few other cases, I testified—again probably no more than two or three times—in support of prosecutors who wanted to rebut the plea of "not guilty by reason of insanity." In most such cases, exemplified by the trial of John W. Hinckley, Jr., the prosecutor in effect colludes with the defense, both parties satisfied with having the defendant incarcerated as insane.

Albert Meloling was not such a prosecutor. He was personally incensed by the deliberate, carefully planned, racially motivated murder of a black boy, especially since the crime was committed in the largely black

---

[18] Don Martinez, "Jury Finds Cromer Guilty of Killing Boy," *San Francisco Chronicle* (18th January, 1981).

[19] Press and Abramson, *ibid.*

city of Oakland, California. Meloling was familiar with my views and contacted me. I agreed to testify, provided he was willing to meet one condition: I would not participate in the charade of "examining the patient." Let me briefly explain why I regard this non-participation—which my critics interpret as medical incompetence and irresponsibility or worse—as crucially important for me, both morally and scientifically.

When a defendant pleads insanity to a charge of murder and when the fact that he committed the murder is not contested, the psychiatric expert is expected to testify about the "mental state" of the defendant not at the time of the examination but at the time when the defendant committed the crime—typically many months before the "examination." In the Cromer case, the interval between the crime and the defense psychiatrists' examination of the defendant was at least ten months.

Psychiatrists regard this practice as objective and scientific, and courts and society accept it as similar to expert testimony given by other medical specialists, for example forensic pathologists. I regard the practice as the epitome of junk science and refuse to participate in it. In the first place, there is no objective test for mental illness, as there is for melanoma or pneumonia. What psychiatrists pretentiously call an "examination" is a conversation with the subject and observation of his behavior. The psychiatrist's conclusion is his opinion about the subject's mental state, at the time of the examination. The claim that a psychiatrist is able to determine the mental state of a defendant, say, on January 15th, whom he first encounters and examines, say, on November 15th, is, in my view, *prima facie* absurd. However, our legal-psychiatric system accepts this fiction as truth. Few people—and hardly any psychiatrists—are interested in questioning, much less rejecting, this charade. Thus, for the prosecutor determined to prevail against the insanity defense, the best tactic is to confront and unmask the defense psychiatrists as quacks, hired guns masquerading as "medical experts." (The prosecutor could also risk having a conventional psychiatrist testify for him, agree that the defendant was "psychotic," but try to convince the jury that he was nevertheless responsible for his criminal act.) Meloling agreed with my suggestion. He had no respect for the insanity defense and for the psychiatrists always ready to call criminals "crazy."

As will soon become apparent, my insistence on not examining the defendant and rejecting the option of offering another retroactive diagnosis, different from the diagnosis proferred by the defense experts, proved crucial in convincing every one of the twelve jurors that the defense psychiatrists were deceiving them. The day after the Cromer trial ended, *the San Francisco Chronicle* reported:

The last witness, called by the prosecution yesterday at a cost of $3,000 was an eminent New York psychiatrist who brought defense lawyers to the edges of their seats when he disputed the previous testimony of four defense experts. . . . Called on rebuttal, Dr. Szasz is author of seventeen books, a recognized authority on psychiatry and legal issues and a professor at the State University of New York. He based his testimony on a review of Cromer's extensive medical records. He added that it would not assist him to examine the defendant. When asked why by Meloling, Szasz said: "Because I could only determine [what] her mental state is now, not on the day of the murder. That is the nature of psychiatry." The long list of defense psychiatrists . . . offered a retroactive diagnosis that Cromer was suffering from psychotic delusions.[20]

I should add here that Meloling knew of me because of my behind the scenes participation in one of the most sensational trials of our times, the 1969 trial of Leslie van Houten, one of the Manson girls. Van Houten's lawyer called several psychiatrists to testify that she was patently crazy: she believed that Manson was god, carved a large X on her forehead, and committed brutalities that "no sane person could commit." The prosecutor solicited my help. I flew to Los Angeles, discussed the case with him, and suggested that he needed no psychiatric expert on his side at all. There was no need for him to put me on the stand. Instead, he could simply concentrate on undermining the credibility of the defense psychiatrists, expose them as quacks always ready to testify that the defendant is not responsible for his crimes and "needs treatment," and rely on the jury's common sense that our basic moral sense demands that such cold-blooded and brutal crimes ought to be punished, and not "excused" by psychiatrists. That is what happened. Leslie van Houten is still in prison. That is the context against which my testimony in the Cromer trial must be viewed.

*   *   *

For reasons I shall describe presently, in 1982 the *American Journal of Forensic Psychiatry* reprinted the verbatim transcript of my entire testimony in the Cromer trial. It begins with the so-called "Direct Examination." I am on the witness stand and the prosecutor, Albert Meloling, is asking me questions.

Q: Have you previously testified in the courts in this country on the subject of psychiatric conditions and responsibility?

---

[20] Martinez, *op. cit.*

A: Yes, I have, on a few occasions.

Q: Did you assist the District Attorney in Los Angeles County in the case involving one of the Manson Group, that is, the case involving Leslie van Houten?[21]

Like any good lawyer, Meloling asked his witness only questions to which he knew the answer. Note that he used the term "assist" instead of "testify." The defense objected to the question as "irrelevant," the judge sustained the objection, and I did not answer the question. After a brief "Voir Dire" examination by Dean Beaupre for the defense, Meloling resumed questioning me. After letting me answer questions about how I became familiar with the circumstances of the crime, he continued:

Q: Now you haven't examined the defendant, have you?

A: No, sir.

Q: Would it assist you in testifying to examine her now?

A: No, sir.

Q: You understand that what we are concerned with is her mental condition on February 5th of last year?

A: That is my understanding.

Q: Why would it not help you to examine her now to determine what her mental condition was on February 5th, last year?

A: Because I could only determine by examining her now what her mental condition is now.

Q: What is the reason for that?

A: That is the nature of a psychiatric examination. I don't know what her mental condition was six months ago. I wouldn't know what it would be six months from now.[22]

Note that this information—elicited from me by the prosecutor for whom I was testifying—was essential for showing the jury that the defense experts had no way of knowing what Cromer's mental condition was at the time of her offense. My fellow psychiatrists in the Cromer trial considered my behavior morally dishonorable medical malpractice in the courtroom. They regarded my acknowledging that I had not examined Cromer as an "admission of guilt" for a medical misdeed. I regarded it as

---

[21] "The Psychiatrist in Court," p. 6.

[22] *Ibid.*, p. 12.

an explanation of my reason for rejecting participation in the mendacious charade of psychiatric exculpatory testimony based on "examining" defendants months after the commission of a crime, for their mental state and "criminal responsibility" at the time of the crime.

Why, then, do psychiatrists and other supporters of psychiatric coercions and excuses continue to accuse me of "failure to examine the defendant" and define my behavior as an "admission" of a wrongdoing? Why does Simon repeat this canard? There are three possible answers. One is that my accusers are so convinced of their being in possession of the truth about mental illness that they are deaf to what I say. They simply do not "hear" what I am saying. Another possibility is that the critics seize on my deliberate departure from standard forensic-psychiatric practice as evidence, *ipso facto*, of psychiatric malfeasance. The third possibility is that they hear my message and understand it only too well, and believe that the best defense is an offense and, instead of engaging my argument, slander me.

After a series of other questions, Meloling asked:

Q: You said that the question of whether or not a person was suffering from schizophrenia is really not relevant to the question of whether or not they are responsible?

A: That is correct. . . . Schizophrenics can be and are responsible . . . it is now general practice not to lock them up. So they have all the rights and freedoms of you and me and, therefore, all the responsibilities of you and me to be held responsible for what they do.[23]

After a series of questions intended to clarify for the jury Cromer's reference to blacks as animals, and her wanting to eat her victim, Meloling asked:

Q: You said it is quite common in everyday language to call items by different names?

A: We all do that, all the time, sooner or later we call things by some figure of speech, some so-called metaphor, some other image. I mean if you don't like somebody, you say "You are a son of a bitch." We don't mean that literally he is the son of a bitch. We call somebody "The apple of my eye." We don't mean that you are an apple.

(*Laughter*)

---

[23] *Ibid.*, p. 14.

A: (*Continuing*) We say to our daughter, "You look so sweet, I can eat you up." That's a figure of speech. The fact that she [Cromer] may have said something like that, obviously she didn't eat the person, so a statement she was going to eat it becomes, in my opinion, an outright lie. If she wanted to eat the person, she had plenty of time to eat him.

(*Laughter*)

(*Continuing*) And when people use figures of speech, that becomes a matter of speech *for juries to determine, not for psychiatrists.*[24]

Meloling then turned to the issue of Cromer referring to blacks as animals, one psychiatrist claiming that "she was grossly delusional and that her believing things about blacks and Chinese far exceeds simple prejudice."

Q: . . . What is the difference between prejudice and a delusion? Is there a difference?
A: Yes. . . . But obviously this is an utterly subjective and politically and morally loaded question because the idea that blacks are not human or that Jews are not human or that non-Christians, for that matter, are not human, I mean this is what history has been all about, that people see other people as animals, and are ready to kill them. . . .[25]

At long last, Meloling asked the ritually required question of his expert.

Q. You have an opinion as to what Ms. Cromer was suffering from, if anything, on February 5th of this year?
A. Yes, I do.
Q. What is that opinion?
A. That opinion is that she was suffering from the consequences of having lived a life very badly, very stupidly. Very evilly; that from the time of her teens, for reasons which I don't know, she had, whatever she had done, she has done very badly. She was a bad student. There is no evidence that she was a particularly good daughter, sister. She was a bad wife. She was a bad mother. She was a bad employee insofar as she was employable. Then she

---

[24] *Ibid.*, pp. 18–19, emphasis added.
[25] *Ibid.*, p. 19.

started to engage [in taking] illegal drugs, then she escalated to illegal assault, and finally she committed this murder. . . . Life is a task. You either cope with it or it gets you . . . If you do not know how to build, you can always destroy. These are the people that destroy us in society, our society, and other people.[26]

Once again, I was questioned by Beaupre. He rejected my assertion about the validity of psychiatric diagnoses, and tried to discredit me and my testimony by establishing that I had not read all of the records pertaining to the case, and had been paid three thousand dollars for my work on the case, plus expenses. Meloling didn't let that go unchallenged.

> Q: Dr. Szasz, is a psychiatric diagnosis as accurate as a medical diagnosis?
> A: Not usually, no.
> Q: What is the reason for that?
> A: Medical diagnoses deal with objective and demonstrable lesions of the body, broken bones, diseased livers, kidneys, and so on. Psychiatric diagnoses deal with behaviors that human beings display, and they have to be interpreted in moral, cultural, and legal terms and, therefore, different interpreters will arrive at different judgments. . . . Homosexuality was recognized as a mental disease until a few years ago. And now it is no longer a mental disease. . . . but last year, smoking is a disease.
> Q: Smoking is now a psychiatric condition?
> A: Not condition, sir, a disease.
> Q: A disease?
> A: A disease. Since January 1980. So is gambling.
> Q: Pardon?
> A: Gambling is also a disease.
> Q: How do you treat that, that is, gambling, do you take away the money?
>
> (*Laughter*)

At this point, the judge was so amused by the absurd humor intrinsic to what psychiatrists call a disease, that he answered the question:

Court: You win.

(*Laughter*)

---

[26] *Ibid.*, pp. 20–21.

Witness: That's right. That's my recommendation also.

(*Laughter*)

Mr. Meloling: I have nothing further.[27]

I was questioned further by Beaupre, Meloling, and the judge, but the remarks I cited suffice to show that it was not a good day for the defense.

In 1989, the public defender's office appealed Cromer's conviction. "Deputy public defender Colleen Rohann said . . . Cromer had a twenty-year history of mental illness and belonged in a psychiatric institution, not a prison."[28] The appeal charged that "Albert Meloling had committed gross misconduct when he called defense psychiatrists 'con men' who were a 'social cancer in society that has to come out.' . . . Cromer had a nearly two-decade history of mental problems and four defense experts said she was insane."[29] The state Supreme Court refused to overturn the murder conviction.

*   *   *

As might be expected, my testimony enraged the local psychiatric community. Donald Lunde was one of the most famous and respected forensic psychiatrist in America. My contradicting his expert opinion was an impertinence. Cromer was a certified lunatic. Who could doubt that she was crazy and "belonged" in a mental hospital, not prison?

Psychiatrists are sore losers. After the trial, they had no trouble overturning the jury's verdict, in the court of expert psychiatric opinion, and, in effect, indicting me of psychiatric malpractice: I didn't "examine" the "patient," and perhaps worse still, I instilled humor into the proceedings.

Obviously, every trial—and surely every sensational murder trial—is theater, *par excellence*. It is not possible to understand or appreciate the play without seeing it performed or at least reading the text of it.

Apparently, Lunde viewed the Cromer trial as a duel in which I bested him by foul means. He wrote a letter to the editor of the *American Journal of Forensic Psychiatry*, suggesting publishing the transcript of my testimony, accompanied by critical comments by experts in forensic psychiatry. Entitled "The Psychiatrist in Court: People of the State of California v. Darlin June Cromer," this material was published in the

---

[27] *Ibid.*, pp. 26–27.

[28] Seth Rosenfeld, "Conviction of Child-killer Upheld: Woman Strangled Tot out of Racial Hatred," *San Francisco Examiner* (March 29th, 1990), p. A8.

[29] Nina Martin, "Conviction Challenged in 1981 Racial Slaying: Prosecutor Inflamed

American Journal of Forensic Psychiatry in 1982.[30] It is not possible to arrive at a judgment of this trial without reading this article. Yet it appears that neither Simon nor the authors of the source she cites read it.

The document runs to forty-one pages. I will try to summarize its highlights, in the order in which they appear. In his letter to Ed Miller, the editor of the journal, Lunde suggests that "a reviewer might address . . . the facts that: (1) Dr. Szasz admits [*sic*] that he never examined the defendant, yet renders an opinion about her. (2) Dr. Szasz admits [*sic*] that he did not review all her medical records, yet renders an opinion. (3) Dr. Szasz testifies as an expert in psychiatry that there is no such thing as mental disease."[31]

Note how naturally the language of the KGB agent comes to Lunde's lips. To say that a person "admits" X, implies that doing X is immoral, illegal, in a word, wrong. A person does not admit to doing good. We don't say that a person admits that he told the truth; we only say that he admits that he has lied.

I have commented already about why I regard "examining the defendant" in such cases and testifying under oath about his mental state many months or years earlier as scientifically contemptible and morally wicked. Regarding Lunde's second charge against me, it was noted that Cromer had been a mental patient for at least twenty years. Examining all of her records—assuming that all of them were available, which is doubtful—would probably have taken weeks. Lunde's third charge is, perhaps, the most telling: I am an expert in theology, yet say there is no God.

The forensic psychiatric establishment decided to rewrite the Cromer case, with the murderer cast as an innocent, sick patient, and me as a callous and irresponsible psychiatrist. After the transcript of my testimony, Selwyn M. Smith, M.D., Professor of Psychiatry and Psychiatrist-in-Chief at Royal Ottawa Hospital, offered this opinion:

> Dr. Thomas Szasz's views are well known . . . disagreements concerning [his] views have been well documents in the psychiatric literature. . . . The preparation by Dr. Szasz prior to giving testimony was in my opinion extremely superficial and contrary to acceptable standards of practice. . . . he came to court to testify and in many ways utilized the witness box as a forum for a presentation of his particular views. . . . This flippancy was

---

Jurors, Appeal Says," *San Francisco Examiner* (January 17th, 1990), p. A1.
[30] "The Psychiatrist in Court: People of the State of California v. Darlin June Cromer," *American Journal of Forensic Psychiatry* 3 (1982), pp. 5–46.
[31] *Ibid.*, p. 7.

compounded by his own statement that he saw no need to examine the defendant. Surely when requested to offer an opinion involving one's expertise as a physician and psychiatrist, one should indeed be prepared to examine the defendant . . . This is particularly true if one is being handsomely paid as was the situation here. I found Dr. Szasz's stance particularly troubling and certainly demeaning to the profession of medicine in general, and psychiatry in particular.[32]

As my testimony shows, I said nothing demeaning about medicine. To be sure, I said demeaning things about psychiatrists excusing the crimes of murderers by means of their expert testimony. That was the whole purpose of my testimony. Smith's comments—and the whole article on the Cromer trial—illustrate that psychiatrists, like inquisitors of yore, will not tolerate disagreement. If the person who disagrees with them is a mental patient, they punish him with more serious diagnoses and more destructive "treatments." If the person is a fellow professional testifying in a courtroom—where he is safe from the psychiatrists' direct retribution—they punish him by slander and declaring his conduct "unprofessional" and hence "harmful for patients."

"Dr. Szasz," Smith continued, "is a Professor of Psychiatry, and yet I found his comments pertaining to psychiatry in general and schizophrenia in particular, simplistic, unrealistic, and unscientific. . . . In my opinion, such comments were not helpful to the court. . . . His testimony in general exhibited a poor command of medical-legal principles and a callous disregard for an ill person."[33] Unwittingly, Smith here offers a typical example of psychiatric arrogance, indeed impertinence. A white person charged with the crime of the racially motivated murder of a black child is here transformed, by psychiatric fiat, into an "ill person," and I am slandered as showing "callous disregard" for the ill. A neat trick, if you can get away with it. Psychiatrists have gotten away with it for the better part of three hundred years, never more successfully than today.

The next contributor to this offensive against me was Joseph C. Finney, LL.B., M.D., Loyola University Medical Center, Maywood, Illinois. Before I turn to his critique, I want to say a few words about the charge that I had inappropriately injected humor into what ought to have been a somber proceeding. I am blessed with a good sense of humor and am quite capable, if I want to, of introducing witticism into virtually any verbal communication, spoken or written. However, in this case, laugh-

---

[32] *Ibid.*, pp. 35–36.
[33] *Ibid.*, p. 37.

ter in the courtroom began—as the transcript shows—not because I said something witty. Instead, it began when I described how psychiatrists make and unmake diagnoses of mental illnesses, citing smoking and gambling as newly minted dieases, and Meloling then asked: "How do you treat that, that is, gambling, do you take away of the money?" The judge then joined the laughter in the courtroom, answering Meloling's question: "Court: You win," which provoked more laughter. I then answered the question: "That's right. That's my recommendation also," and there was more laughter. Ridicule is, of course, the most effective response to pretentious nonsense. The psychiatrists were not amused.

Finney began his criticism of my testimony by psychoanalyzing me. "It may be," he explained, "that the nature of the Cromer crime—murder that was racially motivated, turned Dr. Szasz against the defendant as it turned the prosecutor and the jury. . . . This manifest content [of racial motivation] is irrelevant to the issue of the insanity plea, but it was not irrelevant to Dr. Szasz's willingness to testify. He specifically associated from killing blacks to killing people of his own ethnic group, thus identifying himself with the victim." At least now I know why I testified in this case. Finney probably never read a word I wrote and is unaware of my principled opposition against acquitting any defendant charged with murder on the ground of insanity. Equally clearly, Finney has managed to discredit me and my testimony with what must be one of the most subtle, yet perhaps most persuasive, anti-Semitic comments in contemporary American psychiatric literature.

Finney was a good choice as critical commentator. He did not like what I said and was happy to articulate all his objections. "I find it inappropriate, offensive, and alarming that Dr. Szasz testified that Dr. Lunde's testimony was not only false, but so false as to border on perjury. . . . I am appalled that he said such a thing."[34] Being appalled is not a substitute for showing how or why my claim is false that a psychiatric examination of Jones's mental state conducted in December cannot detect his mental state the previous February. I do not doubt that many psychiatrists believe they have such powers of divination. I don't see how this deprives a psychiatric skeptic of his right to characterize such testimony as "bordering on perjury."

Finney retried the Cromer case in his own mind and found her not guilty of murder: "I strongly suspect that under our laws, Mrs. Cromer was entitled to be found not guilty by reason of insanity. . . . I conclude that the defense attorney did not do a competent job in defending Mrs.

---

[34] *Ibid.*, p. 44.

Cromer . . . He did not cross-examine adequately. . . . I believe an appeal could be taken . . ."[35] An appeal was taken, as I noted earlier, but the verdict of the court was upheld.

A few years ago, when I had occasion to make a study of the life and work of Rudolf Virchow (1821–1902), I came across an episode in his life that closely resembles my refusal to examine Darlin June Cromer.

Virchow, the founder of modern pathology and scientific medicine, was nominally a Protestant, but actually an atheist. The publication of his *magnum opus*, *Cellular Pathology*, in 1858, quickly made him one of most famous medical scientists in the world. "I have dissected thousands of corpses," he declared, "but found no soul in any." He was in the habit of mockingly asking his students engaged in dissection: "Mr. Candidate, have you found a soul already?"[36]

In 1868, Virchow was asked to examine a "patient" and refused. I describe the circumstances and import of this episode in detail in *Pharmacracy*, from which I quote: "In 1868, a Belgian novitiate was supposed to have miraculously survived for three years with 'no sustenance except water and the communion host.' Asked by the Vatican to examine the woman and render an expert medical opinion about the claim, Virchow recognized that there was nothing to examine and refused."[37]

Virchow believed there was no soul that survives the body, or, if there is one, it is the concern of miraculous theology, not scientific medicine. He viewed the claim that a young woman lived for three years without food as, *prima facie*, absurd, if not a deliberate deception. Supposing he undertook to examine the woman in question: what was he supposed to look for?

I see my position regarding the "diagnosis" of mental illness in similar terms. I believe there is no mental illness. No medical examination can detect such a mythical disease. I regard the psychiatrist's claim that he can examine a cold-blooded murderer, detect that he suffered, when he committed the crime, from a mental illness (so severe that it annulled his guilt for his deed), and that his so testifying in court, under oath, is "scientific truth" as a false belief, if not a calculated lie. That the person who utters such an untruth sincerely believes that his lie

---

[35] *Ibid.*, pp. 45–46.
[36] http:// uni-wuerzburg.de/pathologie/virchow/v2/v2_kirche.htm. My translation.
[37] Szasz, *Pharmacracy: Medicine and Politics in America* (Westport: Praeger, 2001), p. 16.

serves the noble cause of "saving a life" does not alter the fact that it is a deliberate falsehood.

*   *   *

It is time now to say a few words about Simon's source for her slanderous attack on my views and behavior. As I noted, her source is a paper published in the *American Bar Association Journal* in 1982. The three authors of the article entitled "Less Insanity in the Courts" were T.L. Clanon, a psychiatrist in San Francisco and a former superintendent of the California Medical Facility at Vacaville, the name a euphemism for what used to be called institutions or hospitals for the criminally insane; Lois Shawver, a clinical psychologist also on the Vacaville staff; and Douglas Kurdys, a lawyer and a doctoral candidate in clinical psychology at the California School of Professional Psychology. The affiliation of the first two authors identifies them as professional advocates and defenders of psychiatric slavery.

The authors begin by asserting: "The present standards by which criminal defendants are considered not guilty by reason of insanity are unsatisfactory. . . . The public is dismayed by the battles of experts the present system produces . . ." However, today more than ever, psychiatrists insist that they are, first of all, physicians, and that mental illnesses are brain diseases. A battle of medical experts is standard practice in tort litigation in cases of medical negligence: neurologists battle other neurologists; pathologists, other pathologists; orthopedic surgeons, other orthopedic surgeons. Once again, the psychiatrists ask for special status, much as they ask and receive special status to incarcerate "patients" and treat them without their consent. "The present system," they state, "deals with the mentally ill in ways that . . . deny mentally ill offenders the opportunity for treatment." That is simply not true. Criminals suffering from diabetes or cancer receive treatment in prison hospitals or, if necessary, in hospitals; following the treatment, they go back to prison. If mental illnesses are like other illnesses, why should mentally ill persons who commit crimes not be punished and imprisoned, and treated in prison, provided they consent to treatment?

The authors then describe "three alternative pictures of criminal insanity": the first they call the "liberal picture of insanity"; the second, the "reactionary picture of insanity"; and the third, which they favor, the "clinical picture of insanity . . . [which] arises largely from our own vantage point and is shared by many others who treat mentally disordered offenders." To demonstrate the unsatisfactory character of present standards of insanity, they focus on the "reactionary picture" of it. They write:

This is an increasingly popular view. It prevailed, for example, in a recent California case, the murder trial of Darlin June Cromer. The defendant was portrayed by the defense in terms of the liberal picture of insanity. She had killed a child and the defense argued that she was innocent because she was insane. It would be hard to construct a case more tailored to the requirements of the liberal picture of insanity. The defendant had been hospitalized frequently for severe mental illness and was under continuous care for many years, and her crime was unquestionably authored by a severely disturbed mind.[38]

Clanon *et al.* have retried Cromer in their own heads and came up with the "right" verdict. Evidently, they are unhappy that no one at the trial was interested in their opinion, because they continue:

> But the prosecution got the jury to accept the reactionary picture of insanity. The psychiatrist for the prosecution, Thomas Szasz, who believes that mental illness should never be exculpating in a criminal trial, testified, without examining Cromer, that she was simply stupid, evil, and bad. Perhaps because of the inhumanity of her crime and her rigid lack of remorse for it, the jury felt that she deserved to be stigmatized and punished, and only by accepting the reactionary picture could they ensure that she was. . . . This trial brings out clearly why the current law is unworkable.

Here, *in statu nascendi*, is the slander of my being guilty of medical negligence for failing to examine a person whom Clanon *et al.* define as a sick patient. This slander of my person is typical of the way in which apologists for psychiatric slavery defend themselves against my criticisms of their ideas and interventions. Once made, the slander is then cited and recited from paper to paper, book to book.

Conclusion

Since the 1950s, when I began to criticize psychiatric ideas and interventions, I have made it clear that my views rest on a rejection of psychiatry's core concept, mental illness, and the psychiatrist's paradigmatic procedures, depriving innocent persons of liberty (civil commitment), and excusing guilty persons of legal responsibility for their crimes (the insanity defense). Simon ignores all that, interprets my objections to the insanity defense in the framework of traditional psychiatry, and concludes that the insanity defense is scientifically valid and morally

---

[38] T.L. Clanon, Lois Shawver, and Douglas Kurdys, "Less Insanity in the Courts," *American Bar Association Journal* 825 (July, 1982), pp. 824 ff.

praiseworthy. She concludes by citing the opinions of Alan Stone, one of the most respected psychiatric traditionalists. Citing an eminent authority, however, is not a substitute for evidence and reasoning.

In less than one thousand words, Simon dismisses the conceptually and empirically problematic nature of the idea of mental illness and my critique of the moral and social legitimacy of civil commitment and the insanity defense, and repeats a slanderous falsehood regarding my testimony in a murder trial.

Lord Acton wisely warned: "To renounce the pains and penalties of exhaustive research is to remain a victim of ill-informed and designing writers, and to authorities that have worked for ages to build up the vast tradition of conventional mendacity."[39]

Simon is not merely a victim of "ill-informed and designing writers" and of "authorities that have worked for ages to build up the vast tradition of conventional mendacity." She is herself an ill-informed and designing writer, an authority who zealously reinforces the vast tradition of conventional mendacity.

---

[39] Lord Acton, quoted in, Damien McElrath, with James Holland, Ward White, and Sue Katzman, *Lord Acton: The Decisive Decade, 1864–1874, Essays and Documents* (Louvain: Publications Universitaires de Louvain, 1970), p. 10.

7

Pharmacracy or Phantom?

E. JAMES LIEBERMAN

A theory is good; but it doesn't prevent things from existing.
—J.-M. CHARCOT, 1886

Psychoanalysis occupies a "middle position between medicine and philosophy," Freud wrote in 1925.[1] A few years later ex-Freudian psychologist Otto Rank declared "one no longer approaches the problem of the neurotic purely medically. . . . they are not sick in the medical sense. Their sufferings are emotional."[2] Freud's assertion codifies what Thomas Szasz deplores in American medicine and psychiatry: the drift away from strictly scientific values. In light of his writings, from *The Myth of Mental Illness* (1961) to *Pharmacracy: Medicine and Politics in America* (2001), Szasz might take Rank's statement as a call to remove emotional suffering from the category of illness or disease and therefore from the purview of scientific and ethical medicine. I would not go that far: emotional and medical problems may be different, but they often are inseparable.

Szasz has done singular service to psychiatry in asserting the rights of patients, and fighting abuses perpetrated in the name of treatment. He is rightly concerned about the power of doctors and courts to take away freedom of individuals who are considered a danger to themselves or others by well-meaning—or conniving—powers-that-be. Ironically,

---

[1] S. Freud, The Resistances to Psychoanalysis. In *SE*19 (1925), p. 216.
[2] O. Rank, *Will Therapy* (1936 [1929]), p. 1.

because his forty-year crusade has been so successful, the dangers of which he warns have now been greatly reduced, though he will not be satisfied until the insanity defense and involuntary commitment are history. But his continuing tirade against medicine and psychiatry seems to ignore the progress for which he deserves so much credit. By exaggerating the power of his opposition, and the dangers of the medical establishment, he may jeopardize his influence on related issues such as the "war on drugs." Meanwhile what many—including me—consider a civilized advance in humane treatment of the mentally ill is seen by him as either coddling criminal misbehavior or punishing nonconformity by medicalizing it. He derides efforts at suicide prevention, gun control, and smoking restrictions as governmental meddling in personal freedom.

My starting point in considering the philosophy of Thomas Szasz dates back to my learning about Otto Rank (1884–1939), Freudian disciple, defector, and critic. Having spent my psychiatric residency with mostly traditional Boston analysts and a few renegades, I discovered Rank in mid-career. After breaking with Freud and the psychoanalytic establishment, Rank called himself a psychotherapist and philosopher of helping. Many of his pioneering ideas are now mainstream, though often without due credit: the importance of the mother, separation-individuation, death-fear and life-fear, brief therapy and end-setting, and the real versus transference relationship in therapy.[3] But above all, Rank's insistence on conscious will as key in therapy and psychology generally, where Freud has dismissed or disguised it in wish and the unconscious, connects with Szasz's insistence on responsibility, and the importance of treating people as competent adults. I, but not Szasz, would add: unless convincing evidence to the contrary exists. For Szasz there is no such exemption: mental illness is a myth. We probably agree that psychotherapists are philosophers of helping—a definition to make health insurance companies balk. But so are physicians, and experts estimate that half the traffic in medical offices comes from psychosomatic or frankly emotional sources. Doctors treat conditions that have no pathological proof of existence and insurance pays, as long as the diagnostic codes are entered and the procedure codes fit.

Szasz has little to say about the doctor-patient relationship, except where he warns about the undue power of the former. Rank's therapy was egalitarian rather than authoritarian, and he was the first of Freud's inner circle to put the nurturing mother at the center of the child's world rather than the menacing father. Rank teaches that the therapist alternates

---

[3] E.J. Lieberman, *Acts of Will: The Life and Work of Otto Rank* (1993 [1985]).

between two roles, assistant ego and assistant reality. But he emphasizes conscious choice, and, though occasionally making suggestions, holds the patient responsible for adopting, rejecting, or modifying them. He saw a "will conflict" between therapist and patient as inevitable and necessary; unlike Freud, who ruled that resistance must be analyzed and overcome, Rank would congratulate a patient who resists and reframe the episode in terms of will expression, whether active, tentative or passive. Suicide is respected as a choice, not reflexively condemned: refusal of suicide is, after all, affirmation of responsibility for one's own life. I am not alarmed that half of American high school students have thought about it. Unlike Szasz, I actively treat depression and try to prevent suicide, but not by force. Again, unlike him, I support physician aid-in-dying as permitted in Oregon since 1996. Szasz speaks of it harshly because killing cannot be "treatment" of a disease, even if the intervention is consensual. I endorse it because physicians control access to the most benign methods of euthanasia, and because they are, or should be, in a special relationship to their patients and knowledgeable about, and sensitive to, issues surrounding death and dying.

Szasz insists on pathological proof of diagnosis to justify the use of the term 'disease', and does not seem concerned with the art of medicine compared with the science (and politics). A purist, he agrees with Roy Porter's characterization of him as "an old-school medical materialist."[4] Frustrated by the casual use of "disease" and "illness" in lay circles, Szasz holds health professionals and journalists in contempt for being careless with these terms. Though also a stickler for accurate and responsible use of language, I accept a less strict and more realistic standard for definitions. Call it pragmatic.[5] Pragmatism holds that the consequences of a belief determine its truth value in whole or in part. This adherence to a particular definition is balanced by the outcome of its use. Otto Rank fits the pragmatic philosophical school, a branch of which one scholar calls "Romantic Science," including, along with Rank, William James, Ludwig Binswanger, Erik Erikson, and Oliver Sacks as examples.[6]

Romantic science, stemming from Goethe and Novalis, brings back the spirit of German romanticism that embraced, and refused to sepa-

---

[4] Thomas Szasz, *Pharmacracy: Medicine and Politics in America* (2001), p. 123. Page references to Szasz in the text, unless otherwise noted, are to *Pharmacracy*.

[5] Daniel B. Fishman, *The Case for Pragmatic Psychology* (1999). For a view of schizophrenia, see pp. 127–29.

[6] Martin Halliwell, *Romantic Science and the Experience of Self* (1999).

rate, natural science and art. A flexible method as seen in James's radical empiricism, it was a response to positivistic and materialistic science that excluded much of what is fundamentally human. Romantic science eschews the mystical while valuing subjective experience, and warns against objectifying people for the sake of measurement and prediction. Only about a century ago did medicine advance enough scientifically to be significantly helpful for the majority of consumers. In the last half-century we have seen unimaginable medical progress from the side of science and technology, while the art languishes somewhat in the shadows. Perhaps because of his focus on individual privacy and the right to be left alone, Szasz seems to minimize the subjective element in medicine, leaving one to wonder what he thinks of the placebo phenomenon, the evolution of the doctor-patient relationship, the role of increased consumer sophistication, malpractice actions as a factor in medical practice, and the humanistic-forensic doctrine of informed consent.

Medicine and Psychiatry Today

It used to be that physicians told patients what was wrong with them and what must be done to treat them. Medicine was a self-regulating profession built on the illusion that self-dealing and greed did not intrude upon the ethical practice of medicine and anyone who suggested otherwise was insulting doctors. Meanwhile Sidney Wolfe, M.D., of the Health Research Group (affiliated with Ralph Nader's Public Citizen) has goaded state regulators and medical societies to do more about incompetent doctors, including naming those who have bad records. And the rise of managed care has put doctors under the scopes of dollar-pinching administrators who have trained lay people to question diagnoses and procedures, especially expensive ones.

The situation has evolved in this country to the point where doctors are struggling to stay in the saddle at all, much less to ride on any high horse. The American Medical Association could not stave off the incursions of managed care or the rise of "alternative medicine." Economic pressures shorten the average time for conversation, and the more sensitive doctors are either soon burned out or they hire a caring nurse or social worker to assist in the office and on the telephone—a function which may not be covered by insurance. The mental health system is broken into pieces, with managers pushing psychiatrists to spend little time with patients and prescribe drugs, while the labor-intensive talking therapy is to be provided by less expensive members of the team, psychologists and social workers. Non-psychiatric physicians, who see plenty of emotional disturbance, or mental illness—a term I use without flinching—actually prescribe ninety percent of psychotropic drugs in the U.S. This is not surprising in view of the fact that perhaps five percent of physicians are psychiatrists, and that medications for depression and anxiety have fewer side-effects than before, and drug companies promote their use by as many doctors as possible. Only the more complicated cases, the severe mood disorders and psychoses, are left entirely to psychiatry.

One rarely hears of someone being committed involuntarily to a mental hospital, and Szasz provides no statistics. Debates continue between the civil liberties champions and psychiatrists like Fuller Torrey and Paul Chodoff, who defend involuntary treatment on some unwitting or unwilling people deemed dangerous to themselves or others. Szasz insists this must be an expression of self-interest on the part of the psychiatrists. De-institutionalization, the emptying of large mental hospitals, in the wake of promises—largely unfulfilled—of community-based treatment, has left us with many people on the streets who fit the more serious categories. Jails and prisons have become the holding institutions for many such sufferers. Public schools have long been the main, if not sole, locale of observation and support for emotionally disturbed children, only a small proportion of whom ever have sophisticated evaluation and treatment. For children, competent evaluation and treatment must include their families. Again, the push is to use drugs, to save time and money.

Is this Pharmacracy? The therapeutic state is stumbling along. Patients have more questions and the gumption to ask them. Doctors are more receptive to sharing decision-making, but are pressed for time to listen and talk. People are getting too many antibiotics, and women are getting too many Caesarian sections, and many are hustled out of hospitals too quickly. Patients delve into alternative medicine, they do research on the Internet, and are less malleable than in the past, less intimidated.

Regarding public health, it was citizens and their lawyers, not doctors, who led the successful fight to make abortion legal and safe, and are doing the same with regard to end-of-life care, including advance directives and the right to physician aid-in-dying. This does not seem to be a country of sheep-like patients acquiesceing to a powerful pharmacracy.

Major changes, not noted by Szasz, came in 1958, with the introduction of informed consent. What a radical idea: patient suffrage! A wise and eloquent statement on these developments comes from psychoanalyst and Yale law professor Jay Katz.[7] Echoing (but not mentioning) Szasz, he writes, "The idea that patients may also be entitled to liberty, to sharing the burdens of decision with their doctors, was never part of the ethos of medicine. Being unaware of the idea of patient liberty, physicians did not address the possible conflict between notions of custody and liberty. . . . Anglo-American law has, at least in theory, a long-standing tradition of preferring liberty over custody . . ."[8] Katz emphasizes autonomy for patients as a value, along with a critique of physicians' assumption that they know the best interests of patients and need not consult them as partners.

> In the absence of any one clear road to well-being, identity of interest cannot be assumed, and consensus on goals, let alone on which paths to follow, can only be accomplished through conversation. Two distinct and separate parties interact with one another—not one mind (the physician's), not one body (the patient's) but two minds and two bodies. Moreover, both parties bring conflicting motivations and interests to their encounters. . . . Conflicts within and between the parties are inevitable.[9]

Szasz does not cite Katz, either. I suspect he does not share the latter's humble optimism about the physician's capacity to improve medical practice through a better relationship. Katz is as much concerned with intersubjectivity as with objectivity.

Disease by Definition

For Szasz disease must be proven by physical evidence, the kind to which pathologists—tissue judges—can testify. To him only this is science, compared to which clinical medicine, cluttered with social constructions, is a political, economic, and moral juggernaut, wholly unaccountable to the "purely materialist-scientific" standards enunciated by pioneer pathologist Rudolf Virchow. Modern technology allows for sophisticated physical, chemical and radiological analysis, but the "criterion of disease remains the same: functional or structural abnormality of cells, tissues, or organs." The corollary: "Because the mind is not a bodily organ, it can be diseased only in a metaphorical sense." Therefore, "The claim that a mental illness is a brain disease is pro-

---

[7] Jay Katz, *The Silent World of Doctor and Patient* (1984).

[8] *Ibid.*, p. 2.

[9] *Ibid.*, p. xviii.

foundly self-contradictory: a disease of the brain is a brain disease, not a mental disease" (pp. 12–13).

While this strict defining may conform to Websterian logic (Szasz likes to cite the dictionary), it remains dehumanized. This is not a problem for Szasz, who quotes French surgeon René Leriche: "If one wants to define disease it must be dehumanized. . . . In disease, when all is said and done, the least important thing is man" (p. 12) But it is a problem for many of us; granted, the mind is not the brain, but the brain has everything to do with the mind and there is no mind without it. Szasz uses the term "mind," while insisting that "disease" can be applied only metaphorically. Since the mind's functions depend on brain functions, logic leads us to assume that malfunction of the former is probably reflected in changes in the latter. One big caveat: mental activity may affect the brain, even as brain activity affects whatever is mental. Szasz wants to place the source in the tissue; when the source of malfunction comes from mind, he classifies it as a problem of living, philosophy, malingering, or socially induced behavior. To call behavioral anomalies disease is, for Szasz, to dehumanize in a different way by stripping away the person's responsibility. Hence his contempt for the insanity defense in criminal matters and his challenge to the likes of E. Fuller Torrey, who wants more latitude to treat seriously disturbed patients. (Torrey insists that schizophrenia *is* a brain disease, and chides psychiatrists who treat less severe cases with psychotherapy as wasting their medical education in areas best left to psychology and social work—problems of living.)

Which form of dehumanization is worse? Having spent a few years working with hospitalized psychiatric patients, I think Szasz trivializes devastating malfunction—serious mental illness—by dismissing such patients as attention-seekers, imposters, and so forth. I always assume that responsibility resides in the individual until demonstrated otherwise. Szasz denies that exemption: murder is criminal, not "sick," nor can lunatic behavior justify involuntary hospitalization. He makes no exception for a woman who drowns her five children. Punishment, not therapy; post-partum psychosis has no defining anatomical-pathological findings, so it cannot be called a disease. Szasz rails at a system corrupted by pharmacratic politics, but he fails to state *how often* criminal acts are redefined as illness, or how often "dangerous to self or others" results in involuntary commitment and enforced treatment.

In a major essay on "Health and Disease," the distinguished medical historian Owsei Temkin emphasizes the complexity of the problem of definition. "A person suffering from an ordinary cold may declare himself ill, whereas the same person laid up with a broken leg may claim to be in perfect health."[10] Hippocrates was aware of socially motivated behavior by physicians, for example a doctor might prognosticate pessimistically to protect himself against criticism in case of a bad outcome. Socially constructed notions of right and wrong, sin and virtue, give meaning to disease in a moral sense: "Disease was punishment for trespass or sin, ranging from involuntary infraction of some taboo to willful crime against gods or men. Disease could also be due to the evil machinations of sorcery."[11] Although naturalistic and rational factors emerged, "no arbitrary end can be assigned to the archaic ways of looking upon health and disease; many features even survive in the superstitions and the unconscious motivations of modern man."[12] He points out that with the spread of Christianity, suffering and disease "could appear as chastisement of those whom the Lord loved. Disease could be a portal through which man acquired eternal salvation. Jesus told the sufferer from a palsy that his sins were forgiven."[13] Descartes, whose separation of body and soul led to difficulty in the area of mental disorder, introduced the idea of reflex action to explain "acts which were seemingly purposeful yet independent of, or even contrary to, man's will."[14] Anticipating Szasz, Temkin describes the scene when Cartesian dualism reigned: "It was logically absurd to think of the soul, a *res cogitans*, as being prone to sickness in the manner of the body; this could only be done metaphorically in the manner in which crime, sin, heresy had long been called diseases of the soul."[15]

Szasz seems to leave off with cellular pathologist Virchow, whereas medical thinking progressed toward physiological thinking, with Claude Bernard, who wrote in 1865: "The words life, death, health, disease, have no objective reality."[16] Process, in terms of bodily equilibrium, became the focus rather than identifiable tissue changes. The person-patient loomed larger as it became clear that different individuals became healthy or sick under quite varying conditions. Meanwhile Szasz leans on the dictionary and the certainties of anatomic-pathological demonstration to the point that he denies, or will not see, certain

---

[10] Temkin, Owsei. "Health and Disease," in Philip P. Wiener, ed., *Dictionary of the History of Ideas* (1973), II, p. 395.

[11] *Ibid.*, p. 396.

[12] *Ibid.*

[13] *Ibid.*, p. 399.

[14] *Ibid.*, p. 400.

[15] *Ibid.*

[16] *Ibid.*, p. 404.

aspects of reality. Ironically, this echoes Freud, who objected to the "mid-air" psychology of Friedrich Nietzsche, who lacked the "indispensable organic foundation."[17]

Temkin's remarkable essay "Health and Disease" includes a summary statement with which Szasz seems to agree, but not happily:

> The prevailing tendency at the present moment seems to merge disease once more with much that formerly was considered distinct from it and to take so broad a view of health as to make it all but indistinguishable from happiness."[18]

Temkin supports a conceptual breadth beyond what Szasz allows: "health and disease have not shown themselves to be immutable objects of natural history. Health and disease are medical concepts in the broadest sense. . . . Thus they are distinguished from purely scientific concepts on the one hand and from purely social ones on the other."[19] He allows for respectable metaphoric extension of the concept of disease. Szasz tries to define mental illness out of existence; he can only do that if all concerned accept his narrow definitions. Some of the most important things—family, music, life itself—are more easily recognized than defined. The same is true of health and disease.

Responses to Szasz

Szasz has met with much criticism, resistance, misperception, and antagonism, as well as enthusiastic support. I struggle with ambivalence about him: he's on the right track, but he goes too far and too straight; life does not fit in that narrow compass, nice as the logic may be. And his assumption that underlying the resistance is a power and greed conspiracy of a self-serving pharmacracy strikes me as a half-truth. Thinking about these issues, I surveyed some sources other than those included in two excellent books about him and his work.[20]

In the second edition of *Core Readings in Psychiatry*,[21] Szasz has three mentions: under "Schizophrenia," the 1976 paper is "much less

---

[17] Freud-Jung letter, 19th April, 1908, paraphrased in Lieberman, *Acts of Will*, p. 102.

[18] *Op. cit.*, p. 406.

[19] *Ibid.*

[20] Richard E. Vatz, and Lee S. Weinberg, eds., *Thomas Szasz: Primary Values and Major Contentions* (1983); Keith Hoeller, ed., *Thomas Szasz: Moral Philosopher of Psychiatry*, special issue of *Review of Existential Psychology and Psychiatry* XXIII (1997), 1–3.

[21] M.H. Sacks, et al., eds. (American Psychiatric Press, 1995).

influential today than it first was but his eloquent elaboration and
[M.] Roth's brilliant critique of his theories are worthwhile reading"
(p. 133). Under "Ethics," his 1987 paper "The Religion Called
Psychiatry" is listed with Paul Chodoff's 1984 paper on involuntary
treatment. Under "Forensic Psychiatry," *Law, Liberty, and Psychiatry*
(1963) is acknowledged as "one of the first to expose psychiatric
practices that allegedly compromised the rights of mentally ill persons. It became the rallying point for a generation of civil liberties
attorneys who radically changed commitment practices and treatment
of mentally ill patients" (p. 757). There is some irony in the last three
words of that comment, but the tone of these references is at least
respectful.

Karl Menninger wrote:

> The use of pejorative labels is a sin of which I have myself been guilty. I
> began to see how much harm it caused and consequently I have discontin-
> ued it. Dr. Thomas Szasz of New York State goes further than I; he will not
> even concede the existence of *any* "mental disease," psychosis, neurosis,
> and the like.[22]

Sidney Walker is a neuropsychiatrist concerned with recognizing underlying physical illness in psychiatric patients. He agrees with Szasz about
the DSM, and the over-medicalization of misbehavior, but asserts, *contra* Szasz, that *"the brain is the organ of behavior . . . all aberrant behavior stems from brain dysfunction. There is no mind without the brain—
and there is no true psychiatric treatment that doesn't treat the brain."*[23]
Walker states that even malingerers

> generally are suffering from brain dysfunctions. I've found, over my
> decades of practice, that people with normal brains rarely pretend to be
> crazy. In claiming that "mental illnesses do not exist; indeed they cannot
> exist, because the mind is not a body part or bodily organ," Szasz would
> have us dismiss millions of patients—many of whom have genetic diseases,
> tumors, medication-induced psychosis, infections, and other brain disor-
> ders—as incompetent, lazy, or bad. He would have us leave them to die on
> the streets, or in our jails. In my book, that view is as bad as the misguided
> psychiatric treatments Szasz rightly attacks.[24]

---

[22] *Whatever Became of Sin?* (1973), p. 171.
[23] *A Dose of Sanity: Mind, Medicine, and Misdiagnosis* (1996), p. viii.
[24] *Ibid.*, p. 157. Citation from *The Therapeutic State* (1984).

In a major new history of recent American psychiatry three different writers address Szasz.[25] In the chapter on "Antipsychiatry," historian Norman Dain calls him "The most influential ideologist of the 'new' antipsychiatry of the 1960s and 1970s. . . . His influence was greatest among the lay public, ex-mental patients, and the political left (whom Szasz, a conservative libertarian, disdained, and who, as Szasz did not, wanted public funding for mental health facilities); his fellow psychiatrists generally regarded him with anger, if not contempt."[26]

Psychiatrist John O. Beahrs, writing on "The Cultural Impact of Psychiatry," addresses patient autonomy, with credit to Szasz for starting a movement that

> led to a shift in the philosophy of involuntary treatment from *parens patriae* to the doctrine of police powers: the deprivation of liberty cannot be justified by need alone, but instead requires that one also be in imminent danger of harming oneself or others. Beginning in the 1960s, involuntary commitment proceedings became increasingly criminalized, and due process safeguards were established similar to a criminal defendant's right to counsel, right to confrontation of witnesses, and privilege against self-incrimination. Defense of patient autonomy has continued to expand to the point that it has become a central ethical tenet of all health care.
>
> Indeed, patient autonomy was dramatically increased, but at significant cost both to patients themselves and to society. Nondangerous patients unable to make rational decisions were increasingly denied the effective treatments they had long received, and mainstream society became less shielded from aberrant behavior.[27]

Finally, psychiatrist Seymour Halleck regards Szasz, "the most prominent, and certainly the most influential, critic of modern psychiatry," as a "powerful intellectual ally of the civil liberties movement. . . . He developed a substantial following in the Western world among attorneys, humanists, and libertarians. Although rejected by most of his own profession, his ideas and writings provided intellectual inspiration to those seeking to change the influence of psychiatry on the mental health and criminal justice systems"[28]

---

[25] Roy W. Menninger and John C. Nemiah, eds., *American Psychiatry After World War II: 1944–1994* (Washington, D.C.: American Psychiatric Press, 2000).

[26] *Op. cit.*, p. 284.

[27] *Op. cit.*, p. 326.

[28] *Op. cit.*, p. 526, chapter on Forensic Psychiatry.

Like Karl Menninger, psychiatrist and ethicist Paul Chodoff agrees with Szasz up to a point, but maintains that involuntary hospitalization is occasionally justified and humane.[29] There are occasions when it can be life-saving, which for Szasz is not a sufficient justification to limit another person's freedom—the slippery slope begins with enforcible suicide prevention. Most suicide prevention is voluntary: psychotherapy and pharmacotherapy. To avoid hospitalization, a suicidal patient will often make a contract with a therapist, whose judgment should favor patient autonomy unless there is evidence of danger. Some therapists resort to legal force (or threat thereof) if the contract fails or is refused. Patients can, of course, reassure therapists falsely, giving lip service to a contract in order to forestall confinement and then proceed with a suicide plan. Szasz seems to underestimate this ability, focusing on the victimization of patients by force.

Electro-convulsive therapy (ECT or "shock" treatment) is a prime example of unpleasant psychiatric intervention. It has certainly been applied without patient consent, though this is now rare, as is medication without consent. ECT can be very beneficial, but remains controversial because it is distasteful, is mysterious, and has been overused. This problem exists in many areas of medicine, from caesarian sections to arthroscopic surgery; for these reasons a promising intervention may be vetoed by patients, doctors, or their families.

Arguments Begged

In several areas I question the soundness of *Pharmacracy* or its perspective.

Definitions

Weaknesses in the argument begin with the title. Readers are likely to think that "Pharmacracy" means domination by pharmaceutical companies. Szasz defines the term historically, from the Greek *pharmakon*, for drug, and *kratein*, rule or control. But he means "rule by medicine or physicians." This illustrates that rigorous standards in the use of language may result in quite different usages and definitions. Metaphors may be dangerous, but are useful, indeed essential in rhetoric, and cannot be silenced; even good science depends on them for progress and innovation. If "mental illness" is a metaphorical extension of terms used

---

[29] Paul Chodoff, "Involuntary Hospitalization of the Mentally Ill as a Moral Issue," *American Journal of Psychiatry* 141 (1984), 384–89.

in physical medicine, so be it. There is a gray area—not just for metaphorical illness, but also for old fashioned physical illness—where pragmatic rather than materialistic philosophy rules, with its mingling or merging of laboratory science and social custom or policy. Szasz repeats his definitions stridently and often, but, to paraphrase Charcot, they do not prevent things from existing.

Evidence

Szasz gives no statistics suggesting increases in the tendencies he deplores. Ironically, thanks in considerable measure to his own success, involuntary confinement has been reduced, and the insanity defense seems to have been shaken. John W. Hinckley, Jr. used it successfully but not Andrea Yates. I doubt that Hinckley would be successful with the insanity defense today. That former Leviathan, the American Medical Association, lost 12,000 members in 2001, and now includes only 29 percent of U.S. physicians and medical students; thirty years ago that figure was 75 percent.[30] As for state medicine, condemned by Szasz, he has no horrible examples of abuses in those countries (most advanced industrial nations) that have national health services. We have limited government medicine—Medicare, Medicaid, the military and veterans and members of Congress (who enjoy the highest quality American socialized medicine, including 75% of drug costs).

Analogies

Szasz, so careful with definitions, runs wild with historical analogy. He likens pharmacracy in the Western world today to that in Hitler's Germany, reminding us along the way that calling Nazis fascist is incorrect, since the term belongs properly to Mussolini and Franco, neither of whom "exhibited [Hitler's] kind of interest in health or genocide . . ."[31] He cites *The Nazi War on Cancer* (1999) by historian Robert N. Proctor, who does not believe our situation is analogous with Nazi Germany. Szasz likes Proctor's facts, not his conclusions. Proctor says (and I appreciate Szasz's willingness to quote): "My intention is not to argue that today's anti-tobacco efforts have fascist roots, or that public health measures are in principle totalitarian—as some libertarians seem to

---

[30] *Psychiatric News* (19th July, 2002), p. 25.
[31] *Pharmacracy*, p. 148.

want us to believe."[32] Szasz, the libertarian, insists on the comparison. Were there any medical malpractice suits in Nazi Germany? Or managed care, as we know it? Or medical ethics that explicitly refer to informed consent? Szasz says:

> The truth is that the Nazi health ideology closely resembles the American health ideology. Each rests on the same premises—that the individual is incompetent to protect himself from himself and needs the protection of the paternalistic state, thus turning private health into public health. . . . It was not fascism, which was not genocidal, but medical Puritanism that motivated the Nazis to wage therapeutic wars against cancer and Jews. This is a crucial point. Once we begin to worship health as an all-pervasive good—a moral value that trumps all others, especially liberty—it becomes sanctified as a kind of secular holiness.[33]

Szasz points to our Surgeon General and his "bully pulpit" as further evidence of overweening public health power. He also says the modern Surgeon General is "a medical hack whose job is to serve his political masters" (p. 39) But Drs. C. Everett Koop, Joycelyn Elders, and David Satcher were well out in front of, and challenging to, politicians, even the presidents who appointed them.

Who listens to health advice? It competes with myriad messages of temptation and outright deception. Szasz sees governments and doctors as deceivers, but seems not to be worried about the big powers in the marketplace. In present-day America one-third of adults still smoke, and sixty percent are overweight or obese (a huge increase). Health hardly trumps other values, such as the pleasures of eating, avoiding exercise, and smoking. Public health values are often trumped by venal politics. Funds collected from tobacco companies through citizen action in the courts are often diverted from health and education budgets to entirely unrelated needs of states, even while some 2,000 youngsters start smoking every day in the U.S. A banker and longtime Director of Philip Morris Co. proudly serves as a Trustee of a leading U.S. cancer hospital.[34] Asthma increases rapidly while automakers and other industries fight successfully against emission reduction. Meanwhile Szasz complains that commemorative postage stamps devoted to health themes—

---

[32] *Ibid.* Note also that Proctor applies "fascist" to Nazis.
[33] *Ibid.*, p. 149.
[34] John Reed, formerly head of Citibank and Citigroup; Memorial Sloan-Kettering Cancer Center.

breast and prostate cancer, dental health—are small symbols of a tyrannical therapeutic state (p. 128).

Money trumps health all the time in the U.S. Clean air and water cannot be considered free any more. The airwaves, which belong to the citizenry and are rented to the networks that make huge profits giving the people "what they want" now are channels for slanted and misleading information; but Szasz can only see the government as the source of deception as in the case in which the drug czar rewarded certain television producers when dramatic material was politically correct.[35] Szasz fails to note that, when uncovered, the scandal stopped. Reporters were not jailed for exposing the truth. The government was embarrassed and is far less likely to repeat such an intrusion. Meanwhile, corporations and the media saturate our airwaves with half-truths about things that do a great deal of harm: fast foods, fast cars, beer, sun tans, and so on. The government is moderately effective on some health issues like tobacco and alcohol, but hardly resembles an effective tyrant.

Pharmaceutical manufacturers, among the most profitable companies in America, have found ways to extend patent protection and hamper the production of competing generic drugs. Very expensive drugs can be bought cheaper abroad, where governments have imposed price control. Viagra and Rogaine now belong to one company—a victory for investors, based on the treatment of erectile dysfunction and baldness, respectively: non-diseases for the most part. These medicines are never forced on patients. How much money and effort are these companies devoting to rarer conquerable diseases compared with developing cousins of best-selling drugs for common ills like arthritis and allergy?

Interpretation

Szasz notes that Americans have higher *per capita* health expenditures than other comparable nations, but unlike them we have forty million citizens uninsured, and many more only partly insured. We fall behind a number of countries in some important measures of public health, so are we inefficient in our spending? Frivolous? Or simply showing the results of a two-tiered health delivery system? He doesn't say. And his outcry against increased federal expenditures for health and mental health depends on an interpretation that civilian health care is no business of the government; he opposes even voluntary health care if the government is involved.

---

[35] *Pharmacracy*, p. 136.

Szasz correctly cites war as the universal threat to liberty, because it allows governments to curtail individual freedom in the name of security. He cannot be faulted for failing to predict the terrorist attack of 2001, but he was too optimistic when he wrote

> Although we have little to fear from the traditional foes of freedom, commentators across the political spectrum lament the creeping loss of our liberties. How can this be?
> Our foreign policies have not failed: America is more secure than ever from foreign aggression. (p. 161)

Szasz explains that, absent real wars, our liberties are eroded by "entrusting our health to the state" (p. 162). He concludes:

> The evidence presented in this book confirms that most Americans indeed prefer health—or what they think is "health"—over liberty, forgetting Benjamin Franklin's warning, "They that can give up essential liberty to obtain a little temporary safety, deserve neither liberty nor safety." . . .
> The first casualty of all wars is clear thinking and personal independence, replaced by the collective stupidity and timidity of a people united by fear and hatred against a common enemy. The sacrifice of liberty is perceived as liberation, whether the enemy is Communism or cancer . . . (p. 163)

Or Osama Bin Laden.

Szasz castigates the government, but holds the people responsible, as befits a society claiming to uphold democratic values. There is some blurring in the interpretation, as he insists on the one hand that people can make choices about their health-related and other conduct, but on the other, cowed by fear, they become stupid and vulnerable.

Conclusion

Paul Chodoff recently discussed, and, like Thomas Szasz, deplores, "The Medicalization of the Human Condition."[36] Like Otto Rank, Chodoff recognizes that the medical model can be stifling and that psychiatry and the other helping professions must transcend it. I agree, and see this as a balancing act, not a power-grab. Patients increasingly are coming to share control of their medical care with a formerly authoritarian medical

---

[36] *Psychiatric Services* 53(2002), pp. 627–28.

establishment. Threats to personal autonomy and privacy exist, but are also constantly challenged: information on genetics for example, might lead to rejection by health insurers. Carriers of transmissible diseases must be treated sensitively while any related threat to the community be considered. The community is grappling with such issues quite openly. This is not Nazi Germany. If there is any similarity to be found to Nazi Germany, it is in the response to terrorism that justifies imprisonment without charges, denial of legal counsel, and racial, religious, or national stereotyping. We can hope these sequlae of September 11th, 2001 become only temporary embarrassments to a free society, and that we citizens and our government soon get back to nourishing the true roots of homeland security in an insecure world: education, health, full employment, a safety net for the less fortunate, and vigorous protection of individual liberty.

Reply to Lieberman

THOMAS SZASZ

I

Lieberman states: "One rarely hears of someone being committed involuntarily to a mental hospital . . ."

This an astounding assertion. Not a day passes without the media reporting that this or that person has been detained for "psychiatric evaluation." As I sat down to compose my reply to Lieberman, the Associated Press reported:

> TAMPA, Fla., Aug. 24 (AP)—A doctor suspected of hatching a plot to blow up dozens of mosques and an Islamic education center had enough expertise and firepower to carry it out. . . . Deputies also found a typed list of about 50 Islamic places of worship in the Tampa and St. Petersburg area and elsewhere in Florida . . . . When the police searched Dr. [Robert J.] Goldstein's home in Seminole, near St. Petersburg, they found a cache of up to 40 weapons, including .50-caliber machine guns and sniper rifles and two M72 rocket launchers. . . . Dr. Goldstein . . . was placed in custody under a state law that allows involuntary commitment for psychiatric evaluation.[1]

Brushing aside the ubiquity of psychiatric coercion and my voluminous writings about it, Lieberman complains that I offer "no statistics" and fail "to state . . . how often 'dangerousness to self or others' results in involuntary commitment and enforced treatment." *Law, Liberty, and Psychiatry, Psychiatric Justice, The Manufacture of Madness, The Therapeutic State, Psychiatric Slavery, and Liberation By Oppression*

---

[1] Associated Press, "Police Say Man Accused in Plot Had Explosives," *New York Times* (25th August, 2002); http://ad.doubleclick.net/adi/N339.nytimes.com/B922384;sz=720x300;ord=2002.08.25.18.49.47

242

are devoted partly or wholly to the subject of involuntary mental hospitalization. I cite cases and offer documented evidence of the frequency of the procedure. According to the latest statistics, "Each year in the United States well over one million persons are civilly committed to hospitals for psychiatric treatment. . . . It is difficult to completely separate discussions of voluntary and involuntary commitment because voluntary status can be converted efficiently to involuntary status, once the patient has requested release."[2]

Lieberman knows, or ought to know, that, in reality, there is no such thing as voluntary mental hospitalization, that the adjective "voluntary" is a brazen mendacity. In an often-quoted 1972 article, I showed that *all so-called voluntary mental hospitalizations* are, actually or potentially, involuntary incarcerations, instances of an officially "unacknowledged practice of medical fraud."[3] The *New England Journal of Medicine* considered this criticism important and valid enough to merit publishing my paper. Today, as Lieberman's repeated remarks indicate, conventional wisdom decrees that involuntary mental hospitalization is a thing of the past.

II

Alas, the opposite is the case. David Healy—Reader in Psychological Medicine at the University of Wales College of Medicine and a true believer in mental illness—writes:

> The community mental health centers did nothing to reduce rates of admission to public hospitals; indeed, these rose dramatically, in some cases tripling and others rising by even greater amounts. . . . Compared with 1900, when Kraepelin and Freud were putting forward the ideas that would shape modern psychiatry, by 2000 there had been a fifteen-fold increase in rates of admission to psychiatric wards. There had also been a three-fold increase in rates of detention for psychiatric disorders. And psychiatric patients afflicted with schizophrenia and manic-depressive disorder, the disorders at

---

[2] Mary L. Durham, "Civil Commitment of the Mentally Ill: Research, Policy, and Practice," in Bruce D. Sales and Saleem A. Shah, eds., *Mental Health and Law: Research, Policy, and Services* (Durham, N.C.: Carolina Academic Press, 1996), pp. 17–40 (p. 17).

[3] Thomas Szasz, "Voluntary Mental Hospitalization: An Unacknowledged Practice of Medical Fraud," *New England Journal of Medicine* 287 (10th August, 1972), pp. 277–78.

the core of psychiatric business, were likely to spend more time in a service bed during their psychiatric illness than they would have done a century ago."[4]

Yet, Lieberman states: "One rarely hears of someone being committed involuntarily to a mental hospital . . ." I suppose that in 1842, a comfortable, upper-middle class American rarely heard of a slave being mistreated, and in 1942, a similarly situated German rarely heard of a Jew being gassed.

Almost every week, I receive one or more letters from victims of involuntary psychiatric incarceration seeking my help. My efforts and those of others to help one such person were reported in a feature article in *Time,* in July 2002.[5] Lieberman does not mention it, even though his essay was contributed after that date. I summarize the story below.

Rodney Yoder is an inmate in the Chester (Illinois) Mental Health Center. In 1979, he hit his girlfriend, was sentenced to four years in prison, and served his sentence. Subsequently, he went to school, married, had two children, and got divorced. In January 1990, he assaulted his former wife, pleaded guilty, and went to prison. A psychiatrist who examined him in prison stated that "Yoder . . . didn't meet the standard for involuntary hospitalization. He wasn't a danger and there was no indication of acute psychopathology." After Yoder had served his time, he was committed to the neighboring madhouse, the Chester Mental Health Center. That was in 1991. He is still there. John Cloud writes in *Time*:

> Yoder's case is unusual but perhaps not unique. . . . Even though some of his fellow residents at the Chester hospital committed murders of breathtaking brutality, he [Yoder] has lived at the state's only maximum-security facility for the criminally insane more than twice as long as the average patient. . . . [If] Yoder lived in a different place—say, New York City—his life might have followed a different path. He might be the loud guy who bugs you on the subway or one of the city's wearisome politicians. Instead, he lives in rural Illinois, and it is the citizens of Randolph County who form the juries that decide every year or two whether he should stay at the institution. . . . The creator of the cartoon character Popeye was born in the town

---

[4] David Healy, *The Creation of Psychopharmacology* (Cambridge, Massachusetts: Harvard University Press, 2002), pp. 150, 329.

[5] John Cloud, "They Call Him Crazy," *Time* (15th July, 2002) http://www.time.com/time/magazine/printout/0,8816,300661,00.html

of Chester in 1894, and its major annual event is a picnic next to a 900-lb. bronze statue of the sailor man. Popeye's innocent charm somehow coexists with Chester's other landmarks, the Menard prison and the Chester Mental Health Center next door. *Of the town's 8,400 residents, more than 3,000 are incarcerated. . . .*

[At Yoder's last commitment hearing, jurors] heard that Yoder always refused to take psychiatric drugs. But jurors never heard that Yoder had been given multiple, seemingly haphazard diagnoses. For instance, bipolar disorder was diagnosed in 1991, but that diagnosis vanished from his records in 1998—even though Yoder never took part in treatment. Jurors also never heard from . . . a Chester employee who wouldn't testify for fear of losing his job. That employee, who retired not long ago from his position as a guard supervisor but still fears retribution if identified, told me that Chester staff members sometimes provoke Yoder in hopes that he will become violent and provide grist for his next commitment hearing. "[The administration] had a vendetta against him because he beat them in court," says the former supervisor. "Some guards take his property. They taunt him." The ex-employee says Yoder never started fights on his unit. "I'm an ex-police officer. I know violence. Rodney's not violent."

Several years ago, Rodney Yoder contacted me and I have been trying to help him regain his freedom. Cloud writes:

Dr. Thomas Szasz has been the most controversial psychiatrist in the nation for years, so perhaps it's no shock that he has become Yoder's biggest defender. . . . Szasz's most famous book, *The Myth of Mental Illness,* was published in 1961. As the *Atlantic Monthly* said, the book argued "that both our uses of the term 'mental illness' and the activities of the psychiatric profession are often scientifically untenable and morally indefensible." . . . Although he once enjoyed great influence, Szasz is usually dismissed as a crank these days. His foes say he opposes all psychiatry or that he wants to free even incompetent patients who can't feed themselves. Neither is true. But at a time when psychiatry's power has grown dramatically—when it seems normal to grow up taking Ritalin and then graduate to Prozac, when even shyness is treated with pharmaceuticals—his views are worth revisiting. . . . Because of his views, Szasz is often contacted by disgruntled patients "there have been thousands," he sighs. But Yoder was different. "He's extraordinary in the amount of information he amassed," says Szasz. The psychiatrist was impressed that Yoder had tried to go to prison rather than Chester, since Szasz has argued for decades that it's more humane to imprison lawbreakers for a set number of years rather than forcibly treat them in a mental hospital indefinitely. Yoder's calls and letters touched many. Reporter George Pawlaczyk of the Belleville News-Democrat began writing stories about Yoder, and other papers followed. A columnist for the *Natal Witness*, South Africa's oldest newspaper, took up Yoder's cause.

And so have many others. Lieberman is not among them. Worse, he ignores the fact that many people who have served their prison sentences and have been exemplary inmates—but whom the authorities wish to keep imprisoned—are now routinely recommitted to mental hospitals for an indeterminate sentence.

In 1997, in *Kansas v. Leroy Hendricks,* the U.S. Supreme Court declared: "States have a right to use psychiatric hospitals to confine certain sex offenders once they have completed their prison terms, even if those offenders do not meet mental illness commitment criteria."[6]

In February 2000, Wisconsin's oldest prison inmate, a 95-year-old man, was "resentenced" as a sexual predator. A psychologist "testified for the state and said psychological tests performed on Ellefson indicated if he was given a chance, he would commit a [sex] crime. . . . After only minutes of deliberation, the jury found that Ellef J. Ellefson should be committed for mental treatment under the sexual predator law."[7]

III

Often, Lieberman does not hear me or hears me say something I have never said. I shall discuss this problem later. Here I want to note that when Lieberman does hear me, he simply states my view as if its invalidity or absurdity were self-evident and required no further comment from him.

This is Lieberman's answer to my critique of the concept of mental illness: "Some of the most important things—family, music, life itself—are more easily recognized than defined. The same is true of health and disease." If that is not enough of a refutation, here is Lieberman *coup de grâce*: "If 'mental illness' is a metaphorical extension of terms used in physical medicine, so be it. . . . Szasz repeats his definitions stridently and often, but, to paraphrase Charcot, they do not prevent things from existing." What things? *Mental* diseases? But it is precisely the defini-

---

[6] *Kansas v. Leroy Hendricks, No. 95-1649.* "Excerpts from Opinions on Status of Sex Offenders," *New York Times* (24th June, 1997), p. B11.

[7] Associated Press, "Jury: 95-year-old Sexual Predator Is Still a Threat," *Syracuse Herald-Journal* (2nd February, 2000), p. A8.

tion of illness as an attribute of the physical body or parts of it that prevents *mental* illnesses from existing.

"For Szasz," Lieberman writes, "disease must be proven by physical evidence, the kind to which pathologists—tissue judges—can testify. To him only this is science, compared to which clinical medicine, cluttered with social constructions, is a political, economic and moral juggernaut . . ." What is wrong with this view? Lieberman answers: "While this strict defining may conform to Websterian logic (Szasz likes to cite the dictionary), it remains dehumanized." This is an often-repeated argument against my views: My defense of freedom from psychiatric coercion "dehumanizes" the patient. How? By "depriving" him of "life-saving treatment."

Lieberman approvingly cites Chodoff who "maintains that . . . there are occasions when it [involuntary hospitalization] can be life-saving, which for Szasz is not a sufficient justification to limit another person's freedom . . ." Lieberman seems to believe that the mere assertion that psychiatrists claim that psychiatric imprisonment saves the patient's life proves that my views are fallacious and that my policy suggestions are inhumane.

Instead of engaging my argument against the uses of psychiatric power unlimited by the rule of law or a similar safeguard, Lieberman affirms and reaffirms his conventional psychiatric beliefs and practices, especially that it is "humane" to lock up certain people in mental hospitals. What is his evidence? "[H]aving spent a few years working with hospitalized psychiatric patients . . ." In my view, Lieberman has never "worked *with*" hospitalized psychiatric patients. He has worked *against* them. Moreover, the inmates were prisoners, not patients; they were imprisoned, not hospitalized; and Lieberman's "work" consisted of helping the captors, not the captives.[8] I have never committed anyone and my "work" with psychiatric prisoners has been limited to efforts at freeing them from psychiatric slavery.

Lieberman continues: "I think Szasz trivializes devastating malfunction—serious mental illness . . . I always assume that responsibility resides in the individual until demonstrated otherwise. Szasz denies that exemption: for him a murderer cannot be deemed sick, nor can lunatic behavior justify involuntary hospitalization. He makes no exception for a woman who drowns her five children."

---

[8] See for example, Mindy Lewis, *Life Inside: A Memoir* (New York: Atria Books/Simon and Schuster, 2002). There are many similar books by psychiatric survivors.

This is not an argument. It is a restatement of conventional psychiatric wisdom and standard psychiatric practice. Lieberman says nothing
to support his contention that a mother who systematically murders her
children and then calls 911—his allusion is to Andrea Yates—should be
considered not responsible for her behavior and declared "not guilty" in
the eyes of the law and the public.

Repeatedly, Lieberman asserts an erroneous "fact." For example, he
writes that "John W. Hinckley, Jr. used it [the insanity defense] successfully . . ." Hinckley wanted to plead guilty, not insane. The insanity plea
was imposed on him against his will.[9] Ironically, Hinckley has been violated and victimized, with the active collusion of his parents, not once or
twice but three times: first, by invalidating the meaning of his act as the
product of a mad mind; second, by denying him his constitutional right
to trial; and third, by sentencing him to an indefinite term of psychiatric
imprisonment. Yet, Lieberman cites the Hinckley case as an instance of
the humane use of the insanity defense.

Here is another example of Lieberman's "false facts": "Most suicide
prevention is voluntary." This statement is untrue. It also makes it seem
as if I object to voluntary psychiatric interventions, which Lieberman
knows is not the case.[10]

Some of Lieberman's assertions betoken a pathetic blindness to the
political-psychiatric horrors of our age and a lamentable lack of appreciation for the true meaning of phrases such as "state medicine" and
"national health service." He writes: "As for state medicine, condemned
by Szasz, he has no horrible examples of abuses in those countries (most
advanced industrial nations) that have a national health service." The
health care systems of Nazi Germany and the Soviet Union are prime
examples of national health services. *State* mental hospitals are paradigms of "state medicine." With respect to civil commitment, American
and British practices are indistinguishable.[11] As for state medicine today,
is Lieberman unaware that thousands of Canadians come to the United
States to receive the treatment they are denied at home by rationing-by-
waiting-list? That there is a flourishing private-sector medicine in the
United Kingdom?

---

[9] Thomas Szasz, "On Hinckley's 'Innocence By Insanity'," in *The Therapeutic State:
Psychiatry in the Mirror of Current Events* (Buffalo: Prometheus, 1984), pp. 152–54.

[10] Thomas Szasz, *Fatal Freedom: The Ethics and Politics of Suicide* (Syracuse: Syracuse
University Press, 2002 [1999]).

[11] Thomas Szasz, *Liberation by Oppression: A Comparative Study of Slavery and
Psychiatry* (New Brunswick: Transaction, 2002).

There are other oddities in his essay. He characterizes electroconvulsive therapy as "a prime example of unpleasant psychiatric intervention. It has certainly been applied without patient consent . . ." Does this help to support my views? No. "ECT can be very beneficial, but remains controversial because it is distasteful, mysterious, and has been overused . . . [like] arthroscopic surgery."

Lieberman minimizes the harmfulness of pharmacratic-psychiatric social controls in our society. At the same time, he applauds such measures and favors expanding their use. In the process, his socialist impulses lead him to make some embarrassingly naive comments, such as:

> Money trumps health all the time in the U.S.

Only in the U.S.? In Bangladesh, Somalia, and Switzerland it doesn't? In the U.S.S.R., poor and rich got the same kind of health care?

> Clean air and water cannot be considered free anymore.

In biblical times, did people living downwind from erupting volcanoes enjoy access to free clean air? Did the Founding Fathers have access to free clean water?

> Pharmaceutical manufacturers, among the most profitable companies in America . . .

Doesn't Lieberman make a profit from his practice? Does he invest his savings only in unprofitable companies?

Communism (International Socialism) and Nazism (National Socialism) were brutal, unsubtle forms of socialism. Pharmacracy is a milder and subtler form of it. That is why it has proved to be so successful and that is why it is so dangerous. Lieberman seems to be oblivious that this is crux of my criticism of the therapeutic state.

IV

Lieberman's insensitivity to linguistic nuances infects virtually all of his interpretations of my writings. Examples abound:

> [M]ental illness [is] a term I use without flinching.

That is not an answer to my critique of the term and its uses.

Thomas Szasz deplores in American medicine and psychiatry the drift away from strictly scientific values.

This is nonsense. There are no scientific values: politically, science is value free. The values of the scientific enterprise are honesty and truth. Science and medicine may be used to save lives or take lives. What I deplore and oppose is psychiatrists coercing individuals and excusing their misbehavior. This has nothing to with "scientific values."

Szasz might take Rank's statement as a call to remove emotional suffering from the category of illness or disease and therefore from the purview of scientific and ethical medicine.

I eschew the inane use of the adjective "emotional" in psychiatry, and reject Lieberman's categorization of psychiatry as a part of scientific medicine and his absurd characterization of it as "ethical medicine."

Lieberman's linguistic insensitivity leads him to crass misinterpretation of my principles and practices. "Unlike Szasz," he writes, "I actively treat depression and try to prevent suicide, but not by force." Does Lieberman believe that, in my nearly fifty years of private practice, I never "treated" anyone who was depressed? That I encouraged my patients to commit suicide?

Lieberman enthuses about "romantic science," *à la* Goethe. But science is neither romantic nor unromantic. Goethe was a great artist and a great man. He was not a scientist. To Lieberman, Goethe was great because he "embraced, and refused to separate, natural science and art." Lieberman uses Goethe to "warn(s) against objectifying people for the sake of measurement and prediction." By implication, I am one of these unromantic persons who objectifies people.

Lieberman derides my opposition to physician-assisted suicide (PAS), which he enthusiastically supports, without any understanding of my reasons for opposing it. Why does Lieberman support PAS? Because "physicians control access to the most benign methods of euthanasia." Why don't non-physicians have access to lethal drugs? Because doctors, allied with the state, have deprived them of that right. No wonder Lieberman cannot find evidence for pharmacracy, scoffing, "Is this Pharmacracy?"

I oppose psychiatric coercion. Ralph Nader, Sidney Wolfe, and their Health Research group are enthusiastic supporters of psychiatric slavery. As such, they are prime examples of powerful battalions in the army of the Therapeutic State. Lieberman lauds them all. "Is this Pharmacracy?" Yes.

I believe schools ought to educate children, not stigmatize them as mentally ill and force them to submit to "counseling" and drugging. Lieberman lauds these practices. "Is this Pharmacracy?" he asks. Yes.

V

Before concluding, I want to thank Lieberman for his candor. He tells us where he stands. He and I disagree, but do so civilly.

I loathe pharmacracy. Lieberman loves it. When it stares him in the face he thinks he sees the visage of democracy, humanism, and universal health care, and incredulously asks: "Is this Pharmacracy?" Yes, indeed.

"This does not seem," he happily concludes, "to be a country of sheep-like patients acquiescing to a powerful pharmacracy." I have never said that the American people "acquiesced" to an alliance of medicine and the state. That verb implies a resigned acceptance of an onerous duty. A young man not eager to go fight in Vietnam is said to acquiesce to being drafted.

At the end of the last chapter of *Pharmacracy* I write: "Formerly, people rushed to embrace totalitarian states. Now they rush to embrace the therapeutic state."

Pious Jews, Christians, and Muslims do not feel *oppressed* by their respective theocracies; they feel *liberated* by them. They do not *acquiesce* in what they believe to be the Word of God; they rush to *embrace* it, because they find wisdom and security in it. The word "Islam" means submission. Pharmacracy is "medical Islam," exalted submission to the Therapeutic State.

Lieberman systematically distorts my language. He can't or doesn't want to hear me. I hope the reader can and does.

8

Bombing the Cradles: The Disordering Mental Effects of Off-the-Chart Life Experiences

MARGARET A. HAGEN

CHRISTA AND AVA WORTHINGTON, CAPE COD, MASSACHUSETTS, JANUARY, 2002

Worthington was stabbed in the chest at least once and could have been dead for up to 36 hours before a former boyfriend found her bloody body with her daughter on top of her Sunday afternoon, a source close to the case confirmed yesterday.

> — FRANCI RICHARDSON AND JESSICA HESLAM, *The Boston Herald*
> (January 9th, 2002)

On Sunday, Arnold said, he walked into Worthington's home and found her dead on the floor in her nightgown, with her curly-haired $2^{1}/_{2}$-year-old attempting to nurse on her. One investigator told the Associated Press that Worthington, 46, may have been dead for up to 36 hours.

> — Ellen Barry and John Ellement, *The Boston Globe*
> (January 9th, 2002)

Among the welter of news reports on this sensational case, the pundits weighed in heavily. Eileen McNamara, Pulitzer Prize-winning columnist for *The Boston Globe* opined a week after the discovery of the mother's dead body attended by her little girl,

It has been only a week since Christa Worthington was found dead in her Truro home, her daughter at her side. Isn't an immediate assessment of Ava's psychological health a more pressing concern than the ultimate determination of her custody? This child's psychological state needs to be addressed at least as urgently as any issue of custody.

Ava was in the same house, perhaps the same room, when her mother was stabbed to death. She spent the next 36 hours alone with her mother's body. Whatever her outward appearance, she is not fine. Shouldn't a psychological evaluation of Ava Worthington for post-traumatic stress disorder take precedence over a DNA test of Tony Jackett for paternity?

The fact that Ava suffered no physical injuries during the fatal attack on Worthington, a 46-year-old fashion writer, does not mean that she escaped unharmed. 'Age does not protect against trauma like this; we have seen trauma in children even younger who witness violence,' notes Betsy McAlister Groves, director of the Child Witness to Violence Project at Boston Medical Center. (Excerpt: Eileen McNamara, *Boston Globe* [January 16th, 2002], p. B1)

Proposition

Disregarding the sensationalism, what is the mental health proposition underlying the coverage of the two-year-old child left alone with her mother's body for a day and a half after her death, a child who most likely witnessed both the violent assault on her mother and the death itself? Clearly, it is that the child is mentally ill, at least temporarily, that she is suffering from some sort of "mental disorder" induced by the awfulness of her experience. Implicit in this proposition—and explicit in published opinions—is the conjoint claim that the child stands in need of the healing that can be afforded her only by psychotherapy.

What would Dr. Thomas Szasz say to this proposition?

Many people today take it for granted that living is an arduous affair. Its hardship for modern man derives, moreover, not so much from a struggle for biological survival as from the stresses and strains inherent in the social intercourse of complex human personalities. In this context, the notion of mental illness is used to identify or describe some feature of an individual's so-called personality. Mental illness as a deformity of the personality, so to speak, is then regarded as the cause of human disharmony. (Szasz 1960, p. 14)

And, continuing a bit further along in the same essay, Dr. Szasz writes:

What kinds of behavior are regarded as indicative of mental illness, and by whom? The concept of illness, whether bodily or mental, implies deviation from some clearly defined norm. In the case of physical illness, the norm is the structural and functional integrity of the human body. Thus, although the desirability of physical health, as such, is an ethical value, what health is can be stated in anatomical and physiological terms. What is the norm, deviation from which is regarded as mental illness? This question cannot be easily answered. But whatever this norm may be, we can be certain of only one thing: namely, that it must be stated in terms of psychosocial, ethical, and legal concepts. (Szasz 1960, p. 15.

It is clear from these passages, and from many others published elsewhere, that Dr. Szasz sees the issue of modern mental illness primarily as one of pejorative cultural labeling of those who are deviant from the norms, whose conduct fails to conform to the "psychosocial, ethical, and legal" norms of the cultural environment in which they live.

But what happens if we define environment—and environmental norms—in a broader and more primitive sense, in a sense drawn directly from the science of evolution and biological adaptation.? Of particular value to the present analysis is a conceptualization of "environment" first proposed by Egon Brunswick (1956) and then thoroughly developed by James J. Gibson of Cornell in books from 1950, 1967, and 1979, as well as in numerous articles. Gibson's formulation of the environment, and of man-environment relations—what he called the "mutuality of animal and environment—goes as follows:

The fact is worth remembering because it is often neglected that the words "*animal*" and "*environment*" make an inseparable pair. Each term implies the other. No animal could exist without an environment surrounding it. Equally, although not so obvious, an environment implies an animal (or at least an organism) to be surrounded. This means that the surface of the earth, millions of years ago before life developed on it, was not an environment, properly speaking. The earth was a physical reality, a part of the universe, and the subject matter of geology. It was a potential environment, prerequisite to the evolution of life on this planet. We might agree to call it a world, but it was not an environment. (Gibson 1979, p. 8)

Gibson explained further the mutuality of animal and environment thusly:

The "*affordances*" of the environment are what it "*offers*" the animal, what it "provides" or "furnishes," either for good or ill. The verb "*to afford*" is found in the dictionary, but the noun "affordance" is not. I have made it up. I mean by it something that refers to both the environment and the animal in a way that no existing term does. It implies the complementarity of the animal and the environment. (Gibson 1979, p. 127)

Having described examples such as horizontal, flat, extended, rigid surfaces that, for many animals, afford support—they are stand-on-able—Gibson extends the concept of affordances to substances and other objects.

The different substances of the environment have different affordances for nutrition and for manufacture. The different objects of the environment have different affordances for manipulation. The other animals afford, above all, a rich and complex set of interactions, sexual, predatory, nurturing, fighting, playing, cooperating, and communicating. What other persons afford comprises the whole realm of social significance for human beings. We pay the closest attention to the optical and acoustic information that specifies what the other person is, invites, threatens, and does. (Gibson 1979, p. 128)

Szasz has had us consider mental illness as a social construct applicable when the conduct of an individual fails to conform to the psychosocial, ethical and legal norms of the cultural environment in which he or she lives. Let us turn this conceptualization left-to-right, if you will.

Now, holding in mind a Gibsonian—"ecologically valid"—conceptualization of the relations between human beings and their environment, what might we suppose would logically happen to conforming individuals when they are confronted with *environments* that are "deviant from the norms"? What happens to an animal—to a child—when the affordances of the environment take a turn toward furnishing the child with "ill" on a monumental scale, on a scale for which successful adaptation for the species at large did not and, indeed, could not have existed?

If "child" (animal) and "environment" are mutually defined through their interactive complementarity, then what might we anticipate for the child when crucial aspects of the environment are wildly abnormal, when they are off-the-chart in what they afford?

In consideration of this question, it is important to keep in mind further that although the child is, by definition, a member of a species adapted to the general environment of the species, the adaptation skills of the individual child are presumably, like all other inborn skills, subject to much modification through training and experience. And opportunities to learn, to expand their coping skills, their abilities to adapt to the highly deviant must be, of necessity, in short supply for the very young. Perhaps, as with alcohol, tolerance to highly stressful situations must be built up over time.

Put as baldly as possible, the question is this: When normal children are exposed to events greatly outside the normal parameters of life, can they be pushed into a state properly characterized as mentally disordered? Can they be driven "mad"? When they are too young and too inexperienced with environmental stressors that are off-the-chart for them to have developed the more mature coping mechanisms that would characterize their older siblings or their parents in such situations, is it not reasonable to expect a disordering of the normal functioning of the child to mirror the abnormal functioning of the environment?

Let us move from the realm of assumption and argument, and consider rather what evidence is offered to answer the question from the existing research literature on this question. What does the scientific literature say about the ability of young children to adapt to supranormal stressors?

Mother-Assault as a Traumatic Stressor

This chapter began with an horrific account of the presumably highly traumatic experience of young Ava Worthington, the Massachusetts two-year-old who witnessed a fatal assault on her mother and remained with her body alone for some thirty-six hours afterward. It should go without saying that any loss of one's mother, and particularly under such dreadful circumstances, will arouse the professional interests of the psychological community. Indeed, a fairly large literature does exist to examine the effects on children of witnessing assaults both fatal and recurrent—on their mothers. Do the findings support the argument that witnessing maternal assault is traumatic enough to exceed the adaptive skills of the young child?

Lehmann (2000) gives us a preliminary hint of an answer to this question. He performed a meta-analysis of twenty-eight studies, both what he calls "clinical/descriptive" and "empirical" ones, to try to determine how frequently children witnessing "mother-assault" exhibited the signs of Post Traumatic Stress Disorder (PTSD). PTSD is the American Psychiatric Association's current formulation of the expected and frequently occurring mental condition that follows the experience of overwhelming trauma. The incidence of PTSD varied considerably across the groups making up the twenty-eight studies.

Acknowledging that much of this variability may have been introduced by combining groups of children who witnessed non-fatal assaults into the same analysis as children who witnessed the murders of their mothers, Lehmann split the analysis into the two groups of studies. Looking then just at the studies that examined cases of children who witnessed the homicide of their mothers—as opposed to nonfatal assaults—Lehmann found that the incidence of the witnessing children who met PTSD criteria varied from 50 percent to 100 percent wherever final statistics were available. This wide range suggests considerable variability but, in fact, a 100-percent incidence of PTSD among children who witnessed the murders of their mothers was the modal value across the studies reviewed.

Lehmann notes that despite these fairly consistent findings, there is still the misperception that the witnessing children are resilient and do not suffer long term effects. He writes: "Understanding the traumatic impact on children and adolescents exposed to mother-assault is timely and critical for a number of reasons. Primarily, intrafamilial abuse, neglect, and emotional violence account for the majority of the physical and emotional violence suffered by children in the United States" (Carnegie Council on Adolescent Development 1995). (Indeed, it is hard to imagine how it could be otherwise.) Presumably, among this very large group of children exposed to mother-assault, the number of children who actually witnessed the murders of their mothers is rather small.

In a further study on the effects of parental loss on children, Stoppelbein and Greening (2000) chose to compare children who had lost a parent to children who had experienced a fatal tornado disaster. They used as a no-trauma control a group of children coping with an ongoing social or academic stressor. Eighty-five percent of the parent-loss children had lost their fathers, rather than their mothers, and, on the average, were slightly less than ten years old at the time of the death. Death was caused by either disease (71 percent) or accident (29 percent). None of the children either witnessed the parent's death or saw the deceased parent's body at the time of death. The three groups of children were assessed for incidence of PTSD symptoms as well as for anxiety and depression.

Stoppelbein and Greening identified significantly more PTSD symptoms in children who had lost a parent than in children who experienced the tornado or in those who had a problem socially or scholastically. Moreover, the percentage of parentally-bereaved children who score in the severe PTSD range of symptoms was significantly larger than the corresponding percentages for the tornado-experiencing group (14 percent) or the school/social problems group (13 percent).

Bereaved girls, younger children, and children whose surviving parents also scored higher on a measure of PTSD tended to score higher than their counterparts. The authors suggest that the age differences might be "attributed to younger children possessing less mature cognitive coping skills to deal with a personal loss or to their willingness to endorse symptoms" (pp. 1116–17) They note too that the significance of the surviving parent's emotional adjustment for the bereaved children's well-being illustrates the importance of providing an emotionally stable environment for children coping with severe stress.

Stoppelbein and Greening conclude, not surprisingly, that children who have lost a parent could be highly vulnerable to PTSD symptoms because the loss of a parent may threaten a child's sense of invulnerability to threats. It is notable that the children in this study, however, had not lost the parent to homicide, nor had they witnessed a fatal assault on the parent. The traumas in these cases were more matters of ongoing loss, than a discrete event that accords with the DSM formulation of a critical traumatic stressor. Nevertheless, the loss of a parent is not commonplace for young children and may indeed on its own represent a bereavement and a threat that exceeds the grasp of normal coping mechanisms.

Like Stoppelbein and Greening, Kitayama et al. (2000) also chose to use a natural disaster that greatly exceeded normal dimensions to examine children's ability to successfully adapt to possibly overpowering disruption. In this case, that natural disaster was the Hanshin-Awaji Earthquake. Children from both heavily and lightly damaged areas were studied immediately following the earthquake, and then one and then two years later. They found that the children from the heavily damaged sites exhibited significantly more symptoms of PTSD such as persistent re-experiencing, persistent avoidance, and increased arousal. Nevertheless, they also found that all children had returned to "normal" functioning after two years.

Perhaps the earthquake did not rise to the threshold of "off-the-chart." Or, perhaps, over the two year period following it, the children learned to adapt to the stressful event and its aftermath. A quick look at exactly how the DSM defines the "T" in PTSD is in order, as well as a quick description of the behaviors that are said to indicate this disorder.

DSM Description of PTSD

According to the DSM-IV, a diagnosis of PTSD requires first and fore-most a traumatic stressor or stressors and, second, a combination of clus-tered diagnostic criteria. The clustered "symptoms" must include: 1. Persistent re-experiencing of the traumatic event: through recurrent and intrusive distressing recollections including images, thoughts and per-ceptions, and, for children, repetitive play involving themes or aspects of the trauma, distressing dreams, acting or feeling as if the traumatic event were re-occurring, and/or psychological and physiological distress at reminders that symbolize or resemble the event; 2. Avoidance of stimuli associated with the trauma or numbing of general responsiveness: avoid-ing thoughts, feelings, or conversations associated with the event, avoid-ance of activities associated with the event, inability to recall an impor-tant aspect of the event, behavioral regression, diminished interest in normal activities, feelings of detachment, restricted affect, and a sense of a foreshortened future, and 3. Persistent symptoms of increased arousal, such as difficulty falling or staying asleep, irritability, startle response, difficulty concentrating (school problems), and/or hypervigi-lence (pp. 428–29)

Of course, no one is expected to exhibit all of these symptoms; indeed, of the seventeen listed, the diagnosis depends on the appearance of only six of the seventeen.

Although the PTSD criteria, appearing for the first time in DSM-IV, were not identified solely with adult patients in mind, it is unde-niable that the adaptation of what is essentially an adult-based syn-drome despite its frequent extrapolation to young children is occa-sionally awkward in that the adult symptoms do not fit childish behavior, and, in most cases, a commonly observed child symptom lacks any real counterpart in adult patients. For example, flashbacks to an earlier time are extremely unlikely in young children, whereas regression to an earlier developmental level is unlikely to occur in adults.

PTSD Criteria Adapted to Children

A number of clinician-researchers, therefore, have attempted to tailor the DSM criteria for PTSD to fit children while, at the same time, they have attempted to establish reliable and valid instruments for an assess-ment of PTSD specific to childhood trauma.

Foa, Johnson, et al. (2001) report on their efforts to develop and validate an instrument they call the "Child PTSD Symptom Scale" (CPSS). They find that their instrument is internally consistent and reliable over time. Moreover, it correlates more highly with a pre-existing childhood PTSD scale than with measures of depression or anxiety. Thus the authors conclude that they are on the track of establishing a reliable instrument for the assessment of PTSD in children.

It must be noted, however, that the children comprising the test sample had been exposed to the putative trauma, the 1994 Northridge, California earthquake, fully two years before the reported PTSD assessment. Absent the determination of then-current traumatic reaction, it is problematic to argue that the event two years in the past was in any way reliably associated with the behaviors measured on the CPSS. It is far more prudent to examine the effects of a trauma experienced in the more recent past, a course followed by the next researchers.

Ruggiero and McLeer (2000) examined the utility of yet a third proposed measure of childhood PTSD, the PTSD subscale of the Child Behavior Check List, comparing sexually abused children to two groups of non-sexually abused children, one of non-clinic-referred schoolchildren and the other of psychiatric outpatients. They found that the CBCL PTSD subscale lacked concurrent validity and did not reliably distinguish between sexually abused children and psychiatric patients who were not sexually abused.

Clearly, the fundamental assumption that childhood sexual abuse (CSA) is a principle cause of PTSD in children failed to receive unqualified support in the present study. However, it is not clear whether the instrument's failure to discriminate sexually abused from psychiatric patients indicate the lack of trauma in the abuse cases, the presence of trauma in the non-abuse psychiatric cases, or neither of the above.

Not incidentally, both labels—"sexually abused" and "psychiatric"—employed to unify highly diverse groups of children for the purposes of research may simply mask so much variability as to render any discrimination between the groups close to impossible. Ruggiero and McLeer themselves suggest that the failure of the instrument to discriminate among the child groups may lie in the overlap of characteristics across groups. Certainly, the present research does not compel us to the conclusion that sexual abuse per se leads independently to the massive breakdown of coping mechanisms that characterizes PTSD. But we await variables and groups more clearly defined and unconfounded to reach any firm conclusions.

The failings of the field are noted more specifically and directly in a study by Morrissette (1999) who writes of the "definitional problems plaguing the diagnosis" of posttraumatic stress disorder among sexually abused children. In his review of the literature, Morrissette noted repeated difficulties encountered in obtaining an appropriate comparison group for sexually abused children, the lack of consensus in defining sexual abuse, and, again, the lack of standardized outcome measures and adequate instruments.

Perhaps recognizing that the extreme variability in definitions of childhood sexual abuse (see, for example, Kendall-Tackett, Williams, and Finkelhor 1997) makes it unlikely that clear cause and effect relationships between CSA and PTSD can be identified, Kilpatrick and Williams (1998) take the tack of looking at the effect on children not of directly experiencing abuse but of witnessing domestic violence. However, they found that despite their best efforts they could identify no effects at all of some half a dozen or so putatively "mediating variables"—including such fairly abstruse criteria as feelings of guilt or self-blame—on the incidence of symptoms of PTSD exhibited by the witnessing children.

More surprisingly, Kilpatrick and Williams also failed to discover any connection at all between any of their various measures of the intensity and frequency of the violence witnessed and the symptoms of PTSD exhibited by the witnessing children. Kilpatrick and Williams concluded that "all domestic violence may have severe and long-term impact on child witnesses" no matter how mild or extreme the experiences.

They may be correct in this conclusion but they have not provided the evidence to support it. The implication is that the range of severity and duration of the domestic violence experienced by the children was great and must clearly, at least for children at the upper end of the scale, have exceeded the limits of "normal" domestic (Australian) strife.

But it must be noted that the principle source of information about the nature of the alleged violent acts was provided by the mothers in these cases and, to some extent, corroborated by interviews with the children. Neither source is truly objective. It may very well be the case that however distressing to the participants, the mean level of violence experienced by the witnessing children simply did not rise to the threshold of trauma. It is very hard otherwise to argue that the intensity and frequency of the supposedly traumatic experiences had no effect on the traumatic sequelae. However, because domestic violence, like child sexual abuse, is defined so broadly and variably, it is highly likely that the mean level of stressful violence witnessed may not have risen to a critical level. (Most of the children in the present study had not been removed from their mothers' custody.) Likewise, it seems far more parsimonious to conclude that the child behaviors reported and observed were normal coping reactions to stress, and not pathological reactions to intolerable stressors.

Scheeringa et al. (2001), perhaps acknowledging the open question of the special vulnerability of very young children, chose to examine children, all under forty-eight months of age, who had experienced a number of traumas, mostly in and around the home. Scheeringa et al. (2001) discovered that using both a standardized procedure and a semistructured diagnostic interview—videotaped and blind reviewed—only 12 percent of the PTSD diagnostic criteria supposedly present in these children could be detected by clinical observation or interaction with the children. The rest of the symptoms were reported present by parental caregivers. The authors note that parental reporting of child behavior is problematic in a number of respects.

Interestingly, the traumatized children showed significantly more "alternative" PTSD symptoms than criteria noted in the DSM. Scheeringa et al. argued that the standard DSM criteria rely "excessively on verbalizations of subjective experiences." Since they were working with children so young, most of whom were pre-verbal or barely verbal, it was necessary to devise PTSD indicia more objectively observable than subjects' reports on feelings. Reliable alternatives were sleep disturbances, irritability, temper tantrums, hypervigilance, exaggerated startle response, avoidance of reminders of the traumatizing event(s), recurrent recollections of the event, upset over reminders, physiological reactivity to reminders, new fears and new aggressive acts.

It should go without saying that it is quite problematic for researchers to label non-DSM symptoms as indicia of PTSD except for the purpose of proposing hypotheses for further empirical work. If PTSD is to be subject to reliable empirical investigation of its validity, it must be consistently defined. While definitions of disorders may evolve, they cannot simply shift arbitrarily from study to study. At least, they cannot do so and remain within the realm of scientific discourse.

It does not follow, however, that the findings of studies dealing with children who have experienced extreme trauma are not themselves worthy of interest simply because the goal of attempting empirically to apply a DSM disorder label reliably to young children may be off target. In response to extreme trauma, children may exhibit, reliably, a cluster of behaviors indicative of coping breakdown whether or not such cluster meets any present or proposed DSM label. The question is exactly that: do children reliably exhibit indicia of coping/adaptation breakdown in the face of overwhelming stress? All we can tell from the present study is that high, but relatively inconsistent, numbers of children exhibit behavior patterns in response to identified stressors that seem likely to interfere with the accomplishment of developmental tasks like those involved in attending school (for instance "decreased concentration" versus "constriction of play").

The children in the Scheeringa et al. study were undeniably subject to stress. Unfortunately, as with so many of these studies of children and PTSD, children who have experienced a range of stress in terms of severity, frequency, or duration are all lumped into one group for purposes such as validating a new instrument or alternative criterial attributes. Traumatic intensity is almost never considered as an independent variable— presumably because the N in the study would then be very small. So, we find in the present study a range of traumas experienced stretching from unspecified sexual abuse to a dog attack —also of an unspecified nature—to escaping from a home fire to seeing two relatives shot, one of whom was killed. It seems presumptuous in the extreme to assume any sort of equivalence across these putative "traumas" beyond the label given to them.

Certainly it is not possible, given the variety of putative traumas, to reach conclusions about the role of severity of trauma in inducing childhood breakdown.

Research by Soliman (1999), however, moves us indisputably beyond the outer limits of the normative parameters of a child's life, and into the abnormal climate of political violence and wars. What happens when we look at the mental well-being of children who have witnessed the destruction or loss of homes, villages, towns, of every familial and cultural anchor in their lives? Soliman himself examined war's effects on a single child, a Kuwaiti twelve-year-old who experienced the invasion of his country by Iraq, and, while not generalizing beyond this case, suggests that the children of war warrant a much longer and more comprehensive look. He notes in his review of past literature on the subject of the vulnerability of children to the experiences of political violence and wars that research indeed has shown that their reactions are influenced by the nature of the conflict, the magnitude of destruction, and the degree to which children are directly involved in events. (This last is a factor that probably should be considered in the domestic violence research.)

Soliman writes:

> Short-term symptoms associated with these experiences include anxiety, sleep problems, school refusal, loss of appetite, somatic symptoms, paralysis and panic. Long-term symptoms may influence the child's ability to fulfill critical developmental tasks. These symptoms include difficulties in concentration, loss of developmental skills, and flashbacks associated with anxiety, depressed mood, conduct difficulties and lack of confidence in the future. (p. 164)

Soliman noted that a previous researcher considered children's PTSD reactions within the ethological context of theory of attachment and loss.

The case Soliman used for illustration was that of an eleven-year-old boy, Hamad, who lived with his family during the Iraqi invasion of Kuwait in August 1990. As the Iraqi army crossed the Kuwaiti border, news about its atrocity and inhumane treatment of people was spread. During the six months of Iraqi occupation, Hamad, eight-years-old at that time, lived with his parents and his siblings, in the family home and avoided leaving the house unless it was absolutely necessary. It was just a matter of time before the Iraqi soldiers broke into the family home during the night and searched the home, forcing the family to remain in a corner in the living room under the close watch of armed soldiers. After searching the home for weapons, the soldiers forced Hamad's father to go with them for interrogation. The family reacted with shock, fear, disbelief, and horror. While Hamad's siblings remained close to their mother, he kept a psychological distance from everyone in the family.

After two months, Hamad's father was released and returned home in a devastated physical and emotional condition. During the period following the war, Hamad acted normally, but seemed to avoid conversations about the war. He also showed a lack of interest in social activities and seemed withdrawn. After a period of two years, family members observed more behavioral changes in Hamad. His mother indicated that he would wake up several times during the night. He experienced nightmares, but could not remember them in detail. Teachers reported his loss of concentration and inability to stay on task, causing his grades to drop. Hamad avoided social contacts at school and responded with aggressive outbursts when other children tried to approach him. Initially, the family tried different methods to engage Hamad in normal activities but failed. He continued to avoid conversations, news reports, or celebrations regarding the liberation of Kuwait (p. 166).

It does not seem much of a stretch to argue that a child engaged in so many dysfunctional behaviors cannot at the same time be engaged fully in moving forward developmentally, in dealing with the ever-changing array of tasks life presents.

Soliman points out that Hamad's case is not one where the patient—the child or his family—was seeking out the secondary gains associated with being in psychotherapy, or even sometimes, of having been identified as needing psychotherapy. To the contrary. Soliman writes:

> [Hamad's case] is typical of Middle-Eastern perceptions toward therapy. Confusion about treatment options and a lack of understanding of the validity of mental health intervention caused delay in the client receiving appropriate intervention. Initially, the family considered medical intervention for the patient's behavioral changes. Fear of stigmatization and labeling the client as "crazy" were reflected in the family's reluctance to seek therapy. (p. 165)

More generally, Soliman notes that in Third World countries, cultural constraints and lack of awareness of the impact of mental disorders on children have precluded opportunities to receive needed interventions.

Hamad's case strongly suggests that most of the existing research is not looking far enough outside familiar and comfortable cultural parameters, and the contrasting findings of the work on children who have witnessed the murders of their mothers (Lehmann 2000) and the work on abused children suggests similarly that existing research is not focused often enough much beyond the normal parameters of adaptive coping. This is particularly true of American research that tends to look at broadly, and often politically, defined stressful phenomena in children's lives. Davis and Siegel (2000), however, in their review of the expanding interest in applying and adapting diagnostic criteria for PTSD to child samples, point out that literature is increasingly looking at cases of horrific natural disasters, war, and political violence.

What do we find when we look at children's response to life's experiences that are incontrovertibly off-the-chart for normal life's expectations?

Off-the-Chart Traumas and PTSD in Children

According to the DSM, the criterial stressor for PTSD is defined as a traumatic event in which both were present:

the person experienced, witnessed, or was confronted with an event or events that involved actual or threatened death or serious injury, or a threat to the physical integrity of self or others; and the person's response involved intense fear, helplessness, or horror. (pp. 427–28.)

There must certainly be numerous cases of child assault and domestic violence that entail threatened death or serious injury, but the grouping of child subjects together without regard to the severity of the stressor makes it impossible to examine the incidence of PTSD in children so stressed.

Stress, after all, is a normal part of life, and adaptation to or coping with stress is likewise a normal part of life. The fact that the CSA and DV children studied in the research reviewed above failed to reveal any differential effects due to severity of the stressor just tells us about the limits of the research, not about whether the normal coping mechanisms of children can be stressed to the point of mental disorder by exposure to extreme stressors outside the normal range.

PTSD may be a highly suspect diagnosis because in much of the research we find the aggregation into a single sample of a number of individuals whose experiences of psychological stress vary wildly. The diagnosis is also suspect not least in part because of its frequent appearance in tort or liability cases. Also, in many if not most cases, the claimed trauma itself cannot be validated. Moreover, the variety of criteria listed—which frequently include both a symptom *and* its opposite or absence—makes careful research under the existing DSM criteria highly problematic. Indeed, the listing in DSM of PTSD symptoms along with their opposites calls to mind Szasz's apt but humorous comments on the determination of psychiatric problems in schoolchildren:

> I have discussed and documented elsewhere that there is no behavior or person that a modern psychiatrist cannot plausibly diagnose as abnormal or ill. Instead of belaboring this subject I shall cite a set of guidelines—conforming closely to the rule, "Heads I win, tails you lose,"—offered by a psychiatrist for finding psychiatric problems in schoolchildren. In a paper advocating psychiatric services in public schools, the author lists the following types of behavior as "symptomatic of deeper underlying disturbances": 1. Academic problems—under-achievement, over-achievement, erratic, uneven performance. 2. Social problems with siblings, peers—such as the aggressive child, the submissive child, the show-off. 3. Relations with parental and other authority figures, such as defiant behavior, submissive behavior, ingratiation. 4. Overt behavioral manifestations, such as tics, nail-biting, thumb-sucking, (and) interests more befitting to the opposite sex (such as tom-boy girl and effeminate boy).

Clearly, there is no childhood behavior that a psychiatrist could not place in one of these categories. To classify as pathological academic performance that is "under-achievement," "over-achievement," or "erratic performance," would be humorous were it not tragic. When we are told that if a psychiatric patient is early for his appointment, he is anxious, if he is late, he is hostile, and if on time, compulsive, we laugh, because it is supposed to be joke. But here we are told the same thing in all seriousness. (1970, p. 35)

And so it is with PTSD. One may sleep too much or sleep too little. Be hypervigilant or apathetic. Have no memory of the precipitating trauma or endure countless intrusive recollections.

Nevertheless, however "loose" the proposed criterial attributes of the DSM definition of PTSD may be, it does not obviate the central question of whether an extreme, off-the-chart, environmental trauma can indeed disrupt the adaptive functioning of a young child to the point that it is reasonable to call the child "disordered" or "dysfunctional," whatever the establishment term for the condition may be or how consistent across children the "disorder" turns out to be, except in so far as it interferes with the accomplishment of ongoing developmental tasks.

In examining the validity of the hypothesis that the "off-the-chart" life experience can indeed trigger not the normal coping mechanism in the face of stress but a dysfunctional response due to inability of the child to adapt to the extreme abnormality of the situation, it seems far more conservative to look only at unambiguously statistically abnormal experiences such as the maternal homicide with which this chapter began.

A number of candidates for off-the-chart, in addition to witnessing maternal homicide, appear in the literature on children and trauma: chief among these are War and Natural Disasters. Let us look briefly at whether a clearer picture arises of the putatively traumatized child when there is little controversy about the extremity of the validated stressor.

Beyond Maternal Homicide: War and Natural Disasters

Does the research clearly identify at least the experiences of War and serious Natural Disasters as Off-the-Chart, PTSD-inducing, stressors for young children?

Hosin (2001) looked at two children who are war survivors at one remove. Their parents witnessed near death experiences and assaults and the father manifests what the researcher saw as clearly PTSD symptoms. The father also exhibited episodic rage and violent behavior. Hosin points out that "refugee experiences devastate individual well-being and coping mechanisms if there is no hope, support and faith in one's potential." Yet, he finds that although the children of these survivors have developed what he calls "separation problems" and "psychosomatic complaints," they are free of the PTSD and rage symptoms exhibited by the father. (So too is the mother symptom-free.) Hosin discusses these differences in terms of factors that influence "resilience," but at least in the case of the children, it must be noted here that their experience of the war was not as severe as that of their parents, and it is not at all clear what "refugee" status means to a child, whereas the devastating, comprehensive and complex loss invoked by the term is obvious to all adults.

Vizek-Vidovic et al. (2001) looked at groups of schoolchildren who themselves were directly traumatized to different degrees during the war in Croatia. They found that children's reactions to war trauma varied according to the level of traumatization, measured by the number and type of war experiences. Younger children, particularly those who survived more war experiences, reported even more PTSD symptoms than older children.

Ahmad and his colleagues (2000) examined children from forty-five families in two displacement camps who were among the survivors of the "Anfal" military operation in Iraqi Kurdistan. They found that eighty-five percent of the children exhibited symptoms characteristic of PTSD. For brevity's sake, the stressor in this case will be termed "war," but subsumed under this term is all of the destruction and chaos of war as well as the loss of home, livelihood, community, village or town associated with refugee status in a camp for displaced persons. So, clearly, there is no single "stressor" in the lives of these children but a complex of correlated traumatic events. In this study, the extremity of the "trauma" experienced was objectively measured as was the duration of captivity. Severity and duration both predicted, significantly, the symptoms of PTSD in these survivor children.

In a related study, Ahmad et al. (2000) looked at both PTSD-related symptoms and symptoms not grouped under PTSD and determined that it was possible to distinguish between them for groups of children who were war orphans, survivors of a military campaign, and war refugees in another country. The incidence of PTSD among their war survivor group—children who directly experienced the traumatizing violence of war at first-hand—was about eighty-seven percent. They say that the cross-cultural instrument they are devising to measure PTSD in children produces results in accord with existing monocultural instruments.

Berman (2001), in a broad ranging review of recent literature on the effects of war and its correlated disruptive phenomena, points out that despite its almost ubiquitous presence in our daily newspapers, the cataclysmal phenomenon that is modern warfare is not a common experience in the history of humanity. He notes that

> When the United Nations High Commission for Refugees was first established during the 1950s to provide international protection to refugees following World War II, it was estimated that there were 1.5 million refugees and displaced persons. Today there are approximately 14 million, about three-fourths of whom are women and children. Although the experiences of refugee children and adolescents vary considerably, many have witnessed or experienced the death or murder of loved ones. Upon resettlement, they face numerous challenges. (p. 243)

Again, for the purposes of this chapter, the complex of experiences of these children in the present context will be termed the trauma of "war."

Berman's study is a review of recent findings, not an attempt by himself to establish particular cause and effect relationships, but he finds convincing the empirical claim that many of these extremely and repeatedly traumatized children experience long-term "emotional health problems" that are frequently conceptualized by clinicians as Post Traumatic Stress Disorder. The massive and comprehensive evidence certainly seems to support the notion that for many of the child survivor/witnesses to war, the complex experiences exceed their ability to cope, or to adapt.

Conclusions

There will be many more studies of the effects, long-and short-term, on children of war and its myriad associated horrors. Each year the adults of the world create hundreds of thousands of more potential research subjects. Yet, the results of the existing research are so far quite consistent.

We have no more reason to assume that the ability to adapt to highly unusual situations is any more built-in than the ability to figure skate.

The necessary preconditions are there but the skill is not. Absent the skill, an amateur-naïf on the ice can easily break an ankle or fracture a psyche.

The horrific strains of war in its various forms and degrees frequently, for many children, prove to be too much for the inborn adaptive mechanisms to successfully meet. Many children lack the coping strategies, or resilience, or simply the ability to assimilate the experienced events in ways that permit the continued integration of the self. They become so consumed with dysfunctional behaviors like the inability to sleep, constant nightmares, inability to concentrate, loss of belief in a future, that they cannot accomplish the developmental tasks that face them every day.

The American Psychiatric Association chooses to call such a response Post Traumatic Stress Disorder and attempts through means both admirable and short-sighted to establish reliable criteria for its diagnosis. It makes no difference what the label is. Nor does a focus on the specific "symptoms" considered criterial seem useful.

However, to the extent that children are crippled mentally, psychologically, or spiritually—to the extent that they are mired in a developmentally dysfunctional present—then to that extent should we acknowledge the psychological impact of war on the minds—or hearts or souls—of our children and embrace the necessity of ameliorating its effects by whatever means necessary.

As Szasz wrote some time ago when considering the tasks of childhood,

> I submit that "Paradise Lost" is a myth. The pleasurable qualities of childhood experiences and of regressive goals generally have been vastly overrated. Dispensing with the whole vexing problem of how happy or satisfying childhood gratifications are, I shall adhere, instead, to a position concerning psychosocial gratification essentially similar to Langer's. However, I wish to supplement her basic thesis, that man has a need for symbolization and symbolic expression, by adding two complementary notions to it: first, that man has a primary (further irreducible) need for object contact or human relationships; (monkeys, Harlow) ; second, that the notions of objects, symbols, rules and roles are intimately tied together, so that man's growth toward personal identity and integrity on the one hand, and toward social tolerance and decreasing need for group narcissism on the other, go hand in hand with increasing sophistication in regard to the understanding and use of symbols, rules, roles and games. (Szasz 1961, pp. 185–86)

Man's growth toward personal identity and integrity may indeed go hand in hand with increasing sophistication in regard to the understanding and use of symbols, rules, roles and games unless there are too many symbols of helplessness, too many broken rules, and too many roles productive of ill for the individual, until for the child the game is simply lost.

R E F E R E N C E S

Ahmad, A, M.A. Sofi, V. Sundelin-Wahlsten, A.L. von Knorring. 2000. Posttraumatic Stress Disorder in Children after the Military Operation "Anfal" in Iraqi Kurdistan. *European Child and Adolescent Psychiatry* 9:4 (December, 2000), pp. 235–243.

Ahmad, A., V. Sundelin-Wahlsten, M.A. Sofi, J.A. Qahar, A.L. von Knorring. 2000. Reliability and Validity of a Child-specific Cross-cultural Instrument for Assessing Posttraumatic Stress Disorder. *European Child and Adolescent Psychiatry* 9:4 (December, 2000), pp. 285–294

Barry, Ellen and John Ellement. 2002. Friends Say Truro Victim Lived No Ordinary Life. *The Boston Globe*. Third edition. Section: Metro/Region (January 9th), B1.

Berman, H. 2001. Children and War: Current Understandings and Future Directions. *Public Health Nursing* 18:4 (July–August, 2001), pp. 243–252.

Brunswick, Egon. 1956. *Perception and the Representative Design of Psychological Experiments*. Berkeley: University of California Press.

Davis L., and L.J. Siegel. 2000. Posttraumatic Stress Disorder in Children and Adolescents: A Review and Analysis. *Clinical Child Family Psychology Review* 3:3 (September, 2000), pp. 135–154.

Foa, Edna B., Kelly M. Johnson, Norah C. Feeny, R. Kimberli, and H. Treadwell. 2001. The Child PTSD Symptom Scale: A Preliminary Examination of Its Psychometric Properties. *Journal of Clinical Child Psychology* 30:3 (August, 2001), pp. 376–384.

Frances, Allen. 1994. *Diagnostic and Statistical Manual of Mental Disorders*. Fourth edn. Washington, D.C.: American Psychiatric Association.

Gibson, James J. 1950. *The Visual World*. Boston: Houghton Mifflin.

———. 1967. *The Senses Considered as Perceptual Systems*. Boston: Houghton Mifflin.

———. 1979. *The Ecological Approach to Visual Perception*. Boston: Houghton Mifflin.

Hosin, A.A. 2001. Children of Traumatized and Exiled Refugee Families: Resilience and Vulnerability. A Case Study Report. *Medical Conflagration Survivors* 17:2 (April–June, 2001), pp. 137–145

Kendall-Tackett, K. A., L.M. Williams, and D. Finklehor. 1993. Impact of Sexual Abuse on Children: A Review and Synthesis of Recent Empirical Studies. *Psychological Bulletin* 113:1, pp. 164–180.

Kilpatrick, Kym L., and L.M. Williams. 1998. Potential Mediators of Post-traumatic Stress Disorder in Child Witnesses to Domestic Violence. *Child Abuse and Neglect* 22:4 (April, 1998), pp. 319–330.

Kitayama, S., Y. Okada, T. Takumi, S. Takada, Y. Inagaki, and H. Nakamura. 2000. Psychological and Physical Reactions on Children after the Hanshin-Awaji Earthquake Disaster. *Kobe Journal of Medical Science* 46:5 (October, 2000), pp. 189–200.

Lehmann, Peter. 2000. Posttraumatic Stress Disorder (PTSD) and Child Witnesses to Mother-Assault: A Summary and Review. *Children and Youth Services Review* Vol. 22, 3–4 (March–April, 2000), pp. 275–306.

McNamara, Eileen. 2002. Child's Needs Come First. *The Boston Globe.* Third edition (January 13th, 2002).

Morrissette, Patrick J. 1999. Post-traumatic Stress Disorder in Child Sexual Abuse: Diagnostic and Treatment Considerations. *Child and Youth Care Forum*, Vol. 28, 3 (June, 1999), pp. 205–219.

Richardson, Franci, and Jessica Heslam. 2002. Police Say Killer Targeted Truro Fashion Writer. *The Boston Herald.* All editions. Section: News (January 9th, 2002), p. 4.

Ruggiero, Kenneth J., and Susan V. McLeer. 2000. PTSD Scale of the Child Behavior Checklist: Concurrent and Discriminant Validity with Non-Clinic-Referred Sexually Abused Children. *Journal of Traumatic Stress*, Vol. 13, 2 (April), pp. 287–299.

Scheeringa, M.S., C.D. Peebles, C.A. Cook, and C.H. Zeanah. 2001. Toward Establishing Procedural, Criterion, and Discriminant Validity for PTSD in Early Childhood. *Journal of the American Academy of Child and Adolescent Psychiatry* 40:1 (January), pp. 52–60.

Soliman, Hussein H. 1999. Post-traumatic Stress Disorder: Treatment Outcomes for a Kuwaiti Child. *International Social Work*, Vol. 42, 2 (April), pp. 163–175.

Stoppelbein, L., and L. Greening. 2001. Posttraumatic Stress Symptoms in Parentally Bereaved Children and Adolescents. *Journal of the American Academy of Child and Adolescent Psychiatry* 39:9 (September), pp. 1112–19

Szasz, Thomas. 1960. The Myth of Mental Illness. Reprinted in *Ideology and Insanity: Essays on the Psychiatric Dehumanization of Man* (Garden City: Anchor, 1970).

Szasz, Thomas. 1961. *The Myth of Mental Illness.* New York: Harper and Row.

Szasz, Thomas. 1970. *The Manufacture of Madness.* New York: Harper and Row.

Vizek-Vidovic, V., G. Kuterovac-Jagodic, and L. Arambasic. 2000. Post-traumatic Symptomatology in Children Exposed to War. *Scandinavian Journal of Psychology* 41:4 (December), pp. 297–306.

Reply to Hagen

THOMAS SZASZ

Margaret Hagen's essay addresses the role of the potentially deforma-
tive nature of the human environment on human behavior in general, and
on the child's development in particular. Her reflections afford an opportunity for further clarification. Hagen asks:

> [What] might we suppose would logically happen to conforming individu-
> als when they are confronted with *environments* that are 'deviant from the
> norms'? What happens to . . . a child when the affordances of the environ-
> ment take a turn toward furnishing the child with 'ill' on a monumental
> scale, on a scale for which successful adaptation for the species at large did
> not and, indeed, could not have existed?

The answer lies in observation, not in logic. Human environments—
that is, families, societies, religions, cultures—vary greatly and cannot
be said to be either normal nor abnormal. They are what they are. We
don't have, and cannot have, *objective criteria* for what constitutes a
normal family or society or religion or culture. We have, and can have,
only *conventional criteria* for them. By definition, every group regards
its customs and laws as "normal."

Hagen wonders about what happens to a child when his environment
is extremely unfavorable to what we regard as normal development.
Calling such an environment "ill," even if the word is between quotation
marks, moves us in the direction of conceptualizing the phenomenon
and its consequences in psychopathological terms. Hagen asks: "Can
they [children exposed to such an environment] be driven 'mad'?", and
answers by citing the results of a "meta-analysis of twenty-eight studies," that show an increased incidence of PTSD (Post Traumatic Stress
Disorder) among traumatized children. Here, Hagen embraces the psychopathological perspective on human behavior that I reject. There are

no objective tests for mental illnesses, PTSD included. As a result, mental health professionals can easily construct "studies" to prove their prejudices. Then, after several such "studies" are published in the professional literature, psychiatrists and psychologists study the "studies," call the new study a "meta-analysis," and, presto, we have "scientific data." The whole enterprise is a sham.

Hagen's conclusion that "the loss of a parent is not commonplace for young children" is parochial. It is not true at all times, in all places. Her addendum that such loss "may indeed on its own represent . . . a threat that exceeds the grasp of normal coping mechanisms," is oversimplified and erroneous. The important thing with respect to a personal loss is not only what the subject has lost but also what he still has, what replaces his loss, and what he then does with his resources. This is especially true for young children and infants. If a child loses a parent before he is born or in the first two years of life, he may experience no loss at all. His well-being or lack of it will depend on how well he is cared for by the persons who nurture him. Albert Camus and Jean-Paul Sartre both lost their fathers before they were born. They were well cared for by their mothers and other relatives and the human environment in which they grew up was probably more favorable for their development than is the environment that many intact families provide for their children. Bertrand Russell lost both parents when he was an infant and was raised by his grandmother, nannies, and tutors. Insofar as his development was impaired, which it was in some respects but not in others, it was probably largely attributable to the influence of his grandmother, rather than to the loss of his parents *per se*.

However, all this may seem as if I am caviling about minute disagreements. Hagen agrees with my contention that the DSM is a colossal fraud. PTSD is not a disease in the same sense that pneumonia is a disease.

People often torture, injure, and kill their fellow human beings. The result is not mental illness but spiritual crippling, physical deformity, or death.

9

What Kind of Freedom?
Szasz's Misleading Perception of
Physician-Assisted Suicide

MARGARET P. BATTIN

and RYAN SPELLECY

Like other social theorists whose analyses are punctuated with periodic brilliance, Thomas Szasz offers genuine insight into the ethical issues in physician-assisted suicide. Szasz's view of the practice attends to the larger social setting of medicine, and sees the physician as an agent of power in an institution that is deeply socially entrenched. The practice of physician-assisted suicide must play itself out within this institution, undercutting the claim of liberty made by those who favor—or actually seek—physician aid in their own dying.

For Szasz, medicine as an institution carries with it the awesome, often-abused power to define health and illness, to identify and label who counts as well and who is ill. This power is particularly evident in the area of mental illness—where, Szasz thinks, virtually all such discrimination and labeling is fraudulent—but it is nonetheless part of those areas of medicine concerned with "physical" health as well. Who counts as a "patient"? Who shall be "treated"? Who is "under observation," or "in remission," or "developing abnormally"? Ssasz does not deny that people have physical differences, including differences in function and comfort, but resists medicine's global claim to distinguish persons on the basis of such differences as "well" or "ill."

Szasz is surely right that medicine carries with it an awesome power that raises a number of concerns, particularly when this power is manifested in physician-assisted suicide. His work injects a healthy skepticism into the debate surrounding physician-assisted suicide and what role, if any, medicine should play. He warns of the potential for corrupting the practice of medicine that physician-assisted suicide brings, noting parallels some have drawn between euthanizing an animal for humane reasons and physician-assisted suicide (and euthanasia for that matter). In veterinary medicine, a veterinarian recommends euthanasia as the humane option, or even as the preferred treatment. We will address this claim later, but if such recommendations became common practice in medicine, the results would be terrible indeed.

In recent years, since approximately the late 1970s, the issue of physician-assisted suicide has been under broad public discussion. When a patient is nearing the end of his or her life and suffers from irremediable pain, may the patient request and the physician provide direct aid in dying? More plainly put, may the terminally ill patient seek and receive active assistance from the physician in committing suicide? Proponents of this practice and of the legalization of it argue that this is a matter of fundamental liberty: that just as a competent person is recognized in a society based on individual freedom to have the right to determine the course of his or her life, subject only to the proviso that this not cause harm to others, so the person who is dying must also have the right to determine how the very end of his or her life shall go. Choices open to the dying person about how his or her dying process shall conclude include whether it shall end "naturally" as the disease overwhelms medical efforts to forestall it, or in "negotiated" death as life-prolonging treatment is removed, or by means of aid-in-dying as the physician provides the patient the means for actually bringing death about. Thus proponents argue that the dying patient should be able to choose among continuing treatment (even though it will eventually fail), or withholding or withdrawing treatment so that death occurs, or causing their own death directly with the physician's help. This is a matter of fundamental, basic liberty.

Opponents, on the other hand, have made numerous arguments against the practice and legalization of physician-assisted suicide. Critics, including Szasz, have argued against the claim that physician-assisted suicide is a matter of fundamental, basic liberty, and relatedly, that there is no 'right' to physician-assisted suicide, whether that right is seen as positive or negative, moral, or constitutional. Szasz does not oppose suicide generally. He favors the legalization of drugs so that one may preform suicide without the assistance of a physician.

By far the most prevalent and accessible argument against the legalization of assisted suicide is the slippery slope. Such arguments are used,

"to resist the acceptance, performance, or legalization of specific practices" (Battin 1994, p. 21). A slippery slope argument (at least, a good
one) claims that we stand at the edge of a slippery slope. At the bottom
of this slope is a clearly immoral outcome, such as the killing of mentally retarded persons in Nazi Germany, or as Szasz calls it in his discussion in Chapter 6 of *Fatal Freedom*, physician-assisted murder. If we
take a step down the slope we will be unable to stop ourselves and will
find ourselves at the bottom, engaging in the immoral practice. Thus, we
begin with just one step down that slope which seems innocuous
enough, or at least not nearly as objectionable as the bottom of the slope.
That first step might be the legalization of physician-assisted suicide
only in cases involving competent, terminally ill adults. However, we
will slide inexorably down the slope to the Nazis' practice of physician-
assisted murder. This might occur because there is no principled manner
in which to distinguish between permissible and impermissible cases,
because the reasons used to justify the permissible cases must also apply
to and permit the impermissible cases. Such a slippery slope is often
referred to as a logical slippery slope. On the other hand there are empirical slippery slope arguments. These arguments appeal to past experiences, such as the horrors committed by the Nazis, to motivate the idea
of an inevitable slide down the slope. If we relax our vigilance even
slightly, we will begin a slide down the slope . . . again.

Szasz advances many interesting arguments concerning physician-
assisted suicide. We would like to begin by focusing on two of these:
a slippery slope argument and an argument that patients have no need
for physician-assisted suicide. We will begin by addressing the latter,
arguing that Szasz is mistaken when he claims there is no need for
assistance in suicide, and that the physician may in many cases be an
appropriate source of that needed assistance. We will then address
Szasz's slippery slope argument, clarifying the debate and correcting
factual errors made by Szasz in setting up his argument, and question
what role his slippery slope argument really plays. Next, we will turn
to Szasz's objections to physician-assisted suicide based upon the role
of the physician and power. While Szasz's concerns stem from reasonable motivations, his conclusions are unsupported. Finally, we
conclude by examining Szasz's own proposal for how suicide and
assisted suicide might be practiced without the involvement of physicians, weighing concerns of the medicalization of everyday life and
autonomy against the need for safeguards to protect against abuse and
coercion.

The Need for Assistance in Suicide

Part of the brilliance of Szasz's critique lies in the fact that he addresses a number of different approaches to physician-assisted suicide. He does not address merely the liberty interest arguments or arguments that seek to justify the legalization of physician-assisted suicide through an appeal to rights. Rather, he considers a number of different claims, advanced in both scholarly and popular media.

One approach criticized by Szasz argues that physician-assisted suicide is a service, and that patients *need* this service. Szasz counters though that,

> A person has no *need* for another to perform a service that he could perform for himself, provided, of course, that he wants to and is allowed to perform the service for himself. If a person knows how to drive but prefers to be driven by someone else, he has no *need* for a chauffeur, he *wants* a chauffeur. (Szasz 1999, p. 64)

Szasz clarifies his position, noting that he does not deny that the assistance of a physician might be *helpful* in committing suicide, but that that alone cannot mitigate the fact that a person has no need for another person to perform a service that he could perform for himself.

Of course, there is a contingent sense in which persons do have a need for a physician's assistance in suicide. Given U.S. drug laws, patients do not have ready access to the types of drugs used in physician-assisted suicide, and thus need a prescription. Szasz is aware of this and notes that a person has no need for another to provide a service provided he is allowed to perform it for himself. Since individuals require a prescription to gain access to the drugs needed for this type of suicide, they are not allowed to perform it for themselves.

Szasz favors deregulation of (at least) these drugs. Szasz draws an analogy between prohibition and current U.S. drug policy, arguing:

> When [alcohol] Prohibition was the law, physicians prescribed liquor to patients who had a 'medically legitimate' need for it, and people were happy to accept that evasion. Now drug prohibition is the law, physicians want to prescribe barbiturates to patients who have a 'medically legitimate' need for them, and people are happy to accept that evasion. The proper remedy for Prohibition was repeal, restoring control over drinking to the citizen, not the intensified medicalization of drinking. The proper remedy for the 'war on drugs' is repeal, restoring control over drug use to the citizen, not the intensified medicalization of suicide. (Szasz 1999, pp. 66–67)

This is an ii
argument by
tion, in this c
applies to on
must be nearl
are Prohibitioi
thus must shov
barbiturates) p
and so forth, to
could not demo
argument is to c
hibition of barbi
prohibition, the j
therefore the proj
biturate prohibitic
premise—there is
hibition was effect
bade the sale, poss
alcohol with a pres

Szasz's choice of chauffeurs and chau
analogy is the most vexing element of h
physician-assisted suicide. Comparii
nical operation as suicide with s
by a chauffeur misses the coi
Suicide and chauffeuring a
driving oneself and kil
er their centrality t
relative ease. Ki
One of th
cide is th
ly. Th
a

...ould obtain ...z needs to show is that the *reasons* for repealing the prohibition of alcohol should also apply to barbiturates. If these reasons apply equally, then Szasz might modify his argument. We will return to Szasz's argument for de-regulation of these drugs later when we discuss alternatives to legalization of physician-assisted suicide and Szasz's views.

There is a more problematic sense of need in Szasz's argument that there is no need for physician-assisted suicide. Recall that the core of Szasz's argument is that a person has no need for another person to perform a service which he could perform for himself, provided that he wants and is allowed to perform the service for himself. Szasz's inclusion of the caveat that the person has no need for another to perform a service provided he *wants* to provide that service for himself cannot mean that if one wishes to have the service performed but does *not* wish to perform it himself, then that person has need of assistance; otherwise, the chauffeur example would not make sense, as this is an example where a person wants driving performed but does not wish to perform the driving himself. Perhaps Szasz means only that one must want to perform the service for oneself, and this is a prerequisite to avoid coercion. But this would have no bearing on need. Regardless, Szasz's definition of need is unclear. If a condition for "no need" is that I am able and willing to perform the action in question for myself, does this mean that my mere unwillingness to perform an action for myself generates need?

feur-assisted driving for an

s argument against the need for

g such a complex, grave, and tech-

ch a trivial operation as being driven

plexity of the situation and thus the need.

e dissimilar in a number of ways. First of all,

ing oneself are vastly different when we consid-

one's life. Furthermore, one can drive oneself with

ling oneself is not as simple a matter.

e reasons a person might ask for and need assistance in sui-

t committing suicide can be very difficult to perform *correct-*

chance for a mistake is somewhat high, and the consequences of

istake are even higher. Instead of killing oneself, one might rather take too much of a medication and vomit, or take the wrong combination of medications and recover, but with significant mental impairments. The latter can occur in any number of methods used in suicide.

The point here is that there *is* a need for assistance in suicide—a need for technical assistance in order to avoid grave errors and even graver consequences. Requesting assistance in suicide is not akin to assistance in driving. Rather, it is more akin to preparing one's taxes. Certainly I *can* prepare my own taxes. I am also legally allowed to prepare my own taxes. I suppose I might want to prepare my own taxes as well. Nonetheless, I do not prepare my own taxes. I have need for assistance in preparing my taxes because tax codes are extraordinarily complex and I want my taxes done correctly. If one prepares one's taxes oneself, one might pay too little, be audited, and be fined heavily. In my own case, out of fear of audits, I would likely overpay, or perhaps miss many deductions. Either operation, taxes or suicide, generates a need for assistance because the task is so complex and the risks associated with error are so grave.

Perhaps a better analogy can be made with abortion. It is surprising that Szasz misses this analogy, since he discusses abortion in several places, countering arguments made by proponents of physician-assisted suicide. As Szasz notes, there is no need for assistance in suicide because one can perform the action for oneself. Furthermore, people have been performing suicide for themselves, free of assistance, throughout history. In fact, assistance in suicide (or specifically giving a patient a deadly drug) and abortion are singled out and prohibited in the Oath of Hippocrates, which suggests that assistance in suicide and assistance in abortion have been an issue in medicine since nearly its inception. Technically speaking, a woman can in principle perform an abortion for herself, and in fact many women did before access to assistance in abortion was legalized, for example in cases like *Roe v Wade*. Many of these women died because such an operation is complex and the consequences of errors are grave, just as they are in suicide. In unassisted abortion, the result of a mistake can mean the death of the woman. In unassisted suicide, where death is the goal, the result of a mistake can mean life a deeply unwanted outcome, either a painful, bad death or a life of permanent disability.

Socrates as a Model for Suicide

When Szasz discusses arguments made by Timothy Quill, he cites the example of Socrates. Quill suggests that doctors ought not to abandon their patients in suicide: if the patient needs and asks for the physician's help, the patient should not be left to face death alone. Szasz agrees that while Socrates's death is an example of how a person ought not to die alone, those present and assisting ought to be close friends and family, not a physician. It is not the place of physicians to "be there" for patients at the end of life; it is the place of family and friends. Szasz counters that Quill's argument is "an argument for involving family and friends in voluntary death, not for giving more power to physicians. Socrates did not die alone. He was assisted by his friends and pupils, not by physicians" (Szasz 1999, p. 82). Of course, this does not address patients without family and friends, or without family and friends who are able and willing to assist in suicide. Furthermore, should we ask why it must be the case that physicians are necessarily excluded from this circle of loved ones? If a doctor is a friend to a patient perhaps that doctor *should* be present at death. None of Socrates's companions were physicians, but if one had been, why should he not have been permitted to assist as Socrates's other companions did? In this sense, a physician might assist not only technically, but emotionally as well.

More importantly, Szasz has left out the role of the jailor in Socrates's death. Twice, Socrates has need for the technical assistance of the man who was to administer the poison. At 63d, Crito informs Socrates that the man suggests Socrates speak as little as possible, since speaking will warm his body, counteracting the effects of the poison and possibly making extra doses of poison necessary. Socrates famously replies (our own translation follows), "That matter is his own. But have him make his preparations to give me a double dose, triple if necessary." This is important because, given his desires regarding ending his life, Socrates needs the technical assistance of the man to ensure that his desires are met. Later, at 117a when Socrates is finally to drink the poison, he again defers to the technical expertise of the jailor, asking, "Tell me my good friend, for you are knowledgeable in these matters, what must I do?" The man replies, instructing Socrates to drink the poison and walk around until his legs feel heavy, and then lie down.

Thus, even in an example Szasz considers ideal, there is need of technical assistance. Socrates was indeed surrounded by friends, and at times family as well, but he still needed the assistance of someone familiar with the administration of the poison. We have shown that technical assistance is needed in suicide, and that Szasz's argument that a person does not have a need for another to perform a service that he could perform for himself is mistaken. What we have not shown, however (yet?), is that there is a need for *physician*-assisted suicide.

Legitimacy, Medicine, and the Slippery Slope

Perhaps Szasz's most compelling argument is a slippery slope argument made concerning the legitimization of physician-assisted suicide and the role medicine might play in that legitimization. At the bottom of Szasz's slope is a world wherein physician-assisted suicide is prescribed as treatment for disease. Referring to Oregon's Death With Dignity Act, Szasz argues that

> The physician who performs physician-assisted suicide does not merely render a clinical judgment and perform a medical intervention . . . he *defines* prescribing a lethal drug as a *therapeutic response to a medical crisis* rather than a *pseudomedical evasion of drug prohibition.* (Szasz 1999, p. 71)

Szasz also warns against redefining killing as a "type of healing" (Szasz 1999, p. 75), something he sees as a consequence of physician-assisted suicide. For Szasz, the bottom of this slope is a world in which the terminally ill do not simply seek physician-assisted suicide, but rather upon being diagnosed with a terminal illness, are *prescribed* physician-assisted suicide, just as a patient diagnosed with pneumonia is prescribed a course of antibiotics. However, Szasz provides no evidence for the first part of this claim.

On the contrary, advocates of physician-assisted suicide, even if they sometimes speak loosely of "treatment," do not advance the view that physician-assisted suicide is a treatment in any conventional sense. Advocates do not imagine that physician-assisted suicide will "cure" pain, as an appendectomy cures appendicitis. What advocates understand is that physician-assisted suicide will terminate pain or avoid pain that is about to occur. It cannot "cure" pain. Advocates are fully aware that physician-assisted suicide entails the death of the patient, and do not make the simple error that supposes that a patient will survive pain-free if they engage in physician-assisted suicide, though this is the view Szasz seems to attribute to them.

Of course, advocates are also aware that pain is not typically the primary reason for choosing physician-assisted suicide (or euthanasia for that matter). In fact, according to data from both Oregon and the Netherlands, pain may be a factor in some cases, but is comparatively rarely the primary or sole reason for such choices. Indeed, other studies show that patients in severe pain are *less* likely to seek physician-assisted suicide. One such study showed that:

> Patients experiencing pain were not inclined to euthanasia or physician-assisted suicide. This finding is consistent with data from the Netherlands demonstrating that pain was the only reason for euthanasia in just 10% of cases and a contributing factor in fewer than 50% of cases. (Emanuel et al. 1996, p. 1809)

Other studies have found similar results, suggesting that the primary concern among patients requesting aid in dying is not pain or physical concerns, but rather loss of control, dignity, or other non-physical concerns.[1]

Thus, Szasz's claim that advocates for the legalization of physician-assisted suicide view it as a treatment to be prescribed is false . . . but might it also be dangerous? That is, since it is not an accurate portrayal of the views of advocates, is it merely a necessary warning, or something much worse? Care must be taken to ensure that by suggesting (even if erroneously) the view that physician-assisted suicide is treatment, one does not create a self-fulfilling prophecy that encourages people to view the practice in just such a manner. Could Sasz's warning create the very circumstances he fears?

Physicians and Power

Szasz is also critical of the power relationship between physician and patient in the case of physician-assisted suicide. He suggests that the

---

[1] See for example Back et al. 1996, pp. 919–925.

term physician-assisted suicide is "intrinsically mendacious" (Szasz 1999, p. 65) as well as "cognitively misleading and politically mischevious" (Szasz 1999, p. 66), in part because the physician engaging in physician-assisted suicide is the principal, superior to the patient, instead of the assistant. Szasz says that "He [the physician] determines who qualifies for the 'treatment' and prescribes the drug for it" (Szasz 1999, p. 65). There is an extraordinary mix of truth and falsehood at work here. In physician-assisted suicide, the physician does determine whether a patient meets the criteria the law sets (must be terminally ill, must be competent, must make both oral and written requests over a specific length of time) in order to determine whether he, the physician, may legally assist; but this is very different sense from determining who "qualifies for treatment," as if every patient were eager to have it and only some could get it. The physician prescribes the drug in the sense that he writes out a prescription form that the patient can take to the pharmacist in order to receive the drug, but this is a very different matter from prescribing a drug in the sense of ordering a patient to take it. That Szasz appears unable to see this distinction suggests that his vision of the practice is clouded.

Szasz argues that, "*dying is not a disease*; it may, *inter alia*, be a consequence of disease (or other causes, such as accident or violence). More important, *killing (oneself or someone else) is not, and by definition cannot be, a treatment*" (Szasz 1999, p. 64). Szasz rightly points out that not everything performed by physicians is treatment. He notes that while a doctor may give a patient advice concerning the game of golf, simply because the advice proceeds from doctor to patient is insufficient to make the advice treatment (Szasz 1999, p64–65). Yet, while Szasz is certainly right that merely because an action or some advice originates from a doctor is not sufficient to make that action or piece of advice *treatment*, he is wrong to assume that the treatment of disease (and we assume injury as well) is not necessary to qualify an action as treatment. An obvious example can be found in palliative care. Pain is not a disease, though it may, *inter alia*, be a consequence of disease (or other causes, such as accident or violence). Nonetheless, palliative care is indeed treatment.

Szasz also objects to the "bureaucratizing" of physician-assisted suicide (Szasz 1999, p. 66). This too has elements of truth and falsehood. Physician-assisted suicide is "bureaucratized" in the sense that the state sets safeguards (competence, terminal illness, repeated requests, and psychological evaluations if needed), but not at all bureaucratized in the sense that the state shuffles patients to this practice for reasons of its own. The state plays no role in deciding *whether* a patient will choose physician-assisted suicide, though it does play a role in trying to ensure that the patient's choice is voluntary and informed.

Finally, Szasz makes misleading factual claims. For example, Szasz states that "supporters and opponents of PAS alike acknowledge that *neither the Constitution nor any other American law recognizes a right to suicide*" (Szasz 1999, p. 66), and he discusses this point in some detail. He is referring to the landmark joint U.S. Supreme Court decisions *Glucksberg v. Washington* and *Vacco v. Quill*, but he makes the same mistake many commentators have made. In fact, the Court did not make a blanket finding that there exists *no* right at all to assisted suicide; rather the Court held in effect that there is no *positive* right to assistance in suicide, that is, that a patient cannot assert a claim to such assistance. The Court did hold that states were free to legalize physician-assisted suicide if they wished; in this sense, the judgment asserts that a state could recognize patients' *negative* rights to receive such help if they could find a willing provider.

Szasz's Alternatives

By now it is clear that Szasz's criticisms of physician-assisted suicide, though motivated by a healthy skepticism of medicine, are mistaken. The force of his criticisms is severely weakened by numerous factual and logical mistakes. However, to his credit and unlike some commentators, Szasz offers an alternative to the current practice of physician-assisted suicide. Instead of merely condemning the practice, Szasz offers a model of how he thinks suicide *ought* to be practiced in the United States. In what follows, we will sketch and challenge two aspects of Szasz's views regarding how suicide should be practiced: the legalization of the drugs required for suicide and the role of friends and families.

While Szasz does not think there should be such a thing as *physician*-assisted suicide, given his discussion and emphasis on the death of Socrates as recorded in the *Phaedo*, Szasz does not object to *assisted* suicide generally. As discussed above, Szasz thinks that there is no need for assistance, but assistance in suicide by non-physicians is permissible because the various negative effects (the medicalization and legitimization of suicide, excessive government and physician control, the violation of medical principles such as "first do no harm", and so forth) do not accompany suicides assisted by non-physicians.

Szasz summarizes his own position regarding how suicide might be carried out when he notes that, "If both suicide and access to drugs were *unconditionally legal*, there would be no technical need for a physician's assistance with it: People could kill themselves or could be helped to do so by family and friends" (Szasz 1999, p. 66).

But then what are the alternatives? Since Szasz opposes the involvement of physicians in assisted suicide, both the legalization of physician-assisted suicide and the current, underground practice of physician-assisted suicide are out of the question. But Szasz also opposes a return to the criminalization of suicide. From the above remarks, it seems that Szasz favors a combination of legalizing at least the drugs necessary for suicide and decriminalization of assistance in suicide (by non-physicians).

On a practical level, one wonders how Szasz might envision the practice of suicide after the necessary drugs have been legalized. Above, Szasz notes that if drugs were unconditionally legal a person would have no need for assistance from a physician, in the sense that the person would not need a prescription. However, one would still need advice regarding which drugs to take. This is not an objection to Szasz's position, but rather a request for clarification. How indeed might an individual gain the requisite information to commit suicide effectively and in a manner she finds acceptable? Might she simply look on the Internet for a "cocktail recipe" and then proceed to her local pharmacy? This approach, as anyone who has attempted meaningful research on the Internet can attest, would be prone to dizzying numbers of search results and, more seriously, numerous sources of poor or even disinformation. Perhaps she could do her own detective work, deducing an effective means for suicide from warning labels. This may not work, since the appropriate doses for suicide are not included on warning labels. Perhaps companies might market kits, or combinations of pills, in a not too dissimilar manner from mega-doses of birth control pills as emergency contraception. However this might proceed, further clarification from Szasz on the specifics of the actual practice would be beneficial.

More serious questions can be raised regarding Szasz's suggestion that "People could kill themselves or could be helped to do so by family and friends." Now, in the case of Socrates, he was blessed by the presence of benevolent and loving friends. This is not necessarily always the case, though.

Szasz raises concerns, and rightly so, regarding the potential for abuse and coercion if physician-assisted suicide is practiced. What Szasz overlooks is the potential for abuse by friends and families. He seems to view physician-assisted suicide as a state-controlled practice with doctors wielding enormous powers, turning away patients who want their assistance in suicide, and the few patients that doctors allow behind the velvet rope are forced to jump through numerous hoops, controlled by physicians. If drugs are legalized and suicide (and non-physician assistance) is fully legal, individuals will finally be able to make free, competent choices regarding suicide; autonomous agents who have thrown off the shackles of physician dominance. But this simply may not be the case. There is also risk of coercion and abuse from friends and family members who after all have much more at stake in whether the person lives or dies. Simply removing physicians from assisted suicide will not eliminate the risk of abuse and coercion.

Szasz does see many of the dilemmas of the practice of legalized physician-assisted suicide. He writes, "the legal definition of PAS as a procedure that only a physician can perform expands the medicalization of everyday life, extends medical control over personal conduct, especially at the end of life, and diminishes patient autonomy" (Szasz 1999, p. 67). Surely this is in part right, and it is a cost of the need for safeguards. What he sees less clearly are the costs of the alternative he favors, open access to suicide.[2]

---

[2] EDITOR'S NOTE: The authors made minor verbal changes in this chapter after Dr. Szasz had written his reply (but before the reply was seen by the authors).

REFERENCES

Back, Anthony L., Jeffrey I. Wallace, Helene E. Starks, and Robert Perlman. 1996. Physician-Assisted Suicide and Euthanasia in Washington State: Patient Requests and Physician Reponses. *Journal of the American Medical Association* 275:12, pp. 919–925.

Battin, Margaret Pabst. 1991. Euthanasia: The Way We Do It, The Way They Do It. *Journal of Pain and Symptom Management* 6:5.

———. 1995. *Ethical Issues in Suicide*. Englewood Cliffs: Prentice Hall.

———. 1998. Physician-Assisted Suicide: Safe, Legal, Rare? In Battin, Rhodes, and Silvers 1998, pp. 63–72.

Battin, Margaret P., Rosamond Rhodes, and Ani Silvers, eds. 1998. *Physician Assisted Suicide: Expanding the Debate*. New York: Routledge.

Baumrin, Bernard. 1998. Physician, Stay Thy Hand! In Battin, Rhodes, and Silvers 1998, pp. 177–181.

Callahan, Daniel. 1992. When Self-Determination Runs Amok. *Hastings Center Report* 22 (March–April), pp. 52–55.

Caplan, Arthur, ed. 1992. When Medicine Went Mad: Bioethics and the Holocaust. Totowa: Humana Press.

Chin, Arthur, Katrina Hedberg, Grant K. Higginson, and David W. Fleming. 1999. Legalized Physician-Assisted Suicide in Oregon: The First Year's Experience. *New England Journal of Medicine* 340, pp. 577–583.

Cranford, Ronald. 1992. The Contemporary Euthanasia Movement and the Nazi Euthanasia Program: Are there Meaningful Similarities? In Caplan 1992, pp. 201–210.

Emanuel, Ezekiel J., Diane L. Fairclough, Elisabeth R. Daniels, and Brian R. Clarridge. 1996. Euthanasia and Physician-Assisted Suicide: Attitudes and Experiences of Oncology Patients, Oncologists, and the Public. *The Lancet* 347, pp. 1805–810.

Gaylin, Willard, Leon R. Kass, Edmund D. Pellegrino, and Mark Siegler. 1988. Doctors Must Not Kill. *Journal of the American Medical Association* 259:14, pp. 2139–140.

Humphry, Derek. 1997. *Final Exit: The Practicalities of Self-Deliverance and Assisted Suicide for the Dying*. Los Angeles: Hemlock Society.

Macklin, Ruth. 1992. Which Way Down the Slippery Slope? Nazi Medical Killing and Euthanasia Today. In Caplan 1992, pp. 173–200.

Oregon Department of Human Services. 2004. *Sixth Annual Report on Oregon's Death with Dignity Act*.

Rhodes, Rosamond. 1998. Physicians, Assisted Suicide, and the Right to Live or Die. In Battin, Rhodes, and Silvers 1998, pp. 165–176.

Szasz, Thomas. 1999. *Fatal Freedom: The Ethics and Politics of Suicide*. Westport: Praeger.

Stell, Lance K. 1998. Physician-Assisted Suicide: To Decriminalize or Legalize, That Is the Question. In Battin, Rhodes, and Silvers 1998, pp. 225–251.

Reply to Battin and Spellecy

THOMAS SZASZ

I

Battin and Spellecy advocate physician-assisted suicide (PAS) and support political efforts to "legalize" the procedure. I oppose PAS and efforts to enact legislation empowering physicians to kill certain persons under certain circumstances. Battin and Spellecy's candor sharpens and clarifies the facts and premises each of us uses to support our respective positions.

I reject PAS because I regard both suicide and free access to drugs as *basic human rights* and because I oppose *giving physicians power over people called "patients."* My opposition to PAS thus rests on very different grounds than does the opposition of most of its critics. Virtually all opponents of PAS reject the principle of self-ownership and accordingly reject the right to suicide and the right to drugs; indeed, they define the exercise or attempted exercise of these rights as symptoms of mental illness requiring that the subject be deprived of liberty to protect him from himself.[1]

II

It is essential to remember that when we assert that a person has a right to X we do not necessarily mean that we regard X as a good thing to have or to do. In a free society, a person has the right to do many things that may not be good for him or others, as others see "right" or even as he himself sees it. We often engage in activities—religious, ethical, politi-

---

[1] Thomas Szasz, *Fatal Freedom: The Ethics and Politics of Suicide* (Syracuse: Syracuse University Press, 2002 [1999]); *Our Right to Drugs: The Case for a Free Market* (Syracuse: Syracuse University Press, 2002 [1992]).

cal, professional, personal—that others condemn as wrong. Sometimes, we engage in pleasurable activities that we ourselves recognize may be wrong in the long run, but feel right at the moment.

When I say that a person has a right to suicide, I do not mean that suicide is an abstract good or that we should abstain from trying to prevent particular persons or people in general from killing themselves. What I mean is that whether a person kills himself or not is none of the government's business. Justice Louis D. Brandeis's famous declaration about the right to be let alone is particularly relevant in this connection. He stated:

> The makers of our Constitution undertook to secure conditions favorable to the pursuit of happiness. They recognized the significance of man's spiritual nature, of his feelings and of his intellect. They knew that only a part of the pain, pleasure and satisfactions of life are to be found in material things. They sought to protect Americans in their beliefs, their thoughts, their emotions and their sensations. They conferred, as against the government, *the right to be let alone—the most comprehensive of rights and the—right most valued by civilized men.* To protect that right, every unjustifiable intrusion by the government upon the privacy of the individual, whatever the means employed, must be deemed a violation of the Fourth Amendment.[2]

If being let alone is a fundamental right, so is the right to be let alone to commit suicide. I believe that people who announce that they want to kill themselves ought to have a right to be recognized by the state as fully human. Psychiatrists ought to have the right to regard wanting to kill oneself as a manifestation of mental illness, but ought not to have the power to *forcibly* prevent people from committing suicide.

Why do I emphasize the importance of the right to suicide? Because we are disposed to regard "rights" that, as Americans, we view as self-evident—such as the right to freedom of religion—as *reasonable*, but are disposed to regard "rights" framed in radically different terms—such as the right to suicide—as *unreasonable*. In the therapeutic state, being unreasonable resonates with being insane, and the insane person—like the infant and the imbecile—is believed to need help, not liberty.

I maintain that we cannot properly examine our social policies concerning suicide and PAS without attending to the underlying conflict

---

[2] Louis D. Brandeis, *Olmstead v. U.S.*, 277 U.S. 438, 478 (1928) (Brandeis, J., dissenting), emphasis added; http://caselaw.lp.findlaw.com/scripts/getcase.pl?court=US&vol=277&invol=438

between autonomy and authority, that is, between *the rights of the individual over himself versus the duties of the state to protect individuals from aggression and injury by others.* Authorities are fond of granting individuals or groups *permission* to engage in generally prohibited actions, both self-regarding and other-regarding. For example, totalitarian governments permit certain persons to leave the country, normally called "emigration." Democratic governments permit certain persons to obtain certain drugs, normally called the "purchase of a product." Collectively, God grants permission for large-scale murder and mayhem, provided that his appointed officials properly request it. I offer these remarks to underscore the differences between dependence on authority for permission to do X and dependence on the self to exercise the right to do X. The following examples illustrate this difference.

> If you cut off your penis, psychiatrists say you have a mental illness and lock you up in a mental hospital. But if psychiatrists say you have the disease called "transsexualism" and you give consent to a surgeon to cut off your penis, then you are receiving treatment for an illness.

> If you cut off your life, psychiatrists say you did it because you were mentally ill. If you try to cut off your life and fail, psychiatrists say you are mentally ill and dangerous to yourself and lock you up in a mental hospital. If the state cuts off your life, you are receiving capital punishment.

> If you request a physician to cut off your life, and if psychiatrists approve your request, then you are receiving "physician-assisted suicide" (PAS), a form of killing that the advocates of PAS want to add to the repertoire of medical treatments.[3]

III

Although Battin and Spellecy strive to present my views fairly, they frequently misstate them, probably because of the fundamental differences in our viewpoints. They begin their essay by complimenting me for offering "genuine insight into ethical issues in physician-assisted suicide," a statement that implies that I have special interest in the ethics of PAS. That is not the case. My interest in the ethics and politics of PAS is an integral part of my interest in the ethics and politics of suicide and,

---

[3] See especially Thomas Szasz, *Ceremonial Chemistry: The Ritual Persecution of Drugs, Addicts, and Pushers* (Holmes Beach: Learning Publications, 1985 [1976]).

more generally, of all the problematic behaviors that we now conceptualize in medical terms and regulate by pharmacratic means.[4]

The mental health laws of all western nations rely on some version of the formula "mental illness and dangerousness" as the legal basis of civil commitment. Psychiatrists attribute suicide to mental illness (typically depression) and use the combination of mental illness and the threat of suicide ("dangerousness to self") as the medical-legal justification for depriving innocent persons of liberty. *De jure*, civil commitment as suicide prevention is authorized by mental health laws; de *facto*, it is mandated by the "standard of care" requirement of psychiatric practice.[5]

> I oppose "suicide prevention" because the term refers to the practice of using the coercive apparatus of the state to deprive persons of liberty, without acknowledging—indeed, implicitly denying—that fact.

> I oppose "physician-assisted suicide" because the term refers to the practice of augmenting the physician's power to prevent suicide by adding to it the power to provide suicide.

Battin and Spellecy ignore the legal-social milieu in which the current debate on suicide and PAS must be situated. One result is that—perhaps unwittingly and unwillingly—they become guilty of the sin of *Qui tacet consentit* (He who remains silent consents). Another result is that virtually everything they say about my views is distorted and inaccurate. I shall document this conclusion, point by point. The authors write:

> For Szasz, medicine as an institution carries with it the awesome, often-abused power to define health and illness, to identify and label who counts as well and who is ill. This power is particularly evident in the area of mental illness—where, Szasz thinks, virtually all such discrimination and labeling is fraudulent—but it is nonetheless part of those areas of medicine concerned with "physical" health as well.

I have no objection to physicians defining health and disease. That is an exercise of their right to free speech. Nor is the fraudulent character of

---

[4] Thomas Szasz, *Pharmacracy: Medicine and Politics in America* (Syracuse: Syracuse University Press, 2003 [2001]).

[5] There is a vast literature on the subject. See for example David F. Greenberg, "Involuntary psychiatric commitments to prevent suicide," in Rem B. Edwards, ed., *Psychiatry and Ethics: Insanity, Rational Autonomy, and Mental Health Care* (Buffalo: Prometheus, 1982 [1974]), pp. 283–298.

psychiatric nosology the focus of my critique regarding PAS. My focus is the power of the psychiatrist, exemplified by the paradigmatic psychiatric procedures of civil commitment and the insanity defense-and-disposition.

The authors' sin of consent goes to the heart of the subject: They accept as an immutable fact that American laws prohibit drugs and suicide:

> Proponents of this practice [PAS] and of the legalization of it argue that this is a matter of fundamental liberty: that just as a competent person is recognized in a society based on individual freedom to have the right to determine the course of his or her life, subject only to the proviso that this not cause harm to others, so the person who is dying must also have the right to determine how the very end of his or her life shall go.

If an American adult had "the right to determine the course of his or her life, subject only to the proviso that this not cause harm to others," then he would have access to any drug he wants and would have a right to kill himself whenever he pleases. The fact is that drug prohibition and suicide prohibition—composed in part of prescription laws and mental health laws—deprive Americans of these rights.[6] Battin and Spellecy ought to know this.

As if all this were not bad enough, Battin and Spellecy misrepresent my critique of PAS by lumping my argument with the arguments of those who oppose suicide not *because it is physician-assisted* (as I do), but *because all suicide is morally wrongful* (prohibited by the monotheistic religions):

> Critics, including Szasz, have argued against the claim that physician-assisted suicide is a matter of fundamental, basic liberty, and relatedly, that there is no "right" to physician-assisted suicide, whether that right is seen as positive or negative, moral, or constitutional, though Szasz himself holds a view far more broadly libertarian than most advocates of legalization of physician-assisted suicide.

The person reading this sentence would probably be surprised to learn that I oppose the right to PAS *because* I support the right to *physi-*

---

[6] Thomas Szasz, *Ceremonial Chemistry*; *Fatal Freedom*; *Our Right to Drugs*; *The Theology of Medicine: The Political-Philosophical Foundations of Medical Ethics* (Syracuse: Syracuse University Press, 1988 [1977]), *The Therapeutic State: Psychiatry in the Mirror of Current Events* (Buffalo: Prometheus, 1984), *The Untamed Tongue: A Dissenting Dictionary* (La Salle: Open Court, 1990).

cian-unassisted suicide, and that I regard the advocates of PAS as being anti-libertarian. PAS and coerced suicide prevention epitomize the fruits of statist medicine. The authors continue:

> Of course, there is a contingent sense in which persons have a need for a physician's assistance in suicide. Given U.S. drug laws, patients do not have ready access to the types of drugs used in physician-assisted suicide, and thus need a prescription. Szasz is aware of this and notes that a person has no need for another to provide a service provided he is allowed to perform it for himself. Szasz thus favors deregulation of (at least) these drugs. Since individuals require a prescription to gain access to the drugs needed for this type of suicide, they are in effect not allowed to preform it for themselves.

Although Battin, Spellecy, and I inhabit the same geographic space, we don't inhabit the same political space. I maintain that, in the United States today, we live under drug prohibition, called "the war on drugs," and compare it to an earlier system of alcohol prohibition, called "Prohibition." They object:

> Szasz draws an analogy between prohibition and current U.S. drug policy . . . This is an interesting analogy, even though it is obviously wrong. . . . The next step in his argument is to claim that current U.S. drug policy is tantamount to prohibition of barbiturates . . . Of course, Szasz's argument depends upon a false premise—*there is no such thing as barbiturate prohibition"* (emphasis added).

I wonder when was the last time Battin and Spellecy went to a drug store and tried to buy a bottle of Seconal? Suppose they did so and, when refused to be served, would demand the drug because "there is no such thing as barbiturate prohibition." Would they like to try that experiment? Ensconced in jail or mental hospital, they could tell themselves that "there is no such thing as barbiturate prohibition."

Battin and Spellecy's assertion, *"there is no such thing as barbiturate prohibition,"* illustrates how unthinkingly mental health professionals—and people generally—accept the ideology of the therapeutic state. There *is* barbiturate prohibition, but people feel so at one with it that they experience it not as prohibition, but as protection. In his famous dystopian novel, *Facial Justice*, Leslie P. Hartley foresaw and described this mind-set as follows: "As you know"—declares the Dictator, addressing his subjects, called Patients and Delinquents—"our Constitution is based on . . . equality of the most deep-seated and all-embracing order. . . . *it is not imposed, it is, in the good sense of the word, voluntary, the expression, through my Edicts, of your own Free Will.*[7]

At every turn, Battin and Spellecy misunderstand or misrepresent my views. They write: "Szasz does not oppose suicide generally. He favors the legalization of drugs . . ." This is about as accurate or elegant as writing: "Frederick Douglass did not oppose freeing the slaves generally. He favored the legalization of liberty . . ." Battin and Spellecy's objection to my comparing PAS with chauffeur-assisted driving is equally gauche:

> Comparing such a complex, grave, and technical operation as suicide with such a trivial operation as being driven by a chauffeur misses the complexity of the situation and thus the need. . . . one can drive oneself with relative ease. Killing oneself is not as simple a matter.

I did not realize that driving a car is easier than falling off a cliff. Battin and Spellecy, like many other evangelists for PAS, think the proper model for understanding and "legalizing" PAS is abortion:

> Perhaps a better analogy can be made with abortion. It is surprising that Szasz misses this analogy, since he discusses abortion in several places . . . As Szasz notes, there is no need for assistance in suicide because one can perform the action for oneself. Furthermore, people have been performing suicide for themselves, free of assistance, throughout history . . . Technically speaking, a woman can in principle perform an abortion for herself, and in fact many women did before access to assistance in abortion was legalized, for example in cases like by *Roe v. Wade*. Many of these women died because such an operation is complex and the consequences of errors are grave, just as they are in suicide. In unassisted abortion, the result of a mistake can mean a deeply unwanted outcome, the death of the woman. In unassisted suicide, where death is the goal, the result of a mistake can mean a deeply unwanted outcome, either a painful, bad death or a life of permanent disability.

In one sentence, the authors assert that "a woman can *in principle* perform an abortion for herself" (emphasis added), and in the next sentence acknowledge that, *in practice*, she cannot: "Many of these women died." Battin and Spellecy's views regarding the right to suicide are equally idiosyncratic. They state:

---

[7] Leslie P. Hartley, *Facial Justice* (Harmondsworth: Penguin, 1966 [1960]), p. 150, emphasis added.

Finally, Szasz makes misleading factual claims. For example, Szasz states that "supporters and opponents of PAS alike acknowledge that *neither the Constitution nor any other American law recognizes a right to suicide*" . . . and he discusses this point in some detail. . . . By now it is clear that Szasz's criticisms of physician-assisted suicide, though motivated by a healthy skepticism of medicine, are mistaken. The force of his criticisms is severely weakened by numerous factual and logical mistakes.

Battin and Spellecy do not mention suicide prevention policies, avoid the term "coercive psychiatric suicide prevention," and ignore that psychiatrists incarcerate, and are expected to incarcerate, persons they or others consider "suicide risks." They do not identify my "numerous factual and logical mistakes." Instead, they state:

> Szasz summarizes his own position regarding how suicide might be carried out when he notes that, "If both suicide and access to drugs were *unconditionally legal*, there would be no technical need for a physician's assistance with it: People could kill themselves or could be helped to do so by family and friends.

I see no factual or logical mistakes in this statement. Battin and Spellecy continue:

> But then what are the alternatives? Since Szasz opposes the involvement of physicians in assisted suicide, both the legalization of physician-assisted suicide and the current, underground practice of physician-assisted suicide are out of the question. *But Szasz also opposes a return to the criminalization of suicide.* . . . Szasz favors a combination of legalizing at least the drugs necessary for suicide and decriminalization of assistance in suicide (by non-physicians) (emphasis added).

I repeat. Battin and Spellecy write "*Szasz favors . . . legalizing at least the drugs necessary for suicide . . .*" The reader must decide whether Battin and Spellecy intend to misinform the reader or do so because they have misinformed themselves about my position regarding drug prohibition, suicide prohibition, and legalized physician-assisted suicide. There is evidence to suggest that they have misinformed themselves—perhaps because they are inattentive readers or find my views too alien—as they confusedly and confusingly write: "*But Szasz also opposes a return to the criminalization of suicide.*" If, as Battin and Spellecy maintain, suicide has all along been legal, how can I *oppose a return to a criminalization of it*? In a secular society, a corpse cannot be tried and convicted of a crime. In such a society, suicide, properly speaking, cannot be a crime. Instead, what can and is treated as a crime—a violation of mental health law—is the status of a person whom others have accused and successfully condemned as constituting a "danger to himself." Such a "convict" is duly punished by deprivation of liberty and involuntary psychiatric treatment.

Battin and Spellecy's confusion masks their refusal to acknowledge something they must know, namely, that suicide is neither illegal nor legal, a point I discuss at length in *Fatal Freedom*. Briefly put, suicide is legal in the sense that it is not prohibited by the criminal law. But it is illegal in the sense that mental health law authorizes depriving persons of liberty provided they are successfully accused of being "suicidal," and are incarcerated in prisons called "hospitals," by jailers called "doctors."

Finally, Battin and Spellecy add, "He [Szasz] seems to view physician-assisted suicide as a state-controlled practice with doctors wielding enormous powers . . ." No doubt they view this statement as still another factual error.

III

Battin and Spellecy are so committed to defending PAS that they do not recognize that some of their objections to my support of the right to suicide apply to their support of a right to PAS as well. If people had a right to suicide, they note, instead of killing themselves, they "might rather take too much of a medication and vomit, or take the wrong combination of medications and recover, but with significant mental impairments." This is also true for physician-prescribed barbiturates: they too may be taken incorrectly or vomited with undesirable results. What Battin and Spellecy are saying here is that they are concerned *lest patients try to kill themselves and fail.* But if they want to make sure that when a person tries to kill himself he succeeds, we need not physician-assisted suicide but physician-assisted execution, on the model of the lethal injection with which prisoners condemned to death are "helped" to die surely and painlessly. Battin and Spellecy conclude:

> Szasz, does see many of the dilemmas of the practice of legalized physician-assisted suicide. He writes, "the legal definition of PAS as a procedure that only a physician can perform expands the medicalization of everyday life, extends medical control over personal conduct, especially at the end of life, and diminishes patient autonomy." Surely this is in part

right, and it is a cost of the *need for safeguards*. What he sees less clearly are the costs of the alternative he favors, open access to suicide. (emphasis added)

Assuredly, we need safeguards against dangers. But Battin and Spellecy do not identify which policy they consider dangerous, requiring safeguards: the medicalization of everyday life? physician-assisted suicide? the repeal of drug prohibition? the abolition of psychiatric slavery?

What Battin and Spellecy call "open access to suicide," I—following Locke, Hume, and other philosophers of liberty—call "the right to own and kill oneself."

10

Sideshow? Schizophrenia as Construed by Szasz and the Neo-Kraepelinians

RICHARD P. BENTALL

The psychoses (conditions in which individuals experience hallucinations or delusional beliefs or show evidence of grossly abnormal thinking or incoherent speech) have always had a special place in the theory and practice of psychiatry. Whereas the medical pretensions of the profession can easily be challenged in the domains of sexual preference (many people now regard homosexuality to be part of normal human variation), antisocial behaviour (perhaps better managed within a legal than a medical framework), or even the neuroses (which may be more responsive to psychological intervention than medication), it is commonly assumed that psychotic disorders are different. Even many critics of conventional psychiatry assume that these conditions are true diseases that are unlikely to wither away in the face of psychological or sociological analysis. It is for this reason that 'schizophrenia', the most common diagnostic category within the psychotic spectrum, has, as Thomas Szasz (1979) has famously suggested, acquired the status of a sacred symbol of the profession. Hence, critiques that undermine the conventional psychiatric understanding of the condition are of special importance. Striking at the very heart of the discipline, they have the potential to deprive advocates of medical psychiatry of a last redoubt, to which they might otherwise retreat in the face of sustained criticisms of their practice in other areas.

For Szasz, therefore, rejection of the very idea of 'schizophrenia' has a special place in his wider project of challenging the conceptual and ethical framework of medical psychiatry (Szasz 1960). In this chapter, I will consider some of the reasons he gives to justify this rejection, focusing especially on those presented in his book *Schizophrenia: The Sacred Symbol of Psychiatry* (Szasz 1979). Although I am on record as being at least as sceptical about the concept of 'schizophrenia' as Szasz (see Bentall 1990; 1998; Bentall, Jackson, and Pilgrim 1988), I will attempt to show that some of the arguments he has used to reach what I believe to be essentially accurate conclusions do not stand up to careful scrutiny. Indeed, some of these arguments will be shown to be identical to those used by biological psychiatrists when defending the schizophrenia concept. This observation, if correct, must have important implications for Szasz's wider project as outlined in his celebrated paper, "The Myth of Mental Illness" (Szasz 1960).

Was Schizophrenia Discovered or Invented?

An important claim by Szasz (1979) is that 'schizophrenia' was invented rather than discovered. In order to evaluate this claim, it will be necessary to briefly examine the historical origins of the schizophrenia concept, the facts about which Professor Szasz and I are in substantial agreement.

Although the term schizophrenia was first introduced by Bleuler (1911/1950), the concept it refers to can be traced to the work of Emil Kraepelin, a distinguished academic psychiatrist who worked first in Heidelberg and then in Munich in the final years of the nineteenth century and the early years of the twentieth (Berrios and Hauser 1988; Hoff 1995). Kraepelin believed that progress in psychiatry, which he assumed to be a branch of medicine, would be slow without an agreed upon system of classifying the phenomena encountered in the psychiatric clinic. Assuming that psychiatric disorders would eventually be explained as brain diseases, but recognising that progress in the neurosciences had been insufficient to realise this goal, he hit on an idea that is most clearly expressed in the following quotation:

> Judging from our experience in internal medicine it is a fair assumption that similar disease processes will produce identical symptom pictures, identical pathological anatomy and an identical aetiology. If, therefore, we possessed a comprehensive knowledge of any of these three fields—pathological anatomy, symptomatology, or aetiology—we would at once have a uniform and standard classification of mental diseases. A similar comprehensive knowledge of either of the other two fields would give us not just as uni-

form and standard classifications, but *all of these classifications would exactly coincide.* (Kraepelin 1907, italics mine)

This argument was important because it suggested that a classification based on symptoms (particular classes of behaviours and experiences) would lead to discoveries about the presumed cerebral pathology and etiology associated with particular psychiatric conditions. In practice, Kraepelin relied not only on data on symptoms, but also on information about the course of conditions over long periods (whether they got better or worse) to create his diagnostic system. In this way, over a period of decades, he gradually persuaded himself (and others who read the various editions of his textbook) that there were just three major categories of psychosis—dementia praecox (literally senility of the young, but relabelled schizophrenia by Bleuler), manic depression (a category that subsumed the modern concepts of unipolar depression and bipolar disorder) and paranoia (now often referred to as delusional disorder). Dementia praecox/schizophrenia, according to this model, is a disease that leads to progressive deterioration (it is literally a dementia), which is associated with severe cognitive dysfunction, and which often causes hallucinations (perceptions of events that are not in fact occurring, especially 'voices') and delusions (bizarre and irrational beliefs, for example fears of persecution). Manic depression, by contrast, is a disease in which abnormal mood (either depression or manic episodes) is usually evident, and from which a complete recovery is possible.

Szasz's main reason for believing that schizophrenia was invented rather than discovered is Kraepelin's failure to identify a lesion or pathology associated with schizophrenic behaviour. Szasz is unsympathetic towards the difficulties faced by Kraepelin and his followers, and sometimes his attitude towards the pioneers of psychiatric taxonomy borders on hostility (see for example Chapter 1 of Szasz 1979). In part, this reflects his more general assumption that disease equates to physical pathology, about which I will say more later. However, it also reflects a failure to judge the early psychiatrists by the standards of their own time rather than ours. As Szsaz himself acknowledges, some psychiatric disorders, notably Alzheimer's dementia (named after one of Kraepelin's colleagues, who discovered the histological abnormalities associated with the disease) and general paresis (which proved to be caused by an advanced syphilitic infection) did *eventually* yield to biological explanation. However, the critical term here is 'eventually'—both senile dementia and general paresis were held to be diseases long before their biological origins were discovered. Working during the period in which these advances occurred, it was reasonable for Kraepelin to assume that the debilitating cluster of symptoms to which he assigned the term dementia praecox would similarly prove to be the consequence of some kind of insult to the central nervous system.

Kraepelin's classification system has proven to be enormously influential, justifying the historian Edward Shorter's (1997) observation that it is Kraepelin rather than Freud who should be seen as the central figure in the history of psychiatry. Reflecting this influence, the designers of the third edition of the American Psychiatric Association's diagnostic manual (DSM-III) took to describing themselves as 'neo-Kraepelinians'. One, Gerald Klerman (1978), even wrote a neo-Kraepelinian manifesto in which it was asserted that "there is a boundary between the normal and the sick", that "there is not one, but many mental illnesses", and that "the focus of psychiatric physicians should be particularly on the biological aspects of mental illness"—all assumptions that Kraepelin would have happily embraced.

The first of these assumptions is particularly pertinent to our present discussion, because it was implicitly rejected by Szasz, who has repeatedly (and sometimes humorously) pointed to examples of 'normal' behaviour that seem impossible to distinguish from psychotic symptoms on grounds that are not arbitrary. For example:

> *Delusions*. We know what they are: believing that you are the one of the Chosen People; or that Jesus is the son of God who died, but has been resurrected and is now still alive . . ." (Szasz 1979, p. 18)

and

> *Hallucinations*. No problem here, either: communicating with deities or dead people (and being successful at claiming a 'divine calling' or being a spiritualist) . . . (Szasz 1979, p. 19)

Szasz's intuition in this regard is undoubtedly correct. In the last thirty years, a large volume of evidence collected by psychologists such as Jean and Loren Chapman in the United States (see, for example, Chapman and Chapman 1980; 1988) and Gordon Claridge (1985; 1987) in Britain, has convincingly demonstrated that schizophrenic behaviours lie at one end of a spectrum of personality characteristics, and that a sizeable minority of the ordinary population, if asked, will report quasi-psychotic experiences. More recently, several large-scale epidemiological studies, in which random samples of the population have been interviewed using standardised psychiatric assessments, have established that a surprising number of people have experienced hallucinations (11–13 percent lifetime prevalence according to Tien 1991; about 8 percent current prevalence according to van Os, Hanssen, Bijl, and Ravelli, 2000) or delusions (approximately 20 percent lifetime prevalence according to Poulton et al. 2000; 12 percent current prevalence according to van Os et al. 2000) defined according to DSM or equivalent criteria. Obviously, there is not "a boundary between the normal and the sick" as the neoKraepelinians assumed.

However, as Gordon Claridge (1990) has pointed out, these observations alone do not allow us to reject the idea that schizophrenia is a disease. After all, there are widely recognised physical conditions that lie at the far end of a normal distribution of human characteristics. A good example is essential hypertension, a disorder that is asymptomatic (people suffering from high blood pressure are usually unaware of it) and which exists at the tail end of a normal distribution of blood pressures. The dividing line between normal and abnormal blood pressure is arbitrary, but high blood pressure is considered to be a disease because patients suffering from it are likely to experience life-threatening consequences (strokes or heart disease) later on. In practice, physicians often consult tables that estimate the risks of these complications in the light of an individual patient's blood pressure and other factors (age, weight, cholesterol level) before discussing with the patient whether some kind of medical intervention is appropriate and desirable.

Of course, Szasz would no doubt claim that essential hypertension is different from schizophrenia because physical pathology is identifiable in principle, even if it is often missed in practice. I will discuss this argument shortly, but before doing so I would like to draw the reader's attention to an important criticism of Kraepelin and his followers that Szasz appears to have overlooked, but which is central to my own critique of modern psychiatric theory. Although earlier I suggested that it was quite reasonable for the pioneers of psychiatry to attempt to define psychiatric illnesses in terms of symptoms, and that they set about this project honestly, it is doubtful whether Kraepelin and his followers succeeded in achieving a system of classification that is scientifically valid. My reasons for making this claim are empirical and have been outlined in detail elsewhere (Bentall 1990; 1993; 1998). Briefly, research has established that the majority of patients suffering from psychotic symptoms do not fall clearly into the major psychiatric categories of schizophrenia and manic depression as defined by Kraepelin, but rather suffer from a mixture of schizophrenic and affective symptoms. Moreover, Kraepelinian or neoKraepelinian diagnoses are very poor predictors of the long-term outcome of patients' symptoms or their response to specific types of treatment. In short, psychiatric diagnoses are rather similar to astrological star signs: it is widely assumed that they are meaningful, tell us something useful about people, and allow us to predict what will happen in the future, but they fail on all these counts.

It is important to note that this argument, like the observation that psychotic behaviours and experiences exist on a continuum with normal functioning, does not, on its own, require us to reject the idea that psychosis is disease. After all, it might be possible to develop a new system of psychiatric classification that better fulfils the main functions of diagnosis. (For evidence that dimensional classification systems may have some utility in this regard, see van Os et al. 1999).

Could Psychosis Be a Disease?

The central assumption of Szasz's (1960) famous critique of the concept of mental illness was that the attribution of illness requires the demonstration of some kind of biological pathology or disease. On his view, in the absence of pathology, the concept of mental illness is incoherent and self-contradictory, in much the same way that it is self-contradictory to speak about married bachelors or meat-eating vegetarians. This argument is repeated by Szasz (1979), for example:

> Kraepelin and Bleuler discovered no histopathological lesions or pathophysiological processes in their patients. Instead, they acted as if they had discovered such lesions; named their 'patients' accordingly; and committed themselves and their followers to the goal of establishing a precise identification of the 'organic' nature and cause of these diseases. (Szasz 1979, p. 9)

I will return to the substance of this argument later on. However, it is first important to note a remarkable coincidence of opinion between Szasz and many of the strongest advocates of a medical approach to psychiatric problems. Like Szasz, such advocates have typically assumed that the concept of illness implies biological pathology. This is true of the nineteenth-century pioneers working during the period that Edward Shorter (1997) has dubbed the "first era of biological psychiatry", and also of modern practitioners, notably the neoKraepelinians who devised the DSM system.

For example, when in 1867 Wilhelm Griesinger founded the *Archives for Psychiatry and Nervous Disease*, one of the first academic journals in the discipline, he published an opening editorial in which he stated that:

> Psychiatry has undergone a transformation in its relation to the rest of medicine. This transformation rests principally on the realization that patients with so-called 'mental illnesses' are really individuals with illnesses of the nerves and brain. (Quoted in Shorter 1997)

Nearly a century later, in their famous account of *Three Hundred Years of Psychiatry*, Hunter, and McAlpine (1963) argued that:

> The lesson of the history of psychiatry is that progress is inevitable and irrevocable from psychology to neurology, from mind to brain, never the other way round.

This approach to understanding psychiatric disorders perhaps reached its zenith with the neoKraepelinians, one of whom wrote an editorial for the journal *Psychological Medicine* that simply asserted:

> There can be no such thing as a psychiatry that is too biological. (Guze 1989)

If we accept this assumption at face value, therefore, the dispute between Szasz and many conventional psychiatrists about the nature of schizophrenia should be resolvable by determining whether the behaviours and experiences subsumed by the diagnosis are, in fact, associated with physical pathology. Surprisingly, just as Szasz failed to offer a comprehensive review of the biological data when making his claim that pathology was absent in schizophrenia patients, few of those who responded to the publication of either Szasz 1960 or Szasz 1979 rose to his challenge by providing evidence that pathology was present. Perhaps this failure to debate the issue empirically reflected the fact there was very little biological data available at the time. However, in the years since, there have been enormous advances in the neurosciences. Although it would be impossible to review all of the findings that have been obtained from schizophrenia patients as a consequence of these advances, it will be instructive to look at two of the most significant developments.

Aberrant Chemistry and the Dopamine Hypothesis

Although Otto Loewi and Henry Dale received the Nobel Prize for medicine in 1936 for their demonstration that the sympathetic and parasympathetic nervous systems utilise noradrenaline and acetylcholine, the idea that neurotransmitters played an important role in the central nervous system only became widely accepted in the 1960s (Finger 2000; Healy 1997), approximately forty years after Kraepelin's death. As Szasz (1979) has noted, theories that implicate the various neurotransmitter systems in psychosis have generally followed from serendipitous observations of the effects of drugs. However, this has been the normal course of progress in pharmacology. The beta-blockers stand out as the only major class of drugs synthesised entirely on the basis of a well worked-out physiological theory (Le Fanu 1999).

Even the most enthusiastic biological psychiatrist will accept that many avenues of psychopharmacological research have proven to be dead ends. For example, in 1938 the Swiss chemist Albert Hoffman, who was searching for compounds derived from ergot in the hope that these would prove useful for controlling muscle spasms during pregnancy, first synthesized lysergic acid diethylamide (LSD). The drug appeared to have little effect on animals and it was only after accidentally inhaling it that Hoffman discovered that it was a powerful hallucinogen. This discovery encouraged some researchers to argue that schizophrenia might be caused either by some kind of endogenous (self-created) hallucinogenic substance (Wooley and Shaw 1954). In 1962, a dramatic breakthrough was reported which seemed to support this hypothesis. Researchers saw a 'pink spot' when the urine of schizophrenia patients was allowed to diffuse on chromatography paper, and this spot was absent when the procedure was repeated with urine from ordinary people (Friedhoff and van Winkle 1962). The spot was thought to be an endogenous hallucinogen but was later discovered to be of dietary origin and could be found in the urine of anyone who ate institutional food.

The pink spot debacle no doubt contributed to researchers losing interest in the possible role of endogenous hallucinogens in schizophrenia, but more important still was the emergence of a viable alternative hypothesis that proved to be more enduring. In 1951, Henry Laborit, a French naval surgeon, accidentally stumbled on the psychological effects of a synthetic antihistimine, 4560 RP, which seemed to induce a curious state of indifference in his patients (Healy 1996; 1997). The next year, Jean Delay and Pierre Deniker conducted the first substantial trials to establish that the new drug, soon to be known as chlorpromazine, had a genuine antipsychotic effect. Arvid Carlsson's subsequent demonstration that dopamine was an important neurotransmitter soon led to the suggestion that the therapeutic effects of chlorpromazine were attributable to its capacity to block dopamine receptors, and the demonstration that all of the then available antipsychotic drugs had this effect (Carlsson and Lindqvist 1963).

In the following decades, the dopamine hypothesis has so dominated the search for a neurobiological substrate of schizophrenia that some have considered questioning it a heresy. (When I recently gave a talk about the incoherence of the schizophrenia concept at a British university, someone in the audience angrily challenged me to draw a circuit diagram of the dopamine system.) Indeed, on first sight, the evidence supporting the hypothesis seems fairly impressive. First, there can be no doubt that antipsychotic medication, when compared to placebos or compounds such as barbiturates that have similar sedative effects, produces in perhaps the majority of patients a marked reduction in hallucinations and delusions (Joy, Adams, and Lawrie 2004; Kane 1989; Thornley, Adams, and Award 2004). On the negative side, the drugs are also associated with distressing side effects, of which the most obvious are the extra-pyramidal effects, which include Parkinsonian symptoms (stiffness and tremor), akathisia (severe subjective restlessness), dystonias and tardive dyskinesia (see Day and Bentall 1996 for a review). Second, drugs that are known to increase dopamine turnover in the brain, for example amphetamine, sometimes produce psychotic reactions in ordinary people (Angrist and Gershon 1970; Connell 1958). Third, the same is sometimes true of drugs administered to treat idiopathic Parkinson's disease, for example levo-dopa (Leonard 1992). Together, these observations seem to suggest that an increase in dopaminergic activity can precipitate psychosis whereas a reduction in activity leads to Parkinsonian symptoms.

Although the logic of this theory is attractive, it has not survived the test of time particularly well. This is partly because, on close examination, the crucial observations that appear to support the theory are not as clear-cut as was once believed. For example, it is known that a complete blockade of the crucial dopamine D_2 receptors is achieved within a few hours of taking an adequate dose of medication, but that the effects of antipsychotic drugs on positive symptoms do not become apparent before several weeks of treatment (Trimble 1996). Some of the more recently discovered atypical antipsychotics, notably clozapine, do not seem to have a specific affinity for dopamine receptors. Moreover, the specificity of antipsychotic drugs for schizophrenia is highly question-able. Whereas a proportion of schizophrenia patients consistently fail to respond to this kind of treatment (Brown and Herz 1989; Kinon, Kane, Johns, et al. 1993), antipsychotic drugs are sometimes effective in the treatment of mania (Johnstone, Crow, Frith, and Owens 1988).

More importantly, perhaps, an expensive and sustained search for dopamine abnormalities in schizophrenia patients has so far drawn a blank. Attempts to measure dopamine levels in patients' brains at post-mortem, or to measure the metabolites of dopamine in living patients, have consistently indicated that dopamine turnover is *not* elevated in schizophrenia (McKenna 1994). Early demonstrations of abnormally high dopamine receptor density in drug-naive schizophrenia patients (Wong et al. 1986) have been impossible to replicate (Fadre et al. 1987). As the search for other kinds of neurochemical abnormalities (for exam-ple in brain pathways utilizing GABA or glutimate) has so far proven to be equally inconclusive, neurochemical research has not supported the assumption that pathology is present in schizophrenia patients, and appears to favour Szasz rather than the followers of Kraepelin.

In fact, this conclusion may be too simple, as two recent studies have indicated. In one, abnormal levels of an enzyme that converts ampheta-mine to dopamine were found in trauma victims who had become psy-chotic (Hamner and Gold 1998). In the other, the dopamine system of schizophrenia patients was observed to be over-responsive to a dose of amphetamine, but only in patients who were symptomatic and not in those whose symptoms were in remission (Laruelle, Abi-Dargham, Gil, Kegeles, and Innis 1999). Whether these findings can be replicated remains to be seen. However, they raise the possibility that abnormal biochemistry, even if found in patients, may be the brain's response to adverse experiences, or a *correlate* of symptoms rather than a primary cause of them. Neurochemistry may be a less clear-cut indicator of pathology than is often assumed.

The Anatomy of Madness: Evidence from Structural Neuroimaging

Perhaps research on the structure of the nervous system will prove to be more conclusive. Investigations of this kind were advocated by Kraepelin, who encouraged his colleague Alois Alzheimer to carry out postmortem studies of psychiatric patients. Although he accepted Alzheimer's conclusion that the brains of dead psychotic patients looked more or less normal, this did not stop him from asserting that, in dementia praecox: "Partial damage to, or destruction of, cells of the cerebral cortex must probably occur . . . which mostly brings in its wake a singular, permanent impairment of the inner life" (Kraepelin 1907).

Research on the neuroanatomy of psychotic patients was revolutionised by Geoffrey Hounsefield's invention of computerised tomography (CT) scanning which, in the early 1970s, allowed cross-sectional slices through the body to be depicted for the first time. More recently, the development of even more sensitive methods, particularly magnetic resonance imaging (MRI) has added to this impetus. Many different kinds of neuroanatomical abnormalities have been reported in psychotic patients as a consequence, including enlargement of the sulci (crevices in the folded tissue of the cortex), focal lesions in different cortical areas, and atypical asymmetries of the cerebral hemispheres. However, in this review I focus on reports of enlarged cerebral ventricles (the fluid-filled cavities in the centre of the brain) in schizophrenia patients, a type of abnormality that has received considerable attention from researchers, perhaps because the ventricles were the only structures that could be easily depicted by early CT scanners.

Eve Johnstone and her colleagues at Northwick Park Hospital published the first report of enlarged lateral ventricles in schizophrenia patients (Johnstone, Crow, Frith, Husband, and Kreel 1976), a finding that seemed to indicate that their patients had suffered from some kind of atrophy of the cerebral cortex. Later studies, carried out in many different countries with both CT and MRI scanners, reported similar findings, making ventricular enlargement one of the best replicated findings in biological psychiatry (Woodruff and Lewis 1996). On the surface, then, these findings strongly support the neoKraepelinian assumption that schizophrenia is associated with neuropathology, and allow biological psychiatrists to reject Szasz's assertion that the diagnosis does not identify a disease.

Once again, however, closer examination of the evidence reveals a more complex picture. The early CT scan studies almost certainly overestimated the extent of ventricular enlargement in schizophrenia patients, probably because they failed to recruit well-matched control participants (Smith and Iacano 1986). More recent and more carefully controlled investigations have reported less dramatic differences between patients and ordinary people, although differences still seem to exist (van Horn and McManus 1992; Woodruff and Lewis 1996). Interestingly, recent studies have also reported evidence of ventricular enlargement and other anatomical abnormalities in the brains of patients diagnosed as suffering from bipolar disorder and psychotic depression

(Dolan and Goodwin 1996). Consistent with my earlier comments about Kraepelin's distinction between dementia praecox/schizophrenia and the affective psychoses, abnormal neuroanatomy does not seem to be specific to schizophrenia.

It is not clear whether these differences between patients and ordinary people reflect some kind of causal degenerative process, as is usually assumed. In the short term, ventricular volume can change in response to alcohol consumption, water retention and even pregnancy (Woodruff and Lewis 1996). (It is perhaps not surprising, therefore, that patients who at first appear to have large ventricles sometimes show a reduction of ventricular volume to within normal limits when scans are repeated at a later date, as observed by Piri et al. 1997.) Longer term correlations between ventricular volume and age, head size, educational achievement, social class, and ethnicity probably reflect the way in which neurodevelopment is driven by the environment. Our brains literally rewire themselves in the light of our experiences and sometimes these changes are large enough to be detectable by scanner. For example, the volumes of the hippocampus (an area of the brain that plays an important role in memory) and the corpus callosum (the bundle of fibres that connects the two cerebral hemispheres) are reduced in people who have experienced post-traumatic stress following warfare or sexual assault, or who have been victims of sexual abuse during childhood (Bremmer et al. 1995; Teicher 2000). Conversely, the volume of the posterior hippocampus seems to increase as taxi drivers learn to find their way around London (Maguire et al. 2000).

This analysis of the neuroimaging data allows me to elaborate on a conclusion I hinted at after surveying the research on the dopamine hypothesis. Whereas hippocampal enlargement in taxi drivers is considered to be quite normal, the structural changes in the brains of schizophrenia patients are widely seen as evidence of disease. Perhaps this is because driving taxis is seen as a socially valuable form of behaviour, whereas experiencing hallucinations and expressing strange beliefs is not. The biological facts alone, it seems, do not determine whether biological differences between individuals are pathological.

An Etiological Conundrum

So far I have whittled away at the distinction between pathology and normal biology by examining the biological correlates of psychosis. An obvious objection to this approach is that I have not really said anything about the *causes* of psychotic behaviours and experiences. Perhaps a neurobiological difference between schizophrenia patients and ordinary people might be described as pathological if biological etiology can also be demonstrated.

(As an aside, it is worth mentioning that it is quite difficult to determine which antecedent factors out of a rich network of events can be said to play a causal role in the etiology of a disease. The problem is not just that it is difficult to isolate events and prove that they are necessary for a disease to develop. It is also that different kinds of events, described in different ways, will be prioritised according to the purpose of the etiological theory that is being constructed. Take lung cancer for example. Geneticists are likely to look to gene sequences that confer vulnerability to the development of malignant carcinoma. Physicians are likely to point to the effect of inhaled tobacco fumes on the process of cell division in lung tissue. However, psychologists are likely to point to the roles of personality and peer-pressure in determining the decision to smoke, whereas sociologists may focus more on the influence of cigarette advertisements, or the failure of governments to regulate the tobacco industry.)

One of the foremost researchers into psychiatric genetics, Seymore Kety (1974) once remarked that, "If schizophrenia is a myth, it is a myth with a strong genetic component". Estimates of the percentage of variance in schizophrenic symptoms that can be attributed to genes have often been higher than 70 percent (Gottesman and Shields 1982). Although the steps taken by geneticists when reaching figures of this sort have not gone unchallenged (Marshall 1990), and although attempts to implicate specific genetic loci in psychosis have so far proven fruitless (Moldin 1997), it is hard to deny that heredity plays a role at least in conferring vulnerability to symptoms. For example, in dizygotic (nonidentical) twins the pairwise concordance rate for schizophrenia (the proportion of affected individuals whose twin is also affected) has been conservatively estimated at 6 percent, whereas the corresponding figure for monozygotic twins seems to be about 28 percent (Torrey, Bowler, Taylor, and Gottesman 1994). To many minds (for example, Kety's), findings of this sort unequivocally establish that schizophrenia is a disease.

However, this argument falls for exactly the same reason that the neurobiological evidence fails to provide an objective criterion for pathology. The presence of a biological determinant alone does not establish that a human characteristic is a disease. It is easy to point to characteristics that are genetically influenced but which are not classified in this way. The most obvious example is intelligence, for which heritability estimates at least equal those given for schizophrenia (Dickins and Flynn 2001).

What if some kind of direct insult to the nervous system has occurred to schizophrenia patients, for example, some kind of physical damage to the brain as might occur following a blow to the head? Would this provide a scientific and morally unambiguous criterion for deciding that pathology is present? When considering this most clear-cut example of biological causation, it is worth noting that, on the one hand, physical damage of this sort is absent in many recognised diseases, for example essential hypertension, and that, on the other hand, there is considerable circumstantial evidence of damage of this sort in schizophrenia patients. For example, the well-replicated finding that people born in late winter or early spring are at elevated risk of psychosis (Fuller, Miller, Rawlings, and Yolken 1997) is most likely explained by the effects of viruses on early brain development. Consistent with the hypothesis that early brain damage confers a risk of psychosis in later life, children born during periods of famine are at increased risk of later becoming psychotic (Susser and Lin 1992). Also consistent with this hypothesis, some children who later become psychotic show motor abnormalities in the first few years of life (Walker, 1994), and have delayed developmental milestones (Jones and Done 1997).)

Even in the case of a clear causal connection between a wound to the brain and aberrant behaviour, however, it remains the case that the wound is only regarded as evidence of pathology because the behaviour in question is viewed as undesirable. Imagine a situation in which a wound to the brain produces desirable consequences. (In his science fiction novel *Jem*, Fredrick Pohl suggests that callosotomy operations might be offered to professional linguists in order to facilitate their simultaneous translation skills.) In these circumstances, it is unlikely that the wound would be considered evidence of pathology.

The Mental Illness Debate as Sideshow

I began this essay by noting that Szasz and the neoKraepelinians agree on a criterion for disease, arguing that there must be demonstrable physical pathology. According to this viewpoint, the question of whether schizophrenia is a disease should be empirically resolvable. However, when we have looked at specific examples of neurobiological research, the data appear to be ambiguous, and can easily be interpreted either way.

This difficulty does not arise simply because (as biological psychiatrists often assert) schizophrenia is a complex illness, and because the brain is the most complex organ in the human body. Rather, the problem seems to be that we have no clear *empirical* criterion for deciding whether biological deviations from the norm are pathological and hence evidence of disease. Indeed, it seems that we regard such deviations as evidence of pathology only when the characteristics that they are seen to cause are regarded as undesirable. This is as true in physical medicine as in psychiatry. In physical medicine an illusion that judgements of pathology are value-free is created by the fact of almost universal agreement about which consequences of biological deviation are undesirable (almost no one wants to suffer shortness of breath, an inability to move without pain, or the risk of sudden death). In psychiatry, by contrast, agreement is not so universal. Homosexuality, which may well be influenced by biological factors, was once considered an undesirable characteristic but is now widely accepted as 'normal'. Even in the case of the psychoses, many people seem to live relatively happy lives without seeking treatment for their hallucinated voices or unconventional beliefs (Poulton *et al.* 2000; Tien 1991; van Os *et al.* 2000). (Indeed, arguing that people who hallucinate are more in need of liberation than cure, the Dutch social psychiatrist Marius Romme and his partner Sondra Escher (1993) have formed a mutual-support organisation for 'voice hearers'.)

At first sight, this conclusion may seem more comforting to Szasz than to the neoKraepelinians, as it concords with his view that judgements about mental illness are always value-laden. Indeed, to my mind, Szasz's greatest and most important contribution has been to highlight the moral dimension of psychiatric care, and the ethical problems inherent in compulsory psychiatric treatment. However, he has reached this position on the basis of a false premise—that there is such a thing as 'real pathology', which can be defined in a manner that lies outside anybody's value system.

This analysis suggests that the argument about whether or not mental illness is a myth is, at best, a sideshow in the fight to develop more ethical psychiatric services. Such services should meet the moral requirements of any medical system (including those designed to help people who suffer from the kinds of physical conditions that Szasz would recognise as true illnesses). These requirements, which have been clearly articulated by medical ethicists, include obligations to offer interventions that improve quality of life (sometimes called the principle of beneficence), to avoid causing harm (the principle of non-maleficence), to respect patients' autonomy (including their judgements about whether their difficulties require medical intervention), and to distribute health resources justly (Beauchamp and Childess 1979; Gillon 1985). It is perhaps ironic that these principles are considered uncontentious in physical medicine (which Szasz considers to be a poor model for psychiatry), but are routinely flouted by services for the 'mentally ill'.

REFERENCES

Angrist, B.M., and S. Gershon. 1970. The Phenomonenology of Experimentally Induced Amphetamine Psychosis: Preliminary Observations. *Biological Psychiatry* 2, pp. 95–107.

Beauchamp, T.L., and J.F. Childress. 1979. *Principles of Biomedical Ethics*. Oxford: Oxford University Press.

Bentall, R.P. 1990. The Syndromes and Symptoms of Psychosis: Or Why You Can't Play 20 Questions with the Concept of Schizophrenia and Hope to Win. In R.P. Bentall, ed., *Reconstructing Schizophrenia* (London: Routledge). pp. 23–60.

———. 1993. Deconstructing the Concept of Schizophrenia. *Journal of Mental Health* 2, pp. 223-238.

———. 1998. Why There Will Never Be a Convincing Theory of Schizophrenia. In S. Rose, ed., *From Brains to Consciousness: Essays on the New Sciences of the Mind* (London: Penguin), pp. 109–136.

Bentall, R.P., H.F. Jackson, and D. Pilgrim. 1988. Abandoning the Concept of Schizophrenia: Some Implications of Validity Arguments for Psychological Research into Psychotic Phenomena. *British Journal of Clinical Psychology* 27, pp. 303–324.

Berrios, G., and R. Hauser. 1988. The Early Development of Kraepelin's Ideas on Classification: A Conceptual History. *Psychological Medicine* 18, pp. 813–821.

Bleuler, E. 1950 [1911]. *Dementia praecox or the Group of Schizophrenias*. Translated by E. Zinkin. New York: International Universities Press.

Bremmer, J.D., P. Randall, T.M. Scott, R.A. Bronen, J.P. Seibyl, S.M. Southwick, R.C. Delaney, G. McCarthy, D.S. Charney, and R.D. Innis. 1995. MRI-based Measurement of Hippocampal Volume in Patients with Combat-related Post-traumatic Stress Disorder. *American Journal of Psychiatry* 152, pp. 973-981.

Brown, W.A., and L.R. Herz. 1989. Response to Neuroleptic Drugs as a Device for Classifying Schizophrenia. *Schizophrenia Bulletin* 15, pp. 123–28.

Carlsson, A. 1995. The Dopamine Theory Revisited. In S.R. Hirsch and D.R. Weinberger, eds., *Schizophrenia* (Oxford: Blackwell), pp. 379–400.

Carlsson, A., and M. Lindqvist. 1963. Effect of Chlorpromazine or Haloperidol on Formation of 3-Methoxytyramine and Normetanephrine in Mouse Brain. *Acta Pharmacologica et Toxicologica* 20, pp. 140–44.

Chapman, L.J., and J.P. Chapman. 1980. Scales for Rating Psychotic and Psychotic-like Experiences as Continua. *Schizophrenia Bulletin* 6, pp. 477–489.

———. 1988. The Genesis of Delusions. In T.F. Oltmanns and B.A. Maher, eds., *Delusional Beliefs* (New York: Wiley), pp. 167–183.

Claridge, G.S. 1985. *The Origins of Mental Illness*. Oxford: Blackwell.

———. 1987. The Schizophrenias as Nervous Types Revisited. *British Journal of Psychiatry* 151, pp. 735–743.

———. 1990. Can a Disease Model of Schizophrenia Survive? In R.P. Bentall, ed., *Reconstructing Schizophrenia* (London: Routledge), pp. 157–183.

Connell, P. 1958. *Amphetamine Psychosis*. London: Chapman and Hall.

Day, J.C., and R.P. Bentall. 1996. Neuroleptic Medication and the Psychosocial Treatment of Psychotic Symptoms: Some Neglected Issues. In G. Haddock and P.D. Slade, eds., *Cognitive-Behavioural Interventions with Psychotic Disorders* (London: Routledge), pp. 235–274.

Dickins, W.T., and J.R. Flynn. 2001. Heritability Estimates versus Large Environmental Effects: The IQ Paradox Resolved. *Psychological Review* 108, pp. 346–369.

Dolan, R.J., and G.M. Goodwin. 1996. Brain Imaging in Affective Disorders. In S. Lewis and N. Higgins, eds., *Brain Imaging in Psychiatry* (Oxford: Blackwell).

Fadre, L., F.A. Wiesel, H. Hall, C. Halldin, S. Stone-Elander, and G. Sedvall. 1987. No D2 Receptor Increase in PET Study of Schizophrenia. *Archives of General Psychiatry* 44, pp. 671–72.

Finger, S. 2000. *Minds Behind the Brain: A History of the Pioneers and Their Discoveries*. Oxford: Oxford University Press.

Friedhoff, A., and E. van Winkle. 1962. The Characteristics of an Amine Found in the Urine of Schizophrenic Patients. *Journal of Nervous and Mental Disease* 135, pp. 550.

Fuller, E.T., J. Miller, R. Rawlings, and R.H. Yolken. 1997. Seasonality of Births in Schizophrenia and Bipolar Disorder: A Review of the Literature. *Schizophrenia Research* 28, pp. 1–38.

Gillon, R. 1985. *Philosophical Medical Ethics*. London: Wiley.

Gottesman, I.I., and J. Shields. 1982. *Schizophrenia: The Epigenetic Puzzle*. Cambridge: Cambridge University Press.

Guze, S. 1989. Biological Psychiatry: Is There Any Other Kind? *Psychological Medicine* 19, pp. 315–323.

Hamner, M.B., and P.B. Gold. 1998. Plasma Dopamine Beta-hydroxylase Activity in Psychotic and Non-psychotic Post-traumatic Stress Disorder. *Psychiatry Research* 77, pp. 175–181.

Healy, D. 1996. *The Psychopharmacologists: Interviews with David Healy*. London: Chapman and Hall.

———. 1997. *The Anti-depressant Era*. Cambridge, Massachusetts: Harvard University Press.

Hoff, P. 1995. Kraepelin. In G. Berrios and R. Porter, eds., *A History of Clinical Psychiatry* (London: Althorne Press), pp. 261–279.

Hunter, R., and I. McAlpine. 1963. *Three Hundred Years of Psychiatry.* London: Hogarth Press.

Johnstone, E.C., T.J. Crow, C.D. Frith, J. Husband, and L. Kreel. 1976. Cerebral Ventricular Size and Cognitive Impairment in Chronic Schizophrenia. *Lancet* ii, pp. 924–26.

Johnstone, E.C., T.J. Crow, C.D. Frith, and D.G.C. Owens. 1988. The Northwick Park 'Functional' Psychosis Study: Diagnosis and Treatment Response. *Lancet* ii, pp. 119–125.

Jones, P.B., and D.J. Done. 1997. From Birth to Onset: A Developmental Perspective of Schizophrenia in Two National Birth Cohorts. In M.S. Keshavan and R.M. Murray, eds., *Neurodevelopment and Adult Psychopathology* (Cambridge: Cambridge University Press), pp. 119–136.

Joy, C.B., C.E. Adams, and S.M. Lawrie. 2004. *Haloperidol versus Placebo for Schizophrenia (Cochrane Review),* In the Cochrane Library (Chichester: Wiley).

Kane, J. 1989. The Current Status of Neuroleptic Therapy. *Journal of Clinical Psychiatry* 50, pp. 322–28.

Kety, S.S. 1974. From Rationalization to Reason. *American Journal of Psychiatry* 131, pp. 957–963.

Kinon, B.J., J.M. Kane, C. Johns, et al. 1993. Treatment of Neuroleptic Resistant Relapse. *Psychopharmacological Bulletin* 29, pp. 309–314.

Klerman, G. L. (1978). The Evolution of a Scientific Nosology. In J.C. Shershow, ed., *Schizophrenia: Science and Practice* (Cambridge, Massachusetts: Harvard University Press, pp. 99–121.

Kraepelin, E. 1907. *Textbook of Psychiatry.* Seventh edition. Translated by A.R. Diefendorf. London: Macmillan.

Laruelle, M., A. Abi-Dargham, R. Gil, L. Kegeles, and R. Innis. 1999. Increased Dopamine Transmission in Schizophrenia: Relationship to Illness Phases. *Biological Psychiatry* 46, pp. 56–72.

Le Fanu, J. 1999. *The Rise and Fall of Modern Medicine.* London: Little, Brown.

Leonard, B.E. 1992. *Fundamentals of Psychopharmacology.* London: Wiley.

Maguire, E.A., D.G. Gadian, I.S. Johnsrude, C.D. Good, J. Ashburner, R.S.J. Frackowiak, and C.D. Frith. 2000. Navigation-related Structural Changes in the Hippocampi of Taxi Drivers. *Procedings of the National Academy of Science.*

Marshall, R. 1990. The Genetics of Schizophrenia: Axiom or Hypothesis? In R.P. Bentall, ed., *Reconstructing Schizophrenia* (London: Routledge), pp. 89–117.

McKenna, P.J. 1994. *Schizophrenia and Related Syndromes.* Oxford: Oxford University Press.

Moldin, S.O. 1997. The Maddening Hunt for Madness Genes. *Nature Genetics* 17, pp. 127–29.

Piri, B.K., N. Saeed, A. Oatridge, J.V. Hajnal, S.B. Hutton, L.-J. Duncan, M.J. Chapman, T.R.E. Barnes, G.M. Bydder, and E.M. Joyce. 1997. A Longitudinal MRI Study of First-episode Schizophrenia: Assessment of Cerebral Changes and Quantification of Ventricular Changes. *Schizophrenia Research* 76.

Poulton, R., A. Caspi, T.E. Moffitt, M. Cannon, R. Murray, and H. Harrington. 2000. Children's Self-reported Psychotic Symptoms and Adult Schizophreniform Disorder: A 15-year Longitudinal Study. *Archives of General Psychiatry* 57, pp. 1053–58.

Romme, M., and S. Escher, eds. 1993. *Accepting Voices*. London: MIND Publications.

Shorter, E. 1997. *A History of Psychiatry*. New York: Wiley.

Smith, G.N., and W.G. Iacano. 1986. Lateral Ventricular Enlargement in Schizophrenia and Choice of Control Group. *Lancet* i, p. 1450.

Susser, E.S., and S.P. Lin. 1992. Schizophrenia after Prenatal Exposure to the Dutch Hunger Winter of 1944–1945. *Archives of General Psychiatry* 49, pp. 938–988.

Szasz, T.S. 1960. The Myth of Mental Illness. *American Psychologist* 15, pp. 564–580.

———. 1979. *Schizophrenia: The Sacred Symbol of Psychiatry*. Oxford: Oxford University Press.

Teicher, M.H. 2000. Brain Abnormalities Common in Survivors of Childhood Abuse. *Cerebrum* 2, pp. 50–67.

Thornley, B., C.E. Adams, and G. Award. 2004. *Chlorpromazine versus Placebo for Schizophrenia, (Vol. 3)*. In the Cochrane Library (Chichester: Wiley).

Tien, A.Y. 1991. Distribution of Hallucinations in the Population. *Social Psychiatry and Psychiatric Epidemiology* 26, pp. 287–292.

Torrey, E.F., A.E. Bowler, E.H. Taylor, and I.I. Gottesman. 1994. *Schizophrenia and Manic-Depressive Disorder*. New York: Basic Books.

Trimble, M. 1996. *Biological Psychiatry*. Second edition. Chichester: Wiley.

van Horn, J.D., and I.C. McManus. 1992. Ventricular Enlargement in Schizophrenia: A Meta-analysis of Studies of Ventricular Brain Ratio. *British Journal of Psychiatry* 160, pp. 687–697.

van Os, J., C. Gilvarry, R. Bale, E. van Horn, T. Tattan, I. White, and R. Murray. 1999. A Comparison of the Utility of Dimensional and Categorical Representations of Psychosis. *Psychological Medicine* 29, pp. 595–606.

van Os, J., M. Hanssen, R.V. Bijl, and A. Ravelli. 2000. Strauss (1969) Revisited: A Psychosis Continuum in the Normal Population? *Schizophrenia Research* 45, pp. 11–20.

Walker, E.F. 1994. Neurodevelopmental Precursors of Schizophrenia. In A.S. David and J.C. Cutting, eds., *The Neuropsychology of Schizophrenia*. Hove: Erlbaum.

Wong, D. F., H.N. Wagner, L.E. Tune, R.F. Dannals, G.D. Pearlson, and J.M. Links. 1986. Positron Emission Tomography Reveals Elevated D2 Dopamine Receptors in Drug-naive Schizophrenics. *Science* 234, pp. 1558–563.

Woodruff, P.W.R., and S. Lewis. 1996. Structural Brain Imaging in Schizophrenia. In S. Lewis and N. Higgins, eds., *Brain Imaging in Psychiatry* (Oxford: Blackwell).

Wooley, D.E., and E. Shaw. 1954. A Biochemical and Pharmacological Suggestion about Certain Mental Disorders. *Proceedings of the National Academy of Sciences USA* 40, pp. 228–231.

Reply to Bentall

THOMAS SZASZ

I

"I will attempt to show," writes Bentall, "that some of the arguments he [Szasz] has used to reach what I believe to be essentially accurate conclusions do not stand up to careful scrutiny." This kind of yes-but statement makes me uneasy.

Bentall calls my assertion that mental illness is a myth my *conclusion*. That is an error: it is my *premise*. After the sentence quoted above, Bentall comments, with implied criticism: "Indeed, some of these arguments will be shown to be identical to those used by biological psychiatrists when defending the schizophrenia concept." That is right. The scientific standard for what counts as a disease is an objectively demonstrable bodily lesion or process that deviates from an objectively defined biological norm. That is why biological psychiatrists search for brain lesions in schizophrenics: they want to show that certain so-called mental illnesses are neurological diseases. It seems to elude Bentall and biological psychiatrists alike that success in such an endeavor would prove that the person with a brain lesion has a *bodily disease;* it would not prove that mental diseases are bodily (literal) diseases.

When I assert that (mis)behaviors are not diseases I assert an analytic truth, similar to asserting that bachelors are not married, or that consecrated bread is not the body of Jesus. It is a symptom of our living in a therapeutic state that many people are unable to recognize the medical version of such a conflation of symbol and symbolized, metaphoric and literal meaning. In 1976, in the Introduction to *Heresies,* I wrote:

> The literalization of the metaphor of the Last Supper creates the image that Jesus is alive. If so, He can be killed again. Incredible as it may sound to the contemporary reader, this belief was actually held in Europe until relatively

recent times. For about three hundred years, from the thirteenth until the sixteenth centuries, there were repeated episodes of Jews being accused of stabbing the sacramental wafer and making it bleed—justifying the killing of thousands of Jews. Moreover, the colloquial characterization of Jews as "Christ-killers," even in modern anti-Semitism, also points to the power that literalized metaphors exercise over the human mind: for this epithet must be read as casting blame for the death of Jesus not only on some Jews who lived a long time ago, but also on Jews who are the speaker's contemporaries. The story of the "bleeding" Eucharist is a fascinating, but astonishingly neglected, chapter of medieval history.

According to Eugene Gaughran, the first authentic reference to mysterious blood appearing on bread is the report of classical historians concerning the siege of Tyre, in what is now Lebanon, in 332 B.C. Diodorus Siculus, the Greek historian, gave this account of the phenomenon: "At the distribution of the rations on the Macedonian side, the broken pieces of bread had a bloody look."[1] The exact cause of this reddish coloration, which was often mistaken for blood, was not discovered until 1823, when the Italian naturalist Bartolomeo Bizio identified, named, and described the saprophytic bacterium *Serratia marcescens* as its cause. This widely distributed bacterium, which grows readily in starchy foods, produces a blood-red pigment. To those who believed that the Host was the body of Christ and not just a piece of bread, the occurrence of this pigment in the bread thus had momentous significance. One of the earliest reports of such bacterial discoloration of the sacramental wafer was reported in 1247. In the village of Berlitz, in Germany, "A maid held the Host in her mouth during communion. Later she sold it to Jews who stabbed it, kept the blood which flowed from it, and gave the Host back to her. The Miraculous blood made the Church of Berlitz famous."[2]

In *The Myth of Mental Illness,* I argued that mental illness does not exist not because no one has yet found such a disease, but because *no one can find such a disease:* the only kind of disease medical researchers can find is literal, bodily disease. Bentall's confusion on this score is reflected in the title of his essay: he brackets me with neo-Kraepelinians. True, Kraepelin, neo-Kraepelinians, and I share the belief that only bodily diseases are diseases. However, Kraepelin regarded putative diseases as proven diseases, and neo-Kraepelinians do the same thing; whereas I

---

[1] E.R.L. Gaughran, "From Superstition to Science: The History of a Bacterium." *Transactions of the New York Academy of Sciences,* Series II, 30, pp. 3–24 (January 1969), p. 3.

[2] Thomas Szasz, "Introduction," in *Heresies* (Garden City: Anchor-Doubleday, 1976), pp. 1–12; and Gaughran, "From Superstition to Science," p. 7.

count only proven diseases as real diseases.[3] Also, Kraepelin supported involuntary mental hospitalization and coerced psychiatric treatment, and so do neo-Kraepelinians; whereas I reject such interventions as deprivations of liberty and crimes against humanity.

Without stating his criterion for illness, Bentall finds fault with my use of the Virchowian-pathological criterion. He writes:

> sometimes his [Szasz's] attitude towards the pioneers of psychiatric taxonomy borders on hostility. In part, this reflects *his more general assumption that disease equates to physical pathology* . . . (emphasis added)

It is true that my criterion for disease is physical pathology. I don't know what else it could be, without improperly inflating the class of phenomena called "diseases."[4]

II

Bentall is undecided about what counts as a literal, bodily disease. After repeatedly criticizing the Virchowian criterion, he writes:

> it is first important to note a remarkable coincidence of opinion between Szasz and many of the strongest advocates of a medical approach to psychiatric problems. Like Szasz, such advocates have typically assumed that the concept of illness implies *biological pathology*.

This is not a "coincidence" and there is nothing remarkable about it. The only kind of *literal* pathology there is, is biological pathology. Bentall flirts with the idea of regarding *psychopathological terms* as designating the same kinds of phenomena that pathologists find at autopsy, but does not commit himself to that view. He also neglects to mention that I explicitly reject the use of the misleading term "medical model" in reference to biological psychiatry. Typically, physicians treat adults who seek their services. Only pediatricians and psychiatrists treat persons who do not seek their services. In *Insanity: The Idea and Its Consequences*, I emphasize that "both psychiatry and antipsychiatry rest on a coercive pediatric model characterized by relations of domination

---

[3] Thomas Szasz, *Insanity: The Idea and Its Consequences* (Syracuse: Syracuse University Press, 1997 [1987]), pp. 48–45.

[4] Thomas Szasz, *Pharmacracy: Medicine and Politics in America* (Westport: Praeger, 2001).

and subjection, rather than on a noncoercive medical model of respect for persons characterized by relations of mutual cooperation and contract."[5]

Again and again, Bentall simultaneously asserts his agreement with, and disavowal of, my views. He writes: "Szasz's intuition in this regard [about delusions and hallucinations] is undoubtedly correct," but then continues: "After all, it might be possible to develop a new system of psychiatric classification that better fulfills the main functions of diagnosis." What do psychiatric diagnoses identify and what is their main function? Bentall doesn't say. *De facto,* the function of psychiatric diagnoses is to stigmatize the subject as "crazy," justify incarcerating and treating him against his will, excusing him of responsibility, and paying him for his alleged disability "caused" by his fictitious illness.

Bentall dwells on "advances in neuroscience" that have no bearing on my views about schizophrenia and coercive psychiatric interventions. He believes that forcibly drugging psychotics relieves them of symptoms and is therapeutic:

> there can be no doubt that antipsychotic medication . . . produces in perhaps the majority of patients a marked reduction in hallucinations and delusions.

I do not regard hallucinations and delusions as "symptoms" requiring "treatment." I view hallucinations as disowned self-conversations and delusions as stubborn errors or lies.[6] Both are created by "patients," and could be stopped by them. By the same token, I do not regard the responses of incarcerated mental patients to neuroleptic drugs as improvements. The majority of patients agree with me. If they agreed with Bentall, it would not be necessary to forcibly medicate them, nor would so many of them discontinue taking antipsychotic drugs as soon as they are at liberty to do so.

After discussing the dopamine hypothesis of schizophrenia at length, Bentall writes: "an expensive and sustained search for dopamine abnormalities in schizophrenic patients has so far drawn a blank." If so, why doesn't he dismiss psychopharmacological claims about the therapeutic properties of neuroleptics as well?

After repeatedly asserting that he agrees with me, Bentall ends his essay by dismissing "the mental illness debate" as a "sideshow." Why?

---

[5] Szasz, *Insanity*, p. 91.

[6] Thomas Szasz, *The Meaning of Mind: Language, Morality, and Neuroscience* (Syracuse: Syracuse University Press, 2002 [1996]).

Because "whether schizophrenia is a *disease* should be empirically resolvable (emphasis added)." That has been precisely my position. However, the question is empirically resolvable *only* if by disease we mean bodily disease. No amount of empirical study can establish that schizophrenia is a *mental* disease. Bentall concludes:

> This analysis suggests that the argument about whether or not mental illness is a myth is, at best, a *sideshow in the fight to develop more ethical psychiatric services*. (emphasis added)

I disagree. I have not argued that mental illness is a myth to develop, as Bentall quaintly puts it, "more ethical psychiatric services." More ethical than what? There is no need for Bentall to interpret why I have argued that mental illness is a myth. I have made my reasons abundantly clear: to combat the false belief that problems in living are diseases and to abolish psychiatric slavery.

III

Bentall's sudden introduction of the phrase "ethical psychiatric services" at the end of his essay suggests that his assertions of agreement with my views conceal a profound disagreement. The history of psychiatry is the history of "ethical psychiatric services," as psychiatrists and the society in which they have lived defined what was ethical. Euthanasia of crippled children and mental patients was an ethical psychiatric service in Nazi Germany. Coerced lobotomy in the free West was an ethical psychiatric service, recognized as such by the Nobel awards committee. In the United States today, acquitting John W. Hinckley, Jr. of the attempted assassination of President Reagan and imprisoning him in a mental hospital for an indefinite period is an ethical psychiatric service, and so is giving Ritalin to five million children.

Who determines what is ethical medical practice?[7] Is performing abortions ethical? Is prohibiting the use of birth control, or eating pork, or drinking wine, or smoking marijuana ethical? Is depriving a person of liberty to prevent him from killing himself ethical? Is providing tax

---

[7] Thomas Szasz, "Medical Ethics: An Historical Perspective." *Medical Opinion and Review* 4, pp. 115–121 (February 1968); and *The Theology of Medicine: The Political-Philosophical Foundations of Medical Ethics* (Baton Rouge: Louisiana State University Press, 1977; New York: Harper Colophon, 1977); with a new Preface (Syracuse: Syracuse University Press, 1988).

payer-funded physician-assisted suicide ethical? Bentall ignores that psychiatrists deliver what they regard as "ethical medical services," that is, they adhere to the practices endorsed by their professional association and the law, called "the standard of care." We call pharmaceutical agents available by prescription only "ethical drugs," and the pharmaceutical companies that develop and manufacture such drugs "ethical drug companies."[8] But we consider free trade in drugs unethical.

---

[8] See entries under "ethical drugs" and "ethical drug companies" at www.google.com; and Melody Petersen, "Suit Says Company Promoted Drug in Exam Rooms," *New York Times* (May 15th, 2002), http://www.nytimes.com/2002/05/15/business/15DRUG.html

11

Moving Beyond the "Myth" of Mental Illness

RONALD PIES

If sick men fared just as well eating and drinking and living exactly as healthy men do . . . there would be little need for the science [of medicine].

—HIPPOCRATES

A physician is but a consoler of the mind.

—PETRONIUS ARBITER, *Satyricon*

Introduction

Any visitor to the website honoring the work of Dr. Thomas Szasz (www.szasz.com) will immediately appreciate that the debate over Dr. Szasz's ideas continues to this day. In 1979, in an article entitled, "Myths and Countermyths," I attempted to refute some of the major contentions put forth in Szasz's book, *The Myth of Mental Illness*. Excerpts from that paper (Pies 1979) are now posted in the "Critics Corner" of the Szasz website, for which courtesy I must thank Professor Jeffrey Schaler. A number of correspondents have challenged many of the points I make in that paper, and I have been inspired by their intellectual prodding to prepare a rather long "coda" to my original article. I have deliberately avoided quoting individuals in this piece, with a few exceptions, since this sort of debate can quickly become both personalized and rancorous.

It is my hope that by dealing with ideas, rather than with personalities, I can shed some light on some of the very contentious issues raised by Dr. Szasz and those who propound various versions of his views. My intention is not to disparage the many valuable contributions Dr. Szasz's writings have made to the debate over the civil liberties of the "mentally ill." Rather, I want to focus on more theoretical issues raised in Szasz's early work, pertaining to what we mean by the term "disease". I also want to re-examine the basis for considering schizophrenia and related disorders (such as schizoaffective disorder) legitimate "diseases," worthy of both medical investigation and medical treatment. To do this, I will discuss some ideas about "disease," "disorder," and related terms, from the linguistic, philosophical, historical, and "practical" standpoints. By "practical", I have in mind the nature of everyday medical praxis in specialities outside clinical psychiatry. Specifically, I will aim to show that a purely *Virchovian-Szaszian* (V-S) view of "disease" is inconsistent with (a) most of the history of medicine over the past two millennia; (b) ordinary language, or what Wittgenstein calls "the language game"; and (c) standard medical practice in a variety of specialties, such as neurology. Indeed, I will argue that a purely V-S view of disease creates logical absurdities and wreaks havoc with ordinary language. I will review some of the etymological underpinnings of the physician-patient "dyad," and show how these word origins fundamentally inform medical treatment. I will then discuss a number of common "myths" regarding psychiatric practice and nosology. Specifically, I will try to show that the issue of what counts as a "disease" is logically distinct from the civil liberties concerns of so many opponents of psychiatry. To this end, I will argue that the decision to detain or "commit" an individual involuntarily is not a function of any specific diagnostic scheme or medical speciality. Finally, I will suggest some ways that disagreements over these many issues may be resolved constructively, by encouraging dialogue and compromise rather than obdurate rhetoric.

The views of Michel Foucault—sometimes regarded as another "anti-psychiatry" figure—are extremely complicated and often difficult to interpret. While I will not discuss Foucault in the body of this paper, I do offer some comments in an appendix.

A Very Brief Synopsis of the Virchovian-Szaszian Position on Disease

In the preface to the second edition of *The Myth of Mental Illness*, Szasz avers that "disease or illness can affect only the body (Szasz 1974, p.

xii). Hence, there can be no such thing as mental illness." Psychiatric interventions, according to Szasz's view, "are directed at moral, not medical, problems." Thus, whereas "medical diagnoses are the names of genuine diseases, psychiatric diagnoses are stigmatizing labels." (Szasz 1974, p. xii).

Szasz does not deny that many so-called schizophrenics "often behave and speak in ways that differ from the behavior and speech of many (though by no means all) other people . . . "and that this behavior may be "gravely disturbing either to the so-called schizophrenic person, or to those around him, or to all concerned" (Szasz 1976, p. 191). But Szasz insists that all this has nothing to do with illness: "The articulation of diverse aspirations and the resolution of the conflicts which they generate belong in the domains of ethics and politics, rhetoric and law, aggression and defense, violence and war" (Szasz 1976, p. 191).

Moreover, in his book, *Schizophrenia*, Szasz (1976, p. 3) argues that:

> The claim that some people have a disease called schizophrenia . . . was based not on any medical authority. . . . it was, in other words, the result not of empirical or scientific work, but of ethical and political decision making.

Furthermore,

> Until the middle of the nineteenth century and beyond, illness meant a bodily disorder whose typical manifestation was an alteration of bodily structure . . . [a] lesion, such as a misshapen extremity, ulcerated skin, or a fracture or wound." (Szasz 1974, p. 11)

This "original meaning" of illness, on Szasz's view, was established by the great nineteenth-century pathologist Rudolph Virchow. Before Virchow "the concept of disease was abstract and theoretical, rather than concrete and empirical" (Szasz 1976, p. 8). Subsequently, because of Virchow's discoveries:

> The accepted scientific method for demonstrating diseases consisted, first, of identifying their morphological characteristic by post-mortem examination of organs and tissues; and second, of ascertaining, by means of systemic observations and experiments, their origins and causes." (Szasz 1976, p. 131)

A more recent, succinct summation of Szasz's views is presented on the website for The Thomas S. Szasz MD Cybercenter for Liberty and Responsibility (http://www.szasz.com):

Mental illness is a metaphor (metaphorical disease). The word "disease" denotes a demonstrable biological process that affects the bodies of living organisms (plants, animals, and humans). The term "mental illness" refers to the undesirable thoughts, feelings, and behaviors of persons. Classifying thoughts, feelings, and behaviors as diseases is a logical and semantic error, like classifying the whale as a fish. As the whale is not a fish, mental illness is not a disease. Individuals with brain diseases (bad brains) or kidney diseases (bad kidneys) are literally sick. Individuals with mental diseases (bad behaviors), like societies with economic diseases (bad fiscal policies), are metaphorically sick. The classification of (mis)behavior as illness provides an ideological justification for state-sponsored social control as medical treatment. . . . If we recognize that "mental illness" is a metaphor for disapproved thoughts, feelings, and behaviors, we are compelled to recognize as well that the primary function of Psychiatry is to control thought, mood, and behavior. (from *Thomas Szasz's Summary Statement and Manifesto*)

Finally, for Szasz, there can be no treatment without illness. Hence, the medical "treatment" of so-called diseases like schizophrenia has no scientific basis. I have tried to show (Pies 1979) that these arguments fail on a number of philosophical and historical grounds, and will not repeat those arguments here. I have also suggested that *Virchow himself* left some doubt as to what he considered the *sine qua non* of "disease." The reader is directed to the complete text of the February 1979 *Archives of General Psychiatry* article on these points.

The Meaning of "Disease" in the History of Medicine

I have argued that there has never been a single, universally accepted definition of "disease" in the last two millennia of medical history, and that two competing views have held sway since the time of Hippocrates; namely, the "organic" view of disease as disordered structure (or more recently, as "pathophysiology"); and the "phenomenal" view of disease as an enduring disturbance in the overall well-being of the individual, characterized by *suffering* and *incapacity*. I now want to argue that throughout the history of medicine, the concept of "mental illness" or "diseases of the mind" has always been prevalent; and that this concept was *not* metaphorical. While I do not intend to defend a theory of "mind" as distinct from brain, I do want to argue that physicians throughout history have used various versions of the term "mental illness" to name a very real kind of affliction.

Moses ben Maimon—known as Maimonides (ca. 1138–1204 C.E.)—was arguably the greatest Jewish physician of the Middle Ages. It is quite clear that Maimonides recognized "mental illness" as a real, and not a metaphorical, clinical entity. (The reader is referred to Kranzler 1993 for details). Maimonides built his concept of mental illness atop the scaffolding provided in the Talmud. There, the *shoteh* [insane person] was defined in strictly phenomenal or behavioral terms (Kranzler 1993, p. 51): "Who is an insane person [*shoteh*]? One who goes out alone at night; one who spends the night in a cemetery and one who rends his garments" (Hagigah 3b). Maimonides recognized that this description did not do justice to the clinical phenomena of mental illness, which he defines as follows:

> By *shoteh* is to be understood not only one who walks around naked, breaks things and throws stones, but anyone whose mind has become disturbed so that his thinking is consistently confused in some domain. (*Mishneh Torah*, Laws of Witnesses 9:9–10; in Kranzler 1993, pp. 50–51)

Note that the recognition of mental illness is essentially *cognitive-behavioral*: it is based on what the individual *does or does not do*, and how he is observed to think or speak. As Kranzler shows, Maimonides expanded the legal definition of insanity to include any symptoms of confusion or psychosis, "whether the etiology is mental illness, mental retardation, or a physical illness" (Kranzler 1993, p. 51). Maimonides also recognized that "there are many biological conditions, as well as psychological states, that can influence the functioning of the mind" (Kranzler 1993, p. 52). Anticipating modern nosology, Maimonides differentiated psychotic and confusional states from affective disorders and depression. But Maimonides was, of course, more than a physician. He was also arguably the foremost Jewish ethicist and philosopher of the Middle Ages. In his *Eight Chapters*, Maimonides utilizes an Aristotelian perspective to argue that mental health is the "middle way" between extremes of any emotion or character trait. Conversely, "*illness of the soul* and character is defined as any deviation from the balanced middle way" (Kranzler 1993, p. 53, italics mine). In Chapter 3 of this work, Maimonides states, "The ancients maintained that the soul, *like the body*, is subject to good health and illness. . . . Those whose soul becomes ill should consult the sages, the moral physicians, who will advise them" (Kranzler 1993, p 54, italics mine). Maimonides did not necessarily have in mind what we would now call an M.D. as his "moral physician" (or "physician of the soul"; *Rofe ha-Nefesh*). He seems to have envisioned a kind of compassionate philosopher-sage, who would guide the patient back to a state of mental health. But Maimonides certainly would not have excluded "medical doctors" from this select group, so long as they possessed the requisite moral or philosophical qualities. Indeed, Kranzler sees Maimonides himself as just such a "physician of the soul." It is no accident that the etymology of our term *psychiatrist* is, literally, "Soul (or mind) physician." Maimonides seems to have practiced something quite like our modern "biopsychosocial" model of psychiatric care. When one of the royal family (the Vizier Al-Malik al Fadil) presented with clinical depression,

> In addition to providing all the prescriptions for diet, exercises, syrups, and electuaries for the vizier's depression, anxiety, and constipation . . . Maimonides provides the guidance for his ethical growth in an effort to help him achieve some degree of moderation and inner balance. (Kranzler 1993, p. 57)

In short, Maimonides recognized depression as a real illness, worthy of medical treatment, and provided a "holistic" treatment regimen that anticipated our own "biopsychosocial" approach by some eight centuries. There is no basis for asserting that Maimonides used the term "illness of the soul" as a *metaphor*. In many other contexts, Maimonides makes clear that for him, the soul is a "real" entity, with its own internal workings and structures. For example, in the *Guide of the Perplexed* (Part 3, Chapter XII), Maimonides describes the soul as "a force residing in the body" such that "the properties of the soul depend on the condition of the body" (Maimonides 1956, p. 270). Note also that the diagnosis of depression, for Maimonides, does not rest on the identification of a specific lesion or pathophysiological process. The Vizier had complained to Maimonides of "occasional gloom, bad thoughts, nervous anxiety, and fear of death" (Heschel 1991, p. 233). *Depression is recognized in the suffering and incapacity of the one who asks for help.* As Maimonides famously observed, "The physician does not cure a disease, he cures a diseased person."

Some four centuries later, the English physician Thomas Sydenham (1624–89) continued and expanded the Maimonidean model of clinical medicine. Sometimes known as "The English Hippocrates", Sydenham was a soldier before he became a physician and had little patience for theorizing. He emphasized the meticulous observation of clinical signs and symptoms, and was among the first to differentiate scarlet fever from measles. Today, we know him from the term "Sydenham's chorea" (St. Vitus's Dance). Sydenham's view of disease is clearly opposed to the patho-anatomical (V-S) model. He argues that the physician discovers the causes of diseases by careful clinical observation, not by anatomical investigation, and that the latter is unlikely to aid the physician in his treatment of the patient:

> How regulate [the patient's] dose, to mix his simples and to prescribe all in a due method? All this is only from history and the advantage of a diligent observation of these diseases, of their beginning, progress, and ways of cure, which a *physician may as well do without a scrupulous enquiry into the anatomy of the parts* . . . (Dewhurst 1966, p. 86; italics mine)

Moreover, contrary to the Szaszian view that "mental illness" is merely the construction of modern-day psychiatrists, Sydenham explicitly recognizes several "functional" disorders *as diseases*, despite their having no clear patho-anatomical basis. Sydenham states:

> Hence, a fright which causes such *diseases* as epilepsies, hysterical fits, and fatuity often cures others as agues. . . . 'tis probable in these cases 'twould puzzle the quickest sighted anatomist, assisted too by the best microscope, to find any sensible alteration made either in the juices or solid parts of the body. (Dewhurst 1966, p. 92)

The observational-phenomenal approach to disease continued in the work of Hermann Boerhaave (1668–1738), who was famous for the admonition that "theoretical discussion ended at the patient's bedside" (McGrew, p. 68). To this day, the concept of "disease" in clinical medicine retains its essentially phenomenal character; that is, disease is initially recognized and treated *on the basis of the patient's presentation*. It is fascinating to note that in the most recent (14th) edition of *Harrison's Principles of Internal Medicine,* the term "disease" does not appear in the index, and—so far as I can see—is *never actually defined in the entire text.* And yet, the emphasis on *suffering and incapacity* is evident in the editors' introductory chapter:

> Tact, sympathy, and understanding are expected of the physician, for the patient is no mere collection of symptoms, signs, disordered functions, damaged organs, and disturbed emotions. He is human, fearful, and hopeful, seeking relief, help, and reassurance . . . the misanthrope may become

a smart diagnostician of organic disease, but he can scarcely hope to succeed as a physician. (Fauci et al. 1998, p. 1)

If we wish further evidence of the phenonmenal model of disease, we
can look back to the eighth edition of Harrison's text (1977), where we
find this breathtakingly broad definition:

> The clinical method has as its object the collection of accurate data con-
> cerning all the diseases to which human beings are subject; namely, *all con-
> ditions that limit life in its powers, enjoyment, and duration.* (italics mine)

The editors go on to say that the physician's ". . . primary and traditional
objectives are utilitarian—the prevention and cure of disease and the *relief
of suffering, whether of body or of mind*" (Isselbacher 1977, p. 1).

In summary, while the detection of lesions and disordered biochemical processes is almost always a desideratum in clinical medicine, it is
not necessary for the recognition and treatment of disease. Indeed, as I
shall argue below, it is the *formation of the physician-patient dyad* that
sets in motion the treatment of disease, based on the recognition of the
patient's suffering and incapacity. The search for lesions or pathophysiological processes comes *after* the recognition of disease and the decision to treat it.

Disease, Syndrome, Malady, Disorder, and so Forth

Nomenclature in clinical medicine is confusing and inconsistent, and
must be distinguished from the underlying *philosophy of disease* that we
have adumbrated. As the Oxford scholar, Robert Burton lamented in his
classic work, *The Anatomy of Melancholy*, "What a disease is, almost
every physician defines." (Incidentally, Burton divided all diseases into
those ". . . of the body *and mind*."). One problem is the profusion of so-
called "eponymous" diseases, such as Addison's Disease, Cushing's
Disease, Graves's Disease, and so forth. In theory, when a physician
observes a set of symptoms and signs occurring together in an individual, he or she tries to assimilate these phenomena into a recognized *syndrome*. While a syndrome "embodies a hypothesis concerning the
deranged function of an organ, organ system or tissue," it usually "does
not identify the precise cause of an illness" (Fauci et al. 1998, p. 3).
Later, when the pathophysiology of a syndrome is "parsed" into one or
more subtypes, the syndrome may be refined into a *specific disease*.

(Note that this does not speak to the underlying philosophical basis of disease as a *generic* term). Thus, Cushing's *Syndrome* (central obesity, muscle weakness, hypertension, amenorrhea, and so forth.) was only later refined so as to contain Cushing's *Disease* as a subtype (Cushing's syndrome due to a *pituitary lesion*). In reality, the nomenclature is littered with entities that are known as either a syndrome, a disease, or both, for instance Adams-Stokes disease *or* syndrome, Behcet's disease *or* syndrome. (Dorland's 1974).

Technically, schizophrenia as currently understood might better be classified as a syndrome, rather than as a "disease" in the sense just explained. Thus, we might well have begun with a term like "Bleuler's Syndrome" to describe the collection of signs and symptoms originally observed by Bleuler; and later developed the term "Bleuler's Disease" as a *subtype* of schizophrenia definitively identified with a specific neuro-anatomical lesion. In clinical terms, however, this is largely an academic distinction. Schizophrenia, on the view I have put forth, remains a "disease" in so far as it entails *prolonged suffering and incapacity in the absence of a clear exogenous agent that sustains such suffering and incapacity.* This definition is quite close to Clouser et al.'s (1981) description of a "malady", that is, as "a condition . . . such that [the person] is suffering, or at increased risk of suffering . . . pain, disability, loss of freedom or opportunity, or loss of pleasure" in the absence of an external sustaining cause (Clouser et al. 1981, p. 36). Thus, neither my definition of *disease* nor Clouser et al.'s concept of *malady* would include, for example, suffering and incapacity due to being buried by an avalanche, or tortured by terrorists. We may refine this concept of disease by augmenting it with the criterion of *reduced agential capacity*, as defined by Daly (1991): the seriously diseased individual has a reduced ability to pursue "his prudential interests" (Daly 1991, p. 379). (Daly, however, does not reach the conclusion that "madness" is an illness).

Finally, the term "disorder" is often used synonymously with "disease" or "illness", and is sometimes defined broadly as "a morbid physical or mental state" (Dorland's, p. 465). However, as I will use the term, *a disorder is a specific pathophysiologic process that explains, or is believed to explain, a given disease.* Thus, it may turn out that schizophrenia represents a *disorder* of dopamine metabolism, a *disorder* of neuronal migration, or something else. On the other hand, I am not opposed to a more comprehensive notion of disorder, that might posit, for example, that schizophrenia is a disorder of "internal objects." Ironically, this was precisely the hypothesis put forth by Thomas Szasz in his paper "A Contribution to the Psychology of Schizophrenia"

(*A.M.A. Archives of Neurology and Psychiatry* 77, pp. 420–436). As Arieti explains, "Szasz believes that schizophrenia is largely the result of a deficiency in internal objects, or deficiency of introjected objects" (*Interpretation of Schizophrenia*, p. 335). Of course, there is no reason, in principle, why an underlying biochemical disorder could not *predispose* an individual to become "deficient" in internal objects. It is one of the great losses in the history of psychiatry that Szasz's original and very promising formulation of schizophrenia was not pursued and integrated with biological models, but was instead buried under the spurious "myth" of mental illness.

This discussion only hints at the complexities and ambiguities surrounding the evolution of medical nosology, as nicely detailed by Feinstein (1977). Feinstein notes, for example, that what counts as a "disease" in one era may be "demoted" in a later era to the status of "symptom." Thus, whereas angina pectoris was once considered a disease, it is now considered a symptom of ischemic heart disease. Indeed, it is only partly in jest, I think, when Feinstein—an epidemiologist—states that "the only workable definition of disease is that it represents whatever the doctors of a particular era have defined as a disease" (Feinstein 1977, p. 190). Actually, this definition makes two serious points that we will elaborate below: 1. It is not at all clear that we can ever arrive at an "essential" definition of disease, that is, one that *infallibly specifies the necessary and sufficient criteria* for using the term, now and forever more; and 2. The meaning of a word is, at least in part, a function of how various individuals or groups of individuals *use* that word—a point made in much more rigorous fashion by the philosopher Ludwig Wittgenstein. (Arguably, Feinstein's point also speaks to some of the concerns regarding "power" raised by Michel Foucault, and discussed briefly in my appendix to this chapter).

Essential Definitions, Ordinary Language, and Disease

For Plato, to grasp the meaning of a word was to understand the "ideal form" that underlies our particular use of the word. Thus, for Plato, there is an independently existing ideal form of "redness," of which any particular "red" object is merely a reflection. Plato's ideas led to the concept of *essential definitions* of words; the notion that words have *fixed meanings* derived from their ideal forms. Thus, "triangle" is defined by its ideal form, in terms of certain necessary and sufficient conditions: a triangle exists if and only if a geometric form contains three angles. On this view, we should be able to determine whether any particular condition is a *disease* by holding it up, as it were, to the "ideal form" called *Disease*, and seeing if the two coincide—rather like seeing if a round peg fits into a round hole. This Platonic-essentialist view is essentially the one put forth by Szasz when he insists that the Virchovian definition of disease is, in effect, *the only legitimate one, now and forever more*. On this view, if a condition does not involve a lesion or a specific pathophysiologic process, then it cannot be a disease, for it does not correspond to the Virchovian-Platonic "ideal form."

Anyone is entitled to espouse this view, but it is by no means the only viable theory of "meaning". In his later work (such as *Philosophical Investigations* and *The Blue and Brown Books*), Wittgenstein argued that there are no such "essential" meanings in words, and that "words have those meanings which we have given them" (Wittgenstein 1958, p. 27). For Wittgenstein,

> many words in this sense then don't have a strict meaning. But this is not a defect. To think it is would be like saying that the light of my reading lamp is no *real* light at all because it has no sharp boundaries. (Wittgenstein 1958, p. 27, italics mine)

In this one sentence, Wittgenstein lays bare the glaring underlying fallacy of the entire Szaszian argument about what counts as a "real" disease. But this is not to say that words have no meaning at all, or that meaning is completely arbitrary. We can find what Wittgenstein called "family likenesses" (Wittgenstein 1958, p. 17). For instance, suppose we wanted to learn the meaning of the word 'comparing', as in the mental experience of comparing two things. Wittgenstein teaches us that we may never arrive at a single essential meaning of 'comparing'. Nevertheless:

> We find that what connects all the cases of comparing is a vast number of overlapping similarities, and as soon as we see this, we feel no longer compelled to say that there must be some one feature common to them all. What ties the ship to the wharf is a rope, and the rope consists of fibers, but it does not get its strength from any fiber which runs through it from one end to the other, but from the fact that there is a vast number of fibers overlapping. (Wittgenstein 1958, p. 87)

This is precisely the case when one examines the "rope" of medical nosology. It is difficult, if not impossible, to find a single "fiber" that constitutes the necessary and sufficient conditions for calling something a disease (or disorder, or illness). Rather, there are hundreds of overlapping fibers, such as fever, inflammation, rash, weakness, lethargy, swelling, pain, dizziness, numbness, decreased acuity of the senses, and so on. The definition I have proposed for "disease"—*prolonged suffering and incapacity in the absence of a clear exogenous cause*—is by no means a perfect definition, and is certainly not the only reasonable one. It is simply the definition that seems most suitable to the "language game" not only of clinical medicine, but of ordinary discourse.

To understand how unsuitable a purely Szaszian-Virchovian definition of disease is to ordinary language, consider the following dialogue:

SMITH: Hello, there, Jones. Did I tell you that my brother is in the hospital?

JONES: No, what's the matter?

SMITH: He came back from Africa with a terrible disease. He's got dizziness, disorientation, numbness all over his body, loss of taste, and the absolutely fixed belief that he is the Flying Nun.

JONES: My, that sounds serious, but tell me: have the doctors found the underlying lesion yet?

SMITH: The what?

JONES: Come, now, Smith, the lesion! The lump or bump that explains your brother's problem. Or, at the very least, have the doctors established the underlying and specific pathophysiology?

SMITH: The *what*?

JONES: The pathophysiology, man! The underlying biochemical basis for all these symptoms he's having!

SMITH: Well, no, actually. In fact, they did a million dollar work up with CAT scans, PET scans, MRIs, spinal taps, the whole bit. They said they couldn't find a single thing wrong with him.

JONES: Well, that's good news indeed! You understand, of course, that your brother cannot *possibly* have a disease—or at least, *not yet*.

SMITH: Are you crazy? Of course he's got a disease! I'm telling you, he can't even get out of bed! He's at death's door!

JONES: Oh, that's all well and good, but I'm afraid none of that counts as having a *real* disease.

SMITH: I just don't think you get it!

Indeed, a purely Szaszian-Virchovian concept of disease creates all manner of trouble for ordinary language. If we know only fifty percent of the pathophysiology or abnormal anatomy behind a putative disease, does the patient have only half a disease? If we are eighty percent certain we have identified the specific lesion underlying a putative disease, does the patient have eighty percent of a disease, or an eighty percent chance of *having* a disease—even if the patient is one hundred percent incapacitated? Did HIV-associated dementia (HAD) not become a "real" disease until neuropathologists discovered that glial cells and macrophages in the nervous system are the primary site of viral attack? If new investigations were suddenly and completely to overturn the results of these studies, would patients who are still suffering with HAD *no longer have a disease*? What, precisely, *would* they have at that point? We are reminded of Feinstein's comment that a simple way to eliminate cancer overnight is to give it another name. The Szaszian-Virchovian view of disease does, indeed, eliminate schizophrenia overnight—by cleverly renaming it as a "metaphorical disease."

Finally, these words from Wittgenstein:

> It is wrong to say that in philosophy, we consider an ideal language as opposed to our ordinary one. For this makes it appear as though we thought we could improve on ordinary language. But ordinary language is all right. (Wittgenstein 1958, p. 28)

Not all philosophers fully agree with Wittgenstein, of course—but Wittgenstein's analysis of ordinary language provides us with a reasonable basis for rejecting the Szaszian-Virchovian position.

The Physician-Patient Dyad: Some Etymologies

If the meanings of words relate to their use, it behooves us to examine the *history* of how a word has been used, and how that word was first conceived. Such historical and etymological investigations clearly do not reveal to us the "real" or "essential" meaning of a word—nor do they always tell us how a word is being used today. I would argue, however, that we cannot divorce ourselves from the history of a word, for it often turns out to have important "resonances" with how our *patients* think and feel.

Let's consider the word 'patient'. One might think, from the Herculean labors of Szaszian-Virchovian philosophizing, that the word 'patient' might have something to do with having a *lesion*, or some clearly-defined *pathophysiologic process*. Perhaps, in our investigations, we might find that the word originally meant something like, "One who has a lesion or wound." On the contrary: the term 'patient' is derived from the Latin *pati,* meaning 'to suffer' or 'to bear'.

The term 'physician' is derived from the Greek *physike*, meaning "science of nature"; and *ian,* meaning "one who engages in." A physician, then, is fundamentally "One who assists nature." The role of the physician in the physician-patient dyad is to help the patient back to his or her "old self"—to the patient's "natural" state of good health. *It is this dyad that forms the foundation for legitimate medical treatment*—not a metaphysical or physical theory of disease; not the presence of a lesion; and not the *a priori* knowledge of a specific pathophysiologic process.

And finally, what of the etymology of "disease"? As late as 1615, the word was hyphenated as "dis-ease" (*Oxford English Dictionary*). We also had the word "diseasy", meaning, "marked by discomfort." Even in Shakespeare's time, disease was widely understood in *phenomenal* terms. In Macbeth, Act V, scene 1, when the physician observes Lady Macbeth's sleepwalking, he says, "This *disease* is beyond my practice." Similarly, in Act V, scene 3, Macbeth asks the physician, "Canst thou not minister to a mind *diseased*?" There is no reason to suppose that Shakespeare was employing a "metaphor" in describing Lady Macbeth's behavior: Elizabethan usage allowed for a straightforward, literal use of the term, to mean "uneasiness, discomfort . . . disquiet, disturbance . . ." (*Oxford English Dictionary*). Now, I do not mean to argue that these archaic uses of the word should *determine our current usage*, or that we can establish the "correct" meaning of a word by unearthing its etymology. I *do* mean to argue that the meaning of the term "disease" as Shakespeare knew it is probably closer to our *patients'* understanding than is the microscopically over-specialized Virchovian-Szaszian notion of "disease."

Some Myths About Psychiatric Nosology and Practice

The following claims about psychiatry are from a variety of critics, and do not necessarily reflect statements made by Thomas Szasz. When they do reflect Dr. Szasz's views directly, this will be indicated.

> Psychiatrists diagnose mental illness solely on the basis of a person's "thoughts, feelings, and behaviors."

Contrary to this claim in Szasz's "manifesto," psychiatrists and other clinicians do not ordinarily classify "thoughts, feelings, and behaviors" per se as *diseases*. It is only when certain types of thoughts, feelings and behaviors coalesce in the context of *suffering and incapacity* that a *dis-*

ease is formally diagnosed. Indeed, virtually all the major mental disorders in DSM-IV (schizophrenia, bipolar disorder, major depression) require not only certain "thoughts, feelings, and behaviors," but demonstrable *impairment* in social, interpersonal, or vocational function. To be sure, it might be argued that such "impairment" resolves merely into various socially unacceptable *behaviors*—for example, not showing up at work, not coming out of one's room, refusing to converse with others, and so forth.—but then the charge of "behaviorally-based" diagnosis must be leveled at other medical specialties as well. For example, Chronic Fatigue Syndrome (CFS) is discussed under *neurologic* disorders in Harrison's *Principles of Internal Medicine*, 14th edition. The Center For Disease Control (CDC) criteria for CFS include persistent fatigue that "results in substantial reduction of previous levels of *occupational, educational, social, or personal activities*" (Fauci et al. 1998, p. 2484). In the end, if we completely eliminate "behaviors" as one acceptable criterion for the diagnosis of disease, we must cast aside the neurologist's use of "ataxia" as a defining feature of, say, Friedreich's ataxia. After all, the concept of "ataxia" ("irregularity of muscular action") requires some normative idea of "regular" muscular action—and the latter is nothing more than a kind of *behavior*, no different in principle from the catatonic posturing of some patients with schizophrenia.

Psychiatrists (and only psychiatrists) "commit" patients against their will.

This notion represents a distortion of the relationship between psychiatry and the law. It also ignores the role of other professionals, paraprofessionals, and even "ordinary citizens" in the commitment process. As Dr. Robert Simon points out in his book, *Psychiatry and Law for Clinicians*, "mental health professionals must understand that *it is not they who make commitment decisions about patients*. Commitment is a judicial decision that is made by the court or by a mental health commission. The clinician files a petition or medical certification that initiates the process of involuntary hospitalization." (Simon 1998, p. 127, italics mine). This is not a trivial or semantic distinction. True: most states provide for brief, emergency hospitalizations (for example 48–72 hours) *before* a judicial hearing is held, at which time it is a *judge*—not a psychiatrist—who determines whether sufficient grounds exist for continuing the hospitalization. But the initial petition for involuntary civil commitment, in many states, may be initiated by "police officers, next of kin, psychiatrists, other physicians, psychologists, social workers, or even 'interested parties'" (Simon 1998, p. 128). Of course, one might argue that in so far as these other parties "behave" like psychiatrists, the whole motley crew constitute agents of "state-sponsored social control" (Szasz manifesto, *op. cit.*). This argument turns the concept of "agency" on its head. In fact, when a court authorizes a commitment, *it is acting as the agent of the doctor, the social worker, or, in many cases, the parent of the sick individual.* This is as it should be in a democracy, where the "state" (state and national government) exists to carry out the will of the people. To be sure, there are countries in which—at various times in their history—psychiatrists and other physicians truly have acted as agents of the state. This was clearly the case in Nazi Germany, the old Soviet Union, and arguably, in present-day China. I would submit that such "political" uses of psychiatry are very rare in the United States, and certainly not part of every day clinical practice. (I am aware that a few very high-profile cases, such as the confinement of Ezra Pound in the 1940s, may be exceptions to this general conclusion). The persistent failure of some critics of psychiatry to distinguish the system of civil commitment in *this* country from involuntary confinement in totalitarian countries greatly undermines the credibility of their moral claims.

> Other non-psychiatrist medical specialists—those who deal with "real" diseases—do not involuntarily hospitalize patients.

In part, this is a corollary of the previous myth. In reality, other medical specialists *do* hospitalize patients involuntarily, and the diseases these patients have, or are reasonably believed to have, are not necessarily those traditionally considered "mental illnesses." It is only contingently true that psychiatrists are much more often involved in involuntary commitment procedures. In New York State, where the consent of any two *physicians* can initiate the commitment process, non-psychiatric physicians often do so, particularly in counties with few psychiatrists (M. Dewan M.D., personal communication, April 2001). Emergency detention of dehydrated, demented patients with admission to the general *medical* ward—*not* the psychiatric unit—has been carried out in some states (Schneidermayer et al. 1982). In rare cases, neurologists may initiate the commitment process for demented patients with severe behavioral disturbance (J. Cummings M.D., personal communication, April 2001). Of course, one may protest that, in so far as these other physicians "act like psychiatrists," they, too, are not "real" doctors, and are also acting as "agents of the state." In the end, this becomes simply a political and rhetorical argument—there is no empirical study or experiment that can possibly refute it. But consider the following vignette:

> An 84-year-old man with no previous "psychiatric" history falls and hits his head. He feels alright at first, but over the ensuing week, he notices some difficulty walking and urinating. He sees a neurologist who performs a CT scan of the brain, and determines that the man is developing normal pressure hydrocephalus, which often develops after a head trauma. The neurologist urges the man to undergo surgical treatment, and cautions him that his condition will probably worsen without the installation of a "shunt." The man refuses and goes home. Three weeks later, he becomes confused, irritable, and verbally threatening to his wife and next-door neighbor. In the middle of January, the man runs outside in the snow, wearing only his pajamas. He absolutely refuses to see the neurologist or any other doctor. The man's wife phones the neurologist and begs for help. The neurologist says that the patient's behavior is "likely due" to the untreated hydrocephalus, though he "can't be certain." He recommends an emergency hospital admission, against the patient's will.

Now: what is the Szaszian position with respect to the neurologist's recommendation? If it is one of *assent*, then we must acknowledge that under certain circumstances, we *do* deprive some individuals of their liberty on the basis of "disapproved behaviors," *even when there are no criminal offenses involved, and even when we can't be certain the behaviors are due to brain disease*. Indeed, in Israel, involuntary hospitalization of senile and arteriosclerotic dementia patients is permitted under the 1991 Israeli Mental Health Act (Heinik and Kimhi 1995).

If the Szaszian position is to *disagree* with the neurologist, even when the patient's behavior is likely due to *clearly documented brain dysfunction,* then the Szaszian quarrel is *not* with psychiatry or psychiatric diagnosis *per se*, but with the *police power of the state* and the doctrine of *parens patriae* (which asserts that the state may act on behalf of those citizens who are unable to take care of themselves; Simon 1998, p. 121).

The vignette also demonstrates that *involuntary hospitalization is not intrinsically a function of psychiatric diagnosis*. Rather, it results from the convergence of three factors: *mental derangement* of a very general type (loosely defined in most jurisdications, and "certifiable" by many non-psychiatric personnel); *dangerousness* to self or others; and the invocation of either the state's *police power* or the doctrine of *parens patriae*. In some countries—for example, in England and

Wales—involuntary detention of individuals with *tuberculosis* has also been permitted, when an individual is thought to pose a "serious risk of infection" to others (Coker 2000). Such uses of the state's police power may be criticized on human rights grounds (Coker 2000)—but this is *not* a matter inherently related to psychiatric diagnosis or disease categories.

> Psychiatry is a "pseudoscience" if it insists that something can remain a "disease" and yet have no specific, known pathophysiology.

This claim misunderstands not only the "phenomenal" medical model of disease, but also the nature of the scientific method. Since I have already dealt with the former, I shall focus on the issue of "pseudoscience." A discipline is a science if it meets the following criteria: (1) It systematically collects information on a particular phenomenon; (2) It organizes that information into hypotheses and theories, using both inductive and deductive reasoning; (3) It tests these hypotheses and theories by means of empirical observation, study, and experimentation (not necessarily in a "laboratory" setting); (4) It continuously revises its theories in light of new, and often contradictory, empirical evidence. (5) If it is a clinical discipline, it uses empirical studies and experiments to guide treatment. As L.S. King (1983, p. 2476) has succinctly put it, "The essence of the scientific mind is the ability to evaluate evidence and to withhold assent until the evidence proves adequate." I believe that modern-day psychiatry easily meets these standards. Psychiatry does not require a microscopic substratum of "pathophysiology" to remain scientific, though it may earnestly seek such hidden processes as a practical means of enhancing its therapeutic power.

> Only psychiatrists believe that schizophrenia is a "real" disease.

This claim is quite easy to refute. We have only to listen to this statement from *neurobiologist* Katherine Taber Ph.D., at Baylor College of Medicine: "I think what we presently define as schizophrenia does result from brain insult and so would be considered to be a real disease." (personal communication, March 2001). All critics of "biological psychiatry" should take the time to read the piece by Taber and colleagues ("Schizophrenia: what's under the microscope?") in the Winter 2001 issue of the *Journal of Neuropsychiatry and Clinical Neurosciences*. In that piece, the authors summarize our present neurobiological understanding of schizophrenia, and conclude that "schizophrenia may be the functional end result of various combinations of brain abnormalities"

(Taber et al. 2001, p. 2). We can also turn to the most recent edition of Harrison's *Principles of Internal Medicine*, where we find a chapter on "Mental Disorders" that includes a discussion of schizophrenia. We can turn to Professor of Neurology M.-M. Mesulam's excellent text, *Principles of Behavioral Neurology* (F.A. Davis 1985), in which schizophrenia is discussed several times. (Dr. Mesulam specifically points out abnormalities in frontal lobe function in patients with schizophrenia). Finally, we can look at Professor of Physiology William F. Ganong's classic text, *Review of Medical Physiology* (18th edition, Appleton and Lange, 1997), to learn that "in patients with schizophrenia, MRI studies have demonstrated reduced volumes of gray matter on the left side in the anterior hippocampus-amygdala" (Ganong 1997, p. 257). One can multiply examples from other general medical and even pediatric texts without difficulty.

> If what is called "schizophrenia" cannot be traced to a single, specific anatomical or pathophysiologic abnormality, it cannot be counted as a real disease.

This might be characterized as the "single lesion, single syndrome" fallacy (K. Taber Ph.D., personal communication). It makes much of the fact that the biological research on schizophrenia and related illnesses has turned up a variety of neuro-anatomical and neurochemical abnormalities (See Taber et al. *op cit.*), but has not discovered a *single* underlying physical basis for the putative illness. The proponents of this fallacy have failed to understand modern neurobiological thinking about mental illness, as well as how the human brain "works" or fails to work. Again, let us hear not from a psychiatrist, but from a *neurobiologist*:

> It does not appear that there is a single or specific lesion for all schizophrenics, at least in the gross anatomical sense. Given that the brain can be thought of as a set of interacting circuits, it would not be at all surprising to get similar symptoms from damage/dysfunction in more than one area. This, of course, will make it a great deal more difficult to figure out what is really going wrong to produce the symptoms, but is, to me, a lot more believable than the "single lesion, single syndrome" approach." (K. Taber, Ph.D., personal communication, March 2001).

We have precedents for this understanding in everyday neuropathology. For example, the syndrome of "global aphasia" may result from *either* a middle cerebral artery occlusion, *or* from two small branch occlusions—one affecting Wernicke's area and the other affecting Broca's area (J. Cummings M.D., personal communication, April 2001). We would be naïve, indeed, if we claimed that global aphasia was not a "real" disease (or syndrome) because there was no "single" neuroanatomical lesion involved. Similarly, Mesulam describes how the syndrome of transcortical motor aphasia (TCM) may result from lesions in (1) the lateral convexity of the frontal lobe, *or* (2) the supplementary motor area in the medial parasagittal region of the frontal lobe. Mesulam adds, "Other mechanisms may yet be elucidated" (Mesulam 1985, p. 211).

Finally, while at least some advocates of the Szaszian position would probably agree that Alzheimer's Disease (AD) is a "real" disease, *we still do not know the precise pathophysiology of this condition.* For example, while the classical findings of amyloid plaques and neurofibrillary tangles are considered hallmarks of the disease, "the pathologic basis of the neuropsychiatric symptoms of AD is not fully understood" (White and Cummings 1997, p. 827). It may be that *numerous* poorly-characterized neurotransmitter abnormalities in AD—affecting acetylcholine, serotonin, and perhaps other brain chemicals—are more closely related to some neuropsychiatric symptoms than are plaques and tangles. Despite this ambiguity, we do not find books written about "the myth of Alzheimer's Disease." Indeed, the diagnosis of AD remains essentially a *clinical* one, albeit supported by brain imaging and other studies.

"Real" doctors do examinations. Psychiatrists do conversation.

It is richly ironic that detractors of psychiatry should take aim at "conversation." For many centuries, long before physicians had any effective "somatic" treatments for their patients' maladies, the therapeutic effects of "conversation" were well known. As Zvi Lothane, M.D., reminds us:

> Operationally speaking, we should properly call psychotherapy 'word therapy', which is awkward. For we think and speak with words: it is not just the proverbial pen, it is the spoken word that is mightier than the sword. It is words that connect us as speakers and listeners, both in everyday dialogue and in that special conversation we call psychotherapy, words that speak of love or hatred, words that hurt and words that heal. (Lothane 1996, p. 50)

In recent years, we have learned that so-called "conversation" may be associated with important changes in brain function. For example, one study (Schwartz et al. 1996) found that among patients with obsessive-compulsive disorder, those who responded to cognitive-behavioral therapy had greater reductions in brain metabolic activity in the caudate—a region known to be "hyperactive" in many OCD patients—than did poor responders. While we can't infer that psychotherapy "caused" these changes in brain function, there are many lines of evidence suggesting that this may be the case. In any event, there is no empirical basis for denigrating the role of therapeutic "conversation" in the alteration of brain function.

The old canard that psychiatrists do not do physical examinations is probably a remnant of the stereotypical "psychoanalyst," so energetically lampooned in the popular media (Pies 2001). True, it would be very unusual for a psychoanalyst—who may or *may not* be a physician—to perform a complete physical examination on a patient he or she is treating. But anyone with the slightest experience in hospital-based psychiatry knows that in that setting, both resident and attending psychiatrists are frequently called upon to do limited or complete physical examinations. Furthermore, neurological examinations are routinely performed by psychiatrists in hospital settings, and even office-based "outpatient" psychiatrists frequently check the patient's pulse and blood pressure, examine the patient to rule out abnormal involuntary movements, and so on. Most outpatient psychiatrists will periodically order laboratory testing, such as thyroid functions, electrocardiograms, and various kinds of brain imaging. The emerging fields of *behavioral neurology* and *neuropsychiatry* have begun to break down the artificial Cartesian boundaries between "mind" and "body," brain and behavior.

And consider what goes on in the following scenario: Mr. Brown has been seeing a neurologist for some years, owing to chronic sciatic nerve problems. One day, while on a business trip, Mr. Brown experiences an excruciating, left-sided headache, accompanied by nausea, sensitivity to light, and strange "picket fence" like flashes in his visual field. Having never experienced this before, Brown phones his neurologist and describes the symptoms. The neurologist says, "Sounds like you're having a migraine. I'll phone in a prescription for some sumatriptan [Imitrex]."

What has gone on here? *Was there a lesion detected? Was there a specific pathophysiologic process uncovered? Is such a process even known with certainty, in our understanding of migraine headaches?* The answer to the last three questions is *no*. What has gone on is *conversation*—no other diagnostic procedure was necessary. The only other element that needed to be in place for medical treatment to occur was the presence of a "sufferer" and an "assister of nature"—the patient and the physician.

Conclusion

While the statement "Joe, who has been diagnosed with schizophrenia based on DSM-IV criteria, has demonstrable brain disease" is, in principle, an empirically falsifiable proposition (by doing SPECT, MRI, and so forth), the statement "Schizophrenia is a disease" is not empirically falsifiable. That is because "disease" is not an empirical term, or a term with an *essential definition*, but an existential-historical construct derived from multiple, overlapping, and sometimes competing world-views; for example, the Virchovian model of "lesions" versus the Hippocratic model of suffering and incapacity. In this paper, I have argued that schizophrenia may reasonably be considered a disease because it involves significant and enduring suffering and incapacity, including diminished "agential capacity," in the absence of a clear exogenous cause. Schizophrenia may also be regarded as a "syndrome", since it presents with a reasonably consistent set of signs and symptoms; tends to run in families; is associated with increased morbidity, mortality, and so forth. While there are very compelling data supporting an underlying neurobiological basis for schizophrenia, such data are neither necessary nor sufficient for the clinical diagnosis and treatment of this, or related, psychiatric illnesses.

A Bridge to Compromise

Thomas Szasz has taught us many things over the past forty years. First, he has pushed us all to examine the basic premises upon which our clinical philosophy and treatment are based. He has taught us to examine our language carefully and critically. He has taught us to question the received wisdom of self-appointed "authorities". He has pushed us to re-examine our approach to the civil liberties of psychiatric patients. And he has constantly prodded the field of psychiatry to clarify its approach to defining and diagnosing disease. From my own standpoint, Dr. Szasz's most compelling message is that *we must never bully our patients*. For this teaching alone, we owe him a debt of gratitude. *And yet*—what of the young man, rocking back and forth in a pool of his own urine, responding to voices from "a CIA computer" that are instructing him to kill himself? To bring this young man into the hospital against his wishes is not to "bully" him, but to begin the process of restoring his humanity. To do less is to collude in the destruction of his very soul.

Somehow, we must find a way to infuse Szasz's fervent humanitarian impulses into the realities of modern-day psychiatric practice, which occurs in a complex matrix of medical and legal obligations. Denunciations of psychiatric nosology and psychiatric practitioners will *not* improve the care of those diagnosed with mental illness. To be sure: psychiatry must refine its diagnostic criteria, and seek out the pathophysiologic bases of the diseases we treat—but these conditions will remain terrible diseases whether we discover those bases or not. And yes, psychiatric practice must take every reasonable step to ensure that the civil liberties of the mentally ill are maintained and respected—but securing these liberties must not prevent us from caring for the gravely ill. Critics of psychiatry would spend their time most wisely by working *with*, rather than against, clinicians, to achieve these goals. These critics, in my view, would also benefit by working directly with organizations such as the National Alliance for the Mentally Ill, both to appreciate the struggles of the mentally ill and their families, and to engage in a productive dialogue with these individuals. Finally, in our own discourses, those on both sides of this intense debate must find a way to honor that Talmudic maxim to "Judge all individuals charitably."

Appendix: Foucault's Critique of Psychiatry

In the introduction to Michel Foucault's *Madness and Civilization*, Jose Barchillon, M.D., writes that this work "more effectively than many previous attempts . . . [dispels] the myth of mental illness." And yet, it is not clear from this work that Foucault has done anything other than attributing malign motives to the founders of the early psychiatric asylums. Before pursuing this line of argument, however, it may be helpful to place Foucault's work in the broader context of post-modernist thinking. Michel Foucault (1926–1984) used to describe himself as an "archaeologist" whose task it was to "uncover the latent structures of knowledge and power" that are responsible for various Western cultural phenomena (*Critical Theory*, http://www.smpcollege.com/litlinks/critical/foucault.htm). Foucault analyzed culture in terms of what he called "discourses." These are essentially the "complex[es] of credentials, protocols, jargon, and specialized knowledge that defines theory and practice within the human sciences" (Rohmann 1999, pp. 142–43). On this view, it might be argued that the DSM-IV is a prime example of a "discourse." For Foucault, when such discourses coalesce around a dominant, socially-defining paradigm—not unlike Thomas Kuhn's notion of a "paradigm" in science—the result is an *episteme* (the Greek root for "epistemology"). For Foucault, such epistemes are society's vehicles of power. He argues that "all disciplines—be they scientific, legal, political, or social—operate through a network of self-legitimizing power and knowledge" (*Critical Theory, op cit.*). "Truth", therefore, cannot be absolute: claims of objectivity are impossible "in a domain in which truth itself is always a discursive construct. Any given historical period shares unconscious formations that define the right way to reason for the truth" (*Critical Theory, op cit.*). In *Madness and Civilization*, as Rohmann (1999, p. 143) summarizes it,

> Foucault maintained that the definition and treatment of "insanity" constitutes a form of social control. Once "madness" was defined as abnormal, rather than simply eccentric, its victims were separated from the "sane" population by exile or incarceration; then, in the nineteenth century, physicians created a science of mental disease, parallel to physical medicine, with institutionalized procedures to restore patients to sanctioned standards of normalcy.

Foucault aimed to show that in the Classical Age (the seventeenth and eighteenth centuries), the dominant "episteme" was one in which madness was seen not as an inherent part of the human condition, but in terms of an anti-natural "animality" (Foucault 1973, p. 78). The *asylum*—ostensibly an attempt to humanize the treatment of the insane—was really a coercive attempt to confine and marginalize the "animality of madness." As Barchillon puts it, "as the madman had replaced the leper, the mentally ill person was now a subhuman and beastly scapegoat" (Foucault 1973, vii).

It does not take much imagination to see how Foucault's arguments have been used to create a modern stalking-horse, behind which the opponents of psychiatry can stage their attacks; for instance, psychiatry is a "covert agent of the state," an "agent of social control," and so forth. But, returning to Foucault's premises, we can immediately see some historical and conceptual problems. In the first place, whereas the *asylum* may well have arisen *de novo* from the "episteme" of eighteenth-century rationalism, there was ample historical precedent for "marginalizing" insanity and keeping the putatively insane individual at bay. In Plato's time, we learn that, "Even at Athens, the mentally afflicted were still shunned by many, as being persons subject to a divine curse, contact with whom was dangerous: you threw stones at them to keep them away, or at least took the minimum precaution of spitting" (Dodds 1951, p. 68). Foucault himself acknowledges that "there existed throughout the Middle Ages and the Renaissance a place of detention reserved for the insane" (Foucault 1973, p. 9). Indeed, as historian Jacques LeGoff (1988, p. 319) notes, Bethlehem or "Bedlam" Hospital in London was just such a place, founded in the late thirteenth century. To be sure, one can cite differences in attitude toward madness between, say, the Middle Ages and the eighteenth century. The medieval invention of the gargoyle was arguably that age's way of both taming the demonic and yet of keeping it within sight of the general populace—outside the cathedral, safely transformed into a water spout. Foucault may be right in arguing that in the Age of Rationalism, insanity was exiled and suppressed to a greater degree—but this hardly touches on the *ontological or clinical reality of mental illness.* Indeed, I find nothing in *Madness and Civilization* that impugns the claim that mental illness is "real" or that it is a "disease." As an "archaeologist" of ideas, Foucault was not in a position to make such a claim. His analysis may shed light on how differing "epistemes" affect society's *management* of mental illness—but this does not touch the ontological claim that mental illness is "real." And as Ian Hacking (1986, p. 29) suggests, "Despite all the fireworks, *Madness and Civilization* follows the romantic convention that sees the exercise of power as repression, which is wicked." Hence, *Foucault's work becomes merely another episteme,* wherein the author asserts his own "self-legitimizing power and knowledge." Like Szasz's objections to modern methods of involuntary confinement, Foucault's arguments about the "asylum" are essentially implicit *moral judgments,* aimed at establishing the "wickedness" of certain behaviors. This is not, then, a scientific argument, nor one merely about "the latent structures of knowledge and power." Rather, Foucault's argument with psychiatry, like Szasz's, is fundamentally one of *how people ought to behave toward their fellow citizens.* This is perfectly respectable political advocacy—but it should not be confused with a "scientific" or "objective" critique of psychiatry or psychiatric nosology.[1]

---

[1] The author would like to thank Mr. David Herman, Dr. Robert Daly, Dr. Mantosh Dewan, and Dr. Zvi Lothane for their ideas and comments, at various stages of this work. However, the author alone is responsible for the conclusions in this chapter.

REFERENCES

Burton, R. 1986. *The Anatomy of Melancholy*. New York: Classics of Modern Medicine Library.

Clouser, K.D., C.M. Culver, and B. Gert. 1981. Malady: A New Treatment of Disease. *The Hastings Center Report* (June, 1981), pp. 29–38.

Coker, R.J. 2000. The Law, Human Rights, and the Detention of Individuals with Tuberculosis in England and Wales. *Journal of Public Health Medicine* 22, pp. 263–67.

Daly, R.W. 1991. A Theory of Madness. *Psychiatry* 54, pp. 368–385.

Dewhurst, K. 1966. *Dr. Thomas Sydenham, 1624–1689*. Berkeley: University of California Press.

Dodds, E.R. 1951. *The Greeks and the Irrational*. Berkeley: University of California Press.

Dorland's. 1974. *Dorland's Illustrated Medical Dictionary*. 25th edition. Philadelphia: Saunders.

Fauci, A.S., E. Braunwald, K.J. Isselbacher, et al., eds. 1998. *Harrison's Principles of Internal Medicine*, 14th edition. New York: McGraw-Hill.

Feinstein, A.R. 1977. A Critical Overview of Diagnosis in Psychiatry. In V.M. Rakoff et al., eds. *Psychiatric Diagnosis* (New York: Brunner/Mazel), pp. 189–206.

Foucault, M. 1973. *Madness and Civilization*. New York: Vintage.

Ganong, W.F. 1997. *Review of Medical Physiology*. 18th edition. Stamford: Appleton and Lange.

Hacking, I. 1986. The Archaeology of Foucault. In D.C. Hoy, ed., *Foucault: A Critical Reader* (Oxford: Blackwell).

Heschel, A.J. 1991. *Maimonides*. New York: Image Books.

Heinik, J., and R. Kimhi. 1995. Psychiatric Hospitalization of Senile and Arteriosclerotic Dementia Patients by Commitment Order under the 1991 Israeli Mental Health Act. *Medicine and Law* 14, pp. 471–78.

Isselbacher, K., ed. *Harrison's Principles of Internal Medicine*. Eighth edition. New York: McGraw-Hill.

King, L.S. 1983. Medicine Seeks to Be 'Scientific'. *Journal of the American Medical Association* 249, pp. 2475–79.

Kranzler, H.N. 1983. Maimonides' Concept of Mental Illness and Mental Health. In F. Rosner and S.S. Kottek, eds. *Moses Maimonides: Physician, Scientist, and Philosopher* (Northvale: Jason Aronson), pp. 49–58.

Le Goff, J. 1988. *Medieval Civilization, 400–1500*. Oxford: Blackwell.

Lothane, Z. 1996. Psychoanalytic Method and the Mischief of Freud Bashers. *Psychiatric Times* XIII: 12, pp. 49–50.

Maimonides, M. 1956. *The Guide for the Perplexed*. New York: Dover.

McGrew, R.E. 1985. *Encyclopedia of Medical History*. London: Macmillan.

Mesulam, M.-Marsel. 1985. *Principles of Behavioral Neurology*. Philadelphia: Davis.

Pies, R. 1979. On Myths and Countermyths. *Archives of General Psychiatry* 33, pp. 139–144.

———. 2001. Psychiatry in the Media: The Vampire, the Fisher King, and the Zaddik. *Journal of Mundane Behavior*, www.mundanebehavior.ogg/issues/v2n1/pies.htm.

Rohmann, C. 1999. A World of Ideas. New York: Ballantine.

Schneidermaye, D.L., E.H. Duthie, M.V. Shelley, et al. 1982. Emergency Detention of the Elderly: Demographics, Diagnoses, and Outcome. *Journal of the American Geriatric Society* 30, pp. 383–86.

Schwartz, J.M., P.W. Stoessel, L.R. Baxter, et al. 1996. Systematic Changes in Cerebral Glucose Metabolic Rate after Successful Behavior Modification Treatment of Obsessive-Compulsive Disorder. *Archives of General Psychiatry* 53, pp. 109–113.

Simon, R.I. 1998. *Psychiatry and the Law for Clinicians.* Washington, D.C.: American Psychiatric Press.

Szasz, T.S. 1974. *The Myth of Mental Illness.* Second edition. New York: Harper and Row.

———. 1976. *Schizophrenia: The Sacred Symbol of Psychiatry.* New York: Basic Books.

Taber, K.H., D.A. Lewis, and R.A. Hurley. 2001. Schizophrenia: What's Under the Microscope? *Journal of Neuropsychiatry and Clinical Neuroscience* 13, pp. 1–3.

White, K.E., and J.L. Cummings. 1997. Neuropsychiatric Aspects of Alzheimer's Disease and Other Dementing Illnesses. In S.C. Yodofsky and R.E. Hales, eds., *The American Psychiatric Press Textbook of Neuropsychiatry* (Washington, D.C.: American Psychiatric Press).

Wittgenstein, L. 1958. *The Blue and Brown Books.* New York: Harper and Row.

Reply to Pies

THOMAS SZASZ

I

Pies writes as if he were a philosopher-king, looking down from his Olympian perch on his quarreling child-subjects. His conclusion is emblematic: "Finally, in our own discourses, those on both sides of this intense debate must find a way to honor that Talmudic maxim to 'Judge all individuals charitably.'"

Instead of engaging the conflict between the supporters and opponents of forced psychiatric treatment, Pies quotes the Talmud, devotes three pages to Moses Maimonides, endorses psychiatric coercion as a service self-evidently beneficial for the involuntary patient, and advises me to "compromise" and endorse it as well.

II

Religious maxims must be situated in their cultural contexts, not used as shields against the systematic abuse of psychiatric power. Pronouncements such as Jesus's often-quoted admonition, "Judge not, that ye be not judged" (Matthew 7:1), must be seen as originating from a people steeped in piety, who believed in a personified, all-powerful God. That deity owned and controlled the universe and everything in it. Making moral judgments is his privilege. That is why Jews, Christians, and Muslims spend so much time and effort trying to figure out the will of the Heavenly Father.

Why is this such an all-important project? Because the person ignorant of God's will cannot please him. Pies appears to share that viewpoint. He dwells on the writings of Moses Maimonides, as if this twelfth-century Jewish mystic's ideas about medicine were relevant to the issue of whether coercive psychiatry is a force for good or evil.

According to *The Catholic Encyclopedia*, "The most characteristic of all his [Maimonides's] philosophical doctrines is that of acquired immortality. 'Oh, God, *Thou has appointed me* to watch over the life and death of Thy creatures.'"[1] I do not value this sort of boundless conceit masquerading as pious humility and leave its exercise to the psychiatrists who seek to "help" their unhappy patients with incarceration and forcibly administered lobotomy, electroshock, and Haldol. In his enthusiasm for religious maxims, Pies forgets Lord Acton's warning: "Morality must be set up apart from religion: *for every religion in its turn has promoted its own cause by crimes.*"[2]

The modern scientist, in his role as scientist, is not interested in god's will. He is interested in how nature works, not in how god works. I am not a scientist but try to think as one. I believe that judging human behavior—our own and that of our fellow man—is our moral duty, not the duty of a nonexistent deity. Bearing in mind that obligation, I have nevertheless endeavored—in my writings as well as in my personal relationships—to avoid *ad hominem* arguments. I have condemned certain social policies I regard as harmful to individual liberty and personal responsibility and the actions of persons who implement them, rather than individuals *qua* persons. To be sure, since an individual is what he does, the separation between judging the action and the actor is contrived. My psychiatric critics have been less restrained: for decades, they have sought to defame me with a long list of slanderous mischaracterizations.

III

Pies heads his essay with epigraphs from Hippocrates and Petronius, as if the ideas of such ancient healers about the proper role of the physician were relevant to modern, high-tech American medicine and the roles assigned to physician-agents of the Therapeutic State. He then mischaracterizes my work by praising my "many valuable contributions . . . to the civil liberties of the 'mentally ill.'" But I have made no contributions to the "to the civil liberties of the 'mentally ill.'" I have tried to show that

---

[1] William Turner, "Teaching of Moses Maimonides," in *The Catholic Encyclopedia*, Volume IX, Online Edition Copyright © 1999 by Kevin Knight, http://www.newadvent.org/cathen/09540b.htm, emphasis added.

[2] John E.E.D. Acton, *Essays in the Study and Writing of History*, edited by J. Rufus Fears (3 vols.; Indianapolis: Liberty Classics, 1988), vol. 3, p. 649, emphasis added. See also Omer Bartov and Phyllis Mack, eds., *In God's Name: Genocide and Religion in the Twentieth Century* (New York: Berghahn, 2000).

the term "mental illness" is an oxymoron and have sought equal legal treatment for persons regardless of psychiatric-diagnostic labels and regardless of whether psychiatrists seek to incriminate or excuse them as "mentally ill."

Pies continues: "I want to re-examine the basis for considering schizophrenia and related disorders . . . legitimate diseases, worthy of both investigation and medical treatment." Pies ought to know that I have no objection to anyone investigating anything, provided the research entails neither force nor fraud and is neither sponsored nor funded by the state. Similarly, I have no objection to any competent adult "treating" any other competent adult—regardless of whether one party is a physician and the other a sick patient—provided the relationship is consensual and contractual.

The most important issue before us, about which Pies equivocates, consists of two parts: one part is our criterion of bodily illness and, derivatively, the precise criteria we use to designate some deviant behaviors, but not others, as the manifestations of mental illnesses; the other part pertains to the practical, personal and social consequences of a psychiatrist's calling another person "mentally ill," and thus implying or asserting that, because of his illness, he is "dangerous to himself or others."[3] If the legal and social consequences of being diagnosed "mentally ill and dangerous to self or others" were as theoretically unimportant and socially inconsequential as diagnosing him as, say, "having a mild fungus infection of his toenails," then I would not care whom psychiatrists label mentally ill. Like the coercive psychiatrists for whose barbarities he fronts, Pies in effect denies the legal and social implications of calling people "mentally ill" or "schizophrenic": he fills page after page with historical commonplaces, known to anyone with a decent high school education.

"I will aim to show," Pies writes, "that a purely Virchowian-Szaszian (V-S) view of 'disease' is inconsistent with (a) most of the history of medicine over the past two millennia." There is no need to "show" this. I have gone out of my way to contrast the modern, pathological concept of disease with the older, humoral concept of it, as well as with the spiritual-religious concept of disease, still held by Christian Scientists, Jehovah's Witnesses, and other god-intoxicated persons.

Does Pies really believe that scientific progress since the Enlightenment should have had no effect on our concept of disease? The ancient Greeks'

---

[3] Thomas Szasz, *Insanity: The Idea and Its Consequences* (Syracuse: Syracuse University Press, 1997 [1987]).

ideas about the laws governing falling objects differed from Isaac Newton's. Is that an argument against the concept of gravitation?

Pies declares that "the issue of what counts as a 'disease' is logically distinct from the civil liberties concerns of so many opponents of psychiatry." This is correct, as far as it goes. *The connections between madness (mental disease or disorder) and psychiatric slavery are empirical, not logical, in much the same way that the connections between blackness and chattel slavery were empirical, not logical.* Chattel slavery rested on social custom and law, not on a logical connection between blackness and involuntary servitude. Psychiatric slavery rests on social custom and law, not on a logical connection between psychiatric diagnosis and psychiatric incarceration.[4]

Pies's premise is that whatever is called a mental illness is a disease. For Pies, it matters not whether the term "disease" predicates the body, the mind, or the soul. Perhaps because of this premise, he does not understand the distinction between a literal and a metaphorical illness and misrepresents the history of psychiatry. He writes: "*It is quite clear that Maimonides recognized 'mental illness' as a real, and not a metaphorical, clinical entity. . . .* Maimonides built his concept of mental illness atop the scaffolding provided in the Talmud" (emphasis added).

The Talmud is not a medical text. There was no biological-scientific concept of disease in the twelfth century. Hence, in the medical world of Maimonides, there could have been no distinction between literal and metaphorical disease. Pies's assertion that "Maimonides recognized 'mental illness' as a real, and not a metaphorical, clinical entity," is patently false. To boot, Maimonides's views on mental illness are as irrelevant to modern medicine and modern psychiatry as are Leucippus's views to modern physics. (Leucippus of Miletus, fifth century B.C., coined the term "atomos" [non-cuttable] for what he believed were the smallest particles of matter.)

Pies is unwilling to distinguish literal from metaphorical disease. He writes: "The Szaszian-Virchovian view of disease does, indeed, eliminate schizophrenia overnight—by cleverly renaming it as a 'metaphorical disease'." Pies was trained in Syracuse and must have heard me, more than once, offer the following example of the difference between literal and metaphorical disease.

Typhoid fever is a literally febrile, literal disease. Spring fever is a metaphorically febrile, metaphorical disease: it is not febrile and is not

---

[4] Thomas Szasz, *Liberation by Oppression: A Comparative Study of Slavery and Psychiatry* (New Brunswick: Transaction, 2002).

a disease. This assertion does not, and is not intended to, "eliminate," spring fever. It merely distinguishes spring fever as a condition radically different from typhoid fever. Not long ago, psychiatrists insisted that masturbatory insanity, drapetomania, and homosexuality were literal diseases. Now they insist that they are not diseases at all. It is they, not me, who create and eliminate diseases, by means of revisions of the American Psychiatric Association's *Diagnostic and Statistical Manual*.

Pies does not admit that any mental illness ever was or is now a metaphorical disease. He writes: "I now want to argue that *throughout the history of medicine, the concept of "mental illness" or "diseases of the mind" has always been prevalent; and that this concept was not metaphorical*" (emphasis added). I disagree. Consider the record:

> In 1845, the Viennese psychiatrist, Ernst von Feuchtersleben (1806–1848), wrote: "The maladies of the spirit alone, *in abstracto*, that is, error and sin, can be called diseases of the mind only *per analogiam*. They come not within the jurisdiction of the physician, but that of the teacher or clergyman, who again are called physicians of the mind only *per analogiam*".[5]

> Theodor Meynert (1833–1892)—one of the founders of modern neuropsychiatry and one of Freud's teachers—began his textbook, *Psychiatry* (1884), with this statement: "The reader will find no other definition of 'Psychiatry' in this book but the one given on the title page: *Clinical Treatise on Diseases of the Forebrain*. The historical term for psychiatry, i.e., 'treatment of the soul,' implies more than we can accomplish, and transcends the bounds of accurate scientific investigation."[6]

> In his classic, *Lectures on Clinical Psychiatry* (1901), Emil Kraepelin (1856–1927), the creator of the first modern psychiatric nosology, stated: "The subject of the following course of lectures will be the Science of Psychiatry, which, as its name [*Seelenheilkunde*] implies, is that of the treatment of mental disease. It is true that, in the strictest terms, we cannot speak of the mind as becoming diseased."[7]

---

[5] Ernst von Feuchtersleben, *Medical Psychology,* in Daniel Schreber, *Memoirs of My Nervous Illness,* edited and translated by Ida MacAlpine and Richard Hunter (London: Dawson, 1955), p. 412.

[6] Theodor Meynert, *Psychiatry: Clinical Treatise on Diseases of the Forebrain* [1884], translated by Barbara Sachs (New York: Putnam's, 1885), p. v, emphasis in the original.

[7] Emil Kraepelin, *Lectures on Clinical Psychiatry* [1901] (New York: Hafner, 1968), p. 1, emphasis added.

In 1913, Karl Jaspers (1883–1969)—famed psychiatrist-turned-philosopher—observed: "Admission to hospital often takes place against the will of the patient and therefore the psychiatrist finds himself in a different relation to his patient than other doctors. . . . Rational treatment is not really an attainable goal as regards the large majority of mental patients in the strict sense."[8]

Pies's assertion "that throughout the history of medicine, the concept of 'mental illness' or 'diseases of the mind' . . . was not metaphorical" is mendacity masquerading as scholarship. The truth is exactly the opposite of Pies's statement.

Repeatedly, Pies attributes views to me that I do not hold and statements that I have never made, such as: "This Platonic-essentialist view is essentially the one put forth by Szasz when he insists that the Virchowian definition is, in effect, *the only legitimate one, now and forever more*" (emphasis in the original). Pies appends no citation. Instead, he adds an appendix about Foucault to smear me with Foucault's ideas, most of which I reject. It would have been more relevant to add an appendix on Virchow or Acton.

Pies offers this platitudinous observation by Wittgenstein as the definitive refutation of my views about mental illness and opposition to psychiatric coercion: "'many words in this sense don't have a strict meaning. But this is not a defect.' . . . In this one sentence, Wittgenstein lays bare the glaring underlying fallacy of *the entire Szaszian argument about what counts as a 'real' disease*" (emphasis added). I fail to see how Wittgenstein's sentence does all this. Evidently, Pies also doubts it: instead of ending his essay at this point, he goes on for another eighteen pages of apologetics for psychiatric paternalism and coercion.

IV

Pies refers approvingly to the National Alliance for the Mentally Ill (NAMI) and suggests that I collaborate with that group. Let us be clear about the sort of psychiatric practices NAMI advocates and, by implication, Pies supports. The following text appears on the NAMI website:

> Sometime, during the course of your loved one's illness, you may need the police. By preparing now, before you need help, you can make the day you

---

[8] Karl Jaspers, *General Psychopathology* [1913, 1946], 7th edition, translated by J. Hoenig and M.W. Hamilton (Chicago: University of Chicago Press, 1963), pp. 839–840.

need help go much more smoothly. . . . It is often difficult to get 911 to respond to your calls if you need someone to come & take your MI relation to a hospital emergency room (ER). They may not believe that you really need help. And if they do send the police, the police are often reluctant to take someone for involuntary commitment. . . . When calling 911, the best way to get quick action is to say, "Violent EDP," or "Suicidal EDP." EDP stands for Emotionally Disturbed Person. This shows the operator that you know what you're talking about. Describe the danger very specifically. "He's a danger to himself "is not as good as "This morning my son said he was going to jump off the roof." . . . Also, give past history of violence. *This is especially important if the person is not acting up.* . . . When the police come, they need compelling evidence that the person is a danger to self or others before they can involuntarily take him or her to the ER for evaluation. . . . Realize that you & the cops are at cross purposes. You want them to take someone to the hospital. They don't want to do it. . . . Say, "Officer, I understand your reluctance. Let me spell out for you the problems & the danger. . . . *While AMI / FAMI is not suggesting you do this, the fact is that some families have learned to "turn over the furniture" before calling the police.* . . . If the police see furniture disturbed they will usually conclude that the person is imminently dangerous. . . . THANK YOU FOR YOUR SUPPORT WHICH MADE IT POSSIBLE FOR US TO PROVIDE THIS INFORMATION TO THOSE WHO COULD BENEFIT FROM IT.[9]

Filing a false report with the police is a felony. The Eighth Commandment states: "Thou shalt not bear false witness!"

Most psychiatrists, including Pies, support forced psychiatric treatment. Yet, he rejects my contention that psychiatrists commit mental patients. "[M]ental health professionals must understand," he explains, "that *it is not they who make commitments decisions about patients. Commitment is a judicial decision that is made by the court*" (emphasis in the original). Psychiatrists say lawyers commit, lawyers say they merely implement the psychiatrists' medical request for commitment: "*[T]he petition is filed by doctors. . . . they filed the petitions asking that he be recommitted.*"[10] Thus spoke an Illinois State Public Prosecutor, commenting on the predicament of an innocent person

---

[9] D.J. Jaffe, "How to Prepare for an Emergency," (2000). http://www.nami.org/about/naminyc/coping/911.html.

[10] Michael Burke, Illinois State Prosecutor, "All Things Considered," National Public Radio Profile, "Case of Rodney Yoder, who is fighting the whole system of forced mental health facility sentences," October 23rd, 2002, emphasis added. http://search.npr.org/cf/cmn/segment_display.cfm?segID=152183

who has been incarcerated for more than eleven years in a state mental hospital.

Legally, psychiatrist and prosecutor are both right. The psychiatrist cannot incarcerate a patient *without judicial approval*, and the judge cannot order a patient incarcerated *without a psychiatric diagnosis and recommendation to* commit.[11] Recognizing the wrongfulness intrinsic to chattel slavery, slaveholders appealed to God as the agent responsible for the institution; they were merely "following orders." Recognizing the wrongfulness intrinsic to psychiatric slavery, psychiatrists appeal to Medicine, and lawyers to Psychiatry, as the agents responsible for the institution; they, too, are merely following orders.[12]

How do judge and mental patient meet? The psychiatrist introduces them to one another. How does the judge know whom to commit? The psychiatrist tells him. Does Pies believe that depriving innocent persons of liberty, under mental health auspices, is a good thing or a bad thing? He does not tell us in plain words. We must infer his values from his comments. He writes: "In fact, when a court authorizes a commitment, *it is acting as the agent of the doctor, the social worker. Or, in many cases, the parent of the sick individual.* This is as it should be in a democracy, where the 'state' (state and national government) carry out the will of the people" (emphasis in the original).

Pies believes that tyranny by a majority is admirable social policy. John Stuart Mill didn't believe that. I also don't believe that. Pies wraps his love of tyranny by an American majority in patriotism: "The persistent failure of some critics of psychiatry to distinguish the system of civil commitment in *this* country from involuntary confinement in totalitarian countries greatly undermines the credibility of their moral claims" (emphasis in the original).

In the end, Pies descends from his Olympian height and flaunts his willingness to bear the burden of the white man, a.k.a., psychiatric slave master. First, he again mischaracterizes my views: "Dr. Szasz's most compelling message is that *we must never bully* our *patients*"

---

[11] Szasz, *Liberation by Oppression.*

[12] Thomas Szasz, *Cruel Compassion: The Psychiatric Control of Society's Unwanted* (Syracuse: Syracuse University Press, 1998 [1994]); *Ideology and Insanity: Essays on the Psychiatric Dehumanization of Man* (Syracuse: Syracuse University Press, 1991 [1970]); *Insanity: The Idea and Its Consequences* (Syracuse: Syracuse University Press, 1997 [1987]); *The Manufacture of Madness: A Comparative Study of the Inquisition and the Mental Health Movement* (Syracuse: Syracuse University Press, 1997 [1970]); and Thomas Szasz, ed., *The Age of Madness: A History of Involuntary Mental Hospitalization Presented in Selected Texts* (Garden City: Doubleday Anchor, 1973).

(emphasis in the original). That is wrong: my message is that psychiatrists ought to be stripped of the power to coerce patients. (It goes without saying that no decent person ever bullies anyone.) Pies then cites the case of a hypothetical "young man, rocking back and forth in a pool of his own urine," and declares: *To bring this young man into the hospital against his wishes is not to 'bully' him, but to begin the process of restoring his humanity. To do less is to collude in the destruction of his very soul"* (emphasis added). It is morally wicked to describe taking a person in handcuffs to a building where he is incarcerated as "bringing him into a hospital." Also, I reject the proposition that saving souls—"not colluding in the destruction of souls," as Pies puts is—is a form of medical treatment. If it is, then psychiatric practice is a flagrant violation of the principle of the separation of church and state.

V

"Finally," Pies concludes, "I will suggest some ways that disagreements over these many issues may be resolved constructively, by encouraging dialogue and *compromise* rather than obdurate rhetoric. . . . These critics, in my view, would also benefit by working directly with organizations such as the National Alliance for the Mentally Ill." Since Pies's comments are addressed to me, I assume that his phrase "these critics" refers to me.

This is a disingenuous suggestion. I maintain there is no mental illness; there is only behavior, good or bad, legal or illegal, permitted or prohibited by criminal law or mental health law. In the October 7th, 2002 edition of NAMI's newsletter, *E-News,* the group restated its commitment to the belief that "No one is immune" from mental illness and called for more "screening, evaluating, diagnosing and treating mental illnesses"—code words for advocating more psychiatric slavery in the name of freedom from mental illness:

> One out of five Americans will experience a mental illness, but no more than a third get *the treatment they need*. The cost to society of untreated mental illness is more than $100 billion a year. . . . The nation experiences 30,000 suicides each year—more than the number of homicides . . . *We need to build a comprehensive, efficient system to screen, evaluate, diagnose and treat mental illnesses at every stage of life. We need a system that affirms principles of individual liberty and freedom*—which are as old as the values

in our nation's Declaration of Independence. We must act now to build a new revolution.[13]

Pies denies the profound moral gulf that separates the psychiatric slaveholders from the psychiatric abolitionists. In contrast to Pies's defense of psychiatric slavery by a pretense at conciliation, Columbia psychology professor Ethan E. Gorenstein offers these forthright remarks in his essay, "Debating Mental Illness":

> The issues raised are enormously controversial, and the depth of disagreement between adversaries cannot be minimized. Szasz's position, for example, is fundamentally irreconcilable with that of the medical establishment. Whereas Szasz denounces involuntary commitment categorically, the medical establishment generally supports it as legitimate and even desirable. .... When can treatment be applied forcibly? When can an individual's rights be abridged? When is an individual absolved from responsibilities? These are serious questions, difficult questions, but what ultimately must be faced is that they are not theoretical or empirical questions. They are questions of social regulation that must be addressed directly, not concealed within a specious debate over the existence of an undefined abstraction.[14]

I am a lone individual who has devoted himself to abolishing psychiatric force and fraud and separating psychiatry and the state. NAMI is a large, well-financed organization that works in tandem with the American Psychiatric Association and international pharmaceutical companies to promote the practice of psychiatric force and fraud and the union of psychiatry and the state. I do not share Pies's belief that betraying my moral principles would benefit me. I am committed to opposing NAMI's revolution.

---

[13] "NAMI Calls for Political Revolution to End Broken Promises," *NAMI ENews* (7th October, 2002); http://www.irshad.org/idara/qadiani/mirzphas.htm (emphasis added).
[14] Ethan E. Gorenstein, "Debating Mental Illness: Implications for Science, Medicine, and Social Policy," http://www.pages.drexel.edu/grad/kld22/index240sz.html

12

Mental Illness as a Myth: A Methodological Re-interpretation

H. TRISTRAM ENGELHARDT, Jr.

I The Myth of Mental Illness as a Practical Postulate

There are insights that illumine a time and books that aid a culture to see its practices afresh. Such has been the contribution of Thomas S. Szasz. His critical assessment of the medicalization of mental problems correctly recognizes the profound moral and cultural dangers involved in assimilating all mental problems to a medical model. As he appreciates, such assimilation threatens to deny human freedom and obscure the responsibility persons have to come to terms with their problems in living. Szasz makes this point by employing a rhetorically powerful and engaging claim: mental illness is a myth.

As I argue, this should not be regarded as an empirical or metaphysical claim that mental diseases do not or cannot exist. Instead, the claim that mental illness is a myth should be interpreted as indicating the importance of treating "mental problems," bad habits, and problems in living within a social practice or institution of psychotherapy understood within a moral, not medical, model. In this context, they are problems in living, not mental illnesses. In short, Szasz's work should be interpreted as reminding us that core to human life is the retrieval and maintenance of moral autonomy. The retrieval and maintenance of autonomy require taking personal responsibility for how one decides to solve, live with, or deny one's problems in living. Szasz construes psychotherapists as heal-

ers of the soul, not as physicians addressing problems that lie within the
brain, even when these express themselves in mental diseases, and even
if all mental processes have a biological substratum. Seen from the perspective of this moral practice, it is a myth that "mental problems," bad
habits, and problems in living are simply mental illnesses or diseases.

Provocative phrases can be heuristic. They can as well have pernicious side effects. Such has surely been the case with Szasz's claim that
mental illness is a myth. When engaging its heuristic power, its claims
about reality must carefully be put in context. Otherwise, the claim is
outrageously and manifestly false. Not just physicians and patients, but
persons generally know that mental illnesses exist. People have breaks
with reality, hallucinate, and lose control of themselves in ways that can
increasingly be explained and treated within biological models. Mental
illnesses are a fact of medicine and of life. Since the publication of *The
Myth of Mental Illness* in 1961,[1] advances in the understanding of brain
function and in the biological treatment of mental diseases have made
this even more obvious by eroding the barrier between organic and functional mental disorders. The appreciation of the biological bases of
behavior and of mental illness has become clearer over these forty years.
Szasz's injunction that psychotherapists not provide biologically-based
treatments seems to deny the obvious benefits of the important treatments now available. This is not how Szasz should be read.

Szasz's core claims are best viewed as methodological and moral, not
empirical or metaphysical. Szasz should be read as holding that, for
important moral and cultural reasons, a methodological separation
should be established between the role of psychotherapists and the role
of physicians. This approach recasts Szasz's position in the image and
likeness of a Kantian *als-ob* practical postulate, namely, that the moral
importance of psychotherapy can be maintained only if psychotherapists
consistently act *as if* mental illnesses were a myth. This as-if commitment does not deny the empirical truth that mental illnesses exist or that
biological treatments are effective. Instead, Szasz's brilliantly critical
work correctly recognizes that there is in our culture an often pernicious
confusion between the commitment to treat disease and the commitment
to recognize individuals as free moral agents. On the one hand, influenced by the medical model, courts have been tempted both to confine
some mental patients indefinitely and to excuse some criminals too easily on the grounds of mental illness. Explaining behavior in medical
terms seems to undercut claims on behalf of autonomy and responsibil-

---

[1] Thomas S. Szasz, *The Myth of Mental Illness* (New York: Hoeber-Harper, 1961).

ity, making the behavior a caused phenomenon rather than a chosen action. The medicalization of mental problems threatens the recognition of personal autonomy and responsibility. On the other hand, the courts have recognized that accountability and freedom are central both to the criminal system and to the constitutional rights of free citizens.[2] Still, the success of biologically-based psychiatry appears to give grounds for bringing these convictions into question. Szasz recognizes psychotherapy's special role in preserving human responsibility in the face of the power of the medical model.

II A Methodological Dualism

Through his article, "The Myth of Mental Illness,"[3] and his book with the same title, Szasz engaged an issue core to moral theory. He has done so in a way that can best be understood as a continuation of one of Immanuel Kant's core philosophical insights: humans are destined to consider themselves not only as objects of scientific research, but most importantly also as moral agents. On the one hand, humans are the object of their own scientific investigations. As empirical investigators, they understand their own behavior as determined in conformity with scientific laws. On the other hand, humans as moral beings must consider themselves as free and responsible. Imagine the observant orthodox deterministic behaviorist who holds that all of his actions are causally determined. Were one to ask him if this were true, he could only answer that "given my hard-wiring and all my past experiences and the stimulus of your question, I am caused to say that I am causally determined." He cannot claim on rational grounds, within the constraints of behaviorism, that it is true that he is in fact determined. He could only state that he is caused to state that he is determined. The human self-referential standpoint leaves humans with no option, if they are to be consistent, but to treat themselves as if they were free.

This position should not be read as a Cartesian dualism of substances with two diverse universes of predicates, such that bodies have illnesses and minds have problems in living. Such a Cartesian dualism could lead one to conclude that it is a category mistake to claim that persons have mental illnesses, for illnesses and diseases can only be predicated of

---

[2] Thomas S. Szasz, "The Insanity Plea and the Insanity Verdict," *Temple Law Quarterly* 40 (Spring, 1967), pp. 271–282.

[3] Thomas S. Szasz, "The Myth of Mental Illness," *The American Psychologist* 15 (February, 1960), pp. 113–18.

bodies. Instead, the more metaphysically modest approach is to con-
strue Szasz in the image and likeness of John Hughlings Jackson
(1835–1911), who claimed that one must separate medicine with neurology from introspective psychology and psychiatry.[4] Jackson's
methodological proposal is not metaphysical in the sense of making an
a priori claim about the existence of two kinds of substances, minds
and bodies, which can be bearers of quite different sorts of predicates.
Rather, Jackson's proposal is a programmatic or methodological one:
for neurology to achieve success as a physical science and practice, it
must not confuse itself with psychology. The introduction of psychological terms and explanations would undermine the integrity of neurological investigation and treatment. For Jackson, one must focus on the
integrity of neurology over against psychology. Because of this
methodological commitment, Jackson is thoroughgoing in his commitment to exorcising from neurology and neurophysiology all psychological language and explanation.

> The current explanation of the post-epileptic comatose patient's immobility
> is, that he does not move, because he is unconscious. This, I submit, is a
> metaphysical explanation. We want, in scientific matters, realistic explana-
> tions. My belief is that the post-epileptic immobility is paralysis. . . . No
> man was ever conscious without there being at the same time some physi-
> cal change in at least the highest arrangements of his highest centres.[5]

Given its character as a physical science and practice, so Jackson argues,
neurology must be committed to physiological explanations. It is not
that Jackson denies the possibility or usefulness of psychological language, terms, and explanations. Rather, he recognizes them as belonging to a different category of explanation.

Both Jackson[6] and Szasz would have benefited from a strong dose of
Kant's resolution of the Third Antinomy, namely, the conflict between

---

[4] H. Tristram Engelhardt, Jr., "John Hughlings Jackson and the Mind-Body Relation,"
Bulletin of the History of Medicine 49 (Summer, 1975), pp. 137–151.

[5] John Hughlings Jackson, *Selected Writings of John Hughlings Jackson*, ed. James
Taylor (London: Staples Press, 1958), vol. 2, p. 59.

[6] There is no evidence that John Hughlings Jackson ever read Kant, or for that matter
was even indirectly influenced by Kantian philosophical reflections. However, a reliable
judgment in this matter is made difficult by the circumstance that Jackson tended to rip
pages from books as he read them and to jettison books once he had read them completely. "But books, as books, he treated with the greatest disrespect. As Jonathan
Hutchinson says, he had no compunction about tearing out of a book any portion which

scientific explanations of humans as determined objects in the world versus moral accounts of persons as free and responsible agents. Thus, with regard to immoral behavior, Kant holds that one can give a fully encompassing, deterministic, scientific explanation of that behavior, while at the same time holding that we are obliged to treat these persons as having freely chosen their actions and as therefore being responsible for their consequences. As Kant puts it,

> First of all, we endeavour to discover the motives to which it [the immoral action] has been due, and then, secondly, in the light of these, we proceed to determine how far the action and its consequences can be imputed to the offender. As regards the first question, we trace the empirical character of the action to its sources, finding these in defective education, bad company, in part also in the viciousness of a natural disposition insensitive to shame, in levity and thoughtlessness, not neglecting to take into account also the occasional causes that may have intervened. We proceed in this enquiry just as we should in ascertaining for a given natural effect the series of its determining causes. But although we believe that the action is thus determined, we none the less blame the agent.[7]

Kant is not advancing a metaphysical claim about two kinds of substances. Instead, Kant is making a methodological distinction between the kinds of explanations given in the sciences and the accounts of action provided by morality. This heuristic, methodological distinction between the world of empirical science and that of moral concerns, which is reflected in John Hughlings Jackson's distinction between the interests of scientific medicine and those of psychology, had an important influence on Sigmund Freud (1856–1939), who in his early writings

---

interested him, and would frequently send to a friend a few leaves torn out of a book dealing with any subject in which he knew the friend to be interested. A curious incident happened after his death, illustrating this. A set of the London Hospital Reports, consisting of the only volumes—four—which were issued, which had belonged to him, was bought from his cousin by a colleague of Dr. Jackson's, chiefly, of course, on account of the contributions of Jackson contained in these volumes. One can imagine the chagrin of the buyer on finding that the only things those volumes did not contain were Jackson's papers! These had evidently been torn out by him at some time and for some particular purpose, so that the volumes, so far as his writings were concerned, were absolutely blank." James Taylor, "Biographical Memoir," in J. Hughlings Jackson, *Neurological Fragments* (Oxford: Oxford University Press, 1925), p. 20.

[7] Immanuel Kant, *Kant's Critique of Pure Reason*, translated by Norman Kemp Smith (London: Macmillan, 1964), A554 = B582, p. 477.

expresses gratitude to Jackson for warning against the "confusion of the physical with the psychic."[8] Szasz is best understood in a similar light: he is underscoring the difference between medicine's concerns with diseases versus psychotherapeutic concerns with bad habits and problems in living.

This interpretation of Szasz's work in terms of a methodological dualism is needed in order to bring plausibility to his many important criticisms of the misuse of psychiatry. They depend on a distinction between physicians who take care of bodies, and true psychotherapists who help persons with their difficulties in living. This distinction depends neither on a claim about two kinds of substances (mind and body) nor on a denial of the existence of mental illness. Instead, it involves a claim about the integrity of different areas of explanation and therapy. Jackson put this distinction clearly in his warning, "There is no physiology of the mind any more than there is psychology of the nervous system."[9] Szasz should appreciate the conclusion that Jackson draws from this perspective, namely, "Our concern as medical men is with the body. If there be such a thing as disease of the mind, we can do nothing for it."[10] Jackson anticipates Szasz in holding that medicine has to do with diseases and illnesses, and psychotherapy has to do with a domain of problems associated with autonomy, and therefore not with diseases and illnesses.

III Psychotherapy Reconsidered: Beyond the Medical Model

Thomas Szasz's distinction between illnesses and problems in living becomes clearer in light of his account of the moral and methodological bases of psychoanalysis. In *The Ethics of Psychoanalysis*,[11] Szasz clearly sets the concerns of psychotherapy in contrast with those of medicine. Indeed, Szasz is skeptical of any benefit conveyed to the psychotherapist from also being a physician. As he notes, "The fact that the therapist is a physician is largely a historical accident; his medical training and credentials help him little, if at all, with his task as psychotherapist."[12] Considering what might be the medical value of psychoanalysis, he

---

[8] Sigmund Freud, *On Aphasia*, translated by E. Stengel (London: Imago, 1953), p. 56.

[9] Jackson, *Selected Writings*, vol. 1, p. 417.

[10] *Ibid.*, vol. 2, p. 85.

[11] Thomas S. Szasz, *The Ethics of Psychoanalysis* (New York: Basic Books, 1965).

[12] *Ibid.*, p. 135.

states that it is "scant".[13] Given his methodological commitments, he should have stated that it is irrelevant. The difficulty is that he fails to provide a sufficient, theoretical account of why psychotherapeutic concerns are categorially different from that of medicine as a whole. Had he drawn on the resources of Immanuel Kant or John Hughlings Jackson, he could have more clearly underscored that his claim is not a metaphysical one (that is, it is not the claim that there are no mental illnesses), but a methodological one: in order for psychotherapy to function successfully as a moral therapeutic intervention aimed at enlarging "the patient's choices and hence his freedom and responsibility,"[14] psychotherapists must act *as if* mental illness were a myth. To accomplish this, psychotherapists must be warned that theirs is a moral, not a medical endeavor, so that illnesses are irrelevant to their task. As Szasz puts it, "The purpose of psychoanalysis is to give patients constrained by their habitual patterns of action greater freedom in their personal conduct."[15]

It is because of a methodologically-based categorical difference that the psychotherapist does not provide medical diagnoses, but rather "a better understanding of ethics, politics, and social relations generally."[16] Psychotherapy functions as a moral practice with moral therapeutic rather than medical therapeutic aims. He correctly recognizes psychotherapy as a relationship between two free individuals. As Szasz states, "Accordingly, the psychotherapist does not 'treat' mental illness, but relates to and communicates with a fellow human being."[17] After all, physicians treat bodies; psychotherapists help persons to meet the challenges they confront as autonomous beings. Szasz puts this bluntly; it is for this reason that Szasz proceeds to give an account of the psychiatric symptom as a restriction of freedom. "The analyst does have special skills, but they are entirely nontechnological; as for special equipment, the analyst needs none and uses none."[18] The skill of the psychotherapist turns out to be, according to Szasz, not implausibly the psychotherapist's moral character and insights. "His special skills are his self-discipline and self-awareness, his critical and inquiring attitude, and his ability to understand and decode the patient's communications and the meaning of

---

[13] *Ibid.*, p. 12.
[14] *Ibid.*, p. 16.
[15] *Ibid.*, p. 18.
[16] *Ibid.*, p. 13.
[17] *Ibid.*, p. 30.
[18] *Ibid.*, p. 32.

his 'mental illness'."[19] Szasz relocates the Freudian psychoanalytic endeavor fully within a moral praxis freed of Freudian assumptions regarding the causally determined character of human behavior. Instead, psychoanalysis presupposes personal autonomy and is directed to it. The goal of psychoanalysis is "to extend the control of the ego over certain areas of the id, as they [Freudians] put it, or to augment the client's capacity for self-determination and making choices, as I prefer to put it."[20]

The role of the psychotherapist can then be understood as that of a special form of educator: an educator who provides an equal with meta-advice, ways of looking at different possibilities for free and responsible choice. In this, the psychotherapist is also like a travel agent who has knowledge of the terrain of different possible destinations. The travel agent describes what is involved in visiting particular locations, given the ways in which individuals are enmired in bad habits and problems of living, but leaves it to the would-be traveler to book a particular trip.

> Education, in this special sense, means meta-advice. Much of the teaching and learning in analysis belongs in this class. For example, through the analyst's decoding of the patient's symptoms and dreams, the patient learns about his unacknowledged ('unconscious') transferences; the patient obtains an inventory of his major interpersonal strategies, their origins, and aims. In all these ways, the analytic teacher (therapist) gives more to his student (patient) than does the therapist who gives advice. And yet, in a sense, he also gives less, for he requires the student to work his own way from meta-advice to advice.
>
> Psychoanalytic insight or understanding may be put to various uses; the choice rests with the patient. Once more, this is like giving a tourist a map of a strange city: the analytic traveler may, with a map, orient himself, but not find out where he *should* go.[21]

In playing the role of meta-educator, the psychotherapist does not so much give treatment as instruction about the various possibilities for free and responsible choice, for the resolution of bad habits and difficulties in living.

As meta-educator, the psychotherapist makes a very particular kind of cultural contribution. Psychotherapy can only make this contribution to certain people under particular circumstances. Just as fine art may not

---

[19] *Ibid.*, p. 38.
[20] *Ibid.*, p. 6.
[21] *Ibid.*, pp. 51–52.

be for everyone, so, too, what the psychotherapist has to offer is not necessarily appropriate for everyone. Szasz is refreshingly frank about the culturally elite character of what psychotherapy or psychoanalysis has to offer. "The poor need jobs and money, not psychoanalysis. The uneducated need knowledge and skills, not psychoanalysis."[22] The special meta-education offered by psychotherapists can only have meaning for those who already enjoy a significant background level of freedom from constraint so that they may engage in a special focus on and exploration of the possibilities for autonomy and responsibility. "The kind of *personal* freedom that psychoanalysis promises can have meaning only for persons who enjoy a large measure of economic, political, and social freedom."[23]

IV Taking Autonomy Seriously: The Background Ethics of Szaszian Psychotherapy

Szasz demands a watertight seal between the role of psychotherapists as moral educators and the role played by physicians, including biologically oriented psychiatrists. He argues for this separation on the basis of a moral distinction between autonomous and heteronymous psychotherapists. It is not enough if psychotherapists simply eschew the use of drugs and hospitalization. In addition, the psychotherapist is for Szasz to be moved by an ethic of autonomy that respects the psychotherapist and the psychotherapist's clients or patients as fully autonomous individuals. "The ethic of the analytic relationship is communicated by what actually occurs between analyst and analysand. What distinguishes this enterprise from others is that, although the analyst tries to help his client, he does not 'take care of him.' The patient takes care of himself."[24]

Unlike the heteronymous therapist who claims, "I will take care of you," the autonomous therapist instead offers the analysand an opportunity "to look at himself in a new light, then, by small steps, there will be some change in the patient's personality."[25] In this encounter, the psychotherapist and the analysand meet as free and equal. Szasz bluntly states that the "primary duty of the autonomous therapist is to take care of himself; by this I mean that he must protect the integrity of his

---

[22] *Ibid.*, p. 28.
[23] *Ibid.*
[24] *Ibid.*, p. 24.
[25] *Ibid.*, p. 59.

therapeutic role,"[26] rather than take care of the patient. The cardinal goal of this process is the increase of personal autonomy. "[The analysand] learns that only self-knowledge and responsible commitment and action can set him free. In sum, autonomous psychotherapy is an actual small-scale demonstration of the nature and feasibility of the ethic of autonomy in human relationships."[27]

Like Kant, Szasz insists that, although we can understand ourselves as beings determined according to the laws of science, we must also understand ourselves as free and responsible moral agents. The psychotherapist for Szasz becomes one of the cardinal defenders in our culture of the role of persons as autonomous, free, moral agents. Psychotherapy and the role of the psychotherapist are thus defined in moral, rather than medical and scientific expectations. His claim that mental illness is a myth must then be interpreted as an injunction about how psychotherapists are to act. Unlike those who treat diseases, psychotherapists act as if diseases, or at least mental diseases and illnesses, did not exist so as without confusion to invite autonomous individuals responsibly to confront their problems in living.

In this light, one can understand Szasz's injunction that psychotherapists, appropriately understood, should not take on the role of prescribing drugs or hospitalizing patients. Somewhat on the analogy of the priest's absolute commitment to the seal of confession, whatever the consequences, in order to protect a cardinal role of the priesthood, so, too, for Szasz the therapist must protect the autonomy that grounds the role of psychotherapist so as to make possible the growth of the autonomy of the analysand. Should the analysand appear to need medication or hospitalization, the psychotherapist can recommend where such services can be found. However, for Szasz the role of psychotherapist is defined and sustained through an adamant refusal to allow the psychotheraputic role to be conflated with any other relationship with the patient or client, in particular a physician/patient relationship. It is for this reason that Szasz construes suicide threats in terms of the free choices that confront a patient. As he puts it, "only if the patient is deeply convinced that the analyst respects his autonomy, including his right to take his own life, can he engage effectively in the analytic exploration and mastery of his ideas about suicide."[28] The same goes for any "mental illness." Psychotherapists are to treat "mental illnesses" as bad habits or problems in living for patients to confront as matters of personal responsibility.

---

[26] *Ibid.*, p. 44.

[27] *Ibid.*, p. 24.

[28] *Ibid.*, p. 175.

Given this Kantian-Jacksonian recasting of Szasz, Szasz can provide a theoretical basis for holding that psychotherapy has a very special role that is strategically brought into question when the psychotherapist also plays the role of physician and addresses problems as if they were illnesses. However, as just noted, this heuristic, methodological distinction between treating disease and aiding autonomous persons with their bad habits and problems in living does not exclude biologically oriented psychiatrists from diagnosing a patient's problem as a disease and then treating it biologically. It is simply that this is not the role of a psychotherapist. Psychotherapists, *sensu stricto à la* Szasz, are persons who do not prescribe drugs or hospitalize patients, but instead give meta-education. Szasz is not committed to denying the obvious, namely, that various forms of biologically-based therapy do indeed treat psychiatric diseases, which appear to be illnesses on a close analogy with those treated in other areas of medicine. The advances in biological psychiatry demonstrate that it is a myth to hold that mental illness is a myth in this straightforward sense. That is, Szasz need not be taken as denying the obvious (e.g., there are mental diseases amenable to biological therapies), but as underscoring the importance of free and responsible choices and relationships.

Szasz's reflections concerning mental illness as a myth provide the basis for recognizing psychotherapy's unique status and its important contributions to our culture. As has been argued, the force of Szasz's research and scholarship cannot be clearly appreciated until they are embedded in a methodological dualism such as that found in John Hughlings Jackson, which allows on the one hand the pursuit of empirical science and on the other hand the affirmation of the integrity and place of moral practices that take autonomy seriously. The insights of Szasz, so recast, help us to understand better why psychotherapy can never be reduced to biologically-based psychiatry. Unlike biology and the biological sciences, which are aimed at empirically understanding and through efficient causal means changing life processes, psychotherapy is a moral practice aimed at offering an enhanced opportunity to act freely and responsibly. The price of this protection is that psychotherapy becomes distinct in its foundations from medicine, including biologically-based psychiatry and deterministic psychology. Here lies its primary cultural and moral significance: psychotherapy offers an opportunity for self-knowledge towards the goal of enhancing autonomy. Without denying the existence of mental diseases or the efficacy of biologically-based psychotherapeutic interventions, humans as self-conscious moral agents cannot escape affirming that mental illness is a myth insofar as it denies the possibility of responsible choice.

Reply to Engelhardt

THOMAS SZASZ

I

Tristram Engelhardt is one of the most philosophically sophisticated psychiatric scholars writing today. I am grateful for his appreciative representation of the theses of two of my early works, *The Myth of Mental Illness* and *The Ethics of Psychoanalysis*. His contribution rightly focuses on the moral concerns I address in these books.

II

Engelhardt emphasizes that "the claim that mental illness is a myth should be interpreted as indicating the importance of treating 'mental problems,' bad habits, and problems in living within a social practice or institution of psychotherapy understood within a moral, not medical, model. In this context, there are problems in living, not mental illnesses." This is exactly right, so far as it goes.

However, Engelhardt qualifies his agreement: he states that my claim that mental illness is a myth "should not be regarded as an empirical or metaphysical claim that mental diseases do not or cannot exist." This is partly right. My claim asserts an analytic, not a synthetic, truth; as such, it is not based on empirical observation. Nevertheless, it is empirically valid. The claim that there are no ghosts or mermaids is not empirically based, but is empirically valid.

Engelhardt rightly refers to the work of Immanuel Kant and its influence on my writings. Yet, he fails to mention that it was Kant who famously suggested distinguishing between "analytic truths" and "synthetic truths." Today, this distinction is common knowledge, albeit it is often overlooked. The meaning of these terms may be summarized as follows. The truth of an analytic proposition is due to the meanings of the words involved. We know that bachelors are unmarried without having to investigate their marital status. In contrast, the truth of a synthetic proposition depends on its relation to facts in the world. We know that the capital of New York State is Albany only by reference to appropriate records.

To restate: In an analytic proposition, the predicate is contained in the subject; in a synthetic proposition, the predicate cannot be arrived at by an analysis of the terms employed. *Analytic truths are "truths of reason": they result from reasoning and the precise use of language. Synthetic truths are "truths of fact": they result from experience of the world.* We need rationalist methods to verify analytic statements, empirical methods to verify synthetic statements.

When, in 1960, I first asserted that mental illness is a myth, I meant to remind people that, according to strict medical definition, disease is a predicate of *(human) bodies.* If we grant that definition, then we need not examine any particular person to know that he does not have a mental illness. The mind can be ill only in a metaphorical sense.[1]

Why is this simple proposition so difficult to accept and why is it so often misunderstood and misrepresented? Three reasons spring to mind. One is that a person "diagnosed" as ill—that is, said to have a disease or believed to have a disease—may or may not have a disease. We cannot know whether the statement, "John Doe has acute appendicitis," is true or false without examining him. And even if we examine him, our conclusion that he does or does not have appendicitis may be erroneous. People assume that the same considerations apply to the person suspected of being mentally ill.

The second reason for misunderstanding the meaning of my claim that mental illness is a myth is obvious cognitively, but obscured linguistically. The claim *re-asserts an analytic truth that people perceive as if it were a synthetic truth, subject to falsification by means of empirical observation.* In addition, the claim is misunderstood because people, especially educated people, equate mental disease with brain disease. Psychiatry is a branch of medicine. Psychiatrists and other authorities regularly assert that mental diseases are brain diseases. Thus, when a "normal" person hears me say that there is no such thing as mental illness, he is likely to counter: "But I know persons who were diagnosed as mentally ill and have turned out to have X (neurosyphilis, multiple

---

[1] In this connection, see my "Reply to Simon" in Chapter 6 above, especially the transcript of my testimony for the prosecution in a criminal trial where the defendant pleaded insanity.

sclerosis, brain tumor). In due time, with refinements in medical technology, psychiatrists will be able to show that all mental illnesses are
bodily diseases."

Let me try to clarify this fashionable conundrum by recourse to the
familiar example of the bachelor as an unmarried person. Suppose that
my interlocutor were to misinterpret this definition, which asserts an
analytic truth, as if it were a synthetic truth. He might then reply: "But I
know several bachelors who were secretly married. Hence, there are
married bachelors." This is fallacious. There may well be persons in the
world who claim to be bachelors, or whom others believe to be bachelors, who in fact are married. But regardless of how many such persons
there may be in the world, the word "bachelor" denotes an unmarried
person.

Foolishly, psychiatric loyalists nowadays often engage in precisely
such a tactic, trying to prove the *existence of mental illnesses:* they look
for married bachelors, in an effort to prove that the word "bachelor"
does not mean unmarried person. One of the highlights of the 2001
meeting of the American Psychiatric Association (APA) was a session
devoted to helping "psychiatry educators hone their skills and learn new
teaching techniques." Ronald O. Rieder, M.D.—director of residency
education and vice chair for education in the department of psychiatry
of Columbia University and an APA-certified master-teacher—presented a demonstration "focus[ing] on the 'myth of mental illness' propos-
als of Thomas Szasz, M.D., and relevant biological data such as brain-
imaging findings. Rieder will discuss these and other methods of getting
students who have not yet had direct clinical experiences and are skeptical of the concept of psychiatric illness excited about psychiatry and
interested in learning more about psychiatric illness."[2] The believer in
psychiatric miracles has replaced the believer in religious miracles: seeing signs of mental illness in the brain is like seeing signs of bleeding in
the Eucharistic host.[3]

---

[2] "Leading Educators Share Secrets at Annual Meeting Sessions," *Psychiatric News*
36:18 (16th March, 2001).

[3] See E.R.L. Gaughran, "From Superstition to Science: The History of a Bacterium,"
Transactions of the New York Academy of Sciences, Series II, 30 (January, 1969), pp.
3–24. For details, see Thomas Szasz, "Introduction," in *Heresies* (New York: Doubleday
Anchor, 1976), pp. 1–22. Also, Ruth Gledhill, "Body of Christ Wafers Sacrilege," *The
Times* (London, 10th March, 2001), Internet edition; Lauren F. Winner, "Killing Jesus
All Over Again: How Medieval Stories about Desecrating the Eucharist Were Used to
Justify the Murder of Jews," *Books and Culture* (May–June 2001), http://www.chris-
tianitytoday.com/bc/2001/003/10.24.html; "Messages from Heaven," members.aol.com/

Undoubtedly, there are persons who claim to be, or whom others believe to be, mentally ill who have a disease of the brain or some other part of the body. My critics conclude that this proves that mental illnesses are genuine diseases. This is fallacious. If a person has a disease of the brain or some other organ, then he has a neurological illness or some other disease, not a mental illness. Regardless of how many such persons there may be in the world, the word "disease" denotes a condition of the body.

Whenever we analyze an argument that contains words with contested meanings, it is essential that we keep the distinction between analytic truth and synthetic truth in mind. If we argue that something is true, we need to be clear about whether we are saying something about the empirical world, or whether we are clarifying the meanings of words.[4]

The third reason for misunderstanding and misrepresenting the meaning of my claim that mental illness is a myth is, broadly speaking, existential. For psychiatrists, abandoning the idea of mental illness would require and entail relinquishing the advantages that society bestows on persons it credits with medical authority; for lay persons, it would require and entail relinquishing the resources that the mental health industry offers in dealing with their personal problems and the personal problems of their relatives.

Religious symbolism is saturated with what believers view as miracles, and non-believers regard as oxymorons, literalized metaphors, or deceptions and self-deceptions. Catholics assert that the consecrated host is the body of Christ. Non-believers know, *a priori*, that it is not. How do they know this? By adhering to the definition of the word "body," used to refer to a human body, as an object—an organism, composed of organs, tissues, and cells. A consecrated ceremonial wafer is not a body. However, a Catholic priest cannot deny the miracle of transubstantiation and remain a priest.

In our Therapeutic State, the concept of mental illness and the psychiatrist occupy a similar status and role. In the religion of "mental health," a psychiatric diagnosis of mental illness—masturbation, homosexuality, smoking cigarettes or marijuana, depression, hearing voices—is miraculously transformed into a disease of the brain. The psychiatrist who "denies" this miracle is not only cast out of the profession, his views are ignored as uninformed criticisms of psychiatry unworthy of

---

bjw1106/marian9.htm 8k; "Daniel Sanford's Miraculous Host Page: Welcome to the Burning & Bleeding Host of Betania," dsanford.com/miraclehost.html

[4] See Roger Jones, "The Enlightenment," http://www.philosopher.org.uk/enl.htm

attention. It is small wonder that few psychiatrists have taken that step. Even the "antipsychiatrist" Ronald Laing recoiled from denying the reality of mental illness, rejected my opposition to psychiatric coercions, and reasserted his loyalty to psychiatry as medicine.[5]

An example borrowed from contemporary politics further illustrates the point. Writing about the Stalinism still fashionable among left-liberal London intellectuals in the 1970s, the noted Russian-Jewish emigré author Zinovy Zinik, observes: "I share Chekhov's opinion that it takes more guts to dissent within your circle of friends and ideological bedfellows than it does to protest against some far-distant regime or future catastrophe."[6] Before the fall of the Berlin Wall, my psychiatric critics never tired of denouncing psychiatric abuses in the Soviet Union, while praising the uses of psychiatry at home. Now they rail against psychiatric abuses in China, while praising the uses of psychiatry at home. Yet, they scorn my books and revile my persona. Why? Because I am a "traitor": I wash dirty linen in public.

Clearly, Engelhardt is familiar with the distinction between analytic truths and synthetic truths. Nevertheless, he writes: "This position [my labeling mental illness a myth] should not be read as a Cartesian dualism of substances with two diverse universes of predicates, such that bodies have illnesses and minds have problems in living. Such a Cartesian dualism could lead one to conclude that it is a category mistake to claim that persons have mental illnesses, for illnesses and diseases can only be predicated of bodies."

I agree that "illnesses and diseases can only be predicated of bodies," and that my position "should not be read as a Cartesian dualism of substances." But I do not agree "that bodies *have* illnesses and minds *have* problems in living" (emphasis added). The use of the verb "have" here is inappropriate and misleading. Our bodies exhibit properties that we, *qua* medically informed or uninformed observers, interpret as diseases. As sentient persons, we perceive some of our life experiences as problematic—unpleasant, painful, depressing—and interpret them in religious, moral, philosophical, psychological, sociological, political, and medical (psychiatric) terms. The gist of my thesis —summed up in the phrase "myth of mental illness"—is an argument against reducing "problems in living" to diseases as biological processes and a plea to

[5] See Thomas Szasz, "Cleansing the Modern Heart: Is There a Place for a Pacific-Secular Cure of Souls in the Therapeutic State?," *Society* 40 (2003), pp. 52–59.
[6] Zinovy Zinik, "With Friends Like Us," *Times Literary Supplement* (23rd August, 2002), p. 5.

separate psychiatry as the "cure of souls" from medicine as the treatment of bodies. Engelhardt does not want to bring about such a divorce. He writes:

> Provocative phrases can be heuristic. They can as well have pernicious side effects. Such has surely been the case with Szasz's claim that mental illness is a myth. When engaging its heuristic power, its claims about reality must carefully be put in context. Otherwise, the claim is outrageously and manifestly false. Not just physicians and patients, *but persons generally know that mental illnesses exist.* People have breaks with reality, hallucinate, and lose control of themselves in ways that can increasingly be explained and treated within biological models. *Mental illnesses are a fact of medicine and of life.* Since the publication of *The Myth of Mental Illness* in 1961, advances in the understanding of brain function and in the biological treatment of mental diseases have made this even more obvious by *eroding the barrier between organic and functional mental disorders* (emphasis added).

These comments are unworthy of a psychiatrist with Engelhardt's philosophical sophistication.

"Persons generally know that mental illnesses exist." As Josh Billings famously remarked: "It ain't so much the things we know that get us into trouble. It's the things we know that just ain't so." People know lots of things that ain't so, for example that hell and heaven and angels and saints exist.

"Mental illnesses are a fact of medicine and of life." Homosexuality as mental illness was a fact of medicine and of life. Now smoking—a.k.a. nicotine addiction—is such a fact.

". . . the biological treatment of mental diseases ha[s] made this even more obvious by eroding the barrier between organic and functional mental disorders." Here, Engelhardt uses the vocabulary of psychiatry, which forms an integral part of the subject matter of my critique of psychiatry, as evidence for his premise, that mental illnesses are diseases.

Perhaps a difference in lifestyle explains our differing emphases. I have long ago embraced the risk of impairing my credibility by rejecting the role of the correct psychiatrist *qua* physician who "believes in mental illness." I did so because I love medicine, not because I hate it; and because I feel secure enough in my medical identity, which I earned by hard work and maintained by vigilant interest in the subject, without feeling the need to bask in the glory (or shame) it reflects on me when what I do is *not done in my role as a physician.* In short, I have not looked to my medical credentials as a means for validating my work. Engelhardt has made a more conventional career choice. Still, the agreements between Engelhardt's psychiatric views and mine are many, the disagreements few. I focus on the latter in the hope that doing so will help us think more clearly about the problems that face psychiatrists and a public that mistake medical myths for scientific truths.

Many of Engelhardt's most penetrating comments display the mixture of agreement and disagreement to which I allude. Recognizing the profound influence of Kantian ethics on my work, Engelhardt writes:

> Through his article, "The Myth of Mental Illness" [1960], and his book with the same title, Szasz engaged an issue core to moral theory. He has done so in a way that can best be understood as a continuation of one of Immanuel Kant's core philosophical insights: humans are destined to consider themselves not only as objects of scientific research, but most importantly also as moral agents. On the one hand, humans are the object of their own scientific investigations. As empirical investigators, they understand their own behavior as determined in conformity with scientific laws.

I agree with the first three sentences, but disagree with the fourth. As empirical investigators, we can learn to understand the behavior of our organs "as determined in conformity with scientific laws." However, I do not believe that as empirical investigators we can, or ever will, understand our behavior as moral agents in conformity with scientific laws. Here is another example of a large agreement combined with a small but significant disagreement. Engelhardt summarizes:

> On the one hand, influenced by the medical model, courts have been tempted both to confine some mental patients indefinitely and to excuse some criminals *too easily* on the grounds of mental illness. Explaining behavior in medical terms seems to undercut claims on behalf of autonomy and responsibility, making the behavior a caused phenomenon rather than a chosen action. The medicalization of mental problems threatens the recognition of personal autonomy and responsibility. On the other hand, the courts have recognized that accountability and freedom are central both to the criminal system and to the constitutional rights of free citizens. *Still, the success of biologically-based psychiatry appears to give grounds for bringing these convictions into question* (emphasis added).

This passage obscures that my claims are much more radical than this. I believe that a diagnosis of mental illness should *never* be a ground for depriving a competent adult of liberty, that both civil commitment and the insanity defense should be abolished.

Engelhardt refers to the work of Hughlings Jackson as if it supported his (Engelhardt's) belief in the reality of "mental illnesses" *qua* diseases. I believe it supports my denial of that claim. Engelhardt writes:

> This interpretation of Szasz's work in terms of a methodological dualism is needed in order to bring plausibility to his many important criticisms of the misuse of psychiatry. They depend on a distinction between physicians who take care of bodies, and true psychotherapists who help persons with their difficulties in living. This distinction depends neither on a claim about two kinds of substances (mind and body) nor on a denial of the existence of mental illness. Instead, it involves a claim about the integrity of different areas of explanation and therapy. Jackson put this distinction clearly in his warning, "There is no physiology of the mind any more than there is psychology of the nervous system." Szasz should appreciate the conclusion that Jackson draws from this perspective, namely, "Our concern as medical men is with the body. If there be such a thing as disease of the mind, we can do nothing for it." Jackson anticipates Szasz in holding that medicine has to do with diseases and illnesses, and psychotherapy has to do with a domain of problems associated with autonomy, and therefore not with diseases and illnesses.

I interpret Jackson's statement, "If there be such a thing as disease of the mind, we can do nothing for it," as synonymous with the statement "diseases of the mind are not diseases in the medical sense of the term." Indeed, this is not a new idea and I never claimed that it was. On the contrary, it was the contention of many classical psychiatrists whose views I have repeatedly cited in my work.

As early as 1845, the Viennese psychiatrist, Ernst von Feuchtersleben (1806–1848), declared: "The maladies of the spirit alone, *in abstracto*, that is, error and sin, can be called diseases of the mind only *per analogiam*. They come not within the jurisdiction of the physician, but that of the teacher or clergyman, who again are called physicians of the mind only *per analogiam*."[7]

Theodor Meynert (1833–1892)—one of the founders of modern neuropsychiatry and one of Freud's teachers—began his textbook, *Psychiatry* (1884), with this statement: "The reader will find no other

---

[7] Ernst von Feuchtersleben, *Medical Psychology,* in Daniel Schreber, *Memoirs of My Nervous Illness,* edited and translated by Ida MacAlpine and Richard Hunter (London: Dawson, 1955), p. 412.

definition of 'Psychiatry' in this book but the one given on the title page: *Clinical Treatise on Diseases of the Forebrain.* The historical term for psychiatry, i.e., 'treatment of the soul', implies more than we can accomplish, and transcends the bounds of accurate scientific investigation."[8]

In his classic, *Lectures on Clinical Psychiatry* (1901), Emil Kraepelin (1856–1927), the creator of the first modern psychiatric nosology, stated: "The subject of the following course of lectures will be the Science of Psychiatry, which, as its name [*Seelenheilkunde*] implies, is that of the treatment of mental disease. It is true that, in the strictest terms, we cannot speak of the mind as becoming diseased. [*Allerdings kann mann, streng genommen, nicht von Erkrankungen der Seele sprechen*]."[9]

III

I owe a special debt of gratitude to Engelhardt for discussing my old book on psychoanalysis or, more precisely, what I saw as the moral core of the human relationship misnamed "psychoanalysis."

Engelhardt acknowledges that psychotherapists do not deal with illnesses but fails to recognize the consequences of taking that proposition seriously. Summarizing my view of the task of the "autonomous psychotherapist," he writes: "To accomplish this, psychotherapists must be warned that theirs is a moral, not a medical endeavor, so that illnesses are irrelevant to their task. As Szasz puts it, 'The purpose of psychoanalysis is to give patients constrained by their habitual patterns of action greater freedom in their personal conduct.'" Yet, oddly, he complains that

> The difficulty is that he [Szasz] fails to provide a sufficient, theoretical account of why psychotherapeutic concerns are categorically different from that of medicine as a whole. Had he drawn on the resources of Immanuel Kant or John Hughlings Jackson, he could have more clearly underscored that his claim is not a metaphysical one (that is, it is not the claim that there are no mental illnesses), but a methodological one: in order for psychotherapy to function successfully as a moral therapeutic intervention aimed at

---

[8] Theodor Meynert, *Psychiatry: Clinical Treatise on Diseases of the Forebrain* [1884], translated by Barbara Sachs (New York: Putnam's, 1885), p. v, emphasis in the original.
[9] Emil Kraepelin, *Lectures on Clinical Psychiatry* [1901] (New York: Hafner, 1968), p. 1, emphasis added.

enlarging "the patient's choices and hence his freedom and responsibility," psychotherapists must act as if mental illness were a myth. It is because of a methodologically based categorical difference that the psychotherapist does not provide medical diagnoses, but rather "a better understanding of ethics, politics, and social relations generally." Psychotherapy functions as a moral practice with moral therapeutic rather than medical therapeutic aims. He correctly recognizes psychotherapy as a relationship between two free individuals. As Szasz states, "Accordingly, the psychotherapist does not 'treat' mental illness, but relates to and communicates with a fellow human being." After all, physicians treat bodies; psychotherapists help persons to meet the challenges they confront as autonomous beings. Szasz puts this bluntly; it is for this reason that Szasz proceeds to give an account of the psychiatric symptom as a restriction of freedom. . . . Szasz relocates the Freudian psychoanalytic endeavor fully within a moral praxis freed of Freudian assumptions regarding the causally determined character of human behavior. Instead, psychoanalysis presupposes personal autonomy and is directed to it.

For the most part, this is an accurate and sensitive interpretation of what I have written. The sole inaccuracy lies in Engelhardt's effort, which seems to me contrived, to reassert that my views and practices need not entail a rejection of the idea of mental illness. However, ideas have consequences. One of the consequences of the idea of (mental) illness is that it places its management in medical hands. Engelhardt knows this. I knew it and never forgot it. It is a social fact that the idea of mental illness as a real illness is even more firmly rooted in the modern American mind than is the idea of God. That is one of the reasons why the moral promise of psychoanalysis as a secular cure of souls failed and was fated to fail.

My aim in *The Ethics of Psychoanalysis* was to articulate what I regarded and still regard as the moral and political-economic core of, and conditions for, the psychoanalytic situation. As I recently restated,

the elements of this core are: the inviolable privacy of the therapist-patient relationship; the patient's willingness to assume responsibility for his behavior and pay for the service he receives; the analyst's willingness to eschew coercion justified by the legal-psychiatric principle of the "duty to protect" (the patient from himself and the community from the patient); the legal system's willingness to exempt the analyst from this principle (at present an integral part of the mental health professional's mandate); and the public's willingness to accept that a secure guarantee of privacy and confidentiality—similar to that granted the librarian and priest—as an indispensable condition for the proper conduct of psychoanalysis as a secular "cure of souls." These conditions are absent in the Therapeutic State. The result is a tragic loss of liberty for patient, therapist, and society.[10]

Let me now return to Engelhardt's fine restatement of my views about psychotherapy, a restatement that ironically illustrates that hardly anyone else today uses the word "psychotherapy" as he and I do. Engelhardt approvingly summarizes my characterization of psychoanalysis as meta-education. He writes: "The role of the psychotherapist can then be understood as that of a special form of educator: an educator who provides an equal with metaadvice, ways of looking at different possibilities for free and responsible choice. In this, the psychotherapist is also like a travel agent who has knowledge of the terrain of different possible destinations. The travel agent describes what is involved in visiting particular locations . . . but leaves it to the wouldbe traveler to book a particular trip." And he quotes me as writing in *The Ethics of Psychoanalysis*:

> Education, in this special sense, means meta-advice. Much of the teaching and learning in analysis belongs in this class. For example, through the analyst's decoding of the patient's symptoms and dreams, the patient learns about his unacknowledged ("unconscious") transferences; the patient obtains an inventory of his major interpersonal strategies, their origins, and aims. In all these ways, the analytic teacher (therapist) gives more to his student (patient) than does the therapist who gives advice. And yet, in a sense, he also gives less, for he requires the student to work his own way from meta-advice to advice. Psychoanalytic insight or understanding may be put to various uses; the choice rests with the patient. Once more, this is like giving a tourist a map of a strange city: the analytic traveler may, with a map, orient himself, but not find out where he *should* go.[11]

Engelhardt adds: "In playing the role of meta-educator, the psychotherapist does not so much give treatment as instruction about the various possibilities for free and responsible choice, for the resolution of bad habits and difficulties in living." None of this is possible in a culture whose laws regard psychotherapy as "therapy." Engelhardt knows this and he values the therapist's privilege to serve as the patient's agent. He writes:

---

[10] Thomas Szasz, "Cleansing the Modern Heart: Is There a Place for a Pacific-secular Cure of Souls in the Therapeutic State?," *Society* (2003), op. cit.
[11] Thomas Szasz, *The Ethics of Psychoanalysis: The Theory and Method of Autonomous Psychotherapy* [1965], with a new preface (Syracuse: Syracuse University Press, 1988), pp. 51–52, emphasis in the original.

It is not enough if psychotherapists simply eschew the use of drugs and hospitalization. In addition, the psychotherapist is for Szasz to be moved by an ethic of autonomy that respects the psychotherapist and the psychotherapist's clients or patients as fully autonomous individuals. . . . Unlike the heteronymous therapist who claims, "I will take care of you," the autonomous therapist instead offers the analysand an opportunity "to look at himself in a new light, then, by small steps, there will be some change in the patient's personality." . . . The psychotherapist for Szasz becomes one of the cardinal defenders in our culture of the role of persons as autonomous, free, moral agents. Psychotherapy and the role of the psychotherapist are thus defined in moral, rather than medical and scientific expectations. *His claim that mental illness is a myth must then be interpreted as an injunction about how psychotherapists are to act.* Somewhat on the analogy of the priest's absolute commitment to the seal of confession, whatever the consequences, in order to protect a cardinal role of the priesthood, so, too, for Szasz the therapist must protect the autonomy that grounds the role of psychotherapist so as to make possible the growth of the autonomy of the analysand. . . . for Szasz the role of psychotherapist is defined and sustained through an adamant refusal to allow the role to be conflated with any other relationship with the patient or client, in particular a physician/patient relationship. It is for this reason that Szasz construes suicide threats in terms of the free choices that confront a patient. As he puts it, "only if the patient is deeply convinced that the analyst respects his autonomy, including his right to take his own life, can he engage effectively in the analytic exploration and mastery of his ideas about suicide" (emphasis added).

This is a faultless representation of my approach to therapy. Again, my only disagreement with Engelhardt is that he recasts my categorical rejection of the concept of mental illness as a tactically necessary "as-if" proposition. We must pretend, but not claim, that mental illness does not exist:

> Given this Kantian-Jacksonian recasting of Szasz, Szasz can provide a theoretical basis for holding that psychotherapy has a very special role that is *strategically brought into question* when the psychotherapist also plays the role of physician and addresses problems as if they were illnesses. However, as just noted, this heuristic, methodological distinction between treating disease and aiding autonomous persons with their bad habits and problems in living *does not exclude biologically oriented psychiatrists from diagnosing a patient's problems a disease and then treating it biologically*" (emphasis added).

Engelhardt's last remark is a *non-sequitur*. In a free society, client and therapist ought to be free to regard the patient's problem any way they choose, as medical, moral, religious, legal, political, whatever. Engelhardt's next interpretation of my views is inaccurate in ways I have discussed earlier. Again, the reason, I believe, is his desire to defend the validity of the concept of mental illness as a disease in the medical sense. He writes:

> Szasz is not committed to denying the obvious, namely, that various forms of biologically-based therapy do indeed treat psychiatric diseases, which appear to be illnesses on a close analogy with those treated in other areas of medicine. The advances in biological psychiatry demonstrate that it is a myth to hold that mental illness is a myth in this straightforward sense. That is, Szasz need not be taken as denying the obvious (for example, there are mental diseases amenable to biological therapies), but as underscoring the importance of free and responsible choices and relationships. Szasz's reflections concerning mental illness as a myth provide the basis for recognizing psychotherapy's unique status and its important contributions to our culture.

IV

Engelhardt insists on using the term "mental illness" in much the same way that psychiatrists, journalists, and lay persons use it, that is, without defining it, without clearly saying what sorts of phenomena qualify as mental illnesses and why. As I noted, this may be because, in our therapeutic culture, the polarization between accepting and rejecting the reality of mental illness possesses a ceremonial-religious quality similar to the polarization, in a religious culture, between accepting and rejecting the reality of God. In the religious culture, the person who rejects God is shunned by the opinion-makers of society. In the therapeutic culture, the person who rejects mental illness suffers a similar fate.

Not by coincidence, neither the idea of God nor the idea of mental illness is susceptible to definition. Jews cannot—are not even permitted to—name their deity. That willful inability to name the "sacred" characterizes ideas, words, and symbols whose function is purely ceremonial-social: their aim is to identify and unite a community of believers, not convey cognitive content.

Like theists unable and unwilling to define god, psychiatrists are unable and unwilling to define mental illness. Not only does Engelhardt use the term "mental illness" without defining it, he does not mention that psychiatrists do not and cannot define it. In fact, with a kind of perverse twist of logic, psychiatrists are proud of their inability to define the characteristics of the "species" that they place in the genus they call "mental disorders."

In the Introduction to the fourth edition of the American Psychiatric Association's *Diagnostic and Statistical Manual of Mental Disorders—IV*, the authors state: "Although this volume is titled the *Diagnostic and Statistical Manual of Mental Disorders,* the term *mental disorder* unfortunately implies a distinction between 'mental' disorder and 'physical' disorder, that is a reductionistic anachronism of mind/body dualism."[12] Allen J. Frances, professor of psychiatry at Duke University Medical Center and Chair of the *DSM-IV* Task Force, writes: "*DSM-IV* is a manual of *mental* disorders, but it is by no means clear just what *is* a mental disorder . . . There could arguably not be a worse term than *mental disorder* to describe the conditions classified in *DSM-IV.*"[13]

If the word "mental," as Frances says, "implies a mind-body dichotomy that is becoming increasingly outmoded,"[14] then we would expect a special catalogue of *mental* diseases to be phased out, instead of being steadily enlarged. Frances, speaking for the APA, laments the inappropriateness of the term "mental illness," yet both insist on preserving it. It is a sacred symbol they dare not cast off.[15]

The view that psychiatric diagnoses are the names of "neurobiological diseases," treatable with drugs, is now a defining element of what counts as correct psychiatric practice. In the 1999 Annual Report of the Eli Lilly Company, Prozac, Zyprexa, and Olanzapine are classed as drugs used for *"Neuroscience Disorders,"*[16] a remarkable honorific for chemical stimulants and straitjackets. Lilly's other products are categorized as drugs used in "Animal Health," "Diabetes Care," "Oncology," and "Primary Care." The terms "Science" and "Disorder" appear only in connection with psychiatric products. The disorders Lilly classifies as "Neuroscience Disorders" not only match the names of disorders listed in the *DSM,* but include "treatment resistant depression," evidently treatable—with a drug.

---

[12] American Psychiatric Association, "Introduction," in *Diagnostic and Statistical Manual of Mental Disorders—IV* (Washington, D.C.: American Psychiatric Association, 1994), pp. xxi, xxv.

[13] Allen J. Frances, "Foreword," in J.Z. Sadder, O.P. Wigging, and M.A. Schwartz, eds., *Philosophical Perspectives on Psychiatric Diagnostic Classification* (Baltimore: Johns Hopkins University Press, 1994), pp. vii–ix; p. viii.

[14] *Ibid.*

[15] Thomas Szasz, *Schizophrenia: The Sacred Symbol of Schizophrenia* (Syracuse: Syracuse University Press, 1988 [1976]).

[16] Lilly, *1999 Annual Report*, (Indianapolis: Eli Lilly and Company, 2000), pp. 14–15, emphasis added. See also www.lilly.com.

The use of the term "mental illness" requires piling inconsistencies upon inconsistencies. Since the first edition of the DSM, each successive edition contained more illnesses than its predecessor. Nevertheless, at a meeting of the New Clinical Drug Evaluation Unit of the National Institute of Mental Health in 2002, Dr. Arif Khan—associated with the Northwest Clinical Research Center in Bellevue, Washington—presented the goals for drafting *DSM-V*. In first place, he listed: "Basic Nomenclature Issues of DSM-V. . . . How to define 'mental disorder.' DSM has never contained a detailed definition that is useful as a criterion for deciding what is, or is not, a mental disorder. A useful definition should be developed."[17] A laudable idea, indeed.

Similar problems of definition plague the term "psychoanalysis." Physics is the study of matter and energy. Biology is the study of living things. But what is psychoanalysis? Who speaks for psychoanalysis?

We are familiar with the many contradictory things Freud said about it and the many diverse practices he engaged in, calling them all "psychoanalysis." The term is used to refer to a method of diagnosing mental illnesses, treating such alleged maladies, explaining and influencing the behaviors of human beings, detecting mental illnesses in historic personages and other dead persons as well as in characters invented by poets and writers, interpreting the "meaning" of works of art, and to many other ideas and interventions as well. My point is that, although the term "psychoanalysis" is widely used, it is never used to name the kind of human helping situation that I describe in *The Ethics of Psychoanalysis*. The situation reminds me of Gilbert K. Chesterton's famous remark, "Christianity has not been tried and found wanting; it has been found difficult and not tried."[18] My ideal (or idealized) version of psychoanalysis has never been embraced by psychoanalysts or any other group of practitioners and, in that sense, has never been tried.

Actually, organized psychoanalysis is moving away as fast as it can from the image that I painted of it.[19] Dick Fox, president of the American Psychoanalytic Association in 2001, proudly declares: "Psychoanalysis today is a far cry from what it was thirty to forty years

---

[17] Quoted in Carl Sherman, "Antisuicidal Effect of Psychotropics Remains Uncertain," *Clinical Psychiatry News* 30:8 (August, 2002); http://www2.eclinicalpsychiatrynews.com/scripts/om.dll/serve

[18] http://www.quotegallery.com/asp/quotesalpha.asp?letter=C&curpage=4

[19] See Irving Louis Horowitz, "Szasz Against the Theorists," *Chronicles* (January, 1996), pp. 23–26.

ago . . . We lobby in Washington . . . We work with other groups such as the ACLU to further our goals."[20] What goals? One of the goals of the ACLU is to formulate commitment laws, the better to justify incarcerating individuals accused of mental illness.[21] Fox also tells us that the American Psychoanalytic Association no longer bars psychologists and other non-physicians from membership: "We have extended our membership . . . We have shed our medical orthodoxy . . ."[22]

Yet, it would be a grave mistake to conclude that psychoanalysts acknowledge that problems in living are not diseases and that listening-and-talking is not a medical procedure. On the contrary, analysts have expanded the concepts of disease and treatment and claim that "psychotherapy changes the brain," which in turn proves that they are treating real diseases. In a paper titled, "Psychoanalysis and psychotherapy: Long-term outcome," delivered at the 2002 annual meeting of the American Psychiatric Association, Glen Gabbard, M.D., Professor of Psychiatry and Director, Baylor Psychiatry Clinic and one of the leading psychoanalysts in the United States, explained that recent studies "suggested that behavior therapy and drug therapy were affecting the same brain areas and in the same manner. . . . Psychotherapy seems capable of favorably influencing the minds and bodies of persons with bodily diseases and perhaps is even capable of countering those diseases. . . . [It is important] to get scientific results that lend credibility to psychotherapy as a *real treatment*."[23]

Clearly, the labels "psychoanalysis" and "psychoanalytic" continue to be attached to virtually every idea and action that pertains to evaluating, judging, justifying, rationalizing, glorifying, demonizing, and otherwise influencing the beliefs and behaviors of individuals and groups.

The fact that my response to Engelhardt is longer than his contribution is primarily an expression of my esteem for his contributions to the philosophy of medicine and psychiatry. I have written such a long

---

[20] Dick Fox, "Will the Real Psychoanalyst Please Stand Up?" *American Psychoanalyst* 35:27 (2001).

[21] See Charles L. Markmann, *The Noblest Cry: A History of the American Civil Liberties Union* (New York: St. Martin's Press, 1965), and Thomas Szasz, "The ACLU's Mental Illness Cop-out," *Reason* (January 1974), pp. 4–9; reprinted in Szasz, *The Therapeutic State: Psychiatry in the Mirror of Current Events* (Buffalo: Prometheus, 1984), pp. 58–66.

[22] Dick Fox., *op. cit.*

[23] Quoted in Joan Arehart-Treichel, "Evidence Is In: Psychotherapy Changes the Brain," *Psychiatric News* 36:33 (July 6th, 2001), emphasis added.

response to Engelhardt primarily because of the importance of his contributions to the philosophy of medicine and psychiatry and secondarily because I have used it, as I have used some of my other replies in this volume, as an opportunity to clarify subtle but important issues about mental illness and psychotherapy.

Appendix

Documents from the Szasz Affair at Upstate

Spelling and grammatical errors and other infelicities have been retained in the following documents.

Letter from Hoch to Hollender, 21st November, 1962

STATE OF NEW YORK
DEPARTMENT OF MENTAL HYGIENE
ALBANY

November 21, 1962

Marc Hollender, M.D.
Director
Syracuse Psychiatric Hospital
Syracuse, New York

Dear Dr. Hollender:

At our recent meeting in Albany, we discussed the situation relating to Dr. Thomas Szasz. I told you that Dr. Szasz is entitled to his opinion but that I cannot agree that he should teach in the framework of the Department of Mental Hygiene and instruct our residents that, as I understand him, that mental diseases do not exist and therefore installations for the treatment of mental disorders are a detriment to their welfare.

I have no authority about Dr. Szass' teachings in the medical
school, but I hereby direct you to terminate Dr. Szass' to the residents
of the state institutions and to any personnel which is employed by the
Department of Mental Hygiene of the State of New York.

Very truly yours,
(signed)
PAUL H. HOCH, M.D.
Commissioner

Memo from Hollender to Szasz, 26th November, 1962

To: Thomas Szasz, M.D.   November 26, 1962
From: Marc H. Hollender, M.D.

As Director of the Syracuse Psychiatric Hospital, I have been directed
by the Commissioner of the Department of Mental Hygiene of the
State of New York to inform you that you can no longer conduct your
seminar for residents of the Upstate Medical Center at the Syracuse
Psychiatric Hospital.

As Chairman of the Department of Psychiatry at the Upstate
Medical Center, I have asked Dr. Robinson to arrange for another
room in which you can conduct your seminar.

(signed)
Marc H. Hollender, M.D.

Letter from Thirteen Residents to Szasz, 5th March, 1963

Syracuse, N.Y.
March 6, 1963

Dear Dr. Szasz,

We have written 3 letters, all essentially worded the same, protesting the injunction against your teaching at SPH. These letters were addressed to:

Dr. Robert King, Chairman of Committee A of the AAUP.
Dr. Paul Hoch
Governor Nelson Rockefeller

We are enclosing copies of two of these.

Very truly yours,

THE THIRTEEN SIGNERS

"THE THIRTEEN SIGNERS" were Kenneth R. Barney, M.D., Andrew C. Godwin, M.D., Samuel Graceffo, M.D., Steven J. Hirsch, M.D., Arthur P. Kraut, M.D., Jonathan S. Malev, M.D., Barton Pakull, M.D., Norman H. Pearl, M.D., Bennett L. Rosner, M.D., Frank Soults, M.D., William A. Tucker, M.D., Roy M. Waldman, M.D., and Howard Weinberg, M.D. Drs. King, Hoch and Governor Rockefeller were asked to address their correspondence to "THE THIRTEEN SIGNERS," in care of Kenneth R. Barney, M.D., 18 Caton Drive, Syracuse 14, New York.

Letter from Thirteen Residents to Hoch, 5th March, 1963

Dear Dr. Hoch:

On Monday, November 26, 1962, we, the undersigned, were
informed that Professor Thomas S. Szasz was barred from teaching his
course in psychotherapy on the premises of the Syracuse Psychiatric
Hospital by a directive from the Commissioner of Mental Hygiene of
the State of New York. To prevent a university professor from teaching
anywhere is a serious matter.

We find it hard to believe that Professor Szasz was barred from
teaching because he is against the involuntary hospitalization of
mental patients, or because he minces no words in stating his position,
or because there is fear that his views might corrupt the minds of
young residents. We find it hard to believe that the spokesmen for one
of the most progressive state hospital programs in the United States
must resort to fighting theoretical issues or even verbal invective with
political sanctions. We find it hard to believe that the position of the
New York State Department of Mental Hygiene is such that it cannot
defend itself against words with words, but must resort to action. We
find all this hard to believe, but what else can we think.

It is not our purpose to take sides. It seems to us that if Dr. Szasz
is disposed to make embarrassing or even imprudent public statements
about the State Hospital System (thereby perhaps threatening the
availability of State Hospital Staff), you may well consider it in your
best interests to try to silence him.

However, we don't believe your method accomplishes its purpose.
You compromise yourself in the eyes of many by this action, for what
practitioners of our science would be willing to subject themselves to
an institution that curtails freedom of expression? Furthermore Dr.
Szasz is not hurt by your attempts to restrict him as much as we
residents are, because Dr. Szasz' 'political' views in psychiatry are
in no way a reflection of his competence to teach a course in
psychotherapy which is considered by us to be the highlight course
of the residency program.

If it is your purpose to have us, in turn, exert pressure upon Dr.
Szasz to recant, then we must register a vigorous protest at being used

in this way. Also, as physicians, we resent the implication, even if unintentional, that we may somehow be influenced or tainted by Szaszian heresy. We are quite able to evaluate, accept, or reject ideas, even when expounded by the most convincing and influential personalities.

If Dr. Szasz' techniques of criticism result in personal affronts and hurts, then such matters should be handled by the individuals involved, rather than by quasi-political maneuvers involving others. It is our sincere hope that the directive against Professor Szasz will be rescinded, for it is freedom of expression without fear of reprisal that is the real issue, not Dr. Szasz' views. Without freedom of expression, psychiatry can lay no claim to science. We are not so much afraid for Dr. Szasz, we are afraid for psychiatry.

Respectfully,

Residents in Psychiatry
State University of New York
Upstate Medical Center
Syracuse, New York

Letter from Hoch to Barney, 2nd April, 1963

Paul H. Hoch, M.D.
Commissioner
State of New York
Department of Mental Hygiene
Albany

April 2, 1963

Dr. Kenneth R. Barney
18 Caton Drive
Syracuse 14, New York

Dear Dr. Barney:

On receipt of your letter, the entire situation with regard to Dr. Thomas Szasz and the Syracuse Psychiatric Hospital was again reviewed and I would outline the situation in the following manner.

The Syracuse Psychiatric Hospital is one of the institutions of the Department of Mental Hygiene located in the immediate vicinity of the University and the Medical School in order to provide a good liason with the teaching facility, but its primary purpose is to serve as a center for the Upstate Psychiatric Institutions of the Department and to provide instruction and assistance to these institutions in the development of their programs. The organization of the hospital is based on this function and the academic personnel who take part in the program do so by virtue of appointments at the hospital and not by an extension of academic appointment in the Medical School. For this reason any action with regard to such persons is not felt to reflect on their academic position. The arrangement between the Hospital and Medical School is a cooperative one based on mutual respect and consideration and has been very successful over the years, but its basic nature remains unchanged. Particularly, it should be noted, that the Department of Mental Hygiene does not confer academic status, but, through its institutions, makes arrangements with various consultants and instructors to carry on functions at a service level.

This should be kept in mind with regard to the problem raised in connection with Dr. Szasz. The Department had for some time been increasingly disturbed about reports and complaints from a number of reliable sources to the effect that Dr. Szasz was conducting teaching sessions at the Syracuse Psychiatric Hospital in such a way as to embarrass the residents and the other medical personnel of the State institutions who took part in the program, some of them on a full-time basis for a period of months and others on the basis of sessions once a week. These men were profoundly disturbed by various statements from a physician who held Professorial rank in the Medical School.

The Department was reluctant to take action on these complaints or even give them full credence and delayed for some time until Dr. Szasz by his own public and recorded utterances, made is quite clear that these were really his opinions and that he felt very strong about them and there could no longer be any doubt about the substance of the complaints which had been made.

Dr. Szasz, speaking of State hospitals, said that, '. . . there are hospitals in this country where there are three or four or 10,000 patients in the hands of so-called psychiatrists.'

Speaking of New York State psychiatrists, he said, ' . . . and the only less qualified, less well-recommended, psychiatrists go to the State hospitals. The better psychiatrists have become psychoanalytical in their private practice where they can make three times as much more money, have more prestige, have a nicer life.' Speaking again of State hospital psychiatrists, he said, 'I think they harm patients.' Further on he said, 'No, I don't believe in diagnosis, no. I know how to make one. It is an article of faith. I disbelieve in it. I know what it is, just like I know what witches are.'

Elsewhere in his testimony, he stressed, 'I am expressing a personal opinion to which I have given much thought,' and the Department must conclude that these opinions are indeed his considered opinions.

Speaking of a psychiatric evaluation presented in the courtroom, he characterized it as 'gobbledygoop,' 'hot air,' and 'junk' and defined 'psychiatric hot air' in the following answer: 'Psychiatric hot air is this——cremating (creating?) worthless psychiatric terms which they relate with sneering, palpebral fissure—junk. Those terms which create the feeling that you are dealing with some sort of monster who is flexing his eyelids.'

Subsequently, he made a comment concerning treatment which could be extremely disruptive if taken literally by the medical staffs of the State hospitals, 'I would consider that blocking the laws of liberty, being called a psychiatric patient, when one does not want to be called a psychiatric patient, being give drugs—psychiatric drugs when one doesn't want psychiatric drugs—I would consider all of these things together as brutality, yes.'

Finally, he was asked 'even though you think that there is psychiatric brutality in Marcy State Hospital, even though you think that there are psychiatrists that are fairly incompetent in Marcy State Hospital, even though you think a person may be half sane when goes into Marcy Satate Hospital and when he comes back he is more insane than when he went in, you have not made any recommendations to the authorities in Marcy State Hospital, is that correct?' He answered, 'That's correct. I was never asked for any.'

He finally made the remark that he would not want to be caught dead as an employee in a mental hospital or as a patient.

Certainly, in spite of all protests about his opinions, it is understandable that in an academic setting it is necessary to give them very wide latitude as expressions of academic opinion. However, the Department of Mental Hygiene feels that the setting of the Syracuse Psychiatric Hospital does not confer a degree of freedom which permits instruction that it finds medically unacceptable and needlessly embarrassing to those who come for instruction, and for this reason the Department asked the Director to take the necessary action in the interests of the many thousands of patients who must be served by these psychiatrists and must be cared for in these institutions. This action was considered to be in relation to the service functions of the Department and has no implications with regard to academic status elsewhere.

In closing, I would say that the Department feels strongly that the difference between academic freedom and license should be clearly defined. They express some doubt whether even in academic circles a teacher should be permitted to speak about a school and its personnel and its procedures in terms parallel to those which Dr. Szasz has used in establishing his thesis that 'mental illness is a myth' and that psychiatry in the State mental hospital is a 'threat to civil liberties.'

Dr. Henry Brill, Deputy Commissioner of the Department, discussed these matters at great length with one of the groups of

psychiatric residents shortly after the question arose and I believe
he would be willing to meet also with your group in order to explain
more fully the Department's attitude and the action which it felt forced
to take in making this very difficult decision.

>Very truly yours,
>(signed)
>PAUL H. HOCH, M.D.
>Commissioner

Letter from Halpern to Eugene Kaplan, 11th May, 1963

A.L. Halpern, M.D.
502 Scott Avenue
Syracuse 3, N.Y.

Granite 6-8030

May 11, 1963

Dear Doctor Kaplan,

As you undoubtedly know, a rapidly spreading anti-mental
health movement is interfering with the development of psychiatric
services in some of our states. This problem is of particular interest
to me in my capacity of director of community mental health services
for Onondoga County.

Before leaving for the American Psychiatric Association meeting
last weekend, I decided to mail a number of copies of the pamphlet
"Mind Tapping," even though I did not have time to write an
explanatory note. I wanted to better acquaint people with the role
played by one of our own colleagues in this movement. The additional
pamphlet I sent was intended to show the affiliation of the American
Opinion Library with the John Birch Society.

I am now enclosing a copy of Professor Weihofen's letter published in the March, 1963, issue of the American Journal of Psychiatry; it points out some of the fallacies contained in the "Mind Tapping" article.

I would welcome any comments you may have on the subject of the opposition to psychiatry within our own ranks.

Sincerely yours,
[signed Abe Halpern]

Bibliography of Thomas Szasz

Compiled by Jeffrey A. Schaler,
with the assistance of Antonio F. Mastroniani

1947a.　The "Schemm Regime" in the Treatment of Extreme Congestive Heart Failure: A Case Report. With S. Elgart. *Ohio State Medical Journal* 43 (September), 926–28.

1947b.　The Role of Hostility in the Pathogenesis of Peptic Ulcer: Theoretical Considerations, with the Report of a Case. With E. Levin, J.B. Kirsner, and W.L. Palmer. *Psychosomatic Medicine* 9 (September–October), 331–36.

1948a.　Psychiatric Aspects of Vagotomy: A Preliminary Report. *Annals of Internal Medicine* 28 (February), 279–288.

1948b.　Psychiatric Aspects of Vagotomy: II. A Psychiatric Study of Vagotomized Ulcer Patients with Comments on Prognosis. *Psychosomatic Medicine* 11 (July–August), 187–199.

1949a.　Factors in the Pathogenesis of Peptic Ulcer. *Psychosomatic Medicine* 11 (September–October), 300–04.

1949b.　Psychiatric Aspects of Vagotomy: IV. Phantom Ulcer Pain. *Archives of Neurology and Psychiatry* 62 (December), 728–733.

1950a.　Psychosomatic Aspects of Salivary Activity: I. Hypersalivation in Patients with Peptic Ulcer. *Proceedings of the Association for Research in Nervous and Mental Disease* 29, 647–655.

1950b.　A Theory of the Pathogenesis of Ordinary Human Baldness. With A. Robertson. *Archives of Dermatology and Syphilology* 61 (January), 34–48.

1950b.　Psychosomatic Aspects of Salivary Activity: II. Psychoanalytic Observations concerning Hypersalivation. *Psychosomatic Medicine* 12 (September–October), 320–331.

1951a.　Physiological and Psychodynamic Mechanisms in Constipation and Diarrhea. *Psychosomatic Medicine* 13 (March–April), 112–16.

1951b.　Oral Mechanisms in Constipation and Diarrhea. *International Journal of Psychoanalysis* 32, 196–203.

1952a.　On the Psychoanalytic Theory of Instincts. *Psychoanalytic Quarterly* 21 (January), 25–48.

1952b.   Psychoanalysis and the Autonomic Nervous System. *Psychoanalytic Review* 39 (April), 115–151.

1952c.   Psychiatric Aspects of Vagotomy: III. The Problem of Diarrhea After Vagotomy. *Journal of Nervous and Mental Diseases* 115 (May), 394–405.

1952d.   The Psychosomatic Approach in Medicine. With Franz Alexander. In Franz Alexander and Helen Ross, eds., *Dynamic Psychiatry* (Chicago: University of Chicago Press), 369–400.

1952e.   Psychosomatic Research. In Franz Alexander and Helen Ross, eds., *Twenty Years of Psychoanalysis* (New York: Norton), 268–280.

1955a.   Entropy, Organization, and the Problem of the Economy of Human Relationships. *International Journal of Psychoanalysis* 36, 289–297.

1955b.   The Nature of Pain. *A.M.A. Archives of Neurology and Psychiatry* 74 (August), 174–181.

1955c.   The Ego, the Body, and Pain. *Journal of the American Psychoanalytic Association* 3, 177–200.

1956a.   On the Experiences of the Analyst in the Psychoanalytic Situation: A Contribution to the Theory of Psychoanalytic Treatment. *Journal of the American Psychoanalytic Association* 4, 197–223.

1956b.   Is the Concept of Entropy Relevant to Psychology and Psychiatry? *Psychiatry* 19, 199–202.

1956c.   Some Observations on the Relationship between Psychiatry and the Law. *A.M.A. Archives of Neurology and Psychiatry* 75 (March), 297–315.

1956d.   A Contribution to the Philosophy of Medicine: The Basic Models of the Doctor Patient Relationship. With Marc Hollender. *A.M.A. Archives of Internal Medicine* 97 (May), 585–592.

1956e.   Malingering: Diagnosis or Social Condemnation? *A.M.A Archives of Neurology and Psychiatry* 76 (October), 432–443.

1956f.   Comments on The Definition of Psychosomatic Disorder. *British Journal for the Philosophy of Science* 7, 231–34.

1957a.   Some Observations on the Use of Tranquilizing Drugs. *A.M.A Archives of Neurology and Psychiatry* 77 (January), 86–92.

1957b.   The Psychology of Bodily Feelings in Schizophrenia. *Psychosomatic Medicine* 19,1116.

1957c.   A Contribution to the Psychology of Bodily Feelings. *Psychoanalytic Quarterly* 26, 25–49.

1957d.   A Critical Analysis of the Fundamental Concepts of Psychical Research. *Psychiatric Quarterly* 31, 96–108.

1957e.   On the Theory of Psycho-Analytic Treatment. *International Journal of Psychoanalysis* 38, 166–182.

1957f.   A Contribution to the Psychology of Schizophrenia. *A.M.A Archives of Neurology and Psychiatry* 77 (April), 420–436.

1957g.   *Pain and Pleasure: A Study of Bodily Feelings*. New York: Basic Books.

1957h. Commitment of the Mentally Ill: Treatment or Social Restraint? *Journal of Nervous and Mental Disease* 125 (April–June), 293–307.

1957i. Review of *The Criminal, the Judge, and the Public*, by Franz Alexander and Hugo Staub. *A.M.A Archives of Neurology and Psychiatry* 78 (July), 109–111.

1957j. The Concept of Testamentary Capacity: Further Observations on the Role of Psychiatric Concepts in Legal Situations. *Journal of Nervous and Mental Disease* 125 (July–September), 474–77.

1957k. Psychiatric Expert Testimony: Its Covert Meaning and Social Function. *Psychiatry* 20 (August), 313–16.

1957l. Review of Psychiatric Research Reports Nos. 2, 4, and 6. *Mental Hygiene* 41 (October), 583–84.

1957m. Normality, Neurosis, and Psychosis: Some Observations on the Concepts of Mental Health and Mental Illness. With Marc Hollender. *Journal of Nervous and Mental Disease* 125 (October–December), 599–607.

1957n. The Problem of Psychiatric Nosology: A Contribution to a Situational Analysis of Psychiatric Operations. *American Journal of Psychiatry* 114 (November), 405–413.

1957o. Review of *Psychical Research* by R.C. Johnson. *American Journal of Psychiatry* 114 (November), 475–76.

1958a. Psychiatry, Ethics, and the Criminal Law. *Columbia Law Review* 58 (February), 183–198.

1958b. Scientific Method and Social Role in Medicine and Psychiatry. *A.M.A. Archives of Internal Medicine* 101 (February), 228–238.

1958c. Men and Machines. *British Journal for the Philosophy of Science* 8 (February), 310–17.

1958d. Psychoanalysis as Method and as Theory. *Psychoanalytic Quarterly* 27, 89–97.

1958e. The Role of the Counterphobic Mechanism in Addiction. *Journal of the American Psychoanalytic Association* 6, 309–325.

1958f. Reply to Ian Stevenson, M.D. [Letters] *American Journal of Psychiatry* 114 (March), 847–48.

1958g. Recent Books on the Relation of Psychiatry to Criminology. *Psychiatry* 21 (August), 307–319.

1958h. Psycho-Analytic Training: A Socio-Psychological Analysis of Its History and Present Status. *International Journal of Psychoanalysis* 39, 598–613.

1958i. The Doctor-Patient Relationship and Its Historical Context. With Mark Hollender and Fritz Knoff. *American Journal of Psychiatry* 115 (December), 522–528.

1958j. Review of *Studies on Hysteria*, by Joseph Breuer and Sigmund Freud. *American Journal of Psychiatry* 115 (December), 568–69.

1958k.   Politics and Mental Health: Some Remarks Apropos of the Case of Mr. Ezra Pound. *American Journal of Psychiatry* 115 (December), 508–511.

1959a.   A Critical Analysis of Some Aspects of the Libido Theory: The Concepts of Libidinal Zones, Aims, and Modes of Gratification. *Annals of the New York Academy of Sciences* 76 (23rd January), 975–990. Discussion, 990–1009.

1959b.   The Classification of Mental Illness. A Situational Analysis of Psychiatric Operations. *Psychiatric Quarterly* 33 (January), 77–101.

1959c.   Law for the Mentally Ill. [Letters] *New York Times* (20th February), 24.

1959d.   Psychoanalysis and Medicine. In Morton Levitt, ed., *Readings in Psychoanalytic Psychology* (New York: Appleton-Century-Crofts), 355–374.

1959e.   Pound, Politics, and Mental Health. [Letters] *American Journal of Psychiatry* 115 (May), 1040–41.

1959f.   Review of *Economics of Mental Illness*, by Rashi Fein. *A.M.A. Archives of General Psychiatry* 1 (July), 116–18.

1959g.   Language and Pain. In S. Arieti, ed., *American Handbook of Psychiatry* (New York: Basic Books), vol. 1, 982–999.

1959h.   Introduction. In Ernst Mach, *The Analysis of Sensations and the Relation of the Physical to the Psychical*. Trans. from the First German Edition by C.M. Williams; Revised and Supplemented from the Fifth German Edition by S. Waterlow (New York: Dover), v–xxxi.

1959i.   Recollections of a Psychoanalytic Psychotherapy: The Case of Prisoner K. In A. Burton, ed., *Case Studies in Counseling and Psychotherapy* (Englewood Cliffs: Prentice-Hall), 75–110.

1959j.   What Is Malingering? *Medical Trial Technique Quarterly* 6 (September), 29–40.

1959k.   Psychiatry, Psychotherapy, and Psychology. *A.M.A. Archives of General Psychiatry* 1 (November), 455–463.

1959l.   The Communication of Distress Between Child and Parent. *British Journal of Medical Psychology* 32, 161–170.

1960a.   Mach and Psychoanalysis. *Journal of Nervous and Mental Disease* 130 (January), 6–15.

1960b.   Psychiatry Shouldn't Interfere with the Law. [Letters] *New York Herald Tribune* (5th February), 10.

1960c.   The Myth of Mental Illness. *American Psychologist* 15 (February), 113–18.

1960d.   Freedom and the Physician's Role. [Letters] *Journal of the American Medical Association* 173 (7th May), 84–85.

1960e.   Hospital Refusal to Release Mental Patient. *Cleveland Marshall Law Review* 9 (May), 220–26.

1960f.   Moral Conflict and Psychiatry. *Yale Review* 49 (June), 555–566.

1960g. Three Problems in Contemporary Psychoanalytic Training. *A.M.A. Archives of General Psychiatry* 3 (July), 82–94.

1960h. Civil Liberties and Mental Illness: Some Observations on the Case of Miss Edith L. Hough. *Journal of Nervous and Mental Disease* 131 (July), 58–63.

1960i. Civil Liberties and the Mentally Ill. *Cleveland-Marshall Law Review* 10 (September), 399–416.

1960j. The Right to Commit a Crime. *Current* (September), 53–54.

1960k. The Ethics of Birth Control—Or: Who Owns Your Body? *Humanist* 20 (November–December), 332–36.

1961a. The Uses of Naming and the Origin of the Myth of Mental Illness. *American Psychologist* 16 (February), 59–65.

1961b. Hospital-Patient Relationships in Medicine and Psychiatry. *Mental Hygiene* 45 (April), 171–79.

1961c. Review of *The Couch and the Circle* and *One for All,*, by Hyman Spotnitz. *New York Times Book Review* (14th May), 7.

1961d. The Meaning of Suffering in Therapy: A Round Table Discussion. *American Journal of Psychoanalysis* 21, 12–17.

1961e. *The Myth of Mental Illness: Foundations of a Theory of Personal Conduct.* New York: Paul B. Hoeber.

1961f. Two Types of Therapy. [Letters] *New York Times Book Review* (11th June), 28–30.

1961g. Criminal Responsibility and Psychiatry. In H. Toch, ed., *Legal and Criminal Psychology.* New York: Holt, Rinehart, and Winston, 146–168.

1962a. Who Has a Right to an Abortion? *Current* (December), 52–53.

1962b. The Problem of Privacy in Training Analysis: Selections from a Questionnaire Study of Psychoanalytic Practices and Opinions. *Psychiatry* 2 (August), 195–207.

1962c. Psychiatry as a Social Institution. In H. Schoeck and J.W. Wiggins, eds., *Psychiatry and Responsibility* (Princeton: Van Nostrand), 1–18.

1962d. Review of *Pain: Its Modes and Functions*, by F.J.J. Buytendijk. *A.M.A Archives of General Psychiatry* 7 (September), 220.

1962e. Bootlegging Humanistic Values through Psychiatry. *Antioch Review* 22 (Fall), 341–49.

1962d. Mind Tapping: Psychiatric Subversion of Constitutional Rights. *American Journal of Psychiatry* 119 (October), 323–27.

1962e. Human Nature and Psychotherapy: A Further Contribution to the Theory of Autonomous Psychotherapy. *Comprehensive Psychiatry* 3 (October), 268–283.

1962f. Open Doors or Civil Rights for Mental Patients? *Journal of Individual Psychology* 18 (November), 168–171.

1963a. Psychiatry's Threat to Civil Liberties. *National Review* (12th March), 191–93.

1963b. Mind Tapping. [Letters] *American Journal of Psychiatry* 119 (March), 900.

1963c. Psychiatry in Public Schools. *Humanist* 23 (May–June), 89–93.

1963d. Freud as Leader. *Antioch Review* 23 (Summer), 133–144.

1963e. Psychoanalytic Treatment as Education. *A.M.A. Archives of General Psychiatry* 9 (July), 46–52.

1963f. Foreword. In N.H. Pronko, *A Textbook of Abnormal Psychology* (Baltimore: Williams Wilkins), vii–viii.

1963g. Psychoanalysis and Suggestion: An Historical and Logical Analysis. *Comprehensive Psychiatry* 4 (August), 271–280.

1963h. A Questionnaire Study of Psychoanalytic Practices and Opinions. With Robert Nemiroff. *Journal of Nervous and Mental Diseases* 137 (September), 209–221.

1963i. *Law, Liberty, and Psychiatry: An Inquiry into the Social Uses of Mental Health Practices.* New York: Macmillan.

1963j. The Concept of Transference. *International Journal of Psychoanalysis* 44, 432–443.

1963k. Discussion of "Papers on Schizophrenia," by Arieti, Bychowski, and Sechehaye. *Psychiatric Research Report APA* 17 (November), 57–60.

1963l. Should Insanity Be an Excuse for Crime? *North American Newspaper Alliance* (28th December).

1964a. What Psychiatry Can and Cannot Do. *Harpers Magazine* 228 (February), 50–53.

1964b. What Psychiatry Can Do. *Harpers Magazine* 228 (April), 100, 50–53.

1964c. A Question of Identity. *New York Times Book Review* (5th April), 14–16.

1964d. Review of *The Birth and Death of Meaning* and *The Revolution in Psychiatry*, by Ernest Becker. *The Behavior Sciences Book Service* (October).

1964e. Psychoanalysis and Taxation: A Contribution to the Rhetoric of the Disease Concept in Psychiatry. *American Journal of Psychotherapy* 18 (October), 635–643.

1964f. Criminal Insanity: Fact or Strategy? *New Republic* (21st November), 19–22.

1964g. The Moral Dilemma of Psychiatry: Autonomy or Heteronomy? *American Journal of Psychiatry* 121 (December), 521–28.

1965a. Psychiatry as Ideology, In Hector Hawton, ed., *The Rationalist Annual* (London: Pemberton), 43–52.

1965b. Legal and Moral Aspects of Homosexuality. In Judd Marmor, ed., *Sexual Inversion: The Multiple Roots of Homosexuality* (New York: Basic Books), 124–139.

1965c. A Strategy of Freedom: The Moral Dimension of Freudian Therapy. *Trans-Action* 2 (May–June), 14–19.

1965d. *The Ethics of Psychoanalysis: The Theory and Method of Autonomous Psychotherapy*. New York: Basic Books.

1965e. A Note on Psychiatric Rhetoric. *American Journal of Psychiatry* 121 (June), 119–293.

1965f. *Psychiatric Justice*. New York: Macmillan.

1965g. Portrait of a Secular Moralist. *New Republic* (27th November), 32–33.

1965h. Toward the Therapeutic State. *New Republic* (11th December), 26–29.

1965i. Review of *The Addict and the Law*, by Alfred R. Lindesmith. *American University Law Review* 15 (December), 163–68.

1966a. Review of The Addict and the Law, by Alfred R. Lindesmith. *International Journal of the Addictions* 1 (January), 150–55.

1966b. Equation of Opposites. *New York Times Book Review* (6th February), 6.

1966c. Discussion of "The New Technology and Our Ageless Unconscious," by Martin Grotjahn. *Psychoanalytic Forum* 1, 15–16.

1966d. Unending Challenge. *New York Times Book Review* (17th April), 18, 20, 22.

1966e. The Mental Health Ethic. *National Review* (14th June), 570–72.

1966g. Is Mental Illness a Myth? [Letters] *New York Times Magazine* (3rd July), 433.

1966h. Is Mental Illness a Myth? [Letters] *New York Times Magazine* (10th July), 2.

1966i. Psychotherapy: A Socio-Cultural Perspective. *Western Medicine* 7 (December), 15–21.

1966j. Review of *Medical Orthodoxy and the Future of Psychoanalysis*, by K.R. Eissler. *Village Voice* (1st September), 5, 10–11.

1966k. The Ethics of Abortion. *Humanist* 26 (September–October), 147–48.

1966l. The Social Situation of the Hospitalized Mental Patient. *AAUW Journal* 60 (October), 31–32.

1966m. Whither Psychiatry? *Social Research* 33 (Autumn), 439–462.

1966n. There Was No Defense. *New York Times Book Review* (13th November), 4, 34.

1966o. Ezra Pound. [Letters] *New York Times Book Review* (11th December), 65.

1966p. Alcoholism: A Socio-Ethical Perspective. *Western Medicine* 7 (December), 15–21.

1966q. Discussion of "A Historical Review of Classification of Behavior and One Current Perspective," by Lewis L. Robbins. In Leonard D. Eron, ed., *The Classification of Behavior Disorders* (Chicago: Aldine), 38–41.

1966r. The Psychiatric Classification of Behavior: A Strategy of Personal Constraint. In Leonard D. Eron, ed., *The Classification of Behavior Disorders* (Chicago: Aldine), 123–170.

1967a. There Was No Defense. *Psychiatry and Social Science Review* 1 (January), 21–24.

1967b. Review of *The Trial of Ezra Pound*, by Julien Cornell. *Rutgers Law Review* 21 (Winter), 367–374.

1967c. Review of *Thomas Woodrow Wilson: Twenty-Eighth President of the United States*, by Sigmund Freud and William C. Bullitt. *Psychiatry and Social Science Review* 1 (February), 5, 10–12.

1967d. The Hazards of Zeal. *National Review* (21st March), 307–310.

1967e. Murder and Violence in the Affluent Society. *Boston Sunday Herald* (30th April), 18.

1967d. How Sick Is Sick? *New Republic* (6th May), 21–23.

1967e. The Doctor in the Case. *New York Times Book Review* (28th May), 8.

1967f. The Destruction of Differences. *New Republic* (10th June), 21–23.

1967g. Behavior Therapy and Psychoanalysis. *Medical Opinion and Review* 3 (June), 24–29.

1967h. Mental Illness. [Letters] *Economist* (17th June), 1192.

1967i. The Insanity Plea and the Insanity Verdict. *Temple Law Quarterly* 40 (Spring–Summer), 271–282.

1967k. Moral Man: A Model of Man for Humanistic Psychology. In James F.T. Bugental, ed., *Challenges of Humanistic Psychology* (New York: McGraw-Hill), 44–51.

1967k. Reply to Dr. Wladimir G. Eliasberg. [Letters] *American Journal of Psychiatry* 124 (September), 163.

1967l. Freedom and Goals. [Letters] *Medical Opinion and Review* 3 (September), 119–123.

1967m. Mental Illness as an Excuse for Civil Wrongs. With George J. Alexander. *Notre Dame Lawyer* 43 (October), 24–38.

1967n. The Psychiatrist: A Policeman in the Schools. *This Magazine Is About Schools* (October), 114–134.

1967o. Psychoanalysis and the Rule of Law. *Washburn Law Journal* 7 (Fall), 25–34.

1967q. College Psychiatrists. [Letters] *Transaction* 5 (December), 4.

1967q. Involuntary Mental Hospitalization: A Crime Against Humanity. *Exchange* (December), 14.

1968a. The Painful Person. *Lancet* 88 (January), 18–22.

1968b, Some Remarks on Autonomous Psychotherapy. *Psychiatric Opinion* 5 (January), 4, 68.

1968c. College Psychiatry: A Critique. *Comprehensive Psychiatry* 9 (January), 81–85.

1968d. Medical Ethics: An Historical Perspective. *Medical Opinion Review* 4 (February), 115–121.

1968e. Subversion of the Rule of Law. *National Review* (12th March), 247–48.

1968f. Science and Public Policy: The Crime of Involuntary Mental Hospitalization. *Medical Opinion Review* 4 (May), 24–35.

1968g. Mental Illness as an Excuse for Civil Wrongs. With George J. Alexander. *Journal of Nervous and Mental Disease* 147 (August), 113–123.

1968h. Justice and Psychiatry. *Atlantic* (October), 127–132.

1968i. Review of *The Insanity Defense*, by Abraham S. Goldstein, and *Criminal Justice*, by Abraham S. Blumberg. *Boston University Law Review* 48 (Winter), 151–55.

1968j. Problems Facing Psychiatry: The Psychiatrist as Party to Conflict. In E. Fuller Torrey, ed, *Ethical Issues in Medicine: The Role of the Physician in Today's Society* (Boston: Little, Brown), 265–284.

1968k. The Psychology of Persistent Pain: A Portrait of L'Homme Douloureux. In A. Soulairac, J. Cahn, and J. Charpentier, eds., *Pain* (London: Academic Press), 931–33.

1968l. Hysteria. In David L. Sills, ed., *International Encyclopedia of the Social Sciences* (New York: Macmillan), 7, 47–52.

1969a. The Crime of Commitment. *Psychology Today* 2 (March), 55–57.

1969b. The Right to Health. *Georgetown Law Journal* 57 (March), 734–751.

1969c. An Unscrewtape Letter: A Reply to Fred Sander. *American Journal of Psychiatry* 125 (April), 143–235.

1969d. The Right to Health. *Freeman* 19 (June), 352–362.

1969e. Psychiatry, the Law, and Social Control. *University Review* 2 (Summer), 8–13.

1969f. Interview: Thomas S. Szasz, M.D. *New Physician* 18 (June), 453–461, 476.

1969g. Enigmas of Violence. [Letters] *Science* (June 27th), 164, 1465.

1969h. Social Control and Legal Psychiatry. *Journal of the Albert Einstein Medical Center* 17 (Summer), 52–59.

1969i. Abortion Law Reform. [Letters] *Humanist*, 20 (September–October), 34.

1969j. Justice in the Therapeutic State. *Indiana Legal Forum* 3 (Fall), 14–34.

1969k. Mental Illness Is Not a Disease. *Science Digest* 66 (December), 7–14.

1970a. The Mad Scene: Who Is Dangerous to Whom? *Medical Opinion and Review* 6 (February), 111.

1970b. A Psychiatrist Views Mental Health Legislation. *Wabash Law Journal* 9 (Winter), 224–243.

1970c. Blackness and Madness. *Yale Review* 59 (Spring), 333–341.

1970d. *Ideology and Insanity: Essays on the Psychiatric Dehumanization of Man*. Garden City: Doubleday.

1970e. Justice in the Therapeutic State. In *The Administration of Justice in America*. The 1968–69 E. Paul du Pont Lectures on Crimes, Delinquency, and Corrections (University of Delaware), 75–92.

1970f. *The Manufacture of Madness: A Comparative Study of the Inquisition and the Mental Health Movement*. New York: Harper and Row.

1970g. The Mad Scene: Brothers' Keepers. *Medical Opinion and Review* 6 (April), 52–53.

1970h. Introduction. In Lucy Freeman and Lisa Hoffman, *The Ordeal of Stephen Dennison* (Englewood Cliffs: Prentice Hall), ix–xii.

1970i.   Blackness and Madness: Images of Evil and Tactics of Exclusion. In
         John F. Szwed, ed., *Black Americans* (New York: Basic Books), 67–77.

1970j.   Psychiatry as Tactic. [Letters] *New York Times* (25th July), 22.

1970k.   The Right to Drugs: A Matter of Freedom? *Newsday* (21st October),
         3B.

1970l.   R.F.K. Must Die! *New York Times Book Review* (15th November), 874.

1971a.   "Mental Illness" Myth Cruel Fraud. *Twin Circle* (14th March), 15.

1971b.   Fairness and Folly. *Medical Opinion* 7 (April), 65.

1971c.   From the Slaughterhouse to the Madhouse. *Psychotherapy* 8 (Spring),
         64–67.

1971d.   The Sane Slave: An Historical Note on the Use of Medical Diagnosis
         as Justificatory Rhetoric. *American Journal of Psychotherapy* 25
         (April), 228–239.

1971e.   The Ethics of Suicide. *Antioch Review* 31 (Spring), 7–17.

1971f.   The Negro in Psychiatry: An Historical Note on Psychiatric Rhetoric.
         American Journal of Psychotherapy 25 (July), 469–471.

1971g.   The American Association for the Abolition of Involuntary Mental
         Hospitalization, *Abolitionist* 1 (Summer), 12.

1971h.   Involuntary Commitment: A Form of Slavery. *Humanist* 31
         (July–August), 11–14.

1971i.   In the Church of America, Psychiatrists Are Priests. *Hospital
         Physician* (October), 44–46.

1971j.   The Ethics of Addiction. *American Journal of Psychiatry* 128
         (November), 541–556.

1971k.   Under Mind. Review of *A Question of Madness*, by Zhores A.
         Medvedev and Roy A. Medvedev. *New Society* (London, 16th
         December), 1213–15.

1972a.   Scapegoating Military Addicts: The Helping Hand Strikes Again.
         Trans-Action 9 (January), 46.

1972b.   Drugs, Doctors, and Deceit. [Letters] *New England Journal of
         Medicine* 286 (13th January), 111.

1972c.   The Ethics of Addiction. *Harpers Magazine* 244 (April), 74–79.

1972d.   Psychosis, Psychiatry, and Homicide. [Letters] *Journal of the
         American Medical Association* 220 (8th May), 864–65.

1972e.   A Dissent. [Letters] *National Catholic Reporter* (12th May), 10.

1972f.   Tragic Failures. Review of *In a Darkness*, by James A. Wechsler.
         National Review (26th May), 591, 593.

1972g.   Reply to J.W. Goppelt. [Letters] *American Journal of Psychiatry* 128
         (June), 1588.

1972h.   Reply to R.D. Blair [Letters] *American Journal of Psychiatry* 128
         (June), 1589.

1972i.   Remarks. In Symposium on the Aging Poor. *Syracuse Law Review* 23,
         78–82, 84–85.

1972j. Law, Property, and Psychiatry. With George J. Alexander. *American Journal of Orthopsychiatry* 42 (July), 610–626.

1972k. Bad Habits Are Not Diseases: A Refutation of the Claim that Alcoholism Is a Disease. *The Lancet* 2 (8th July), 83–84.

1972l. Voluntary Mental Hospitalization: An Unacknowledged Practice of Medical Fraud. *New England Journal of Medicine* 287 (10th August), 277–78.

1972m. Introduction. In Bruce Ennis, *Prisoners of Psychiatry: Mental Patients, Psychiatrists, and the Law* (New York: Harcourt, Brace), xi–xix.

1972n. Psychiatric Stigmatization. [Letters] *New York Times* (26th December), 32.

1973a. Fanaticism. [Letter to the Editor} *Times Literary Supplement* 3 (February), 124.

1973b. Medicine and the State: The First Amendment Violated. An Interview with Thomas Szasz. *Humanist* 33 (March–April), 305–07.

1973c. The Physician as a Spy. [Letter to the Editor] *New York Times* (24th March), 32.

1973d. Mental Illness as a Metaphor. *Nature* 242 (30th March), 305–07.

1973e. La Liberta del Malato Mentale. In *Enciclopedia della Scienze e della Tecnica Mondadori*. (Milano: Mondadori), 368–69.

1973f. From Contract to Status via Psychiatry. With George. J. Alexander. *Santa Clara Lawyer* (Spring), 537–559.

1973g. *The Second Sin*. Garden City: Doubleday.

1973h. *The Age of Madness: The History of Involuntary Mental Hospitalization Presented in Selected Texts*. Garden City: Doubleday.

1973i. Panel Discussion: Do Solutions to Drug Problems Threaten Our Civil Liberties? *Villanova Law Review* 18 (May), 875–895.

1973j. Drugs and Freedom. Transcript of the "Firing Line" Program Taped at WKPC in Louisville, Kentucky, 16th May, 1973; originally telecast on PBS, 15th July, 1973. Host: William F. Buckley, Jr., Guest: Dr. Thomas S. Szasz. Columbia, South Carolina: Southern Educational Communications Association.

1973k. The Dominion of Psychiatry. *New York Times* (5th August), E15.

1973l. Interview. *Penthouse* (October), 68–74.

1974a. The A.C.L.U.'s "Mental Illness" Cop-Out. *Reason* 5 (January), 49.

1974b. Freedom for Patients: A Dialogue. *Bulletin of the New York State District Branches of the American Psychiatric Association* 16 (January), 1, 9.

1974c. Language and Humanism. *Humanist* 34 (January–February), 25–30.

1974d. Illness and Indignity. *Journal of the American Medical Association* 227 (February), 543–45.

1974e. When History Comes Home to Roost. *New York Times* (6th March), 33.

1974f. The A.C.L.U. and Involuntary Commitment: A Reply. *Reason* 5 (April), 29.

1974g. Crime, Punishment, and Psychiatry. In Abrahamn S. Blumberg, ed., *Current Perspectives on Criminal Behavior: Original Essays on Criminology* (New York: Knopf), 262–285.

1974h. Medicine and Madness. Special Report in *The Encyclopedia Britannica Yearbook* (Chicago: Encyclopedia Britannica), 454–55.

1974j. Objectionable Psychologizing. [Letter to the Editor] *New York Times Magazine* (21st April), 8.

1974k. The Psychiatric Perspective on Pain and Its Control. In F. Dudley Hart, ed., The Treatment of Chronic Pain (London: Medical and Technical), 39–61.

1974l. *The Myth of Mental Illness: Foundations of a Theory of Personal Conduct.* Revised edition (New York: Harper and Row).

1974m. Psychiatry: A Clear and Present Danger. *Mental Hygiene* 58 (Spring), 17–20.

1974n. *Ceremonial Chemistry: The Ritual Persecution of Drugs, Addicts, and Pushers.* Garden City: Doubleday.

1974o. The Myth of Mental Illness: Three Addenda. *Journal of Humanistic Psychology* 14:3 (Summer).

1974p. ECT. [Letter to the Editor] *The Listener* (25th July).

1974q. Introduction. In John Rublowsky, *The Stoned Aged: A History of Drugs in America* (New York: Putnam's), 9–11.

1974r. Might Makes the Metaphor. *Journal of the American Medical Association* 229 (2nd September), 13–26.

1974s. Straight Talk from Thomas Szasz. An Interview. *Reason* 6 (October), 4–13.

1974t. The Myth of Psychotherapy. *American Journal of Psychotherapy* 28 (October), 517–526.

1974u. Your Last Will and Your Free Will. *The Alternative* 8 (November), 10–11.

1974v. Our Despotic Laws Destroy the Right to Self-Control. *Psychology Today* 8 (December), 1929, 127.

1974w. Review of *About Behavior*, by B.F. Skinner. *Libertarian Review* 3 (December), 67.

1975a. Sargant and Szasz. [Letter to the Editor] *Spectator* (22nd February), 197.

1975b. The Moral Physician. *The Center Magazine* 8 (March–April), 29.

1975c. Stop Poking Around in Your Patients' Lives! [Interview] *Medical Economics* (9th June), 106–128.

1975d. The Age of Madness. [Letter to the Editor] *Times Literary Supplement* (25th July), 841.

1975e. On Involuntary Psychiatry. [Op-Ed] *New York Times* (4th August), 19.

1975f. Medical Metaphorology. *American Psychologist* 30 (August), 859–861.

1975g. The Age of Madness. [Letters to the Editor]. *Times Literary Supplement* (29th August), 971.

1975h. To Review Stand on Drugs. [Letters to the Editor] *New York Times* (31st August), 14E.

1975i. The Danger of Coercive Psychiatry. *American Bar Association Journal* 61 (October), 617–622.

1975j. The Control of Conduct: Authority vs. Autonomy. *Criminal Law Bulletin* 11 (September–October), 617–622.

1975k. Preface. In J. Renard, *Poil de Carotte* (*Carrot Top*) (New York: Stonehill).

1976a. Some Call It Brainwashing. *The New Republic* (6th March), 10–12.

1976b. Mercenary Psychiatry. *The New Republic* (13th March), 112.

1976c. APA and Zionism. [Letter to the Editor] *Psychiatry News* 11 (2nd April), 2.

1976d. Psychiatry in Courtrooms. [Letter to the Editor] *The New Republic* (8th May).

1976e. *Heresies*. Garden City: Doubleday.

1976f. Anti-Psychiatry: The Paradigm of the Plundered Mind. *The New Review* [London], 314.

1976g. Male Women, Female Men. *The New Republic* (9th October), 89.

1976h. Ezra Pound. [Letter to the Editor] *Times Literary Supplement*, 1306.

1976i. Abortion: Punish the Women? [Guest comment] *Daily Orange of Syracuse University* (9th October), 68.

1976j. Political Torture and Physicians. [Letter to the Editor] *New England Journal of Medicine* 295 (28th October), 1018.

1976k. Schizophrenia: The Sacred Symbol of Psychiatry. *British Journal of Psychiatry* 129 (October), 308–316.

1976l. *Schizophrenia: The Sacred Symbol of Psychiatry*. New York: Basic Books.

1976m. Patriotic Poisoners. *Humanist* 36 (November–December), 57.

1976n. Anti-Psychiatry. [Letter to the Editor] *The New Review* (November), 71.

1976o. *Paresis and Plunder: The Models of Madness in Psychiatry and Anti-Psychiatry*. The Noel Buxton Lecture. Colchester: University of Essex.

1976p. *Karl Kraus and the Soul-Doctors: A Pioneer Critic and His Criticism of Psychiatry and Psychoanalysis*. Baton Rouge: Louisiana State University Press.

1976q. Involuntary Psychiatry. *University of Cincinnati Law Review* 45, 347–365.

1976r. The Right to Die. *The New Republic* (11th December), 89.

1976s. The Theology of Therapy: The Breach of the First Amendment through the Medicalization of Morals. In Bernard Schwartz, ed., *American Law: The Third Century* (Hackensack: Rothman), 365–376.

1976t.   A Different Dose for Different Folks: We Should Treat Drug Taking in the Same Way We Treat Speech and Religion, as a Fundamental Right. *Skeptic* (January–February), 47–49, 63–70.

1977a.   *Psychiatric Slavery: When Confinement and Coercion Masquerade as Cure*. New York: The Free Press.

1977b.   *The Theology of Medicine: The Political-Philosophical Foundations of Medical Ethics*. Baton Rouge: Louisiana State University Press; New York: Harper Colophon.

1977c.   A Dialogue on Drugs. *Psychiatric Opinion* 14 (March–April), 10–12, 44–47.

1977d.   Szasz on Schizophrenia. [Letter to the Editor] *British Journal of Psychiatry* 130 (May), 520–24.

1977e.   Donaldson. [Letter to the Editor] *Psychiatric News* 12 (2nd May), 2.

1977f.   What Do Psychiatrists Know About Terrorism? [Letter to the Editor] *New York Times* (19th June), 16E.

1977g.   Aborting Unwanted Behavior: The Controversy on Psychosurgery. *Humanist* 37 (July–August), 7, 10–11.

1977h.   The Child as Involuntary Mental Patient: The Threat of Child Therapy to the Child's Dignity, Privacy, and Self-Esteem. *San Diego Law Review* 14, 1005–027.

1977i.   On the Incarceration of Martha Mitchell. [Letter to the Editor] *New York Times* (25th September), 14E.

1977j.   Christmas Book Recommendations. *American Spectator* 11 (December), 29.

1977k.   Models of Madness. *The Listener* [London] (1st December), 721–23.

1977l.   Soviet Psychiatry: The Historical Background. *Inquiry* (5th December), 67.

1977m. Foreword. In Carl Goldberg, *Therapeutic Partnership: Ethical Concerns in Psychotherapy* (New York: Springer), vii–viii.

1977n.   Psychiatric Diversion in the Criminal Justice System: A Critique. In Randy E. Barnett and John Hagel, III., eds., *Assessing the Criminal: Restitution, Retribution, and the Legal Process* (Cambridge, Massachusetts: Balinger), 99–120.

1977o.   The Concept of Mental Illness: Explanation or Justification? In H.T. Engelhardt, Jr. and S.F. Spicker, eds., *Mental Health: Philosophical Perspectives* (Dordrecht: Reidel), 235–250.

1977p.   Healing Words for Political Madness: A Conversation with Dr. Thomas Szasz. *The Advocate* (28th December), 37–40.

1978a.   Soviet Psychiatry: Its Supporters in the West. *Inquiry* (2nd January), 45.

1978b.   Drug Prohibition. *Reason* 9 (January), 14–18.

1978c.   The Soviets Are Worse. [Letter to the Editor] *Inquiry* (20th February), 32.

1978d.   State Mental Hospitals: Orphanages for Adults. *Pacific News Service Syndicate* (23rd February).

1978e.   *The Myth of Psychotherapy: Mental Healing as Religion, Rhetoric, and Repression*. Garden City: Doubleday.

1978f.   Condoning Psychiatric Slavery. *Inquiry* (6th March), 34.

1978g.   Why Do We Fear the Retarded? *Newsday* (16th March), 93.

1978h.   The Psychiatrist as Accomplice. *Inquiry* (3rd April), 45.

1978i.   Prescription for Control. *Inquiry* (1st May), 45.

1978j.   The Case Against Compulsory Psychiatric Interventions. *The Lancet* (13th May), 1035–36.

1978k.   New Addictions for Old. *Inquiry* (29th May), 45.

1978l.   The Rapist as Patient. *Inquiry* (June), 34.

1978m.   Criminal Intent. [Letter to the Editor] *Inquiry* (26th June), 32.

1978n.   The Ethics of Therapy. *National Forum* 58 (Spring), 25–29.

1978o.   Schizophrenia: A Category Error. *Trends in NeuroSciences* 1 (July), 26–28.

1978p.   Nobody Should Decide Who Goes to the Mental Hospital: Dr. Thomas Szasz Talking with Governor Jerry Brown and Dr. Lou Simpson. *Co-Evolution Quarterly* (Summer), 56–69.

1978q.   Should Psychiatric Patients Ever Be Hospitalized Involuntarily Under Any Circumstances? No. In J.P. Brady and H.K.H. Brodie, eds., *Controversy in Psychiatry* (Philadelphia: Saunders), 965–977.

1978r.   The Abortionist as Fall Guy. *Inquiry* (24th July), 45.

1978s.   The Psychiatric Presidency. *Inquiry* (18th September), 46.

1978t.   Pilgrim's Regress. *The Spectator* (23rd September), 72–73.

1978u.   Psychiatry: The New Religion [Interview with Professor Thomas Szasz] *Cosmos* [Australia] 6 (October), 67.

1978v.   Twice-Brainwashed. *The New Republic* (23rd October), 68.

1978w.   Peter Bourne's Quaalude Caper. *Inquiry* (30th October), 47.

1978x.   A Dialogue about Drug Education. *Psychiatric Opinion* 15 (October), 10–14.

1978y.   The Concept of Schizophrenia. [Commentary] *Trends in Neuroscience* 1 (November), 129.

1978z.   Bourne's Quaalude Caper. *Inquiry* (27th November), 46.

1978za.   Gifts that Could Change the World. *Newsday* (24th December), 8.

1978zb.   The Devil's Fool. *Inquiry* (25th December), 45.

1978zc.   Behavior Therapy: A Critical Review of the Moral Dimensions of Behavior Modification. *Journal of Behavior Therapy and Psychiatry* 9, 133–34.

1979a.   Insanity and Irresponsibility: Psychiatric Diversion in the Criminal Justice System. In Hans Toch, ed., *Psychology of Crime and Criminal Justice* (New York: Holt) 133–144.

1979b.   Psychiatric Diversion in the Criminal Justice System. In Nancy J. Beran and Beverly G. Toomy, eds., *Mentally Ill Offenders and the Criminal Justice System* (New York: Praeger), 54–73.

1979c. Power and Psychiatry. In Donald W. Harward, ed., *Power: Its Nature, Its Use, and Its Limits* (Cambridge: Schenkman), 153–58.

1979d. Jones as Jesus. *Libertarian Review* (January), 34–35.

1979e. The Freedom Abusers. *Inquiry* (5th February), 46.

1979f. What Is Most Humane Commitment to the Mentally Ill? [Letters] *Milwaukee Journal* (8th February), 8.

1979g. Torsney and Our Psychiatric Executioners. [Letters] *New York Times* (24th February), 20.

1979h. Should the FDA Ban H20? *Inquiry* (April), 32–33.

1979i. Mental Illness and Police Brutality. *Libertarian Review* (April), 32–33.

1979j. Male and Female He Created Them. *New York Times Book Review* (10th June), 11–39.

1979k. An Exchange of Letters with W.B. Grant. *Mental Health in Australia* 1 (July), 44–45.

1979l. J'Accuse: How Dan White Got Away with Murder, and How American Psychiatry Helped Him Do It. *Inquiry* 20 (6th August), 17–21.

1979m. Critical Reflections on Child Psychiatry. *Children and Youth Services Review* 1, 7–29.

1979n. The Lying Truths of Psychiatry. In R. Duncan and M. Weston Smith, eds., *Lying Truths: A Critical Scrutiny of Current Beliefs and Conventions* (London: Pergamon).

1979o. Dreyfus Redux, in Reverse. *New York Times* (4th August), 19.

1979p. The Lying Truths of Psychiatry. *Journal of Libertarian Studies* 3 (Summer), 121–139.

1979q. A.A.A.I.M.H—R.I.P. *Abolitionist* 9 (September), 14.

1979r. Psychodrama in the White House. *Libertarian Review* (December), 24–31.

1980a. *Sex by Prescription: The Startling Truth about Today's Sex Therapy.* Garden City: Doubleday.

1980b. Ein Kritischer Blick auf die Psychiatrie. *Neue Zurcher Zeitung* (18th February), 17–18.

1980c. Therapeutic Tyranny. *Omni* (March), 43.

1980d. Our Fear and Trembling through the Ages. *Saturday Review* (15th March), 39–40.

1980e. Would You Give Tranquilizers to King Lear? [Interview] *New Zealand Listener* [Auckland] (19th April), 38–39.

1980f. Backwards to the Back Streets. *TV Guide* (17th–23rd May), 32–36.

1980g. Das Recht des Menschen auf Sein Heroin. *Penthouse* [Germany] (June), 52–53.

1980h. Voyeurism as Science. *Inquiry* (9th–23rd June), 15–16.

1980i. Diagnostician or Accuser? *Spectator* (13th September), 20–22.

1980j. Schlechte Gewohnheiten Sind Keine Krankheiten. [Letters] *Penthouse* [Germany] (October), 82.

1980k. A Critical Look at Psychiatry. *News from Gracie Square Hospital* 11 (December), 14.

1980l. The Political Use of Psychiatry in the United States: The Case of Dan White. *American Journal of Forensic Psychiatry* 2, 1–11.

1980m. The ACLU vs. Walter Polovchak. *Inquiry* (27th October), 68.

1981a. The Case Against Sex Education. *Penthouse* (January), 124–25.

1981b. Tea and Sympathy on the Way to Mecca. *Free Inquiry* 1 (Spring), 16–17.

1981c. A Talk with Thomas Szasz, by Lawrence Mass, M.D. *Christopher Street* (March–April), 32–39.

1981d. Criminals' Sickness Is in Our Minds. Interviews. *Post-Standard Syracuse* (6th April), C1.

1981e. The Sadness of Sex. *Inquiry* (27th April), 22–24.

1981f. Reagan Should Let the Jurors Judge Hinckley. *Washington Post* (6th May), A19.

1981g. Power and Psychiatry. *Society* 18 (May–June), 16–18.

1981h. The Protocols of the Learned Experts on Heroin. *Libertarian Review* (July), 14–17.

1981i. The Case of John Hinkley. *Spectator* (11th July), 9–10.

1981j. Mental Illness: A Myth? In L. Kristal, ed., *The ABC of Psychology* (London: Michael Joseph), 150–53.

1981k. Szasz on the Dangerous Patient. Discussion. *American Journal of Forensic Psychiatry* 2, 67, 17.

1981l. Interview: Thomas Szasz. *High Times* (September), 32–38, 69–70.

1981m. Le Combat de Thomas Szasz Contre les Tortures Psychiatriques. Interview with Alexandre Szombati. *Le Monde Dimanche* (11th October), xii–xii.

1981n. On Preventing Psychopathology: A Libertarian Analysis. In Justin M. Joffe and George W. Albee, eds., *Prevention through Political Action and Social Change* (Hanover and London: University Press of New England), 26–33.

1981o. Conversazione con Thomas S. Szasz. Colettivo/R (Guigno, 1981–Maggio, 1982), 26, 28.

1982a. Viewpoint: From Pathogenic to Therapeutic. *Sexual Medicine Today* (10th February), 33.

1982b. The Lady in the Box. *New York Times* (16th February), A19.

1982c. The War Against Drugs. *Journal of Drug Issues* 12 (Winter), 115–122.

1982d. The Psychiatrist as Moral Agent. *Whittier Law Review* 4, 77–85.

1982e. Purifying America. *Inquiry* (12th April), 26–30.

1982f. Building the Therapeutic State. *Contemporary Psychology* 27 (April), 297.

1982g. Writing People Off as Crazy. *Washington Post* (16th April), A29.

1982h. Shooting the Shrink. *The New Republic* (16th June), 11–15.

1982i. Interview. *The Review of the News* (14th July), 39–48.

1982j. The Psychiatric Will: A New Mechanism for Protecting Persons Against "Psychosis" and Psychiatry. *American Psychologist* 37 (July), 762–770.

1982k.   The Right to Refuse Treatment: A Critique. In Nora K. Bell, ed., *Who Decides? Conflicts of Rights in Health Care* (Clifton: Humana Press), 109–118.

1982l.   On the Legitimacy of Psychiatric Power. *Metamedicine* 3 (October), 315–324.

1982m.   Foreword. In "Psychiatry and Freedom." *Metamedicine* 3 (October), 313.

1982n.   Speaking About Sex: Sexual Pathology and Sexual Therapy as Rhetoric. *Syracuse Scholar* 3 (Fall), 15–19.

1982o.   Tylenol Killer: Mad or Just Bad? *Washington Post* (3rd November), A23.

1982p.   Was Virginia Woolf Mad? *Inquiry* (December), 44–45.

1982q.   Literature and Medicine. *Literature and Medicine* 1, 36–37.

1982r.   Lunatic Reform. *The Spectator* 4 (December), 16.

1982s.   Foreword. In *Psychiatric Drugs: The Need to Be Informed* (Sydney, Australia: The Committee on Mental Health Advocacy), iii.

1982t.   The Concept of Psychosis: A Cause and a Consequence of Certain Medical-Ethical Dilemmas. In Bart Gruzalski and Carl Nelson, eds., *Value Conflicts in Health Care Delivery* (Cambridge: Ballinger), 720.

1983a.   Foreword. In Richard E. Vatz and Lee S. Weinberg, eds., *Thomas Szasz: Primary Values and Major Contentions* (Buffalo: Prometheus), 910.

1983b.   Objections to Psychiatry: Dialogue with Thomas Szasz. In Jonathan Miller, ed., *States of Mind: Conversations with Psychological Investigators* (London: British Broadcasting Corporation), 270–290.

1983c.   The Psychiatric Will: II. Whose Will Is It Anyway? *American Psychologist* 38 (March), 344–46.

1983d.   Learned Psychotics. *American Spectator* (April), 32–33.

1983e.   Psychiatric Self-Defense. *Reason* (May), 41–43.

1983f.   Speaking about Sex: Sexual Pathology and Sexual Therapy as Rhetoric. In Clive M. Davis, ed., *Challenges in Sexual Science* (Publication of the Society for the Scientific Study of Sex), 17.

1983g.   A Look at John Hinckley's Parents. *Washington Times* (12th May), C1.

1983h.   Foreword. In Irwin Silverman, *Pure Types Are Rare: Myths and Meanings of Madness* (New York: Praeger), ix–x.

1983i.   Points/Counterpoints: Should Alcohol and/or Drug Abusers Be Legally Coerced into Treatment? *U.S. Journal of Drug and Alcohol Dependence* (7th June), 7.

1983j.   The Electroshock Dilemma. *Inquiry* (July), 26–29.

1983k.   Feuchtersleben and Szasz: A Rejoinder. *Psychiatry* 46 (August), 290–92.

1983l.   This Week's Citation Classic: Szasz, T.S., "The Myth of Mental Illness," *American Psychologist* 15 (1960), 113–18. *Current Contents* (31st October), 21.

1983m. Psychiatry. In Robyn Williams, ed., *The Best of the Science Show*. (Melbourne: Nelson/Australian Broadcasting Corporation), pp. 155–165.

1983n. Questions About a Clergyman/President. [Letters] *New York Times* (29th January), 18E.

1983o. Though This Be Madness. [Letters] *Sciences* 24 (January–February), 4.

1984a. *The Therapeutic State: Psychiatry in the Mirror of Current Events*. Buffalo: Prometheus.

1984b. Illness and Incompetence. In David J. Schnall and Carl L. Figliola, eds., *Contemporary Issues in Health Care* (New York: Praeger), 112–125.

1984c. Myth of Mental Illness, In Raymond J. Corsini, ed., *Encyclopedia of Psychology*. 4 vols. (New York: Wiley), vol. 2, 414–15.

1984d. Defender of the Faith. *Spectator* (25th August), 20–21.

1984e. Review of *Law, Psychiatry and Morality*, by Alan A. Stone. *Journal of Mind and Behavior* 5 (Summer), 363–64.

1984f. The Insanity Defense Reconsidered. *American Journal of Forensic Psychiatry* 5, 109–117.

1984g. Treat Mental Illness? It Isn't Even a Disease. *USA Today* (11th October), A10.

1985a. New Ideas, Not Old Institutions, for the Homeless. *Wall Street Journal* (7th June), 24.

1985b. Homelessness Is Not a Psychiatric Problem. *USA Today* (17th June), 10A.

1985c. Insurance Against Malpractice and Malresuit Crucial for Patients. *New York City Tribune* (15th July), 1B–4B.

1985d. Why Does Television Grovel at the Altar of Psychiatry? With Richard E. Vatz and Lee S. Weinberg. *Washington Post* (15th September), D12.

1985e. Psychiatry: Rhetoric and Reality. *The Lancet* 2 (28th September), 711–12.

1985f. The Pretensions of the Freudian Cult. *Spectator* (5th October), 32.

1985g. Intentionality and Insanity: Some Lessons from Reflections on Art. *Literature and Medicine* 4, 112.

1985h. Panel Discussion. In Ruth Terrington, ed., *Towards a Whole Society* (London: Richmond Fellowship Press), 55–71.

1985i. A Home for the Homeless: The Half-Forgotten Heart of Mental Health Services. In, Ruth Terrington, ed., *Towards a Whole Society* (London: Richmond Fellowship Press), 39–45.

1986a. A Home for the Homeless: The Half-Forgotten Heart of Mental Health Services. *Freedom* (March), 28–33.

1986b. The Case Against Suicide Prevention. *American Psychologist* 41 (July), 806–812.

1986c. Foreword. In S.L. Sharma, *The Therapeutic Dialogue: A Theoretical and Practical Guide to Psychotherapy* (Albuquerque: University of New Mexico Press), xi–xii.

1986d. What Counts as Disease? *Canadian Medical Association Journal* 135 (15th October), 859–860.

1987a. *Insanity: The Idea and Its Consequences*. New York: John Wiley.

1987b. Comments. The Criminal Justice System: How Well Does It Work? In *Crime in America: Is Anybody Safe?* A Transcript of the Providence Journal/Brown University Public Affairs Conference (1st–11th March), 45–73.

1987c. Justifying Coercion Though Religion and Psychiatry. *Journal of Humanistic Psychology* 27 (Spring), 158–174.

1987d. Myth of Mental Illness. In Raymond J. Corsini, ed., *Concise Encyclopedia of Psychology* (New York: Wiley), 746.

1987e. Justifying Coercion Though Theology and Therapy. In Jeffrey K. Zeig, ed., *The Evolution of Psychotherapy* (New York: Brunner/Mazel), 210.

1987f. Comments. In The War on Drugs: Symposium Proceedings—Round-table Discussion. *Nova Law Review* 11 (Spring), 939–1023.

1987g. Why the Drug War Is Unstoppable. *Nova Law Review* 11 (Spring), 915–18.

1987h. The Morality of Drug Controls. In Ronald Hamowy, ed., *Dealing With Drugs: Consequences of Government Control* (Lexington, Massachusetts: Lexington Books/D.C. Heath), 327–351.

1987i. Criminals Deserve Not So Much Treatment as More Punishment. [Letters] *New York Times* (21st May), A30.

1987j. Mental Illness and Social Policy. *Newsday Magazine* (7th June), 47.

1987k. AIDS and Drugs: Balancing Risk and Benefits. [Letters] *The Lancet* 2 (22nd August), 450.

1987l. The Religion Called Psychiatry. *Second Opinion* 6 (November), 50–61.

1987m. The Case Against Child Psychiatry. *Freedom* 20 (December), 16–21.

1988a. We Have Met the Enemy in the War on Drugs. [Letters] *New York Times* (6th March), E24.

1988b. Homelessness Is Not a Disease. *USA Today* (March), 28–30.

1988c. Afterword. In Szasz, *Psychiatric Justice* (Syracuse: Syracuse University Press).

1988d. Utopia. In Paradise Tossed, by Marion Long. *Omni* (April), pp. 98–99.

1988e. The Man Behind the Couch. Review of *Freud: A Life for Our Time*, by Peter Gay. *Wall Street Journal* (21st April), 28.

1988f. Preface. In Szasz, *The Myth of Psychotherapy* (Syracuse: Syracuse University Press), vii–viii.

1988g. Koryagin and Psychiatric Coercion. [Letters] *The Lancet* 2 (3rd September), 573.

1988h. Preface. In Szasz, *Schizophrenia: The Sacred Symbol of Psychiatry* (Syracuse: Syracuse University Press), xi–xiv.

1988i. Divine Justice. [Letters] *New York Times* (23rd July), 26.

1988j. Preface. In Szasz, *The Theology of Medicine* (Syracuse: Syracuse University Press), ix–x.

1988k.   A Plea for the Cessation of the Longest War of the Twentieth Century: The War on Drugs. *Humanistic Psychologist* 16 (Autumn), 314–322.

1988l.   Review of *A Social History of Madness: Stories of the Insane*, by Roy Porter. *Medical History* 32 (October), 472–73.

1988m.   Preface. In Szasz, *The Ethics of Psychoanalysis* (Syracuse: Syracuse University Press), vi–xvi.

1988n.   Preface. In Szasz, *Pain and Pleasure: A Study of Bodily Feelings* (Syracuse: Syracuse University Press), vii–xvi.

1989a.   A Plea for the Cessation of the Longest War of the Twentieth Century: The War on Drugs. In *CORA: The Cost of Prohibition on Drugs* (Roma: Radical Party).

1989b.   Getting It Backward on Crack Patients. [Letters] *New York Times* (13th June), A26.

1989c.   A Point of Protest. *Salisbury Review* 7 (June), 22–23.

1989d.   Psychiatric Justice. *British Journal of Psychiatry* 154 (June), 864–69.

1989e.   The Myth of the Rights of Mental Patients. *Liberty* 2 (July), 1926.

1989f.   Suicide and Psychiatric Coercion. *Journal of Humanistic Psychology* 29 (Summer), 380–84.

1989g.   Letter to Karl Menninger. In Menninger, K., Reading Notes. *Bulletin of the Menninger Clinic* 53 (July), 351–52.

1989h.   The Politics of Addiction: An Interview with Psychiatrist Thomas Szasz. *Focus* 12 (August–September), 20–21, 32–37.

1989i.   Whose Competence? *National Review* (15th September), 38–60.

1989j.   Preface. In Szasz, *Law, Liberty and Psychiatry* (Syracuse: Syracuse University Press), ix–xvi.

1989k.   The Moral View on Suicide. In D. Jacobs and H.N. Brown, eds., *Suicide: Understanding and Responding* (Madison, Connecticut: International Universities Press), 437–447.

1989l.   L'incapace: Un' attribuzione morale. In M. Mellini et al., eds., *Sotto Il Nome D'Incapace* (Milano: Spirali/Vel), 69–81.

1989m.   A Dialogue on Education for Autonomy. *Interchange* 20, 32–47.

1989n.   Psychiatry in the Age of AIDS. *Reason* 21 (December), 31–34.

1990a.   Psychoanalysis as Religion: Psychoanalytic Theory as Ideology, Psychoanalytic Practice as Cure of Souls. In G.L. Ormiston and R. Sassower, eds., *Prescriptions: The Dissemination of Medical Authority* (Westport: Greenwood Press), 121–139.

1990b.   Dying with Their Rights On. [Letters] *The Lancet* (10th February), 335, 356–57.

1990c.   Lay Down Your Arms. *Free Inquiry* 10 (Spring), 7.

1990d.   Killing as Therapy. *Liberty* 3 (May), 78.

1990e.   *L'incapace: Lo Specchio Morale del Conformiso*. Milano: Spirali/Vel.

1990f.   Preface. In Szasz, *Anti-Freud: Karl Kraus's Criticism of Psychoanalysis and Psychiatry* (Syracuse: Syracuse University Press), xix–viii.

1990g. The Laws He Violated. [Letters] *New York Times* (19th June), A22.

1990h. Szasz on AIDS and Psychiatry. Interview. *Phoenix Rising* 8 (July), S6–7.

1990i. Mental Health System: House of Cards. *AHP Perspective* (July), 5.

1990j. The Myth of Psychotherapy. In J.K. Zeig and W.M. Munion, eds., *What Is Psychotherapy? Contemporary Perspectives* (San Francisco: Jossey-Bass), 171–74.

1990k. Crazy or Different? [Letters] *National Review* (5th November), 48.

1990l. Preface. In Szasz, *Sex By Prescription* (Syracuse: Syracuse University Press), ix–xiii.

1990m. Law and Psychiatry: The Problems that Will Not Go Away. *Journal of Mind and Behavior* 11 (Summer and Autumn), 557–563.

1990n. *The Untamed Tongue: A Dissenting Dictionary.* LaSalle: Open Court.

1991a. Psychiatry and Social Control. *Humanist* 51 (January and February), 24–25, 34.

1991b. Noncoercive Psychiatry: An Oxymoron. *Journal of Humanistic Psychology* 31 (Spring), 117–125.

1991c. Preface. In Szasz, *Ideology and Insanity* (Syracuse: Syracuse University Press), vii–xiii.

1991d. Hinckley and Son. *Reason* 23 (July), 51.

1991e. The Medicalization of Sex. *Journal of Humanistic Psychology* 31, 34–42.

1991f. Gli Stati Uniti Contro la Droga. Translated by Carlo Oliva. *Volonta Milano*, 11–27.

1991g. The Myth of Treatment. *Drug Policy Letter* 3 (Fall), 34.

1991h. Mental Illness? [Letters] *New York Times* (2nd November), 22.

1991i. The Right to Use Drugs. In Arnold S. Trebach and Kevin B. Zeese, eds., *New Frontiers in Drug Policy* (Washington, D.C.: Drug Policy Foundation), 15.

1991j. Diagnoses Are Not Diseases. *The Lancet* 338 (21st–28th December), 1574–76.

1992a. The Socrates Option. *Reason* 24 (April), 47.

1992b. *Our Right to Drugs: The Case for a Free Market.* New York: Praeger.

1992c. Taking Dialogue as Therapy Seriously: Words Are the Eessential Tool of Treatment. *Journal of the Society for Existential Analysis* 3 (July), 29.

1992d. The Fatal Temptation: Drug Prohibition and the Fear of Autonomy. *Daedalus* 121 (Summer), 161–64.

1992e. Discussion of "Toward Better Results in the Treatment of Depression," by Joseph Wolpe. In Jeffrey K. Zeig, ed., *The Evolution of Psychotherapy: The Second Conference* (New York: Brunner/Mazel), 137–38.

1992f. The United States v. Drugs. In Jeffrey K. Zeig, ed., *The Evolution of Psychotherapy: The Second Conference* (New York: Brunner/Mazel), 300–06.

1993a. *A Lexicon of Lunacy: Metaphoric Malady, Moral Responsibility and Psychiatry*. New Brunswick: Transaction.

1993b. Insanity Defense Is, Well, Insane. *Newsday* (9th March), 73.

1993c. Crazy Talk: Thought Disorder or Psychiatric Arrogance? *British Journal of Medical Psychology* 66, 61–67.

1993d. Psychiatry and the Denial of Evil: Defining Misbehavior as a Brain Disease. *Pacific Law Journal* 24 (April), 1103–06.

1993e. The Brain Tenders. Who Picks up the Tab? *Washington Times* (4th May), F1.

1993f. Curing, Coercing, and Claims Making: A Reply to Critics. *British Journal of Psychiatry* 162, 797–800.

1993g. Foreword. In S. Farber, *Madness, Heresy, and the Rumor of Angels: The Revolt Against the Mental Health System* (Chicago: Open Court), xi–xv.

1993h. Le Monopole Medico-Statique. *In Première Journée Internationale du Cannabis: Textes des Intervenants* (Paris: Editions du Lezard), 89–90.

1993i. Prefazione. In G. Antonucci, *Critica Al Guidizio Psichiatrico* (Roma: Sensibili alle Foglie), 79.

1993j. My Views on Psychiatry. *East European Medical Journal* 2, 13–20.

1994a. Therapeutic State Is a Modern Leviathan. [Letters] *Wall Street Journal Europe* (11th January), 9.

1994b. *Cruel Compassion: Psychiatric Control of Society's Unwanted*. New York: Wiley.

1994c. Killing Kindness. *Reason* 26 (May), 40–41.

1994d. Mental Illness Is Still a Myth. *Society* 31 (May–June), 34–39.

1994e. Foreword: Remembering Roy. In R.A. Childs, Jr., *Liberty Against Power: Essays by Roy A. Childs, Jr.* Edited by Joan Kennedy Taylor. (San Francisco: Fox and Wilkes), ix–x.

1994f. Thomas Szasz on Drugs. In F. Batman and S. Lewis, eds., *The Reader's Companion: A Book Lover's Guide to the Most Important Books in Every Field of Knowledge, as Chosen by the Experts* (New York: Hyperion).

1994g. Psychiatric Diagnosis, Psychiatric Power, and Psychiatric Abuse. *Journal of Medical Ethics* 20 (September), 135–38.

1995a. The Origin of Psychiatry: The Alienist as Nanny for Troublesome Adults. *History of Psychiatry* 6, 119.

1995b. Idleness and Lawlessness in the Therapeutic State. [Letters] *Society* 32 (September–October), 5–6.

1995c. In Search of Sanity. [Letters] *The Economist* (30th September), 8, 10.

1995d. Foreword. In F. Tassano, *The Power of Life and Death: A Critique of Medical Tyranny* (London: Duckworth), vii–ix.

1995e. Psychiatric Fictions. [Letters] *New York Times Book Review* (19th November), 4.

1996a. The War on Drugs Is Lost. *National Review* (12th February), 45–47.

1996b.   Audible Thoughts and Speech Defect in Schizophrenia: A Note on Reading and Translating Bleuler. *British Journal of Psychiatry* 168 (May), 533–35.

1996c.   Routine Neonatal Circumcision: Symbol of the Birth of the Therapeutic State. *Journal of Medicine and Philosophy* 21:137–148.

1996c.   A Brief History of Medicine's War on Responsibility. *Journal of Clinical Epidemiology* 49 (June), 609–613.

1996d.   *The Meaning of Mind: Language, Morality, and Neuroscience.* Westport: Praeger.

1997a.   Save Money, Cut Crime, Get Real (Symposium on drug policy). *Playboy* (January), 128, 190.

1997b.   Foreword. In D.A. Levy, *Tools of Critical Thinking: Metathoughts for Psychology* (Boston: Allyn and Bacon), v.

1997c.   Discussion. O.F. Kernberg, "Convergences and Divergences in Contemporary Psychoanalytic Technique and Psychoanalytic Psychotherapy." In J.K. Zeig, ed., *The Evolution of Psychotherapy: The Third Conference* (New York: Brunner/Mazel), 18–20.

1997d.   The Healing Word: Its Past, Present, and Future. In J.K. Zeig, ed., *The Evolution of Psychotherapy: The Third Conference* (New York: Brunner/Mazel), 299–306.

1997e.   Thomas Szasz: In conversation with Alan Kerr. *Psychiatric Bulletin* (Royal College of Psychiatrists, U.K.) 21 (January), 39–44.

1997f.   Medics in the War on Drugs. *Liberty* 10 (March), 47–48.

1997g.   The Case Against Psychiatric Coercion. *The Independent Review* 1 (Spring), 485–498.

1997h.   No Kevorkian Needed. [Letters] *New York Times* (1st April), A14.

1997i.   Preface. In Szasz, *Insanity: The Idea and Its Consequences* [1987] (Syracuse: Syracuse University Press), ix–xi.

1997j.   Preface. In Szasz, *The Manufacture of Madness: A Comparative Study of the Inquisition and the Mental Health Movement* [1970] (Syracuse: Syracuse University Press), xi–xiv.

1997k.   Abortion Law and History. [Review] *Washington Post Health* (8th July), 15.

1997l.   Preface. In D.A. Levy, *Tools of Critical Thinking: Metathoughts for Psychology* (Boston: Allyn and Bacon), v.

1997m. Mental Illness Is Still a Myth. *Review of Existential Psychology and Psychiatry* 23, 70–80.

1997n.   Foreword. In J. Hillman, ed., *Suicide and the Soul.* Second Edition (Woodstock, Connecticut: Spring), 6–10.

1998a.   Interview with the Anti-Christ. By Patrick Hopkinson. *Mental Health Care* (U.K.) 1 (January), 154–55.

1998b.   The Perils of Prohibition. In R. Coomber, ed., *The Control of Drugs and Drug Users: Reason or Reaction* (London: Harwood Academic Publishers), 155–59.

1998c.   The Ethics of Psychoanalysis. *Society* 35 (January–February), 16–21. (Reprint from Transaction, 1965.)

1998d.   The Political Legitimation of Quackery. *Reason* 29 (March), 25–26.

1998e.   The Unapatient Manifesto. *Liberty* 11 (March), 9.

1998f.   The Healing Word: Its Past, Present, and Future. *Journal of Humanistic Psychology* 38 (Winter), 1–13.

1998g.   Freedom and Madness. *Liberty* 11 (May), 33–36, 48.

1998h.   Myth of Mental Illness. In *Encyclopedia of Mental Health* (San Diego: Academic Press), vol. 2, 743–752.

1998i.   Vatican Diagnosis. [Letter] *New York Times* (11th May), A16.

1998j.   Commentary on Aristotle's Function Argument and the Concept of Mental Illness. *Philosophy, Psychiatry, and Psychology* 5 (September), 203–07.

1998k.   Parity for Mental Illness, Disparity for the Mental Patient. *The Lancet* 352, (10th October), 1213–15.

1998l.   When a Killer Blames His Doctor. [Letter] *New York Times* (14th October), A22.

1998m.   What Counts as Disease? Rationales and Rationalizations for Treatment. *Research in Complementary Medicine* 5 (Supp. 1) (October), 40–46.

1998n.   Drug Warriors. *Issues in Science and Technology Online* (Winter).

1998o.   Discretion as Power: In the Situation Called "Psychotherapy." *British Journal of Psychotherapy* 15 (Winter), 216–228.

1998p.   Illusory Euphemism in a Deadly Practice. *Washington Times* (9th December), A19.

1999a.   Parity for Mental Illness, Disparity for the Mental Patient. [Letters] *The Lancet* 353 (2nd January), 74.

1999b.   Facing up to Coercion. *Liberty* 13 (January), 47–48.

1999c.   Alias Dr. Death. *Liberty* 13 (February), 41–42, 45.

1999d.   Gullible Skeptics. *The Freeman* 49 (May), 26–27.

1999e.   Rethinking Suicide. *The Freeman* 49 (July), 41–42.

1999f.   The Hazards of TruthTelling. *The Freeman* 49 (September), 38–39.

1999g.   Medical Incapacity, Legal Incompetence and Psychiatry. *Psychiatric Bulletin* 23 (September), 517–19.

1999h.   *Fatal Freedom: The Ethics and Politics of Suicide*. Westport, Connecticut: Praeger.

1999i.   Is Mental Illness a Disease? *The Freeman* 49 (November), 38–39.

2000a.   Remembering Krafft-Ebing. *Ideas on Liberty* 50 (January), 31–32.

2000b.   Mental Disorders Are Not Diseases. *USA Today* (Magazine) (January), 30–31.

2000c.   On the Future of Psychotherapy. *New Therapist* (January–February), 12–13.

2000d.   Does Insanity Cause Crime? *Ideas on Liberty* 50 (March), 31–32.

2000e. The Case Against Psychiatric Power. In Phil Barker and Chris Stevenson, eds., *The Construction of Power and Authority in Psychiatry* (Oxford: Butterworth/Heinemann), 43–56.

2000f. Remembering Masturbatory Insanity. *Ideas on Liberty* 50 (May), 35–36.

2000g. Mind, Brain, and the Problem of Responsibility. *Society* (May–June), 34–37.

2000h. Curing the Therapeutic State. Interview with Jacob Sullum. *Reason* 32 (July), 26–34.

2000i. Chemical Straitjackets for Children. *Ideas on Liberty* 50 (July), 37–38.

2000j. Creativity and Criminality: The Two Faces of Responsibility. *Ideas on Liberty* 50 (November), 31–32.

2000k. Fiktion als Fakt: Drogenbekaempfung und die Angst vor Selbstbestimmung. In Reiner Matzker and Siegfried Zielinski, eds., *Medienwissenschaft* (Bern: Peter Lang), 143–46.

2000l. Do Humans Have a Nature? *HRP Studies in Human Nature*. Occasional Paper No. 4 (Cambridge, Massachusetts: Harvard Review of Philosophy).

2001a. Public Schools as Drug Delivery Systems. *Ideas on Liberty* 51 (January), 36–37.

2001b. Affirmative Chemical Action. *Ideas on Liberty* 51 (March), 35–36.

2001c. Anatomy of a Teenage Shooting. [Letter] *New York Times* (13th March), A18.

2001d. With Friends Like These, Pity America's Kids. *Los Angeles Times* (15th March), B11.

2001e. Actions Speak Louder Than Words. [Letters] *British Medical Journal*, electronic edition, 17th April, 2001; www.bmj.com/cgi/eletters/322/7291/937#EL12

2001f. *Pharmacracy: Medicine and Politics in America*. Westport: Praeger.

2001g. The Therapeutic State: The Tyranny of Pharmacracy. *Independent Review* 5 (Spring), 485–521.

2001h. Kevorkian, Lies, and Suicide. *Ideas on Liberty* 51 (May), 35–36.

2001i. Diagnosing Behavior: Cui Bono? *Legal Studies Forum* 25, 505–517.

2001j. Foreword. In Carol Hebald, *The Heart Too Long Suppressed: A Chronicle of Mental Illness* (Boston: Northeastern University Press), xi–xiii.

2001k. Placebos, Healing, and a Mother's Kiss. [Letter] *New York Times* (29th May).

2001l. The Person as Moral Agent. In Kirk J. Schneider, James F.T. Bugental, and J. Fraser Pierson, eds., *The Handbook of Humanistic Psychology: Leading Edges in Theory, Research, and Practice* (Thousand Oaks: Sage), 77–80.

2001m. The Bought Mind. *Ideas on Liberty* 51 (July), 33–34.

2001n. The Medical Ethics of Peter Singer. *Society* 38 (July–August), 20–25.

2001o. The Psychiatric Collaborator as Critic. *Ideas on Liberty* 51 (September), 29–30.

2001p. Actions Speak Louder than Words. [Letters.) British Medical Journal, print edition, 323 (1st September), 511.

2001q. Actions Speak Louder Than Words. (Letters] *British Medical Journal*, electronic edition. (7th September); www.bmj.com/cgi/eletters/323/7311/511/a#EL4

2001r. Mental Illness: Psychiatry's Phlogiston. Journal of Medical Ethics, 27 (October), 297301.

2001s. Mental Illness: Psychiatry's Phlogiston. *Ideas on Liberty* 51 (November), 31–32.

2001t. Assisted Suicide Is Bootleg Suicide. *Los Angeles Times* (23rd November).

2001u. Thumbs on the Parity Scale for Psychiatrists. *Washington Times* (9th December).

2002a. Kevorkian Warps the Value He Touts. *Detroit Free Press* (10th January).

2002b. Patient or Prisoner? *Ideas on Liberty* 52 (January), 31–32.

2002c. Mises and Psychiatry. *Liberty* 16 (February), 23–26.

2002d. The Trouble with Self-Esteem. [Letters] *New York Times Magazine* (17th February).

2002e. Rothbard on Szasz. *Liberty* 16 (March), 33–34, 40.

2002f. Parity for Mental Illness, Disparity for Mental Patients. *Ideas on Liberty* 52 March), 33–34.

2002g. Szasz and Mises: In Response to Bettina Bien Greaves. *Liberty* 16 (April), 46, 60.

2002h. Suicide Bomber, to Be Precise. *Washington Post* (18th April), A20.

2002i. The Psychiatrist as Accomplice. *Washington Times* (28th April), B03.

2002j. Reply to Brassington. *Journal of Medical Ethics* 28 (April), 124–25.

2002k. The Maternity Hospital and the Mental Hospital. *Ideas on Liberty* 52 (May), 33–34.

2002l. *Liberation By Oppression: A Comparative Study of Slavery and Psychiatry*. New Brunswick: Transaction.

2002m. Hayek and Psychiatry. *Liberty* 16 (June), 19–20, 24.

2002n. Insanity and Intolerance. *Ideas on Liberty* 52 (July), 34–35.

2002o. Diagnosing Behavior: Cui Bono? In Jonathan D. Raskin and Sara K. Bridges, eds., *Studies in Meaning: Exploring Constructivist Psychology* (New York: Pace University Press), 169–179.

2002p. Sins of the Fathers: Is Child Molestation a Sickness or a Crime? *Reason* 34 (August), 54–59.

2002q. Coercion and Psychiatry. *Liberty* 16 (August), 33–35.

2002r. Straight Talk about Suicide. *Ideas on Liberty* 52 (September), 34–35.

2002s.   Mental Illness: From Shame to Pride. *Ideas on Liberty* 52 (November), 37–38.

2003a.   Taking Drug Laws Seriously. *Ideas on Liberty* 53 (January), 28–29.

2003b.   Opiate of the Masses. [Letters] *The Village Voice* (5th–11th February); www.villagevoice.com/issues/0306/letters.php

2003c.   Parity or Prevarication? *Ideas on Liberty* 53 (March), 28–29.

2003d.   Remember Psychiatric Patients' Civil Rights. The Seattle Post-Intelligencer (3rd April), B9; http://seattlepi.nwsource.com/opinion/115509mentalcon03.shtml

2003e.   Cleansing the Modern Heart. *Society* 40 (May–June), 52–59.

2003f.   The Myth of Health Insurance. *Ideas on Liberty* 53 (May), 30–31.

2003g.   Unequal Justice for All. *Ideas on Liberty* 53 (July), 26–27.

2003h.   Psychiatry and the Control of Dangerousness: On the Apotropaic Function of the Term Mental Illness. *Journal of Medical Ethics* 29 (August), 227–230.

2003i.   Psychiatric Slavery? [Letter] *Psychiatric News* 38 (September), 28.

2003j.   Marijuana Medicalization: Bad Cause, Bad Faith. *Journal of Cognitive Liberties* 4, 83–85.

2003k.   Taking Drug Laws Seriously, II. *Ideas on Liberty* 53 (October), 20–21.

2003l.   Limbaugh's Disease. *Liberty* 17 (December), 15–16.

2003m.   Civil Liberties and Civil Commitment. *The Freeman* 53 (December), 25–26.

2003n.   The Psychiatric Protection Order for the Battered Mental Patient. *British Medical Journal* 327 (20th December), 1449–451.

2003o.   Obesity in the Young. [Letter] *New York Times* (22nd December), A16.

2004a.   The Greatest Poem. *Liberty* 18 (January), 13.

2004b.   Interview with Randall C. Wyatt. Thomas Szasz: Liberty and the Practice of Psychotherapy, by Randall C. Wyatt. *Journal of Humanistic Psychology* 44 (Winter), 71–85.

2004c.   Self-Ownership or Suicide Prevention? *The Freeman* 54 (March), 24–25.

2004d.   Protecting Patients against Psychiatric Intervention. *Society* 41 (March–April), 7–9.

2004e.   On Autogenic Diseases. *The Freeman* 54 (May), 24.

2004f.   *Words to the Wise: A Medico-Philosophical Dictionary.* New Brunswick: Transaction.

2004g.   *Faith in Freedom: Libertarian Principles and Psychiatric Practices.* New Brunswick: Transaction.

2004h.   "Knowing What Ain't So": R.D. Laing and Thomas Szasz. *Psychoanalytic Review* 91 (June), 331–346.

2004i.   Pharmacracy in America. *Society* 41 (July–August), 54–58.

Index